WEST'S
AMERICAN
GOVERNMENT *Updated Edition*

WEST'S
AMERICAN
GOVERNMENT

ABOUT
THE COVER

This 7′×4′ oil painting "Sweet Liberty" by George Sumner was created in an effort to raise money for the restoration and centennial celebration of the Statue of Liberty. The artist's interpretation of our symbol of freedom, the torch burning brightly in a world of turmoil, reflects his optimism that peace and freedom will prevail.

Only three contemporary works of art are permanently installed in the museum at the base of the Statue. Sumner was deeply honored to enshrine "Sweet Liberty" there as part of the celebration on July 4, 1986.

In his environmental impressionist style, George Sumner continues to strive for the conservation and protection of our planet. He has dedicated "Sweet Liberty" to the people of America—in honor of a country and its soul.

West Publishing Company

St. Paul   New York   San Francisco   Los Angeles

COPYRIGHT © 1994 By WEST PUBLISHING COMPANY
610 Opperman Drive
P.O. Box 64526
St. Paul, MN 55164-0526

Library of Congress Cataloging-in-Publication Data

West's American government.
    p.   cm.
Includes index.
    1. United States—Politics and government.   I. Title.
JK274.M59   1992
320.973—dc20   91-30900
Student Edition (Updated Edition): 0-314-02373-9
Teacher's Wraparound Edition (Updated Edition): 0-314-02374-7

ART: Miyake Illustration and Design
COMPOSITION: Parkwood Composition Service, Inc.
COVER IMAGE: "Sweet Liberty . . . in honor of a country and its soul" by George Sumner. Original oil 4′×7′ (miniprints available—please contact Sumner Fine Arts, Sausalito, CA).

Acknowledgments

Unit/Chapter Art Credits

Unit One Independence Hall/Bettmann; Trucks/Image Bank; **Chapter 1** Statue of Liberty/Bettmann; **Chapter 2** Independence Hall/Bettmann; **Chapter 4** Trucks/Image Bank; Soldiers/Bettmann; **Unit Two** Martin Luther King/Bettmann; Man on Strike/Black Star/Steve Leonard; Flag Burning/Bettmann; **Chapter 5** Strikers/Black Star/Steve Leonard; Flag Burning/Bettmann; **Chapter 6** Martin Luther King/Bettmann; Indian Woman/Bettmann; **Unit Three** Convention/Black Star/Rick Friedman; Theo-dore Roosevelt/The Granger Collection, New York; Money/FPG; Ellis Island Immigrants/Bettmann; **Chapter 7** Statue of Liberty/Bettmann; Immigrants/Bettmann; **Chapter 8** Donkey/Bettmann; Elephant/Bettmann; Convention/Black Star/Rick Friedman; Teddy Roosevelt/The Granger Collection, New York; **Chapter 9** National Organization for Women/Black Star/John Troha; Gray Panthers/Black Star/Tom Sobolik; Money/FPG; **Chapter 10** TV/Sony Corporation; Nixon/Kennedy Debate/Bettmann; Campaign Signs/Stock Boston; **Chapter 11** Voting Booth/Bettmann; Suffragettes/Bettmann; **Unit Four** Congress in Session/House of Representatives; Attendance Board/House of Representatives; Man giving speech/Black Star/Dennis Brack; TV/Sony Corporation; **Chapter 12** Foley presiding over House/Sygma/Ron Sachs; New Jersey District Map/State of New Jersey; **Chapter 13** Man giving speech/Black Star/Dennis Brack; Budget meeting/Black Star/Dennis Brack; Impeachment Ticket/The Granger Collection, New York; **Chapter 14** Sample Bill/House of Representatives; Hopper Box/House of Representatives; Attendance Board/House of Representatives; Congress in Session/House of Representatives; TV/Sony Corporation; **Unit Five** Five Presidents/Bettmann; Shuttle Launch/UPI/Bettmann Newsphotos; Nixon's visit to China/UPI/Bettmann; Helicopter/Black Star/Dennis Brack; **Chapter 15** Lincoln Memorial/The Granger Collection, New York; Five Presidents/Bettmann; **Chapter 16** Bush/State of the Union/House of Representatives; Helicopter/Black Star/Dennis Brack; Carter and Panamanian President/Sygma/Tom Zimberoff; Nixon in China/UPI/Bettmann; **Chapter 17** Postal Worker/Black Star/Dennis Brack; Shuttle Launch/UPI/Bettmann Newsphotos; Park Ranger/David Hanover; **Unit Six** Supreme Court Justices/Sygma; John Marshall/Collection of the Curator/Supreme Court; **Chapter 18** John Marshall/Collection of the Curator/Supreme Court; Supreme Court Justices/Sygma; Thurgood Marshall/Supreme Court Historical Society/National Geographic Society; **Unit Seven** United Nations/United Nations/Y. Nagata; Exxon Valdez/Sygma/Alain Keler; Stealth/Sygma; Troops/Reuters/Bettmann—Phillipe Wojazer; Berlin Wall/Sygma/J. Langevin; CIA Seal/Central Intelligence Agency; **Chapter 19** Exxon Valdez/Sygma/Alain Keler; Homeless person/Stock Boston/J. Dunn; **Chapter 20** Troops/Reuters/Bettmann—Phillippe Wojazer; United Nations/United Nations/Y. Nagata; Stealth/Sygma; Berlin Wall/Sygma/J. Langevin; CIA Seal/Central Intelligence Agency; **Unit Eight** Capitol Building/State of Nebraska/Nebraska Land Magazine; Flag/State of Alaska; Flag/State of Illinois; Seal/State of Texas; Court House/Texas Department of Highways and Public Transportation; City Hall & Mayor Dinkins/Sygma/A. Tannenbaum; Mario Cuomo/Office of the Governor of New York; School Children/Black Star/James Suger; Firefighter/Stock Boston/Martin Rogers; **Chapter 21** Capitol (tall one on left)/State of Nebraska/Nebraska Land Magazine; Flag and Seal/State of Nebraska/Nebraska Land Magazine; Flag/State of Illinois; Flag/State of Alaska; State office building/State of Alaska; Constitution and Capitol Building/State of Texas; Texas Flag/Austin American

(Acknowledgments continued following index)

CONTENTS IN BRIEF

Preface viii

▍UNIT ONE
Foundations of American Democracy 1

Chapter 1
Government and the People—The Global
 Connection 2

Chapter 2
Forging the American Dream 22

Chapter 3
The Constitution 52

Chapter 4
Our System of Federalism 74

▍UNIT TWO
The Rights of All Citizens 100

Chapter 5
Personal Freedoms 102

Chapter 6
Equality Under the Law 128

▍UNIT THREE
The Politics of Democracy 154

Chapter 7
Citizenship: Privileges and Responsibilities 156

Chapter 8
Political Parties 180

Chapter 9
Public Opinion and Interest Groups 206

Chapter 10
Campaigns, Elections, and the Media 232

Chapter 11
Voters and Voting Behavior 260

▍UNIT FOUR
The Federal Legislative Branch 280

Chapter 12
The Organization of Congress 282

Chapter 13
The Powers of Congress 312

Chapter 14
How Congress Makes Laws 332

UNIT FIVE
The Federal Executive Branch 352

Chapter 15
The Presidency 354

Chapter 16
The President at Work 376

Chapter 17
The Bureaucracy in Action 400

UNIT SIX
The Federal Judicial Branch 428

Chapter 18
The Federal Courts 430

UNIT SEVEN
American Policy in a Changing World 456

Chapter 19
Economic Policy, Poverty, and the Environment 458

Chapter 20
Defense and Foreign Policy 488

UNIT EIGHT
State and Local Governments 518

Chapter 21
State Constitutions and Legislative Processes 520

Chapter 22
Governors and State Administrators 544

Chapter 23
The State Courts 562

Chapter 24
Local Government 582

Chapter 25
Paying for State and Local Government 606

UNIT NINE
Other Nations 624

Chapter 26
Comparing Governments and Economic Systems 626

The Resource Center 653

Glossary 743

Index 763

PREFACE

You are fortunate to be living in one of the most exciting and challenging periods in history. Political, social, technological, and economic changes are occurring at a faster pace than ever before. Recent events have dramatically altered the face of Europe, Asia, and the world. The empire once called the Soviet Union no longer exists. It has been replaced by a collection of independent republics, some only loosely tied together. Today, news stories are almost instantaneously broadcast around the world, and you can buy computing power in a laptop computer that only 20 years ago would have required equipment that filled an entire room. The impact of these changes has been immediate and wide-ranging, and will undoubtedly have long-lasting effects.

The book you hold in your hands, WEST'S AMERICAN GOVERNMENT, is new. It has been developed to help you understand the fast-changing world in which we all live. It is not just a book of facts, although facts are important. It is not a book of current events, although many of them are used as examples. Rather, you are beginning to read a book that examines the *process* of government and politics. Current events may not remain current for long, but the political process in this country changes very slowly. An understanding of the American political system will serve you well as a point of reference as you strive to understand what is happening elsewhere in the world.

Being informed allows you to enjoy the privileges and understand the responsibilities of citizenship. Knowledge of the Constitution, understanding of how our governmental institutions and the American political system function, and awareness of today's issues are necessary in order for you to make the most of your role as a participant in our living democracy.

In addition to learning about American government and politics, it is also important for you to understand the underlying themes and ideas that are an important part of our American heritage. When the founders, in the Declaration of Independence, stated that all people are created equal and all have the right to life, liberty, and the pursuit of happiness, they were stating the underlying ideals of the American dream. How this dream has changed, been shaped, and expanded is an important theme of this text. Over the course of history, the American dream was forged out of the experiences and hopes of a wide diversity of ethnic groups and cultures. In recent years, this cultural diversity has even been further expanded as America has welcomed many new groups. Incorporating this expanded cultural diversity into American life and making sure that all people have a chance to share the American dream is a challenge for the America of today and certainly of tomorrow.

CONTENTS

Preface viii

UNIT ONE
Foundations of American Democracy 1

Chapter 1
Government and the People—The Global Connection 2

Chapter Objectives 2
Introduction 3
SECTION 1. **The Meaning of Politics and Government 3**
  Government in Action: The French Revolution 9
SECTION 2. **How Do Governments Differ from One Another? 10**
  Citizenship Skills and Responsibilities: The Duties of Citizenship 14
SECTION 3. **The Challenge of Interdependence 15**
  Building Social Studies Skills: Using the Features of This Textbook 16
  Challenge to the American Dream: Do Our Representatives Represent Too Many People? 18
Chapter Review 19

Chapter 2
Forging the American Dream 22

Chapter Objectives 22
Introduction 23
SECTION 1. **European Origins of Our Governmental System 23**
SECTION 2. **The First British Settlements 26**
SECTION 3. **The Colonies Rebel 29**
  Government in Action: The Founding Mothers 33
SECTION 4. **The Articles of Confederation 34**
  Building Social Studies Skills: Using Government Publications 35
  Citizenship Skills and Responsibilities: Making Decisions 38
SECTION 5. **Creating the Constitution 39**
  Architect of the American Dream: George Washington 42
SECTION 6. **Ratifying the Constitution 44**
  Challenge to the American Dream: Holding Another Constitutional Convention 48
Chapter Review 49

Chapter 3
The Constitution 52

Chapter Objectives 52
Introduction 53
SECTION 1. **The Structure of Our Constitution 53**
SECTION 2. **The Constitution's Major Principles of Government 56**
  Government in Action: *Marbury* v. *Madison* (1803) 60
SECTION 3. **The Bill of Rights 61**
  Government in Action: The Bill of Rights Was Not a Foregone Conclusion 62
SECTION 4. **The Formal Process of Amending the Constitution 63**
  Government in Action: Elizabeth Cady Stanton 64
  Citizenship Skills and Responsibilities: Compromise and Negotiation 66
SECTION 5. **The Informal Amending Process 67**
  Building Social Studies Skills: Analyzing Primary Sources 69
  Challenge to the American Dream: The Equal Rights Amendment 71
Chapter Review 72

Chapter 4
Our System of Federalism 74

Chapter Objectives 74
Introduction 75
SECTION 1. **Three Basic Types of Governmental Systems 76**
SECTION 2. **Dividing Governmental Power 78**
  Building Social Studies Skills: Analyzing Political Cartoons 79
  Government in Action: The Family 82
SECTION 3. **The Relations Among the States 85**
  Citizenship Skills and Responsibilities: Community Action Project—Helping the Hungry 88
SECTION 4. **Who Shall Reign Supreme? 89**
  Government in Action: The Sagebrush Rebellion 90
SECTION 5. **The Changing Face of American Federalism 94**
  Challenge to the American Dream: Snowbelt versus Sunbelt 97
Chapter Review 98

■ UNIT TWO
The Rights of All Citizens 100

Chapter 5
Personal Freedoms 102

Chapter Objectives 102
Introduction 103
SECTION 1. **Our System of Personal Freedoms 103**
  Citizenship Skills and Responsibilities: Responsibilities of Citizens 107
SECTION 2. **Freedom of Religion 108**
  Government in Action: Churches and Taxes 111
SECTION 3. **Freedom of Speech 113**
  Government in Action: The Right to Beg? 114
SECTION 4. **Freedom of Speech: The Press 116**
  Building Social Studies Skills: Reading a Newspaper Article Critically 119
SECTION 5. **Freedom of Assembly and Petition 122**
  Challenge to the American Dream: Burning an American Symbol 124
Chapter Review 125

Chapter 6
Equality Under the Law 128

Chapter Objectives 128
Introduction 129
SECTION 1. **Due Process of the Law 129**

SECTION 2. **Rights of the Accused: Searching and Wiretapping 131**
  Government in Action: New Technology, New Questions 133
SECTION 3. **Rights of the Accused: A Fair Trial 134**
  Government in Action: Law in Other Cultures 138
SECTION 4. **Equal Protection Under the Law 139**
  Architect of the American Dream: Martin Luther King, Jr. 140
  Building Social Studies Skills: Identifying Your Own Values and Biases 145
  Government in Action: Rosa Parks 146
SECTION 5. **New Challenges 148**
  Citizenship Skills and Responsibilities: Equal Access for the Differently Abled 149
  Challenge to the American Dream: Does Affirmative Action Result in Reverse Discrimination? 151
Chapter Review 152

■ UNIT THREE
The Politics of Democracy 154

Chapter 7
Citizenship: Privileges and Responsibilities 156

Chapter Objectives 156
Introduction 157

SECTION 1. Who is a Citizen? 157
SECTION 2. Immigration and the Non-Citizen 161
  Government in Action: Taking the Census 162
  Government in Action: Cesar Chávez 165
  Building Social Studies Skills: Reading Bar
    Graphs 168
**SECTION 3. Citizenship Rights and
  Responsibilities 170**
SECTION 4. Tolerance and Open-mindedness 174
  Citizenship Skills and Responsibilities: Applying for
    a Government Job 175
  Challenge to the American Dream: Immigrants,
    American Jobs, and Wages 177
Chapter Review 178

Chapter 8
Political Parties 180

Chapter Objectives 180
Introduction 181
**SECTION 1. The Meaning and Roles of Political
  Parties 181**
  Government in Action: Jesse Jackson 185
  Citizenship Skills and Responsibilities: Joining a
    Political Party 188
**SECTION 2. The Beginning of the Two-Party
  Tradition 190**
  Building Social Studies Skills: Interpreting
    Tables 194
**SECTION 3. Third Parties: Their Impact on
  American Politics 196**
SECTION 4. The Structure of Political Parties 199
  Government in Action: Machine Politics 200
  Challenge to the American Dream: Is the Party
    Over? 202
Chapter Review 203

Chapter 9
Public Opinion and Interest Groups 206

Chapter Objectives 206
Introduction 207
**SECTION 1. Definition and Measurement of Public
  Opinion 207**
  Citizenship Skills and Responsibilities: Writing a
    Letter to the Editor 209
SECTION 2. Factors that Affect Public Opinion 210
  Building Social Studies Skills: How to Read a Public
    Opinion Poll 213
SECTION 3. Categorizing Political Attitudes 214
SECTION 4. Interest Groups 217

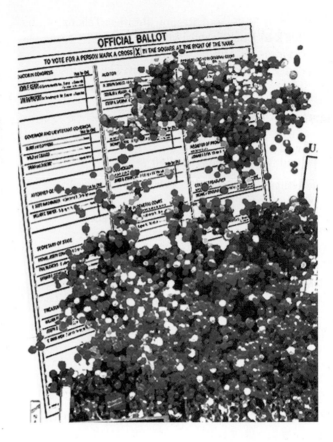

  Government in Action: Ralph Nader: Consumer
    Activist 222
SECTION 5. How Groups Try to Shape Policy 223
  Government in Action: Mothers Against Drunk
    Driving (MADD) 226
  Challenge to the American Dream: Can Lobbying
    Endanger Democracy? 229
Chapter Review 230

Chapter 10
Campaigns, Elections, and the Media 232

Chapter Objectives 232
Introduction 233
SECTION 1. Step One: The Nomination 233
SECTION 2. The Campaign 238
  Government in Action: Criticisms of the Mass Media
    in Campaigns 241
**SECTION 3. The Structure of American
  Elections 244**
**SECTION 4. The Role of the Media in Campaigns
  and Elections 249**
  Building Social Studies Skills: Evaluating Political
    Commercials 250

Citizenship Skills and Responsibilities: Talking Back to Your Television 252

Government in Action: Connie Chung 254

Challenge to the American Dream: The Overwhelming Importance of Campaign Money 257

Chapter Review 257

Chapter 11
Voters and Voting Behavior 260

Chapter Objectives 260
Introduction 261
SECTION 1. History of Voting and Current Requirements 261
Architect of The American Dream: Susan B. Anthony 264
SECTION 2. More Suffrage, Less Participation 268
Government in Action: Voting by Mail 270
Citizenship Skills and Responsibilities: Voting 272
SECTION 3. Why People Vote as They Do 273
Building Social Studies Skills: Analyzing a Photograph 275
Challenge to the American Dream: An Indifferent Electorate 277
Chapter Review 277

Challenge to the American Dream: Limiting Terms Served in Congress 308

Chapter Review 309

Chapter 13
The Powers of Congress 312

Chapter Objectives 312
Introduction 313
SECTION 1. Legislative Powers 313
Building Social Studies Skills: Cause and Effect versus Correlation 318
Government in Action: Who Controls the Federal Budget? 320
SECTION 2. Nonlegislative Powers 321
Government in Action: Congressman Bill Archer 323
Citizenship Skills and Responsibilities: How to Communicate With Members of Congress 325
Government in Action: Daniel Ken Inouye 327
Challenge to the American Dream: Limits on the Congressional Power to Investigate 329
Chapter Review 330

UNIT FOUR
The Federal Legislative Branch 280

Chapter 12
The Organization of Congress 282

Chapter Objectives 282
Introduction 283
SECTION 1. Creation and Evolution of Congress 283
Building Social Studies Skills: Using a Political Map 288
SECTION 2. House and Senate Organization 289
Government in Action: Senator Bob Dole 290
SECTION 3. Members of Congress and Their Responsibilities 293
Government in Action: Patricia Schroeder 295
Citizenship Skills and Responsibilities: How to Find Out What's Going On in Congress 298
SECTION 4. The Structure of Congress 299
Government in Action: The Politics of Congressional Committees 304

Chapter 14
How Congress Makes Laws 332

Chapter Objectives 332
Introduction 333
SECTION 1. Congress Begins Its Work 333
  Government in Action: Ileana Ros-Lehtinen 336
  Government in Action: Many Laws Proposed, Few
    Passed 338
SECTION 2. How a Bill Becomes a Law 340
  Government in Action: Senator Lloyd Bentsen 341
  Citizenship Skills and Responsibilities: Locating and
    Interpreting Congressional Voting Records 344
SECTION 3. The Final Stages 347
  Building Social Studies Skills: Analyzing
    Information 348
  Challenge to the American Dream: Do Members of
    Congress Get the Wrong Signals? 349
Chapter Review 350

UNIT FIVE
The Federal Executive Branch 352

Chapter 15
The Presidency 354

Chapter Objectives 354
Introduction 355
SECTION 1. The Office of President 355
  Architect of the American Dream: Abraham
    Lincoln 360
  Building Social Studies Skills: Analyzing a Political
    Debate 362
SECTION 2. The Office of Vice President 363
  Citizenship Skills and Responsibilities: Discovering
    the Political You 364
SECTION 3. The Cabinet 365
  Government in Action: The Conflicting Roles of
    Cabinet Heads 368
SECTION 4. The Executive Office of the
    President 369
  Challenge to the American Dream: Can the Vice
    President Handle the Job? 373
Chapter Review 374

Chapter 16
The President at Work 376

Chapter Objectives 376
Introduction 377
SECTION 1. Presidential Powers 377

Building Social Studies Skills: Reading
    Biographies 381
SECTION 2. The Many Presidential Roles 382
  Government in Action: President George Bush 384
  Government in Action: The Line-Item Veto 392
SECTION 3. Checks on the President's Powers 394
  Citizenship Skills and Responsibilities: How to
    Contact the President 395
  Challenge to the American Dream: The Abuse of
    Presidential Power 397
Chapter Review 398

Chapter 17
The Bureaucracy in Action 400

Chapter Objectives 400
Introduction 401
SECTION 1. Bureaucracy: Its Nature and Size 401
  Building Social Studies Skills: Reading an
    Organization Chart 403
SECTION 2. The Executive Departments 405
  Government in Action: Your Rights as an
    Employee 408
SECTION 3. Independent Agencies and Government
    Corporations 410
  Government in Action: Secretary of Agriculture
    Edward Madigan 411
  Citizenship Skills and Responsibilities: Using the
    Freedom of Information Act 412

Government in Action: Deregulation and Re-
  regulation 417
SECTION 4. How the Civil Service Works 420
SECTION 5. Bureaucrats as Policymakers 423
  Challenge to the American Dream: Minorities and
  Women in Civil Service 425
Chapter Review 425

UNIT SIX
The Federal Judicial Branch 428

Chapter 18
The Federal Courts 430

Chapter Objectives 430
Introduction 431
SECTION 1. Law and Where It Comes From 431
  Government in Action: Gideon v. Wainwright 433
  Citizenship Skills and Responsibilities: Serving on a
  Jury 434
SECTION 2. The Federal Court System 436
  Architect of the American Dream: John
  Marshall 440
SECTION 3. How Cases Reach the Supreme
  Court 442

Government in Action: Students and the First
  Amendment 444
Government in Action: Sandra Day O'Connor 446
SECTION 4. Supreme Court—Appointments and
  Ideology 447
SECTION 5. Judicial Activism and Judicial
  Restraint 450
  Building Social Studies Skills: Distinguishing
  Between Fact and Opinion 451
  Challenge to the American Dream: Has the Federal
  Judiciary Become Too Conservative? 453
Chapter Review 453

UNIT SEVEN
American Policy in a Changing
World 456

Chapter 19
Economic Policy, Poverty, and the Environment 458

Chapter Objectives 458
Introduction 459
SECTION 1. Monetary and Fiscal Policy 459
  Architect of the American Dream: Franklin Delano
  Roosevelt 462
  Government in Action: Making Sense of Dollars and
  Cents 465
  Building Social Studies Skills: Reading Line
  Graphs 468
SECTION 2. Systems of Taxation 469
SECTION 3. The Government's Attempt at
  Eliminating Poverty 474
  Government in Action: Antonia Coello Novello 478
SECTION 4. Cleaning Up the Environment 479
  Citizenship Skills and Responsibilities: How to Be a
  Waste-Conscious Consumer 482
  Challenge to the American Dream: Can the
  Government Save Our Banking System? 485
Chapter Review 486

Chapter 20
Defense and Foreign Policy 488

Chapter Objectives 488
Introduction 489
SECTION 1. The Development of Our Foreign
  Policy 489
  Building Social Studies Skills: How to Watch TV
  News 494

SECTION 2. Foreign Policy Makers 495
   Citizenship Skills and Responsibilities: How to Influence American Foreign Policy 498
SECTION 3. The Departments of State and Defense 500
   Government in Action: General Colin Powell 502
SECTION 4. American Foreign Policy Goals and the Methods Used to Achieve Them 505
   Government in Action: Nelson Mandela 509
SECTION 5. The United Nations 510
   Challenge to the American Dream: Terrorism 514
Chapter Review 515

UNIT EIGHT
State and Local Governments 518

Chapter 21
State Constitutions and Legislative Processes 520

Chapter Objectives 520
Introduction 521
SECTION 1. The U.S. Constitution and the State Constitutions 521

   Building Social Studies Skills: Reading Maps for Economic Information 527
SECTION 2. The State Legislative Process 528
   Citizenship Skills and Responsibilities: Witnessing a Crime 531
SECTION 3. State Legislators 532
   Government in Action: The ''Congressionalization'' of State Legislatures 533
SECTION 4. How the Legislature Is Organized 536
SECTION 5. How a State Bill Becomes Law 538
SECTION 6. Direct Democracy 540
   Challenge to the American Dream: Limiting Lengthy Stays in the State Legislature 541
Chapter Review 542

Chapter 22
Governors and State Administrators 544

Chapter Objectives 544
Introduction 545
SECTION 1. The Modern Governor 545
SECTION 2. The Governor's Many Roles 548
   Citizenship Skills and Responsibilities: Responsible Driving and Traffic-Law Violations 549
SECTION 3. The Powers of the Governor 550
   Building Social Studies Skills: Improving Your Memory 555
SECTION 4. Other State Administrators 556
   Challenge to the American Dream: Off-Year Election of Governors 559
Chapter Review 560

Chapter 23
The State Courts 562

Chapter Objectives 562
Introduction 563
SECTION 1. A Typical State Court System 563
SECTION 2. How Judges Are Selected 565
   Citizenship Skills and Responsibilities: The Small Claims Court 566
   Building Social Studies Skills: Understanding Contracts 570
SECTION 3. Protection of Life and Property 571
   Government in Action: Protecting the Rights of Minors 572
SECTION 4. Prosecuting Offenders 575
SECTION 5. Sentencing and Prisons 577
   Challenge to the American Dream: The Question of Capital Punishment 579
Chapter Review 579

Chapter 24
Local Government 582

Chapter Objectives 582
Introduction 583
**SECTION 1. The Legality and Functions of Local
    Government 583**
  Citizenship Skills and Responsibilities: Recycling in
      Your Community 588
SECTION 2. How Local Governments Operate 590
  Government in Action: Waging the War on
      Drugs 596
SECTION 3. How Municipalities are Governed 597
  Building Social Studies Skills: Figuring and Using
      Percentages 601
  Challenge to the American Dream: Can
      Overlapping Governmental Units Be
      Avoided? 603
Chapter Review 604

Chapter 25
Paying for State and Local Government 606

Chapter Objectives 606
Introduction 607
**SECTION 1. Limitations on State and Local
    Taxation 607**
**SECTION 2. Sources of State and Local
    Revenues 609**
  Government in Action: State-Run Lotteries on the
      Rise 612
  Citizenship Skills and Responsibilities: Organizing
      for Community Action 614
SECTION 3. Money from Uncle Sam 615
  Building Social Studies Skills: Reading Statistical
      Tables 618
**SECTION 4. State and Local Government
    Spending 619**
  Challenge to the American Dream: Cities and States
      in Need 621
Chapter Review 622

UNIT NINE

Other Nations 624

Chapter 26
Comparing Governments and Economic Systems 626

Chapter Objectives 626
Introduction 627
SECTION 1. Great Britain 627
SECTION 2. France 631
SECTION 3. Japan 634
  Citizenship Skills and Responsibilities: How to
      Support Human Rights 637
SECTION 4. Types of Economic Systems 638
**SECTION 5. Characteristics of the American
    Economy 641**
  Building Social Studies Skills: Understanding Mean
      and Median 642
**SECTION 6. Converging Political and Economic
    Systems 645**
  Government in Action: Technology versus
      Totalitarianism? 646
  Challenge to the American Dream: Can We Ever
      Solve the World's Problems? 649
Chapter Review 650

THE RESOURCE CENTER

Original Source Documents 654

Constitution of the United States of America 654
The Bill of Rights 665
The Magna Carta (1215) 672
Mayflower Compact (1620) 674
Declaration of Independence (1776) 675
Articles of Confederation (1781–1789) 677
Federalist Papers #10 and #51 (1787/1788) 681
Anti-Federalist Writings (1787–1788) 687
Monroe Doctrine (1823) 687
Seneca Falls Declaration (1848) 689
Emancipation Proclamation (1862) 689
Pledge of Allegiance (1892) 690
The American's Creed (1917) 691
Brown v. Board of Education of Topeka (1954) 691
The Preamble to the Charter of the United Nations 692

Annotated Table of Legal Cases 692

How to Read Legal Case Citations and Find Court
    Decisions 692
Table of Court Cases 693

Extended Case Studies 701

Immigration Reform and Control Act of 1986 and
    Amnesty 701
The AIDS Epidemic 703
The War on Drugs 705
Exxon Valdez 707

**Presidents and Vice Presidents of the United
States 710**

**Supreme Court Chief Justices and Associate Justices
Since 1789 721**

State Atlas 726

U.S. and World Maps 737

Map of the United States 738

Map of the World 740

Glossary 743

Index 763

FEATURES

ARCHITECT OF THE AMERICAN DREAM

George Washington 42

Martin Luther King, Jr. 140

Susan B. Anthony 264

Abraham Lincoln 360

John Marshall 440

Franklin Delano Roosevelt 462

GOVERNMENT IN ACTION

The French Revolution 9

The Founding Mothers 33

Marbury v. *Madison* (1803) 60

The Bill of Rights Was Not a Foregone Conclusion 62

Elizabeth Cady Stanton 64

The Family 82

The Sagebrush Rebellion 90

Churches and Taxes 111

The Right to Beg? 114

New Technology, New Questions 133

Law in Other Cultures 138

Rosa Parks 146

Taking the Census 162

Cesar Chávez 165

Jesse Jackson 185

Machine Politics 200

Ralph Nader: Consumer Activist 222

Mothers Against Drunk Driving (MADD) 226

Criticisms of the Mass Media in Campaigns 241

Connie Chung 254

Voting by Mail 270

Senator Bob Dole 290

Patricia Schroeder 295

The Politics of Congressional Committees 304

Who Controls the Federal Budget? 320

Congressman Bill Archer 323

Daniel Ken Inouye 327

Ileana Ros-Lehtinen 336

Many Laws Proposed, Few Passed 338

Senator Lloyd Bentsen 341

The Conflicting Roles of Cabinet Heads 368

President George Bush 384

The Line-Item Veto 392

Your Rights as an Employee 408

Secretary of Agriculture Edward Madigan 411

Deregulation and Re-regulation 417

Gideon v. *Wainwright* 433

Students and the First Amendment 444

Sandra Day O'Connor 446

Making Sense of Dollars and Cents 465

Antonia Coello Novello 478

Colin Powell 502

Nelson Mandela 509

The ''Congressionalization'' of State Legislatures 533

Protecting the Rights of Minors 572

Waging the War on Drugs 596

State-Run Lotteries on the Rise 612

Technology versus Totalitarianism? 646

CITIZENSHIP SKILLS AND RESPONSIBILITIES

The Duties of Citizenship 14

Making Decisions 38

Compromise and Negotiation 66

Community Action Project—Helping the Hungry 88

Responsibilities of Citizens 107

Equal Access for the Differently Abled 149

Applying for a Government Job 175

Joining a Political Party 188

Writing a Letter to the Editor 209

Talking Back to Your Television 252

Voting 272

How to Find Out What's Going On in Congress 298

How to Communicate With Members of Congress 325

Locating and Interpreting Congressional Voting Records 344

Discovering the Political You 364

How to Contact the President 395

Using the Freedom of Information Act 412

Serving on a Jury 434

How to Be a Waste-Conscious Consumer 482

How to Influence American Foreign Policy 498

Witnessing a Crime 531

Responsible Driving and Traffic-Law Violations 549

The Small Claims Court 566

Recycling in Your Community 588

Organizing for Community Action 614

How to Support Human Rights 637

BUILDING SOCIAL STUDIES SKILLS

Using the Features of This Textbook 16

Using Government Publications 35

Analyzing Primary Sources 69

Analyzing Political Cartoons 79

Reading a Newspaper Article Critically 119

Identifying Your Own Values and Biases 145

Reading Bar Graphs 168

Interpreting Tables 194

How to Read a Public Opinion Poll 213

Evaluating Political Commercials 250

Analyzing a Photograph 275

Using a Political Map 288

Cause and Effect versus Correlation 318

Analyzing Information 348

Analyzing a Political Debate 362

Reading Biographies 381

Reading an Organization Chart 403

Distinguishing Between Fact and Opinion 451

Reading Line Graphs 468

How to Watch TV News 494

Reading Maps for Economic Information 527

Improving Your Memory 555

Understanding Contracts 570

Figuring and Using Percentages 601

Reading Statistical Tables 618

Understanding Mean and Median 642

CHALLENGE TO THE AMERICAN DREAM

Do Our Representatives Represent Too Many People? 18

Holding Another Constitutional Convention 48

The Equal Rights Amendment 71

Snowbelt versus Sunbelt 97

CHALLENGE TO THE AMERICAN DREAM—Continued

Burning an American Symbol 124

Does Affirmative Action Result in Reverse Discrimination? 151

Immigrants, American Jobs, and Wages 177

Is the Party Over? 202

Can Lobbying Endanger Democracy? 229

The Overwhelming Importance of Campaign Money 257

An Indifferent Electorate 277

Limiting Terms Served in Congress 308

Limits on the Congressional Power to Investigate 329

Do Members of Congress Get the Wrong Signals? 349

Can the Vice President Handle the Job? 373

The Abuse of Presidential Power 397

Minorities and Women in Civil Service 425

Has the Federal Judiciary Become Too Conservative? 453

Can the Government Save Our Banking System? 485

Terrorism 514

Limiting Lengthy Stays in the State Legislature 541

Off-Year Election of Governors 559

The Question of Capital Punishment 579

Can Overlapping Governmental Units Be Avoided? 603

Cities and States in Need 621

Can We Ever Solve the World's Problems? 649

CHARTS, TABLES, GRAPHS, AND MAPS

Figure 1–1. Four Theories on the Origin of Government 10

Figure 1–2. Forms of Government 13

Figure 2–1. Roanoke Island 26

Figure 2–2. The Thirteen Colonies 28

Figure 2–3. American Government Under the Articles of Confederation 36

Figure 2–4. Weaknesses in the Articles of Confederation 37

Figure 2–5. Ratification of the Constitution 45

Figure 2–6. The Route to Enduring Self-Rule 47

Figure 3–1. Structure of the U.S. Constitution 54

Figure 3–2. Checks and Balances Among the Branches of Government 58

Figure 3–3. Process of Amending the Constitution 65

Figure 4–1. Governmental Units in the United States Today 75

Figure 4–2. The Flow of Power in Three Systems of Government 77

Figure 4–3. Powers Granted by the Constitution 81

Figure 4–4. Powers Denied by the Constitution 84

Federal Ownership of Land in the United States 91*

Population Changes in Selected States, 1950–1990 97*

Figure 5–1. The Bill of Rights 105

Figure 6–1. In the Words of the Court 147

Figure 7–1. How Non-Citizens Become Naturalized Citizens of the United States 160

U.S. Households by Type, 1990 162*

U.S. Cities with Greatest Populations, 1990 163*

Figure 7–2. Highlights of the 1990 Immigration Act 167

Immigration to the United States, 1821–1990 168*

U.S. Population by Age, 1960–1990 169*

Figure 7–3. Incorporating the Bill of Rights into the Fourteenth Amendment 171

Figure 8–1. Party Affiliation by Group—1991 189

Figure 8–2. Evolution of the Major American Political Parties and Splinter Groups 192

Vote by Groups in Presidential Elections, 1960–1992 194*

Political Party Identification, 1937–1991 202*

Figure 9–1. The Political Spectrum 216

Figure 9–2. Profiles of Selected Interest Groups 219

Figure 10–1. Primary Election Ballot 236

Figure 10–2. Typical Presidential Campaign Organization 239

Figure 10–3. Congressional Campaign Spending 1983–1990 242

Figure 10–4. Top 15 PAC Contributions to Congressional Candidates (January 1, 1989–June 30, 1990) 243

Figure 10–5. Electoral Votes for President 1992 248

Cost of Running a Half-Minute Political Commercial During a Highly Rated Prime Time Television Program in Selected Markets 251*

Figure 11–1. Extension of the Right to Vote 263

Figure 11–2. African-American Voter Registration Before and After the Voting Rights Act of 1965 267

Figure 12–1. Reapportionment of House Seats Following the 1990 Census 286

Changes in State Populations, 1980–1990 288*

Figure 12–2. Differences Between the House and the Senate 292

Figure 12–3. Profile of the 103rd Congress 293

Figure 12–4. Occupations of the Members of the 103rd Congress 294

Figure 12–5. Standing Committees in Congress 303

Figure 12–6. Typical Staff of a Member of Congress 306

Figure 13–1. Powers Granted to Congress by Article 1, Section 8, of the Constitution 319

Figure 14–1. Floor Plan of the U.S. Capitol 335

Figure 14–2. Selected Bills From the 102nd Congress 339

Figure 14–3. How a Bill Becomes a Law 346

Figure 15–1. Line of Succession to the Presidency of the United States 359

Figure 15–2. Executive Office of the President 370

Figure 16–1. Media Evaluations of the Bush Administration During 1990 380

Figure 16–2. Presidential Vetoes 390

Figure 16–3. Roles of the President 393

Santa Barbara County Association of Governments 403*

---

*Unnumbered illustrations appearing in boxed features.

CHARTS, TABLES, GRAPHS, AND MAPS—Continued

Figure 17–1. Organization of the Federal Government 404

Figure 17–2. Executive Departments 406

Sample Letter for Requesting Information from an Executive Department or Agency*

Figure 17–3. Selected Independent Executive Agencies 414

Figure 17–4. Selected Independent Regulatory Agencies 416

Figure 17–5. Selected Government Corporations 419

Figure 17 6. General Schedule (GS) Ratings and Their Respective Minimum Salaries, 1992 422

Figure 18–1. The Federal Court System 437

Figure 18–2. U.S. District Courts and U.S. Circuit Courts 438

Hazelwood School District v. Cathy Kuhlmeier 445*

Figure 18–3. Profile of Supreme Court Justices to 1992 449

Figure 18–4. Pay Scale for Federal Judges 450

Figure 19–1. Brief History of our Nation's Banking and Monetary Policies 460

Figure 19–2. Federal Reserve System Districts 461

Figure 19–3. Public Debt of the Federal Government 1940–1993 467

U.S. Public Debt Held by Foreigners 468*

Figure 19–4. Proportional Tax System 470

Figure 19–5. Progressive Tax System 470

Figure 19–6. Major Taxes 471

Figure 19–7. Federal Revenues Accounted for by Personal Income Taxes, 1940–1993 (est.) 472

Figure 19–8. Tax Burdens in Selected Countries 473

Figure 19–9. Major Federal Environmental Legislation 480

Figure 20–1. National Defense Spending as a Percentage of Total Outlays, 1940–1996 (est.) 504

Figure 20–2. National Outlays for Foreign Aid, 1962–1996 (est.) 507

Figure 20–3. The United Nations System 512

Figure 21–1. General Information on State Constitutions 524

Figure 21–2. Provisions for Calling State Constitutional Conventions 526

Estimated Total Tax Bill for Middle-Class Families in the 50 States, 1991 527*

Figure 21–3. Proposed 69th Assembly District in California 532

Figure 21–4. Characteristics of State Legislatures 534

Figure 21–5. How a State Bill Becomes a Law 539

Figure 22–1. Typical State Executive Branch 551

Figure 23–1. Typical State Court System 563

Characteristics of Small Claims Courts in Selected States 567*

Figure 23–2. Selection of State Judges 569

Juvenile Justice System 573*

Figure 24–1. Map of Washington, D.C. 586

Figure 24–2. Special Districts According to Function 595

Figure 24–3. Commission Plan of Municipal Government 598

Figure 24–4. Council-Manager Plan of Municipal Government 599

Figure 24–5. Strong Mayor-Council Plan 600

Property Stolen and Recovered 601*

Figure 24–6. Weak Mayor-Council Plan 602

Figure 25–1. The Importance of Taxes at the State and Local Levels 610

Lottery Ticket Sales 612*

Figure 25–2. Declining Federal Contribution to State and Local Governments 616

Population in Coastal Areas, 1940–1990 618*

Figure 25–3. State Expenditures 619

Figure 25–4. Local Expenditures 620

Figure 26–1. Circular Flow of Economic Activity in the Market 639

Unemployment Rates in Selected Countries, 1990 643*

WEST'S
AMERICAN
GOVERNMENT *Updated Edition*

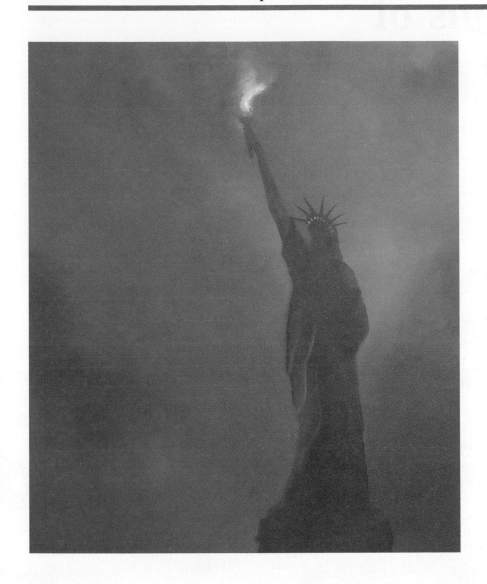

UNIT ONE

Foundations of American Democracy

UNIT CONTENTS

- *Chapter 1* Government and the People–The Global Connection
  - *Chapter 2* Forging the American Dream
    - *Chapter 3* The Constitution
      - *Chapter 4* Our System of Federalism

CHAPTER 1

Government and the People— The Global Connection

CHAPTER OBJECTIVES

To learn and understand

- The meaning of politics and government and the purposes that government serves.
- The different types of government and the main principles of democracy.
- The challenge of interdependence with other nations.

Keynote

"But what is government itself, but the greatest of all reflections on human nature? If men were angels, no government would be necessary."

——— **James Madison**
(1751–1836) Fourth President of the
United States

INTRODUCTION

Even at the time James Madison made the above statement over 200 years ago, he was observing what had been apparent for many centuries. People need an organized form of government and a set of rules by which to live. None of us is an angel. As Madison recognized, human nature requires us to have a form of government.

If someone said that you must have rules in order to be free, what would you say? You might disagree. But imagine for a moment what life might be like if there were no government. Consider this news story of an *imaginary* town called Prosperville that grew up almost overnight after the discovery of gold in the early 1900s:

> Many Prosperville citizens have become virtual prisoners in their own homes. Because there are no courts of law in Prosperville, land and property ownership disputes have become impossible to settle. People have begun to take over one another's land by force. Last week there were seven shootings over such disputes. Dishonest people have moved into town; robberies and violent crimes are committed against citizens almost every day. There is no police force to protect the citizens, so people are becoming frightened to walk in the streets. They have begun to carry weapons. Suspected criminals are being lynched by groups of vigilantes. Through fear and misunderstandings, many innocent people have been hanged. There are no schools for the children of Prosperville, and no postal service for its citizens. Because there are no child labor laws, the owners of some of the gold mines are working the children of the poorer families for fourteen hours a day, at ten cents an hour. Because there is no public health officer, plague is spreading throughout the town. There are rumors that a band of desperadoes is riding toward Prosperville to take it over. One citizen, who owns most of the gold mines, has decided to form his own army and name himself mayor. He wants to outlaw all churches except his own and impose a tax on all citizens to build himself a mansion. He has spies in the town working for

him to seek out his opponents. People have become suspicious of one another; they have stopped caring about what happens to anyone but themselves.

As you can see from the story of Prosperville, life without government would be chaotic. In fact, government is one of humanity's oldest and most universal institutions. History records very few societies that have existed with no government. In order to live together, people need some form of authority and organization. Thus, as the earliest societies developed, so did the need for government.

SECTION 1

The Meaning of Politics and Government

Preview Questions

- What purposes does government serve?
- What is a nation?
- What are the characteristics of a nation?
- What are the theories regarding the origins of the state?

Politics means many things to many people. To some, politics is an expensive and extravagant game played at election time in Washington, D.C., in state capitols, and in city halls. To others, politics involves all the tactics and maneuvers carried out by the president and Congress. Most formal definitions of politics begin with the notion of **social conflict**—(the idea that people in a society disagree over beliefs, values, and what the society's priorities should be) It also includes the idea that conflicts will arise over how the society should use its scarce resources. This conflict is seen as inevitable and

3

natural in any social system. It is not inherently bad. In fact, the process of resolving these conflicts provides good opportunities for positive change.

Political scientist Harold D. Laswell offered a brief but useful definition of **politics:** the process that determines ''who gets what, when, and how'' in a society. Another political scientist, David Easton, defines politics as ''the authoritative allocation of values.'' Both definitions imply that a set of procedures is needed to resolve the questions of who receives which benefits from society. These benefits may include wealth, status, health care, and higher education. Politics, in this case, encompasses all the activities involved in that process.

There are also many different notions about the meaning of government. A political scientist would define **government** as the individuals and processes that make society's rules about who gets what, and that possess the power and authority to enforce those rules. You might view government as a distant group of politicians who campaign loudly for reelection in your hometown and who debate issues in Washington, D.C. A citizen who has broken the law might view government as an interference, while another elderly citizen might view government as a ''rescuer'' that provides public services such as transportation, health care, and protection from crime in her neighborhood. Perhaps the best way to un-

derstand both politics and government is by understanding how they affect you.

Why Study Government and Politics?

One student of politics maintained that to most Americans politics is ''a sideshow on the circus of life.'' Generally, thinking about government and politics ranks well below family, work, romance, and many other activities. Most of us, however, will at some time in our lives enter the political world. People usually enter that world through many different forms of **political participation.** Voting, the most common form, is only one among many. Discussing politics or watching news programs about the government are other forms.

More and more people with common interests are joining together to participate in politics because they see how government affects their own interests. Blacks, whites, Hispanics, women, and the elderly all advocate policies concerning equality in America. Consumers, farmers, small business owners, and corporation managers all want government to make economic and political decisions that favor their interests. These groups have become involved in politics because they realize how far reaching and long lasting government action can be. They see how profoundly politics touches their everyday lives.

▼ Voter registration drives such as the one shown here encourage citizens to participate in our government through voting. What are some other forms of political participation?

▲ Government in its many forms touches our lives on a daily basis. For example, these government inspectors work to ensure that the meat we purchase in supermarkets is safe and of high quality. What are some other ways that government touches our daily lives?

Yet there are many people who say they do not want to be involved in government and politics. These people do not realize that they already are involved. Apathy, or indifference, is as much a political statement as active participation—both positions influence who gets what in society. Good school systems, safe communities, and adequate health standards are the results of political decisions that are influenced by who participates, who is prevented from participating, and who chooses not to participate in government and politics.

Every day of our lives is affected by someone's political choices. The quality of the food you had for breakfast was regulated by a government agency. The cost of the eggs and milk were probably influenced by the government's decisions concerning economic aid to farmers, as well as the farmers' ability to influence government to grant that aid. The quality of the school you attend and the public transportation (or lack of it) in your community are the results of how the government decided to allocate its resources to your city or state.

Thus, the question is not *whether* to become involved in politics and government, but *how* to become involved. The choice is not whether politics and government affect us. They do, and will continue to do so throughout our lives. The choice is how aware we want to be, and how we want to affect politics.

Purposes of Government

The first step in understanding how government works is to understand what it actually does for people and society. Government serves five major purposes: (1) it solves conflicts; (2) it provides public services; (3) it provides for the national security and common defense; (4) it sets goals for public policies; and (5) it preserves culture.

Solving Conflicts Even though people have lived together in groups since the beginning of time, we have not learned how to do so without political conflict— disputes over how to distribute the society's valued resources. These valued resources, such as property, are limited, while people's wants are unlimited. This imbalance creates conflict, and as a result, people need ways to determine who wins and who loses, and how to get the losers to accept that decision. Who has the legitimate power and authority to make these decisions? This is where government steps in.

Governments decide how conflicts will be resolved so that public order can be maintained. Governments have **power**—the ability to influence the behavior of others. Power is getting someone to do something he or she would not do otherwise. Power may involve force

Providing for the common defense can be very expensive. For instance, a great deal of money is required to buy military hardware such as this vehicle used by the United States Army during Operation Desert Storm in 1991. Why do you think defense matters have been given such a high priority throughout history?

(often called coercion), or persuasion, or reward. Governments also have **authority**—legitimate power. In this case, legitimate means even more than legal—it implies moral correctness and a collective recognition and acceptance of this authority. Power and authority are central to government's ability to resolve conflicts by making and enforcing laws, placing limits on what people can do, and developing court systems to make final decisions.

Providing Public Services Another purpose of government is to distribute benefits and provide essential services that people cannot carry out alone. Governments undertake projects that individuals usually would not or could not do on their own, such as building and maintaining roads, providing welfare programs, operating public schools, and preserving national parks. Governments also provide such services as law enforcement, fire protection, and public health and safety programs. As Abraham Lincoln once said:

> The legitimate object of government is to do for a community of people whatever they need to have done but cannot do at all, or cannot so well do for themselves in their separate and individual capacities. But in all that people can individually do for themselves, government ought not to interfere.

Providing for National Security and Common Defense Governments also provide for a nation's security and for common defense against attack from other nations. Historically, defense matters have always been given high priority by governments and have demanded considerable time, effort, and expense. In the twentieth

century, however, national defense has become an especially expensive and complex activity for almost every government in the world.

The government of the United States provides for common defense and security with its Army, Navy, Air Force, Marines, and Coast Guard. The State Department, Defense Department, Central Intelligence Agency (CIA), and other agencies also contribute to this defense network. As part of an ongoing policy of national security, many departments and agencies in the federal government are constantly dealing with other nations. The Constitution gives our national government exclusive power over relations with foreign nations. No individual state can negotiate a treaty with a foreign nation.

Setting Goals for Public Policies Governments set goals meant to improve the lives of their citizens. These goals may affect the people on a local, state, or national scale. Upon setting these goals, governments design plans of action, known as **public policies,** to support or achieve these goals.

There are many issues on which government must make public policy choices. These public policy goals may be short term, such as improving a city's education system by adding new classes, or long term, such as discovering new energy sources. Political and social goals for the United States might include decisions to launch an orbiting space station by the year 2000, to eliminate discrimination against Americans with disabilities, or to clean up the environment in the 1990s.

Preserving Culture A nation's culture includes the customs, language, beliefs, and values of its people.

6

Governments have worked to preserve their nation's culture in ways that citizens cannot. For example, the observance of Independence Day and Thanksgiving in the United States helps carry on a tradition that celebrates our history. In France, Bastille Day is celebrated every July 14th. In the People's Republic of China, National Day is celebrated October 10. Perhaps the ultimate way that governments preserve their national culture and way of life is through defending it against force or attack by other nations that wish to impose their wills on others.

The Nation

Governments exist to serve citizens in the many ways outlined above, but where are governments actually found? You probably have a student government in your school that helps make decisions and rules for your student body. Your city has a government that makes decisions for its local residents. The largest group of people served by a government is the body of people living within a nation. A **nation** is a particular geographic boundary within which an organized government makes and enforces laws *without the approval of a higher authority.*[1]

Characteristics of Nations

Today there are over 170 different nations in the world and no two are the same. Each one has its unique geographical, economic, cultural, and linguistic features. To be a nation, however, they must have four fundamental characteristics: territory, population, sovereignty, and government.

Territory Obviously, a nation must start out with some land on which its people can live and the boundaries of the state must be recognized by other nations. The total area of the United States is 3,615,122 square miles (9,363,123 square kilometers). The People's Republic of China covers 3,691,502 square miles (9,560,990 square kilometers). Both the United States and China have ex-

panded their territory since they were first established. Other nations, such as Mexico, have diminished in size since their beginning.

Recognizing the location of political boundaries between nations is often a source of conflict and has led to many wars throughout history. Wars have also resulted when nations have attempted to take over the territory of other nations. Sometimes stronger nations come to the aid of weaker ones who are invaded. This is what happened when the United States sent troops to the Middle East in reaction to the Iraqi invasion of Kuwait in 1990.

Population A nation contains people who occupy its territory. The number of persons living within each nation varies, ranging from several thousand in Luxembourg to over a billion in the People's Republic of China. The population of the United States is over 250 million.

▼ Indonesia, shown here, is one of over 170 different nations in the world today. What are the four fundamental characteristics of a nation?

---

1. Note that the word *state* and the word *nation* are commonly interchanged in conventional usage. *Webster's Ninth New Collegiate Dictionary* defines *state* as "a politically organized body of people usually occupying a definite territory; especially one that is sovereign," and defines *nation* as "a community of people composed of one or more nationalities and possessing a more or less defined territory and government." For the purposes of clarity we will use *nation* to refer to sovereign nations, such as Mexico or Japan, and use *state* only to refer to states in the United States of America, such as Oregon or Texas.

This painting of the signers of the Declaration of Independence was done by John Trumbull. Trumbull, who served as a soldier in the Continental Army during the War for Independence, was known as "The Patriot Painter." How might a British painter of the same period have depicted this scene?

Sovereignty   The essential feature that determines a nation is **sovereignty**—the right, power, and authority to govern its own people. A nation has complete authority to determine its form of government, its economic and legal systems, and its foreign policy. The United States claimed sovereignty in 1776 through the Declaration of Independence, when it severed any dependence or ties with Great Britain.

Where the sovereignty is located—who holds the power within a nation—is extremely important. Some nations are ruled by one person or a small group of people. As you will learn, in a democratic government the people hold the power and are sovereign.

Government   Every nation has some form of political organization through which public policies are made and enforced. Most nations have several levels of government, which operate according to an overall plan. Most governments today have either a unitary or federal system of government. A **unitary government** is one in which all authority is vested in the central government. A **federal government,** such as in the United States, divides its powers and authority between national and state governments. A third type of government is a confederate government made up of a group of independent states. You will learn more about these systems in Chapter 4.

How Did Government Begin?

What factors first brought about the existence of governments? This question has been examined and debated for many centuries by political thinkers and historians. Over the years, many theories have been proposed, but none provides conclusive answers. Nonetheless, several of these theories have been widely discussed.

Evolutionary   The **evolutionary theory** holds that government developed gradually, step by step. The first stage of human political development was the primitive family, usually headed by the father. Over a period of many years, families joined together and worked cooperatively for protection. The units gradually grew from clans to tribes. Usually one of the older males (or a group of males) led the tribe and was looked upon to make decisions and resolve conflicts between members. As the years went by, the number of families involved grew and the "government" became larger and more formalized. These groups eventually gave up the nomadic life and settled down to an agricultural existence.

Force   According to the **force theory,** governments first originated when strong persons or groups conquered territories, and then forced everyone living in those territories to submit to their will. Then, **institutions**—police, courts, and tax collectors—were created to make people work and to collect all or part of what they produced for the conquerors. The first leader of the German Empire, Otto von Bismark, said in 1862 that "the great questions of our day cannot be solved by speeches and majority votes . . . but by blood and iron." Obviously, Bismark was a strong proponent of the force theory of government.

Divine Right   Prior to the eighteenth century, the theory of divine right was widely accepted in Europe (and in ancient Egypt, China, Greece, and Rome). The **divine right theory** held that God gave those of royal birth the unlimited right to govern other men and women—the "divine right" to rule. According to this theory, only God could judge those of royal birth. Thus, all citizens

CASE STUDY

The French Revolution

GOVERNMENT IN ACTION

Not all countries have as stable a government as we do in the United States. And some countries that do were not always stable, but in fact were created out of revolutions.

A drastic change in a government can be a **revolution.** In a revolution, a government is overthrown by force and a new government is established. Revolutions often occur when many people in a society believe that the government and economy are not meeting their needs.

One of the most important revolutions in the Western world was the French Revolution, which began as a popular uprising in 1789. The result was the overthrow of the monarchy (rulership by a king or queen) of Louis XVI. The causes for the popular uprising were excessively high taxes on the working classes relative to the exceedingly low taxes on the nobility and the Church. In Paris, rebels armed themselves heavily and stormed the Bastille, a prison that had formerly held many famous political dissidents, on July 14, 1789. The uprising was successful and a new constitution was written in 1791. It eliminated the old order, which had created inequality and privilege by nobles, and ensured a new order of basic human rights. The governmental system that grew out of the French Revolution is credited with being the model of popular sovereignty and civil equality that rapidly spread throughout Europe.

As you know, the United States was created by a revolution in 1776. Americans have disagreed sharply over many issues since then. We have even suffered through a nearly devastating civil war. But we have never had to face another revolution. We are fortunate that our government was designed to be flexible and responsive to the demands of its citizens.

THINK ABOUT IT _____

1. Sometimes journalists and social commentators talk about a revolution in *ideas*. Does the term *revolution* in such a phrase have anything to do with the term *revolution* as applied to political change?
2. Why is a revolution virtually impossible in the United States today?

▶ The United States' War for Independence is often credited as being an inspiration for the French Revolution. What is one way in which the French Revolution, as depicted in this painting, differed from our War for Independence?

Four Theories on the Origin of Government

■ **Evolutionary Theory**

Government developed as families joined to form clans, which grew into tribes regulated by older males.

■ **Divine Right Theory**

God gave those of royal birth the unlimited right to govern other men and women.

■ **Force Theory**

Government originated when strong groups conquered territories and then brought the inhabitants under their control.

■ **Social Contract Theory**

Government arose in order to protect people's natural rights to life, liberty, and property; it did so by providing regulation and social stability.

▲ FIGURE 1–1 **Four Theories on the Origin of Government.** The figure above lists four widely discussed theories of how government developed. Which theory would an absolute monarch be most likely to support?

were bound to obey their monarchs, no matter how unfair or unjust they seemed to be.

Social Contract The **social contract theory** was developed in the seventeenth and eighteenth centuries by philosophers such as John Locke and Thomas Hobbes in England, and Jean-Jacques Rousseau in France. According to this theory, individuals voluntarily agree with one another to create a government and in so doing give to that government adequate power to secure the mutual protection and welfare of all individuals. John Locke, one writer who particularly influenced the American colonists, argued that people are born with **natural rights** to life, liberty, and property that no government can take away. He theorized that the purpose of government was to protect natural rights and that any government that abused its power by interfering with those rights should not be obeyed. Human beings, he asserted, would voluntarily give up some of their freedoms in order to gain the benefits of orderly government. The unwritten means by which they did this was a social contract.

Locke's theories greatly influenced many of the leaders in the American Revolution. Benjamin Franklin, James Madison, and Thomas Jefferson were all followers of Locke. His thoughts and even some of his exact words were used in the Declaration of Independence and in the Constitution. Locke's thoughts also influenced many people in France. Like the leaders of the American Revolution, these people found that they had to fight to win popular sovereignty. (See the case study on page 9.)

SECTION 1 REVIEW _____

1. What is government and what purposes does it serve?
2. What are the characteristics of a nation?
3. What are the theories regarding the origin of government?
4. **For critical analysis:** Government in the United States provides many services. What are some services that are currently provided both by government and by business and industry? (Hint: One example is medical care.)

SECTION 2

How Do Governments Differ from One Another?

Preview Questions
- What are the main differences among the various types of government?
- What is the difference between a direct and an indirect democracy?

Through the centuries, governments have been organized in many different ways. A government's structure is influenced by a number of factors such as history, customs, values, geography, climate, resources, and human experiences and needs. No two nations have exactly the same form of government. Over time, however, political analysts have developed different descriptions designed to classify different systems of governments. One of the most meaningful ways of classifying governments is according to *who* governs. Who has the power to make the rules and laws that all must obey?

Rule By One: Autocracy

In an **autocracy,** the power and authority of the government is in the hands of a single person. In ancient times, autocracy was one of the most common forms of government (and still exists in some parts of the world). These autocrats usually obtained their power either by inheriting it (as in the divine right theory of monarchy) or by using force.

Monarchy   One form of autocracy, known as a **monarchy,** is government by a king, queen, emperor, empress, or tsar. The monarch, usually acquiring his or her power through inheritance, is the highest authority in the government. Historically, most monarchies have been **absolute monarchies,** in which rulers held complete and unlimited power. They claimed that their right to absolute power came from God. Challenging this power meant not only treason against the government, but was regarded as a sin against God.

Most modern monarchies, however, are **constitutional monarchies,** in which kings or queens share governmental power with elected lawmakers. Their power is limited, or checked, by other government leaders and by constitutions. In most cases, the people themselves elect these leaders to office. Constitutional monarchs, such as those in Great Britain, Denmark, and Sweden, serve mainly as *ceremonial* leaders of their governments.

Dictatorship   Another form of autocracy is a **dictatorship,** in which a single leader rules, although *not* through inheritance. Dictatorships are **authoritarian,** meaning the dictator can use arbitrary power and is not subject to constitutional limitations. He or she is also not responsible to voters or to their elected representatives. Changes in leadership can only come about by voluntary resignation, death, or forcible overthrow.

Dictatorships can also be **totalitarian,** which means the leader (or group of leaders) seeks to control almost all aspects of social and economic life. The needs of the nation come before the needs of individuals and all citizens must work for the common goals established by the government. Examples of this form of government include Adolf Hitler's government in Nazi Germany

BENT OFFERINGS By Don Addis

ABSOLUTE MONARCHY MEANS NEVER HAVING TO SAY YOU'RE SORRY

© 1991 Creators Syndicate, Inc.

10-1

from 1933 to 1945, Benito Mussolini's rule in Italy from 1922 to 1943, and Josef Stalin's rule in the Soviet Union from 1929 to 1953. More contemporary examples include Saddam Hussein in Iraq and Fidel Castro in Cuba.

Rule by Many: Democracy

The most familiar form of government to Americans is **democracy,** in which the supreme political authority rests with the people. The word democracy comes from the Greek *demos,* meaning ''the people,'' and *kratia,* meaning ''rule.'' The main idea of democracy is that government exists only by the consent of the people, and reflects the will of the majority.

The Athenian Model of Direct Democracy   Democracy as a form of government began long ago. In its purest form, direct democracy was practiced in Athens and other ancient Greek city-states about 2,500 years ago. **Direct democracy** exists when the will of the people is directly translated into public policy. While some consider the Athenian form of direct democracy ideal because it demanded a high degree of participation, others point out that only nonslave males were allowed to participate.

Clearly, direct democracy is possible only in small communities in which citizens can meet in a chosen place

▲ The New England town meeting is a form of direct democracy. Why was direct democracy in Athens considered to have been an ideal form of democracy?

and decide key issues and policies. Some New England town meetings and a few of the smaller political subunits, or cantons, of Switzerland still use a modified form of direct democracy.

Representative Democracy   Although our founders were aware of the Athenian model and agreed with the idea of government based on the consent of the governed, many feared that a pure, direct democracy would deteriorate into mob rule. They believed that large groups of people meeting together would ignore the rights and opinions of people in the minority, and would lead to decisions being made without careful thought. For this reason, they thought that a representative democracy would enable public decisions to be made in a calmer and more fair manner.

In a **representative democracy** (also called **indirect democracy**), the will of the majority is expressed through a smaller group of individuals elected by the people to act as their representatives. These representatives are elected by the people, are responsible to the people for their conduct, and can be voted out of office. Our founders preferred to use the term **republic,** which is essentially the same as a representative democracy. As our population has grown, this republic has become increasingly removed from the Athenian model, as you

will learn by reading Challenge to the American Dream on page 18.

Presidential and Parliamentary Democracy   In the modern world there are two forms of representative democracy: presidential and parliamentary. A **presidential democracy** is one in which the law-making and law-implementing branches of government are separate. For example, in the United States, Congress is charged with the power to make laws and the president is charged with the power to carry them out. In a **parliamentary democracy** the law-making and law-implementing branches of government overlap. In England, for example, the Prime Minister and the Cabinet are members of the legislature and enact the laws as well as carry them out.

Principles of Democracy

> This country, with all its institutions, belongs to the people who inhabit it. Whenever they shall grow weary of the existing government, they can exercise their constitutional right of amending it, or their revolutionary right to dismember or overthrow it.

With these words, Abraham Lincoln underscored the most fundamental concept of American government: that the people, not the government, are ultimately in control.

▼|FIGURE 1–2 **Forms of Government.** While no two nations have exactly the same form of government, most governments can be described by one of the models in the figure below. Which of the models best describes the United States government?

CITIZENSHIP SKILLS AND RESPONSIBILITIES

The Duties of Citizenship

Americans are citizens of a democracy. As you have learned, democracy is government by the people, and citizen involvement is at the heart of democracy. If only a few people decided to become involved in government, public decisions would be left to those few. Such a government would no longer be an effective democracy. Being a citizen in a democratic society requires learning certain skills, some of which include:

1. **Acquiring and using information.** Citizens must know how to find answers to important questions. They do this by reading books, magazines, and government publications, and by using radio and television media. They must know how to ask questions, write letters, and make telephone calls to obtain the information they need. Throughout this book, you will be learning how to gather and use various types of information.
2. **Making decisions.** Citizens need to recognize that there may be more than one solution to any given problem. They must be able to evaluate alternatives and be familiar with the decision-making process.
3. **Making sound judgments.** In order to make sound judgments, citizens must distinguish between fact and opinion, recognize their own biases and values, see both sides of an issue, and identify irrelevant and ambiguous information.
4. **Communicating.** Citizens must be able to express their views and communicate their ideas effectively, both in writing and in speaking.
5. **Cooperating.** Citizens must be able to work together to achieve common goals.

These and many other specific citizenship skills are reviewed throughout this book.

TAKING ACTION

1. Choose a current issue facing your community, such as how to solve the homeless problem or how to reduce illegal drug use. Read as much as you can about the issue for two weeks. Put together a file of the newspaper and magazine articles that you have read about the subject.
2. Over the same period, watch TV or listen to the radio for news on the same topic. Take notes on what you learn.
3. Decide what you think must be done to solve the problem you have chosen. Make a list of your conclusions.

Democracy is based on five principles, all of which will be discussed throughout this text:

- **Equality in voting.** Citizens need equal opportunities to express their preferences about policies or leaders.
- **Individual freedom.** All individuals must have the greatest amount of freedom possible without interfering with the rights of others.
- **Equality of all persons.** The law must entitle all persons to equal treatment within the society.
- **Majority rule and minority rights.** The majority should rule, while guaranteeing minorities' rights.
- **Voluntary consent to be governed.** The people who make up a democracy must agree voluntarily

to be governed by the rules laid down by their representatives.

SECTION 2 REVIEW

1. What is the difference between a monarchy and a dictatorship?
2. What is direct democracy and why did our founders oppose it?
3. What is the difference between a direct democracy and an indirect, or representative, democracy?
4. What are the principles of democracy?
5. **For critical analysis:** How do you think your life would be different if you were living in a country ruled by a monarch?

SECTION 3

The Challenge of Interdependence

Preview Questions
- What does interdependence mean?
- What are the reasons for this growing interdependence?

You have read about how each nation is sovereign, with its own population, territory, and government. This does not mean that each nation is a world in itself. Each nation is one among many nations in the world, all sharing the same planet and the same environment. When you hear people say that "the world is getting smaller," they mean that through increased communications and transportation, people around the world have become more aware of and affected by the goals and problems of others. All of us are becoming more and more interdependent. **Interdependence** means that nations rely on each other for many different reasons. There are several important reasons for this currently increasing interdependence.

The Global Economy

One of the most important ways in which nations are becoming interdependent is through world trade. Nations depend on one another for the products they cannot make or cannot grow for themselves. They also depend on each other for natural resources not found within their own borders. Economic policies in one country can strongly affect the economy and well-being of another. In the United States, for example, we buy cars from Germany, Italy, and Japan; videocassette recorders from Korea and Japan; wool shirts from Scotland; and shoes and other leather goods from Italy, Spain, and Argentina. Other countries buy our cars, our computers, and our agricultural products. If another country's government decides that it wants to prohibit its citizens from purchasing American goods, that decision affects us economically. If we decide to do the same thing, our government's action affects citizens in other countries.

When McDonald's went into business in Moscow, Russian citizens were able to see how it is possible to receive a high quality product at a low price with friendly service. This has had an effect on what they expect from other businesses in their country. The same has happened in the United States. When Americans saw that the Japanese could make cars of higher quality, on average, than American-made cars, American auto makers felt pressured to improve the quality of domestically produced cars.

The Role of Technology

Interdependence has also increased because of the improvements in communication and transportation technologies. Satellites, computers, airplanes, and facsimile (fax) machines have linked nations and their peoples in ways that were only dreamed of years ago. Americans with television satellite dishes can watch news broadcasts from many countries. Radio broadcasts allow people around the world to hear news from other nations. In 1989, when Chinese students demonstrated for democracy in Beijing's Tiananmen Square, the world watched the daily events on television. The Chinese government tried to cut off the world news media, but news continued to flow through long-distance telephone links and satellite broadcasts. When the Iraqis invaded Kuwait in 1990, everyone knew it immediately throughout the world. As Iraqi soldiers carried much of Kuwait's wealth into Iraq, the world knew quickly that Iraq's ruler, Saddam Hussein, was not telling the truth about his

▼ The first McDonald's Restaurant in Moscow is an example of the globalization of business. Such globalization increases the amount that nations rely on each other. What word is used to describe the increasing reliance of nations on one another?

BUILDING SOCIAL STUDIES SKILLS

Using the Features of This Textbook

Within any textbook there is a vast amount of information that you can make your own. To help you, this textbook is divided into many parts, each of which has its own function. Some parts prepare you for information; other parts help you study that information. Using a textbook and its parts wisely is an important first move toward mastering its contents.

How to Use this Textbook

To get the most from this textbook, use the following guidelines.

1. **Study the table of contents to locate information.** Here you can find where each chapter, section, feature, map, graph, and table can be found.
2. **Examine the chapter- and unit-opening pages.** Read the titles and objectives, and ask yourself questions about the photos, such as how each relates to the chapter title. Read the introduction and familiarize yourself with the theme.
3. **Skim the chapter.** Preview the chapter, noting each section title and the subheadings. These will give you clues about how the chapter will progress. Note the maps, photographs, and other visuals to get a feel for the chapter. Read the section guide questions that start each section.
4. **Read the chapter carefully.** Use the headings and subheadings to get clues about the main and supporting ideas. Reread any paragraph that is unclear until you understand what it says. Pay attention to the boldfaced words—they are highlighted because they are important terms. Review the illustrations and relate them to the content of your reading. Use the review questions at the end of the sections to check your understanding.
5. **Read the special features.** Each chapter has special features that will add to your knowledge of government. You will recognize them easily because they will appear in boxes. You may prefer to read them as you go along, which is often a good idea, because many of the features directly relate to the surrounding information. Or you may prefer to read them as part of the previewing step, or before reviewing the section. When you read

them is not as important as being sure you do read them.
6. **Summarize and review the chapter.** Each chapter ends with a summary that will help you recap the main ideas. Each chapter also has a set of review questions, questions for thought and discussion, activities and projects, a communication skill exercise and a social studies skill exercise. All of these review features are designed to help you master the material.
7. **Look at the glossary.** The glossary includes definitions for the important new words found in this book.
8. **Use the Resource Center.** The Resource Center found in the back of this book is loaded with useful material including original source documents and more.

Remember, no textbook can teach you this course. A textbook cannot be a substitute for your instructor's skills and experience. This book, like all textbooks, is a tool. When used properly, it can enhance your knowledge and broaden your understanding.

PRACTICING YOUR SKILLS

1. Turn to the glossary and answer these questions: (a) On what page(s) in the glossary is the term *veto* found? (b) What is the last entry under L?
2. Turn to the table of contents and answer the following questions: (a) Who are the Americans profiled under "Architects of the American Dream"? (b) How many units and chapters does the book have? (c) Name three "Government in Action" features found in the book.
3. List all of the special features used in the textbook.
4. How many individuals are featured in the profiles and the "Architects of the American Dream" combined?
5. What is special about the Constitution as it is presented in the Resource Center?
6. Find your state in the State Atlas in the Resource Center. When was it admitted to the Union?

▲ When Iraq's leader, Saddam Hussein, dumped oil into the Persian Gulf it was an environmental disaster. Why should Americans be concerned with environmental disasters that take place in other parts of the world?

intentions in Kuwait. In 1991, an attempted coup against the government of Mikhail Gorbachev in the Soviet Union was viewed by hundreds of millions of world citizens. Throughout that vast country, citizens immediately responded against the attempted coup. When the popularly elected president of Russia, Boris Yeltsin, stood on top of an army tank in front of the Russian Parliament and told his people to resist, the image was seen by people all over the world.

Virtually no events can go unknown and unseen in the political world today, no matter where they take place. Indeed, some political analysts believe that the worldwide spread of relatively inexpensive telecommunications has been a principal reason why nondemocratic countries have had to change—their citizens know that better forms of government exist elsewhere in the world because they hear about them on the radio or see them on TV or in movie houses.

Our Shared Environment

Nations of the world are also interdependent because they share the same air and water. Pollution in one nation can affect the people and environment of other nations. As a result, the world's nations must depend on each other to protect an environment that knows no national boundaries.

An accident at a nuclear power plant in one country can affect the lives of millions of people thousands of miles away. The clear-cutting of the Brazilian rain forest might affect all of us if the world's oxygen level is severely reduced. In the United States, many of our electric utility plants generate pollution that spreads hundreds of miles into Canada and creates the problem of acid rain, which has a high acid content that harms Canadian forests and lakes.

The depletion of the earth's ozone layer is a global problem. One of the major causes is thought to be the release of chlorofluorocarbons into the atmosphere. Some countries have banned the use of chlorofluorocarbons, for example, in the making of refrigerator coolant. But what happens if one country continues to produce numerous products that cause more and more chlorofluorocarbons to be released into the air? Clearly, there is an interdependence among countries here that cannot be ignored.

Nor can we ignore the problem of dangerous pesticides and chemicals. A country may ban pesticide use domestically, but still allow its manufacturer to sell it to countries where it is not banned. This occurred with the chemical DDT. The same is true with respect to medicines that may not be approved in the country in which they are manufactured, but can be sold elsewhere in the world. What if those pesticides and medicines have dangerous side effects?

The United States is truly part of a global society. Decision makers must always be aware of this fact of modern life.

SECTION 3 REVIEW

1. What does interdependence mean?
2. Why is the world becoming more interdependent?
3. **For critical analysis:** Do you think this growing interdependence will have a positive or negative effect on the United States? Explain your answer.

17

CHALLENGE TO THE AMERICAN DREAM

Do Our Representatives Represent Too Many People?

Everybody accepts the notion that direct democracy as practiced in ancient Greece would not work in a nation of over 250 million people. Even if a small percentage of the total adult population wanted to participate in direct democracy, the result would be a mass meeting that could not be held in even the largest structure in the world. Representative democracy is therefore the most practical democratic system we can use in this country.

Our representative democracy took on a distinct form in 1788 with the ratification of the U.S. Constitution. The first president, George Washington, took office in 1789 when the population numbered about 4 million. During the first election, twenty-two senators and fifty-nine representatives were elected. Therefore, the two senators from each state represented an average of 180,000 citizens. The average member of the House of Representatives represented about 68,000 citizens. The situation in 1789 was, of course, a far cry from the Athenian model of direct democracy.

Consider now the current situation. The population in the United States has grown to over 250 million. There is still one president. The number of senators has increased to 100, however, and the number of representatives to 435. That means that the two senators from every state represent an average of 5 million Americans. The average member of the House represents about 575,000 Americans. At the extreme, the two senators from California represent almost 30 million Americans.

This is a nation of diverse cultures, needs, desires, demands, preferences, and religious beliefs. Is it possible for any one representative to truly reflect the ''will of the people'' when each congressional official in our government represents so many Americans?

Some have begun to question whether representative democracy can still work in the United States because of the continued rate of population growth. Others point out that this nation will probably reach its maximum, stable population sometime between the years 2020 and 2040. While the population will probably increase to about 300 to 330 million, it will not be significantly larger than it is now. In other words, if representative democracy is working today, even with all of its faults, it will certainly work with 50 to 80 million more people. The two senators from each state will represent an average of 6 million people; for representatives, the average will be about 690,000 people. Certainly, the effect and influence any individual citizen has on his or her elected officials will not markedly change with a population that is 25 percent larger.

The challenge to the American dream is, nonetheless, to improve the representative nature of our democracy in spite of an increasing population. This can be done by more voter participation, a greater understanding among all Americans (particularly young people) of the political process, and more limits on the degree to which our representatives are allowed to act in their own best interests rather than in those of the people they represent.

You Decide

1. Do you think that representative democracy worked better at the beginning of our nation's history, when each senator and representative represented fewer Americans? Explain.

2. Some have argued that each member of the House now represents too many Americans and that therefore the number of representatives should be increased. What problems would arise if that occurred?

3. If, indeed, representative democracy is in danger because of an increase in population, what alternatives might work better?

4. Some people look to technology that will allow electronic voting from the home as a way of meeting this challenge. Do you think such technology would increase political participation among Americans? Do you think this would adequately meet the challenge to the American dream just presented?

CHAPTER 1 REVIEW

Key Terms

absolute
  monarchies 11
authoritarian 11
authority 6
autocracy 11
constitutional
  monarchies 11
democracy 11
dictatorship 11
direct democracy 11
divine right theory 8
evolutionary theory 8

federal government 8
force theory 8
government 4
institutions 8
interdependence 15
majority rule 14
monarchy 11
nation 7
natural rights 10
parliamentary
  democracy 12

political
  participation 4
politics 4
power 5
presidential
  democracy 12
public policies 6
representative
  democracy (indirect
  democracy) 12
republic 12

revolution 9
social conflict 3
social contract
  theory 10
sovereignty 8
totalitarian 11
unitary government 8

Summary

1. Government consists of the individuals and processes that make society's rules, and that possess the power to enforce the rules about resolving conflicts over the allocation of resources. Politics is the process that determines "who gets what, when, and how" in society. Government serves several major purposes: solving conflicts, providing public services, providing for the national security and common defense, setting political and social goals, and preserving culture. The nation is the basic political unit in the world today. A nation is a political community with its own population, territory, sovereignty, and government. The force theory of government holds that governments first originated when one person or group conquered a given territory and forced everyone living in that territory to submit to their will. The evolutionary theory holds that government developed gradually, beginning with the family. The divine right theory holds that God gave those of royal birth the "divine right" to rule. The social contract theory holds that government rose out of the voluntary act of free individuals to serve the will of the people.

2. Although all governments carry out the same basic functions, there are tremendous differences in the ways governments can be organized and operated. In an autocracy, power is concentrated in the hands of an individual. In a democracy, the supreme political authority rests with the people. Direct democracy, as practiced in ancient Greek city-nations, exists when the will of the people is directly translated into public policy at mass

meetings. In a representative democracy, popular will is expressed through individuals elected by the people to act as representatives. The basic democratic principles include equality in voting, individual freedom, social equality for all persons, and majority rule and minority rights.

3. Interdependence means that nations rely on each other for many different reasons. One of the most important ways in which nations rely on each other is through world trade. Interdependence has also increased because of the improvements in the technologies of communications and transportation. Nations are also interdependent because they share the same environment.

Review Questions

1. Why do people living in groups need some form of government?
2. What are several forms of political participation?
3. What are the purposes of government?
4. List and explain the characteristics of a nation.
5. List and explain the four major theories of the origins of government.
6. Into what types can governments be classified?
7. How does a monarchy differ from a dictatorship?
8. What is the primary characteristic of any dictatorship?
9. Which form of government best describes the government of the United States?
10. Who holds the supreme political authority in a democracy?

CHAPTER 1 REVIEW—Continued

11. Explain the differences between a direct democracy and an indirect, or representative, democracy. Which type best describes the system used in the United States?
12. What are the basic concepts of democracy and why are they important?
13. Explain why there is a growing interdependence between nations.
14. Name at least four skills required to be a good citizen.
15. How has population growth weakened the representative nature of our democracy?

Questions for Thought and Discussion

1. Give three examples of why you must have rules in order to be free.
2. Historians have speculated that at one time humans lived without a form of organized government. Why do you think early peoples decided to devise laws and governments? What is your own theory of the origin of government?
3. In your opinion, should our democracy be direct or representative? Give reasons for your answer.
4. Compare the three types of government outlined in this chapter and describe what your life might be like living under each one.
5. Consider the decision-making process in your city. Can you identify certain individuals or social groups that seem to control the decision making? How are such "elite" groups controlled by the voters?
6. There are many reasons why nations are becoming more interdependent. The reasons discussed in this chapter were increased international trade, better and less expensive communications technology, and world environmental problems. Can you think of at least one other reason why nations are becoming more interdependent? Develop your answer.

Improving Your Skills
Communication Skills

Listening

Have you ever heard someone talking to you, but couldn't remember anything that he or she said five min-

utes later? The person was probably insulted because you weren't really listening. Many individuals don't really listen to half of what they hear in life. We may hear the words but don't turn them into understandable and useful information. We consciously or unconsciously sort through what we've heard, and focus on only *part* of the information. You may easily remember the scores of every football game last year, or the top five MTV videos for the past six months, but when it comes to remembering what your teacher said in yesterday's class, you draw a blank.

You can become an effective listener at school, at work, and with family and friends by understanding the listening process:

- You hear what's being said.
- You make a decision as to its importance.
- You react to it.
- You file the information or discard it.

To become a more effective listener, you must gain more control over this process. Follow these guidelines:

1. *Tell yourself that you want to retain what you are hearing.* Concentrate on the speaker and tune out outside interferences such as music, telephones, other conversations, and anything else about which you might be thinking. You must discipline yourself to become an active, involved listener because it is easy to be distracted.
2. *Try to organize what you hear by listening to clues from the speaker.* For example, "The main point here is that . . . ; The three reasons this happened are . . . ."
3. *If you know that a lecture or discussion is going to be based on something you have previously heard or learned, review that information ahead of time.* It is much easier to relate new information to knowledge that you already have.
4. *Try to relate what you hear to your own knowledge and experience.* Coming up with concrete examples of what is being explained may help you understand. For example, if you are learning about the concepts of democracy, think of specific situations in which they apply to you.
5. *Ask questions if you don't understand or need more information.* If you need a point repeated or clarified, don't hesitate to ask the speaker.

CHAPTER 1 REVIEW—Continued

Writing

On a sheet of paper, complete the following statements.

1. The qualities most important for a high-ranking government policymaker are . . .
2. The best things about the United States are . . .
3. The president should work toward . . .

Get into teams with three or four of your classmates. Take turns reading your responses to each other. Then take turns trying to repeat exactly how the others in your team have completed the statements.

Social Studies Skills

Learning About Forms of Government

Use Figure 1–2 on page 13 to answer the following questions. This figure shows the forms of government. It simplifies the many complex forms that governments have taken since the beginning of organized society.

1. How does the upper panel on autocracy relate an absolute monarchy with a dictatorship?
2. In the middle panel, what is the distinction between laws developed under direct democracy and those developed under representative democracy?
3. In the bottom panel, what is the distinction between a presidential democracy and a parliamentary democracy?
4. In the bottom panel, what distinguishes a modern constitutional monarchy from a parliamentary democracy?
5. In the bottom panel, why do you think the arrow pointing towards ''monarch'' is a broken line?

Activities and Projects

1. Divide the class into groups of five or six. Assume that each group has founded a new town that is growing quickly but as yet has no form of government. Each group should devise a plan of government for each town. Decide what the town goals will be, how a leader will be chosen, and what rules will be made and enforced.

2. Prepare a series of posters that illustrate each form of government described in this chapter. Use pictures and words.
3. Stage a debate or class forum on one of the following topics:
   (a) People could provide public services better without government interference.
   (b) Representative democracy cannot work because the people don't take enough time to learn about important political issues.
   (c) A dictatorship may be better than a democracy if the dictator is a smart and kind person.
   (d) The United States should only worry about its own problems, not those in any other country.

Forging the American Dream

CHAPTER OBJECTIVES

To learn and understand

- The European origins of the American governmental system.
- The development of the American governmental system through the first British settlements.
- The colonies' push for independence.
- The governmental arrangements set up by the Articles of Confederation.
- The Constitutional Convention and the ratification of the Constitution of the United States.

Keynote

"The Colonies are at so great a distance from England that the members of Parliament can generally have but little knowledge of their business, connections, and interests but what is gained from people who have been there; the most of these have so slight a knowledge themselves that the information they can give are very little to be dependent on, though they may pretend to determine with confidence on matters far above their reach."

———— **Stephen Hopkins**
(1721–1785) Member of First and
Second Continental Congresses

INTRODUCTION

Most people know that the United States first started out as English colonies. As the opening quote makes clear, the distance between the colonies and England was vast. The rulers in Great Britain had difficulty keeping current on what was happening in America and consequently knew little about the colonists' activities or needs. This does not mean that if satellite communications had been available in the 1770s, the American Revolution never would have happened. But perhaps that revolution would have started later had the British Crown known how life really was across the Atlantic.

In spite of our revolutionary break with England in 1776, much of the political thought that has formed the way our nation governs itself has its origins in the theories of European philosophers.

SECTION 1

European Origins of Our Governmental System

Preview Questions
- What is limited government? Where did the concept of limited government come from?
- What is the system of representative government? Where did this system come from?
- What were some early influences on American political philosophy?

The American colonies were settled by individuals from many nations, including France, Spain, Holland, Sweden, and Norway. Nonetheless, the majority of American settlers came from England. The English colonists brought with them the two principles of *limited government* and *representative government*, which became important factors in forming the American political system.

Limited Government

For many years under the British monarchy, the king or queen had virtually unrestricted powers. This changed in 1215, when King John was forced by his nobles to sign the **Magna Carta,** or great charter. (See the Resource Center at the back of this book.) This monumental document provided for a trial by jury of one's **peers** (equals). It prohibited the taking of life, liberty, and property without due process of law. Additionally, the Magna Carta forced the king to obtain the nobles' approval of any taxes he imposed on his royal subjects. Government became a contract between the king and his subjects.

The Magna Carta's importance to England cannot be overemphasized, for it clearly established the principle of **limited government**—a government on which strict limits are placed, usually by a constitution. Hence, the Magna Carta signaled the end of the monarch's absolute power. While it is true that the rights provided under the Magna Carta originally applied only to the nobility, it formed the basis of the future constitutional government for all individuals in England and eventually in the United States.

The principle of limited government was expanded 400 years later, in 1628, when Charles I was forced to sign the Petition of Rights. Among other things, this petition prohibited the king from imprisoning political critics without a jury trial. Perhaps more importantly, the

▲ When King John signed the Magna Carta, the principle of limited government was established. Why do you think the Magna Carta was important to the formation of the United States Constitution?

Representative Government

A system of **representative government** is one in which the people, by whatever means, choose a limited number of individuals to make governmental decisions for all citizens. Those chosen by the citizens are called **representatives.** Usually, these representatives are elected to office for a specific period of time.

In England, this group of representatives is called **Parliament.** As it did in the eighteenth century, Parliament consists of an upper chamber, called the House of Lords, and a lower chamber, called the House of Commons, which was mostly made up of merchants and property owners. Members of the House of Commons were elected by other merchants and property owners. Thus in England, the concept of government by and for the people became reality. It later became a model by which the thirteen American colonies would govern themselves as well. (A more complete explanation of Parliament can be found in Chapter 26.)

Early Philosophical Influences

It may seem obvious to you that government without the **consent** (permission and agreement) of the governed should not exist. Such a notion, however, was still very new and revolutionary in the 1600s. An important English political philosopher, John Locke, who wrote *Two Treatises of Government* in 1689, argued that neither custom nor tradition, nor the fact of being born in a certain society, were sufficient reasons to obey rulers. He stated that ''No one could be subjected to the political power of another, without his [or her] own consent.'' Government, therefore, was only legitimate as long as the people continued to consent to it. Locke further argued that all persons were born free, equal, and independent, and all persons had a **natural right** to life, liberty, and property—rights that everyone possessed even before governments existed. He argued that the primary purpose of government was to protect those natural rights, and believed that government was really a social contract between the people and their government.

Both John Locke and another English philosopher, Thomas Hobbes, theorized that before government existed, people lived in ''a state of nature'' in which they had unlimited freedom and the right to do as they wished. Hobbes argued that this situation led to chaos and violence because the weak could not protect themselves against the strong. Rights could only be won through force. Life in this ''free'' state of nature, therefore, was essentially, as Hobbes put it, ''nasty, brutish, and short.''

petition declared that even the king or queen had to obey the law of the land.

In 1689, the English government passed the English Bill of Rights, which further extended the concept of limited government. Several important ideas were included in this document:

- The king or queen could not interfere with parliamentary elections.
- The king or queen must have Parliament's approval to levy (collect) taxes or to maintain any army.
- The king or queen must rule with the consent of the people's representatives in Parliament.
- The people could not be subject to cruel or unusual punishment or to excessive fines.

Because the British colonists in North America were also British citizens, the English Bill of Rights of 1689 applied to them. Because of this, virtually all the major concepts in the English Bill of Rights became part of the American system of government.

▲ English political philosopher John Locke argued that "No one could be subjected to the political power of another without his [or her] own consent." What did Locke see as the primary purpose of government?

According to Hobbes in his landmark political study *Leviathan,* which was published in 1651, human beings voluntarily agreed to create a powerful government in order to establish security and safety. In exchange for this, they gave up the freedoms they had won in the state of nature, and owed their complete loyalty to the government that protected them. He believed that a government in which a ruler enjoyed absolute authority over the people would end the conflicts waged in the natural state. Although few political thinkers agreed that the individual owed total loyalty to the government, Hobbes' writings contributed to the growing idea that government was based on a negotiated agreement between the rulers and the ruled, rather than on raw force and power.

Like Hobbes and Locke, Jean-Jacques Rousseau, a French philosopher, also believed that people had once lived in a state of nature and freedom, but had many years ago entered into a contractual agreement with their government. He wrote that many governments in more recent times had come under the control of unjust rulers who ruled at the expense of their citizens' personal freedom. He argued that the people alone had the right to

determine how they should be governed. In *The Social Contract,* published in 1762, he wrote that "man is born free, yet everywhere he is found in chains." Rousseau was referring to the large number of people on the European continent living under oppressive governments. He proposed that because all human beings in a state of nature were born free, the main duty of government should be to maintain as much freedom as possible in a civilized society.

A French philosopher, Charles de Secondat, the Baron of Montesquieu, was the first political writer to speak about the idea of dividing government into three separate branches with different duties and the ability to check on each other's power. In his book *The Spirit of the Laws,* published in 1748, Montesquieu pointed out in an examination of English government that no one person was allowed to make the laws, enforce the laws, and interpret the laws. This partial separation of governmental responsibilities helped to prevent the abuse of power and to protect the liberties of the English people. The framers of our Constitution agreed with

▲ In 1762 French political philosopher Jean-Jacques Rousseau commented on the large number of Europeans living under oppressive governments by stating that "Man is born free, yet everywhere he is found in chains." What did Rousseau feel was the main duty of government?

Montesquieu, but wanted to ensure that the American form of government had an even more distinct separation of powers. In this way, they hoped that liberty would be safer in the United States than in England.

As you shall see, the ideas of these philosophers are clearly embodied in the documents that outline the American philosophy of government.

The American way of life is, in many respects, the result of the American system of government, which resulted from many struggles against nature, England, and ourselves. In order to fully understand this system, we must trace its roots back to our nation's beginnings. Between 1600 and 1750, Americans, as we would later be called, developed a **political philosophy,** which is a set of notions or ideas about how people should be governed.

SECTION 1 REVIEW

1. What is the concept of limited government? How did the American way of government evolve out of this concept?
2. What is the system of representative government?
3. How did the theories of European philosophers influence American political thinking?
4. **For critical analysis:** What are some common restrictions on government in the United States that follow the principle of limited government?

SECTION 2

The First British Settlements

Preview Questions
- What was the first British settlement in North America? What were some of the changes that this settlement went through?
- How was the Plymouth Company set up to be governed?
- What was the nation's first written constitution? What kind of government did it establish?

During the 1590s, Britain and Spain were constantly at war. Government officials in Britain decided that their war efforts against Spain would be improved by having British ships along the shores of North America. These ships could then harass the Spanish treasure fleets, which consisted of fast ships that took gold and other precious metals from the New World to Spain. Sir Walter Raleigh,

the adventurer and writer, convinced England's queen, Elizabeth I, to allow him to establish the first British outpost in North America. He did this by sending a ship of settlers in 1585 to Roanoke Island off the coast of North Carolina in an unsuccessful attempt to create a settlement.

The Many British Attempts at Settlement

In 1607 another group from London, the Virginia Company, established a trading post in Virginia, which they called Jamestown. In the first year of its existence, over 60 percent of the colony's 105 inhabitants had died. In 1609, England sent over 800 new arrivals. By the spring of the following year only 60 were left. The survivors, admitting defeat, decided to return to England. Just as they were planning to depart, new supplies and more settlers arrived on three ships. The original 60 colonists changed their plans; together, the colonists all

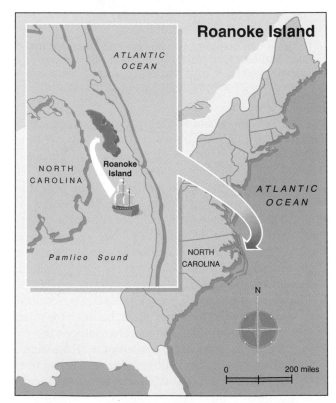

▲ **FIGURE 2–1 Roanoke Island.** The first British outpost in North America was established by Sir Walter Raleigh on Roanoke Island in 1585. Why did Britain want to establish a settlement in North America?

▶ This 19th century engraving depicts the arrival of the first English colonists at Jamestown, Virginia in May, 1607. What happened to these colonists?

rebuilt Jamestown, which became the first permanent British settlement in North America.[1]

Of the six thousand people who left England for Virginia between 1607 and 1623, four thousand died. Those who lived established a type of government that would serve as a model for later colonial adventures.

Representative Assembly The king of England gave the Virginia Company of London a **charter,** a written grant of authority, to make laws "for the good and welfare" of the Jamestown settlement. Jamestown's colonists used this charter to institute a **representative assembly,** a law-making body that is composed of individuals who represent the population. A representative assembly is different from a *direct democracy,* which was discussed in Chapter 1—a type of government in which citizens collectively make the decision.

Pilgrims and the Mayflower Compact The Plymouth Company established the first New England colony in 1620. A group of English Protestants, calling themselves Pilgrims, sailed to North America on the *Mayflower,* a 180-ton, 90-foot (27-meter) ship with three masts and two decks. They landed at what is now Provincetown Harbor, at the tip of Cape Cod in Massachusetts. (They later moved the ship to Plymouth, Massachusetts, which became their new home.) Even before the Pilgrims went ashore, the adult males drew up the **Mayflower Compact,** or agreement, in which they set up a government and promised to obey its laws. (See the Resource Center.) It was signed by 41 of the 44 men aboard on November 21, 1620. No women were allowed to sign it, nor did they have any direct part in developing it, because women at that time did not have any political status. The Pilgrims felt obligated to establish a written document for self-government because their leaders believed that they needed a set of rules to govern themselves. They also wanted to create a government based on the consent of the governed.

The Mayflower Compact, although often referred to as a constitution, was in fact a *social contract,* of the type that Locke had described—an agreement among individuals to establish a government and to abide by its rules. This particular social contract had great historical significance because it served as a **prototype**—a model—for similar compacts in American history.

By 1639 a number of Pilgrims were being persecuted for their religious beliefs, and decided to leave

---

1. It was not the first permanent *European* settlement in North America. That honor goes to St. Augustine, Florida—a city that still exists—which was founded on September 8, 1565, by the Spaniard Pedro Menéndez de Áviles.

In 1620 the Pilgrims sailed aboard the Mayflower to establish a colony in New England. Before going ashore, the Pilgrims drew up the Mayflower Compact, which established a set of rules under which they would govern themselves. Why were no women allowed to sign the Mayflower Compact?

the Massachusetts Bay Colony. They colonized the area that is now Connecticut and in the process developed America's first written constitution—the **Fundamental Orders of Connecticut.** This written document called for a representative assembly, made up of elected representatives from each town to serve in that assembly and to make laws. It also called for the popular election of a governor and judges.

By 1732, all thirteen colonies had been established, each with its own political documents and constitutions. For example, the Massachusetts Body of Liberties was adopted in 1641. It supported protection of individual rights and became part of colonial law. In 1683 the Pennsylvania Frame of Government was passed. This document, along with the 1701 Pennsylvania Charter of Privileges, established at least part of the basis for the U.S. Constitution and the Bill of Rights.

Early Legislatures

Not only did the colonies have constitutions, they also had law-making bodies, called **legislatures.** The first one was the Virginia House of Burgesses, established in 1619. The first laws that this colonial legislature passed were to aid farmers and to impose fines for public idleness and improper dress.

By the time the colonies declared independence from England in 1776, each colony had its own representative

government, and most governments had been operating for over one hundred years. These colonial legislative bodies were the schooling grounds for many of the leaders who later wrote the U.S. Constitution in 1787. The representative legislatures provided leaders with experience in self-government and provided a model for our later political framework.

These colonial groups and their individual members also had extensive contact with the governing methods

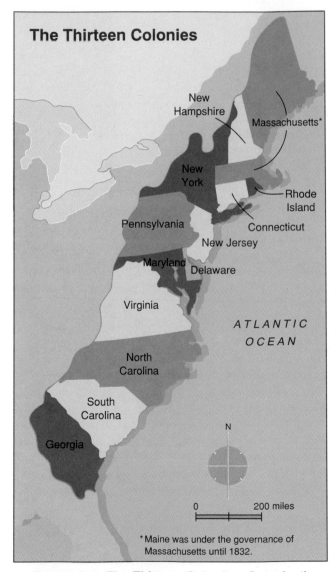

FIGURE 2–2 **The Thirteen Colonies.** Georgia, the last of the thirteen colonies, was established in 1732. By this time, each of the thirteen colonies had developed its own political system complete with necessary political documents and a constitution. Which colony had the first written constitution and what was it called?

of the native peoples. It was out of a rich Native American democratic tradition that some of the distinctive political beliefs of American life emerged.

SECTION 2 REVIEW

1. What were the major political concepts brought to America by early English settlers?
2. What kind of governing body did the Fundamental Orders of Connecticut establish? What was the role of the people under this constitution?
3. **For critical analysis:** Describe the historical significance of the Fundamental Orders of Connecticut. How do we still see its principles in operation today?

SECTION 3

The Colonies Rebel

Preview Questions
- What were some of the restrictions that Britain placed on the colonies? How did the colonists react?
- Why was the First Continental Congress called into existence? What was decided at that meeting?
- What did the Second Continental Congress accomplish?
- What arguments and events led to the Declaration of Independence?
- What concerns did the citizens of the first states have toward their governments?

Even though the thirteen colonies had each been formed differently and were governed differently, they were all under the rulership of the British monarchy. Britain wanted the colonies to act in England's best interest, but the British government did little to manage its outposts in the colonies. After all, they were located more than three thousand miles (4831 kilometers) away and it took almost two months to sail across the Atlantic. Therefore, the colonies gradually became self-governing even though they were still officially ruled by the British Crown in London.

By the mid-1770s the government's responsibilities were limited to the defense of the colonies, a uniform system of money and credit, and a common market for colonial trade (that would benefit England). Otherwise, the colonies were free to do what they wanted. There was little taxation of the colonies to pay for the government in London.

Increasing British Restrictions

This period of limited taxation did not last. The British increased restrictions on the colonists in 1651 when the **Navigation Acts** were passed by the English Parliament. These acts required that only English ships (including ships of its colonies) could be used for trade within the British empire. Similar acts were passed until 1750.

In the early 1760s George III was crowned king of England. More restrictions were applied to colonial trade. The Proclamation of 1763 declared that no colonial settlement could be established west of the Appalachian Mountains. In 1764 the Sugar Act, which raised taxes, was passed to pay for wars that the British had waged. These taxes were also used to support British troops in North America, who were there to protect the colonists from the Indians and the French.

Taxation Without Representation

Further legislation soon followed. In 1765 the British Parliament passed the **Stamp Act,** placing the first direct tax on the colonies. The Stamp Act required the use of tax stamps on all legal documents, newspapers,

▲ This reproduction of a 19th century engraving shows American colonists protesting the Stamp Act by burning the English tax stamps in a bonfire in 1765. Why did the American colonists object to the Stamp Act?

pamphlets, playing cards, and certain business agreements. The colonists denounced the new taxes, not only because the taxes were so severe, but also because they felt it was unfair to be taxed without having an elected official to represent their interests in Parliament. The colonists claimed this was "taxation without representation."

In October of 1765, nine of the thirteen colonies sent **delegates** (representatives) to the Stamp Act Congress held in New York City. The delegates prepared a declaration of rights and **grievances** (complaints) against the new British actions, which was sent to King George III. This action marked the first time that a majority of the colonies joined together to oppose British rule. As a result of the colonists' grievances, the British Parliament repealed the Stamp Act.

The British Crown passed new laws, however, designed to bind the colonies more tightly to the central government in London. Laws that imposed taxes on glass, paint, lead, and many other items were passed in 1767. The colonists protested the taxes by **boycotting**—refusing to purchase—all English goods. In 1773 anger over taxation reached a powerful climax at the famous Boston Tea Party, in which colonists dressed as Mohawk Indians dumped almost 350 chests of British tea into the Boston Harbor as a gesture of tax protest.

The British Parliament was quick to respond to the Tea Party. It passed the Coercive Acts (sometimes called the "Intolerable Acts") in 1774, which closed the harbor and placed the government of Boston under direct British control.

The First Continental Congress

In response to the "Intolerable Acts," Rhode Island, Pennsylvania, and New York proposed the meeting of a colonial congress. The Massachusetts House of Representatives requested that all colonies select delegates to send to Philadelphia for such a congress.

On September 5, 1774, the **First Continental Congress** was held at Carpenters Hall in Philadelphia. Of the thirteen colonies, Georgia was the only one that did not send delegates. The First Continental Congress decided that the colonies should send a petition to King George III to explain their grievances. Other resolutions were passed to continue boycotting British trade and to require that each colony start an army. Almost immediately after receiving the petition, the British government condemned the congress' actions as open acts of rebellion.

The congressional delegates declared that every county and city in the colonies should form a committee

whose mission was to spy on people's actions, and to report to the press the names of those who violated the trade boycott against Britain. The list of names was then printed in the local papers and the individuals so named were harassed and ridiculed. Over the next several months all colonial legislators supported this and other actions taken by the First Continental Congress.

The Second Continental Congress

Britain reacted to the resolution passed by the First Continental Congress with even more strict and repressive measures. On April 19, 1775, British soldiers, called Redcoats, fought with colonial citizen soldiers, called Minutemen, in the towns of Lexington and Concord in Massachusetts. The battle at Concord was the "shot heard around the world," the first battle of the American Revolution. Less than a month later, delegates from twelve colonies (Georgia's delegates did not arrive until the fall) gathered in Pennsylvania for the **Second Continental Congress,** which immediately assumed the powers of a central government. It declared that the militiamen who had gathered around Boston were now a full army. It also named George Washington—a delegate to the Second Continental Congress who had some military experience—as its commander-in-chief.

The delegates to the Second Continental Congress still intended to reach a peaceful settlement with the British Parliament. As one declaration stated, "we [the congress] have not raised armies with ambitious designs of separating from Great Britain, and establishing independent States."

Independence

Public debate raged bitterly about the problems with Great Britain, but the stage was set for independence. One of the most rousing arguments in favor of independence was presented by a former English corsetmaker,[2] Thomas Paine, who wrote a brilliant pamphlet called *Common Sense.* In that pamphlet he mocked King George III, and attacked every argument that favored loyalty to the king. He wanted the developing colonies to become a model nation for democracy, in a world in

---

2. Corsets are close-fitting undergarments that were worn at the time by both men and women to give the appearance of having a smaller waist. Whalebone was inserted in the corsets to make them stiff, and lacing was used to tighten them around the body.

COMMON SENSE;

ADDRESSED TO THE

INHABITANTS

OF

AMERICA,

On the following interesting

SUBJECTS.

I. Of the Origin and Design of Government in general,
with concise Remarks on the English Constitution.

II. Of Monarchy and Hereditary Succession.

III. Thoughts on the present State of American Affairs.

IV. Of the present Ability of America, with some mis-
cellaneous Reflections.

Man knows no Master save creating HEAVEN,
Or those whom choice and common good ordain.
THOMSON.

PHILADELPHIA;

Printed, and Sold, by R. BELL, in Third-Street.

MDCCLXXVI.

▶ Thomas Paine's pamphlet, *Common Sense,* went through 25 editions and sold over 120,000 copies in early 1776. How original were the arguments presented?

which other nations were oppressed by strong central governments.

None of Paine's arguments were new; in fact, most were commonly heard in tavern debates throughout the land. The reason that Paine's *Common Sense* was so effective was because of the near poetry of his words:

A government of our own is our natural right: and when a man seriously reflects on the precariousness [uncertainty] of human affairs, he will become convinced, that it is infinitely wiser and safer, to form a constitution of our own in a cool and deliberate manner, while we have it in our power, than to trust such an interesting event to time and chance.

The Resolution of Independence   Many colonists began to call for independence. Samuel Adams, a patriot from Massachusetts, asked "Is not America already independent? Why not then declare it?" In June of 1776, after more than a year of fighting, Richard Henry Lee of Virginia introduced the Resolution of Independence to the Second Continental Congress. By this time, the congress had already voted for free trade at all American ports for all countries except England. Congress had also suggested that all colonies establish state governments separate from Britain. On July 2 of that year, the congress adopted the Resolution of Independence:

RESOLVED, That these United Colonies are, and of right ought to be free and independent States, that they are absolved from allegiance to the British Crown, and that all political connection between them and the state of Great Britain is, and ought to be, totally dissolved.

Although it was not a legally binding document, the Resolution of Independence was one of the first necessary steps to establish the **legitimacy**—legal authority—of a new nation in the eyes of foreign governments. The new nation required supplies for its armies and commitments of foreign military aid. Unless officials of foreign nations believed that this new land was truly

In CONGRESS, July 4, 1776.

The unanimous Declaration of the thirteen united States of America,

The Declaration of Independence, which was drafted by Thomas Jefferson, proclaimed to the world that Americans had been mistreated under British rule and were therefore severing their political ties with Britain. What did Jefferson, in the Declaration of Independence, name as an individual's inalienable rights?

independent from Britain, they would not support its new leaders.

The Declaration of Independence   Soon after Richard Henry Lee proposed the Resolution of Independence, Thomas Jefferson, a tall redheaded Virginia planter, began writing the draft of the Declaration of Independence. Jefferson worked alone on the document for the last two weeks in June. On June 28, he asked John Adams and Benjamin Franklin to look over his draft. They made few changes.

Immediately after adopting the Resolution of Independence, the congress was ready to pass Jefferson's declaration. Some of his work was amended so that all the delegates would accept it. For example, his condem-

nation of slavery was eliminated to satisfy delegates from Georgia and North Carolina, where slaves were held on many farms and plantations. On July 4, 1776, one of the world's most famous documents, the Declaration of Independence, was adopted. On that day King George III, unaware of events 3,000 miles away, wrote in his diary, "Nothing of importance happened today."

Minor changes were made in the following two weeks. On July 19, the modified draft became the "unanimous declaration of the thirteen United States of America." On August 2, the members of the Continental Congress signed it. The first official printed version carried only the signatures of the congress' president, John Hancock, and of its secretary, Charles Thompson.

CASE STUDY

The Founding Mothers

There is always talk about America's founding fathers, but few of the books written about the colonial era ever mention our country's "founding mothers." While it may be true that no women were present at the Constitutional Convention, women nonetheless contributed significantly to the political changes of those times.

In the years prior to the American Revolution, many women encouraged opposition to the British. Small groups of women who called themselves "Daughters of Liberty" helped spread the boycott of British goods. Some women wrote political pamphlets, which helped turn public opinion in favor of independence. Mercy Ottis Warren (1728–1814) of Massachusetts was one of the first people to urge the Massachusetts delegates to the Second Continental Congress to vote for independence from England. Warren expressed her political ideas in written correspondence with John Adams and Thomas Jefferson, and wrote a three-volume history of the American Revolution called *The History of the Rise, Progress, and Determination of the American Revolution*, which was published in 1805. She also helped encourage pro-revolutionary sentiments by making fun of the British colonial government in her plays, *The Adulateur* (1773), *The Defeat* (1773), and *The Group* (1775).

During the War for Independence, many women served as nurses, seamstresses, and cooks. A few even disguised themselves as men and fought in battle. One such female soldier is buried in West Point Cemetery.

After independence was won many women remained politically active, including Mercy Warren. She campaigned against the proposed constitution because she did not think it allowed people to participate enough in the affairs of government.

THINK ABOUT IT

1. How do you think women's economic status over 200 years ago in this country may have prevented them from participating as actively as men did in the American Revolution?
2. How do you think the roles of women in World War I or World War II might have differed from their roles in the Revolutionary War?

▶ Mary (Molly) McCauley, who was known as Molly Pitcher for the pitcher of water she carried to troops, is revered as the heroine of Monmouth. During the battle of Monmouth in 1778, Molly is supposed to have taken a place at a cannon that was left when her husband was wounded. What were the primary ways that women helped the war effort?

GOVERNMENT IN ACTION

Natural Rights and the Consent of the Governed

The second paragraph of the Declaration of Independence begins with this sentence:

> We hold these Truths to be self-evident, that all Men are created equal, that they are endowed by their Creator with certain inalienable Rights, that among these are Life, Liberty, and the Pursuit of Happiness. . . .

The inalienable—or natural—rights referred to in the Declaration of Independence are the same rights that Locke presented in his political philosophy. Natural rights are *inherent* rights, meaning they cannot be taken away from a person, and are beyond the power of governments to grant or deny.

According to the Declaration of Independence, government exists to protect individuals' natural rights. In a democratic society, government derives its power from the **consent of the governed,** which means that the people give government the power to rule. Because government is based on the will of the people, it can also be abolished by the people. The Declaration of Independence declares that whenever any form of government ''becomes destructive to these ends, it is the Right of the People to alter or abolish it, and to institute a new government.'' (See the Resource Center.)

The American Creed　The ideals and standards set forth in the Declaration of Independence have become known as the **American Creed,** a set of political beliefs that most analysts agree exists in the United States. The American Creed stresses natural rights, limited government, equality under the law, and government by consent of the governed. In some ways, the Declaration of Independence defines the American sense of right and wrong. It presents a challenge to anyone who might wish to overthrow our democratic processes, or deny our citizens their natural rights to life, liberty, and the pursuit of happiness. (See the Resource Center.)

From Colonies to States

Even prior to the Declaration of Independence, some of the colonies had transformed themselves into sovereign states, with their own permanent governments. In May of 1776, the Second Continental Congress had directed each of the colonies to form ''such governments as shall . . . best be conducive to the happiness and safety of their constituents [voters].'' Before then all thirteen colonies had constitutions. Eleven of the colonies had newly drafted their constitutions; the other two, Rhode Island and Connecticut, made minor modifications to old royal charters. Seven of the new constitutions contained bills of rights that defined the personal liberties of all state citizens. All constitutions called for limited governments.

Many citizens were fearful of a strong central government because of their experience under the British Crown. They opposed any form of government that even seemed like monarchy, such as a strong **executive authority**—a person with wide-reaching administrative powers. Consequently, wherever such anti-royalist sentiment was strong, the legislature itself became all powerful. In Pennsylvania and Georgia, **unicameral** (one-house) **legislatures** were unchecked by executive authority. Indeed, anti-royalist sentiment was so strong that the executive branch was weak in most states. This situation would continue until the ratification of the U.S. Constitution.

SECTION 3 REVIEW

1. What kind of relationships had developed between the British Crown and the colonies by the mid-1700s? Why?
2. How did the thirteen colonies respond to the Stamp Act of 1765?
3. What type of resolution did the First Continental Congress pass?
4. Describe the major events and common attitudes that led to the signing of the Declaration of Independence.
5. **For critical analysis:** Do you think the experiences under English rule made it difficult for Americans to form a strong national government? Explain your answer.

SECTION 4

The Articles of Confederation

Preview Questions

- What are the basic provisions and weaknesses of the Articles of Confederation?
- Why were the 1780s a critical period in American history?
- What major events and popular sentiments led to the Constitutional Convention of 1787?

BUILDING SOCIAL STUDIES SKILLS
Using Government Publications

Every year the government prints hundreds of publications, many of which can be useful in understanding American government and politics. Listed below are several government publications that may prove useful in your studies.

The *Statistical Abstract of the United States* is published by the Bureau of the Census. It contains hundreds of tables that give statistics on the social, political, and economic status of government and business in the United States. Its hundreds of charts, graphs, and tables cover topics such as population, law enforcement, immigration, and much more.

The *Book of States* is published by the Council of State Governments. It contains information on state governments, economies, taxes, constitutions, and many other subjects.

The *Congressional Record* is published for every day that Congress is in session. It contains everything that is said and done on the floors of both houses. It is bound and indexed annually.

The *Congressional Directory* is a publication of the Congressional Joint Committee on Printing. It contains autobiographical accounts of the members

of Congress, lists of committees and committee assignments, statistics for recent congressional elections, and maps of congressional districts.

The *United States Government Manual* is a guide to the federal government. It contains information about the legislative, executive, and judicial branches of government and federal agencies and commissions. Addresses and telephone numbers of government offices are also included.

PRACTICING YOUR SKILLS

Go to your local library and use the sources listed above to find the following items and information.

1. A map of your congressional district
2. An autobiographical account of one of the senators in your state
3. The name of the state judicial agency that can give you information about your state's handgun law

Anti-royalist sentiments influenced the thinking of the delegates to the Continental Congress, who formed a committee to draft a plan of confederation. A **confederation** is a voluntary association of *independent* states. In a confederation, the member states agree to let the central government undertake a limited number of activities, such as forming an army. But the member states themselves do not allow many restrictions on their own actions. They typically can still govern most state affairs as they see fit.

On November 15, 1777, the Second Continental Congress agreed on a draft of the plan, which was finally signed by all thirteen colonies on March 1, 1781. The Articles of Confederation, the result of this plan, served as this nation's first national constitution. They represent an important step in the creation of our governmental system. (See the Resource Center.)

The Government of the Confederation

The Congress of the Confederation was the central governing body for all the states. This congress was a

unicameral assembly of ambassadors, as they were called, from the various states. Although the states could send between two and seven ambassadors each to the congress, each state, no matter what the size, had only one vote. The issue of sovereignty was an important part of the Articles of Confederation:

Each State retains its sovereignty, freedom and independence, and every power, jurisdiction, and right, which is not by this Confederation expressly delegated to the United States in Congress assembled.

The structure of our government under the Articles of Confederation is shown in Figure 2–3 on page 36.

The Powers of Congress Under the Articles

Congress had several powers under the Articles of Confederation:

- To enter into treaties and alliances
- To establish and control armed forces

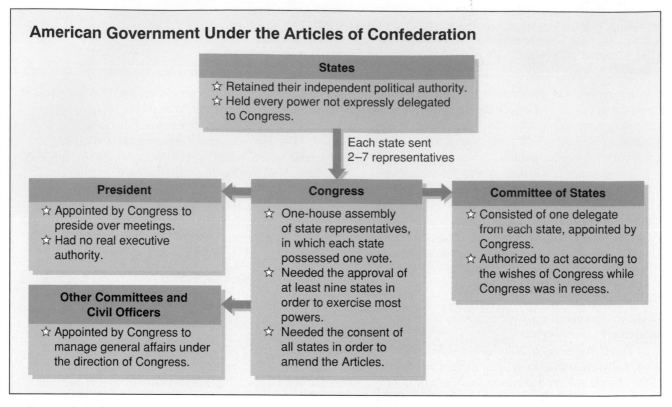

American Government Under the Articles of Confederation

States
☆ Retained their independent political authority.
☆ Held every power not expressly delegated to Congress.

Each state sent 2–7 representatives

President
☆ Appointed by Congress to preside over meetings.
☆ Had no real executive authority.

Congress
☆ One-house assembly of state representatives, in which each state possessed one vote.
☆ Needed the approval of at least nine states in order to exercise most powers.
☆ Needed the consent of all states in order to amend the Articles.

Committee of States
☆ Consisted of one delegate from each state, appointed by Congress.
☆ Authorized to act according to the wishes of Congress while Congress was in recess.

Other Committees and Civil Officers
☆ Appointed by Congress to manage general affairs under the direction of Congress.

▲ **FIGURE 2–3 American Government Under the Articles of Confederation.** As you can see from looking at the figure above, the individual states were supreme in power under the Articles of Confederation. Under the Articles of Confederation, how was a president chosen? Was the president very powerful?

- To declare war and make peace
- To regulate coinage (but not paper money)
- To borrow money from the people
- To create a postal system
- To regulate Indian affairs
- To set standards of weights and measures
- To create courts for problems related to ships at sea
- To settle disputes between the states under certain circumstances
- To guarantee that citizens visiting other states would have the same rights and privileges as the state's resident

Under the Articles, a number of accomplishments were made. Certain states' claims to western land were settled with the **Northwest Ordinance.** It established a basic pattern for how states should govern new territories north of the Ohio River. Additionally, and perhaps most importantly, the United States under the Articles of Confederation won the Revolutionary War. Congress was then able to negotiate a peace treaty with Great Britain

that was signed in 1783. Under the treaty, Britain not only recognized American independence, but also granted the United States all of the territory from the Atlantic Ocean to the Mississippi River, and from the Great Lakes and Canada to what is now northern Florida.

The Articles of Confederation proved to be a good "first draft" for the Constitution of the United States, which was soon to follow. They were an unplanned experiment that tested some of the principles of government set forth earlier in the Declaration of Independence. Some argue that without the experience of government under the Articles of Confederation, it would have been difficult, if not impossible, to arrive at the compromises that were put into the Constitution several years later.

Weaknesses of the Government of the Confederation

In spite of its accomplishments, the government created by the Articles was in fact weak. Due to its lack of power, the central government had a difficult time coping with the problems that the growing nation was facing.

▼|FIGURE 2–4 **Weaknesses in the Articles of Confederation.** The lack of a strong central government and the fierce independence of the states under the Articles of Confederation led to several problems. Each of these problems was due to a weakness in the Articles of Confederation. Which weakness led to financial problems for the central government?

Weaknesses in the Articles of Confederation

Weakness	Result
Congress could not force the states to meet military quotas.	They could not draft soldiers to form a standing army.
Congress could not regulate commerce between the states or with other nations.	Each state was free to set up its own system of taxes on goods imported from other states. Economic quarrels among the states broke out. There was difficulty in trading with other nations.
Congress could enter into treaties, but could not enforce its power or control foreign relations.	The states were not forced to respect treaties. Many states entered into treaties independent of Congress.
Congress could not directly tax the people.	It had to rely on the states to collect and forward taxes, which the states were reluctant to do. The central government was always short of money.
Congress had no power to enforce its laws.	The central government depended on the states to enforce its laws, which they rarely did.
Nine states had to approve any law before it was enacted.	Most laws were difficult, if not impossible, to enact.
Any amendment to the Articles required all 13 states to consent.	The powers of the central government could not be changed in practice.
There was no national judicial system.	Most disputes among the states could not be settled by the national government.
There was no executive branch.	Coordinating the work of the central government was almost impossible.

CITIZENSHIP SKILLS AND RESPONSIBILITIES
Making Decisions

Think of a serious problem facing your community, such as crime, pollution, overpopulation, lack of educational facilities, or inadequate transportation systems. Although everyone might agree there is a problem, chances are everyone does not agree on the same solution.

One vital citizenship skill is making thoughtful decisions about such government matters. Also, some day you may want to make a decision about which candidate to elect for governor, state representative, or school board chair. You may need to decide what to do about one of the problems mentioned above. Remember that there is almost always more than one solution to any problem. To make the best decision, you need to identify all possible alternatives and choose the one that will be the most effective for yourself and others. Doing this means knowing what goals or values are involved in each alternative, and what the consequences of each choice will be.

The process outlined below can help you make wise decisions:

1. **Define what you need or want.** Try to pinpoint what it is you are trying to accomplish or what you need or want from your decision.
2. **Look carefully at your resources.** Be aware of all the resources available to you.
3. **Identify your choices.** There are at least two choices, and usually more, for every decision. Sometimes you need to gather information and do research in order to identify your choices. Try to come up with as many possibilities as you can without eliminating any.
4. **Sort through your choices.** After you've listed all your choices, take a good look at each one. Consider their advantages and disadvantages. Be sure that each option you are considering is legal and ethical.
5. **Compare your choices.** Use the information you have found to evaluate each possible choice. Compare them and see which one makes the most sense.
6. **Make the decision.**
7. **Make a plan to carry out your decision.**

TAKING ACTION

1. Think of a decision you have made recently. Name two options you had and name the advantages and disadvantages of each.
2. Think of a problem facing your community. Recommend a possible solution to the problem by using the decision-making process outlined above. Then send your recommendation to the council, commission, or official in charge of making such decisions.
3. Do you think the founding fathers used any part of this decision-making process while they were drafting the Declaration of Independence or the Articles of Confederation? Explain your answer.

The Articles of Confederation also had other major weaknesses, which are listed in Figure 2–4 on page 37. These weaknesses stemmed from the fact that the government under the Articles was made up of independent states that had no intention of giving up their sovereignty.

As you can see from the figure on page 37, much of the functioning of the government under the Articles basically depended on the goodwill of the states. Article 3, for example, simply established a "league of friendship" among the states, with no central government intended.

A Time of Crisis—the 1780s

The Revolutionary War ended on October 18, 1781. The Treaty of Paris, which confirmed the colonies' independence from Britain, was signed in 1783. Peace with the British may have been won, but peace within the new nation was hard to find. The states bickered among themselves, and refused to support the new central government in almost every way.

As George Washington stated, "We are one nation today and thirteen tomorrow. Who will treat us on such terms?'' States started printing their own money at dizzying rates, which lead to inflated prices. The states also increasingly taxed each other's goods and at times even prevented trade altogether. The intensity of the states' squabbles reached a boiling point in a well-known event that occurred in August, 1786.

Shays' Rebellion   In western Massachusetts, angry farmers protested the state legislature's decision not to issue cheap paper money, as well as the state court's decision to throw debtors in jails. Finally, in 1786, former revolutionary captain Daniel Shays, along with approximately two thousand armed farmers, seized county courthouses and disrupted the debtors' trials. Shays' men then launched an attack on the national government arsenal in Springfield. The rebellion continued to grow into the winter when it was finally stopped by the Massachusetts militia.

Despite the upheaval, the revolt had actually done something important. It had scared American political and business leaders, and caused more and more Americans to realize that a *true* national government had to be created. That central government had to be strong enough to cope with the serious economic problems facing the nation.

The Annapolis Meeting   Unhappy members of the Confederation Congress jumped at the Virginia legislature's call for a meeting of all states at Annapolis, Maryland, on September 11, 1786. Five of the thirteen states sent delegates, two of whom were Alexander Hamilton of New York and James Madison of Virginia. Both of these men favored a strong central government. Thus, they were called **nationalists.** They persuaded the other delegates to issue a report calling on the states to hold a constitutional convention in Philadelphia in May of the following year.

The Confederation Congress at first was reluctant to give its approval to the Philadelphia convention. By mid-February of 1787, however, seven of the states had named delegates to the Philadelphia meeting. Finally, on February 21, the Congress called upon the states to send delegates to Philadelphia ''for the sole and expressed purpose of revising the Articles of Confederation.'' That Philadelphia meeting became the Constitutional Convention.

▼ | This 19th century engraving depicts the battle between Daniel Shays' rebels and the government troops at the arsenal at Springfield, Massachusetts. Why was Shays' Rebellion so important?

SECTION 4 REVIEW _____

1. What were the powers of Congress under the Articles of Confederation?
2. Describe the government set up by the Articles.
3. What were the major weaknesses of the Articles and what were the results of those weaknesses?
4. What did George Washington mean when he stated, ''We are one nation today and thirteen tomorrow. Who will treat us on such terms?''
5. **For critical analysis:** Why do you think Shays' Rebellion scared American business and political leaders?

SECTION 5

Creating The Constitution

Preview Questions
- What basic concepts did the delegates agree upon?
- What compromises were necessary and why?
- What were the final compromises reached?

Although the Philadelphia convention was supposed to start on May 14, 1787, few of the delegates had actually arrived in Philadelphia on that date. It formally opened in the East Room of the Pennsylvania State House (later named Independence Hall), on May 25th. Fifty-five of the seventy-four delegates had arrived. Only Rhode Island, where feelings were strong against creating a more powerful central government, did not send any delegates.

Who Were the Founding Fathers?

The 55 delegates were relatively young by today's standards. James Madison was 36, Alexander Hamilton was 32, and Jonathan Dayton of New Jersey was 26. Thirty-three were members of the legal profession. Fifty percent were college graduates in a country in which less than 1 percent finished college. Seven were former chief executives of their respective states; eight were important businessmen; six were large plantation owners; and three were physicians.

Several men stood out as leaders. George Washington, who served as commander-in-chief during the war for independence, was already a national hero. Among all the prominent men assembled at the Philadelphia convention, Washington was immediately recognized as the leader of the leaders. Benjamin Franklin was a world-famous scientist and diplomat. At 81 years old he played an active role in the debates (even though he had to be carried in on a portable chair held by four prisoners from the local jail). Virginia had sent James Madison, a brilliant supporter of a strong central government. Madison's carefully taken notes are our primary source of information about what happened at the Constitutional Convention. He is often called the "Father of the Constitution" because he authored the basic plan of government that was ultimately adopted by the convention. Thomas Jefferson, unfortunately, could not be at the convention because he was serving as Ambassador to France. John Adams was serving as Ambassador to Great Britain and could not attend either.

Working Conditions

The founding fathers worked for 116 days (of which they actually met on 89) in a room where the windows were usually shut. None of the framers of the Constitution wanted anybody to hear what they were doing, because they did not want rumors spread about the form of government upon which they would ultimately decide. Besides, if they opened the windows, hordes of flies would descend upon them. The air became humid and hot by noon of each day. At the end of each session they retired to the nearby tavern, the Indian Queen.

George Washington was chosen to preside over the meetings. Each state had one vote on all questions and a simple majority rule was used. The **quorum**—the number of members necessary to legally transact business for a group—consisted of delegates from at least seven states. All of the delegates present agreed on a number of basic concepts. They wanted the powers of the national government to be divided among three branches: legislative, executive, and judicial. They wanted the central government to limit the power of the states to make their own money. And they all wanted, in varying degrees, a more powerful central government. The debates within the convention were, therefore, not over these fundamental issues, but rather over how to put them into practice.

The Compromises

James Madison had spent months reviewing European political theory before he went to the Philadelphia Convention. When his Virginia delegation arrived before anybody else, he put them to work immediately. On the first day of the convention, governor Edmond Randolph of Virginia was able to present fifteen resolutions. This was a masterful political stroke on the part of the Virginia delegation. It immediately set the **agenda**—plan of things to be done—for the remainder of the convention.

The Virginia Plan The fifteen resolutions under the Virginia Plan proposed an entirely new national government under a constitution. The plan, which favored large states such as Virginia, called for the following:

- A **bicameral** (two-house) **legislature.** The lower house was to be chosen by the people. The smaller upper house was to be chosen by the elected members of the lower house. The number of representatives would be in proportion to the state's population (the larger states would have more representatives). The legislature could void any state laws.
- A national executive branch, elected by the legislature.
- A national court system, created by the legislature.

The smaller states immediately complained because they would have less representation in the legislature. After two weeks of debate they offered their own plan.

The New Jersey Plan William Paterson of New Jersey presented an alternate plan favorable to the smaller states. He argued that under the Articles of Confederation all states had equality and that therefore the convention had no power to change this arrangement. He suggested the following:

- That Congress be able to regulate trade and impose taxes.
- That each state have only one vote.
- That acts of Congress be the supreme law of the land.
- That an executive office of more than one person be elected by Congress.
- That the executive office appoint a national supreme court.

The Connecticut Plan, or the Great Compromise As the summer grew hotter, so did the tempers of the delegates. Most were unwilling to consider the New Jersey Plan. When the Virginia Plan was brought up again, delegates from the smaller states threatened to leave, and the convention was in danger of dissolving. The Convention was deadlocked. On July 16, Roger Sherman of Connecticut proposed a plan for the legislature that has become known as the Connecticut Compromise, or the Great Compromise:

- A two-house legislature in which the number of state representatives from the lower house (the House of Representatives) would be determined by the number of people in each state.
- An upper house, called the Senate, which would have two members from each state elected by the state legislatures.

The Connecticut Compromise broke the deadlock and, like any good compromise, it gave something to both sides. It resolved the small-state versus large-state controversy.

The Three-Fifths Compromise A second compromise settled a disagreement over how to count slaves for the purposes of determining how many representatives each state would have in the House. Although slavery was legal everywhere except in Massachusetts, most slaves and slaveowners lived in the South. The Southern states wanted slaves to be counted equally in determining representation in Congress, but not in determining taxation. Because they did not have many slaves, the Northern states took the opposite position. They wanted slaves counted for tax purposes but not for representation. The **Three-Fifths Compromise** settled this deadlock.

▲ Despite the fact that the War for Independence was fought for such ideals as the equality of all persons, some 500,000 African Americans were held as enslaved persons in 1776. How did the Three-Fifths Compromise help to continue this exploitation of enslaved people?

Three-fifths of the slaves were to be counted for both tax purposes and for representation. This part of the Constitution was eventually changed by the Thirteenth Amendment, which abolished slavery in 1865.

The Slavery Question Continued The Three-Fifths Compromise did not satisfy everyone present. Many delegates wanted slavery banned completely in the United States. The delegates compromised on this question by agreeing that Congress could limit the number of slaves imported into the country after 1808, but the issue of slavery itself was never addressed. The South won twenty years of unrestricted slave trade and a requirement that escaped slaves in free states be returned to their owners in slave states.

Those delegates who strongly believed that slavery should be banned had to face reality. The Southern states would never accept the Constitution if it interfered with the slave trade. A *tradeoff* was therefore accepted. In order to create a new and stronger government, the

ARCHITECT OF
The American Dream

E ven though George Washington was born more than two and a half centuries ago, he remains one of the foremost architects of the American dream. He was a central figure during the events that shaped the founding of our nation.

George Washington was born in Bridges Creek, Westmoreland County, Virginia, on February 22, 1732. After his father's death in 1743 he lived chiefly at Mount Vernon and worked as a surveyor. He served as a lieutenant colonel in the French and Indian Wars from 1754 to 1758 and in 1759 entered the Virginia colonial legislature, the House of Burgesses. He was a leader in the movement for independence and a delegate to the First and Second Continental Congresses. On June 15, 1775, he was chosen to be general and commander in chief of the Army of the United Colonies. He persevered through the long and difficult years of the Revolution until his secret and rapid march from the Hudson River to the Chesapeake Bay. This resulted in the surrender of British General Cornwallis at Yorktown in 1781, thus ending the war. When he resigned his commission in 1783, he said he was through with public life, but his retirement did not last.

Returning to public life, he supported the movement for a more effective union and presided over the Philadelphia Convention in 1787 that adopted the Constitution. Even though he did not design the Constitution, many believe it would not have taken the shape it did without his commanding presence and leadership.

The framers of the Constitution respected George Washington and wanted him to be the first president. They created the office with him in mind. He had the qualities they thought a chief executive should have: honesty, fairness, wisdom, dignity, natural leadership, and the ability to balance executive authority with the rights of citizens. He was elected unanimously as the first president. George Washington knew the importance of being the first to hold the office. He wrote: ''I walk on untrodden ground. . . . There is scarcely any part of my conduct that may not hereafter be drawn into precedent.'' He did indeed set precedents, including establishing a cabinet and holding regular cabinet meetings. He thought of the United States as ''an experiment entrusted to the hands of the American people'' and knew that it was his responsibility to give that experiment proper direction. During his two terms, he helped to set the new nation on a solid foundation and organized the machinery of government. He declined a third term of office, which set the precedent of limiting the number of presidential terms to two.

HIS WORDS

Farewell Address, September 17, 1796

''The great rule of conduct for us in regard to foreign nations is, in extending our commercial relations to have with them as little *political* connection as possible. So far as we have already formed engagements let them be fulfilled with perfect good faith. Here let us stop.

Europe has a set of primary interests which to us have none or a very remote relation. Hence she must be engaged in frequent controversies, the causes of which are essentially foreign to our concerns. Hence, therefore, it must be unwise in us to implicate ourselves by artificial ties in the ordinary

George Washington

This painting by Howard Chandler Christy depicts the scene at the signing of the Constitution of the United States on September 17, 1787. Why do you think George Washington was chosen to preside over the convention?

HIS WORDS–*continued*

vicissitudes of her politics or the ordinary combinations and collisions of her friendships or enmities.

Our detached and distant situation invites and enables us to pursue a different course. If we remain one people, under an efficient government, the period is not far off when we may defy material injury from external annoyance; when we may take such an attitude as well cause the neutrality we may at any time resolve upon to be scrupulously respected; when belligerent nations, under the impossibility of making acquisitions upon us, will not lightly hazard the giving us provocation; when we may choose peace or war, as our interest, guided by justice, shall counsel.

It is our true policy to steer clear of permanent alliances with any portion of the foreign world, so far, I mean, as we are now at liberty to do it; for let me not be understood as capable of patronizing infidelity to existing engagements. I hold the maxim no less applicable to public than to private affairs that honesty is always the best policy. I repeat, therefore, let those engagements be observed in their genuine sense. But in my opinion it is unnecessary and would be unwise to extend them."

DEVELOPING CRITICAL THINKING SKILLS

1. Washington states that "Europe has a set of primary interests which to us have none or a very remote relation." How has our relationship with Europe changed since the days of George Washington?
2. What do you think Washington meant when he said, "the period is not far off when we may defy material injury from external annoyance"?
3. At what point in history did our nation begin to stray from Washington's advice to "steer clear of permanent alliances with any portion of the foreign world"?

FOR FURTHER READING

Cunliffe, Marcus. *George Washington: Man and Monument.* Boston: Little Brown, 1958.

Davis, Burke. *George Washington and the American Revolution.* New York: Random House, 1975.

Eaton, Jeanette. *Leader by Destiny: George Washington, Man and Patriot.* New York: Harcourt Brace, 1938.

43

CHALLENGE TO THE AMERICAN DREAM

Holding Another Constitutional Convention

The first and last constitutional convention that this country had was over two hundred years ago. Since then, many changes have occurred in the political, economic, social, and technological arenas of our society. Not surprisingly, a number of individuals have called for a second constitutional convention, to incorporate such changes as allowing prayer in the public schools and outlawing the burning of the American flag.

A second constitutional convention might follow the same pattern as the first one in Philadelphia, in which major changes to the basic document were made. But because the Constitution itself does not offer guidelines for a second convention, such a meeting would undoubtedly operate under rules laid down by Congress. Once it got under way, however, the delegates could probably modify those rules or interpret them according to the will of the majority. Let's say, for example, that Congress called a convention for a very narrow purpose, such as passing an amendment to make flag burning illegal. There would be no practical way for Congress to control the convention once it was under way. Who knows what additional proposals might be introduced?

Imagine some of the outrageous possibilities: Tampering with the structure of the executive branch by calling for a plural presidency (say with three individuals holding equal power); eliminating the office of vice president; repealing the right to freedom of speech. Such proposals are of course possible, though highly improbable. The potential for such drastic proposals being incorporated into the Constitution would depend upon the representatives present at the convention.

When all is said and done, the comparison between what happened at the Philadelphia Convention in 1787 and what might occur at a constitutional convention in,

say, 2000, should not be exaggerated. We don't have many Franklins, Washingtons, Jeffersons, Madisons, and Hamiltons in our midst who are going to articulate and craft the political outlines of an entirely new national constitution. Moreover, it would be difficult to duplicate the secrecy with which the Philadelphia Convention met. The prying eyes and ears of the media would make it unlikely that major surprises would be sprung on an unsuspecting nation. The openness of the convention might even prevent any proposals for truly radical changes in the constitutional status quo. Finally, the rest of the world would be watching—something that wasn't happening in 1787.

But a limited convention still is a possibility, and, if it occurred, it could make important changes in our lives, such as requiring that the federal government raise taxes every time it wants to increase spending, or that schoolchildren start every school day with a moment of silence or prayer. To some, such changes would be welcome; to others, they would be seen as threats to the nation's future.

The challenge to the American dream is to ensure that the results of the national and state legislative processes reflect the desires of the majority of Americans. If this is in fact happening, there will be less reason than ever to worry about the problems of a second constitutional convention.

◤ You Decide

1. If there were a second constitutional convention, which special interest groups might be the most powerful and why?
2. The United States Constitution is a model of brevity. Do you think that a new constitution would be as short as the original? Explain.
3. If you were a delegate to a second constitutional convention, what changes to the Constitution would you suggest? Why?

CHAPTER 2 REVIEW

Key Terms

agenda 40
American Creed 34
Anti-Federalists 44
bicameral
  legislature 40
boycott 30
charter 27
confederation 35
consent 24
consent of the
  governed 34
executive authority 34
exports 44
delegates 30

factions 45
Federalists 44
First Continental
  Congress 30
Fundamental Orders of
  Connecticut 28
grievances 30
interstate commerce 44
legislatures 28
legitimacy 31
limited government 23
Magna Carta 23

Mayflower
  Compact 27
nationalists 39
natural right 23
Navigation Acts 29
Northwest
  Ordinance 36
Parliament 24
peers 23
political philosophy 26
prototype 27
quorum 40
ratified 44

representative
  assembly 27
representative
  government 24
representatives 24
Second Continental
  Congress 30
Stamp Act 29
status quo 45
Three-Fifths
  Compromise 41
unicameral
  legislature 34

Summary

1. The English colonists brought with them to North America political ideas that had been developing for centuries. Among these was the idea of limited government that derived from the Magna Carta and from the English Bill of Rights. Other important influences were the English system of representative government and the political philosophy of John Locke.

2. Jamestown became the first permanent British settlement in North America. Jamestown colonists instituted a representative assembly. The Plymouth Company established the first New England colony in 1620. Some of the Pilgrims developed a document called the Fundamental Orders of Connecticut, which provided for an assembly of elected representatives and the popular election of a governor and judges. By 1732, all thirteen colonies had been established, each with its own constitution and legislature.

3. The American colonies banded together against Britain to win independence. Oppressive economic practices imposed by the British heightened the colonists' desire for independence. At the First Continental Congress in 1774, the colonists passed a resolution that banned trade with Britain or purchase of British goods. The British treated the resolution as an open act of rebellion and attacked colonial militiamen at Lexington and Concord in 1775. This signaled the start of the American Revolution. A Second Continental Congress issued the Declaration of Independence in 1776. Even prior to the Declaration of Independence, some of the colonies had already transformed themselves into states.

4. The Articles of Confederation represented an important step in the creation of a national government and our current system. Despite its accomplishments, the national government established under the Articles of Confederation was weak. Financial conflicts, a lack of cooperation among the states, and an armed rebellion of farmers led by Daniel Shays led to a call for a convention to revise the Articles.

5. Our founders replaced the Articles with a new Constitution at a meeting in Philadelphia that lasted from May to September, 1787. Many of the provisions of the Constitution were arrived at through a series of compromises.

6. When the Constitution was submitted to the states for ratification, conflict between the Federalists and Anti-Federalists developed. The Federalists' promise to add the Bill of Rights helped resolve the conflict. On March 4, 1789, the new Congress convened in the Federal Hall on Wall Street in New York City. George Washington was elected president on April 6.

CHAPTER 2 REVIEW—Continued

Review Questions

1. What two aspects of English government most strongly influenced the American style of government?
2. How did the British Parliament affect the way American government was organized?
3. What were the first British settlements?
4. What contribution did the Pilgrims make to the development of American government?
5. Explain the major reasons for the colonists' revolt against Great Britain.
6. Describe the events that led up to the American Revolution.
7. Why were the First and Second Continental Congresses called?
8. Why is the Declaration of Independence important?
9. What is significant about the second paragraph of the Declaration of Independence?
10. How did the Articles of Confederation fail to create a strong central government?
11. What led George Washington to say "We are one nation today and thirteen tomorrow. Who will treat us on such terms?"
12. Explain what the Connecticut Compromise stated and why it was necessary.
13. What major arguments did the Federalists offer in favor of the Constitution? Why did the Anti-Federalists oppose the Constitution?
14. What promise turned the tide in favor of ratifying the Constitution?
15. List and describe the steps that one should normally take to reach an intelligent decision.
16. What are some problems that might be encountered if Congress allows a second constitutional convention?

Questions for Thought and Discussion

1. If you had been a participant at the Constitutional Convention, would you have ended up a Federalist or an Anti-Federalist afterward? Explain why.
2. The Constitution has been described as a "bundle of compromises." When do you think political compromise is justifiable? When is it not justifiable? Support your answers with recent examples of political compromises.
3. Do you think it was right for the delegates to the Constitutional Convention to have met in secret? Would it be right for this to happen today?

Improving Your Skills
Communication Skills
Note Taking

The skills of listening and note taking are closely related. You must listen well in order to take good notes, and you must take notes—either mentally or on paper—in order to gain the most from listening. If you haven't done so already, read the section in Chapter 1 on listening.

There are many methods of note taking. Regardless of the method that you choose, the following guidelines will help you get the most from your note taking.

The Mechanics
1. *Use a loose-leaf binder with notepaper.* This way you can reorganize your notes or insert other materials. If you buy a spiral notebook instead, make sure it has pockets for handouts. Use a pen for easy readability.
2. *Always indicate the date, class, and name of your topic at the top of your notes.*
3. *Divide each page so that you have a 2 1/2-inch column on the right or left.* Use this space to make sketches to illustrate important points, or to write helpful comments such as "T" for possible test question, "see textbook," or "use for term paper."

Prepare Your Mind
1. *Read any assigned work before going to class.* The lecture will make more sense and you will be able to relate the ideas to what you have read.
2. *Review notes from the previous class a few minutes before class starts.*
3. *Reflect for a few minutes on any personal experiences or previous learning that relates to the subject.* New learning "sticks" most readily when it fits into a meaningful context.

CHAPTER 2 REVIEW—Continued

Be a Keen Listener

1. *Get interested.* Rousing interest in the subject matter helps sharpen your attention and concentration, and heightens your learning and remembering. It also helps you shut out distractions.
2. *Sort out the important points and significant details.* Listen for key phrases such as:

   ● *Contrast:* "on the one hand . . ." "on the other hand . . ." "but," "on the contrary"
   ● *Additional points:* "in addition to," "as well as," "another"
   ● *Conclusion:* "in summary," "as a result," "finally"
   ● *Phrases that introduce main points:* "Thus, the important point is . . .," "What is essential to understand is . . .," "The three conditions are . . ."
3. *Be mentally alert.* Listen to changes in a speaker's volume or tone. Pay attention to his or her voice and actions.

Record

1. *Take notes in your own words unless the subject is very technical.* Write in block, paragraph, or outline form, whichever you can manage most accurately and quickly.
2. *Skip a line whenever the lecturer moves on to another topic.*
3. *Keep your notes brief, using words or phrases rather than sentences.* Use common abbreviations and symbols such as:

w = with
w/o = without
+ = and
vs. = versus
def. = definition
ex. = example

Abbreviations can also be used for words that are used consistently. For example:

SC = Supreme Court
C. = Congress
H.R. = House of Representatives
gov. = government

Review

1. *Review your notes as soon as possible after the class.* Fill in missing words and flesh out the concepts based on what you remember. Underline the most important ideas. Make corrections, summaries, and additions in the margin.

Writing

1. Watch an evening news program, taking notes as you watch. Check to see if you have followed the note-taking guidelines listed above.
2. Take notes during a lecture. Afterward, compare your notes with a classmate, and exchange suggestions and tips for improving each other's notes.

Social Studies Skills

Map Reading

Use Figure 2–2 (The Thirteen Colonies) on page 28 to answer the following questions.
1. Approximately what is the distance between the northernmost colony and the southernmost colony?
2. Which is the largest colony?
3. Which are the two smallest colonies?
4. Which colony doesn't have any coastline?

Activities and Projects

1. Divide the class into groups of three or four. Have each group study one of the influential leaders of this period, such as Benjamin Franklin, James Madison, George Washington, Samuel Adams, Thomas Paine, Alexander Hamilton, Thomas Jefferson, Gouverneur Morris, or Patrick Henry. Each group should prepare a short oral report on how the leaders they researched contributed to the development of American government.
2. Prepare a wall chart that lists the major weaknesses of the Articles of Confederation and shows how those matters were remedied by the Constitution.
3. Stage a class Federalist/Anti-Federalist debate on this statement: *A strong federal government leads to violations of personal freedoms.* In the course of the debate, discuss how the issue of balance between a strong central government and people's rights continues to be a major factor in American politics.

CHAPTER 3

The Constitution

CHAPTER OBJECTIVES

To learn and understand

- The structure of the Constitution.
- The Constitution's major principles of government.
- The Bill of Rights and how it was formulated.
- The formal and informal processes of amending the Constitution.

Keynote

"The Constitution of the United States was made not merely for the generation that then existed, but for posterity—unlimited, undefined, endless, perpetual posterity."

————— **Henry Clay**
(1777–1852) United States Senator

INTRODUCTION

If you take the time to sit down and actually read the Constitution, you might be amazed. It is not a dreary and obsolete relic of history that has nothing to do with your life today. It may not be written in a way you are normally accustomed to, but if you look beyond what seems to be its old-fashioned language to the thoughts and convictions of its framers, you might discover how this document relates to your life.

As Henry Clay's quote above states, the Constitution was not written for one generation, but for perpetual posterity. Certainly Clay understood the concept of change. He had served as a U.S. Senator for no less than four separate terms, the first starting in 1806 and the last ending in 1852. He had also served in the House of Representatives for six terms, during which he was Speaker of the House three times and then later became President John Q. Adams' secretary of state.

Clay recognized, along with others, that the framers of the Constitution had the foresight to know that this nation would constantly change. So they made the document general enough for each of the many generations that would follow to interpret it according to their needs and values. This is why our Constitution is often called a living, breathing document, created by people with a vision.

The Constitution serves today as the plan for government in the United States and is the supreme law of the land. It outlines the ideals of American government and describes how they should be achieved. It outlines the rules by which your government must carry out its actions and imposes limits on the powers of government. It tells you what your rights and privileges are. The Constitution affects you, your family, and your friends as much as it affected those who wrote it over 200 years ago.

The Structure of Our Constitution

Preview Questions
- What are the three major parts of the Constitution?
- What is the purpose of the Preamble?
- What are the purposes of the seven articles in the Constitution?

In its original form, the United States Constitution contained only about five thousand words. Today, after twenty-seven amendments were added, there are still only about seven thousand words. Compared to virtually all state constitutions and to constitutions in other nations, ours is brief and to the point. The founding fathers did not attempt to spell out in detail exactly how the government should operate. Rather, they gave us a general

▼ The United States Constitution, which is on display at the National Archives in Washington, D.C., is visited by thousands of people who want to see the document that is the supreme law of the land. Why do you think the U.S. Constitution still works today, even though it was written over two hundred years ago?

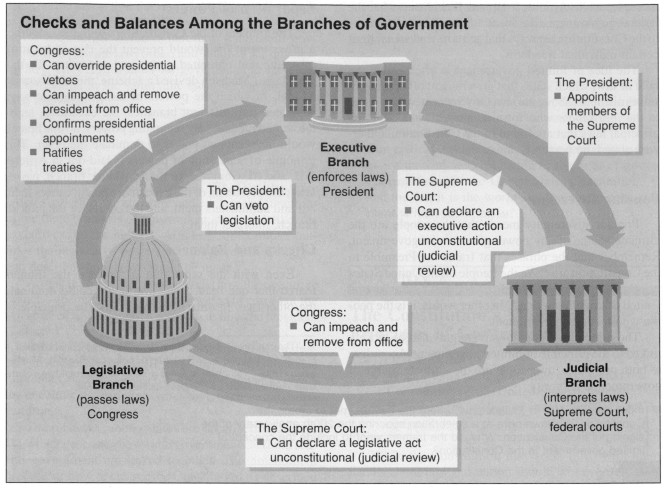

Checks and Balances Among the Branches of Government

Congress:
- Can override presidential vetoes
- Can impeach and remove president from office
- Confirms presidential appointments
- Ratifies treaties

The President:
- Can veto legislation

Executive Branch
(enforces laws)
President

The President:
- Appoints members of the Supreme Court

The Supreme Court:
- Can declare an executive action unconstitutional (judicial review)

Congress:
- Can impeach and remove from office

Legislative Branch
(passes laws)
Congress

Judicial Branch
(interprets laws)
Supreme Court, federal courts

The Supreme Court:
- Can declare a legislative act unconstitutional (judicial review)

▲ **FIGURE 3–2 Checks and Balances Among the Branches of Government**
The above figure details the system of checks and balances among the branches of the United States government. As you can see, each branch of government has some authority over the actions of each other branch. Why did the framers include a system of checks and balances in the Constitution?

checks and balances was introduced into the Constitution. Under this principle, each branch of government is independent of the others, but also exercises power over the actions of the others. Look at Figure 3–2 above and you can see how this is done.

As the figure shows, the president checks Congress by holding **veto power,** which is the ability to refuse to sign congressional bills into law. Congress, in turn, controls taxes and spending and the Senate must approve presidential appointments. For example, the president can appoint justices to the Supreme Court, but only after the advice and consent of the Senate.

Under the system of checks and balances, each branch's independence is protected, yet at the same time the Constitution forces cooperation between at least two

branches at a time, which thereby fosters dependence. For example, Congress can pass a law, but the executive branch must approve, administer, and enforce it.

Judicial Review

Judicial review refers to the court's ability to decide whether an act of a legislature does or does not violate the Constitution. In actual cases that come before the Supreme Court, if the justices find that a federal or state law violates the U.S. Constitution, that law is declared **unconstitutional.** Such a law no longer has any validity or legitimacy—it is as if it did not exist. For example, if your state passes a law that specifically allows the state police to monitor telephone conversations (wiretapping)

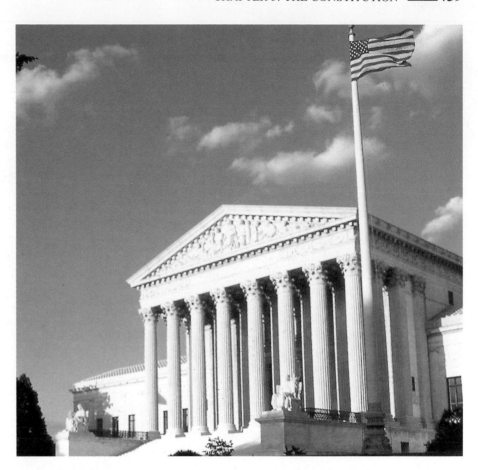

In our system of checks and balances, the United States Supreme Court, which meets in the Supreme Court Building in Washington, D.C. (shown here) has the power of judicial review. How would you describe judicial review?

without formally obtaining permission from a judge, the U.S. Supreme Court might strike down that law as unconstitutional because it violates the Fourth Amendment to the Constitution. If you had been convicted of a crime based on evidence obtained through the illegal wiretapping of your phone lines, your conviction would probably be overturned because of the unconstitutional nature of the law that justified tapping your phones without formal permission from a court.

The Constitution does not *explicitly* state that the principle of judicial review should be put into practice. Most constitutional scholars do believe, however, that the framers *meant* that the federal courts should have that power. In the 1803 case of *Marbury* v. *Madison,* judicial review became part of the United States' system of government. The Supreme Court ruled for the first time that part of an act that Congress had passed was unconstitutional. Chief Justice John Marshall declared that it is ''the province and duty of the Judiciary department to say what the law is.'' (See next page.)

After this important case, the Supreme Court became part of the checks and balances system through its power of judicial review. It now had the right in related court cases to declare the policies of the other two branches of government unconstitutional.

Federalism

In a federal system of government, the national, or federal, government coexists with various state governments. Because the states feared too much centralized control, the Constitution granted states' rights. This **principle of federalism,** which means that some powers belong to the federal government while others belong to the states, has lasted for over two hundred years. This principle was a compromise between delegates to the Philadelphia convention who had strong federalist views and those who felt that the states should retain most of their rights. In the next chapter you will read about the federal system in more detail.

GOVERNMENT IN ACTION

Marbury v. Madison (1803)

John Adams was president from 1797 to 1801. He supported the idea of a strong national government. In 1800 he lost his bid for presidential reelection to Thomas Jefferson. Adams thought that Jefferson's supporters would weaken the power of the national government by asserting states' rights. He also feared that Jefferson's supporters would be anti-business. So during the final hours of Adams' presidency, he worked feverishly to "pack" the judiciary with loyal supporters who favored a strong national government. He made what became known as "midnight appointments" just before Jefferson took office.

All of Adams' judicial appointments had to be certified and delivered. The task of delivery fell on Adams' secretary of state, John Marshall. Out of the fifty-nine midnight appointments, Marshall delivered only forty-two. He assumed that the remaining seventeen would be delivered by Jefferson's new secretary of state, James Madison. Of course, the new administration refused to cooperate in packing the judiciary: Jefferson refused to have Madison deliver the remaining commissions.

William Marbury—who was to be a judge—along with three other Federalists to whom the commissions had not been delivered, decided to sue. The suit was brought directly to the Supreme Court seeking a **writ of mandamus** (an order issued by a court to force a government official to act), authorized by the Judiciary Act of 1789.

Coincidentally, the man responsible for the lawsuit, John Marshall, had stepped down as Adams' secretary of state only to become chief justice of the Supreme Court. He was now in a position to decide the case for which he was responsible.* Marshall was faced with a dilemma: If he ordered the commissions delivered, the new secretary of state could simply refuse. The Court had no way to enforce

its decisions because it had no police force. Also, Congress was controlled by the Jeffersonian Republicans, who might impeach Marshall for such an action.** But if Marshall simply allowed Secretary of State Madison to do as he wished, the Court's power would be severely eroded.

Marshall stated for the unanimous Court that Jefferson and Madison had acted incorrectly in refusing to deliver Marbury's commission. Marshall also stated, however, that the Supreme Court did not have the authority to hear this particular case, because the section of the law that gave it such authority was unconstitutional. The Judiciary Act of 1789 specified that the Supreme Court could issue writs of mandamus as part of its authority. Marshall didn't agree and pointed out that Article III of the Constitution, which spells out the Supreme Court's authority, did not mention writs of mandamus. In other words, Congress did not have the right to expand the Court's jurisdiction, so this section of the Judiciary Act of 1789 was unconstitutional and hence void.

With this decision, the power of the Supreme Court was enlarged when it stated that "A law repugnant [offensive] to the Constitution is void."

THINK ABOUT IT

1. If the Supreme Court has no way to compel action because it has no police force, then how are its decisions put into practice?
2. How did Marshall's use of judicial review prevent the Supreme Court's power from being eroded?

* Today any justice who previously has been involved in the issue before the Court would probably disqualify himself or herself because of a conflict of interest.
** In fact, in 1805, Congress did impeach Supreme Court Justice Samuel Chase, a Federalist, though he was not convicted.

SECTION 2 REVIEW

1. List the basic principles upon which the Constitution was built.
2. How do these principles relate to each other?
3. **For critical analysis:** How does the inclusion of these principles make the Constitution stronger than the Articles of Confederation discussed in Chapter 2?

SECTION 3

The Bill of Rights

Preview Questions
- Why was the Bill of Rights drafted?
- What events led to the ratification of the Bill of Rights?

In order for the Constitution to be ratified in several important states, the Federalists had to provide assurances that amendments would be passed to protect individual liberties against violations by the national government. At the state ratifying conventions, protection of many specific rights was recommended. James Madison considered these recommendations as he labored to draft what became the Bill of Rights (see the *Government in Action* feature on page 62).

Madison's Difficult Job

Ironically, a year earlier Madison had told Jefferson, "I have never thought the omission [of the Bill of Rights] a material defect" of the Constitution. But Jefferson's enthusiasm for a Bill of Rights apparently influenced Madison, as did his own desire to gain popular support for election to Congress. Madison promised in his campaign letter to voters that once they elected him, he would force Congress to "prepare and recommend to the States for ratification, the most satisfactory provisions for all essential rights."

After sorting through more than two hundred state recommendations, the final number of amendments that Madison came up with was sixteen. Congress tightened the language somewhat and eliminated four of the amendments. Of the remaining twelve, two—one dealing with the apportionment of representatives and one on the compensation (payment) of the members of Congress—were rejected by the states. The remaining ten are what now form our Bill of Rights.

▲ The landmark case of *Marbury* v. *Madison* arose when William Marbury (pictured above) sued Secretary of State James Madison. Why is this case important?

The Difference Between *Ought* and *Shall*

Madison worked with the suggested proposals that the state ratifying conventions had provided. All of these proposals were framed in terms of the words *ought* and *ought not*. Those words sound weak to Americans who

▲ This famous painting entitled "Freedom of Speech" was painted by American artist Norman Rockwell, who was known for his moving portraits of American life. Look at how the man who is standing and speaking is dressed. What point do you think Rockwell was trying to make?

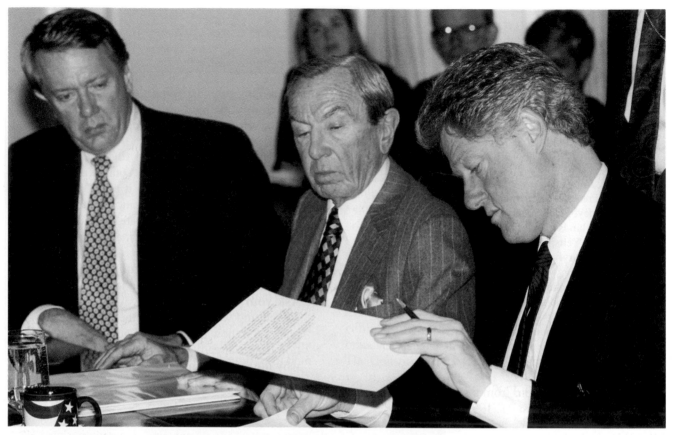

▲ The president's group of closest advisors is known as the cabinet. Here President Clinton is meeting with Secretary of the Interior Bruce Babbitt and Secretary of State Warren Christopher. Where in the Constitution is the existence of a cabinet explained?

For many years there was a tradition that no president would run for a third term. This tradition was started by George Washington. Franklin D. Roosevelt defied this tradition by running for office and winning a third presidential term in 1940, and then winning a fourth term in 1944. Many politicians and ordinary citizens believed that Roosevelt was creating a permanent presidency, almost as if he were setting himself up as a king. As a result, the Twenty-second Amendment was added, which limits the duration of presidential **tenure** (the period of holding office) to two four-year terms. In this way, tradition evolved to become law.

Until the Twenty-fifth Amendment was passed in 1967, the Constitution said nothing about the vice president assuming the office of president in the event of the president's death. Yet on eight occasions that is exactly what happened. The Constitution, though, only conferred the powers and duties of the president, rather than the office itself, to a vice president in such instances (Article II, Section 1, Clause 6).

The Constitution, with its formal and informal amendments, has gone from serving the needs of a small rural republic with no international prestige to providing a political framework for a major world government with immense geographic, natural, and human resources.

SECTION 5 REVIEW

1. How can the Constitution be informally amended?
2. Why is this process important to understanding constitutional change?
3. **For critical analysis:** If custom and usage generate informal amendments to the Constitution, explain how a violation of custom and usage by, say, a president, can lead to a formal change in the Constitution. Give an example.

CHALLENGE TO THE AMERICAN DREAM

The Equal Rights Amendment

The Equal Rights Amendment, or ERA, was the proposed Twenty-seventh Amendment to the U.S. Constitution. Although the problems it meant to solve were (and are) complex, the wording of the amendment was very simple: *Equality of rights under the law shall not be denied or abridged by the United States or by any state on account of sex.*

The ERA was first introduced in Congress in 1923 by leaders of the National Women's Party, which felt that women's obtaining the right to vote was not enough to change women's status in society. After almost fifty years, during which the amendment was not even given a hearing in Congress, it was finally approved by both the House and Senate in 1972.

As noted in this chapter, any constitutional amendment must be ratified by the legislatures (or conventions) in three-fourths of the states before it can become law. Since the early 1900s, most proposed amendments have required that ratification occur within seven years after Congress approves it. Supporters of the ERA initially had until March 22, 1979, to obtain ratification by thirty-eight states.

The ERA had tremendous popular support, especially among those who saw it as a way to invalidate numerous existing state laws that continue to discriminate against women and hold them in inferior status. By March 22, 1973, the ERA had been ratified by thirty states—eight fewer than were needed. At the same time forces opposing the ERA were becoming more organized and militant.

Much of the responsibility for the defeat of the ERA rests with the efforts of Phyllis Schlafly, a housewife from Alton, Illinois, and a law school graduate. Emphasizing the positive and unique qualities of the traditional roles women have played in society,

Schlafly mobilized the sentiments of many women and men against the ERA through the Stop-ERA and the Eagle Forum organizations. Schlafly claimed that pro-ERA groups were hostile to all the values women had traditionally held and to the general welfare of women.

Other opponents of the ERA felt that past instances of discrimination against women were adequately dealt with in Supreme Court rulings, state court rulings, and new legislation at both state and federal levels. Therefore, these opponents felt that the ERA was no longer necessary and would simply "clutter" the Constitution. Some religious groups also came out strongly against the ERA.

The opponents' campaign was effective. The necessary thirty-eight states failed to ratify the amendment within the seven-year period, in spite of the support given to the ERA in numerous national platforms and by six presidents and both houses of Congress. The National Organization for Women (NOW), the principal women's organization in support of the ERA, boycotted states that did not ratify the amendment. A number of pro-ERA associations refused to hold their conventions in Las Vegas, Miami Beach, Atlanta, Chicago, Kansas City, and New Orleans because their states were among those that turned down the amendment. As the 1979 deadline neared, five approvals were still lacking, and three states rescinded their ratification. Although Congress decided to extend the deadline to June 30, 1982, the ERA again failed to receive the required number of ratifications by that deadline.

The challenge to the American dream is whether women need the Equal Rights Amendment to be on equal footing with men throughout society, or whether Congress and state legislatures will pass enough effective legislation to obtain the same result.

You Decide

1. Why do you think such a simply worded amendment would arouse such heated debate?
2. What arguments can be used to support the ERA?

CHAPTER 3 REVIEW

Key Terms

amendments 56
cabinet 68
checks and balances 58
commerce clause 67
executive
  agreements 67

judicial review 58
Madisonian Model 57
preamble 54
principle of
  federalism 59

repeal 65
rule of law 57
supremacy clause 56
tenure 70
tyranny 57

unconstitutional 58
veto power 58
writ of mandamus 60

Summary

1. The Constitution is this nation's fundamental law. It is made up of three parts: the Preamble, the articles, and twenty-seven amendments. In brief, concise language, it establishes the basic organization of the nation's government and the powers of its various branches.

2. The Constitution sets forth the six basic principles upon which the American system of government rests. These are limited government, popular sovereignty, separation of powers, checks and balances, judicial review, and federalism.

3. On December 15, 1791, the Bill of Rights was adopted. It set out the constitutional guarantees of freedom of expression and belief, of security for each individual, and of equal and fair treatment before the law. Additionally, it provided in the Tenth Amendment for the concept of the reserved powers of the states in the federal system of government.

4. The formal amendment process is set out in Article V. It provides for four methods, two of which have never been used. To date, twenty-seven amendments have been added. One reason why only twenty-seven amendments have been added to the Constitution is that passage of an amendment requires widespread support among lawmakers and the public.

5. Informal amendments have also broadened the Constitution. Although informal amendments do not change the written words of the document, they have influenced the way we have interpreted the Constitution in light of new events and concerns. Informal amendments have been brought about through congressional legislation, presidential actions, judicial review, political parties, and custom and usage.

Review Questions

1. Describe the basic structure of the Constitution.
2. What is the Supremacy Clause and why is it important?
3. Identify and briefly describe the six basic principles of the Constitution.
4. How does the Constitution provide for limited government?
5. How does the system of checks and balances work?
6. Explain how the Bill of Rights was added to the Constitution.
7. What are the two methods of proposing an amendment to the Constitution?
8. What are the two methods of ratifying an amendment?
9. Why have only twenty-seven amendments been added to the Constitution?
10. What are the methods by which the Constitution has been informally amended? Give an example of each.
11. What are the four steps to the negotiation process outlined in *Citizenship Skills and Responsibilities* in this chapter? Why is each step an important part of this process?
12. How was the Equal Rights Amendment defeated?

Questions for Thought and Discussion

1. The principle of checks and balances was built into the American system of government. In what ways do you think this system has created conflict between the branches? In what ways has it avoided conflict?
2. Think of an amendment you would like to add to the Constitution. Develop and present an argument, either

CHAPTER 3 REVIEW—Continued

orally or in writing, on why your amendment should be added.

3. What characteristics of the Constitution have enabled it to survive and adapt to the growth and change of our nation?
4. The Constitution has been amended only twenty-six times in over two hundred years, although many more amendments have been proposed. Why do you think the founders made the amendment process so difficult? Develop and present arguments either for or against the present amendment process.
5. What is the difference between a law passed by Congress and an amendment to the Constitution?

Improving Your Skills
Communication Skills
Learning from What You Read:

One of the most common assignments made in high school and college is to study a chapter in a textbook. Yet many students do not know how to read effectively in order to learn. They "read blindly," and when they have finished reading the chapter, they can't remember most of what they read.

Do you want to know how to use your brain for learning? First, you "turn it on" by *wanting* to learn. Second, you become a detective searching for meaning by using the following approach in reading your textbook:

1. *Survey.* Survey the assigned material for an overview of the content. Pay attention to the title, the section heads, the first paragraphs, and the last paragraphs. Read the introduction, the chapter summary, and the chapter objectives.
2. *Question.* Questions create curiosity, improve concentration, give purpose to your search, and make important ideas more visible—all of which improve comprehension. Rephrase the main headings and subheadings into questions. Jot down questions that occur to you while surveying the chapter. Read the review questions at the ends of the sections and the chapter.
3. *Read.* Read each section carefully, actively searching for answers to your questions as you read. You are a detective with a purpose, absorbing ideas more quickly as a result of surveying the chapter and asking questions.

4. *Recite.* At the end of each section, look away from the book for a few seconds. Think about what you've learned and recite it out loud. This makes a deeper impression on your mind. Answer the review questions out loud. Hearing your answers will help you put the information into long-term memory.
5. *Review.* After you've followed the above steps with each section, you're ready to look at the whole chapter and see how all the parts relate to each other. This total review is the final step for organizing the information to understand and remember it.

This method of learning is called the SQRRR (or SQ3R) approach, which stands for *survey, question, read, recite,* and *review.*

Writing

1. Write an explanation of the SQRRR study approach, defining the purpose of each step in your own words.
2. Begin studying the next chapter of this textbook, applying the techniques of surveying and questioning only.

Social Studies Skills
Interpreting a Diagram

Use Figure 3–3 (The Process of Amending the Constitution) on page 65 to answer the following questions.

1. How does the drawing in the upper left-hand corner of the diagram relate to the words directly underneath it about the necessary vote in both houses of Congress for a proposed amendment to pass?
2. Which amendment procedure has never been used?
3. Which amendment procedure has been used only once?

Activities and Projects

1. With a group, make a scrapbook of articles and political cartoons from newspapers and magazines that illustrate the underlying principles of the Constitution: limited government, popular sovereignty, and so on. Write a brief description for each item, explaining how it shows the Constitution in action.
2. Prepare a class report on the reasons and events that led to the adoption of one of the twenty-six amendments. Present the report in class.

CHAPTER 4

Our System of Federalism

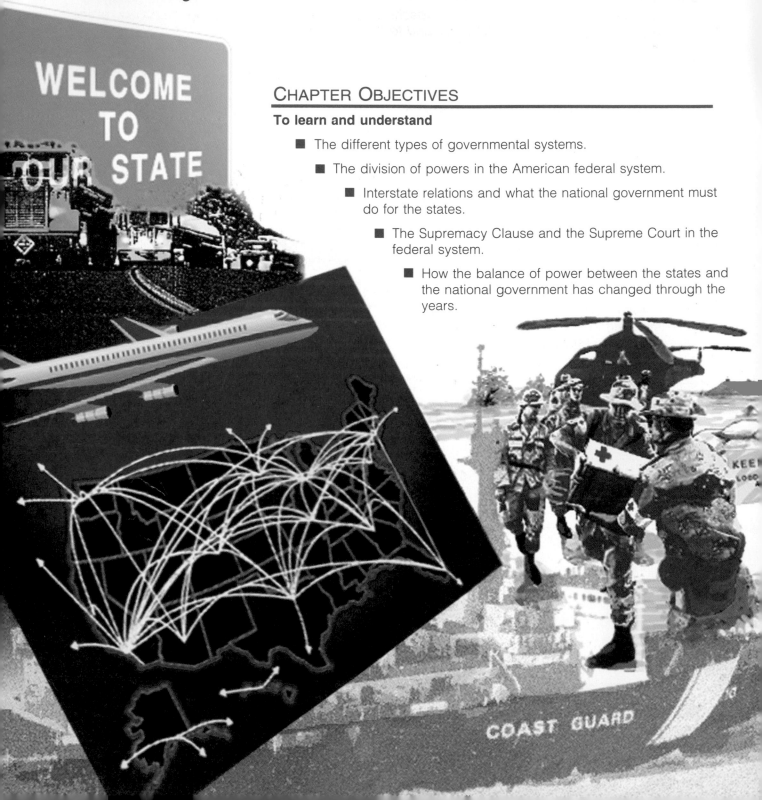

CHAPTER OBJECTIVES

To learn and understand

■ The different types of governmental systems.

■ The division of powers in the American federal system.

■ Interstate relations and what the national government must do for the states.

■ The Supremacy Clause and the Supreme Court in the federal system.

■ How the balance of power between the states and the national government has changed through the years.

Keynote

"We decry the Supreme Court's encroachments on rights reserved to the states and to the people, contrary to established law, and to the Constitution."

———

The Southern Manifesto: A Declaration of Constitutional Principles (1956)

INTRODUCTION

As was discussed in the previous chapter, one of the basic principles upon which the authors of the Constitution based their plan was the concept of federalism. They invented an arrangement that gives the federal government certain powers and reserves others for the states. In addition, there are some powers that are shared by the federal and state governments. Finally, there are powers the Constitution denies to each level of government: local, state, and federal. The authors of the Constitution developed a federal system because they wanted to limit the powers of government and assure that the rights of the people would be protected. They recognized that the federal and state governments serve different purposes.

Identifying and separating federal and state matters, however, has not always been easy. In fact, throughout American history there has been much disagreement over the proper limits of federal and state jurisdictions, or areas of authority. As recently as 1956, 19 senators and 77 representatives from Southern states who were opposed to the Supreme Court's decision concerning desegregation of schools (*Brown v. Board of Education,* 1954) signed *The Southern Manifesto: A Declaration of Constitutional Principles,* in which they made the above statement.

Thus, the American federal system of government has been as controversial as it is complex. It consists of over eighty thousand separate governmental units, as Figure 4–1 illustrates. Those more than eighty thousand separate governments are run by over half a

Governmental Units in the United States Today

The Number of Governments in the United States Today

Government	Number	
Federal Government	1	
State Governments	50	
Local Governments		
Counties	3,042	
Municipalities (mainly cities or towns)	19,205	
Townships (less extensive powers)	16,691	83,149
Special districts (water, sewer, etc.)	29,483	
School districts	14,728	
TOTAL	**83,200**	

Source: U.S. Department of Commerce, *Statistical Abstract of the United States* 1991 (Washington, D.C.: U.S. Government Printing Office, 1991).

Percentage of All Governments in the United States

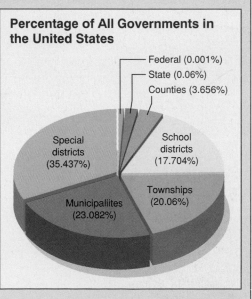

- Federal (0.001%)
- State (0.06%)
- Counties (3.656%)
- School districts (17.704%)
- Townships (20.06%)
- Municipaliites (23.082%)
- Special districts (35.437%)

▲ **FIGURE 4–1 Governmental Units in the United States Today.** There are 83,200 existing governmental units. What percentage of this total do municipalities and townships form?

million elected and appointed government officials. To many Americans our system of federalism is confusing, for it is difficult to keep track of which level of government is in charge of what. But while federalism may not be the easiest or most exciting part of your study of American government, it is surely one of the most important features of our system.

SECTION 1

Three Basic Types of Governmental Systems

Preview Questions
- What are the differences between the different types of governmental systems?
- What is the meaning and nature of federalism?

The United States started with a *confederate* system under the Articles of Confederation. Today we have a *federal* system. In most other countries, neither of these two systems is used. Most countries have a *unitary* system of government.

Unitary System

A **unitary system** is a centralized system in which state and/or local governments exercise only those powers given to them by the central government, which holds ultimate authority. Japan is an example of a unitary system. The Japanese national government, for example, makes the most important decisions for all schools within the nation, and even decides the subjects that must be taught nationwide.

In France today a modified form of the unitary system is in effect. Within France there are departments and municipalities, or local governments, with their own elected and appointed officials. But all decisions by those officials and appointees can, for the most part, be overruled by the national government. Also, the national government in Paris can cut off the funding of many departmental and municipal government activities. Finally, all policies related to police, land use, welfare, and education are determined by the national government, although they are carried out by the departmental and municipal entities.

Confederal System

A **confederal system,** or confederation, is a league of independent states. In the pre-constitutional days of our country, this type of system was put in place under the Articles of Confederation. The central government handled only those matters of common concern expressly delegated to it by the member states. The central government itself, however, could not pass laws that directly applied to individuals unless the member states explicitly supported such laws. The former republics of the Soviet Union now make up the Confederation of Independent States. Certain organizations, such as the United Nations and the North Atlantic Treaty Organization (NATO), also follow a confederate model.

◄ In France, most policies related to the police and police officers (such as the airport police officer shown here) are determined by the national government. What term is used to describe the French system of government?

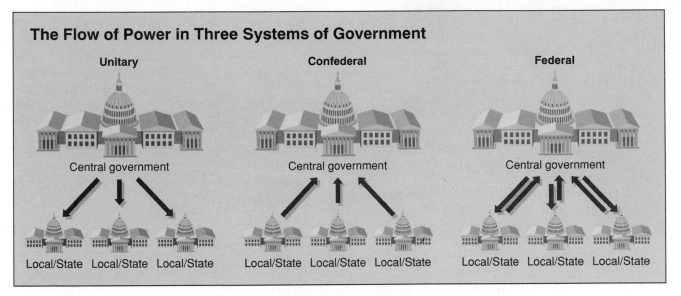

The Flow of Power in Three Systems of Government

▲ FIGURE 4–2 **The Flow of Power in Three Systems of Government.** As you can see in the figure above, in a unitary system the flow of power is from the central government to the local and state governments. In a confederal system, the flow of power is in the opposite direction—from the state and local governments to the central government. Finally, in the federal system, the power flows in both directions. Which of these three systems of government is, in essence, a compromise between the other two?

Federal System

The **federal system** is a compromise between the confederal and unitary forms of government. Authority is usually divided between national and state governments by a written constitution, as in the United States. All levels of government—federal, state, and local—have the power to pass laws that directly influence the people. But while the federal government's laws are supreme, it cannot overrule state and local laws, unless they conflict with federal laws. This is what makes a federal system different from a unitary system.

Keep in mind, however, that *federalism* and *democracy* do not mean the same thing. Federalism, on the one hand, is a system of government in which powers are divided between national and subnational governments, such as states. Democracy, on the other hand, is a system in which the people are involved, either directly or indirectly, in the governing process.

The three systems of government discussed in this section are shown in Figure 4–2 above.

In a confederal system, or confederation, the power of the central government is derived from the state governments. The opposite is true in a unitary system, in which the only power that the state and local governments have is that power that is given to them by the central government. In a federal system power is distributed throughout all levels of government.

Reasons for Federalism

The Articles of Confederation failed because they did not allow for a sufficiently strong central government. The framers of the Constitution, however, were fearful of a central government becoming tyrannical, or too powerful. The natural outcome had to be a compromise—a federal system. The appeal of federalism was that it retained state traditions and local power while establishing a strong national government capable of handling common problems such as national defense.

There were also characteristics specific to the United States that lent themselves to a federal system.

Size and Regional Isolation Even in the days when the United States was only thirteen colonies, the geographic area was larger than that of France or England. Travel was slow and communication was difficult. Given the large geographic spread of our country even then, many regions were isolated within the colonies. The news of any particular political decision might take several weeks to reach everyone. Therefore, even if the framers of the Constitution had wanted a unitary system (which most of them did not), such a system would have been unworkable.

Differences in Political Cultures We have always been a nation of different political subcultures. The

Pilgrims who founded New England were different from those who worked in the agricultural society of the South. Those two groups were both different from those who populated the Middle Atlantic states. The groups who founded New England were religiously oriented, while the groups who populated the Middle Atlantic states were more business oriented. And those who populated the agricultural society of the South were more individualistic than other groups; that is, they were less inclined to accept the authority of the national government.

Any time a nation is composed of numerous political subcultures, the notion of a unitary system of government is difficult to imagine. Typically, such governments have ruled their people with an iron fist.

SECTION 1 REVIEW

1. Describe confederal and unitary systems. How do they differ from a federal system?
2. Why doesn't a federalist system necessarily have to be democratic?
3. Why did the framers create a federal system of government for the United States?
4. **For critical analysis:** Increasingly, the federal government has attempted to make laws that apply to the whole of the United States rather than to specific states. For example, by threatening to withhold federal funding to help rebuild highways, the federal government forced all of the states to raise their minimum age for buying and consuming alcoholic beverages to 21. Why do you think the national government is pushing toward more uniformity in state laws?

SECTION 2

Dividing Governmental Power

Preview Questions
- What are the three kinds of powers delegated to the national government?
- What powers are denied to the national government?
- What powers are reserved for the states? What powers are prohibited?
- What are the concurrent powers?

Although the U.S. has a federal system, the words *federal system* cannot be found in the U.S. Constitution. Nor can you find a systematic explanation of the **division of powers**—the way in which governmental powers are divided between governmental units—between the national and state governments. Nonetheless, the original Constitution, along with the Tenth Amendment, tells what the national and state governments can do. As the Tenth Amendment states:

> The powers not *delegated* to the United States by the Constitution, nor prohibited by it to the States, are reserved to the States respectively, or to the people.

The key word here is *delegated,* which means "giving certain powers to others." Certain powers are delegated to the national government, others to state governments.

The Powers of the National Government

The national government in this country has powers delegated, or granted to it, only by the Constitution. There are three types of delegated powers: *expressed* (or *enumerated*), *implied,* and *inherent.*

The Expressed, or Enumerated, Powers Most of the powers explicitly delegated to the national government are enumerated, or clearly listed, in Article I, Section 8. These are called **expressed,** or **enumerated, powers.** There are eighteen separate clauses enumerating twenty-seven different powers specifically given to Congress. These include:

- Coining money
- Regulating interstate commerce
- Levying and collecting taxes
- Declaring war
- Establishing post offices

Some of the amendments give expressed powers, too. The Sixteenth Amendment, for example, gives Congress the power to impose a federal income tax. Other parts of the Constitution grant expressed powers to the executive branch. Article II, Section 2 enumerates certain powers of the president, which include:

- Making treaties
- Appointing certain federal office holders
- Granting pardons

BUILDING SOCIAL STUDIES SKILLS

Analyzing Political Cartoons

Political or editorial cartoons have appeared in the editorial sections of newspapers and magazines throughout our nation's history. They are often funny, but can also communicate serious messages. Their simplicity, directness, and humor can make them a powerful tool for influencing public opinion. They sometimes present a positive point of view, but more often are critical of a person, group, or issue. Cartoons are an effective way to express a point of view on often complex political issues. Although they may present an issue in simple terms, the reader still must understand the background of the issues to appreciate the cartoon.

Political cartoons often use one of two techniques: *symbolism* and *caricature*. Symbols are objects that are used to stand for something else. Some common symbols in political cartoons are the donkey for Democrats, the elephant for Republicans, Uncle Sam for the government, a dove for peace, the White House for the president, the Capitol for Congress, an eagle for the United States, and a bear for the former Soviet Union. Caricatures are distortions or exaggerations of the physical features of someone or something. Cartoonists will take a slightly prominent feature, such as big teeth or a long nose, and make it more enlarged or comical.

Labels are sometimes used to identify the important features. Captions are also used to either hint at the main idea of the cartoon or to represent the words of the character in the cartoon.

When reading a political cartoon, first examine the entire cartoon to determine the general topic. Then identify the symbols or caricatures used and what they identify. Read all the labels and the caption. Determine the tone of the cartoonist—are the figures presented in a positive or a negative light? Also, try to determine the quality of the humor—is it harsh and angry or is it gently mocking? Then determine whose viewpoint is being expressed. Remember that a political cartoon is an editorial in picture form and the cartoonist is expressing only one point of view. Try to imagine what the other side of the issue would look like in cartoon form.

PRACTICING YOUR SKILLS _____

1. Study the cartoon below and answer the following questions.

   ● What is the cartoonist's point of view?
   ● What is the tone of the cartoon?
   ● Does the cartoonist use symbols or caricatures? If so, identify them.

2. Find and clip out a political cartoon. Interpret the cartoon to the class by using the criteria listed above. Then design a cartoon of your own that would express an alternative point of view.

By Marlette for New York Newsday

"Sometimes, Doctor, I get the feeling nobody's listening!"

Implied Powers Certain powers are given to the national government even though they are not expressly presented in the Constitution. They are *reasonably implied* (suggested or indicated), however, and are therefore called **implied powers.** Their constitutional basis is found in Article I, Section 8, Clause 18, which states that Congress shall have the power

> To make all Laws which shall be necessary and proper for carrying into Execution the foregoing Powers, and all other Powers vested by this Constitution in the Government of the United States, or in any Department or Officer thereof.

The key words in that clause are *necessary and proper.* For this reason it is often called the **necessary and proper clause.** Others have named it the **elastic clause** because it gives elasticity to our constitutional system. The necessary and proper clause gives Congress all those powers that can be reasonably inferred, but are not expressly stated, in the brief wording of the Constitution. Through exercising the power vested in it by this clause, the national government has strengthened the scope of its authority to meet many problems that the founding fathers did not or could not anticipate.

There are thousands of examples of the national government's exercise of implied powers. The Constitution does not expressly state that the national government is responsible for the construction of an interstate highway system. Yet our government has paid money for precisely this purpose. Certainly nowhere in the Constitution is it expressly stated that the national government should involve itself in the disputes between workers and their managers. But Congress does involve itself in such disputes through one of its agencies. Nowhere in the Constitution does it state that Congress should pass laws prohibiting the manufacture, sale, and consumption of certain drugs. Nonetheless, Congress has done so.

Sometimes several expressed powers are added together, and are then called **resulting powers.** As an example, consider the printing of paper money as **legal tender**—legitimate currency for trade and purchasing. The Constitution gives Congress the expressed power to coin money, as well as to borrow money and to regulate interstate commerce. The resulting power gives our national government the authority to designate the money it produces legal tender for the payment of debts.

Inherent Powers The last category of powers is **inherent powers,** the powers that governments have simply because governments exist. Any government of a sovereign nation has to have certain powers or it could not be considered a government.

The inherent powers are few, but important. Each nation's government must clearly have the ability to act in its own interest within the community of nations. Therefore, each national government must have the inherent ability to make treaties, to regulate immigration, to acquire territory, to wage war, and to create peace.

Prohibited Powers

The Constitution prohibits or denies a number of powers to the national government. It does this in several distinct ways.

Expressly Denied Most of the powers expressly denied to the national government can be found in Article I, Section 9, and in the First through the Eighth Amendments. The national government cannot, for example, impose duties (taxes) on **exports**—goods sold to other countries. Moreover, the national government cannot deny freedom of religion, speech, press, or assembly. It cannot conduct illegal searches or seizures.

▼ Demonstrations, such as this anti-war rally held in Austin, Texas, are protected under the Constitution, which bars the government from interfering with freedom of religion, speech, press, or assembly. Where in the Constitution can you find which powers are expressly denied to the national government?

Powers Granted by the Constitution

Federal
- To coin money
- To conduct foreign relations
- To regulate interstate commerce
- To levy and collect taxes
- To declare war
- To raise and support the military
- To establish post offices
- To establish courts inferior to the Supreme Court
- To admit new states
- Powers implied by necessary and proper clause

Concurrent
- To levy and collect taxes
- To borrow money
- To make and enforce laws
- To establish courts
- To provide for the general welfare
- To charter banks and corporations

State
- To regulate intrastate commerce
- To conduct elections
- To provide for public health, safety, and morals
- To establish local governments
- To ratify amendments to the federal Constitution
- To establish a state militia

▲ **FIGURE 4–3 Powers Granted by the Constitution.** The figure above outlines the powers granted by the Constitution to the federal government and to the state governments, and to both the federal and state governments concurrently. According to the Constitution, which level of government is entitled to create and administer courts?

Not Delegated Our national government is one that has only those powers given to it by the Constitution. Any power not delegated, either expressly or implicitly, to it by the Constitution in one of the ways discussed above is prohibited to it. The Constitution does not, for example, give the national government the power to create a national public school system; as a result, our country does not have one. The Constitution does not expressly give the national government the power to create a uniform system of criminal sentencing, which we do not have either.

The Powers of the States

Through the Tenth Amendment, the Constitution reserves certain powers to the states. These **reserved powers** are not given to the national government, nor can they be taken away by it. At the same time, they are not denied to the state governments.

Some of these reserved powers are each state's right to regulate commerce within its borders and to provide for a state militia. In essence, states have the authority over all their internal affairs and over the health, safety, and welfare of their people. The states exercise their reserved powers when they create public school systems and regulate such family law issues as marriage, divorce and child support. They also exercise their reserved powers when they set age limits on purchasing and drinking alcoholic beverages and driving an automobile. The federal government can, however, influence state governments. For example, under the threat of withholding federal highway funds in the 1980s, all states were forced to increase the legal age of drinking to 21.

GOVERNMENT IN ACTION

PERSONAL LAW

The Family

The basic social unit is the family. Not surprisingly, much personal law involves rules and principles applied to the relationship between members of the family unit. These rules and regulations have been enacted principally to protect and to enhance marriage and the family in America.

The Consequences of Marriage

The legalities of marriage are regulated by state law. Typically, a state requires a person to be at least 18 to be married unless there is parental consent. In fourteen states, when a man and a woman continuously live together as husband and wife for a certain period of time, such as seven years, they are considered to have entered into a **common-law marriage** which is treated the same as all other marriages.

Marriage is a serious commitment for both parties. It involves emotional as well as financial obligations. If a married couple has children, then an additional set of responsibilities enters into the arrangement.

Protecting the Rights of Children

To a large extent parents have a right to rear their children any way they want, free from interference from the government. Nonetheless, the government intrudes into the parent-child relationship whenever the health and welfare of the child is threatened. Even at the federal level, the government has tried to give children more rights. In 1984 the Federal Child Abuse Prevention and Treatment Act was passed. This act encourages the fifty states to adopt laws to prevent child abuse.

Some children have no proper parental care or have no home and are without the necessities of life. They typically fall under the jurisdiction of the juvenile court system, a system used to handle the laws as they apply to minors (those under 18). When this occurs, these minors become "dependents" of the court, which may then order their care, supervision, and support. In some cases, a dependent child may be taken from the custody of its lawful parents and placed in a foster home or in the home of a relative.

Rights of Children After a Divorce

Divorce is a common fact of life in the United States. Half of all marriages end in divorce. Consequently, many minors find themselves in a so-called broken-home environ-

Powers Prohibited to the States

Just as the Constitution denies certain powers to the national government, it also denies some to the state governments. The explicit prohibitions are found in Article I, Section 10, as well as in the Thirteenth, Fourteenth, Fifteenth, Nineteenth, Twenty-fourth, and Twenty-sixth Amendments.

One power explicitly prohibited to the states is the taxation of imports or exports to and from other states or with foreign countries. Another denied power concerns treaties: No state is allowed to enter into a treaty on its own with another country.

Because the Constitution lays out a federal system, no state is allowed to endanger that system. Therefore, states are not allowed to tax activities and agencies of the federal government.

What About Local Governments?

As you know by now, the federal system involves a federal government and fifty state governments. But what ment. The courts award **child custody** and visitation rights when a divorce occurs. If both parents demand custody of a child or argue about visitation rights, the court decides what is best for the child. Most states (44) follow the Uniform Marriage and Divorce Act. It specifies how a court should determine custody arrangements in the best interests of the child.

Child Custody and Support Courts granting divorces must also issue orders to provide for the future support of children. Even when such support is provided, the parent who has the child, most or even all of the time, may have difficulty collecting child support payments. The fact is that such payments are not often made after the first several years. If the parent not making the support payments lives in the same state, the other parent can use that state's judicial system to attempt to collect. In contrast, if the parent not making the support payment lives in another state, a more serious problem arises. How can the parent with the child enforce child support payments in another state? Until the late 1960s, this task was almost impossible. In 1968, though, the Uniform Reciprocal Enforcement of Support Act was passed. Under this law the prosecutor in

the local state can cause a formal legal proceeding to be initiated in the state in which the delinquent parent lives. The court in the other state will enter the child support order and enforce it under that state's laws.

THINK ABOUT IT

1. In divorce proceedings, both spouses usually have the help of a lawyer to protect the rights of each. Minor children in divorce proceedings typically do not have anyone arguing their interests in courts, however. Should the situation be altered and if so, how?
2. At the age of 18, in most states, minors legally become adults and therefore can vote, get married without parental consent, join the military, etc. Nonetheless, in no state today can anyone under the age of 21 legally purchase or consume alcoholic beverages. Why does this inconsistency exist?
3. As you have learned, most states follow the Uniform Marriage and Divorce act for determining custody issues. Whose interests should be of primary importance to those determining custody? Explain your answer.

about the over eighty thousand local government units? How are they governed? You will examine this question in more detail in Part 8 of this book. For now, you should understand that nothing in the Constitution refers explicitly to the powers of local government, and that the relationship between state and local governments is unitary; that is, local governments exist at the will of the states. No local government exists independently of its parent state. Through the constitutions and laws of each state, these local units have been created and are allowed to continue to function. When local governmental units

act, they are acting with the power of the state government. That means anything that the states cannot constitutionally do, local government also cannot do.

Concurrent Powers

In certain areas the Constitution gives national and state governments equal rights to pass legislation and to regulate specific activities. These are called **concurrent powers.** Concurrent powers are held separately but equally by both state and national governments. By

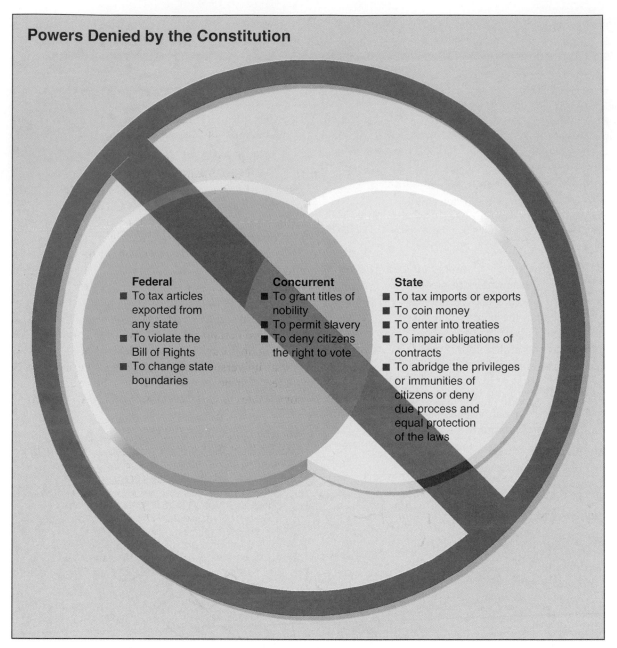

Powers Denied by the Constitution

Federal
- To tax articles exported from any state
- To violate the Bill of Rights
- To change state boundaries

Concurrent
- To grant titles of nobility
- To permit slavery
- To deny citizens the right to vote

State
- To tax imports or exports
- To coin money
- To enter into treaties
- To impair obligations of contracts
- To abridge the privileges or immunities of citizens or deny due process and equal protection of the laws

▲ **FIGURE 4–4 Powers Denied by the Constitution.** The figure above lists the powers denied to the federal government, to state governments, and to both levels of government. According to this, can either the federal government or a state government grant titles of nobility?

definition, all concurrent powers are neither granted exclusively to the national government nor denied to the states.

For example, both state and federal governments have the power to tax. The types of taxation, however, are divided between the levels of government. States may not levy taxes on imported goods, but the federal government may. In addition, neither level of government can tax the facilities of the other. For example, Texas cannot tax the federal government on the fees it charges people to use the federal court building located in Texas.

Certain concurrent powers are implied rather than stated expressly. They include the power to borrow money, to establish courts, and to charter banks. Both the national and state governments share these powers.

SECTION 2 REVIEW _____

1. What is meant by the phrase "division of powers"?
2. What are the three types of powers delegated to the national government? Explain and give examples of each one.
3. What is the significance of the necessary and proper clause?
4. What are the two ways in which the Constitution denies powers to the national government?
5. What are some powers that the Constitution reserves to the states?
6. Where do local governments fit into the federal system?
7. What are the concurrent powers?
8. **For critical analysis:** The Tenth Amendment reserves to the states all those powers not delegated to the national government nor prohibited to the state governments. How can you explain the national government's legislation with respect to the construction of an interstate highway system not mentioned in the Constitution?

SECTION 3

The Relations Among the States

Preview Questions
- What is horizontal federalism?
- What are the constitutional provisions that relate to relations among the states?
- What are the duties of the national government with respect to the states under the Constitution?

So far we have dealt with the relationship between the federal and state governments. The states also have social, commercial, and other dealings among themselves. The citizens of one state travel to other states, and buy various items from other states. All activities, problems, and policies that pass between states make up what is called **horizontal federalism.** The rules of horizontal federalism laid out in the U.S. Constitution prevent any one state from setting itself apart from all the others. The Constitution has three important provisions

that relate to horizontal federalism, each of which was taken almost directly from the Articles of Confederation.

Privileges and Immunities

Article IV, Section 2 indicates that:

The Citizens of each State shall be entitled to all Privileges and Immunities of Citizens in the several States.

The **privileges and immunities clause** prevents states from discriminating against citizens of other states. A resident of one state cannot be treated as an **alien**— a foreigner—when in another state. Each state is required to extend to all U.S. citizens from any other state the protection of that state's laws, the right to work, access to the courts, and any other privileges they may grant their own citizens. A resident of Texas cannot be treated as an alien when that person is in New York. She or he must have access to the courts of each state, the right to travel, and the right to own property.

There are certain instances, however, of "discrimination" against out-of-state residents. For example, at most state universities, out-of-state residents have to pay higher fees than do in-state residents at those universities. In some states a certain amount of residency time is

▼ | The privileges and immunities clause of the United States Constitution prevents states from discriminating against citizens of other states. However, there are certain areas where citizens from other states are treated differently. Out-of-state travelers entering into the State of Arizona must stop at agriculture inspection stations (such as the one shown here) so that inspectors can verify that no banned agricultural products are being brought into the state. Why do you think certain agricultural products would be banned?

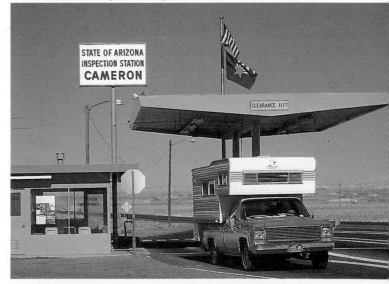

required before public assistance benefits, such as welfare, are obtainable. Some states do not recognize common-law marriages that are recognized in other states.

The Full Faith and Credit Clause

Article IV, Section 1 states that:

Full Faith and Credit shall be given in each State to the public Acts, Records, and judicial Proceedings of every other State.

The **full faith and credit clause** requires states to recognize one another's laws and court decisions. That means that rights that are established, say under a deed of property, will be honored in another state. If you own property in Florida, your ownership rights are valid in Texas, where you may wish to sell the property to a local resident. As another example, if you are legally married in the state of Missouri that marriage will be honored in Montana.

The full faith and credit clause was originally included in the Articles of Confederation in order to promote mutual friendship among the people of the different colonies. As part of the U.S. Constitution this clause has contributed to the unity of American citizens because it allows all Americans to move from state to state without worrying about losing any rights that they have.

Interstate Extradition

The term **extradition** refers to transporting a **fugitive**—an individual wanted for committing a crime—from one state to another. Article IV, Section 2 of the Constitution states that:

A Person charged in any State with Treason, Felony, or other Crime, who shall flee from Justice, and be found in another State, shall on Demand of the executive Authority of the State from which he fled, be delivered up, to be removed to the State having Jurisdiction [authority] of the Crime.

Although the language of this section seems clear, until 1987 state governors were not required by law to extradite fugitives. An 1861 ruling by the U.S. Supreme Court, called the **Dennison Rule**, upheld the right of the governor of Ohio to refuse an extradition request by the governor of Kentucky for a "free man of color," on charges that he had helped a slave escape to freedom.

The Dennison Rule stood for 126 years. Then in 1987 the U.S. Supreme Court reversed itself in a case involving an Iowan, Ron Calder, who was supposed to stand trial in Puerto Rico for alleged homicide in a traffic mishap. The governor of Iowa refused to extradite Calder but was forced to do so after the Supreme Court ruled in favor of the extradition.

In many cases today, the question of extraditing fugitives has little meaning. Congress has made it a federal crime to flee across state lines to avoid prosecution for certain serious crimes. That means that agents of the national government will arrest fugitives regardless of what state they are in. Fugitives are usually turned over to the state from which they fled.

Interstate Compacts

Adjoining states often have common problems and concerns that relate to shared resources and territory. They have to worry about water use, environmental standards, and air-traffic control. States therefore often enter into mutual agreements called **interstate compacts.** One of the best-known examples of an interstate compact was the establishment of the Port of New York Authority. The states of New York and New Jersey entered into this agreement in 1921 to develop and operate the harbor facilities in the area. A number of states in the Southwest entered into the Interstate Oil and Gas Compact in 1935.

What the National Government Must Do for the States

The national government has certain duties with respect to the fifty states. Most of these are listed in Article IV, Section 4:

The United States shall guarantee to every State in this Union a Republican Form of Government, and shall protect each of them against Invasion; and on Application of the Legislature, or of the Executive (when the Legislature cannot be convened) against domestic Violence.

Guarantee of a Republican Form of Government A **republican form of government** is one in which the people are governed by elected representatives. Our national government therefore has had to ensure that each state government was formed according to the will of the majority of its citizens.

The only time that the republican guarantee became truly important was after the Civil War, when a number of Southern states had not ratified the Thirteenth, Fourteenth, and Fifteenth Amendments, nor had they changed their laws to recognize voting rights and other rights of African Americans. As a result, Congress refused to admit senators and representatives from those states until they had made the appropriate reforms.

Protection Against Foreign Invasion   Today, an attack launched against any one state is an attack against all fifty states. While everybody today takes that concept for granted, it was not so well accepted in the 1780s. At that time, the states were not sure if they would stand together if one of them were attacked. Each state agreed, therefore, to give its war-making powers to the national government, only if the government pledged in turn to protect each of the states.

Protection Against Domestic Violence   Each state is obliged to keep the peace within its own geographical boundaries. If for some reason a state cannot do so, the national government may provide help. On a number of occasions presidents have had to send in federal troops, called the National Guard, to control upheavals within various states. For example, in 1967 President Lyndon Baines Johnson sent federal troops to Detroit at the request of Michigan's governor, George Romney. Local and state police personnel were unable to stop riots and looting that were happening in the inner city during that summer. Similarly, President Johnson sent federal troops to the cities of Chicago and Baltimore to help control violent outbreaks that followed the assassination of Dr. Martin Luther King, Jr. in April of 1968.

In all three instances, the president sent the National Guard at the request of local and state officials. The president is not legally bound to wait for such a request, however. Whenever federal property is endangered or federal law is violated, the president can act. Indeed, in 1894, President Grover Cleveland sent federal troops to Illinois, in spite of the objections of Governor William Altgeld, to stop the rioting in the Chicago rail yards that year. The rioters had threatened federal property and had slowed down the flow of mail and interstate commerce.

President Dwight D. Eisenhower sent federal troops to Little Rock, Arkansas in 1957, as did President John F. Kennedy to the University of Mississippi in 1962 and to the University of Alabama in 1963. In each of these instances, these two presidents acted to stop the unlawful obstruction of school integration orders that had been issued by the federal courts.

Territorial Integrity   Under the Constitution, the federal government must guarantee the territorial integrity of each state; that is, it must recognize each state's legal existence and physical boundaries. It must also guarantee the number of votes each state has in Congress. Article IV, Section 3 prevents the national government from geographically dividing a state to make a new state, or from changing boundaries between states. If it wants to do this, both the states involved and Congress have to agree on the changes.

Some argue that the admission of West Virginia to the United States in 1863 violated this guarantee. West Virginia was formed from the forty western counties that had broken away from Virginia during the Civil War. At the time the new state was formed, less than 50 percent of the Virginia legislators agreed to its formation. Congress legitimized the legislators' decision by claiming that they were the only legislators legally capable of acting for the people of Virginia.

▼ When rioting broke out in Baltimore, Maryland in April, 1968, President Lyndon Baines Johnson (shown below) sent in federal troops to help control the disturbance. Under what conditions can the President use federal troops to help keep the peace in individual states?

CITIZENSHIP SKILLS AND RESPONSIBILITIES
Community Action Project—Helping the Hungry

Hunger is one of the most heartbreaking and urgent problems facing the world today. Although it is difficult to believe that people are actually dying of starvation and malnutrition every few seconds, hunger haunts us everywhere—outside our homes, in our own cities, and in faraway countries.

Hunger is being fought by people on many fronts—from short-term solutions, such as providing a hot meal to someone who doesn't know where to turn, to long-term solutions, such as supporting new legislation to alter our policies of food distribution. Helping to feed the hungry in your own community is always a good starting point. Listed below are some actions that can help you begin.

TAKING ACTION

1. Locate the local hunger groups in your area. Start by calling your church, synagogue, or the mayor's office, or look in the Yellow Pages under "Social Service Agencies." If you don't have any luck, there are many national organizations that can help you locate a group. A few of them are listed below:

   National Student Campaign Against Hunger
   29 Temple Place, Boston, MA 02111
   617-292-4823

   The Salvation Army
   799 Bloomfield Avenue, Verona, NJ 07044
   201-239-0606

   Seeds
   222 East Lake Drive, Decatur, GA 07044
   404-378-3566

2. Offer to help out in the office of a local hunger project by answering phones, writing letters, or raising funds.

3. Donate food to a food bank. If you can't locate the food bank nearest you, contact:

   Second Harvest
   116 South Michigan Avenue, Suite 4
   Chicago, IL 60603
   312-263-2303

   Consider volunteering to work in the warehouse sorting contributed food, or assisting with pickups or deliveries.

4. Volunteer two or three hours a week in a soup kitchen that cooks and serves food for homeless people.

If you are interested in starting your own group to fight hunger, order a copy of Seeds' *Hunger Action Handbook—What You Can Do and How to Do It*. It's available from Seeds at the above-listed address.

If you are interested in volunteering to work on a project to end hunger around the world, order Seeds' magazine *Volunteer Opportunities Guide*.

The process of admitting a state to the Union involves several steps. First, people residing in a geographic area desiring statehood apply to Congress for admission. If Congress agrees, it passes an **enabling act,** which directs the proposed state to form a constitution. The state then holds a constitutional convention and obtains approval of the constitution by popular vote. If Congress agrees to statehood when the proposed state constitution is submitted, it passes an **act of admission**. Once a state has entered the Union, it is automatically equal in status to all other states.

Information on when each state was admitted to the Union is included in the Resource Center.

SECTION 3 REVIEW

1. What are the Constitutional provisions that relate to horizontal federalism?
2. What does the full faith and credit clause require?
3. Under the Constitution, what responsibilities does the federal government have toward the states?
4. **For critical analysis:** Two or more states enter into interstate compacts only if all parties benefit. How do you think both New Jersey and New York benefited from the Port of New York Authority Interstate Compact? What would have been an alternative to such an agreement?

SECTION 4

Who Shall Reign Supreme?

Preview Questions

- What is the supremacy clause?
- What decision did the Supreme Court make in *McCulloch* v. *Maryland*? Why was it important?
- What was the issue before the Supreme Court in the case of *Gibbons* v. *Ogden*?
- What issue was at the heart of the controversy that led to the Civil War?

The **supremacy clause,** Article VI, Paragraph 2, gives the federal government supremacy over all state and local governments, and implies that states cannot use their reserved or concurrent powers to counter national policies. Every time a state or local officer, such as a judge or sheriff, takes office, he or she becomes bound by an oath to support the U.S. Constitution. National governmental power always takes precedence over any conflicting state action. For example, when President Eisenhower sent the National Guard to Little Rock High School in Arkansas in 1957, he did so to make sure that the desegregation plan ordered by the federal courts was carried out.

Much of the legal history of the United States has involved conflicts between the supremacy of the national government and the desires of the states to remain independent. The most extreme example of this conflict was the Civil War in the 1860s.

Through the years, because of the Civil War and several key Supreme Court decisions, the national government has increased its power. The first important Supreme Court decision involved a state trying to impose its will on the national government.

McCulloch v. *Maryland*

For several decades after the Constitution was ratified, the states opposed many actions of the national government. When Congress chartered two banks—the First and Second Banks of the United States (1791 and 1816)—and provided part of the money necessary to get them started, a number of states complained. They claimed that the existence of these nationally chartered banks presented unfair competition against state banks. Maryland was one such state to hold this view. The government of Maryland imposed a tax on the Baltimore branch of the Second Bank of the United States. The branch's chief cashier, James McCulloch, decided not to pay the Maryland tax. The state of Maryland took the conflict to its state court, which ruled that McCulloch had to pay the tax. The federal government appealed the case to the U.S. Supreme Court, then headed by Chief Justice John Marshall.

▶ In 1957, when governor Orval Faubus tried to block integration of Central High School in Little Rock, Arkansas, President Dwight D. Eisenhower pressed the Arkansas National Guard into federal service and sent in 1,000 National Guard paratroopers to ensure that the desegregation plan ordered by the United States Federal Court was carried out. The photo here shows the school's first African-American students walking up the steps to the school's entrance flanked by federal troops armed with rifles and bayonets. What Constitutional provision granted Eisenhower the power to make this move?

GOVERNMENT IN ACTION

CASE STUDY

The Sagebrush Rebellion

A federal system, no matter how well thought out, is always going to run into problems. States like to have control over as much as possible. But so do the bureaucrats running the national government. Nowhere has this conflict been more obvious than with the ownership of land in the United States. Look at the map on the next page.

In the Western states, the federal government owns a remarkably high proportion of all land. In Nevada this figure is 80 percent.

Advocates of **decentralization**—a shift of power from federal to state or local governments—argue that states must be allowed to make their own decisions about how their land should be used. The controversy over who should own land in much of the West has been called the Sagebrush Rebellion. It began a number of years ago when the Nevada legislature passed a law declaring that 49 million acres of federal land properly belonged to that state. This idea caught the attention of other Western states, because the federal government owns most of Alaska and Nevada, the bulk of Utah, Idaho, and Oregon, and nearly half of Wyoming and California. A movement began to reclaim lands from federal ownership. The movement united an otherwise maverick group of state activists and rugged individualists with a sense of common cause.

Certain groups in the Western states claimed that the federal government was acting as a powerful absentee landlord, imposing a lot of regulations but never present to deal with their problems. They saw Washington, D.C., as "Big Brother" (referred to in George Orwell's book *1984*) and the Eastern states as unsympathetic to their region's unique vital concerns. As Nevada Attorney General Rich Bryan asserted, "We're tired of being pistol-whipped by the bureaucrats and dry-gulched by federal regulations." Nevada Senator Norm Glaser added: "We're not just a bunch of wild-eyed cowboys out to lynch some federal officials. We're serious people asking for a serious look at the unfair treatment the West is receiving."

Those individuals who prefer the current situation claim that despite the complaints, from meat import quotas to vital water reclamation projects, Westerners often come out quite well under a big federal government. They argue that the West is living in a fantasy if it thinks it can survive without the federal government. "If you pulled the federal presence out of Colorado, the state would collapse," said then Senator Gary Hart from Colorado. Eastern and Western environmentalists argue that if the federal government hadn't stepped in, the West would have sold out and exploited its rare environmental resources. The Idaho Environmental Council said that federal management for the most part "has been far superior to that of the various land boards of the Western states managing state-owned public lands."

Although the Sagebrush Rebellion seemed to subside in the 1980s during President Reagan's administration, it was rekindled in 1990 under President Bush's administration. Fearful of losing control over their own land, and of losing access to natural resources on the West's public lands, a group of ranchers, miners, loggers, and others who rely on the millions of acres of those public lands met in Las Vegas in 1990 to develop a strategy. The Sagebrush Rebellion may be in the headlines again soon.

THINK ABOUT IT

1. To what extent do you think the states, particularly in the West, have the right to claim ownership over lands currently owned by the federal government?
2. What role should the federal government play in land management in this country?

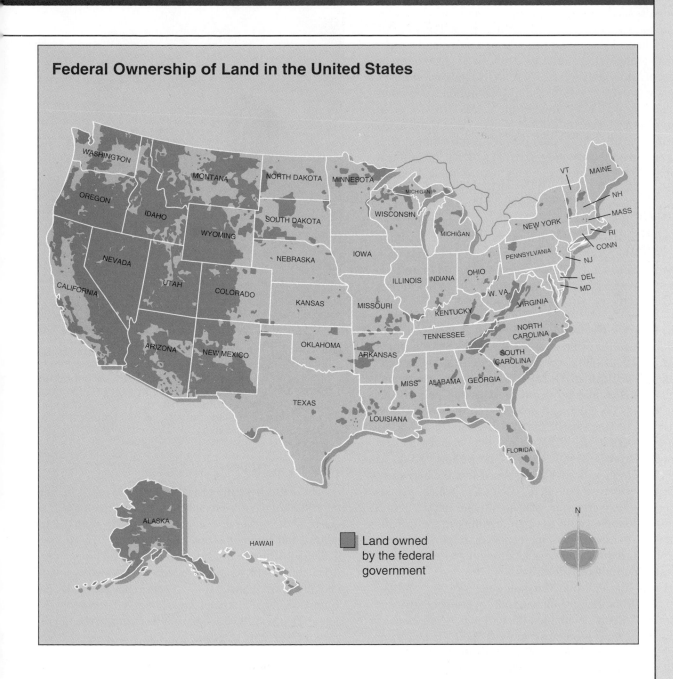

Federal Ownership of Land in the United States

Land owned by the federal government

What role should the state governments play?

3. Should the federal government turn federal lands over to private individuals, such as cattle raisers and oil drillers? Explain.

4. What does the Sagebrush Rebellion tell us about the problems that are a part of our system of federalism today?

The Legal Issue   The issue before the Supreme Court was not simply a question of whether the Second Bank had to pay Maryland's tax. It also had to do with whether Congress had the authority to charter and contribute capital to the Second Bank of the United States. The question was whether the Constitution's necessary and proper clause granted this authority. Those who sided with the state of Maryland were called **strict constructionists.** They wanted the words of the Constitution to be interpreted literally. They thought the words *necessary and proper* referred to only those powers that were *indispensable* for the designated powers of the national government. The Constitution gave the national government the power to coin money and regulate its value. Nothing was specifically stated in the Constitution about the creation of a national bank.

Those who sided with the national government were considered **loose constructionists.** They did not think the words *necessary and proper* should be examined in their strictest sense. They argued that literal interpretation of the necessary and proper clause would mean that it would have no effect at all.

The Court's Decision   Some say that John Marshall had made up his mind about the outcome of *McCulloch* v. *Maryland* (1819) even before he heard the arguments. Marshall decided in favor of McCulloch, who represented the national government. Marshall pointed out that there is no expressed provision in the Constitution to form a national bank, but that if establishing such a bank helped the national government to exercise its designated (expressed) powers, then the authority to do so could be implied. Marshall also said that the necessary and proper clause included ''all means which are appropriate'' to carry out ''the legitimate ends'' of the Constitution. He could not find anything in the Constitution ''which excludes incidental or implied powers; and which requires that everything granted shall be expressly and minutely described.''

From that day on, Marshall's decision became the basis for strengthening our national government's power. Marshall's decision enabled the national government to grow and to meet problems that the founding fathers were unable to foresee. Indeed, today practically every implied power of the national government has been explained by the use of the necessary and proper clause.

Another way that the national government's power has been expanded is through the Court's interpretation of the *commerce clause.* Chief Justice John Marshall was asked to examine an important conflict involving this clause five years after *McCulloch* v. *Maryland.*

▲ Supreme Court Chief Justice John Marshall in his opinion on *McCulloch* v. *Maryland* (1819) stated that the necessary and proper clause of the United States Constitution included "all means which are appropriate to carry out the legitimate ends of the Constitution." Did this decision favor the strict constructionists or the loose constructionists?

Gibbons v. *Ogden*

The states have the reserved power to regulate commerce within their borders. But Article I, Section 8 gives Congress the power to ''regulate commerce with foreign nations, and among the several States. . . .'' The framers of the Constitution did not define the word *commerce.* Strict constructionists had a very narrow view of its meaning, loose constructionists an expanded view. Did commerce include travel by steamboat between two states? That was the issue before the court in the famous case of *Gibbons* v. *Ogden.*

Controlling Steamboat Travel   In 1803 Robert Fulton, the inventor of the steamboat, and the American minister to France, Robert Livingston, obtained from the New York State Legislature the exclusive right, called a **monopoly,** to use steamboats on the waters of New York State. Using this monopoly right, they licensed Aaron Ogden to operate steamboats between New York

In the famous case of *Gibbons* v. *Ogden* (1824) a steamboat monopoly granted by the State of New York was challenged by a competing ferry service operating in the waterways between New York and New Jersey (which are shown as they look today). How did the decision in this case strengthen the power of Congress to regulate interstate commerce?

and New Jersey. Thomas Gibbons also operated steamboats between the two states, but did so without permission from the state of New York. As a result, Ogden sued Gibbons in the New York state courts. Ogden won, and Gibbons issued an appeal to the U.S. Supreme Court.

The Court Decides   The Supreme Court and its Chief Justice Marshall were loose constructionists. They expanded the definition of *commerce* to include all business dealings, such as steamboat travel. The court ruled against the monopoly that Ogden had obtained through license from Fulton and Livingston. Gibbons had to be allowed to compete. Marshall not only used this opportunity to expand the definition of commerce, but also to increase the national government's power to regulate it. He said,

"What is this power? It is the power . . . to prescribe [set down] the rule by which commerce is to be governed. This power, like all others vested in Congress, is complete in itself."

In other words, Marshall said that the national government's power to regulate commerce had only those limitations specifically found in the Constitution and no others.

Since that decision in 1824, the national government has invoked the commerce clause to increase its authority over virtually all areas of economic activity. Few economic activities (even those that take place entirely *within* a state) are outside the regulatory power of the national government. When you buy meat in the supermarket, it is graded according to federal government regulations, which are determined by the U.S. Department of Agriculture. When you ride in a car, many of the safety features in that car were required to be there by an agency of the federal government. When a door-to-door salesperson sells you something, many of the rules governing that sale come from the Federal Trade Commission (FTC). Even when a death occurs in your family, the information you are given about the cost of preparing and burying the body is now regulated by the federal government.

The Battleground of the Civil War

It is easy to think of the Civil War only as a fight to free the slaves. The war, however, can also be viewed as a power struggle between the states and the national government. At the heart of the controversy that led to the Civil War was the issue of national versus state supremacy. That debate was brought to a bloody climax between 1860 and 1865.

In 1824, 1828, and 1832 the national government passed tariff acts, which imposed higher taxes on goods imported into the United States. The Southern states believed that such taxes were against their best interest. One Southern state, South Carolina, attempted to *nullify* the tariffs, or to make them void. It claimed that in cases of conflict between state and national governments, the state should have the ultimate authority to determine the welfare of its citizens. Additionally, some Southerners believed that democratic decisions could only be made when all the segments of society that were affected by those decisions were in agreement. In other words, a **concurrent majority** had to agree. Without that, a decision should not be binding on those whose interest it violates.

93

▲ The American Civil War was fought over many issues including the conflict between national supremacy and states' rights. Did the end of the Civil War bring increased states' rights or increased power for the national government?

Supporters of this concurrent majority concept used it to justify the **secession**—withdrawal—of the Southern states from the union. When the South was defeated in the war, however, the idea that a state can successfully claim its right to secede was defeated with it. We live in an indestructible union of separate states. While the Civil War occurred because of the South's desire for increased states' rights, the result was just the opposite—an increase in the political power of the national government.

SECTION 4 REVIEW

1. If a state law conflicts with a national law, which side must yield?
2. How did the Supreme Court's decision in *McCulloch* v. *Maryland* expand the power of the federal government?
3. How was the Supreme Court's decision in *Gibbons* v. *Ogden* significant?
4. How was the controversy that led to the Civil War related to the concept of federalism?
5. **For critical analysis:** The milestone events discussed in this section—*McCulloch* v. *Maryland, Gibbons* v. *Ogden,* and the Civil War—form part of the trend toward complete supremacy of the national government. What evidence, if any, do you see today that the trend is changing?

The Changing Face of American Federalism

Preview Questions
- What is the concept of dual federalism?
- Why has the era since 1937 been labeled cooperative federalism?
- What is the concept of new federalism?

The balance of political power between the states and the national government has changed through the years. The milestones in the trend toward national government supremacy, described in the previous section, do not tell the full story. There are hundreds, if not thousands, of other court cases and other political actions that both the states and the national government have undertaken. Historically, we can see that the changing model of federalism in our country has passed through three eras: dual federalism, cooperative federalism, and new federalism.

The Era of Dual Federalism

When John Marshall died in 1835, the trend toward national supremacy fostered by him and the loose constructionists on the Court came to an end. During Andrew Jackson's presidency, from 1829 to 1837, he nudged the nation again toward states' rights. At this time in our history political participation increased, particularly among farmers and working men and women. Those individuals were involved in their own local economy. They appealed directly to their state governments for economic benefits. The states as a result took on an increasing sphere of authority over business activities.

The concept of **dual federalism** emphasizes the distinction between national and state spheres of authority, particularly in the area of economic regulation. The Constitution reserves to the states the ability to regulate all **intrastate commerce**—business done wholly within the state. Examples of intrastate commerce include selling fruit from one part of the state to the other, or rendering services within a local region. Under dual federalism, the Supreme Court simply becomes the referee between the national and state governments, which maintain diverse but sovereign powers.

From 1835 to 1864, John Marshall's replacement, Chief Justice Roger B. Taney, allowed the states to increase their power. As he stated in *Abelman* v. *Booth* (1859), he wanted to make sure that the Supreme Court helped to "guard the states from any encroachment upon their reserved rights by the general [national] government."

Except for the period of the Civil War, the doctrine of dual federalism prevailed. For example, in *Hammer* v. *Dagenhart* (1918) the U.S. Supreme Court ruled that a 1916 federal law banning child labor was unconstitutional. It reasoned that child labor was a local problem and the power to deal with it was reserved to the states.

The era of dual federalism came to an end around 1937, when the United States was in the depths of the greatest depression it had ever experienced.

The Era of Cooperative Federalism

In the view of **cooperative federalism,** the national and state governments are seen as complementary parts of a single governmental mechanism, designed to promote the well-being of all of the nation's inhabitants. All of the powers of that mechanism are to be used to solve the problems facing the entire United States. Certainly the Great Depression, which began in 1929, can be described as a period of tremendous national problems. By

▲ When Andrew Jackson was elected to the presidency in 1828, he began to push the nation towards states' rights. This led to the practice of "dual federalism." The system of dual federalism emphasized the distinction between national powers and states' rights. What was the role of the Supreme Court under this system?

the depths of the Great Depression in 1933, over five thousand banks had failed. One-fourth of the people willing to work could not find jobs. During the first three years of the Great Depression, the federal government did very little to solve the nation's economic misery.

A new administration headed by Franklin D. Roosevelt took office in 1933. The first hundred days of FDR's administration ushered in the **New Deal,** a program designed to help the U.S. out of the Depression. It included many government spending and public assistance programs, in addition to thousands of regulations of economic activity. For four years the U.S. Supreme Court, abiding by the doctrine of dual federalism, rejected virtually all of Roosevelt's federal regulation of business as unconstitutional. Then in 1937 Roosevelt threatened to "pack" the Supreme Court by adding new justices. The Supreme Court began to rule in his favor. National laws regulating agricultural prices, general wages, and the relationship between unions and business were passed again and withstood constitutional challenges.

The era since 1937 has been described as an era of cooperative federalism because the state and federal governments cooperated in solving complex mutual problems. It also marked the real beginning of the era of national supremacy, which continues into the present. It is true that today Congress can regulate almost any kind of economic activity no matter where that activity is located. For example, consider a manufacturing business that is located in one state, hires workers only from that state, and sells the products only within that state. The national government, nonetheless, can regulate the hours of work and wages paid to the workers, the safety conditions under which they work, the labeling on the product manufactured, the standards to which the product adheres, and, during certain periods in our history, even the price at which the product can be sold.

During the 1970s and 1980s, several government administrations attempted to revitalize the doctrine of dual federalism, which they renamed new federalism.

The New Federalism

One of the policies of President Richard M. Nixon's administration (1968–1974) was a reduction in the restrictions attached to federal grants to local and state governments. He called this policy the **new federalism.** He wanted local officials themselves to decide how tax revenues should be spent. The centerpiece of this new federalism was a **revenue-sharing program,** which gave local and state officials more freedom in making their spending decisions. The Nixon Administration

▲ By the time that Franklin Delano Roosevelt took office as president in 1933, over 5,000 banks had failed. In an effort to solve this and the other problems of the Depression, President Roosevelt pushed through Congress many new laws regulating agricultural prices, general wages, the banking industry, and the relationship between unions and businesses. FDR's New Deal programs brought about a new era of federalism. What term is used to describe this era of federalism?

asked Congress in 1972 to return a certain percentage of federal tax revenues each year to the state and local governments. Congress passed a general revenue-sharing law in which one-third of the designated funds went to the states and two-thirds were sent directly to local governments. Needless to say, revenue-sharing was quite popular and strongly supported by many governors, mayors, and other state and local officials. It was opposed by the Reagan administration (1980–1988), however, and was abolished due to the growing financial needs of the deficit-ridden federal government.

President Reagan did continue to carry out certain aspects of the new federalism. In 1981, in his first State of the Union Address, President Reagan said that he intended to restore those powers reserved to the states and to the people. His new federalism, similar to Nixon's, was a plan to give the states an increased role in deciding how government revenues should be spent. But Reagan, unlike Nixon, did not want the state and local governments to rely as heavily on the federal government's resources. Reagan wanted the state and local governments to spend as much as they raised themselves, but with less federal regulation on how they spent their own revenues. Reagan's attempt to dismantle forty domestic

programs at the federal level, including social services, transportation, and community development, was strongly opposed by state governors. They saw Reagan's plan as a ploy to cut federal government expenditures on needed programs.

President George Bush continued where Reagan left off. The growing fiscal crisis at the federal level has forced the national government to continue to cut back on financial aid to the states and cities.

SECTION 5 REVIEW _____

1. How has the balance of political power between the state and the federal governments shifted throughout the years?
2. What is the federal government's role under a dual federalism system?
3. Briefly describe the doctrine of cooperative federalism.
4. How did President Reagan's new federalism differ from President Nixon's?
5. **For critical analysis:** Who might be in favor of federal government revenue sharing and why? Who would be against it and why?

CHALLENGE TO THE AMERICAN DREAM

Snowbelt versus Sunbelt

In the past few decades, the population in the United States has shifted away from the Northeast, Midwest, and Northwest states, often referred to as the Snowbelt, to the South and the Southwest, often loosely called the Sunbelt. From 1950 to 1990 population in the Snowbelt increased 36.1 percent, whereas population in the Sunbelt increased 86.2 percent.

The shifting population has generally resulted in a greater amount of federal government benefits going to the Sunbelt than to the Snowbelt. Regional conflict has thereby been intensified. The Snowbelt states have tried to counter this changing power structure, and we can expect to see this battle continue for quite some time.

We continue to see defense and space program industries, funded by national revenues, growing in the Sunbelt states. Many federal anti-poverty programs have been concentrated in such Sunbelt cities as Houston, Atlanta, and Los Angeles. In addition, recent studies have shown that individuals and businesses in the eighteen Snowbelt states pay more in federal taxes than they receive in federal grants and government spending. Sunbelt states, by contrast, receive more from the federal government than they pay in taxes.

The 1982 change in the number of each state's members in the House of Representatives decreased the representation of the Snowbelt states by seventeen seats, giving the South and the West a congressional majority. As a result, the Snowbelt's coalition efforts to secure more federal funds will have to continue.

The power struggle should intensify even further after the effects of another reapportionment from the 1990 census. Nineteen seats have shifted from the East and Midwest to the South and West. Another nineteen will probably shift after the 2000 census. California, Texas, and Florida have been, and will continue to be, the biggest gainers. New York and Pennsylvania will be the biggest losers.

Not all is lost for the Snowbelt states. In recent years many Northeastern states have seen growth in high-technology industries. In contrast, many Sunbelt states suffered economic declines during downturns in the oil industry.

The challenge to the American dream is for Congress to distribute federal projects fairly throughout all of the country in spite of a shifting population.

Population Changes in Selected States, 1950–1990

States with largest population increases:*
1. Nevada (+653.45%)
2. Arizona (+390.7%)
3. Florida (+369.2%)
4. California (+181.9%)
5. Utah (+150.8%)

States with smallest population increases:
1. West Virginia (−10.2%)
2. North Dakota (+3.5%)
3. Iowa (+6.3%)
4. South Dakota (+7.2%)
5. Pennsylvania (+13.6%)

*Study does not consider Alaska or Hawaii.

You Decide

1. Why does a population movement from the colder Northern states to the warmer Southern and Western states necessarily result in a regional conflict within the national government?
2. Why will this regional conflict increase after the 2000 census?
3. How would you go about calculating whether your family receives more or less from the federal government than it pays in taxes?

CHAPTER 4 REVIEW

Key Terms

act of admission 88
alien 85
child custody 83
common-law
  marriage 82
concurrent majority 93
concurrent powers 83
confederal system 76
cooperative
  federalism 95
decentralization 90
Dennison rule 86
division of powers 78
dual federalism 94

elastic clause 80
enabling act 88
exports 80
expressed or
  enumerated
  powers 78
extradition 86
federal system 77
fugitive 86
full faith and credit
  clause 86
horizontal
  federalism 85
implied powers 80

inherent powers 80
interstate compacts 86
intrastate
  commerce 94
legal tender 80
loose
  constructionists 92
monopoly 92
necessary and proper
  clause 80
New Deal 95
new federalism 95
privileges and
  immunities clause 85

republican form of
  government 86
reserved powers 81
resulting powers 80
revenue-sharing
  program 95
secession 94
strict
  constructionists 92
supremacy clause 89
unitary system 76

Summary

1. The Constitution created a federal system—one based on the division of powers between the federal government and the states. Other forms of governmental systems are a unitary system, in which state and/or local governments exercise only those powers given to them by the central government, and a confederal system, which is a league of independent states.

2. Under the U.S. Constitution, the federal government has three types of powers: expressed or enumerated powers, implied powers, and inherent powers. Some powers are expressly denied to the federal government and some powers are reserved to the states. Local governments are created by their states and have no legal existence apart from them. Concurrent powers are those simultaneously held by both the federal and state governments.

3. Horizontal federalism defines relations among the states. Under this system, states may not discriminate against citizens of other states, and are obligated to give full faith and credit to the laws and activities of other states. They must also agree to extradite persons accused of crimes elsewhere. Many states have settled differences among themselves by entering into interstate compacts. The Constitution obligates the federal government to provide the state with a republican form of government, to protect each state against foreign invasion and domestic violence, and to respect each state's territorial integrity.

4. The supremacy clause of the Constitution makes the federal government the supreme governing body of the land. The Supreme Court's decision in *McCulloch* v. *Maryland* (1819) became the basis for strengthening the federal government's power. Since the Supreme Court decision in *Gibbons* v. *Ogden* (1824), the federal government has used the commerce clause to increase its authority over virtually all areas of economic activity.

5. The practice of federalism has changed throughout the years. Historically, we can view the changing model of federalism in the United States as having three eras: dual federalism, cooperative federalism, and new federalism.

Review Questions

1. Explain the differences between the three different types of governmental systems.
2. Explain how federalism creates a two-way system of government.
3. Why did the framers of our Constitution choose a federal framework?
4. What is the source of the national government's expressed powers? What is the source of its implied powers?
5. How has the necessary and proper clause enabled the national government to expand its powers?
6. On what basis does the Constitution deny certain powers to the national government?

CHAPTER 4 REVIEW—Continued

7. Explain the concept of concurrent powers.
8. What does the privileges and immunities clause prevent?
9. Why is the concept of full faith and credit so important to interstate relationships?
10. What is the importance of the interstate compact?
11. What obligations does the Constitution impose upon the federal government with regard to the states?
12. What is the significance of the supremacy clause in our federal system?
13. What was the outcome of the case *McCulloch* v. *Maryland*?
14. Have there been any changes in the balance of political power between the state and national governments throughout the years?

Questions for Thought and Discussion

1. What do you think our government would be like if there were no division of powers between the national government and the states?
2. Should states be given greater power, less power, or do they currently have enough power?
3. Why do you think the powers to wage war and to relate to foreign nations belong to the national government?
4. What factors do you think have been responsible for the national government's growth of power?

Improving Your Skills
Communication Skills

Asking Effective Questions

Asking questions is one of the most important ways for us to learn facts, share ideas, and become informed. Asking effective questions will help you become a better-informed and more responsible citizen. Effective questions are designed to obtain specific information.

To ask effective questions requires preparation. When we don't obtain the information we seek from questions we ask, it is usually because we are asking the wrong source, asking the wrong questions, or asking them in the wrong way. Before you ask questions:

1. Determine the exact information you want to obtain.

2. Determine the best sources of that information.
3. Decide what questions will best draw out the information.
4. Decide how you should ask the questions. Remember that questions that can be answered with only a *yes* or a *no* will not give you much information.

Writing

Follow the four steps above to plan a class interview with a city or county official concerning a current issue in your community.

1. As a group, discuss the kinds of information you would like to obtain from the official. Write down ideas as they occur. Then narrow your ideas to a few specific issues.
2. Decide which city or county official would be the best source for that information.
3. Using the ideas you generated in Step 1, create a formal list of questions for the interview. Have your teacher approve your questions.

Social Studies Skills
Map Reading

Look at the map on page 91 (Federal Ownership of Land in the United States) to answer the following questions.

1. How is federally owned land identified?
2. Do any states have no federally owned land?
3. List the states in which the federal government owns 50 percent or more of the land.

Activities and Projects

1. Stage a debate on the following issue: Federal aid in the form of categorical grants gives the national government too much control over the states and should be abolished.
2. Call or write the district office of your local school district. Find out what kinds of state and federal aid your school district receives. Interview as many school officials as possible (principals, school board members, teachers, etc). Ask them to describe how they feel the aid (or lack of it) affects your school. Report your findings to the class.

The Rights of All Citizens

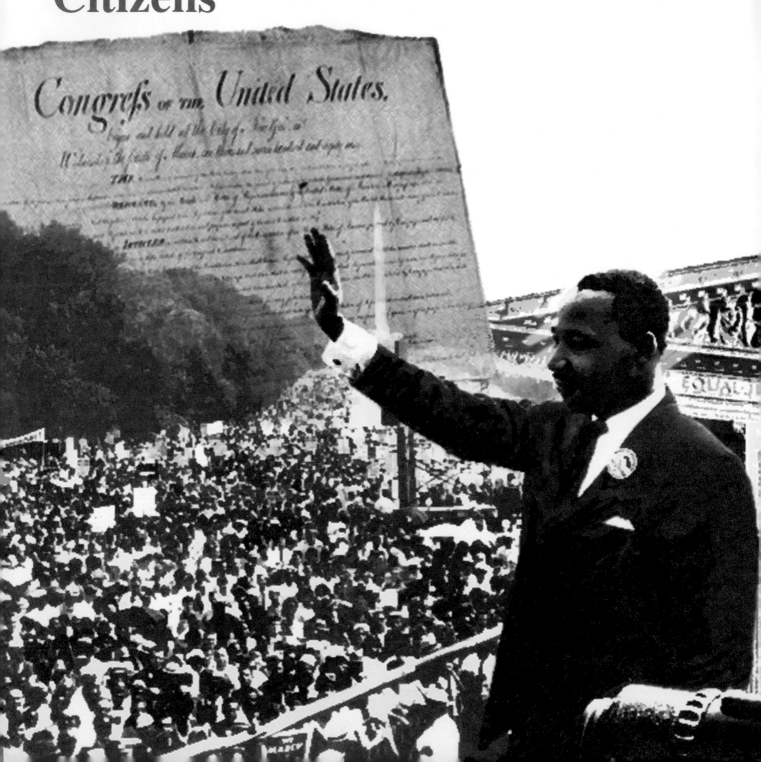

UNIT CONTENTS

- *Chapter 5*   Personal Freedoms
- *Chapter 6*   Equality Under the Law

CHAPTER 5

Personal Freedoms

CHAPTER OBJECTIVES

To learn and understand

■ The origins of our system of personal freedoms and how they are guaranteed under the Bill of Rights.

■ The way the First Amendment guarantees freedom of religion and how the Constitution affects the separation of church and state.

■ The extent to which the government protects as well as limits freedom of speech under the First Amendment.

■ The limits placed on freedom of the press.

What the right to assembly and petition means.

Keynote

"I disagree profoundly with what you say, but I would defend with my life your right to say it."

—— **François Marie Voltaire
(1694–1778) French philosopher**

INTRODUCTION

It is easy to say that all people in the United States should have the right to express themselves— that is, until they say or do something that offends you or someone else. Contrary to that concept, as the opening statement from Voltaire points out, the real test of a democracy is providing freedom of expression for *all* persons, regardless of whether you agree with what they say.

As you have learned, many early settlers came to America to escape religious persecution. Later, the United States was created out of a struggle to guarantee other personal freedoms. The founders dreamed of a country in which everyone could speak freely, write exactly what they felt, and openly practice any religion, all without penalty or interference.

As a result of this commitment, government in the United States has been firmly based on the concept of a *limited government,* which has *only* those powers the people have given to it. In a democracy it is essential that the people retain certain rights.

SECTION 1

Our System of Personal Freedoms

Preview Questions
- What guarantees of freedoms were included in the original Constitution?
- From what does the Bill of Rights protect us?
- Why is the due process clause of the Fourteenth Amendment so important?
- What does the Supreme Court have to do with the Bill of Rights?

Most of us agree that we must have basic freedoms; most of us even agree on what they should be. Most of us also recognize that to maintain order in our society, some lines must be drawn between individual rights and the rights of others or the community as a whole.

We begin to disagree, however, when we try to determine how, where, and when those lines are drawn. Sometimes people's rights seem to conflict with each other. For example, the right of the press to publish information about a crime might interfere with a defendant's right to have a fair trial. You may feel your rights are being invaded if you are forced to listen to music or to a speech that you find offensive.

Civil liberties are legal and constitutional rights that protect citizens *from* government actions. The First Amendment freedoms of religion, speech, press, **assembly** (to gather together for a common purpose), and **petition** (to address the government about its policies) are all civil liberties. Government cannot infringe upon these rights, nor can Congress pass laws **abridging** (diminishing or editing) them.

Constitutional Protections

The founders believed that the constitutions of the individual states had ample provisions to protect their citizens' rights. Most references to individual civil liberties, therefore, were not included in the Constitution until the Bill of Rights was created in 1791. Nonetheless, some safeguards in the original Constitution protected citizens against an overly powerful government.

For example, Article I, Section 9 of the Constitution provides that the writ of *habeas corpus* will be available to all citizens, except in times of rebellion or national invasion. A writ of ***habeas corpus*** (a Latin phrase that roughly means ''you should hand over the body'') is an order that an official must bring the prisoner into court, and the judge must be shown why the prisoner is being

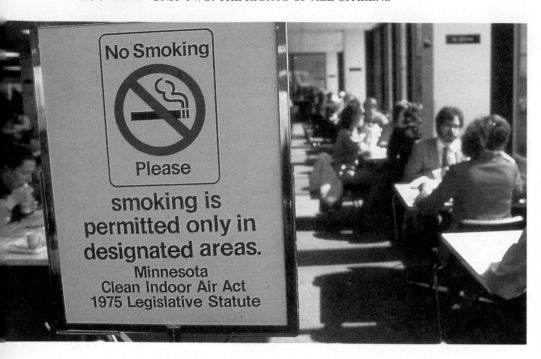

◄ Many of our laws seek to strike a balance between individual rights and the rights of others and the community. In an effort to strike this balance on the issue of smoking, many communities have instituted laws banning smoking in certain areas and requiring certain businesses such as restaurants to establish smoke-free areas for their customers. How does the individual's right to smoke interfere with the rights of others?

kept in jail. If the court finds that the imprisonment is unlawful, it issues such a writ and the prisoner must be released. If our country did not have such a provision, political leaders could jail their opponents without giving them the opportunity to plead their case before a judge. Without this opportunity, many opponents could conveniently disappear, or be left to rot away in prison. The founders realized the importance of the writ of *habeas corpus.*

The Constitution also prohibits the Congress and state legislatures from passing *bills of attainder.* **Bills of attainder** are legislative acts that directly punish a specifically named individual (or a specifically named group or class of individuals) without a trial. A law cannot be passed by any legislature that identifies, convicts, or sentences a person or group of people for a real or imagined offense. For example, a law cannot be passed by your legislature that says students who attend your school and who drive over 35 miles per hour will automatically be sentenced to one night in jail.

The Constitution also prohibits Congress from passing *ex post facto* laws. ***Ex post facto*** roughly means "after the fact." An *ex post facto* law punishes individuals for committing an act that has become retroactively illegal. For example, say you went fishing in a nearby lake last week, when it was still legal to fish in that area. This week a law is passed saying that fishing in that area is illegal. You cannot be prosecuted for fishing there the previous week, because it was still legal to do so.

The *ex post facto* provision also prevents legislatures from increasing the penalty for a crime that was previously committed. You are subject only to the penalty that was in effect at the time.

The Bill of Rights

Even though these few individual protections against government were included in the original Constitution, as you learned in Chapters 2 and 3, there were no general listing of the rights of the people, or bill of rights. Public demand for the bill was strong, and several states ratified the Constitution only with the promise that such a listing would be added.

The first session of Congress in 1789 lived up to that promise with a series of proposed amendments. Ten of them, the Bill of Rights, were ratified by the states and became part of the Constitution on December 15, 1791. The first eight amendments grant the people rights. The Ninth Amendment states that the rights guaranteed in the Constitution are not the only rights the people have. The Tenth Amendment states that if the Constitution does not give a certain power to the federal government, nor denies it to the state governments, then the power belongs to the states or to the people. (This chapter deals mainly with the rights guaranteed under the First Amendment.)

The Bill of Rights protects individuals *against* abuses of power by the federal government. Consequently, the

The Bill of Rights

First Amendment	Guarantees freedom of religion, speech, press, assembly, and petition.
Second Amendment	Guarantees the right to keep and bear arms, since a state requires a well-equipped citizen army for its own security.
Third Amendment	Prohibits the lodging of soldiers in peacetime, without the dweller's consent.
Fourth Amendment	Prohibits unreasonable searches and seizures of persons or property.
Fifth Amendment	Guarantees the rights to trial by jury, due process of law, and fair payment when private property is taken for public use, such as in eminent domain; prohibits compulsory self-incrimination and double jeopardy (trial for the same crime twice).
Sixth Amendment	Guarantees the accused in a criminal case the right to a speedy and public trial by an impartial jury and with counsel; allows the accused to cross-examine witnesses against him or her, and to solicit testimony from witnesses in his or her favor.
Seventh Amendment	Guarantees a trial by jury for the accused in a civil case involving $20 or more.
Eighth Amendment	Prohibits excessive bail and fines, as well as cruel and unusual punishments.
Ninth Amendment	Establishes that the people have rights in addition to those specified in the Constitution.
Tenth Amendment	Establishes that those powers neither delegated to the national government nor denied to the states are reserved for the states.

▲ **FIGURE 5–1 The Bill of Rights.** On September 25, 1789, the Bill of Rights passed both houses of Congress and by December 15, 1791, had been ratified by three-fourths of the states. What does the Bill of Rights do that the original Constitution did not do?

Bill of Rights begins with the words, "Congress shall make no law. ..." According to Justice Hugo Black, who served on the United States Supreme Court from 1937 through 1971, the Bill of Rights is "a collection of 'Thou Shalt Nots'" directed at the government.

In a democracy, government policy tends to reflect the view of the majority. A major role of the Bill of Rights, however, is to protect minority rights against the will of the majority. Justice Robert Jackson, who sat on the Supreme Court from 1941 through 1954, said that "the very purpose of the Bill of Rights was to withdraw certain subjects from the vicissitudes [changes and var-

iations] of political controversy, to place them beyond the reach of majorities." These rights "may not be submitted to a vote." In other words, certain rights should be protected for every citizen, whether the majority agrees on these rights or not.

Who then defines and applies these rights? Who stands guard over our civil liberties?

The Role of the Courts

When disagreements arise over how to interpret the Bill of Rights, it is the courts, especially the United States

Supreme Court, that stand as the major guardians of individual liberties. All officers and agencies of the government are supposed to protect individual rights, but whenever a person claims that government has violated his or her civil liberties, he or she turns to the courts to interpret and apply constitutional guarantees.

Even though the courts stand guard over the rights and liberties of Americans, it is important to remember that ultimate responsibility to protect these rights lies with us, the American people. Each generation must learn anew to uphold its rights by voting, expressing opinions to elected representatives, and bringing cases to the attention of the courts when constitutional rights are threatened. Judge Learned Hand, an often-quoted United States Circuit Court judge, made the point this way:

> I often wonder whether we do not rest our hopes too much upon constitutions, upon laws and upon courts. These are false hopes; believe me, these are false hopes. Liberty lies in the hearts of men and women; when it dies there, no constitution, no law, no court can ever do much to help it.

▲ United States Circuit Court Judge Learned Hand questioned our reliance upon constitutional laws and courts to protect our individual liberties. What do you think Judge Hand meant when he said, "Liberty lies in the hearts of men and women . . . "?

Making the States Comply with the Bill of Rights

For many years the Bill of Rights was not applied to state or local governments. The founders believed that the states, being closer to the people, would be less likely to violate their own citizens' liberties.

State governments are bound to protect their citizens' rights through their state constitutions, most of which usually contain bills of rights. They are also bound to protect civil rights through a clause in the Fourteenth Amendment to the Constitution, known as the **due process clause.** It reads:

> No State shall . . . deprive any person of life, liberty, or property, without due process of law.

Due process is simply the right to be treated fairly under the legal system. That system and its officers are responsible to ensure that "rules of fair play" are

◄ Since being injured by stray bullets from an assassination attempt on President Ronald Reagan by John W. Hinckley, Jr., James Brady and his wife, Sarah Brady, have led a campaign for the control of handguns in this country. Proponents of gun control maintain that the Second Amendment protects the right of the people to keep and bear arms, but only in connection with service in a "well-regulated militia" such as the National Guard. Opponents of gun control argue that the wording of the amendment clearly reflects the founders' desire to protect the right of gun ownership for individual citizens. How do you feel about gun control?

CITIZENSHIP SKILLS AND RESPONSIBILITIES
Responsibilities of Citizens

You have begun to learn about your rights as a citizen. Along with those rights, you also share many responsibilities. These responsibilities help protect your rights and keep the country running smoothly and democratically. Certain responsibilities are required by law. Some of these include:

Attending School.   Every state requires that young people attend school until they reach a certain age, which in most states is age 16. Attending school is vital to democracy, for it is through education that every American becomes an informed and effective citizen. An educated population is essential to our strength as a nation.

Obeying Laws.   All citizens should know as much about the laws as they can. Obeying these laws is one of the most important responsibilities required of Americans. If a law seems unfair or unnecessary, citizens can work through government to change it.

Paying Taxes.   All Americans must pay some amount of taxes. Although this is a duty about which we often complain, it is important to remember our tax dollars are used for services we rely on every day. These include fire and police protection, education, national defense, and protection of the environment.

Defending the Nation.   American citizens have a responsibility to defend the nation. In peacetime, the military is made up of volunteers. Even in peacetime, however, 18-year-old males are required to register for the draft (even though there currently is no draft). **Draft registration** means giving your name, age, and address so that you can be contacted for military service in case the country suddenly needs to increase its armed forces.

TAKING ACTION

1. The list presented above is a list of *required* citizen responsibilities. Make a list of *voluntary* responsibilities that you have as an American citizen.
2. What do you think would happen if the above-listed four legally required responsibilities became voluntary? Write a paragraph explaining your answers.
3. Do you think women should be drafted for military service? If so, what roles do you think women should play in protecting the nation? Explain the reasons for your answer.

followed in making decisions, in determining guilt or innocence, and in punishing those who have been found guilty. Thus, "due process" means that the correct procedures have been followed and that everyone has been given an equal right to be heard.

The Supreme Court has interpreted the due process clause to mean that no state may deny any person any right that is "basic or essential to the American concept of ordered liberty." In a long series of cases, starting in 1925, the Supreme Court gradually began using the due process clause to say that states could not abridge a right that the national government could not abridge. Especially during the 1960s, the Supreme Court broadened its interpretations to limit state action in most areas in which federal action is banned. Many of these decisions, as you will see, have been controversial. For all practical purposes, however, the Bill of Rights guarantees individual rights against infringement by both state and national governments.

SECTION 1 REVIEW

1. What are civil liberties? List the civil liberties each American is guaranteed under the Bill of Rights.
2. What protections did the original Constitution provide against an overly intrusive government?
3. How are the courts one of the principal guardians of personal freedoms in this country?
4. How is the Bill of Rights applied to the states?
5. **For critical analysis:** Reread the quote from Judge Learned Hand on page 106. Explain what you think he means when he says we should not "rest our hopes for our personal liberties too much upon constitutions, laws, and courts."

SECTION 2

Freedom of Religion

Preview Questions
- Why is freedom of religion important in a democracy?
- What does "separation of church and state" mean?
- What distinction is there between the right to believe and the right to practice your religion as you wish?

Imagine for a moment several possible problems that face students and administrators at public schools regarding the practice of religion. Joan, a sophomore at Blue High School, wants permission to leave school during class hours in order to attend religious classes at her church. Should she be allowed to leave? At Oak High

▼ The annual Hare Krishna Festival of Giant Chariots celebrated in Santa Monica, California is just one colorful example of religious freedom in the United States. What does the First Amendment say about religion?

School in a neighboring state, administrators have set aside thirty seconds during homeroom period to allow students to engage in silent prayer. Is this legal? Understanding the Constitution and how it has been interpreted by the Supreme Court can help you answer the questions just posed.

The freedoms guaranteed by the First Amendment of the Constitution are essential for the survival of a democracy. Many nondemocratic governments in Eastern Europe that did not guarantee these rights found out how important they were when, as a result of mass demands for these rights, their governments began to collapse in 1989.

Its not surprising that our Bill of Rights provides for the protection of religious liberty first—many of the colonists came here to escape religious persecution. The First Amendment prohibits Congress from passing laws "respecting an establishment of religion." This is known as the **establishment clause.**

In 1802, President Thomas Jefferson referred to the First Amendment's establishment clause as "a wall of separation between church and state." This makes the United States different from many countries that are ruled by religious governments, such as the Islamic government of Iran. It also makes us different from nations that have in the past strongly discouraged the practice of any religion at all such as the People's Republic of China.

The establishment clause forbids the government to "establish" an official religion. What does this separation of church and state mean in practice?

Separation of Church and State

Church and government, while constitutionally separated by the establishment clause in the United States, have never been enemies or strangers. The establishment clause does not prohibit government from supporting religion *in general*, which remains a part of public life. Most government officials take an oath of office in the name of God, and our coins and paper currency carry the motto "In God We Trust." Clergy of different religions—rabbis, ministers, and others—serve with each branch of the armed forces. The Pledge of Allegiance contains a reference to God. Public meetings and even sessions of Congress open with prayers.

The "wall of separation" that Thomas Jefferson referred to, however, does exist and has been upheld by the Supreme Court on many occasions. The first ruling by the Supreme Court on the establishment clause came in *Everson* v. *Board of Education* (1947). The case involved a New Jersey law that allowed the state to pay for bus transportation of students who attended parochial schools (schools run by churches or other religious groups). The Court upheld the New Jersey law because it did not aid the church *directly,* but provided for the safety and benefit of the students. The ruling both affirmed the importance of separating church and state, and set the precedent that not *all* forms of state and federal aid to church-related schools are forbidden under the Constitution.

The Issue of Released Time In some schools, students are allowed to leave regular classes to attend religious instruction sessions. Some concerned citizens have argued that this policy of **released time** violates the establishment clause. Two cases dealing with this issue have reached the Supreme Court. In *McCollum* v. *Board of Education* (1948), the Court said students could not be released from regular classes in order to attend a religious program in Champaign, Illinois, because public school classrooms and other facilities were being used for religious purposes. Four years later, however, in *Zorach* v. *Clauson,* New York City's released-time program was upheld, because the religious classes were conducted in a private location. The Court held that the schools were doing no more than accommodating the schedules of students to obtain religious instruction.

Education, Prayer, and the Bible On occasion, some schools have promoted a general sense of religion without proclaiming allegiance to any particular one. Whether the states have a right to allow this was the main question presented in *Engel* v. *Vitale* (1962), the ''Regents' Prayer'' case in New York. The State Board of Regents in New York had composed a nondenominational prayer (a prayer not associated with any particular religion) and urged school districts to use it in classrooms at the start of each day. It read:

> Almighty God, we acknowledge our dependence upon Thee, and we beg Thy blessings upon us, our parents, our teachers, and our country.

Some parents objected to the prayer, saying it was a violation of the establishment clause. The Supreme Court agreed and ruled that the Regents' prayer was unconstitutional. Speaking for the majority, Justice Hugo Black wrote that the First Amendment must at least mean ''that in this country it is no part of the business of government to compose official prayers for any group of the American people to recite as part of a religious program carried on by government.''

In 1980, a Kentucky law requiring that the Ten Commandments be posted in all public schools was found unconstitutional in *Stone* v. *Graham.* In 1985, the Supreme Court ruled that an Alabama law requiring a daily one-minute period of silence for meditation and voluntary prayer also violated the establishment clause.

In sum, the Supreme Court has ruled that the public schools, which are agencies of government, cannot sponsor religious activities. It has *not,* however, held that individuals cannot pray, when and as they choose, in schools or in any other place. Nor has it held that the Bible cannot be studied as a form of literature in the schools.

Religion is often a sensitive issue, and public reactions to the Court's rulings have been mixed. In 1984 one group proposed to amend the Constitution to allow Bible reading and recitation of the Christian prayer ''The Lord's Prayer'' in schools. The proposed amendment would have overruled the Supreme Court's decisions, but it did not produce the two-thirds vote in each house of Congress needed to send it to the states for ratification.

Religious Meetings in Schools Cases have arisen around the country in which students who want to pray or hold religious meetings or discussions on public school property have been barred from doing so by public officials. Congress sought to strike a reasonable balance when, in 1984, it passed the Equal Access Act. That law requires public high schools to allow students' religious and political clubs to meet on the same basis as do other extracurricular activity clubs. In 1990, the Supreme Court upheld the Equal Access Act on an 8-to-1 vote in *Board of Education of Westside Community Schools* v. *Mergens*, a case involving a high school in Omaha, Nebraska, in which students sought to form a Christian study group. ''A high school need not permit any student activities not related to the curriculum,'' Justice Sandra Day O'Connor said in the opinion. ''But if it does,'' she continued, ''the school is bound by the Equal Access Act not to discriminate against any student group on the basis of its religious, philosophical, or political viewpoints.''

Aid to Parochial Schools All property owners, except nonprofit institutions, must pay property taxes, of which a large part goes to support public schools. What about the students who attend private schools, which receive no public tax support?

Under certain circumstances parochial schools can constitutionally obtain state aid. Many states have provided aid to church-related schools in the form of

In 1962, it was customary for this San Antonio High School English class to open with a prayer. How did the Supreme Court rule on the issue of prayer in school?

textbooks, transportation, and equipment. Other forms of payment, such as providing for teacher's salaries and payment for field trips have been found unconstitutional.

Those who favor government financial aid to parochial schools argue that 12 percent of all American students attend private schools, 85 percent of which have religious affiliation. These students would otherwise be attending public schools at public expense. They argue that parents must be relieved of some of the double financial burden of paying to send their children to private schools while also paying local property taxes to support public schools.

Opponents argue that parents who send children to parochial schools make their own free choice, knowing full well that such schools are not supported with tax dollars. They should accept the consequences and not expect society to pay for their choice.

Since 1971, the Supreme Court has followed the **excessive entanglement** (involvement) **theory** when deciding cases that involve government aid to religious school groups. To be constitutional, a state's school aid must meet three requirements: (1) the purpose of the financial aid must be clearly secular (not religious); (2) its primary effect must neither advance nor inhibit religion; and (3) it must avoid an "excessive entanglement of government with religion."

The Court first used the test in *Lemon* v. *Kurtzman* (1971). The Court denied public aid to private and parochial schools for the salaries of teachers of secular courses, and for school-building maintenance and repairs. It held that the establishment clause is designed to prevent three main evils: "sponsorship, financial support, and active involvement of the sovereign [the government] in religious activity."

In *Mueller* v. *Allen* (1983), the Court upheld a Minnesota tax law that gave parents a state income tax deduction for costs of tuition, textbooks, and transportation for their elementary and secondary school children. Parents may claim the tax break no matter what schools, public or private, the children attend. Because the deduction was available to *all* parents, the Court found that the law meets the excessive entanglement standards.

The Court has also enforced the separation of church and state in other public places besides schools.

Christmas Displays   Do publicly sponsored displays of religious holidays violate the wall of separation? The answer is not a simple yes or no. In 1984, by a bare majority of 5 to 4, the Supreme Court upheld a display of a Nativity scene depicting the birth of Christ in Pawtucket, Rhode Island, in *Lynch* v. *Donnelly*. It ruled that the display was acceptable because it also included symbols that are not necessarily religious, such as Santa, reindeer, and animals.

In 1989, the Court ruled against another Nativity scene in the Allegheny County Courthouse in Pennsylvania. This one was *not* surrounded by other decorations and *was* found to be in violation of the establishment clause. In the same case the Court ruled that an eighteen-foot modernistic menorah (a religious symbol used in the celebration of Chanukah, a Jewish holiday) at the nearby City-County building during Chanukah *did not*

CASE STUDY

Churches and Taxes

Traditionally, states and cities have not taxed churches and church-owned property used for religious purposes. In other words, such property is *tax exempt.* The Court upheld this practice in *Walz* v. *New York City Tax Commission* in 1970. Walz had challenged the exemption of churches from local property taxes. He argued that these exemptions raised everyone else's property tax bills, and that the exemptions amounted to a public support of religion.

The Court found that the tax exemptions only indicated a state's "benevolent [charitable] neutrality" toward religion, not active support of it. They stated the tax exemptions "create only a minimal and remote [and therefore permissible] involvement between church and state."

In 1990, the Court reached a different sort of decision on state tax and churches. In a defeat for the Jimmy Swaggart Ministries, the Court ruled unanimously that states may require religious groups to pay sales tax on religious materials they sell. It upheld California's tax on Swaggart Ministries' sales of a range of materials, from Bibles and song books to prerecorded audiocassettes.

In an opinion written by Justice Sandra Day O'Connor, the high court rejected arguments that a sales tax on religious materials violates the First Amendment's guarantee of religious freedom. "The collection and payment of the generally applicable tax in this case imposes no constitutionally significant burden" on the Swaggart organization's "religious practices or beliefs," Justice O'Connor said.

Church groups reacted by saying it was the beginning of a disturbing trend that could mean taxing church property and income next. They feared it may be a trend away from treating religion as worthy of special protection under the Bill of Rights.

But a spokeswoman for the American Civil Liberties Union, an organization that fights abuses of constitutionally guaranteed personal freedoms, said the ruling affirms "the neutrality with which government should treat all religions."

THINK ABOUT IT

1. Should *all* types of religious organizations enjoy the same tax-exempt status?
2. Why do you think states have traditionally exempted churches and church-owned property from state and local taxes?

violate the First Amendment's establishment clause. The justices reasoned that it was accompanied by a forty-five-foot Christmas tree and a printed "Salute to Liberty" banner from the mayor linking the menorah and the Christmas tree, which made it acceptable. Justice Harry Blackmun, one of two justices who voted to approve the menorah display while disallowing the Nativity scene, said that unlike Christmas, Chanukah lacks a conventional nonreligious symbol such as a Christmas tree.

Free Exercise of Religion

Another aspect of religious freedom guaranteed by the First Amendment forbids the passage of laws "prohibiting the free exercise of religion." The **free exercise clause** protects individuals' right to worship or believe as they wish, or to hold no religious beliefs at all. No law or act of government may violate this absolute constitutional right.

Belief and Practice are Distinct The free exercise clause does not necessarily mean that individuals can act any way they want on the basis of their religious beliefs. There is an important distinction between belief and practice. The Supreme Court has ruled consistently that the right to hold any *belief* is absolute. The government has no authority to compel you to accept or reject any

▲ The Supreme Court has generally accepted that people are free to believe and practice their religion so long as they don't jeopardize health, safety, or the morals of the community. For example, the Amish are free to follow their religious beliefs. Why then do you think the Supreme Court upheld a state law that forbids the use of poisonous snakes in religious rites (as shown here)?

particular religious belief. The right to *practice* one's beliefs may, however, have some limitations. As the Court itself once asked, "Suppose one believed that human sacrifice were a necessary part of religious worship?"

The first time the Supreme Court dealt with the issue of belief versus practice was in *Reynolds* v. *United States* (1879). Reynolds was a Mormon who had two wives. Polygamy, or the practice of having more than one spouse at a time, was encouraged by the practice and teachings of his religion. It was also prohibited by federal law. Reynolds was convicted and appealed the case, arguing that the law violated his constitutional right to freely exercise his religious beliefs. The Court did not agree. It said that polygamy was a crime, and crimes are not protected by the First Amendment.

Through the years, the Supreme Court has followed the general principle that people are free to believe and to practice their religion as they wish, so long as their conduct does not threaten the health, safety, or morals of the community. For example, it has ruled that Christian Scientists cannot prevent their children from accepting medical treatment, such as blood transfusions, if the children's lives are in danger, even though accepting such treatment is against their religion. It has upheld laws forbidding the use of poisonous snakes in religious rites, as well as laws requiring religious groups to obtain permits before holding a parade.

The Flag-Salute Issue   Can children be forced to salute the flag when this practice is against their religious

beliefs? This question was raised when Lillian and William Gobitis, ages 10 and 12, were expelled from school for refusing to salute the American flag at the start of each day. The children and their parents were Jehovah's Witnesses, who believe that saluting a flag violates the Bible's command forbidding the worship of idols.

In this case, *Minersville School District* v. *Gobitis* (1940), the Court stated that the flag was a symbol of national unity, and ruled that the flag-salute requirement was not an infringement on the free exercise of religion.

Three years later, in a remarkable turnaround, the Court reversed that decision. In *West Virginia Board of Education* v. *Barnette* (1943), it ruled that a compulsory flag-salute law was unconstitutional. Justice Robert H. Jackson, writing for the majority, said:

> To believe that patriotism will not flourish if patriotic ceremonies are voluntary and spontaneous, instead of a compulsory routine, is to make an unflattering estimate of the appeal of our institutions to free minds.

SECTION 2 REVIEW

1. What is the establishment clause?
2. What is meant by separation of church and state?
3. What is the free exercise clause?
4. What are the key differences of opinion that lead some individuals to favor state aid to parochial schools and others to oppose it?
5. **For critical analysis:** In your opinion, where should the line be drawn between belief and practice? Use several examples to explain your answer.

Freedom of Speech

Preview Questions

- Why is freedom of expression important in a democracy?
- What are the limits placed on free speech and press?

How many times have you heard someone say, "I can say what I want. It's a free country"? This common expression reveals the underlying philosophy ingrained in our notion of what democracy in America means.

The right to free speech is the cornerstone upon which a democracy is built. Every person has the right to speak freely and to question its government's decisions. Citizens in a democracy also must have the chance to hear and judge for themselves what others have to say. Our system depends on people's ability to make sound, clear judgments on matters of public concern. In order to do this, people must be free to learn all the facts of an issue, so they can weigh the various interpretations and opinions. This allows people to help shape the decisions and policies of their government. It also makes it difficult for government to cover up any mistakes or injustices. As Supreme Court Justice Oliver Wendell Holmes put it: "The best test of truth is the power of the thought to get itself into the competition of the market." Holmes was simply saying that truth will survive in the free marketplace of ideas.

In many nondemocratic countries throughout the world, individuals do not have the right to free speech. For example, in the People's Republic of China, in Cuba, and in Iraq, most citizens rarely have been allowed publicly to oppose their government's policies. Many have even been executed for doing so. In other countries, such as South Africa, many individuals were jailed for criticizing that government. A government's desire to suppress the free speech of its citizens has resulted in violations of the citizens' basic **human rights**—fundamental rights, such as the right to speak freely, with which no government should interfere. Governments that violate these rights avoid being held accountable for these actions by imprisoning dissenters to silence them.

As we discussed earlier, no one in this country seems to have a problem protecting the free speech of those with whom they agree. The real challenge is protecting unpopular beliefs. The opinions of the majority, after all, need little constitutional protection. The protection needed is, in Justice Holmes' words: "not free thought for those who agree with us but freedom for the thought that we hate."

The First Amendment is designed to especially protect ideas that may be unpopular or different.

Types of Speech

What exactly is free speech? Speech is more than merely the spoken word; it means the broad freedom to communicate, which includes actions and nonverbal means. How far can this freedom go? To what degree are these forms of speech protected? To answer such questions the Supreme Court has distinguished three general categories of speech that are protected by the First Amendment.

Pure speech is the peaceful expression of thoughts, ideas, or opinions before a willing audience. This is the neighborly chat or the local candidate's campaign speech. It is your expression of ideas about a political issue or official. This type of speech is generally protected under the First Amendment.

Speech plus is verbal expression combined with some sort of action, such as marching or demonstrating. Because speech plus involves actions, it may be subject to government restrictions that do not apply to pure speech. The Supreme Court has ruled that while *speech plus* is protected by the First Amendment, it cannot obstruct traffic, block sidewalks, or endanger public safety.

▼ Supreme Court Justice Oliver Wendell Holmes said that we need to protect "not free thought for those who agree with us, but freedom for the thought that we hate." What do you think that Justice Holmes meant by these words?

GOVERNMENT IN ACTION

CASE STUDY

The Right to Beg?

Do the poor have a constitutional right to beg? Is panhandling a form of speech protected under the First Amendment? In January, 1990, a federal judge ruled that people have a right to beg. ''The true test of one's commitment to constitutional principles,'' the judge wrote, ''is the extent to which recognition is given to the rights of those in our midst who are the least affluent, least powerful, and least welcome.'' He argued that begging is informative and persuasive speech.

In May of the same year, another federal court disagreed. It ruled that begging is not a constitutionally protected right, and upheld the power of the Metropolitan Transportation Authority of New York to bar panhandlers from the subways. The judge writing the majority opinion said, ''Whether intended as so or not, begging in the subway often amounts to nothing less than assault, creating in the passengers the apprehension of imminent danger.''

Opponents of begging argue that beggars have become bullies, that panhandlers are often frightening and aggressive. These opponents say that people who work hard for a living, often at low-paying, unpleasant jobs, have the right to be left alone by panhandlers. Beggars disrupt their lives, interfere with their right to privacy, and sometimes harass or scare them into giving money.

Advocates for the beggars say that by silencing the needy, the government would cut off their most effective means of communication. They argue that those frightened or frustrated by the panhandlers should be reminded that silencing a plea for help does nothing to satisfy or eliminate the desperate need for it. They argue that people beg when they are desperate. They have a right to speak and others have the duty to listen.

Panhandling has not historically been protected by the First Amendment, but rather has been regulated, monitored, and sometimes

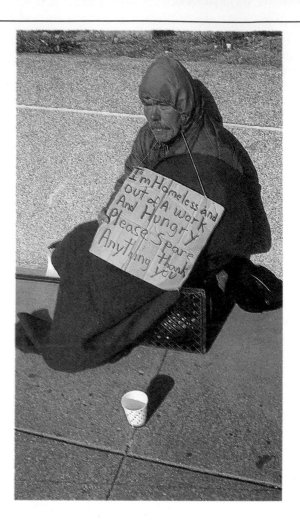

prohibited. Half of the states currently have statutes that limit or ban begging.

THINK ABOUT IT

1. Do you think people should have the right to beg?
2. What restrictions, if any, do you think should be placed on panhandlers?
3. At what point do you think begging becomes harassment?

Symbolic speech involves nonverbal expressions using symbols. Picketing in a labor dispute, or wearing a black armband in protest of a government policy are fairly common examples. During the Vietnam War in the late 1960s and early 1970s, protesters often invoked symbolic speech by burning their draft cards (notices sent to them by the federal government confirming that they were available to be called for military service) to express their opposition to the war. The Supreme Court has given symbolic speech substantial protection. It has ruled, however, that some forms of symbolic speech are not protected under the First Amendment.

Limits Placed on Free Speech

Although Americans have the right to free speech, the Court has also ruled that there are instances when some speech goes too far. Public order must also be considered. Justice Oliver Wendell Holmes argued that "the most stringent protection of free speech would not protect a man in falsely shouting *fire* in a crowded theater."

Supreme Court justices have had different philosophies about what the Constitution means when it says, "Congress shall make no law. . . ." Some Justices have argued that the phrase should be taken literally. Supreme Court Justice Hugo Black observed in 1941 that:

> Freedom to speak and write about public questions is as important to the life of our government as is the heart of the human body. In fact, this privilege is the heart of our government! If that heart be weakened, the result is debilitation [lack of strength]; if it be stilled, the result is death.

Throughout our history, however, most justices of the Supreme Court have taken a more moderate position, arguing that the rights of free speech must be balanced against the need to keep order and preserve the government.

Early Restrictions on Expression At times in our nation's history, there have been individuals who have not supported our form of democratic government. Our government, however, has established a fine line between legitimate criticism and expression of ideas that may seriously harm society. Clearly, government may pass laws against violence, espionage, sabotage, and treason. **Espionage** is the practice of spying for a foreign power. **Sabotage** involves actions normally intended to hinder or damage the nation's defense or war effort. **Treason** is specifically defined in the Constitution as levying war against or adhering (remaining loyal) to enemies of the United States (Article III, Section 3).

But what about **seditious speech,** which urges resistance to lawful authority or advocates overthrowing the government?

Sedition Acts As early as 1798, Congress took steps to curb seditious speech when it passed the Alien and Sedition Acts, which made it a crime to utter "any false, scandalous, and malicious" criticism against the government. The acts were considered unconstitutional by

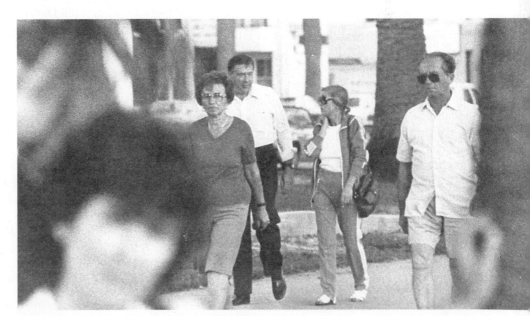

This FBI surveillance photo shows former FBI Agent Richard Miller (wearing white shirt with dark pants) walking with Svetlana Ogorodnikov (wearing jogging suit with sunglasses) in Santa Monica, California. In 1985, Miller was charged with conspiring to sell classified government information to Ogorodnikov, a suspected Soviet spy. What is the name of the crime Miller was accused of?

many, but were never tested in the courts. Under these acts, several dozen individuals were prosecuted and some were actually convicted. In 1801, President Thomas Jefferson pardoned those sentenced under the acts, and Congress soon repealed them.

Congress passed another sedition law during World War I as part of the Espionage Act of 1917. The law made it a crime to "willfully utter, print, write, or publish any disloyal, profane, scurrilous [insulting], or abusive language" about the government. More than two thousand persons were tried and convicted under this act, which was terminated at the end of World War I.

In 1940, Congress passed the Smith Act, which forbade people from advocating the violent overthrow of the United States government. The Supreme Court first upheld the constitutionality of the Smith Act in *Dennis* v. *United States* (1951), in which eleven top leaders of the Communist Party had been accused and convicted of this activity. The Court found that their activities went beyond the permissible line of exercising individual rights of peaceful advocacy of change. According to the Smith Act, these activities threatened society's right to a certain national security. Two justices on the court, Justices Black and Douglas, dissented strongly from the majority opinion. Justice Black closed his dissenting opinion with the observation that:

> Public opinion being what it now is, few will protest the conviction of these Communist petitioners. There is hope, however, that in calmer times, when present pressures, passions and fears subside, this or some later Court will restore the First Amendment liberties to the high preferred place where they belong in a free society.

The statement proved to be correct as both an analysis and a prophecy. By 1957, federal authorities had obtained 145 indictments and 89 convictions under the Smith Act. But that same year the Court significantly modified its position. In *Yates* v. *United States* the Court established a legal distinction between the statement of a philosophical belief and the advocacy of an illegal action. It held that merely advocating the overthrow of the government cannot be made illegal. It would have to be shown that individuals actually intended, now or in the future, to overthrow the government by force and violence, or to persuade others to do so. In *Brandenburg* v. *Ohio* (1969), the Court ruled that advocating the use of force may *not* be forbidden "except where such advocacy is directed to inciting or producing *imminent* [immediate] lawless action and is likely to produce such action."

By the 1960s the court had so narrowed the interpretation of the Smith Act that it is no longer used to prosecute dissenters. The Court has since defined seditious speech to mean only the advocacy of immediate and concrete acts of violence against the government.

SECTION 3 REVIEW

1. When do the rights of free speech and free press become especially challenging to apply?
2. Why is free speech important in a democracy?
3. What are the three types of speech and to what extent is each type protected by the First Amendment?
4. **For critical analysis:** Do you think the American public today would accept the Alien and Sedition Acts of 1798? Explain your answer.

SECTION 4

Freedom of Speech: The Press

Preview Questions

- Under what situations can speech be limited?
- What is meant by prior restraint?
- How does the First Amendment apply to films and other media?
- What speech is not protected?

The framers of the Constitution believed that the press should be free to publish a wide range of opinions and information. They believed that the liberties relating to freedom of speech should be extended to the press.

Guidelines Used in Free-Speech Cases

Over the years the court has developed guidelines or doctrines to use in deciding cases concerning freedom of speech and press. A **doctrine** is a theory or set of principles presented to support a belief.

Clear and Present Danger   One guideline the Court has used resulted from a case in 1919, *Schenck* v. *United States*. Charles T. Schenck was convicted of printing and distributing leaflets urging men to resist the draft during World War I. The government claimed his actions violated the Espionage Act of 1917, which made it a crime to encourage disloyalty to the government or resistance to the draft.

The Supreme Court upheld both the law and the convictions. Justice Holmes, speaking for the Court, stated:

> Words can be weapons . . . The question in every case is whether the words are used in such circumstances and are of such a nature as to create a *clear and present danger* that they will bring about the substantive evils that Congress has a right to prevent. It is a question of proximity [closeness] and degree.

Thus according to the **clear and present danger rule,** government should be allowed to restrain speech only when speech clearly presents an immediate threat to public order. It is often hard to say when speech crosses the line between being merely controversial and being a ''clear and present danger,'' but the principle has been used in many cases since.

The clear and present danger principle seemed too permissive to some Supreme Court justices. Several years after the *Schenck* ruling, in the case of *Gitlow* v. *New York* (1925), the Court held that speech could be permissibly curtailed even if it had only a *tendency* to lead to illegal action. Since the 1920s, however, this guideline, known as the **bad-tendency rule,** has generally not been supported by the Supreme Court.

The Preferred-Position Doctrine   Another guideline, called the **preferred-position doctrine,** states that freedom of speech is so essential to a democracy that it holds a preferred position. According to this doctrine, established by Justice Hugo Black in the 1940s, any law that limits this freedom should be presumed unconstitutional unless the government can show that the law is absolutely necessary. Freedom of speech should rarely, if ever, be diminished, because printed and spoken words are the prime tools of the democratic process.

Prior Restraint   **Prior restraint** means stopping an activity before it actually happens. With respect to freedom of speech, prior restraint involves **censorship,** which occurs when an official removes objectionable material from an item before it is published or broadcast. An example of censorship and prior restraint would be a court ruling that two paragraphs in an upcoming article in the local newspaper had to be removed before the article could be published. The Supreme Court has generally ruled against prior restraint, arguing that governments cannot try to curb ideas *before* they are expressed.

A case involving this issue was *Near* v. *Minnesota* (1931). A newspaper in Minneapolis, Minnesota, had published charges of local corruption, calling officials ''gangsters'' and other ugly names. The State of Min-

▲ Daniel Ellsberg (shown above) was one of thirty-six researchers to work on a Pentagon study of the War in Vietnam. In 1971, he released portions of this study to the *New York Times*. When the government tried to block publication of the study, saying that it threatened national security, the Supreme Court overruled the use of prior restraint in this case. What does prior restraint mean?

nesota closed the paper down. The Supreme Court held that the constitutional guarantee of freedom of press does not allow this kind of prior restraint on a publication. Prior restraint can only be allowed in extreme cases, such as during wartime, or when a publication is obscene or incites readers to violence.

The ban against prior restraint was reaffirmed in *New York Times* v. *United States* (1971), also called the Pentagon Papers Case. The *Times* was about to publish the *Pentagon Papers,* an elaborate secret history of the United States government involvement in the Vietnam War, which had been obtained by a disillusioned former Pentagon official. The government wanted a court order to bar publication of this series, arguing that national security was being threatened and that the documents had been stolen. The *Times* argued that the public had the right to know about the information contained in the papers, and the press had the right to inform them. The Court rejected the government's plea to bar publication, holding that the government had not proven that printing the documents would in fact endanger national security.

On some occasions, however, the Court has allowed prior restraints. In 1988, in *Hazelwood School District* v. *Kuhlmeier,* the Court, noting that students below college level have fewer rights than adults, ruled that high school administrators *can* censor school publications. It ruled that school newspapers are part of the school curriculum, not a public forum. Therefore, administrators have the right to censor speech that promotes "conduct inconsistent with the shared values of the civilized social order."

Confidentiality

Once in a while, a reporter has information that may provide essential evidence in a trial, but reporters want to protect the identities of the people and places the evidence came from. Many reporters argue that if they reveal their sources, their informants will no longer trust them and will not give them the information they need in order to keep the public informed. After all, they argue, much of what is said to them is said in the confidence that the people talking will not be named. State and federal courts have generally rejected this argument, and more than one reporter has gone to jail because she or he refused to reveal the sources of a story.

The Supreme Court held in *Branzburg* v. *Hayes* (1972) that reporters have no constitutional right to withhold information from a court. In the case, a reporter had been allowed to view individuals making hashish from marijuana if he promised to keep their names confidential. He kept his promise and refused to give the names to a grand jury.[1] The Court ruled that *anyone* would have to give such information in a case if called upon to do so. The same rule applies to the news media. If special exemptions are to be given, the Court said, they must come from Congress and the state legislatures.

In response, more than half of the states now have **shield laws** to protect reporters' notes and information from being revealed in court. For the most part, however, reporters have no more right to avoid presenting evidence than do other citizens.

Freedom of the Press and Fair Trial

Where is the line drawn between the right of a free press to comment about and criticize criminal cases, and the duty of the judiciary to ensure a fair trial? The Court

Sidney Harris

has tried to balance suspects' rights with the rights of the press and the public to know.

This issue surfaced in 1954 when Dr. Samuel H. Sheppard was convicted of murdering his wife. He appealed his conviction to the Supreme Court, arguing that during pre-trial media coverage, so many lurid details about his life and behavior had circulated that it was impossible for him to have a fair trial. Finally, in 1966, the Supreme Court agreed, claiming that the press had created a virtual "circus," and reversed Sheppard's conviction.

In the 1970s, judges increasingly issued **gag orders,** which restrict publicity about a trial in progress or even a pre-trial hearing. (A pre-trial hearing is not a trial, but rather a preliminary examination by a judge to determine whether there is enough evidence to hold a person accused of a crime.) In 1976 a man was tried and charged with murdering six members of a neighboring family. A judge issued an order prohibiting the press from reporting information about the pre-trial hearing. The Supreme Court ruled against the judge's gag order, stating that it had violated the First Amendment and was unconstitutional prior restraint.

The Supreme Court ruled in *Gannet Company* v. *De Pasquale* (1979), that both the press and the public *can*

---

1. A grand jury consists of twelve to twenty-three persons who inquire into supposed violations of the law, in order to determine whether the evidence is sufficient to warrant a trial. (See Chapter 23.)

BUILDING SOCIAL STUDIES SKILLS

Reading a Newspaper Article Critically

Newspapers offer detailed information on what is happening all over the world, from Supreme Court cases to events in Eastern Europe to local baseball scores. Newspapers usually present more information about a story than do television or radio reports because they do not have the same constraints. But even newspapers do not have the space to report every detail of every story, nor can they represent all sides of every argument.

When you read newspaper articles, avoid jumping to conclusions. Remember that the article is usually an overview of a situation and may only contain one viewpoint or one aspect of the story. To avoid jumping to conclusions, think about the following as you read an article.

The Evidence   A well-presented argument should always be accompanied and reinforced by some evidence. For example, suppose you were to read an article about the need to ban a certain textbook in your school district because the material in the book would be offensive or harmful to students. The article may thoroughly convince you of its viewpoint. But when you reviewed the article, no evidence was given of the actual contents of the book. It may have been that you were convinced only by a good writer's opinion and an emotional argument. Issues demand evidence, so look for it as you read.

Specificity of the Argument   Is it possible that what seems like an argument is only a generalization? A **generalization** is an oversimplification that doesn't hold true in every specific case. Many political arguments are reduced to generalizations. For example, you may read an article quoting a politician who states, "Standard test scores continue to fall because of the poor attitudes of high-school-age students." Could it really be true that the attitudes of *all* high-school-age students are poor? Could there possibly be many other reasons for falling test scores that have little to do with students' attitudes?

Alternative Explanations   To explain a certain event, an argument may be presented that sounds logically consistent and seems to have evidence to back it up. But other explanations may be equally valid. For example, you may read that stock prices fell yesterday because of a threat of another war in the Middle East. This may be followed by a good explanation with solid evidence that sounds perfectly logical. But there may be hundreds of other reasons why the stock market fell, some of which no one really understands. Just because an argument sounds logical doesn't mean it is wholly true.

Editorials versus News Stories   You must always distinguish between an editorial article and a news story. Editorials are typically found in the editorial section of your newspaper, often toward the end of the first section. They present the opinions of the editorial staff of the newspaper. Regular news articles, in principle, report on actual events or on the opinions of the people interviewed. News stories are not supposed to present a point of view, although some do.

As you are aware, newspapers offer more details and substance than do television or radio news stories. By using the guidelines above, you can critically evaluate what you read in newspapers; thus you can make good political decisions based on the accuracy of the information presented. You might also try to adapt these guidelines for other media, so that you can also critically evaluate the news stories you see and hear on television.

PRACTICING YOUR SKILLS _____

Read one news story about politics and one political editorial. (You can find the latter in the editorial section of your newspaper.) Then compare and contrast the news story with the editorial, asking yourself the following questions:

1. How do the articles use evidence to support the story or issue?
2. If the articles are making arguments one way or another, how specific are the arguments? Where are there generalizations, if any?
3. Are there any alternative explanations for what's being presented?

▲ Radio and television broadcasters such as popular Los Angeles disk jockey Jay Thomas (pictured here) are subject to many more restrictions than are newspaper reporters. Why are radio and television broadcasters more regulated than the print media press?

be excluded from hearings if it was likely that publicity would adversely affect the defendant. Then in *Richmond Newspapers, Inc.* v. *Virginia* (1980), the Supreme Court ruled that judges *cannot* close trials without some (*overriding* need).

Film and Other Media

Our founding fathers could not have imagined the many new ways in which information is disseminated (distributed and made public) today. Nevertheless, the Constitution has proved to be flexible enough to respond to these social and technological changes.

The Supreme Court took its first look at motion pictures in the early days of the movie industry. In 1915 a state law in Ohio barred the showing of any film that was not of "moral, educational, or harmless and amusing character." The Court upheld the Ohio law, ruling that movies were a business, "pure and simple," and *not* part of the press in this country. It said that freedom of press protections did not apply to the movies.

Almost forty years later, the Court reversed itself in *Burstyn* v. *Wilson* (1952). The city of New York had banned a movie from being shown because it was thought to be "sacrilegious." In this case the Supreme Court found that expression by means of motion pictures *is* included within the free speech and free press guarantees.

According to the Court, however, not all censorship of films is unconstitutional. *Teitel Film Corporation* v.

Cusack (1968), established that a state or local government can ban a movie after proving at a judicial hearing that the film is obscene. Today, most audiences generally rely on the motion picture's own rating system to determine the appropriateness of each film. These are the ratings posted along with the movie such as G, PG, PG–13, etc.

Radio and television broadcasting are subject to many regulations because they use electromagnetic airways, which are considered public property. Access to these airways can be gained only through a license issued by the Federal Communications Commission (FCC), which also has the authority to regulate, penalize, and revoke such licenses. The Supreme Court has regularly rejected the argument that the First Amendment prohibits such regulation by the FCC.

The Supreme Court has given the growing cable television industry broader First Amendment freedoms than it has to traditional television. In *Wilkinson* v. *Jones* (1987), the Court ruled that the states cannot regulate "indecent" cable programming. It struck down a state law in Utah that prohibited cable broadcast of any sexually explicit or other "indecent material" between 7 A.M. and midnight each day. The Court's argument was in part that cable does not use public property (i.e., airwaves) to broadcast its material.

The transmission of TV broadcasts via satellite, however, continues to come under close scrutiny. In the early 1990s a number of small satellite broadcasting companies were sued by state governments because of the sexually explicit programs that were picked up in neighboring states. The constitutionality of the resulting restrictions on such companies has yet to be tested.

Advertising

Can advertisers use their First Amendment rights to prevent restrictions on the content of their advertising, otherwise known as **commercial speech**? Until the 1970s the Supreme Court said that advertising was not protected under the First Amendment. Then in *Bigelow* v. *Virginia* (1975), the Supreme Court said that a state law that prohibited the newspaper advertising of abortion services was unconstitutional. In 1976 it struck down another state law that forbade the advertising of prescription drug prices. According to Justice Harry Blackmun, "Advertising, however tasteless and excessive it sometimes may seem, is nonetheless dissemination of information as to who is producing and selling what product for what reason and at what price." Blackmun concluded that consumers are entitled to the "free flow of commercial information."

The government does, however, prohibit false and misleading advertisements as well as the advertising of illegal goods and services. The federal government has even forbidden the advertising of certain legally sold products. For example, in 1970 Congress prohibited the advertising of cigarettes on radio and television. The tobacco industry did not challenge the constitutionality of this action.

Unprotected Speech—Libel, Slander, Obscenity, and "Fighting Words"

Just because you have the right to free speech, does that mean you can say anything you want about anybody or anything at any time? Not exactly. *Not* all forms of expression are protected by the Constitution, and no person has unlimited rights to free speech and free press. Many reasonable restrictions have been placed upon these freedoms. For example, no person has the right to libel or slander another. **Libel** is a published report of falsehoods that tends to injure a person's reputation or character. **Slander** is the public utterance (speaking) of a statement that holds a person up for contempt, ridicule, or hatred. To prove libel and slander, however, certain criteria must be met. The statements made must be untrue, must include intent to do harm, and actual harm must have occurred. The Court has ruled, for example, that public officials cannot collect damages for remarks made against them unless they can prove the remarks were made with "reckless" disregard for accuracy.

Obscenity is another form of speech that is not protected under the First Amendment. Although the dictionary defines it as that which is offensive and indecent, what obscenity is exactly is hard to define. Supreme Court Justice Potter Stewart once said, "I know it when I see it." One problem in defining obscenity is that what is obscene to one person is realistic to another; what one reader considers indecent another reader sees as "colorful." Another problem is that even if a definition were agreed upon, it would change with the times. Major literary works of such great writers as D. H. Lawrence, Mark Twain, and James Joyce were once considered obscene in most of the United States.

After many unsuccessful attempts to define obscenity, the Supreme Court came up with a three-part test in *Miller* v. *California* (1973). It decided that a book, film, or other piece of material is legally obscene if:

1. The average person applying contemporary [present-day] standards finds that the work taken as a whole appeals to the prurient interest—that is, tends to excite unwholesome sexual desire.
2. The work depicts or describes, in a patently [obviously] offensive way, a form of sexual conduct specifically prohibited by an antiobscenity law.
3. The work taken as a whole lacks serious literary, artistic, political, or scientific value.

The very fact that the Supreme Court has had to set up such a complicated test shows how difficult it is to define obscenity. The Court went on to state, in effect, that local communities should be allowed to set their own standards for what is obscene. What is obscene to many people in one area of the country might be perfectly acceptable to those in another area.

One famous case in 1990 that illustrated this issue involved the group 2 Live Crew, a rap music group whose songs contained explicitly sexual lyrics. The group was arrested by sheriff's deputies when it made an appearance at a nightclub in Broward County, Florida. At the same time, a record store owner was arrested for selling 2 Live Crew's albums in violation of the obscenity law. A federal judge upheld the law that the local Broward County sheriff invoked in attempting to prevent the sale of the group's rap albums. Ironically, at two separate trials, 2 Live Crew was acquitted while the record store owner was found guilty.

Another form of speech that is not protected by the First Amendment is what the Supreme Court has called **"fighting words."** This is speech that is so inflammatory that it will provoke the average listener to violence. The Court has ruled that fighting words must go beyond merely insulting or controversial language. The words must be a clear invitation to immediate violence or breach of peace.

SECTION 4 REVIEW

1. What are some of the guidelines the Supreme Court has developed to help it decide what is protected as free expression?
2. How does commercial speech differ from any other type of speech?
3. What kinds of speech are not protected by the First Amendment?
4. What is the difference between libel and slander?
5. **For critical analysis:** Allowing each community to decide what is and is not obscene leads to diversity in obscenity laws. How do you think this diversity affects the entertainment industry?

SECTION 5

Freedom of Assembly and Petition

Preview Questions
- Why is freedom of assembly and petition important in a democracy?
- Why are there limits placed on the freedoms of assembly and petition?
- What are these limits?

It would be impossible to guarantee free speech in a democracy if people were not given the right to assembly and to publicly express their beliefs. An assembly is usually a group of people who gather together for a specific purpose. People, acting as a group, are often more successful in getting their ideas heard than they are acting individually. They are more likely to influence government policies and actions if they organize and collectively display their feelings. Consider, for example, twenty students who each thinks that the school library should have more books. If they act individually, they can talk to their friends, write letters to their principal, and tell their parents. But what if they join together and form "The Committee for School Library Improvement," and create a weekly newsletter, which they distribute to all the parents and school administrators? Certainly, acting as a group, the twenty students have a better chance of improving the library than if they had just acted as individuals.

The Constitution protects the right of people to assemble, or organize, to influence public policy. It also protects their right to petition, to express their views to public officials in the forms of petitions, letters, signs in a parade, or marches on a picketing line.

In 1937, the Supreme Court first ruled on the right to assembly in *De Jonge* v. *Oregon*. De Jonge had been convicted for conducting a public meeting sponsored by the Communist Party. The Supreme Court overturned his conviction, saying that under the First Amendment, "peaceable assembly for lawful discussion cannot be made a crime." The Supreme Court stated the rights of free speech, free press, and free assembly represent the "security of the republic." The case established that the right of assembly was of equal status as the rights of free speech and free press. It also established that the right of assembly was protected by the due process clause of the Fourteenth Amendment.

Limits Placed on Freedom of Assembly

To what extent can demonstrators be regulated? When, in the name of public peace, does the right to assembly end? The Constitution protects the right to assembly as long as it is *peaceable*. It does not give people the right to riot, to incite violence, to block public streets, or to endanger life, property, or public order. The Court has generally agreed that it is reasonable to make and enforce rules covering the time, place, and manner of assemblies. These rules can specify when and where assembly may take place.

Demonstrations are intended to bring issues to public attention. This means that they usually happen in highly visible public places. The more people who see and hear the demonstration, the better it is for the cause. Groups protesting the federal government's cleanup policies on nuclear waste do not demonstrate in someone's backyard. They choose public places, such as a park in New York City.

The need for public exposure also means there is a good chance that the demonstration will interfere with other citizens' rights to use the same places. There is also a good chance of conflict; because most demonstrations are held to protest something, there are usually plenty of people around who support the other side of the issue and may be upset by the demonstration. Therefore, the Supreme Court has often upheld state and local laws that require demonstrators to give advance notice and to obtain permits.

An early case for placing limits on assembly was *Cox* v. *New Hampshire* (1941). Cox was a member of a group that violated a law requiring a permit for a parade. The Supreme Court voted unanimously to uphold the permit law as constitutional, and rejected Cox's argument that the law violated his rights of free speech and assembly.

In 1950, a speaker named Irving Feiner was addressing an outdoor public meeting, inviting the audience to attend a meeting of the Progressive Party. During the speech, he criticized President Truman, the American Legion, and the mayor of Syracuse. He also urged African Americans to fight for civil rights. Feiner's remarks angered the crowd, almost to the point of rioting. He ignored police requests to stop and was arrested and convicted of disturbing the peace. In *Feiner* v. *New York* (1951) the Supreme Court upheld his conviction for unlawful assembly. It concluded that the police had not acted to suppress his speech, but rather had acted to preserve public order. The case set a precedent that police *may* break up assemblies to preserve peace.

Limits on when and where an assembly may take place were tested in 1977 when the American Nazi Party decided to hold a rally and march through the Chicago suburb of Skokie, Illinois. Citizens and city officials objected because about one-half of the residents were Jewish and about 10 percent were survivors or relatives of people who died at the hands of Nazis in German death camps in World War II. They felt the march would cause pain to these people and could lead to violence and rioting.

Skokie's city government required the Nazis to post a $300,000 bond in order to obtain a parade permit. The Nazis claimed that the high-priced bond was set in order to prevent their march and infringed on their freedoms of speech and assembly. The American Civil Liberties Union (ACLU), an organization that negotiates many cases in which such freedoms are in question, defended the Nazis' claim and supported their right to march. The ACLU claimed that the Nazis had the right to hold their march and rally even though many disliked what they said and did.

Opponents said that allowing the group to march was not guaranteeing liberty, but license, or the irresponsible use of freedoms. They also quoted Justice Holmes when he said, ''The most stringent protection of free speech would not protect a man falsely shouting *fire* in a theater and causing panic.''

A federal district court ruled that the city of Skokie had violated the Nazis' First Amendment rights, and the Supreme Court let the lower court's ruling stand. As it turned out, the Nazis never did march in Skokie. Chicago loosened its parade requirements, and the Nazis settled for a couple of poorly attended demonstrations there.

Picketing

Picketing occurs when striking workers patrol a place of business, usually carrying signs protesting the business's policy, and asking workers and the public not to enter the place. The question of how much protection picketers should have under the First Amendment frequently has been debated. Because picketers gather and picketing conveys a message to the public, it is a form of both speech and assembly. Unlike other forms of demonstrations, however, it aims to persuade workers and customers not to deal with a business until the picketers' conditions are met. It can be a strong labor weapon that raises questions about its constitutionality.

In 1940, in *Thornhill* v. *Alabama,* the Supreme Court ruled that peaceful picketing is a form of free speech protected by the First Amendment. Since the *Thornhill*

▲ The Constitution guarantees the right of assembly to all groups regardless of whether or not their views are popular. In this photo, Chicago police (in the background) stand by to see that there is no violence at this rally held by members of the Ku Klux Klan. Have any limits been placed on freedom of assembly?

decision, however, the Court has ruled in a number of cases that labor picketing may be regulated under various national and state laws. The Taft-Hartley Act of 1947, for example, put some restrictions on the right to strike and the right to organize workers. It forbids picketing for such purposes as forcing employees to recognize a union other than the one already lawfully recognized. For example, if the Teamsters already represent the workers, the XYZ Union can't picket to convince employees they should switch unions.

SECTION 5 REVIEW

1. Why is the right to assemble peaceably important in a democracy?
2. What limits may government place on the right to assemble?
3. **For critical analysis:** A 1990 Washington, D.C., rally of fewer than fifty Ku Klux Klansmen required that the D.C. police force spend almost a million dollars on security to prevent violence. Why do you think the government would be willing to spend such sums of money to protect an unpopular group's ability to assemble?

CHALLENGE TO THE AMERICAN DREAM

Burning an American Symbol

While the Republican National Convention was taking place in Dallas in 1984, a group of demonstrators dubbed the "Republican War Chest Tour" was protesting openly the policies of the president and a number of Dallas-based corporations. The demonstrators marched through the streets, chanting political slogans and stopping at several corporate locations to stage "die-ins"—spray-painting buildings and potted plants to dramatize the consequences of nuclear war. During the march, one of the participants, Gregory Lee Johnson, accepted an American flag offered to him by a fellow protestor who had removed it from a flagpole outside one of the targeted buildings.

The demonstrations ended in front of Dallas City Hall, where Johnson unfurled the flag, doused it with kerosene, and set it on fire. While the flag burned, the protestors chanted, "America, the red, white, and blue, we spit on you." After the demonstrators dispersed, one of the witnesses collected the flag's remains and buried them in his backyard. No one was physically injured or threatened, but some witnesses had been seriously offended.

Johnson was charged and convicted with desecration of a venerated object (destroying something that is highly respected), a violation of Texas law. The Texas Court of Criminal Appeals reversed the decision, holding that the state, consistent with the First Amendment, could not punish Johnson for burning the flag under these circumstances. The court found that Johnson's burning of the flag was expressive conduct protected by the First Amendment.

The Supreme Court affirmed this judgment. In a 1990 5 to 4 decision, the Court ruled that the defendant could not be convicted under a statute that was aimed at suppressing his free expression, and there was no evidence that his conduct disturbed the peace. The majority of justices found that flag burning is a form of political expression, and pure speech or expression cannot be punished.

Four justices dissented vigorously—Rehnquist, White, O'Connor, and Stevens. Chief Justice Rehnquist claimed that the Court was ignoring Justice Holmes' familiar saying that "a page of history is worth a volume of logic." He wrote that, "For more than 200 years, the American flag has occupied a unique position as the symbol of the nation, a uniqueness that justifies a governmental prohibition against flag burning. ..." He ended his opinion by saying, "The government may conscript [draft] men into the Armed Forces where they must fight and perhaps die for the flag, but the government may not prohibit the public burning of the banner under which they fight."

In June of 1990, the Supreme Court ruled that a new federal law making it a crime to burn or deface the American flag violated the free-speech guarantee of the First Amendment. The law was declared unconstitutional on the same grounds the Court used to invalidate the Texas statute.

The decisions provoked almost immediate calls for a constitutional amendment to override them and make it possible to prosecute flag burners. The challenge to the American dream here, according to some, is that the "Stars and Stripes" represents all that is good, democratic, and desirable in this country. Therefore, the ability to destroy such a symbol strikes at the very foundations of this nation's greatness.

You Decide

1. Why did the four Supreme Court justices dissent to the constitutional protection of burning the flag?
2. Should the destruction of any other American symbol, such as a replica of the Statue of Liberty, also be protected under the First Amendment? Explain why or why not.
3. Would wearing a picture of the American flag upside down on your tee-shirt be the same thing as burning the flag? Explain.

CHAPTER 5 REVIEW

Key Terms

abridging 103
assembly 103
bad-tendency rule 117
bills of attainder 104
censorship 117
civil liberties 103
clear and present
  danger rule 117
commercial speech 120
doctrine 116
draft registration 107

due process clause 106
espionage 115
establishment
  clause 108
ex post facto 104
excessive entanglement
  theory 110
fighting words 121
free exercise
  clause 111
gag orders 118

generalization 119
habeas corpus 103
human rights 113
libel 121
obscenity 121
petition 103
picketing 123
preferred-position
  doctrine 117
prior restraint 117
pure speech 113

released time 109
sabotage 115
seditious speech 115
shield laws 118
slander 121
speech plus 113
symbolic speech 115
treason 115

Summary

1. Although the original Constitution contains a few protections of personal freedoms, the most important ones are provided in the Bill of Rights. The Bill of Rights protects individuals from an overly intrusive government and protects the rights of the minority against the will of the majority. It is the courts, particularly the U.S. Supreme Court, that defines and applies these rights. The Fourteenth Amendment's due process clause ensures that the states carry out these protections.

2. The First Amendment guarantees freedom of religion. It provides for a separation of church and state in the establishment clause. The Supreme Court has drawn lines on the subject of religion in schools in a series of cases whose subjects range from releasing students for religious activities to prayer in public schools. It has generally ruled that public schools cannot sponsor religious activities. The free exercise clause of the First Amendment protects individuals' rights to worship or believe as they see fit, or to hold no religious beliefs at all. The free exercise of religion may be limited if religious activities are in violation of criminal laws. In contrast, the government may not demand that persons perform certain acts, such as saluting the flag, if these acts violate their religious beliefs.

3. The First Amendment also protects freedom of speech. The Supreme Court has distinguished three kinds of speech that are protected under this amendment: pure speech, speech plus, and symbolic speech. The right to free speech is not absolute and is balanced by the gov-

ernment's duty to maintain public order, preserve the government, and ensure fair trials.

4. The extent to which the government can limit free speech is judged on the basis of three principles: the clear and present danger rule, (rarely) the bad-tendency rule, and the preferred-position doctrine. The Supreme Court has generally ruled against prior restraint. Obscenity, libel, slander, and "fighting words" are forms of speech that are not normally protected under the First Amendment.

5. The Constitution protects the right to assembly as long as it is peaceable. The government may, however, impose reasonable restrictions on such activities in the name of public safety. The Court has generally agreed that it is reasonable for government to make and enforce rules regarding time, place, and manner of assemblies. Some forms of labor picketing have been subjected to restrictions, because they aim to persuade workers and customers not to deal with a business until the picketers' conditions are met.

Review Questions

1. What is meant by the concept of civil liberties?
2. What safeguards in the original Constitution protected citizens against an overly powerful government?
3. What is the Bill of Rights and why was it added to the Constitution?
4. What effect has the due process clause of the Fourteenth Amendment had on the Bill of Rights?

CHAPTER 5 REVIEW—Continued

5. List the rights guaranteed under the First Amendment.
6. What is the establishment clause? What freedom does it provide for the American people?
7. What did Thomas Jefferson mean when he spoke of a "wall of separation between church and state"?
8. What is the excessive entanglement theory? How has it been used by the Supreme Court?
9. What does the free exercise clause protect? What doesn't it protect?
10. Describe the three general categories of free speech generally protected by the First Amendment.
11. What kinds of speech are not protected under the First Amendment?
12. What guidelines does the Supreme Court use when deciding what limits should be placed on free speech?
13. What is prior restraint? Is it constitutional?
14. In what ways has freedom of the press been limited?
15. What types of speech are protected?
16. What is the principal limit that the Constitution places on freedom of assembly?
17. Why are the rights guaranteed by the First Amendment essential in a democracy?
18. Name the four legally required responsibilities that you have as an American citizen.
19. What reasoning have the courts used to protect those who burn the American flag from prosecution?

Questions for Thought and Discussion

1. For many years the Communist Party was strictly outlawed in the United States. Today its candidates can compete openly in presidential and other elections. What activities of the Communist Party do you think should be considered illegal under current laws?
2. The founding fathers certainly could not have predicted the advent of mobile phones, communication satellites, cable television, and the like. At what point do you think that the First Amendment freedom of the press should apply to these and other new forms of communication?
3. Discuss the pros and cons of the constitutionality of regulating videotape rentals to prevent, for example, the spread of pornography to minors.

4. Many issues face the Supreme Court when civil liberties are on trial. The justices must balance the rights of individuals with the rights of society as a whole. Under what circumstances do you believe that the individual's rights must be restricted in order to benefit society? Be specific.
5. Facsimile transmission machines, or FAXs, are becoming increasingly popular in the United States and indeed in the world as their prices fall every month. As a result of this popularity, the glut of advertising via FAX transmission has become a problem. Advertisers send out notices via FAX machines to other businesses, thus occupying those businesses' machines and using up excess amounts of FAX paper. If you were a Supreme Court justice, how might you regulate FAX advertising?
6. How do you think the First Amendment's freedom of the press guarantee should be applied during wartime? Do you think that the government should be allowed to censor press coverage, or that the press should be allowed to report on what it sees? Give reasons to support your answers.

Improving Your Skills
Communication Skills
Summarizing

There was once an old television program called *Dragnet*, in which the star police officer, when trying to get key information from witnesses, would say, "Just the facts, ma'am." He was trying to get the main ideas of the case and did not want witnesses to go off on meaningless tangents. He did not want every detail and opinion; he wanted the witnesses to *summarize* what they knew.

Summarizing is condensing (cutting down) information, while focusing on the main ideas. A summary contains only the most relevant and interesting ideas. Being able to summarize enables you to communicate more effectively. It is also a useful study skill because it helps you keep your focus on the main ideas. Here are some guidelines to use when writing a summary:

1. Read the material carefully. If the material is lengthy, skim it first.
2. Determine the author's point of view as you review the material. (This may involve distinguishing be-

CHAPTER 5 REVIEW—Continued

tween evidence and opinion, or looking for generalizations, as you learned in the feature on reading the newspaper on page 119.)

3. Now rewrite the material in summary style, using your own words.
   a. Be sure to include only the main ideas.
   b. Eliminate all unimportant details.
4. Try to keep your summary to no more than 20 percent of the length of the original text.

Writing

Turn to page 121 under the section entitled ''Unprotected Speech—Libel, Slander, Obscenity, and 'Fighting Words.''' Summarize the section. Then review your summary and ask yourself if you followed each of the four guidelines listed above.

Social Studies Skills

Reading an Information Table

Sometimes lists of information can be presented in a table form such as you see in Figure 5–1, The Bill of Rights on page 105. Use this figure to answer the following questions.

1. How many freedoms are listed for the First Amendment?
2. Which amendment guarantees the accused in a criminal case the right to a trial by jury?
3. Which amendment do you think could be named the ''reserved powers'' amendment?
4. The Seventh Amendment states that a jury trial is guaranteed in a civil case involving more than $20. Do you think $20 could buy more when the Bill of Rights was written than it can today?

Activities and Projects

1. Choose one of the Supreme Court cases mentioned in this chapter to do additional research on in your school or local library. Prepare a report that summarizes the arguments presented on both sides, then write a decision that you would make if you were a justice on the case.
2. Invite a newspaper or television reporter to your class to discuss the freedoms and limitations involved in the press and television. Ask the reporter to discuss how some of the issues mentioned in this chapter, such as libel and slander, are treated in these media.
3. Interview a member of the clergy to find out his or her opinion with respect to the separation of church and state. Prepare a summary of that person's opinion to present in class.
4. Write a letter to the editor of your local newspaper, expressing your views concerning the right to beg.
5. Stage a debate or class forum on this question: Should obscenity be protected as free speech?

6. Give a written explanation of what you think John F. Kennedy meant when he said, ''In giving rights to others which belong to them, we give rights to ourselves and to our country.'' In your explanation, provide three examples of cases in which this statement has proven true.

CHAPTER 6

Equality Under the Law

CHAPTER OBJECTIVES

To learn and understand

■ The concept of due process of law and its important place in the American system of civil rights.

■ The rights of persons accused of a crime.

■ The right to equality under the law.

■ The continuing struggle for equality and the new challenges it brings.

Keynote

"I have a dream that one day this nation will rise up and live out the true meaning of the creed: 'We hold these truths to be self-evident: that all men are created equal.' "

———— **Martin Luther King, Jr.**
(1929–1968) Civil rights leader

INTRODUCTION

On August 28, 1963, Dr. Martin Luther King, Jr. delivered those powerful words before an audience of almost 250,000 in front of the Lincoln Memorial in Washington, D.C. His voice crossed the boundaries of color and religion that day, delivering the message that all Americans are entitled to fair and equal treatment under the law. Though the American democratic system has had many successes since then, it has not been entirely successful in extending those rights to all persons. Equal rights for all continues to be a significant issue in today's society.

In the previous chapter you read about the First Amendment rights that lie at the heart of democratic belief and practice. You may have realized that those rights would do you little good if government officials could judge you unfairly or make decisions about your well-being based on your race, religion, or gender. For example, if you were arrested for disturbing the peace during a demonstration, what good would those rights be if you were not allowed to tell your side of the story, to be treated fairly under the law, and to be judged by people of similar age and social status (otherwise known as your **peers**)? If you were trying to rent an apartment, would you not want to be treated with fairness, not on the basis that you are Hispanic or Jewish or Muslim or Asian or African American or female?

Dr. King looked forward to the day when all Americans would be treated with fairness. He said, "I have a dream that my four little children will one day live in a nation where they will not be judged by the color of their skin but by the content of their character."

In a democracy, there must be fairness and equal treatment afforded to all persons. This is especially critical in the courtroom, which is where the right to *due process* comes into play.

SECTION 1

Due Process of Law

Preview Questions
- What is the meaning of due process?
- What is the difference between procedural and substantive due process?

Our Declaration of Independence proclaims that ''all men are created equal.'' As we all know, this does not mean that everyone is born with the same wealth, intelligence, strength, or ambition. Each one of us has a unique combination of qualities and characteristics. The words of the Declaration mean that all people should have equal *rights,* which is the cornerstone of the democratic ideal. All people, regardless of their physical, racial, ethical, sexual, financial, or religious makeup, should be treated equally before the law.

The Fifth Amendment declares that the federal government cannot deprive any person of ''life, liberty, or property, without due process of law.'' The Fourteenth Amendment places the same restriction on state and local governments. The key words here are *due process,* which means that government must follow a set of **processes** (reasonable, fair, and standard procedures) that the citizen is due (entitled to) by virtue of being a citizen.

The concept of due process of law was originally derived from English common law, probably as early as Henry I (1100–1135), and from the Magna Carta, which was discussed in Chapter 2.

Due process of law has come to mean that government may not act unfairly or arbitrarily (based on individual judgment and impulse, not on reason or law). It may not act capriciously (unstably and undependably) or unreasonably. Of course, disagreements as to the meaning of these commands have plagued us from the

129

Ernesto Miranda (shown here with attorney John J. Flynn) confessed and was convicted of the kidnapping and rape of an 18-year-old woman. This conviction was overturned by the Supreme Court because police officers had not informed Miranda of his Fifth Amendment rights. This decision led to the institution of the Miranda Rules. What are the rights a suspect must be informed of under the Miranda Rules?

of their rights. Later, when Ernesto Miranda himself was murdered, the suspected murderer was read his rights from a Miranda card.

In several cases since *Miranda,* however, the Court has relaxed some of the restrictions of the Miranda Rules. For example, in 1984 the Court ruled that police do not have to read suspects their rights when "public safety" is at risk. In order to find a loaded gun, for example, the police could interrogate a suspect before advising him of his right to remain silent.

The Right to Counsel

The Sixth Amendment guarantees a defendant the right to have the assistance of counsel for his or her defense. This means that people accused of a crime have the right to hire a lawyer to represent their case in court. If they cannot afford to hire a lawyer, the Court will appoint one for them. Even lawyers taken to court hire other lawyers to represent them. (There is an old saying that lawyers who defend themselves have a fool for a client.)

The Sixth Amendment assures the right to counsel in federal courts, but until relatively recently, people who were tried in state courts did not have this right. In 1932, the Supreme Court ordered the states to provide an attorney for indigent (poor) defendants accused of a capital crime (those for which the death penalty could be imposed). Not until 1963, however, did the Supreme Court extend that right to everyone accused of a felony. The change occurred in the case of a penniless drifter from Florida named Clarence Earl Gideon.

Gideon was charged with robbing a pool hall in Florida by stealing change from a vending machine. He did not have any money to hire a lawyer so he asked the court to appoint one, but his request was denied. He was convicted of the crime and sentenced to a five-year jail term.

While in jail, Gideon studied law books and petitioned the Supreme Court himself for a retrial in a handwritten petition. The Court accepted his appeal and ruled unanimously that the due process clause of the Fourteenth Amendment required states to give defendants the Sixth Amendment right to counsel. Justice Black explained that "lawyers in criminal courts are necessities, not luxuries."

Gideon was released and retried with a lawyer. This time he was **acquitted** (released from the charge). More than a thousand other Florida prisoners and thousands more in other states who had been convicted without counsel were also released. As a result of *Gideon* v. *Wainwright* (1963), however poor you are, today you have a right to a lawyer.

The Court has extended the *Gideon* decision to apply not only in felony cases, but whenever there might be a jail sentence involved, even for a minor criminal offense.

The Right to Trial by Jury

The Sixth Amendment also provides defendants the right to be tried by an impartial jury in serious criminal cases. The Supreme Court has defined serious cases as those that could result in six or more months **incarceration** (imprisonment).

The jury is supposed to be impartial, which means those who have made up their mind before the trial should be excluded. It is also supposed to represent a fair cross section of the community, which means no group can be systematically excluded. No persons can be kept off a jury on the grounds of race, religion, color, national origin, or sex (even though the Court allowed the states to exclude women from jury duty until 1975).

The Constitution does not specify the size of a jury. Tradition in England and America has set jury size at twelve persons, and has required a **unanimous** (complete agreement by all) verdict in criminal trials. Some states have experimented with smaller juries and non-unanimous verdicts to save money. The Supreme Court has allowed states to have juries with a minimum of six people serving.

Defendants may waive (give up or relinquish) their right to a jury trial. The judge must be satisfied that the defendant is fully aware of his or her rights and understands what that action means. If the right is waived, a **bench trial**, one heard by a judge alone, is held. Of course a defendant may plead guilty or **no contest**, meaning he or she does not wish to contest the charge, and thereby avoids a trial.

The Grand Jury

The Fifth Amendment provides for a grand jury in federal **capital cases** (ones that might involve the death penalty). A federal grand jury proceeding is the formal process by which a person may be accused of a serious federal crime.

A **grand jury** is a body made up of twelve to twenty-three citizens that examines the evidence presented against a suspect. The purpose of the grand jury investigation is to see if enough evidence exists to hold a criminal trial. If the jury feels there is, an **indictment**, or formal charge of a crime against the accused, is handed down. If the grand jury does not find enough evidence, the charge is dropped.

A grand jury proceeding is not a trial. It does not determine guilt or innocence and is held in secret, unlike normal jury trials. Critics of the grand jury method say that it costs too much time and money for taxpayers.

Double Jeopardy

The Fifth Amendment says that no person shall be "twice put in jeopardy of life and limb." This means that once a defendant is acquitted of a crime, he or she is protected from being tried again for the same crime.

A person can be retried if the jury trial results in a **hung jury**, which means that it cannot reach a unanimous verdict. He or she can also be retried if there is a **mistrial**, an error in the proceedings. If the crime is in violation of both state and federal laws, the person can technically be tried by both a state and federal court.

Speedy and Public Trial

The Sixth Amendment provides that the accused shall enjoy the right to a speedy and public trial. The right to a speedy trial is meant to prevent prisoners

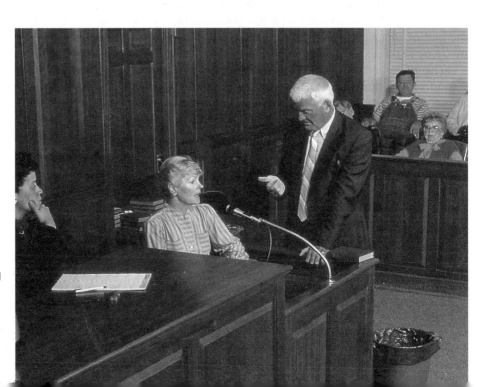

▶ The Sixth Amendment to the United States Constitution grants defendants the right to be tried by an impartial jury in serious criminal cases. What constitutes a serious criminal case?

CHAPTER 6 REVIEW

Key Terms

acquitted 136
affirmative action 148
bail 138
bench trial 137
boycott 145
burden of proof 134
busing 144
capital cases 137
civil disobedience 145
civil rights 142
civil rights
  movement 145
contempt 135
de facto
  segregation 144

de jure segregation 144
denaturalization 139
due process of law 129
equal employment
  opportunity 148
equal protection
  clause 142
exclusionary rule 133
felonies 131
fundamental rights 142
grand jury 137
hung jury 137
incarceration 137
indictment 137

Miranda Rules 135
mistrial 137
no contest 137
peers 129
preventive
  detention 138
probable cause 132
procedural duc
  process 130
processes 129
quota 148
rational-basis test 142
reverse
  discrimination 148

search warrant 132
searches and
  seizures 132
segregation 140
self-incrimination 134
separate-but-equal
  doctrine 143
substantive due
  process 130
suffragists 150
suspect
  classification 142
unanimous 137
waive 135

Summary

1. There are two due process clauses in the Constitution. One in the Fifth Amendment restricts the national government. The second, in the Fourteenth Amendment, restricts state and local governments. These due process clauses require that the government act fairly (procedural due process) under fair laws (substantive due process).

2. The Constitution protects the rights of persons accused of crimes. They cannot be subjected to unreasonable searches and seizures, and evidence illegally acquired by police normally cannot be used against them in a trial. An accused person must be informed of his or her rights. He or she has the right to a fair trial, and the right to an attorney even if he or she cannot afford one. He or she also has the right to remain silent and to not give self-incriminating testimony; to be represented by an attorney before questioning; and to not be subject to cruel and unusual punishment.

3. Civil rights are the protections recognizing that all citizens must be treated equally under the law. The equal protection clause of the Fourteenth Amendment states that unreasonable distinctions cannot be drawn between different classes of people. In the early days of the United States there were widespread segregation laws. In *Plessy* v. *Ferguson* (1896) the Supreme Court ruled that separate-but-equal facilities were constitutional. In *Brown* v. *Board of Education of Topeka* (1954), it unanimously

ruled for complete desegregation. Even though *de jure* segregation laws were illegal, *de facto* segregation continued. The civil rights movement facilitated the passage of the Civil Rights Act in 1964.

4. The struggle for equality continues and has expanded to include many other groups. Affirmative action programs, which grew out of equal employment opportunity programs, are designed to overcome the results of past discrimination. In the late 1980s the Supreme Court issued rulings that rejected some affirmative action policies.

Review Questions

1. What does "due process of law" mean?
2. What is procedural due process? What is substantive due process?
3. When may police conduct a lawful search without a warrant?
4. Why is the exclusionary rule important? Are there any exceptions to the rule? If so, when do they apply?
5. What is self-incrimination?
6. Explain the impact of *Miranda* v. *Arizona* (1966).
7. Explain the concept of double jeopardy.
8. How do the right to counsel, the right to trial by jury, and the right to a speedy and public trial help ensure a fair trial?
9. What is the equal protection clause?

CHAPTER 6 REVIEW—Continued

10. What efforts have been made to deal with *de facto* segregation?
11. What was the civil rights movement?
12. What is the purpose of affirmative action programs?
13. What are some of the ways you can help the differently abled in your community?

Questions for Thought and Discussion

1. Civil liberties for the accused have evolved over the years in various Supreme Court cases. In your opinion, when are such protections appropriate for persons accused of a crime? When are they inappropriate?
2. How do you account for the fact that even though the Fourteenth Amendment was ratified shortly after the Civil War, segregation continued to be widespread for many years?
3. What economic and social changes over the years have lead to the rise of political activism on the part of women?
4. In spite of attempts at desegregating public schools throughout the nation, many school districts continue to be predominantly white or black or Hispanic. What would it take for there to be truly desegregated schools throughout this country?

Improving Your Skills
Communication Skills
Forming an Opinion

Throughout your life you have been asked "What do you think?" or "What is your opinion?" If the question is simple, such as "What is your favorite food?" then your answer is simple. But sometimes the question is more complex, and an opinion is difficult to form. In this case, it is better to form your opinion carefully rather than make a quick "snap judgment" that you may regret later.

An opinion is a belief based on what seems to be true or probable. A good opinion is one made with *reasoned* judgment. Making a reasoned judgment involves investigating all of the available facts, carefully exploring your own feelings, and forming an opinion based on those facts and feelings. Remember these two guidelines:

1. *Be sure that you use facts to form your opinion.* Facts are evidence that can be proven and can support your opinion. Take the time to examine all the evidence.
2. *Consider all sides of an issue with an open mind.* Do not reject the opinions of others without listening to their reasons.

Writing

Re-read the "Challenge to the American Dream" feature in this chapter. Research and read one article on reverse discrimination in your library. Use the information obtained from your research and the guidelines listed above to form an opinion about whether, in the case you researched, reverse discrimination actually occurred. Write a formal opinion that explains your reasoned judgment. Cite the evidence you found, your feelings about the subject, and how you formed your opinion.

Social Studies Skills

Comparing and Contrasting

Reread the three excerpts from the three Supreme Court cases presented in Figure 6–1 on page 147.

1. What is similar about *Gideon* v. *Wainwright* and *Miranda* v. *Arizona*?
2. What is the difference between those two opinions and the first one, *Brown* v. *Board of Education of Topeka*?

Activities and Projects

1. Invite a local police officer to speak to your class. Some of the topics you might ask the officer to discuss could include: (1) the Miranda Rules; (2) procedures followed when dealing with criminal suspects; (3) rules the police follow when obtaining and handling evidence; and (4) how the police work to protect the rights of individuals and of society in general.
2. Research the women's rights movement and the goals it has sought to achieve. Research the philosophies and goals of several women's organizations in your area, then contact these organizations to find out about their current activities. Develop an oral report on your findings to present to the class.

UNIT THREE

The Politics of Democracy

UNIT CONTENTS

- *Chapter 7* Citizenship: Privileges and Responsibilities
- *Chapter 8* Political Parties
- *Chapter 9* Political Opinion and Interest Groups
- *Chapter 10* Campaigns, Elections, and the Media
- *Chapter 11* Voters and Voting Behavior

155

CHAPTER 7

Citizenship: Privileges and Responsibilities

To learn and understand

- What it means to be a citizen.
- The history of America's policies concerning immigration.
- The rights and responsibilities of citizens.
- Why tolerance and open-mindedness are important.

I pledge allegiance to the flag
of the United States of America
and to the republic for which it stands,
one nation under God, indivisible,
with liberty and justice for all.

Keynote

"As citizens of this democracy, you are the rulers and the ruled, the lawgivers and the law-abiding, the beginning and the end."

———— **Adlai E. Stevenson**
(1900–1965) U.S. Presidential
Candidate

INTRODUCTION

Many Americans born in the United States take their citizenship for granted. But to the millions of people around the world from South America to Southeast Asia who struggle to gain entry into the United States, it is a cherished dream. These people understand the precious value of American citizenship perhaps better than those who have always possessed it.

The United States is the first modern nation in which citizens deliberately took governmental power into their own hands. They created a governmental system in which the people, rather than a monarch or dictator or ruling party, have ultimate power. With the above words, Adlai E. Stevenson—who ran for president in 1952 against Dwight D. Eisenhower—summed up the meaning of American citizenship in our democracy.

SECTION 1

Who is a Citizen?

Preview Questions
- When did citizenship in the United States become a *national* issue?
- What is the significance of *Dred Scott* v. *Sandford* (1857)?
- What is the essence of the Fourteenth Amendment?
- What are three ways that American citizenship may be lost?

When the United States first became a nation, the concept of citizenship was not an issue of national concern. Indeed, the Constitution, including the first ten amendments, does not define citizenship. The framers of the Constitution left it up to state governments, rather than the federal government, to decide who was a citizen. Any citizen of a state was automatically assumed to be a citizen of the United States, at least in the minds of the framers. Today, citizenship is decided by the federal government, as you will learn about in this chapter.

The Dred Scott Case

The issue of state versus national citizenship became critical in a famous Supreme Court case, *Dred Scott* v. *Sandford* (1857). A slave named Dred Scott had been moved by his owner to Illinois, where slavery was illegal under state law. Dred Scott sued in court for his freedom. The Supreme Court, which at that time was dominated by Southern judges, ruled that Scott could not be a citizen of the United States because he was a slave and therefore he had no right to sue in court at all. The Supreme Court

▼ Prior to the ratification of the Thirteenth Amendment, which abolished slavery, African Americans, as enslaved persons, were not considered citizens of the United States. Why do you think the Supreme Court ruled this way?

applied this ruling to Scott while he was in Illinois even though slavery was illegal there and African Americans had long been considered citizens in that state (as well as in most other Northern states). The reasoning of the Court was that when the Constitution was adopted, African Americans had not been recognized as citizens of the states. It did not matter whether they were slaves or free at that time. According to the logic of the Court, the only individuals who were United States citizens were those who were directly descended from state citizens in 1787, or immigrants who became citizens through legal means. Slaves, who fell into neither of these categories, were therefore not considered citizens.

The Thirteenth and Fourteenth Amendments
Many individuals in most Northern states did not agree with the *Dred Scott* decision. Some historians believe that the ruling in that case was one of the major causes of the Civil War. As a result of this controversy, the Thirteenth Amendment, which abolished slavery, was passed at the close of the Civil War in 1865. But in passing this amendment, the nation was faced with the need to define who was a citizen. This question was finally answered in 1868 with the Fourteenth Amendment, which begins:

> All persons born or naturalized in the United States, and subject to the jurisdiction thereof, are citizens of the United States and of the State wherein they reside.

In essence, the Fourteenth Amendment reversed the *Dred Scott* decision by making state citizenship an automatic result of national citizenship. The Fourteenth Amendment created the two most common sources of American citizenship: (1) by birth anywhere on land considered American soil and (2) by the legal process called *naturalization*. There is yet a third source—by being born of a parent who is a U.S. citizen.

Citizenship by Birth

Most Americans are citizens simply because they were born in the United States.

Location of Birth—*Jus Soli* The Fourteenth Amendment states that all persons born in the United States are American citizens. This is called citizenship by location. In legal terms this is called citizenship by ***jus soli.*** *Jus soli* are two Latin words that translate as "the law of the soil."

Today, the United States comprises not only the fifty states, but also the District of Columbia, Guam, Puerto

158

▲ Despite the fact that they were the first inhabitants of this land, Native Americans were not immediately recognized as citizens. When were all Native Americans naturalized?

Rico, the Virgin Islands, the Northern Mariana Islands, and American Samoa. Additionally, American embassies in foreign countries and any ship or aircraft operated by agencies of the U.S. government are considered United States soil. Exceptions to the *jus soli* rule are those individuals born in the United States, but not subject to the jurisdiction, or control, of the United States government. These are usually children born to foreign diplomats stationed in the United States.

Surprisingly, at the time the Fourteenth Amendment was passed, Native Americans, who were considered **wards**, or persons under the legal guardianship, of the U.S. government, were not granted citizenship under the Fourteenth Amendment. In 1924, Congress reversed this ruling by granting citizenship to all Native Americans who did not already possess it.

Law of the Blood—*Jus Sanguinis* Since 1790, Congress has included the so-called "law of the blood," or ***jus sanguinis***, as grounds for American citizenship. Under this law, a child born on foreign soil becomes an American citizen at birth if at least one of the parents is a U.S. citizen, and if that U.S. citizen lived in the U.S. (or in an American possession) for at least ten years, five of which occurred after the age of 14.

Citizenship by Choice—Naturalization

The U.S. Constitution in Article I, Section 8 declares that Congress shall have the power to "establish a uniform Rule of Naturalization." **Naturalization** is the process by which individuals who are not yet citizens become United States citizens. These individuals are called **naturalized citizens**, as opposed to native-born citizens described above. There are three ways for naturalization to occur: (1) by act of Congress; (2) by treaty; and (3) by individual action.

By Act of Congress   On rare occasions, the U.S. Congress has passed laws naturalizing entire groups of people. As already mentioned, this was done in 1924 with respect to Native Americans who were not yet citizens. Prior to that, inhabitants of Hawaii and Puerto Rico were granted citizenship by Congress in 1900 and 1917 respectively. The same thing occurred for residents of the Virgin Islands (1927), Guam (1950), and the Northern Marianas (1977). We have already mentioned the collective naturalization of African Americans and others by the Fourteenth Amendment to the U.S. Constitution in 1868.

By Treaty   The largest groups of people to become American citizens through collective naturalization have been naturalized when the United States has acquired new territory. Those living in the areas involved were naturalized by a treaty or a joint resolution of Congress. For example, when the Louisiana Purchase Treaty was signed in 1803, the United States purchased the Louisiana Territory from France. That treaty said that people living in the territory became U.S. citizens. The same occurred in the treaties in which the U.S. acquired Florida (1819) and Alaska (1867). Additionally, a joint resolution of Congress gave citizenship to all inhabitants of Texas in 1845.

By Individual Action   Today naturalization most often occurs through individual action. Every year hundreds of thousands of people apply for citizenship in the United States. Each possible candidate for naturalization must have the following qualifications:

- They must be 18 years or older (except minors who normally become citizens when their parents are naturalized).

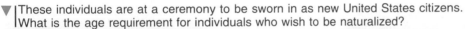

▼ These individuals are at a ceremony to be sworn in as new United States citizens. What is the age requirement for individuals who wish to be naturalized?

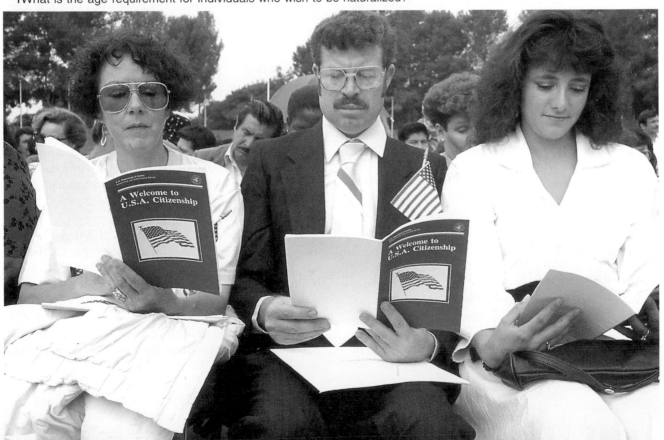

How Non-Citizens Become Naturalized Citizens of the United States

Application	Examination	Final Hearing
Candidates for citizenship must submit an application form, a card of fingerprints, and certain autobiographical data, such as where they were born, who their parents were, etc.	Each candidate appears before an officer at the closest Immigration and Naturalization Service office. The candidate must bring along two U.S. citizens to serve as witnesses. Every candidate must prove his or her qualifications, consistent with those presented previously. Candidates must also demonstrate a basic knowledge of American history and an understanding of our form of government.	The Immigration and Naturalization Service takes a minimum of 30 days to process an application, during which time it may seek additional information about the candidate. The information is presented to a judge in a citizenship court, with the recommendation that the candidate be granted citizenship. If the judge agrees, then the applicant appears before a judge, takes the oath of allegiance, and receives a certificate of citizenship. He or she has become a naturalized citizen of the United States.

▲ FIGURE 7–1 **How Non-Citizens Become Naturalized Citizens of the United States.** As you can see, naturalization is a three-step process. The process appears simple, but usually is not. Why do you think the process usually takes a long time?

- They must have entered the U.S. legally and lived in the United States for at least five years.
- They must demonstrate an understanding of basic English words and phrases.
- They must be able to prove, if necessary, their high moral character.
- They must understand the basic concepts of American government and history.
- They must not have advocated the overthrow of the U.S. government by force or violence within the past ten years.
- They must not have belonged to any subversive organization within the past ten years.
- They must not be a draft evader, a military deserter, an anarchist, or a polygamist (a person with more than one spouse).

How Citizenship May Be Lost

While federal government is the *only* entity that can take away citizenship, state governments do have the right to deny certain privileges of citizenship, such as the right to vote, to their citizens who are convicted of

crimes. The three basic ways Americans can lose citizenship are through *expatriation,* punishment for a crime, and *denaturalization.*

Expatriation The word **expatriation** comes from the prefix *ex-,* meaning "from," and the Latin word *patria,* which means "native country, or fatherland." To expatriate someone is to banish that person from his or her native country. Individuals can voluntarily become expatriates by becoming a naturalized citizen of another country or by renouncing their American citizenship to a representative of the United States government. Once renounced, citizenship cannot easily be regained.

Punishment for a Crime While states may not take away a person's citizenship for just any crime, the federal government can do so if a person is convicted of treason, of inciting rebellion, or of conspiring to violently overthrow the government.

Denaturalization In rare cases, a naturalized citizen may lose citizenship through a process called

denaturalization. Denaturalization occurs if the federal government learns that a naturalized citizen obtained his or her citizenship through fraudulent means.

SECTION 1 REVIEW ⎯⎯⎯⎯⎯

1. What did the Supreme Court rule in the *Dred Scott* case?
2. According to the Fourteenth Amendment, who is a citizen of the United States?
3. In what three ways can American citizenship be lost?
4. **For critical analysis:** Former Justice Earl Warren believed that loss of citizenship as punishment for any crime, even for treason, was a ''cruel and unusual'' punishment, which you have learned is unconstitutional. Do you agree or disagree? Explain your answer. For what reasons, if any, do you think citizens should lose their citizenship? Explain your answer.

SECTION 2

Immigration and the Non-Citizen

Preview Questions

● What is the difference between a refugee and an immigrant?
● According to United States laws, what are the different types of aliens?
● How has the nation's policy on immigration changed over the years?

Not everybody living in the United States is a citizen of this country. Various words have been used to describe people who are not citizens, the two most common of which are *immigrants* and *aliens*. The difference between the two is important. **Immigrants** are individuals who live in the United States with the intention of becoming naturalized citizens and remaining here permanently. During the last decade, immigrants have made up more than one-third of the nation's population growth. **Aliens**, in contrast, are individuals living in this country who are not citizens and who might not have any intention of becoming citizens.

Types of Aliens

According to United States law, there are five different categories of aliens. Each category has important legal distinctions.

1. **Resident aliens** are individuals who have come to the United States to establish permanent residence. These are immigrants and are called resident aliens until they become naturalized citizens. Resident aliens may stay in the U.S. as long as they desire and are not required to seek American citizenship.
2. **Nonresident aliens** are individuals who expect to stay in the United States for a specified period of time. A journalist from Britain who has come to cover the presidential election is a nonresident alien. A Japanese tourist from Tokyo visiting San Francisco for the month of June is a nonresident alien. The head salesperson for a Swiss watch company who is in New York to promote a new line is a nonresident alien.
3. **Enemy aliens** are citizens of those nations with which America is at war. During World War I, when our nation was at war with Germany, German citizens who resided in the continental United States had to register with the U.S. government. During World War II, when Japan was one of our enemies, U.S. residents of Japanese descent living on the West Coast were considered, as a group, enemy aliens, even though more than half could not be technically classified as such. The U.S. government forced over one hundred thousand such individuals to live in ''relocation camps'' for most of the war.
4. **Refugees** are immigrants to the U.S. who are granted entry because they are politically unsafe or unwelcome in their own countries. In recent years, the U.S. has accepted refugees from Southeast Asia, Cuba, El Salvador, Nicaragua, Haiti, and Poland. Currently, fifty thousand refugees may enter the U.S. each year, but Congress can give the president power to waive this limit in emergencies. In 1978, for example, President Carter issued a special order that allowed 117,000 Cuban refugees to legally enter the United States. The Immigration Act of 1990 granted certain refugees from El Salvador temporary ''asylum,'' or political protection, as well as permission to work.
5. **Illegal aliens** are individuals who enter the United States without a legal permit or who enter as tourists (nonresident aliens) and stay longer than their tourist status legally allows. Everyone entering the United

GOVERNMENT IN ACTION

CASE STUDY

Taking the Census

The U.S. Constitution in Article I, Section 2 requires that the federal government take an "enumeration," or census, every ten years. The reason the Constitution requires this is because the number of representatives elected to the House of Representatives by each state depends on the number of its inhabitants. The census results are also used to determine where to build highways, schools, restaurants, and banks, as well as to decide how much money in federal grants should be allocated to local government institutions such as hospitals. In order to be as accurate as possible, the Bureau of the Census made a significant effort to include the homeless and undocumented aliens in the 1990 count.

The Bureau of the Census, which is part of the Department of Commerce, operates within the executive branch of the government. All the census forms sent in are processed by sophisticated optical scanners at lightning speeds. Actually the Census Bureau was the first major institution to use machine-readable punch cards in 1890. (Their inventor, Herman Hollerith, later started the company that became International Business Machines, otherwise known as IBM.)

To get this information for the latest census, almost a half a million part-time employees were hired in 1990, in addition to the Bureau's normal staff of almost ten thousand. Two hundred thousand of these part-time workers were used to survey their home neighborhoods, talking to people from door to door. Here are some of the questions that were asked:

- What is your age, date of birth, and marital status?
- How many years of schooling have you completed?
- How many years' active duty military service have you completed?
- What was your income last year?

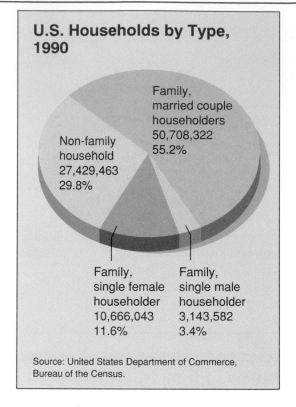

U.S. Households by Type, 1990

Family, married couple householders 50,708,322 55.2%

Non-family household 27,429,463 29.8%

Family, single female householder 10,666,043 11.6%

Family, single male householder 3,143,582 3.4%

Source: United States Department of Commerce, Bureau of the Census.

- Are you of Spanish/Hispanic origin?
- Do you have complete plumbing facilities?
- Do you have complete kitchen facilities?
- Do you have a telephone?
- Which fuel is used most for heating your house or apartment?

All of the canvassers and people who handle census information are sworn to secrecy—they can only reveal the information they gather to authorized personnel. But if you are curious about these numbers, you can buy all of the data from the 1990 census in computer-readable form for only $100,000.* That may

---

* Census records do become public after seventy-two years, when they are sent to the federal achives.

U.S. Cities with Greatest Populations, 1990

Size Rank	City and State	1990 Population
1	New York, NY	7,322,564
2	Los Angeles, CA	3,485,398
3	Chicago, IL	2,783,726
4	Houston, TX	1,630,553
5	Philadelphia, PA	1,585,577
6	San Diego, CA	1,110,549
7	Detroit, MI	1,027,974
8	Dallas, TX	1,006,877
9	Phoenix, AZ	983,403
10	San Antonio, TX	935,933
11	San Jose, CA	782,248
12	Indianapolis, IN	741,952
13	Baltimore, MD	736,014
14	San Francisco, CA	723,959
15	Jacksonville, FL	672,971
16	Columbus, OH	632,910
17	Milwaukee, WI	628,088
18	Memphis, TN	610,337
19	Washington, D.C.	606,900
20	Boston, MA	574,283
21	Seattle, WA	516,259
22	El Paso, TX	515,342
23	Nashville–Davidson, TN	510,784
24	Cleveland, OH	505,616
25	New Orleans, LA	496,938

Source: United States Department of Commerce, Bureau of the Census.

seem expensive, but imagine how much it cost to obtain those numbers! The Census Bureau spent over $3 billion to produce the 1990 census, roughly half of which was spent in that year. The U.S. Postal Service had to deliver 20 million completed forms to the Census Bureau in the first two weeks of April, 1990, at a total cost of $70 million. It takes five thousand miles of microfilm to record all the forms.

THINK ABOUT IT _____

1. Do you think it is an invasion of privacy that Americans be asked so many questions about how they live, even though the Census Bureau keeps all files secret? Explain why or why not.
2. Some cities claim that the Census Bureau undercounted the number of city residents. Why would this be a concern?

These United States Border Patrol Officers work along the United States/Mexico border near Laredo, Texas, to control the entry of illegal aliens into this country. What is meant by the term *illegal aliens*?

States is supposed to have a valid passport, visa, or entry permit. A **visa** is an authorization that allows an alien to enter this country legally, usually an official stamp placed on the inside of an individual's passport. Most visas for nonimmigrants are granted for a specific time period. A tourist, for example, may be allowed to travel legally in the United States for six months.

Illegal aliens can be **deported**, or forced to leave the United States. Over one million illegal aliens are deported each year. The problem of illegal aliens is a serious one that you will read more about at the end of this chapter.

The Rights of Aliens

American citizens have many rights given to them by their state constitutions and by the U.S. Constitution. In particular, the Bill of Rights guarantees the freedom of speech, assembly, and religion. These rights apply equally well to legal aliens whether they be resident or nonresident. In certain circumstances, many of these rights also apply to illegal aliens. In general, all legal aliens can legally own real estate and send their children to public schools; they cannot, however, vote in any election, be it local, state, or federal. Legal aliens normally are not required to serve in the military, nor are they called for jury duty. In exchange for their privileges, resident aliens must pay taxes and obey all laws.

All aliens are protected by the Constitution.

A Nation of Immigrants

According to the 1990 Census, Native Americans (American Indians, Eskimos, and Aleuts) make up less than one percent of the total United States population. This means that almost everyone in the United States can trace his or her roots to another country. The study of immigration in America is therefore a large part of the study of America itself.

Immigration Patterns

As you can see from the figure on page 168, immigration was greatest in absolute numbers from 1901 to 1910. The 1970s and the 1980s were also high periods of immigration, but relative to the percentage of the total population, immigration has been low in the last quarter century. Since 1821, a total of about 60 million people have immigrated to the United States.

Policies on Immigration

In the early days of our country, small numbers of people inhabited vast areas of land. It is not surprising, then, that most early Americans wanted to encourage immigration. During the constitutional debates in Philadelphia, Alexander Hamilton pointed out that immigrants could make an important contribution to the nation, and should be treated as ''first-class citizens.'' Prior to 1800, there were virtually no constraints on immigration except for the Naturalization Act of 1798, which was basically an attempt to prevent members of the Anti-Federalist party from voting. The act had little to do with immigration policy, and was repealed four years after it was passed.

The states believed that there was strength in large numbers. They wanted more people to move to their states, and set up advertising campaigns to lure prospective citizens. By the time the Civil War broke out,

164

PROFILE

Cesar Chávez

GOVERNMENT IN ACTION

Hispanics number over 22 million, about 9 percent of the population, and are second only to African Americans in terms of numbers. It is estimated that they will overtake African Americans as the nation's largest minority in the coming decades.

Most of the Hispanic immigrants, including the undocumented or illegal migrants, came from poor rural areas to seek a better life in the United States by working on large commercial farms. Most could not read or write in English, and had very little or no security in their new jobs. As migrant workers, these men, women, and children labored for very low pay in poor working conditions. They moved, as the crops matured, to Oregon, Washington, Nebraska, and the Great Lakes states, living in substandard shacks or trailers. Social legislation passed to help them was weak and did little to help.

From the early 1900s on, some efforts were made to organize the workers but with little success. In the 1960's, however, Cesar Chávez, born in 1927, finally began making real headway in organizing the workers in the California vineyards and lettuce fields. In 1962 he organized farm workers into the organization called the United Farm Workers and started a five-year strike against California grape growers to force them to recognize the union. The UFW organized a nationwide boycott of table grapes. Sympathetic priests, civic groups, and students aided in Chávez's efforts. In 1965 he launched a strike that led to a nationwide boycott of produce not bearing the label of the United Farm Workers. In 1970, the strikers finally won and the strike ended in a pact with the growers. By 1975, Chávez and the strikers had convinced the California legislature to pass a bill that gave farm workers the same rights held by union members elsewhere.

THINK ABOUT IT

1. Do you think the fact that farm work is often migrant work made the task of organizing a union more difficult? Explain your answer.
2. Do you think this fact helps to explain why there was little effective social legislation enacted to help them? Explain your answer.

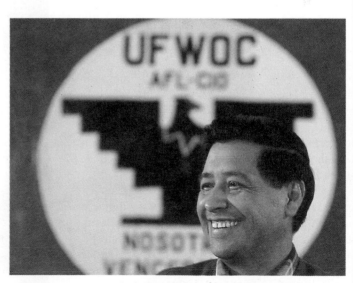

Cesar Chávez is shown here speaking in a meeting hall in Delano, California. In the background is the black Aztec eagle that is the emblem of the United Farm Workers Union.

In the past, many states designed advertising campaigns to entice individuals to immigrate. Shown above is a cover for a guide book for immigrants to Texas from Germany that was published in 1851. This book promoted Texas as a great place for immigrants. Why would states want to encourage immigration?

over thirty states and territorial governments had immigration offices whose purpose was to attract immigrants. Some states passed laws requiring that new immigrants be inspected, particularly for diseases. In New York, for example, sick immigrants were not allowed to enter the state.

The legality of the states' regulation of immigration was upheld in *Mayor of New York* v. *Miln* (1837). In *Henderson* v. *Mayor of New York,* in 1875, however, the Supreme Court declared that state legislation on immigration was unconstitutional because state laws infringed on the exclusive power of Congress to regulate interstate and foreign commerce.

Restricting Immigration The 1880s saw the first true restrictions on immigration. Prior to that time, most immigrants, who were from Northern and Western Europe, blended in easily with the existing population in the United States. Most of these immigrants were Protestants, except for the Irish and a few Germans who were

Catholic. The immigrants who arrived from the 1880s onward were, by contrast, from Eastern and Southern Europe. Their languages were different and their religions were either Jewish, Catholic, or Eastern Orthodox. Their customs seemed strange and foreign to the earlier immigrants.

At the same time as these new European arrivals, the Chinese started entering the Western states, particularly to help build the new railroads. Congress responded to this influx with the Chinese Exclusion Act of 1882, which halted entry of any Chinese immigrants to the U.S. for ten years. That act was the first one to establish the federal government's right to restrict immigration based on **nationalities**. More restrictive acts were passed in 1888 and 1891. They allowed the national government not only to exclude certain individuals—convicts, prostitutes, the insane, and so on—but also to deport aliens who entered the country in violation of these immigration laws.

Quotas The concept of limiting the rights of certain nationalities to immigrate resulted in the Quota Act of 1921. This act limited the annual number of immigrants from each nationality to 3 percent of the number of

This photograph from 1900 shows immigrant women from Southern Europe leaving Ellis Island. These women represent the new immigrants, from Eastern and Southern Europe, who started to arrive in the 1880s. Where were most immigrants from prior to the 1880s?

foreign-born persons of that nationality who were living in the United States in 1910. Most Asian groups were not included in the list of nationalities and, therefore could not legally emigrate to the United States for some time. The law did not apply to certain categories of educated people, such as professors, ministers, doctors, and lawyers. Immigration from the Western hemisphere was also unrestricted. The world responded, with seven hundred thousand immigrants entering the U.S. in 1924. The Immigration Act of 1924 and the National Origins Act of 1929 established a new quota system for each nationality, plus a limit on the total number of immigrants to be allowed entry at all (150,000 per year). The National Origins Quota System thus devised in the 1920s served as the basis for U.S. immigration policy for more than thirty-five years.

Current Immigration Policy Today's immigration policy is based largely on the Immigration Act of 1990, which revised several other acts including ones in 1965 and 1986.

The 1965 law had eliminated quotas based on national origin. As many as 270,000 immigrants could be admitted each year without regard to nationality, country of origin, or race, but not more than 20,000 persons could come from any one country. Close relatives of American citizens were given special status, as were aliens who have specialized occupational talents.

The maximum quota of 270,000 immigrants per year was always exceeded. The Refugee Act of 1980 allowed at least another 50,000 political refugees to legally enter the country each year. Congress and the president have since increased that number to about 100,000 per year. There are 150,000 special immigrants, mostly children and spouses of American citizens, who are also allowed entry. The Immigration Reform and Control Act of 1986 dealt mainly with illegal immigration. It also created a set of preferences for who could become a legal immigrant in the United States.

The big change in immigration law occurred in 1990 with the passage of the Immigration Act of 1990. This act raised the legal immigration levels by about 40 percent annually to 700,000. It stresses family reunification, provides amnesty for certain illegal immigrants (grants these immigrants legal status), and strikes down barriers blocking people with certain political beliefs. The new act's most significant feature was a tripling of the number of visas (to about 140,000 a year) granted to highly skilled professionals such as engineers, researchers, and scientists.

The chart below shows the highlights of the immigration act.

▼|FIGURE 7–2 **Highlights of the 1990 Immigration Act.** The figure below outlines some of the important points from the 1990 Immigration Act. Does the 1990 Immigration Act set country-by-country quotas for immigrants?

Highlights of the 1990 Immigration Act

■ Overall cap of 700,000 visas for legal immigrants. After three years, cap falls to 675,000.

■ 40,000 visas for "priority workers," or aliens with "extraordinary ability" in arts, sciences, education, business, or athletics.

■ 40,000 visas for aliens with advanced degrees or "exceptional ability."

■ 40,000 visas for other skilled workers, such as professionals holding basic degrees.

■ 10,000 visas for investors meeting certain economic criteria.

■ 40,000 visas for three years for aliens from 35 countries with low immigration in recent decades. At least 40 percent of these must come from Ireland.

■ 55,000 visas, in late 1995, for "diversity" immigrants from countries with low immigration in recent decades. Generally requires a high school education or two years of specific work experience.

■ Salvadorans in the United States by September 19, 1990, receive temporary "asylum" and work authorization for 18 months.

BUILDING SOCIAL STUDIES SKILLS

Reading Bar Graphs

A bar graph is a convenient way of showing large amounts of information at a glance. They are often used to show changes in trends that occur over time or to compare data.

When reading a bar graph, first read the title of the graph to find out what information is found there. Bars in a graph can run vertically, such as the one on page 169, or horizontally, such as the one on immigration on the right. One part of the information—ages, dates, percentages, and so on—is usually presented on the left vertical axis. Another part of the information is presented on the bottom horizontal axis. Sometimes, additional information, often indicated with different colors or shading, is presented within the bars themselves. To read graphs, simply note where the bars intersect with the vertical or horizontal axes.

PRACTICING YOUR SKILLS

Use the bar graphs to the right and on page 169 to answer the following questions:

1. In which period did the lowest number of immigrants come to the United States?
2. In which period did the largest number of immigrants come to the United States?
3. Which population group grew the most from 1960 to 1990?
4. Which age group made up a smaller percentage of the total population in 1970 than in 1960?

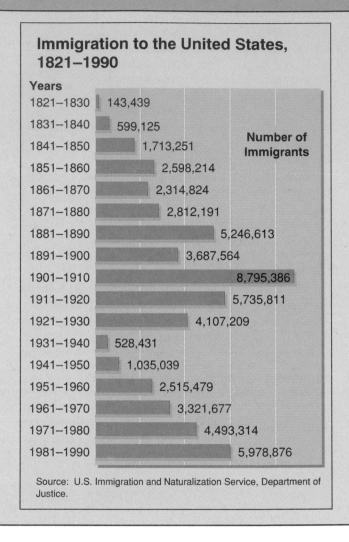

Immigration to the United States, 1821–1990

Number of Immigrants

Years	
1821–1830	143,439
1831–1840	599,125
1841–1850	1,713,251
1851–1860	2,598,214
1861–1870	2,314,824
1871–1880	2,812,191
1881–1890	5,246,613
1891–1900	3,687,564
1901–1910	8,795,386
1911–1920	5,735,811
1921–1930	4,107,209
1931–1940	528,431
1941–1950	1,035,039
1951–1960	2,515,479
1961–1970	3,321,677
1971–1980	4,493,314
1981–1990	5,978,876

Source: U.S. Immigration and Naturalization Service, Department of Justice.

The Immigration Controversy

The number of immigrants legally allowed into the United States does not necessarily represent the actual number of immigrants who come and stay here. This nation has a large flow of illegal aliens, also known as **undocumented aliens**. Many of these are tourists who overstay their visas and start working. Many are from Mexico and other Latin American countries. No one knows for sure how many illegal aliens arrive each year, but the estimate is at 2 million. The number of illegal aliens who permanently live in the United States is estimated to be between 5 and 12 million.

Periodically, the federal government has attempted to remedy the problem of illegal immigration. The latest attempt was in 1986, when the Immigration Reform and Control Act imposed severe penalties on employers who willfully hired illegal aliens (fines range from $250 to $10,000 for each offense). Employers who repeatedly violate this law can be jailed for up to six months.

Another aspect of the 1986 law was an **amnesty** program. (Amnesty means a general pardon for past

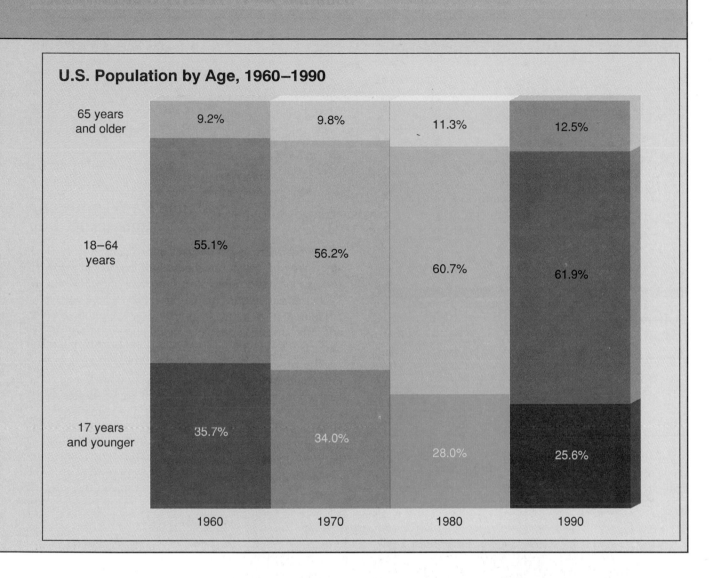

U.S. Population by Age, 1960–1990

	1960	1970	1980	1990
65 years and older	9.2%	9.8%	11.3%	12.5%
18–64 years	55.1%	56.2%	60.7%	61.9%
17 years and younger	35.7%	34.0%	28.0%	25.6%

offenses, in this case illegally residing in the U.S.) From the summer of 1987 to the summer of 1988, illegal aliens who could prove that they had been in this country continuously for at least five years could apply to obtain temporary legal residency status. Eighteen months later they could then apply for permanent residency and eventually for citizenship. (See the Resource Center.)

Immigration policy is the focus of a continuing debate in the United States. Many Americans strongly believe that immigrants, especially illegal immigrants, prevent American citizens from being fully employed.

These critics of liberal immigration policies further believe that increased immigration lowers American wages. Finally, such critics express the fear that new waves of immigrants will have difficulty fitting in with present-day American society.

Supporters of immigration point out the obvious—at one time or another all of us, except for Native Americans, were immigrants. Why should we arbitrarily decide that today immigration is "bad" for America? Additionally, many new immigrants to America take low-paying jobs that Americans leave unfilled anyway. In addition, the majority of immigrants pay taxes and adjust rapidly to the requirements of life in their new country.

SECTION 2 REVIEW

1. List and briefly explain the five types of aliens under United States law.
2. What are the rights of aliens? What are their responsibilities?
3. What were the first restrictions placed on immigration in the United States?
4. **For critical analysis:** A 1986 amnesty program for illegal immigrants allowed many of them to obtain legal residency in this country. How do you think such a program would influence other foreigners wanting to illegally immigrate to the United States? Give reasons for your answer.

SECTION 3

Citizenship Rights and Responsibilities

Preview Questions
● What is meant by the nationalization of the Bill of Rights?
● What are some of the rights and responsibilities of American citizenship?

Citizenship involves both rights and responsibilities. A citizen owes **allegiance,** or loyalty, to her or his nation which, in turn, gives the citizen all the rights and protections of the law. Thus, American citizenship is an implied contract between the nation and the individual for mutual support and assistance.

Rights of Citizens

Citizens' rights are spelled out in the Constitution and in federal and state laws. One right all citizens have is simply to live on American soil. We also have the right to vote, to hold public office, and to travel freely throughout the United States. The federal government also tries to protect American citizens wherever they are in the world. Our major rights are guaranteed by the Bill of Rights as well as several additional amendments.

The Bill of Rights   If you reread the First Amendment to the Bill of Rights, you will notice that it starts with the words "*Congress* shall make no law. . . ." Most citizens do not realize that, as originally presented, the Bill of Rights limited only the power of the federal government, not the power of the states. In other words, a citizen in the state of Virginia in 1795 could not successfully sue in federal court against a law passed in Virginia that violated one of the amendments in the Bill of Rights. Each state had (and still has) its own constitution, normally with its own bill of rights.

Whereas the states' bills of rights were similar to the federal one, there were some differences in content and, perhaps more importantly, differences in interpretation. A citizen in one state effectively had a different set of civil liberties than a citizen in another state. It was not until the Fourteenth Amendment was ratified in 1868 that our Constitution explicitly guaranteed due process

Most of our major rights are protected by the Bill of Rights, shown here as it was taken all over the nation for the public to view. Was the Bill of Rights originally intended to apply to state governments as well as the federal government?

Incorporating the Bill of Rights into the Fourteenth Amendment

Year	Issue	Amendment Involved	Court Case
1925	Freedom of speech	I	*Gitlow* v. *New York, 268 U.S. 652*
1931	Freedom of the press	I	*Near* v. *Minnesota, 283 U.S. 697*
1932	Right to a lawyer in capital punishment cases	VI	*Powell* v. *Alabama, 287 U.S. 45*
1934	Freedom of religion	I	*Hamilton* v. *Regents of the University of California, 293 U.S. 245*
1937	Freedom of and right to petition	I	*De Jonge* v. *Oregon, 299 U.S. 353*
1947	Separation of church and state	I	*Everson* v. *Board of Education, 330 U.S. 1*
1948	Right to a public trial	VI	*In re Oliver, 333 U.S. 257*
1961	No unreasonable searches and seizures	IV	*Mapp* v. *Ohio, 367 U.S. 643*
1962	No cruel and unusual punishment	VIII	*Robinson* v. *California, 370 U.S. 660*
1963	Right to a lawyer in all criminal cases	VI	*Gideon* v. *Wainwright, 372 U.S. 335*
1964	No compulsory self-incrimination	V	*Malloy* v. *Hogan, 378 U.S. 1*
1965	Right to privacy	I	*Griswold* v. *Connecticut, 381 U.S. 479*
1966	Right to an impartial jury	VI	*Parker* v. *Gladden, 385 U.S. 363*
1966	Right to counsel and no compulsory self-incrimination	V, VI	*Miranda* v. *Arizona, 384 U.S. 436*
1967	Right to a speedy trial	VI	*Klopfer* v. *North Carolina, 386 U.S. 213*
1973	No double jeopardy	V	*Colgrove* v. *Battin, 413 U.S. 149*

▲|FIGURE 7–3 **Incorporating the Bill of Rights into the Fourteenth Amendment.** The court cases listed above extended the protections of the Bill of Rights to apply to the citizens of states as well as the national government. Why do you think the Bill of Rights originally applied only to the national government?

of law to people in all states. Section 1 of the amendment provides that:

> No State shall make or enforce any law which shall abridge the privileges or immunities of citizens of the United States; nor shall any State deprive any person of life, liberty, or property, without due process of law; nor deny to any person within its jurisdiction the equal protection of the laws.

Section 5 of the amendment explicitly gives Congress the power to enforce these provisions by appropriate legislation.

Note the use of the terms *citizens* and *person. Citizens* have political rights, such as voting and running for office, but no *person,* citizen or alien, can be denied civil liberties (speech, press, and religion) nor have his or her property taken without equal recourse to the legal system. Note also that there is a distinction between the technical definitions of a civil *right* and a civil *liberty:* Civil rights are granted by the government; civil liberties are inherent.

The Nationalization, or Incorporation, of the Bill of Rights The Fourteenth Amendment (ratified in 1868)

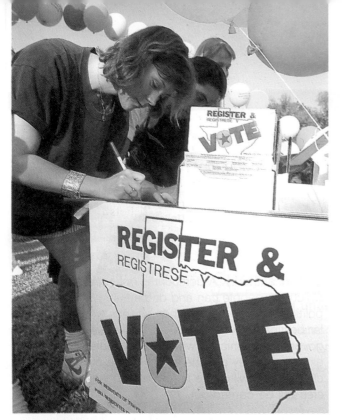

When registering to vote, you have the right to declare your party affiliation. Once you have declared your party affiliation, can you change it?

in-the-electorate, (2) a party as organization, and (3) a party-in-government.

Party-in-the-Electorate The party-in-the-electorate is the largest component, consisting of all those people who describe themselves as Democrats or Republicans. There are no dues, no membership cards, and no obligatory duties. Members of the party-in-the-electorate need never work on a campaign or attend a party meeting. They may register as Democrats or Republicans, but registration is not legally binding and can be changed at will.

Party as Organization Each major party has a national organization with national, state, and local offices. The party organizations are made up of several levels of people who maintain the party's strength between elections, make its rules, raise money, organize conventions, help with elections, and seek candidates.

Party-in-Government The party-in-government consists of all the candidates who won the elections and are now in public office. Even though members of Congress, state legislators, presidents, and all other officeholders almost always run for office as either a Democrat or a Republican, they do not always agree on everything. The

182

party-in-government helps to organize the government's agenda by coaxing and convincing its own party members to vote for its policies. If the party is to translate its promises into public policy, the job must be done by the party-in-government. (Elections normally requiring party affiliation are called **partisan elections**.)

Reasons for America's Two-Party System

In the United States, we have a **two-party system**, which means that two major parties dominate national politics—the Democrats and the Republicans. In a **one-party system**, a single party monopolizes the organization of governmental power and the positions of authority. The single party's functions are controlled by party leaders, and even if elections are held, party members, once on the ballot, have no competition. In most dictatorships, such as Iraq and The People's Republic of China, only one party is officially allowed to exist. Until recently, this was also true of many countries of Eastern and Central Europe, including the former Soviet Union.

Another alternative is a **multiparty system**, in which more than two political parties compete for power and electoral offices. This type of system exists in most European democracies such as France and Germany. In a multiparty system, parties are usually organized around

As Senate Majority Leader, Democrat George Mitchell exemplifies the *party-in-government*. What is the goal of the party-in-government?

different beliefs or interests such as religion, occupation, or political ideology. For example, Italy has nine national parties and several regional parties, including the Christian Democrats, the Socialists, the Radicals, the Liberals, and the Proletarian Unity Party. Israel has more than twenty parties. In the 1990 elections, Czechoslovakia had twenty-two political parties including the Communist Party, the Socialist Party, Public Against Violence, and the Alliance of Farmers and the Countryside.

Why has the two-party system become so firmly entrenched in America? A number of factors help to explain this phenomenon.

National Consensus and Moderate Views A **consensus** is a general agreement among citizens, sometimes defined as 75 percent or more of the people, on matters of public policy. In the United States, most citizens generally agree on certain broad social and economic issues. Most of us believe in the basic principles of government as outlined in the U.S. Constitution. For example, most of us believe that people have a right to own private property and the right to freedom of religion. We also believe that people should be free to choose where they live and work. Our differences usually lie more in *how* to attain the goals, rather than the goals themselves.

Because of this general political consensus, the United States does not have the conditions that would lead to numerous strong rival parties. Even though some Americans have disagreed during our history over many issues, we have not seen the prolonged and intense conflict that some countries have experienced. We have been deeply divided during such times as the Civil War in the 1860s, the Great Depression in the 1930s, and over such issues as civil rights and the war in Vietnam during the 1960s and 1970s. We have not, however, had long-lasting divisions based on religious beliefs as have occurred in the Middle East, nor on issues such as national origins, language, class, or social status, as have occurred in other places.

Unlike many European democracies, in which various radical political parties have strong support, American politics tend more toward center, or moderate, positions. There are no large, long-lasting groups that support radical governmental policies.

Political consensus and moderation in the United States has had another impact on our parties. It has given us two parties that look very much alike. Both tend to be moderate, middle-of-the-road parties built on compromise. For this they have often been criticized: their most stern critics think of them as ''tweedledum'' and ''tweedledee.''[1]

---

1. Two things that have different names, but are practically the same.

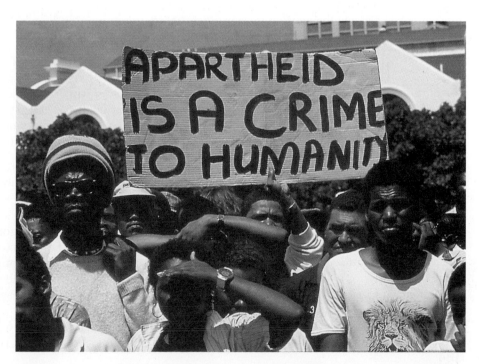

▶ The lack of long-lasting divisions based on national origins, such as those that exist in South Africa, has helped the United States to develop national consensus on certain broad social and economic issues. How has this consensus affected our party system?

Recruiting and nominating candidates for political office is one of the most important functions of our two political parties. For what offices are candidates chosen in a party's national convention, as shown to the left?

Tradition   The first major political division among Americans was between the Federalists and the Anti-Federalists over the ratification of the Constitution. Some people believe that this original two-sided political battle established the domination of the two-party system in this country. In addition, today's established institutions, such as the news media, do not encourage third parties. They do not typically spend much time covering third-party activities, but rather often focus exclusively on the Democrats and Republicans.

Our Elective Process   Our elective process also lends itself to the two-party system. In most elections, only one candidate can win the election to each office, called the **single-member district system**. The candidate who gets the *most* votes obtains a **plurality** (the largest number), and wins the election, even if this means less than 50 percent of the total vote cast. For example, suppose you vote in a local election. There are a total of 1,000 votes available and three candidates are running for mayor: Gomez, Rosenfield, and Gladstone. Gomez receives 450 votes, Rosenfield receives 250 votes, and Gladstone receives 300. Gomez wins even though he received less than 50 percent of the total votes cast. (If a majority vote is required, then sometimes a **run-off election** must take place between the two candidates who got the highest number of votes.)

The single-member district system makes it very difficult for a third-party candidate to win. Most Americans think that voting for a third party candidate is throwing away their vote. They therefore usually vote for either a Democrat or Republican, which discourages third-party candidates from running. Our elective system makes it difficult for minor-party candidates to win elections, and

without election victories parties tend to fade fast. Third parties have neither the numbers, recognition, nor money to endure or win most elections.

American election law also discourages third-party candidates. In most states, the established major parties need only a few signatures to place their candidate on the ballot, while a minor party must get many more signatures. The criterion is often based on the total party vote in the last election, which penalizes a new party that did not enter that election.

What Do Political Parties Do?

The Constitution does not provide for political parties, nor does it even mention them. Yet historically political parties have played a vital role in our democratic system. The main function that political parties perform in a large democracy is linking the people to the government. They link the people's policy preferences to actual government policies. Political parties also perform many other functions that no other body or institution of government performs.

Selecting Candidates   One of the most important functions of the two political parties is to recruit and nominate (to select and approve of) candidates for political office. A party's endorsement for a candidate is called a **nomination**. This function provides a way to simplify voting choices for the **electorate** (voters). Political parties take the large number of people who want to run for office and narrow the field to one candidate. They accomplish this by the use of **primaries**, which is a preliminary election to choose a party's final candidate. In theory, the party chooses the best-qualified member to be the party candidate. It is much easier for voters to choose

GOVERNMENT IN ACTION

PROFILE

Jesse Jackson

Jesse Jackson was born on October 8, 1941, in Greenville, North Carolina. His childhood was one of deep poverty in which he secured his first job at age 6 delivering stove wood. Jackson attended public schools in Greenville and in 1959 enrolled at the University of Illinois where he had a football scholarship. After one year he returned to North Carolina and attended the Agricultural and Technical College of Greensboro. He was ordained as a Baptist minister in 1968 after attending a theological seminary in Chicago.

Jackson played an important role in the civil rights struggles of the 1960s, leading marches, picketings, and sit-ins. He joined Martin Luther King, Jr. in the Southern Christian Leadership Conference (SCLC) and became a close adviser and field organizer. In 1966, as head of the SCLC's Operation Breadbasket, the Conference began a systematic boycott of businesses that, it believed, exploited African Americans.

Soon after King's assassination, which Jackson witnessed, he announced the forma-

tion of operation PUSH (People United to Save Humanity), a Chicago-based civil rights and economic development organization. He also organized programs to increase learning skills among minority students.

Jesse Jackson became in 1983 the first African American to be a serious candidate for a major party's presidential nomination. Although Jackson was given little chance to win the nomination, he carried his campaign to the national convention in 1984. While campaigning, he won two primary elections outright and obtained more than ten percent of the vote in many others. He renewed his campaign to be selected as the Democratic Party's nominee for President in 1988 but was unsuccessful. He has argued that he had insufficient funding to use television advertising. Nonetheless, Jackson won more delegates in the Southern Democratic primaries than any other candidate. Jackson and his supporters, known as the Rainbow Coalition, had arrived as a national political force within the Democratic party.

Jackson, who is no stranger to controversy, has had a profound effect on the Democratic Party and American politics. Through the efforts of Jackson and his Rainbow Coalition, many Americans, who otherwise might have felt left out of the political process, have found a way to participate. These people are becoming able to work from within the system to pursue their American dream.

THINK ABOUT IT

1. How might Jesse Jackson's political success reflect the success of the civil rights movement?
2. Why do you think the name Rainbow Coalition was chosen by Jackson and his supporters?

BUILDING SOCIAL STUDIES SKILLS

Interpreting Tables

What kinds of people are Democrats? What kinds of people are in the Republican Party? The answers to such questions are frequently presented in table form. Tables can effectively present a great deal of information in a limited space; they consolidate information so that it is easier to study. By examining a table, you can compare information and detect trends over time.

Follow these steps when reading a table:

● **Step 1.** *Read the title of the table.*
● **Step 2.** *Notice how the table presents its in-*

formation by reading the vertical (◆) and horizontal (◆) headings.
● **Step 3.** *Note whether the numerical information presented is in whole numbers or percentages. [If the data are percentages, of what are they a part?]*
● **Step 4.** *Analyze the meaning of the percentages or numbers by comparing the various sets of figures.*
● **Step 5.** *See if the numbers are expressed in tens, hundreds, thousands, or larger.*
● **Step 6.** *Read the source for the data.*

Vote by Groups in Presidential Elections, 1960–1992

	1960		1964		1968			1972	
	JFK D	Nixon R	LBJ D	Goldwater R	Humphrey D	Nixon R	Wallace I	McGovern D	Nixon R
NATIONAL	50.1	49.9	61.3	38.7	43.0	43.4	13.6	38	62
SEX									
Male	52	48	60	40	41	43	16	37	63
Female	49	51	62	38	45	43	12	38	62
RACE									
White	49	51	59	41	38	47	15	32	68
Nonwhite	68	32	94	6	85	12	3	87	13
AGE									
Under 30 years	54	46	64	36	47	38	15	48	52
30–49 years	54	46	63	37	44	41	15	33	67
50 years and older	46	54	59	41	41	47	12	36	64
POLITICS									
Republican	5	95	20	80	9	86	5	5	95
Democrat	84	16	87	13	74	12	14	67	33
Independent	43	57	56	44	31	44	25	31	69
EDUCATION									
College	39	61	52	48	37	54	9	37	63
High school	52	48	62	38	42	43	15	34	66
Grade school	55	45	66	34	52	33	15	49	51

*Less than 1 percent

PRACTICING YOUR SKILLS

Look at the table below and answer the following questions:

1. What percentage of women voted for the Democratic candidate in 1984?
2. Does the table support this statement: College graduates have supported Republican presidential candidates since 1968?
3. Do voters under thirty years of age always appear to support the Democrats?

When reading a table, remember that the statistics gathered from the table do not describe individuals. Rather, they describe behavior trends in various groups, or choices made over time. By looking at the tables on these pages, you can conclude that most people with college educations will probably vote for a Republican presidential candidate. You cannot conclude, however, that all people with college educations will vote for a Republican presidential candidate. You also cannot conclude that any one person with a college education will vote for a Republican presidential candidate.

Vote by Groups in Presidential Elections, 1960–1992 (continued)

1976			1980			1984		1988		1992		
Carter D	Ford R	McCarthy I	Carter D	Reagan R	Anderson I	Mondale D	Reagan R	Dukakis D	Bush R	Clinton D	Bush R	Perot I
50	48	1	41	51	7	41	59	45	53	43	38	19
53	45	1	38	53	7	36	64	41	57	41	38	21
48	51	*	44	49	6	45	55	49	50	46	37	17
46	52	1	36	56	7	34	66	40	59	39	41	20
85	15	*	86	10	2	87	13	86	12	NA	NA	NA
53	45	1	47	41	11	40	60	47	52	44	34	22
48	49	2	38	52	8	40	60	45	54	NA	NA	NA
52	48	*	41	54	4	41	59	49	50	NA	NA	NA
9	91	*	8	86	5	4	96	8	91	10	73	17
82	18	*	69	26	4	79	21	82	17	77	10	13
38	57	4	29	55	14	33	67	43	55	38	32	30
42	55	2	35	53	10	39	61	43	56	NA	NA	NA
54	46	*	43	51	5	43	57	49	50	43	36	20
58	41	1	54	42	3	51	49	56	43	NA	NA	NA

*Less than 1 percent
Note: 1976 and 1980 results do not include vote for minor party candidates.

Source: *The Gallup Report*, November 1984, p. 32; *The New York Times*. November 5, 1992, p. B9.

CHAPTER 8 REVIEW—Continued

Summary

1. Political parties are groups of individuals who are organized to win elections, operate the government, and determine public policy. American political parties are sometimes described as three-dimensional, each one consisting of the party-in-the-electorate, the party as organization, and the party-in-government. The United States has a two-party system. Alternatives to this system are the multiparty system, such as in many countries of Europe, which have several major and many lesser parties, or the one-party system, in which only the party of the ruling group is allowed. Our two-party system is the result of our general consensus and moderate views, our political tradition, and our elective process. Political parties select candidates, inform the public, coordinate policymaking, balance competing interests, and run campaigns. Party members have joined parties for material and ideological reasons, and to express solidarity with fellow party members. Taking part in political parties is an important way for citizens to affect government decision making.

2. The founders reacted negatively to the idea of strong political parties, but the first political factions in America—the Federalists and the Anti-Federalists—were formed to support or oppose the Constitution. The Anti-Federalists became the Democratic-Republicans and dominated American politics for the next twenty years and then split into two parties—the Democrats and the Whigs. The Whig Party was absorbed into the new Republican Party in the 1850s. By the end of the Civil War, the Republicans and the Democrats were the most prominent political parties, and continue to be so.

3. Smaller third parties have also competed for power in the nation's two-party system. They are formed because they believe that certain needs and values are not being properly addressed by the major parties. There are three general types of third parties: (1) issue-oriented parties formed to promote particular issues; (2) ideological parties to support a particular set of beliefs or political doctrines; and (3) splinter or personality parties formed from a split with a major party. Many important issues of American politics have been brought to the public's attention by third parties. These parties have also influenced some election outcomes. Third parties fail to win elections because Americans are accustomed to selecting only nominees of the two major parties. They also have difficulty raising enough money to compete in expensive campaigns.

4. In theory, the two major political parties in the United States have standard, pyramid-shaped organizations. In actuality, each major party is fragmented and decentralized. In both the Democratic and Republican parties, state and local organizations are separate from their national organizations. There are four major elements in the structure of both major party national organizations: the national convention, the national committee, the national chairperson, and the congressional campaign committee. Since 1960 there has been a sharp drop in the number of people identifying themselves as Republicans or Democrats; more people are calling themselves Independents.

Review Questions

1. Define what a political party is and explain the roles that parties play in American politics.
2. What factors help to explain America's two-party system? How is this system different from those of other nations?
3. What are the main activities that political parties perform and why are they important?
4. What do party members do and why do people join political parties?
5. Name three minor parties in the United States.
6. What are reasons that individuals identify with political parties?
7. Why did the founders react negatively to the idea of political parties?
8. What were the first political parties in the United States and why were they formed?
9. By the end of the Civil War, what were the dominant parties in the United States?
10. Name the three different types of third parties.
11. What effects have third parties had on American politics?
12. Describe the structure of the national party organization.
13. How can you find the state and local offices of both major parties in your area?
14. Describe the trend over the past thirty years regarding people identifying themselves with the two major parties.

CHAPTER 8 REVIEW—Continued

Questions for Thought and Discussion

1. Some commentators believe that the media have taken over some of the functions of political parties. Discuss what these functions might be and why the media are able to take them over.
2. Although there is a national party structure for both the Democrats and the Republicans, most of the power of political parties lies primarily at the county and state levels. Discuss why the national party apparatus cannot control local politics.
3. Discuss what you believe to be the major differences between the platforms of the Republicans and the Democrats.
4. On at least several occasions, both the Democrats and Republicans have asked the same individual to run as their presidential candidate. This occurred, for example, with Dwight D. Eisenhower. Explain how such a phenomenon could exist.

Improving Your Skills
Communication Skills

Skimming for Information

You have learned the SQ3R reading strategy on page 73, which will help you to thoroughly understand and remember details as you read a textbook. There are certain times when you must read material quickly, such as when deciding which newspaper articles to use in a research project. **Skimming** is a technique that allows you to assess the key concepts of an article or chapter without reading the entire selection. When skimming for information, look at headings, topic sentences, (usually the first or second sentence in a paragraph) and conclusions. Know what information you are looking for ahead of time.

Writing

Practice your skimming techniques by going to the library and researching one of the following religions: Islam, Judaism, Christianity, Hinduism, Buddhism, or any other. Find three books on religion in general and skim them quickly until you find the main facts about the subject. Then write down five facts you learned about the religion you selected.

Social Studies Skills
Reading a Time Line

Information and data are often organized according to when different events occurred. The battles of the Civil War, World War I and World War II can be organized in this fashion. Indeed much of information of an historical nature throughout the field of social studies can be presented in this way. When information is put together in a chart in chronological order (ordered by dates), the chart is called a time line. Look at the time line on the formation of political parties on page 192 and answer the following questions:

1. Over a what year period does the time line extend?
2. The distance between horizontal lines on the time line represent how many years?
3. Which started earlier, the Republican Party or the Democratic Party?
4. If you were reading an updated time line in the year 2010, what might have changed?

Activities and Projects

1. Research a party organization in your state or city. Visit the party headquarters if possible, and find out about its structure, its activities, and how it works with the national party organization. Ask about the main problems it faces in your area, and in which activities you and your classmates could become involved. Write a short report and present your findings to your class.
2. Stage a class debate on the following topic: Resolved—The two-party system in the United States shall be centered around one party called the Conservatives and the other called the Liberals.
3. Determine through research whether your state is predominantly controlled by Democrats or by Republicans. Do this by finding out how many years out of the last twenty-five each party has controlled the state legislature and how many years each party has controlled the governorship. Write a short report.
4. Try to determine whether the city (or county) in which you live is controlled by Democrats or Republicans. List the reasons for your conclusion.
5. Invite an election official to discuss political party participation in your county or plan a panel discussion of local party leaders focusing on community issues.

CHAPTER 9

Public Opinion and Interest Groups

CHAPTER OBJECTIVES

To learn and understand

- The nature of public opinion and how it is measured.
- The many factors that affect public opinion.
- The purposes and goals of interest groups and their many different types.
- The various strategies used by interest groups to affect public policy.

Keynote

"A government can be no better than the public opinion that sustains it."

———— **Franklin D. Roosevelt
(1882–1945) Thirty-second President of
the United States**

INTRODUCTION

Above all else, the aim of a democratic government is to convert the will of the people into public policy. When President Roosevelt spoke the words in the quotation above, he was reminding both the people and the government of this. He was reminding them of their responsibilities to make our democratic system work. In order to translate the will of the people into public policy, citizens must form opinions and openly express them to their elected public officials. Unless Americans make clear to their senators, representatives, and state and local officials where they stand on important issues, these officials will never know what the people want. Only when the people's *opinions* are communicated effectively can they be translated into public policy.

SECTION 1

Definition and Measurement of Public Opinion

Preview Questions
- What is public opinion and why is it important in American politics?
- What is a public opinion poll and how does it work?

The public holds opinions—sometimes very strong ones—about a range of issues, from the ethics of capital punishment to the appearance of the latest fashion. In this chapter, however, we are concerned with **public opinion:** the individual attitudes or beliefs shared by a significant portion of adults about politics, public issues, and public policy. Notice that the definition implies that there is rarely a *single* public opinion. If everyone were of one mind about some question, it would not be much of an issue.

Public opinion is important in American politics because opinions can determine how government handles such issues as gun control, abortion, and the death penalty. Public opinion is the sum total of a complex collection of opinions held by many people. When you hear a news report or read a magazine article stating that "a significant number of Americans" feels a certain way about an issue, you are probably hearing that a particular opinion is held by a large enough number of people to make government officials turn their heads and listen. For example, in the 1990s, as polls began showing that Americans were concerned about environmental problems, many politicians began voicing strong public stances on environmental issues. Public opinion is most often cast in terms of percentages: 62 percent feel this way, 27 percent do not, and 11 percent have no opinion.

Remember that public opinion is limited to only those issues that are in the public arena, such as taxes, health care, social security, clean-air legislation, unemployment, and so on. The issue must be of interest to a significant number of people, and must be cause for some kind of political action, social action, or media coverage.

Measuring Public Opinion

If public opinion is to affect public policy, then public officials must be made aware of it. They must know how strongly people feel about the issues. They must also know when public opinion changes. Of course, the most common ways public officials learn about public opinion are through election results, personal contacts, interest groups, and media reports. The only *relatively* precise way to measure public opinion, however, is through the use of public opinion polls.

A **public opinion poll** is a numerical survey of the public's opinion on a particular topic at a particular moment. Because a poll cannot, of course, survey the entire population, polls are based on scientific polling tech-

207

Demonstrations such as this are designed to shape public opinion. What is meant by the term *public opinion*?

niques that use **samples**—groups of people who are typical of the general population.

Early Polling Efforts During the 1800s, one way to spice up a magazine or newspaper article was by doing a **straw poll,** or mail survey, of readers' opinions. Straw polls try to read the public's collective mind simply by asking a large number of people the same question. Straw polls are still used today: Some newspapers have interviewers who ask adults in shopping centers and other central locations to "cast ballots" on certain issues. Many newspapers and magazines still run "mail-in" polls but more and more of this type of polling makes use of telephone technology and "900" telephone numbers.

The major problem with straw polls is that there is no way to ensure that the opinions expressed are representative of the larger population. Generally speaking,

such opinions usually represent only a small portion of the population. For example, opinions gathered at a yacht club might differ from opinions gathered at a thrift store. A survey of readers of the *Wall Street Journal* will likely differ from a *Reader's Digest* survey.

The most famous of all straw-polling errors took place in the *Literary Digest* in 1936. The magazine sent out millions of postcard ballots for the purpose of predicting the presidential election outcome. The *Digest* predicted that Alfred Landon would easily defeat incumbent Franklin D. Roosevelt. Instead, Roosevelt won by a landslide.

How did the magazine go so wrong? The *Digest* had drawn a **biased sample**, one which did not accurately represent the population. Its editors had sent mail-in cards to citizens whose names appeared in telephone directories, to its own subscribers, and to automobile owners—in all a staggering 2,376,000 people. In this mid-Depression year of 1936, however, people who owned a car or a telephone or who subscribed to the *Digest* were certainly not representative of the majority of Americans. The vast majority of Americans were on the opposite end of the socioeconomic ladder. Despite the enormous number of people surveyed, the sample was unrepresentative and consequently inaccurate.

Several newcomers to the public opinion poll industry, however, did predict the Roosevelt landslide victory. These organizations are still at the forefront of the poll-taking industry: the Gallup poll of George Gallup and Roper Associates, founded by Elmo Roper.

Sampling How can interviewing a small sample of 1,500 to 2,000 voters possibly indicate what *millions* of voters think? Clearly, the sample must be representative of all the voters in the population. A sample must consist of a group of people who are *typical* of the general population, so that, if the sample is properly selected, the opinions of those in the sample will be representative of the opinions held by the population as a whole. If the

Reprinted by permission of UFS, Inc.

CITIZENSHIP SKILLS AND RESPONSIBILITIES

Writing a Letter to the Editor

Too often, we think that the only way to partici-pate in politics is by voting, but there are many forms of political participation. One of the many ways in which public opinion is expressed in this country is by writing a letter to the editor of a news-paper or magazine. Letters to the editor are usually printed on the opinion and editorial (op-ed) page of the newspaper, and on the pages immediately follow-ing the table of contents in a magazine. Usually, newspapers and magazines print letters that best rep-resent a variety of their reader's opinions. Use the following guidelines to help you compose your letter:

- **Know your purpose for writing.** Before you begin writing, be sure to know whether you are trying to inform, persuade, inquire, or complain.
- **Know your subject.** Research your subject before you write your letter so you can back up your opinions with facts.
- **Make sure your letter is neat and well-organized.**
- **Use precise language.** Don't try to impress anybody with your vocabulary. Avoid harsh, sarcastic language. The important thing is to convey your message.

- **Get to the point.** There is not enough space available for long-winded introductions or ex-planations. Plan your opening sentence care-fully for the best initial impact. Deal with only one topic.
- **Use correct grammar and spelling.**
- **Appeal to your readers' sense of fair play and justice.** Challenge them to think about and respond to the issue.
- **Try to be optimistic and practical.** If your letter is in response to a problem, offer poten-tial solutions.

For the final draft, type your letter on one side of the paper using double spacing. Sign your name and give your address and telephone number. You can use a pen name or initials if you wish.

TAKING ACTION

1. Select an issue affecting your school that you would like to write about for a local newspaper. Write a draft of your letter and read it to the class. Ask for constructive criticism from students and teachers.
2. Locate the address of the local newspaper and send it a neatly typed copy of your finished letter.

---

sample is not properly chosen, then the results of the poll may not reflect the ideas of the general population.

The most important principle in sampling is random-ness. A **random sample** means that each person within the entire population being polled has an equal chance of being chosen. For example, if a poll is trying to mea-sure how women feel about an issue, the sample should include respondents in proportion to the entire female population. That is, if 10 percent of all women in the United States are Hispanics, then 10 percent of the re-spondents should be Hispanic women. If 25 percent of the female population is between the ages of 25 and 40, then 25 percent of the sample must be in this age group.

Polls can be surprisingly accurate when they are con-ducted properly. Politicians, the news media, and the public place a great deal of faith in the accuracy of poll results. Policymakers use polls to determine how the

majority feels on issues. Supporters of polling argue that it is a tool for democracy. In contrast, critics of polling think that it makes politicians reactors rather than leaders. Others argue that polls can discourage voters from voting if the numbers predict that their candidates will lose.

Problems with Polls The methods used by public-opinion pollsters have improved dramatically since the days of *Literary Digest,* but they are not entirely without limitations or faults. For example, the wording of ques-tions can slant answers toward a certain bias. Consider a question about whether a new library should be built in town. One way to poll opinions about this issue is simply to ask, ''Do you believe the town should have a new library?'' Another way to ask the same question is, ''Are you willing to pay higher property taxes so that the town can build a new library?'' Undoubtedly,

▲ During the 1980s, a group of very prominent entertainers recorded "We are the World." This event, which was designed to raise money for famine relief efforts, also went a long way toward shaping public opinion on the issue. Can you think of a recent issue that has been brought to the public's attention by entertainers?

and others low priority, the media decide the relative importance of issues. They help determine what people will talk and think about, and which issues politicians will therefore act upon.

For example, due in part to a prolonged famine in Africa, millions of people, particularly Ethiopians, have died of starvation since 1982. The famine got little media coverage at first, and for several years little was done by the U.S. government to help. When the television networks finally broadcast dramatic film footage of corpses and suffering, they called attention to the tragedy. The United States and other Western countries began contributing food and money. The publicity led rock singers to collaborate on a record—"We Are the World"—which brought further public attention and more donations.

Likewise, television played a significant role in shaping public opinion about the Vietnam War, which has been called the first "television war." Part of the public opposition to the war in the late 1960s came from the daily scenes and narrative accounts of destruction, death, and suffering. The war to free Kuwait from Iraqi occupation in 1991 also had extensive media coverage, though some critics feel that this coverage may have shown only the better side of the United States' efforts.

Clearly, the media play an important role in shaping public opinion. The *extent* of that role, however, is often debated. Some studies have shown that the media may not have as much power to influence the opinions of people as has been thought. Generally, people watch television and read articles with preconceived ideas (already established beliefs) about the issues. These ideas act as a screen to block out any information that does not fit with them. For example, if you are already firmly convinced that being a vegetarian is beneficial to your health, you probably will not change your mind if you watch a TV show that asserts that vegetarians live no longer on average than people who eat meat. Apparently, the media are most influential with those persons who have not yet formed an opinion about certain issues or political candidates.

Opinion Leaders Every state and community has well-known citizens who are able to influence the opinions of their fellow citizens. These people might be public officials, religious leaders, teachers, or celebrities. They

BUILDING SOCIAL STUDIES SKILLS

How to Read a Public Opinion Poll

We are flooded with information from public opinion polls reported to us by television, newspapers, and magazines. They claim to tell us a variety of things: whether the president's popularity is up or down; how people feel about government regulation; whether people feel more strongly about environmentalism than they did a few years ago; and who is ahead in the next presidential nomination.

As you are bombarded with this information, keep in mind that not all poll results are equally reliable. Before you believe what the poll is leading you to conclude, ask the following questions:

1. **Who paid for the poll?** If a poll is known to be sponsored by a particular candidate, interest group, or party, the results may be presented in a misleading way. Take this into account and look carefully at how the poll results are worded.

2. **Who was interviewed?** A poll should reveal something about the population sampled. The best samples are scientifically random samples in which everyone has an equal chance of being interviewed. As a rule, you should be skeptical of person-in-the-shopping-mall interviews that you might hear about on local television news. Almost certainly, the people in the mall are not an accurate cross section of all the people in the community. Shopping malls tend to attract younger, middle-class, and female shoppers.

3. **How were the interviews obtained?** By telephone? By mail? In person? Many pollsters think that people are less honest over the telephone than in person, but because telephone surveys cost less than person-to-person interviews, they are often used. Also be wary of mail questionnaires because only a small percentage of people, those who tend to have higher incomes, better jobs, and more education, complete and return them. They are therefore not representative of the general population.

4. **When were the interviews conducted?** If they were conducted a year ago, the results may be outdated. This is particularly true if a change has taken place that would cause people to feel differently.

5. **How were the questions worded?** Elmo Roper, a famous pollster, once said:

> If you ask people about any subject that they've got very strong opinions on, how you word the question really doesn't matter. When they don't have convictions, how you ask the questions and in what sequence you ask them are critical. You can flip-flop the answers ten points one way or the other just because of a relatively subtle phraseology difference or the context in which you ask the questions.

6. **Be skeptical of raw statistics.** It is possible to use raw statistics to slant a story. Raw statistics don't take account of any biases built into the way the data were collected. For example, if only men were interviewed about their opinions on increased taxes to pay for a new stadium, the raw statistics would be suspect.

PRACTICING YOUR SKILLS

1. Look through at least three news or business magazines such as *Time, Newsweek, U.S. News and World Report,* and *Business Week.* Make photocopies of all of the opinion polls, then analyze them in terms of the following questions:
   a. How many individuals were polled each time?
   b. What percentage of the adult population does this represent?

2. Determine whether any of these opinion polls were done over the phone or by person-to-person interviews. Decide which of the polling techniques has the most credibility.

3. Watch the TV news for seven consecutive days. Write down the number of times the newscasters refer to the results of opinion polls. Can you tell by the statements concerning the polls whether the number of individuals polled was small or large? Can you determine whether the polls were done over the phone or in person? After answering these questions, decide how much credibility you wish to give to each poll result.

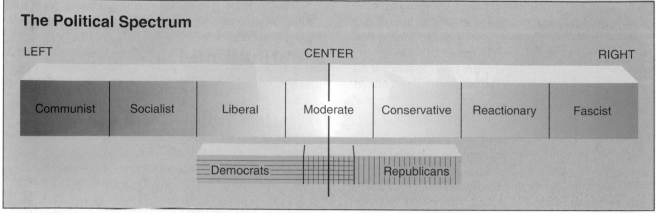

The Political Spectrum

LEFT   CENTER   RIGHT

| Communist | Socialist | Liberal | Moderate | Conservative | Reactionary | Fascist |

Democrats   Republicans

▲ **FIGURE 9–1 The Political Spectrum.** The figure above shows the political spectrum from the left to the right. Where do most Democrats and Republicans fall on this scale?

Look at the diagram of the political spectrum shown in Figure 9–1.

Democrats and Republicans fit somewhere in between liberals and conservatives, although generally Democrats tend to be liberal and Republicans conservative. There are, however, Democrats who are more conservative than certain liberal Republicans. Both radicals (extreme left) and reactionaries (extreme right) favor extreme and immediate change and may be willing to use violence.

The Average American versus the Ideologues

Most Americans, when asked, can typically identify themselves as liberal, conservative, or somewhere in between. Surprisingly enough, however, more people identify themselves as moderates than either liberals or conservatives. The Gallup polling organization, along with the *New York Times* and CBS News, routinely ask individuals what their ideological self-identification is. During the last two decades, between 35 to 50 percent of those polled have considered themselves moderate, between 17 and 21 percent have considered themselves liberal, and between 26 and 33 percent have considered themselves conservative. (The remainder held no opinion.)

Many Americans consider individuals who are extremely liberal or extremely conservative to be **ideologues**, people who hold very strong political opinions. Most Americans, however, are not interested in *all* political issues, and have a mixed set of opinions that do not fit under a conservative or liberal label. Research shows that only about 10 percent of Americans could

conceivably be identified as ideologues. The rest of the population looks at politics more in terms of party lines— Democratic or Republican—or from the viewpoint of their own economic well-being.

Ideology versus Self-Interest

Public opinion polls do certainly show that political issues are not as important to people as the problems that impose themselves on their daily lives. In other words, it is one thing to support more aid to the poor if you in fact are poor; it is quite another if you are extremely well off. It is one thing to support increased government funding for long-term medical care if you are a bedridden elderly person. It is quite another to support such a political program if you are young, healthy, and making a high income.

Some researchers have determined that self-interest is a great motivator of public opinion. Individuals who have suffered at the hands of a criminal often express harsh opinions about issues such as capital punishment or building more prisons. People who have been suddenly laid off will often express negative opinions about the current president's ability to manage the economy.

In any event, the evidence suggests that the majority of Americans hold the strongest political convictions about issues which have a direct effect on their own lives.

SECTION 3 REVIEW _____

1. How do liberals differ from conservatives?
2. What kinds of people are considered ideologues?
3. **For critical analysis:** Of what use are the labels *conservative* and *liberal*?

SECTION 4

Interest Groups

Preview Questions

- What is an interest group? What purposes do interest groups serve in American politics?
- How do interest groups differ from political parties?
- What are the various types of interest groups?

Every single one of us has interests we want represented in government: Farmers want higher prices for their products; young people want good educational opportunities; environmentalists want clean air and water; the homeless want programs for food and shelter; and criminals want fair trials. Throughout our nation's history, organizing to protect these interests has been a natural part of democracy. As the French political observer Alexis de Tocqueville wrote in his often-cited book *Democracy in America* (1835), Americans have a tendency to form "associations," and have perfected "the art of pursuing in common the object of their common desires." The old adage "there is strength in numbers" is true in American politics. The right to organize groups is even protected by the Constitution, which guarantees

people the right "peaceably to assemble, and to petition the Government for redress of grievances." The Supreme Court has defended this important right over the years.

Defining Interest Groups

To define an interest group seems simple enough. *Interest* refers to objectives and policy goals that people have in common; a *group* is an accumulation of people. An **interest group** is therefore an organization of people sharing common objectives who actively attempt to influence government policymakers through direct and indirect methods. They are also called **pressure groups**, which refers to their attempts at putting pressure on government to act in their interests.

Whatever their goals—more or fewer social services, higher or lower prices—interest groups pursue them on every level and in every branch of government. On any given day in Washington, you could catch national interest groups in action. If you breakfasted in the Senate dining room, you might see congressional committee staffers reviewing testimony with representatives from women's groups. Later that morning you might visit the Supreme Court and watch a civil rights lawyer arguing over a discrimination suit. Lunch in a popular Washington restaurant might find you listening in on a conversation between an agricultural lobbyist and a

▲ In his book *Democracy in America,* Alexis de Tocqueville, wrote that Americans tend to form "associations" for "pursuing in common the object of the common desires". What did he mean?

▲ Molly Yard, shown here, is the former president of the National Organization for Women, one of many interest groups that can be found in our nation's capital. What is meant by the term *interest group*?

GOVERNMENT IN ACTION

PROFILE

Ralph Nader: Consumer Activist

Some of the most well-known and perhaps the most effective public interest groups were organized under the leadership of consumer activist Ralph Nader. Nader's rise to the top began when, as a young attorney, he wrote *Unsafe at Any Speed,* a critique of General Motor's purported attempt to prevent the public from learning detrimental information that linked its Corvair car to highway deaths. When General Motors hired a detective to spy on Nader, he sued and won a $280,000 settlement. Partly as a result of Nader's book, Congress began to consider testimony in favor of an automobile safety bill.

Nader became a recognized champion of consumer interests and used the settlement money to help start Public Citizen, Inc., a consumer advocacy group, as well as numerous other organizations protecting consumers' rights.

Nader and Public Citizen's staff, commonly referred to as "Nader's Raiders," challenged not only the automobile industry but many other industries, as well as the Federal Trade Commission and Congress itself. The actions of Nader and his raiders have brought about changes in many industrial practices and a number of consumer protection laws.

Since the time when Public Citizen, Inc. was formed, Nader has turned over much of his income to other public interest groups he has formed or sponsored. In all, there are more than fifteen national "Naderite" organizations promoting consumer interests.

THINK ABOUT IT

1. What problems might someone trying to make changes in the community face? How could these problems be overcome?
2. Think of two consumer-related problems or issues you would like to change. How could you go about changing them?

resource and wildlife conservation. They have organized to oppose strip-mining, nuclear power plants, logging activities, chemical waste dumps, and many other environmental hazards.

Professional Groups Most professions that require advanced education or specialized training have organizations to protect and promote their interests. These groups are concerned mainly with the standards of their professions, but they also work to influence government policy.

Four major groups are the American Medical Association (AMA), representing physicians; the American Bar Association (ABA), representing lawyers; and the National Education Association (NEA) and the American Federation of Teachers (AFT), both representing teachers. Each has an impact on public policy in their areas. In addition there are dozens of less well-known and less politically active professional groups such as the Screen Actors Guild and the National Association of Social Workers.

Women's Groups Groups advocating women's equality have swelled with the women's rights movement. The National Organization for Women (NOW) is the largest women's group with almost three hundred thousand members. With a national board made up of national salaried officers as well as regional representatives, NOW is well organized. NOW has established the Legal Defense and Education Fund, which focuses on education and public information concerning women's rights.

Church-Related Organizations Many church-related organizations try to influence public policy in several important areas. The National Council of Churches, for example, has spoken out on civil rights, human rights, and other social issues.

Ethnic Organizations A number of ethnic groups in the United States have formed organizations to influence public policy at all levels of government. The National Association for the Advancement of Colored People (NAACP) lobbies for improvement in the political, social, and economic status of African Americans. Hispanics have a number of organizations to do the same. They include the Mexican-American Legal Defense and Education Fund and the League of United Latin American Citizens. Asian Americans have the Organization of Chinese Americans and the National Asian Pacific American Legal Consortium.

As America becomes more culturally diverse and economically complex, we will most likely see an even greater array of interest groups.

SECTION 4 REVIEW _____

1. How do interest groups fit into American politics?
2. How does an interest group differ from a political party?
3. Name four different types of interest groups.
4. **For critical analysis:** One individual may belong to several different interest groups at one time. Is it possible that the goals of one group may conflict with those of another to which this same individual belongs? Explain.

SECTION 5

How Groups Try to Shape Policy

Preview Questions
- At which level or levels of government do interest groups operate?
- What are some of the methods used by lobbyists to influence public policymakers?
- What is the difference between the direct and the indirect techniques used by lobbyists?
- What are some of the indirect techniques that interest groups employ?
- How have government regulations affected lobbyists?

Interest groups operate at all levels of government and use a variety of strategies to steer policies their way. They sometimes attempt to directly influence the policymakers themselves, while at other times they try to shape public opinion, which indirectly influences policymakers. The extent and nature of their activities depend on their goals and their resources.

Direct Techniques

Lobbying, providing election support, and rating legislative behavior are some of the direct techniques used by interest groups.

Lobbying The term *lobbying* comes from the foyer or lobby of the legislature itself, where petitioners used to

GOVERNMENT IN ACTION

CASE STUDY

Mothers Against Drunk Driving (MADD)

The formation of this interest group began with a tragedy. On May 3, 1980, Cari Lightner, age 13, was walking in a bicycle lane near her home in Fair Oaks, California. She was on her way to a church carnival when she was struck from behind by a swerving car. She was hit so hard that she was hurled 120 feet down the road. The driver of the car never stopped, but was arrested four days later.

The driver was drunk at the time of the accident. In fact, when he killed Cari, he had been out of jail on bail for only two days because of another hit-and-run drunk driving accident. Although he had been convicted of drunk driving and related offenses three times in four years, he had served only forty-eight hours in jail. The police told Candy Lightner, Cari's mother, that the driver would probably never go to jail because drunk driving was not considered a serious crime in California. The driver, in fact, never did go to prison, but served eleven months in a work camp and halfway house.

Candy Lightner was shocked and angry. After extensive research she found out that nothing effective was being done to keep drunk drivers off the road and that drunk drivers could literally ''get away with murder'' without fear of being punished. ''Death caused by drunk driving is the only socially acceptable form of homicide,'' she concluded.

Candy Lightner decided to do all she could to help other victims and to prevent such tragedies from happening again. She quit her job to form an interest group called Mothers Against Drunk Driving, or MADD. She began her campaign by convincing the California governor and legislature that stiffer penalties were needed for drunk driving offenses. She quickly gained the support of other parents who had experienced similar tragedies.

Once launched, MADD proved to be a powerful force. Members wrote letters, gave speeches, and issued press releases. MADD sponsored community-awareness meetings and educational seminars. They circulated petitions calling for state and federal action. They applied for corporate and foundation grants. They took their fight to Washington, D.C., where they held press conferences, lobbied, and urged stronger legislative action on drunk driving.

Now headquartered near Dallas, the organization has 383 chapters and 600,000 members. Since the founding of MADD, all fifty states have tightened their drunk driving laws. Media coverage, stiffer penalties and laws, and commissions and task forces to study the problem are all accomplishments of which MADD can be proud.

THINK ABOUT IT

1. Drunk driving has been a problem for many years in the United States. Why do you think organizations such as MADD hadn't been formed prior to 1980?
2. Who might be in favor of *not* passing harsher legislation against drunk drivers? Why?

think will benefit them the most. (PACs are discussed in greater depth in Chapter 10.) The number of PACs has grown astronomically, along with the amounts of money they spend on elections. Although campaign contributions do not guarantee that officials will vote the way the groups wish, it usually does ensure that they will have the ear of the public officials they have helped to elect. PACs have also succeeded in bypassing campaign-contribution limits, which has created the same type of "vote-buying" privileges that wealthy individual contributors enjoyed in the past.

The Ratings System Some interest groups try to directly influence legislators through their **ratings system**. They select legislative issues that they feel are important to their groups' goals and rate legislators on the percentage of times they vote favorably on that legislation. For example, one environmental group identifies twelve members of Congress whose voting record on environmental issues is unacceptable and labels them the "Dirty Dozen." The Communication Workers of America (CWA) label policymakers who take a position consistent with their own as "heroes," and those who take the opposite position as "zeroes." Needless to say, legislators do not want to earn membership on the "zeroes" lists of these groups.

Indirect Techniques

Interest groups also try to influence public policy indirectly through third parties or the general public. Such indirect techniques may appear to be spontaneous, but are equally well planned. Public officials also are often more impressed by contacts from voters than from lobbyists.

Shaping Public Opinion Public opinion ultimately trickles back to policymakers, so interest groups cultivate their public image carefully. If public opinion favors a certain group's interests, then public officials will be more obligated to listen and more willing to pass legislation favoring that group. This is often referred to as bringing grass-roots pressure to bear on officials, or mounting campaigns for the people back home. Such efforts may include television publicity, newspaper and magazine advertisements, mass mailings, and public relations techniques to improve the group or industry's public image. For example, environmental groups run television ads to dramatize threats to the environment. Oil companies respond to criticism about increased gas

prices with advertising showing their concern about public welfare. The goal of all these activities is to convince both the public and the policymakers that the public overwhelmingly supports the interest group's position.

Mobilizing Constituents Interest groups sometimes urge members and other constituents to write letters or call government officials to show their support for or opposition to a certain policy. Large interest groups can generate hundreds of thousands of letters and calls. They often provide letter forms or postcards for constituents to fill out and mail. The NRA has successfully used this tactic to fight strict federal gun-control legislation by delivering a half a million letters to Congress within a few weeks. Policymakers recognize that such opinions were initiated by interest groups, but they are still made aware of an issue that is important to that group.

The Court System Achieving policy goals through the legal system offers another avenue for influencing the political process. Civil rights groups paved the way for litigation in the 1950s and 1960s with major victories in cases concerning equal housing, school desegregation, and labor market equality. Litigation is also used by environmental groups such as the Sierra Club. For example, an environmental group might challenge in court developers who threatens to pollute the environment. The legal challenge will force the developers to bear the costs of defending themselves and possibly delay the project. The next time, developers might be more willing to make concessions and avoid lengthy and costly legal battles. In fact, much of the success of environmental groups has been linked to their use of lawsuits.

Groups also try to influence courts indirectly by lobbying the Senate to support or oppose judicial nominees. For example, in 1987 nearly two hundred groups mobilized to support or oppose President Reagan's Supreme Court nominee, Robert Bork. Their actions resulted in the Senate rejecting Bork's nomination.

Demonstration Techniques Some interest groups stage protests to make a statement in a dramatic way. The Boston Tea Party of 1773, in which American colonists dressed as Native Americans and threw tea into the Boston Harbor to protest British taxes, is testimony to the fact that the tactic has been around for a long time.

In recent years, many groups have generated protest marches and rallies to support or oppose issues such as legalized abortion, busing, American support for the *contras* in Nicaragua, nuclear weapons, and government assistance to farmers, and many other interests. Greenpeace, an environmental and peace activist group, has staged many creative protest activities to generate publicity for their causes such as protests against whaling operations.

Why Do Interest Groups Get Bad Press?

Despite their importance to democratic government, interest groups, like political parties, are sometimes criticized by both the public and the press. Our image of interest groups and their special interests is not very favorable. You may have run across political cartoons depicting lobbyists prowling the hallways of Congress, briefcases stuffed with money, waiting to lure representatives into a waiting limousine.

These cartoons are not entirely factual, nor are they entirely fictitious. President Richard Nixon was revealed to have yielded to the campaign contributions of milk producers by later authorizing a windfall increase in milk subsidies. In 1977, "Koreagate," a scandal in which a South Korean businessman was accused of offering lavish "gifts" to several members of Congress, added to the view that politicians were too easily susceptible to the snares of special interests. In the early 1990s, it was revealed that a number of senators who received generous contributions from one particular savings and loan association turned around and supported a "hands off" policy by savings and loan regulators. The savings and loan association in question later got into financial trouble, costing the federal government billions of dollars to bail it out.

Despite these incidents, a few bad apples do not spoil the whole interest group barrel. For every dishonest action, there are hundreds of honest transactions between interest group leaders and public officials. For every lobbyist who attempts to bribe a public official, there are hundreds who try only to provide public officials with solid facts that support the goals of their groups.

Regulation of Interest Groups

Interest groups are not free to do whatever they choose. In principle, they are regulated. In 1946 Congress passed the Federal Regulation of Lobbying Act in an attempt to control lobbying. It is the only major law regulating interest groups, and it applies only to those that lobby Congress. The act states:

1. That any person or organization that receives money to be used principally to influence legislation before

Congress must register with the clerk of the House and the secretary of the Senate.
2. That any group or person registering must identify their employer, salary, amount and purpose of expenses, and duration of employment.
3. That every registered lobbyist must give quarterly reports on his or her activities, which are published in the *Congressional Quarterly*.
4. That anyone failing to satisfy the specific provisions of this act can be fined up to $10,000 and receive a five-year prison term.

The act is very limited and has not regulated lobbying to any great degree. First, the Supreme Court has restricted the application of the law to only those lobbyists who *directly* seek to influence federal legislation. Any lobbyist indirectly seeking to influence legislation through efforts to shape public opinion does not fall within the scope of the law. Second, the act requires only that persons or organizations whose principal purpose is to influence legislation need register. Any interest group or individual claiming that their principal function is something else need not register. Many groups can avoid registration in this way. Third, the act does not cover lobbying directed at agencies in the executive branch or those that testify before congressional committees. Fourth, the public is almost totally unaware of the information in the quarterly reports and no agency that oversees interest-group activities has been created by Congress.

The problem, of course, is that any stricter regulation of lobbying may run into constitutional problems because of the potential abridgment of First Amendment rights. As long as the Supreme Court does not view indirect lobbying as falling within the scope of the law, lobbying will be difficult to control.

SECTION 5 REVIEW _____

1. Name three methods used by special interest groups to directly influence policymakers.
2. How do lobbyists attempt to influence policymakers throughout the electoral process?
3. Describe four techniques by which lobbyists indirectly influence legislators.
4. What federal regulation of interest groups exists?
5. **For critical analysis:** What additional restrictions, if any, do you think should be placed on interest groups? Explain whether you think any further restrictions would violate the First Amendment rights of these groups.

CHALLENGE TO THE AMERICAN DREAM

Can Lobbying Endanger Democracy?

One of this nation's founding fathers, James Madison, seemed to be referring to interest groups when he wrote about the danger of factions. Madison defined a faction as a group "united and actuated [activated] by some common impulse of passion, or of interest, adverse to the rights of other citizens, or the permanent and aggregate [total] interest of the community."

If this is true of factions, or interest groups, then what is to be done about them? James Madison considered this question and came up with a mixed answer. "Liberty is to faction," he said, as "air is to fire." Air may feed fire, but it is also "essential to animal life." Madison believed that the formation of these factions is inevitable in a democracy, but he also believed that the cure—eliminating them—is worse than the disease.

Today there are both those who defend interest groups and those who condemn them. Those who defend them say that interest groups make government more responsive. They provide necessary and important services by communicating the people's wishes to their representatives. They allow certain groups of Americans to be represented according to their economic, social, or occupational interests. They also enable Americans to organize and participate in the American political system, and are a means through which citizens can pressure the government to follow policies they want. Interest groups act as "watchdogs" and protest government policies that are harmful to their members. Proponents also argue that since there are many interest groups competing for power, lawmakers are kept from being controlled by one interest group. Competition among interest groups prevents any one group or combination of groups from dominating American politics.

Critics of interest groups argue that some interest groups are too large and too powerful. They feel that

some have vast amounts of resources that enable them to directly influence the decisions of public officials. Some have an influence on government far beyond their proportionate size or their relative influence on the public. Opponents of interest groups argue that the groups represent only a small portion of Americans. Moreover, the minority who are represented by these groups are generally more affluent, better educated citizens. Critics maintain that less advantaged members of our society do not have the resources to organize and advance their interests. As a result, interest groups do not adequately represent the public interest.

Critics also argue that these groups do not in fact represent the views of all the people for whom they claim to speak, and are often dominated by a limited group of leaders. Critics further claim that some groups use tactics that, if they were to become widespread, would undermine the whole political process. These practices—bribery, threats, and other illegal or unethical means—are not common, but the danger is there.

The potential challenge to the American dream that interest groups pose cannot be taken lightly. As long as the costs of interest-group–sponsored legislation is spread out over a large number of Americans but the benefits are concentrated in a small number of individuals or companies, interest groups will always have the upper hand. They will always be the ones who can raise money to influence legislation. While interest groups are clearly part of the democratic process, they may also potentially threaten its long-term viability.

You Decide

1. Give two arguments in favor of and against interest groups.
2. What did James Madison mean by the statement, "liberty is to faction as air is to fire"?
3. Given what you have learned about interest groups, do you agree with Madison's claim that they are inevitable in American society? Why would the cure be worse than the disease?

CHAPTER 9 REVIEW

Key Terms

agents of political
  socialization 210
biased sample 208
conservatives 215
ideologues 216
interest group 217
labor force 220
liberals 215
liberalism 215

lobbying 224
lobbyist 224
mass media 211
moderates 215
peer group 214
political action
  committee
  (PAC) 225

political
  socialization 210
pressure groups 217
public interest
  groups 218
public opinion 207
public opinion poll 207
radical left 215

random sample 209
ratings system 227
reactionaries 215
samples 208
sampling error 210
straw poll 208
trade and product
  organizations 218

Summary

1. Public opinion is the beliefs and attitudes about politics and public policy shared by a large portion of the population. The most common ways that public officials learn about public opinion is through election results, personal contacts, interest groups, and media reports. One way to measure public opinion is through the use of scientific public opinion polls which, in order to be useful, must use a random sample.

2. Many factors affect public opinion. Most views that are expressed as political opinions are acquired through a learning process called political socialization, which is a complex, lifelong learning process. Some of the agents of political socialization include the family, the educational establishment, the mass media, opinion leaders, and peer groups. Economic status and age can also influence one's political socialization process.

3. Liberals have a viewpoint toward public policy that tends to involve change, and believe in expanding the federal government. Conservatives believe that public policy should maintain tradition, and that state and local governments should rely less on the federal government. Most Americans consider themselves moderates, neither liberal nor conservative.

4. Interest groups are organizations of people sharing common objectives who actively attempt to influence government policymakers through direct and indirect methods. Although both interest groups and political parties are banded together for political purposes, they are very different. Most interest groups seek change based on specific issues, whereas political parties must support a wider range of causes. Private interest groups primarily seek economic benefit for their own members, but public interest groups are formed with the broader goal of working for the "public good." Both public and private groups represent a wide range of interests.

5. Interest groups operate at all levels of government and use a variety of strategies to affect public policy. Some of the direct techniques used by these groups include lobbying, providing election support, and rating legislative behavior. Interest groups also try to influence public policy through indirect methods such as shaping public opinion, mobilizing constituents, litigation, and demonstrations. In principle, lobbying has been regulated by the Federal Regulation of Lobbying Act of 1946, but this act is very limited.

Review Questions

1. What is meant by public opinion?
2. What are the most common ways by which public officials learn about public opinion?
3. Explain what went wrong with early polling efforts.
4. What are the factors that help explain how public opinion is formed?
5. Explain how four of the agents of political socialization influence our political opinions.
6. What distinguishes a conservative from a liberal?
7. What purposes do interest groups serve in American politics and how do they operate?
8. Briefly describe three types of private interest groups.

CHAPTER 9 REVIEW—Continued

9. In what ways do interest groups try to directly influence policymakers?
10. Describe four methods of influencing legislation used by lobbyists.
11. What are the requirements of the Federal Regulation of Lobbying Act of 1946?
12. Briefly describe the guidelines for writing a letter to a newspaper or magazine editor.

Questions for Thought and Discussion

1. What individuals in your life do you think have had the most influence on your political perspectives? In what ways have they influenced you?
2. What kinds of interest groups, if any, do you think could be seen as either public interest or private interest groups? What arguments could you present for them to be classified either way?
3. Why might stricter regulation of lobbying endanger First Amendment rights?

Improving Your Skills

Communication Skills

Formulating a Thesis Statement

Many times throughout your studies, you will be asked to write about your ideas or what you have learned. Before writing an essay, and even before researching a topic, you should write a thesis statement, which should explain the reason for your essay. Here is a sample thesis statement from Section 3 of this chapter:

Most political attitudes are often labeled as either conservative or liberal.

Just as this statement expresses the main idea of that section, writing a thesis statement for your essay will help you clarify your topic and thus focus your research.

The following steps will help you formulate a thesis statement:

1. *Choose a general topic that interests you.* Begin to gather and list facts and information about the general topic.

2. *Gradually narrow the topic in stages.* As you gather more information and facts, look for related facts and make choices about which are really important.
3. *Organize the facts.* Discard the information that has no bearing on your topic, keeping only those that are directly related.
4. *Decide what you believe the facts mean.*
5. *Formulate a thesis statement that can be fully proven by the collected facts.*

Writing

Using your own words, rewrite each of the following thesis statements taken out of the chapter:

1. Above all else, the aim of a democratic government is to convert the will of the people into public policy.
2. Public opinion is important in American politics because opinions can determine how government handles such issues as gun control, abortion, and the death penalty.
3. Most political socialization is informal, almost accidental, and other political socialization is formal.
4. Education is a powerful influence on an individual's political attitudes.
5. The media can also determine what issues, events, and personalities are in the public eye.

Social Studies Skills

Understanding a Pictogram

Look at the pictogram on page 216, Figure 9–1. Why does it have a right side, a left side, and a center? Are there any elements of those on the extreme right—fascists—which also apply to those on the extreme left—communists?

Activities and Projects

1. Develop your own schoolwide "straw poll" on three issues facing high school students in the United States today. Report to the class on your findings and describe the techniques you used.
2. Identify an important national issue that is currently under debate. Research two interest groups that are involved with the issue. Write a summary page on each.

CHAPTER 10

Campaigns, Elections, and the Media

CHAPTER OBJECTIVES

To learn and understand

- The nominating process and the various methods of nomination used throughout the United States.
  - How campaigns are organized and financed.
    - How elections are organized and carried out.
      - The role of the media in campaigns and elections.

Keynote

"The press in America . . . determines what people will think and talk about—an authority that in other nations is reserved for tyrants, priests, parties, and mandarins."

———— **Theodore H. White**
(1915–1986) Political Commentator

INTRODUCTION

The very nature of our government is representative democracy, a system in which the people elect officials to represent them in making laws and running the government. Because over 250 million Americans cannot all gather in one place to make laws and run the government, we need a means by which we can choose representatives who will govern with our consent and truly act on our behalf. We also need a method for holding chosen officials responsible to the people. Popular election is the method we use to accomplish these democratic goals.

Participating in elections today involves more than spending a few minutes voting for someone to represent us. Voters elect over five hundred thousand people each year to a multitude of federal, state, and local offices.

At the turn of the century, a presidential candidate and his entourage piled into a train to carry information to voters at railroad stops across the country. Today the media, not the railroad, carry the candidate and the issues to us. As illustrated by the above quote by Theodore H. White, a political commentator who has written many books on recent presidential campaigns, the media in the United States have a power equivalent to that held by kings and tyrants in other countries. The media are extremely influential in the United States and must be reckoned with by every political candidate. After all, the name recognition given by the media can determine whether the candidate wins or loses.

In this chapter we will look at three very important parts of our representative democracy. These parts are campaigns, elections, and the media. From the day the first candidate announces his or her intention to run for an office, through the endless photo opportunities and the overwhelming media blitz, to the day of the election, campaigns, elections, and the media are irrevocably tied to one another in modern America.

Step One: The Nomination

Preview Questions
- What are the methods by which candidates are nominated in the United States?
- What are direct primaries and what different forms do they take?
- How are presidential candidates nominated?

American political campaigns are usually long, complicated, and expensive events, producing hours of film, volumes of newsprint, thousands of posters and buttons, and finally a winning candidate who becomes a public official for the next few years. The first step in this long process is the **nomination**, the choosing of the candidates within each party who will then seek office by running against the candidates chosen by the other party.

Nominations are a critical step in the election process because they narrow the field of possible candidates and limit a party's choice to one person. The methods by which candidates are nominated have varied from time to time and from state to state. They can be grouped in general categories.

Self-Nomination and Petition

Until the early 1800's, **self-nomination**, or simply announcing one's own desire to run for public office, was the most common way of becoming a candidate. This method is still used at the small-town and rural political levels in many parts of the country.

Self-nomination does not mean that a person's name will automatically appear on the **ballot**—the card or other object on which voters indicate their choices in the election. The candidate must first file a **petition**, a formal request to be listed on the ballot with a certain number

233

▲ This 1824 cartoon shows Andrew Jackson being attacked by dogs, who represent supporters of the caucus system. Why did Jackson protest the caucus system?

of signatures determined by the state to show that the candidate has some public support.

A self-nominated candidate might not be able to gather enough signatures to win a place on the ballot. In this case, she or he may decide to run as a **write-in candidate**, someone who will campaign without being listed on the ballot, and will ask voters to write his or her name on the ballot on election day. For these votes to count, most states require the write-in candidate to register with the local board of elections. Write-in candidates have rarely been successful at winning public office.

Party Caucus

The Constitution gives no instructions for nominating candidates for the presidency and vice presidency. Thus, in 1797 the leaders of the two parties decided to keep political power in their hands by holding congressional conferences later called **caucuses**.[1] In these early meetings the party leaders, who were wealthy and influential members of the community, would choose the candidates in secret. The voters at large would have no part in choosing those who were nominated. The caucus

---

1. This word apparently was first used in the name of a men's club called the *Caucus Club* of colonial Boston sometime between 1755 and 1765. It comes from a Latin word meaning "drinking vessel." Many early political and government meetings took place in a pub.

was frequently referred to as "the smoke-filled room," because meetings were often held in small rooms that soon filled up with smoke because the windows were closed to guarantee secrecy.

By the presidential race of 1820, the caucus method of nomination had become a controversial issue. The system was called "King Caucus" by Andrew Jackson and other presidential candidates who felt it was undemocratic and too powerful. Party leaders were faced with rising opposition and were forced to find other methods of nominating candidates. As it faded away in presidential politics, the caucus system soon diminished at the state and local levels as well.

The caucus is still used for some local nominations, especially in New England. These modern caucuses, however, are open to the general public and bear little resemblance to the original caucus.

Party Nominating Convention

As the caucus method diminished around the country, it was replaced in many states by party conventions. A **nominating convention** is an official meeting of a political party to choose its candidates and to select **delegates**, persons sent to a higher level convention to represent the people of one geographical area. For example, delegates at a local party convention would nominate candidates for local office, and would also choose delegates to represent the party at the state convention. By 1840, the convention system had become the most common way of nominating candidates for government offices at every level.

A party convention was intended to be more democratic than a party caucus because more people were allowed to take part. Yet, like the party caucus, the convention method was abused. Historian Charles Beard described the corruption of party leaders in the late 1840s:

> They packed [conventions] with their henchmen, who drove out or overwhelmed dangerous opponents. They padded the rolls of party members with the names of dead men. . . . They stuffed the ballot boxes, and they prepared the slates which were forced through the nominating convention in the face of opposition.

These practices soon came to the attention of the public. Amidst mounting criticism, state legislatures turned away from conventions as a means of nominating local and state party candidates. The convention is still used, however, in some states such as Connecticut, Delaware, Michigan, and Utah. At the national level, the

This illustration depicts the first Republican convention, which was held under the oak trees at Jackson, Michigan on July 6, 1854. What system of nominating candidates was replaced by the party conventions?

party convention is used to select the presidential candidates of the two major parties from the winners of the state primaries and conventions.

The Direct Primary

In most states the convention method was gradually replaced by the **direct primary**—an election held *within* each party to pick its candidates for the general election. This is the method most commonly used today to nominate candidates for office.

Although the primaries are *party* nominating elections, they are now closely regulated by the states. The states usually set the dates and conduct the primaries. They also provide polling places, election officials, registration lists, and ballots, in addition to counting the votes.

Most state laws require that the major parties use the primary to choose their candidates for the Senate and the House, for the governorship and all other state offices, and for most local offices, as well. In a few states, however, different combinations of nominating conventions and primaries are used to pick candidates for the top offices.

Because state laws vary, there are several different kinds of primaries used throughout the country.

Closed Primaries In a **closed primary**, only party members can vote to choose that party's candidates, and they may vote only in the primary of their own party. Thus, only Democrats can vote in the Democratic primary to pick candidates of the Democratic party. Only Republicans can vote for the Republican candidates. A person usually establishes party membership when he or she registers to vote. In some states such as Illinois, a person may register right at the polling place.

Regular party workers favor the closed method because it promotes party loyalty; independent voters oppose it because it excludes them from the nominating process.

Open Primaries An **open primary** is a direct primary in which voters can vote for a party's candidates whether or not they belong to the party. In most open primaries, all voters receive both a Republican and Democratic ballot. Voters then choose either the Democratic or the Republican ballot in the privacy of the voting booth.

Primary Election Ballot, 1988

DEMOCRATIC
PRESIDENT OF THE UNITED STATES

PRESIDENTIAL PREFERENCE
Vote for One

LYNDON LAROUCHE	Democratic	2→ ○
MICHAEL S. DUKAKIS	Democratic	3→ ○
AL GORE	Democratic	4→ ○
PAUL SIMON	Democratic	5→ ○
JESSE JACKSON	Democratic	6→ ○

UNITED STATES SENATOR

Vote for One

ROBERT J. BANUELOS — Communication Specialist	Democratic	11→ ○
LEO McCARTHY — Lt. Governor of California	Democratic	12→ ○
CHARLES GREENE — Los Angeles County Commissioner	Democratic	13→ ○
JOHN HANCOCK ABBOTT — Political Science Teacher	Democratic	14→ ○

NONPARTISAN JUDICIAL
JUDGE OF THE SUPERIOR COURT

Office No. 1 — Vote for One	JEROLD A. KRIEGER — Judge of the Municipal Court	132→ ○
	JOE BARILLA — Deputy District Attorney	133→ ○
Office No. 2 — Vote for One	J. MICHAEL BYRNE — Judge of the Municipal Court	134→ ○
		→○
Office No. 3 — Vote for One	JEWELL (JUDY) JONES — Superior Court Commissioner	136→ ○
	SHERRILL D. LUKE — Judge of the Los Angeles Municipal Court	137→ ○
Office No. 4 — Vote for One	ALLAN A. NADIR — Los Angeles City Prosecutor	138→ ○
	TERRY SMERLING — Judge of the Municipal Court	139→ ○
Office No. 10 — Vote for One	REGINALD A. DUNN — Chief Assistant Prosecutor	140→ ○
	MALCOM H. MACKEY — Judge of the Los Angeles Municipal Court	141→ ○
Office No. 52 — Vote for One	SHERMAN W. SMITH, JR. — Judge of the Los Angeles Municipal Court	142→ ○
		143→ ○
Office No. 74 — Vote for One	HENRY PATRICK NELSON — Judge of the Superior Court	144→ ○
	JOE INGBER — Attorney at Law	145→ ○

▲ FIGURE 10–1 **Primary Election Ballot, 1988.** The figure above is an excerpt from a primary election ballot. In what type of primary was this ballot used?

A different version of the open primary is used in Alaska, Louisiana, and Washington, where it is known as the "wide open" primary, or **blanket primary**. In each of these states, the voters receive a single large ballot listing each party's candidates for each nomination. Voters may choose candidates from different parties. This means that a voter may help choose a Democratic candidate for one office, and a Republican candidate for another office.

Runoff Primaries Candidates for most offices must win only a **plurality** of votes—more votes than any other candidate—to be declared the winner. They do not need to win a majority of the votes. In some states, however, candidates are required to win by a majority. If none of the candidates receives a majority in the primary election, a **runoff election** is held, in which the two candidates who won the most votes in the first primary election run against each other. The person who wins the runoff election becomes the party's candidate in the general election.

Nonpartisan Elections In most states, some offices are filled in **nonpartisan elections**—elections in which candidates do not run under party labels. Nonpartisan elections are most often used at the local level to choose, for example, candidates for the school board, hospital board, city council, and other local offices. Nonpartisan ballots are also used to elect about half of all state judges.

Nominating Presidential Candidates

In some respects, being nominated for president is tougher than being elected. The nominating process narrows a very large number of hopefuls down to a single candidate from each party. Choosing presidential candidates is unlike nominating candidates for any other office. One reason for this is that the nomination process combines several different methods.

State Primaries About three-fifths of the states hold presidential primaries, held between February and June of a presidential year, to select delegates to attend the national convention. For a candidate, a good showing in early primaries means plenty of media attention as television networks and newspaper reporters play up the results. The other state primaries that follow shortly after the big primaries tend to serve as contests to eliminate unlikely candidates.

Because the results of early primaries tend to influence later primaries, some large states that have late primaries have tried to hold them earlier. For example, California, the state with the most electoral votes, holds its primary in June, well after the nominating process has begun in most other states. By then, the identities of the presidential nominees have virtually been assured. In 1990, Democratic lawmakers tried to move the California primary date to March, but failed to win legislative approval. In 1991, California Democrats devised a plan calling for nearly one-third of the Democratic delegates to be selected at caucuses three months before the primary election. That number is about the same as the combined total chosen in February in the Maine and Iowa caucuses and in the New Hampshire primary.

Attempts at moving the primary to March continue. By the time you read this, California may have one of the earliest primaries.

The array of laws that determine how the primaries are set up, who may enter them, and who may vote in them are made up by state legislatures and state parties. For example, several different methods of voting are used in presidential primaries. In some states, primary voters only select delegates to a party's national convention and do not know which candidates the delegates intend to vote for at the convention. In other states, the delegates' names, along with the names of the candidates they support, appear on the ballot. In still other states, the names of the candidates for the nomination and the delegates appear separately. Voters may then cast separate votes for candidates and for delegates. This is known as a **preference poll**.

Some states, Texas among them, use a form of the preference poll in which delegates are selected at a state convention. The voters then cast ballots for candidates, and the delegates must vote for the winning candidate at the national convention. This method is called the **mandatory preference poll**.

In some states, instead of presidential primaries, delegates to the convention are chosen by caucuses or conventions. Iowa, for example, holds caucuses to choose delegates to local conventions. These delegates, in turn, choose those who will attend the state and national conventions. Other states use a combination of conventions and primaries.

National Party Conventions Presidential nominating conventions have been described as giant pep rallies, or "the Fourth of July of American politics." Despite the hats, conga lines, and blaring horns and sirens, each convention's task is a serious one—to adopt the official party platform and to decide who will be the party's presidential candidate.

▶ National party conventions have been described as giant pep rallies. Despite this outward appearance, national party conventions do manage to complete some important tasks. What tasks are accomplished at the national party conventions?

For four days in late July or August, the two or three thousand delegates at the convention theoretically represent the wishes of the voters and political leaders of their home states. On the first day of the convention, delegates hear the reports of the **Credentials Committee**, which inspects each prospective delegate's claim to be seated as a legitimate representative of his or her state. (This does not mean physically seated, but rather accepted as a legitimate delegate.) When the eligibility of delegates is in question, the committee decides who shall be seated. In the evening there is usually a **keynote speaker**—someone of national importance—to whip up enthusiasm among the delegates. The second day includes committee reports and debates on the party platform. Of course, other things are happening on an unofficial agenda: Backers of certain candidates are seeking to influence uncommitted delegates and change the minds of those pledged to other candidates. Delegates from state caucuses also are meeting to discuss strategies and how they will vote.

The third day is devoted to nominations and voting. Balloting begins with an alphabetical roll call in which states and territories announce their votes. By midnight, the convention's real work is over and the presidential candidate has been selected. The vice presidential nominations and the acceptance speeches occupy the fourth day.

Conventions today are not as important in the nominating process as they once were. There is the same hoopla, extravagance, long speeches, and demonstrations, but because so many delegates are selected by primaries, we usually know who will be nominated before the convention begins. There are only a few delegates who are actually uncommitted when they arrive at the convention. Even though conventions may be less important in determining nominations, they are important in developing the party platform and in promoting political representation.

SECTION 1 REVIEW

1. Why are nominations an important part of the electoral process?
2. Briefly explain the different methods of nomination used throughout the country.
3. What is the nominating method most commonly used today and how does it work?
4. What is the process by which a candidate for president is nominated?
5. **For critical analysis:** Which nomination method do you think is most appropriate for a representative government? Explain your answer.

SECTION 2

The Campaign

Preview Questions
- How are campaigns typically organized and planned?
- What are the basic provisions of the Federal Election Campaign Act?
- What is the purpose of PACs and how do they function?

Once nominated, candidates concentrate on campaigning. The term *campaign* was not always a part of Americans' political vocabulary. It was originally a military word: Generals mounted campaigns, using their scarce resources (soldiers and materials) to achieve military objectives. In political campaigns, resources are also scarce, and have to be timed and targeted carefully.

There are many different ways to campaign. Which method a candidate uses often depends on the particular office sought and the amount of competition for that office. A candidate running for the school board may put up posters, talk to voters door-to-door, and speak at several luncheons. In contrast, for a candidate running for a higher office, a campaign becomes much more complicated, much more time consuming, and many times more expensive.

The goal of any campaign is to win the election. To accomplish this, a campaign must be organized and carefully planned, and must have sufficient funds.

Campaign Organization

The success of any campaign depends on the people who organize it. In a small local election, a campaign may be handled by a few friends, while in a national race thousands of individuals are involved. A presidential campaign, for example, may have as many as five hundred paid staff and one million volunteers.

Candidates for major offices set up campaign organizations similar to the one in Figure 10–2 on page 239. As you can see, the **campaign manager** coordinates and plans the campaign strategy, while other staff members provide leadership in specific areas such as print publicity or weekly polling. Critical to any major campaign are the volunteers, who make up the great majority of campaign workers. Volunteers handle the bulk of day-to-day work such as putting up posters, handing out pamphlets, answering phone calls, helping register voters, and seeing that voters get out on election day.

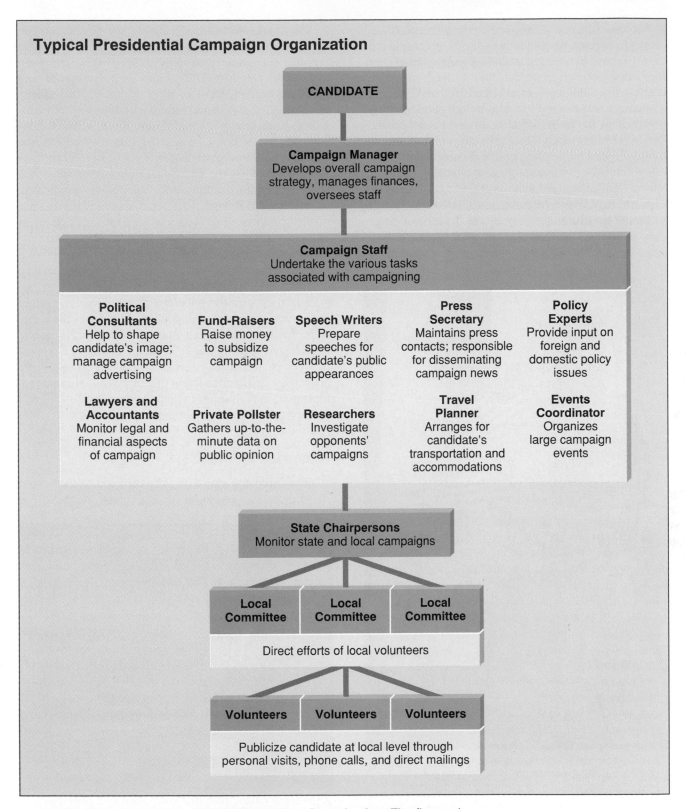

▲ FIGURE 10–2 Typical Presidential Campaign Organization. The figure above presents a look at how people involved in a presidential campaign are organized for action. What is the role of the campaign manager?

To run a successful campaign today, the candidate's organization must be able to raise funds, get media coverage, produce commercials, convey the candidate's position, hire pollsters, research the opposing candidate, schedule the candidate's time effectively, make sure the candidate's name is well known by the public, and get the voters to the polls. What is different about today's campaigns is that often these tasks are put into the hands of paid professionals called **political consultants**, rather than volunteers, political parties, or amateur politicians. Political consultants are paid large fees to devise a campaign strategy, create a campaign theme, and manage the **image building** of the candidate. Image building is using public and private polls to mold the candidate's image to meet the particular needs of the campaign.

▲ Bill Clinton made effective use of public appearances during the 1992 campaign. Who do you think is generally responsible for planning the candidate's public appearances?

Any serious candidate running for governor, state legislator, U.S. Congress or the presidency has a paid political consultant who daily suggests new campaign ideas to the candidate and decides what new advertising spots are needed. Most of these campaign consultants are not politically neutral—they will only work for candidates from one particular party. Some political consultants have become so popular that they choose the candidates they wish to handle. Two California firms—Whitaker and Baker and Spencer-Roberts—have had great success in handling only Republican candidates, such as Ronald Reagan, who decided to run for governor of California in 1965 and won against the incumbent Governor Edmond G. ''Pat'' Brown. At the national level, Democratic political consultants include Patrick Caddell, Peter Heart, and Joseph Napolitan Associates.

Some critics of professional campaign managers argue that they are only concerned with personalities rather than with issues and philosophies, but this is their job. A professional campaign manager is simply a public relations person who looks at each election as a contest between personalities rather than between two opposing principles. Critics also argue that professional campaign managers, in their quest to help their candidate win, will reshape the candidate's public image so that it bears little relation to reality.

Campaign Planning

The campaign plan is usually centered on the voters. A strategy is needed to decide many matters. For

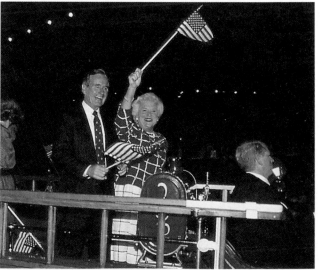

▲ In some cases, paid political consultants plan nearly every move the candidate makes. How do you think this affects the choices available to voters?

CASE STUDY

Criticisms of the Mass Media in Campaigns

GOVERNMENT IN ACTION

Originally, television and radio were seen as a democratizing force. They helped break down party machines and let candidates speak directly to the electorate.

But now another effect of television is becoming clear. "The rise of electronic media has had an effect of draining content out of campaigns," according to Arthur Schlesinger, Jr., a prominent American historian.

One of the main criticisms of current mass-media campaigns is that they reduce the personal element in American politics. Because TV and radio media allow only 30-second spots to cover most issues, the issues are often presented in shortened or oversimplified form. Complex issues such as environmental policy or military spending are reduced to mere slogans that fit the designated time frame. As a result, in-depth discussions about issues are avoided and voters may consequently not be properly informed.

Another criticism of mass-media campaigns is that they are run by campaign consultants normally located in cities not very close to where the campaigns are targeted. These consultant-run campaigns are some-times called "cookie-cutter" campaigns in which the candidates simply use computerized preformed commercials and fill in the blanks with their particular information. The problem with these campaigns is that they are removed from the lives of the people who have a stake in the community in which the candidate is running for office.

Another criticism is that the mass media have dramatically darkened the tone and content of political campaigns. Thomas Patterson, professor of political science at the Maxwell School of Government, said that in the 1960 presidential campaign, 60 percent of the coverage of the presidential candidates in *Time* and *Newsweek* was favorable. In 1988, only 30 percent was favorable. The same trend is found in newspapers and television.

THINK ABOUT IT

1. Do you think it is difficult for critics of mass-media campaigns to propose reforms? Explain your answer.
2. Do you agree or disagree with these criticisms? Explain your answer.

---

example, should the candidate wage an aggressive or a low-key campaign? What stand should the candidate take on issues such as the environment, schools, water, highways, and a variety of other problems? What theme or campaign slogan should be adopted? How much money should be spent on television, radio, or newspaper advertising?

Door-to-Door Techniques Over the years, a variety of standard campaign techniques have been developed and are included in most campaigns. Door-to-door campaigning requires that the candidate knock on voters' doors and talk with them briefly. Campaign workers also use these techniques to talk with voters. Candidates also go to factory gates or shopping centers to seek out voters and talk with them.

Mass Media and Computerized Techniques Although the traditional campaign techniques mentioned above are still widely used, one of the major developments in contemporary American politics is the rise of a new style of campaigning based mainly on reaching the voter through the use of mass media—television, radio, and newspapers. Modern campaigns also use computers and polls to constantly keep track of and use campaign information. Experts estimate that some three hundred companies currently specialize in computer services and software for political campaigns.

In order to find out what is most important to the voters, information based on opinion polls—both public and private—becomes a major part of campaign strategy. Often presidential hopefuls will have private polls taken. In the 1980 presidential campaign, for example, Jimmy

Congressional Campaign Spending, 1983–1990

	House of Representatives (amount in millions of dollars)				Senate (amount in millions of dollars)			
	1983–1984	1985–1986	1987–1988	1989–1990	1983–1984	1985–1986	1987–1988	1989–1990
Total Disbursements	203.5	239.3	256.5	265.1	170.5	211.6	201.1	180.1
Disbursements by Party:								
Democrats	111.0	128.7	145.1	150.8	82.0	89.0	107.6	87.6
Republicans	91.8	110.5	110.5	113.2	88.3	122.6	93.2	92.5
Others	.7	.1	.9	1.1	.2	(z)	.3	(z)
Disbursements by Position:								
Incumbents	114.9	132.5	156.5	163.0	72.1	89.3	101.3	113.5
Challengers	54.7	48.8	51.0	46.7	38.3	66.2	55.9	54.6
Open Seats	33.9	58.0	49.0	55.4	60.1	56.1	44.0	11.9

(z) = Less than $50,000, or .05 percent.
Source: Federal Election Commission

▲ FIGURE 10–3 Congressional Campaign Spending 1983–1990. As you can see from the figure above, campaigning for a congressional seat has become very expensive in this country. Do you think it would be more expensive to run a presidential campaign? Why?

Carter relied on polls conducted by his personal pollster, Patrick Caddell. Ronald Reagan relied on private pollster Richard Wirthlin in 1980 and 1984. By polling the potential voters in the state or nation, the candidate can find out his or her strengths and weaknesses and try to fix problem areas in his or her public image through advertising. As the election approaches, many candidates use **tracking polls**, which are polls taken almost every day, to find out how well they are competing for votes. They enable the campaign organization to fine tune the candidate's speeches and advertising in the last critical days.

Campaign Financing and Regulation

The sophisticated vote-getting techniques that candidates employ have made campaigning very expensive. Huge sums are spent for television and radio time, printing costs, advertising, travel, and office rent, to list only a few expenses. The more important the office sought, the more money is likely to be spent. It is estimated that over $2 billion was spent at all levels of government campaigning in 1988 (a presidential election year) and over $1 billion in 1990. Some candidates are able to use part of their own money to run for office, but most rely on contributions from individuals and organizations.

The connection between money and campaigns gives rise to some of the most difficult problems in American politics. The biggest fear is that contributors might be able to influence people running for office by giving large gifts or loans. There is also the possibility that some special interest groups will try to buy favored treatment from those who are elected to office. To prevent these abuses, laws have been passed to regulate campaign finances.

In the wake of the scandals uncovered by the Watergate break-in in 1972, Congress and the Supreme Court restructured campaign financing rules. Although not related to the Watergate scandal, President Richard Nixon's questionable campaign financing brought about calls for campaign reform, notably from such public interest lobbies as Common Cause and the National Committee for Effective Congress. In 1974, the House and Senate passed the Federal Election Campaign Act, which in essence did the following:

● **Established an independent agency known as the Federal Election Commission (FEC) set up by Congress in 1974 to carry out this act.** The Commission has six members, appointed by the president, subject to the approval of the Senate.

● **Provided public financing for presidential primaries and general elections.** Presidential candidates who raise some money on their own in at least twenty states can get a check from the U.S. Treasury to help pay for primary campaigns. For the general election campaign, presidential candidates get federal funding for almost all expenses *if* they are willing to accept campaign spending limits.

● **Limited presidential campaign spending.** Any candidate accepting federal support must agree to limit expenditures to amounts set by federal law.

● **Required disclosure.** Candidates must file periodic reports with the FEC that list who contributed to the campaign and how the money was spent.

● **Limited contributions.** Citizens can contribute up to $1,000 to each candidate in each federal election or primary. The total limit for any individual in one year is $25,000. Groups can contribute a maximum of $5,000 to a candidate in any election.

The Growth of PACs

The 1974 reforms and their subsequent amendments encouraged a new way of contributing to campaigns by allowing corporations, labor unions, and special interest groups to set up political action committees (PACs) to raise money for candidates.

Top 15 PAC Contributions to Congressional Candidates (January 1, 1989–June 30, 1990)

Group	Amount in millions
Democratic-Republican Independent Voter Education Committee (International Brotherhood of Teamsters)	$6.4
American Medical Association	3.0
National Association of Realtors	2.7
National Congressional Club (Senator Jesse Helms' political organization)	2.6
American Federation of State, County, and Municipal Employees	2.4
Voter Guide (bipartisan California group)	2.3
American Telephone and Telegraph Company, Inc.	2.3
Association of Trial Lawyers of America	2.3
United Automobile Workers	2.0
Committee on Letter Carriers Political Education	1.9
National Rifle Association Political Victory Fund	1.8
American Citizens for Political Action (a conservative fund-raising committee)	1.7
National Education Association	1.7
Machinists Nonpartisan Political League	1.6
C.W.A.-COPE Political Contributions Committee (Communications Workers of America)	1.5

Source: Federal Election Commission

▲ |FIGURE 10–4 **Top 15 PAC Contributions to Congressional Candidates (January 1, 1989–June 30, 1990).** The above figure lists the 15 political action committees that made the largest contributions to congressional campaigns over an 18-month period ending in 1990. What was the total contribution of all 15 of these PACs during that period?

This is how a PAC works. A union, corporation, or interest group decides to channel some of its money into the political campaign of a candidate who supports their goals. They create a PAC by registering with the FEC. The PAC can then collect money from executives, employees, stockholders, or members to donate to the campaign of their choosing. No PAC may give more than $5,000 to each candidate for each election, but there is no overall limit on PAC giving. Each may contribute up to $5,000 to as many different candidates as it chooses. There are over 4,600 PACs and they are estimated to have put more than $380 million into the presidential and congressional campaigns of 1992. They also spend money to defeat candidates whose positions they oppose.

PACs are not limited to making campaign contributions. They may conduct their own campaigns for presidential and congressional candidates. They also spend hundreds of thousands of dollars for television commercials and other independent efforts to praise or attack candidates they support or oppose. They may spend as much money as they choose, providing the candidates themselves don't control how the money is spent. A sample of what PACs spent in a recent year is shown in Figure 10–4 on page 243.

Campaign Spending   Most of the spending limits imposed by the current laws apply only to presidential campaigns. Presidential candidates campaigning for office can choose whether or not to accept federal funding. If they do not accept, they must then raise all campaign monies on their own, and can spend as much as they choose. If they do accept, they are limited in the amount they may spend. In 1988, for example, no candidate could spend more than $23.05 million in the preconvention period. After the conventions, presidential candidates Dukakis and Bush could spend $46.1 million each on their campaigns.

Public funding of presidential campaigns was provided for in the Revenue Act of 1971, which set up the Presidential Election Campaign Fund. Under this act, persons who file a federal income tax return may request that $1 of their tax payment go to the fund. The monies in the fund are to be used to pay for preconvention campaigns, national conventions, and presidential election campaigns. Presidential hopefuls must raise at least $100,000 in contributions from individuals in order to receive money from the fund. It must be gathered in $5,000 lots, from each of at least twenty states, with each lot built from individual donations of not more than $250. The FEC will then match qualifying contenders the first $250 of each individual's donation up to a total of half

of the overall limit. This requirement is meant to discourage candidates who are not seriously committed to campaigning.

Upon applying, both major parties automatically receive a grant to pay for their national convention. This has been true for every convention since 1976. In 1988, both parties received $9.22 million each from the FEC. Every presidential nominee from a major party automatically qualifies for a public subsidy to cover some of the costs of the general election campaign. In 1988, the Bush and Dukakis campaigns each received $46.1 million from the FEC. A third-party candidate qualifies only if he or she received more than 5 percent of the popular vote in the previous presidential election or 5 percent in the current election.

Candidates for the Senate and House of Representatives receive no public funding for their campaigns. They must raise money from private individuals and organizations. There are no ceilings on how much they may spend.

SECTION 2 REVIEW _____

1. Describe how a typical campaign is structured.
2. What are some techniques used in campaigning?
3. What are the provisions of the Federal Election Campaign Act?
4. How do PACs function and what is their purpose?
5. **For critical analysis:** The Revenue Act of 1971 allows individuals to earmark $1 of their tax payment for presidential election campaigning. This doesn't seem like much, so why would a person choose not to check the $1 box on his or her income tax returns?

SECTION 3

The Structure of American Elections

Preview Questions
● What are the various types of elections in the United States and how do they differ?
● What is a ballot and what forms does it take?
● How does the electoral college system work?

There finally comes the time when the last debate is debated, the last poll is reported, and the last television reporter has commented: It is time for the elections. Democratic government cannot succeed unless elections are free, honest, and accurate. Because most of the elective offices in the United States are at the state and local level, most of the election law in the United States is state law. The Constitution grants the power to fix "the times, places, and manner of holding elections" to the state legislatures, but the Constitution gives Congress the power to alter such regulations. Congress has required the use of secret ballots and has passed several laws to protect the right to vote for certain groups of people. Congress also has the power to regulate certain aspects of the presidential election process, to forbid certain corrupt practices, and to regulate campaign finances.

Kinds of Elections

Two important kinds of elections in the United States are general elections and special elections.

General Election   The most familiar kind of election is the **general election**, a regularly scheduled election at which voters cast their final votes for selection of public officeholders. General elections are held in even-numbered years on the first Tuesday after the first Monday in November for the president, the vice president, and senators and representatives of Congress. The president and vice president are elected every four years, senators every six years, and representatives every two years. General elections are also held to choose state and local government leaders, often at the same time as those for national offices. The fact that American elections are held at these fixed intervals—every two or four years, for example—may seem too obvious to mention, but it is not that way in most democracies. In parliamentary systems, elections may be called irregularly. In Great Britain, for example, elections must be called every five years, but may be called earlier if the majority party thinks it can boost its control of Parliament or if the government loses the support of its parliamentary coalition.

Special Elections   A **special election** is held whenever an issue must be decided before the next general election. For example, an important city official might resign or die before the end of his or her term. The city may decide to hold a special election to fill the vacancy.

In each of these kinds of elections, voters elect both federal and state office holders. In many states voters also participate in direct lawmaking through the initia-

tive, referendum, and recall processes described on page 540.

Polling Places

State law divides local units of government into smaller voting districts, or precincts. State law usually restricts the size of precincts and local officials set the boundaries. Within each precinct, voters cast their ballots at one *polling place.*

A precinct election board supervises the polling place and the voting process in each precinct. It sets hours for the polls to be open according to the laws of the state and sees that ballots or voting machines are available. In most states it provides the list of registered voters and makes certain that only qualified voters cast ballots in that precinct. When the polls close, the board counts the votes and reports the results, usually to the county clerk or board of elections.

Representatives from each party, called poll watchers, are allowed at each polling place to make sure the election is run fairly.

▼ Voters in Santa Cruz, California can cast their votes in this bakery that serves as a polling place for each election. Name some other possible polling places.

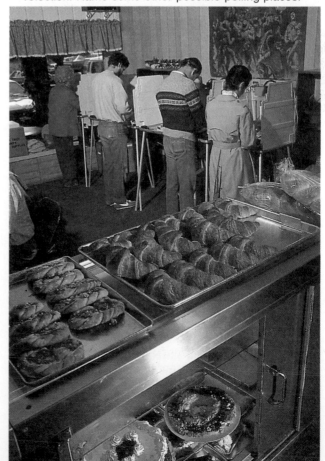

Ballots

In the early days of our country, voters gathered in a central place and called out their vote. They could be applauded or booed as they voiced their preferences. Of course, with this method of voting, people were unduly influenced by others and many people wanted the system changed. By the mid-1800s, political parties passed out paper ballots to voters. The ballots were different colors to symbolize different parties, and the ballot box was in public view; thus, anyone watching still knew who voted for whom.

Because voters were still subject to vote-buying and political pressure, many local and state governments came under the control of **political machines**, highly organized party organizations that were very powerful in many large cities in the nineteenth and early twentieth centuries. These political machines won elections by giving government favors—well-paying public jobs or public construction contracts—instead of competing fairly. They put their own interests before the interests of the public.

Australian Ballot The balloting system was improved in 1888 when a new method of voting was introduced from Australia. The **Australian ballot** had four main features: (1) it was printed by election officials at public expense; (2) it listed the names of all candidates in an election; (3) it was distributed only at the polling places to qualified voters; and (4) the actual voting was done in secret. There are two variations of the Australian ballot used in the United States today.

- **Office-group ballot.** With the **office-group ballot**, all candidates for each office are listed together. For example, all candidates for state senator are listed under that heading along with their party affiliation. Initially it was common for the names to appear in alphabetical order. Today, in most states, the names are now rotated, so that each candidate has a chance to be listed first. Sometimes this ballot is called the *Massachusetts ballot,* because that state first used it in general elections in 1888.
- **Party-column ballot.** The **party-column ballot** lists candidates under their party label. For example, the Republican candidates for senator, representative, governor, state legislator, and local office are listed under the Republican column. There is often a place at the top of the ballot where a voter, with one mark, can vote for all of one party's candidates. This encourages ''straight-

party'' voting, especially if the party has a strong candidate at the head of the ticket. This style is losing favor because differences between the two parties seem to be less apparent, and voters' identification with party labels appears to be weakening.

Length of Ballots Besides selecting many public officials, voters must often vote on a number of local and statewide issues as well. Because all of these choices must be listed on the ballot, the ballot is typically lengthy, and has been called the ''bedsheet ballot.'' Many people criticize such ballots today because they believe they are too long. In 1990, for example, the California ballot had over eight pages. Critics feel it is almost impossible to make intelligent and informed decisions on so many candidates and issues and complain of ''ballot fatigue.'' They argue that the smaller the number of elected officials on a ballot, the better chance there is that voters will know the candidates' qualifications.

Others argue that the greater the number of officials elected to office, the more democratic the system. They argue that the public has the right to get as involved as it can in government decision making.

Voting Machines

Thomas Edison took out the first patent for a voting machine in 1868, and his invention was initially used in an election in Lockport, New York, in 1892. Now, over half of all voters in the United States cast ballots on voting machines, which have steadily replaced paper ballots.

Voting machines differ in some details, but all work in much the same way. By pulling a large lever, the voter encloses himself or herself within a curtain. The ballot appears on the face of a machine and voters make choices by pulling down the small levers over the names of the candidates they choose. The machine is programmed so that voters can cast only one vote per contest. Once all the levers are in the desired positions, the voter opens the curtain. This action records the votes and clears the machine for the next voter.

Many election districts use computerized voting machines. The voter marks a square or punches a hole on a card and the computer reads the card, then totals the votes for each candidate and prints out the results. Voting machines speed up the voting process by doing away with the need for manual counting. They reduce the number of persons needed to administer elections and increase the amount of voters that can be handled per precinct. They can also minimize fraud and counting errors.

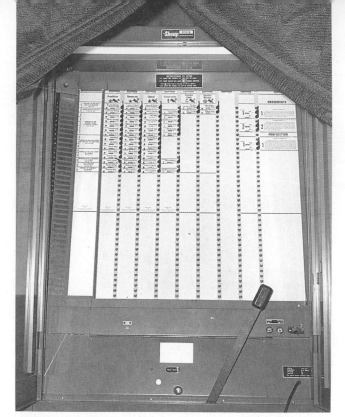

This voting machine was first used in the 1964 presidential elections in New York City. What do you think are the advantages of using voting machines in elections?

Electing the President

It is true that *nominating* the presidential and vice presidential candidates is different from nominating officials for any other office. The same is true of *electing* the president and vice president: It is a complex system with its own set of rules.

The Electoral College System   The writers of the Constitution argued long and hard about the method of electing the president. Many did not want the president to be directly elected by the people because they did not trust the average person's judgment, and feared that citizens scattered all across the new country would have a hard time learning enough about the candidates to make a wise choice. At that time there were, after all, problems with time lapses in communication and transportation. They wanted the president to be elected by the nation's elite (a small group of wealthy, powerful, and hopefully reasonable leaders), and not by the people directly, so they provided for presidential *electors*. The result was the **electoral college system**, in which direct votes by the citizens do not actually elect the president.

Fortunately, over time, political practice has made the electoral vote more responsive to popular majorities. In the early days electors could vote any way they chose,

but today virtually all electors vote for the candidate who got the most votes in their state; some states have even made it illegal for electors not to vote this way. These changes have helped democratize the electoral system. (The electoral vote could, however, be won by the candidate receiving fewer popular votes but the majority of electoral votes.)

The Electoral College System Today   The first step in the electoral college process is the general election in which all registered voters may vote for the president and vice president. This is called a **popular vote**, or the vote of the people.

Most voters today believe that they actually vote directly for a president or vice president, when in fact they are choosing a slate of **electors**, people who will cast the official votes for them. These electors are chosen by the states' political parties, subject to the laws of the state. Each state has as many electoral votes as it has United States senators and representatives. In addition, there are three electors from the District of Columbia.

The electoral college system is a **winner-take-all system**, in which the candidate who receives the largest

The popular vote, which is open to all registered voters, is only one step in electing a president and vice president. Who actually casts the votes that decide presidential elections?

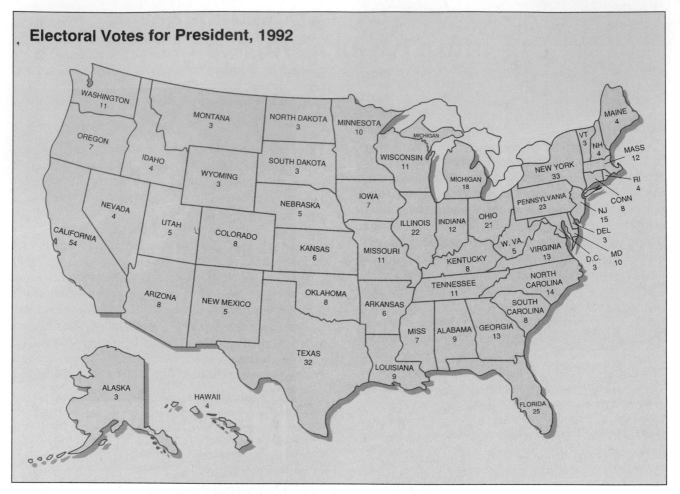

Electoral Votes for President, 1992

▲ FIGURE 10–5 **Electoral Votes for President, 1992.** Each state has the same number of electors as it has United States senators and representatives. Why did the founders of our country choose to use the electoral college system for electing the president?

popular vote in a state is credited with *all* that state's electoral votes—one vote per elector. This is true no matter what the margin of victory.

In December, after the general election, members of the electoral college meet in their state capitals to cast their votes for president and vice president. Although they are not legally bound to do so by Article 1, Section 2 of the Constitution, the electors usually vote for the candidate who won popular support in their state. In 1976, an elector from Seattle, Washington, voted for Ronald Reagan even though Gerald Ford had won the majority of popular votes in that state. It has only been on rare occasions that an elector breaks a pledge to vote for the party's nominee. It has never affected the outcome of an election.

The votes are sealed and then sent to the Senate. The ballots are counted and certified before a joint session of Congress early in January. The candidates who receive a majority of the electoral votes are officially declared president and vice president.

To be elected, a candidate must receive more than half of the 538 electoral votes available.[2] This means that a candidate needs 270 votes to win. If no candidate gets an electoral college majority, the House of Representatives votes on the candidates, with each state delegation casting only a single vote. (This has happened twice—in 1800 and in 1824.)

The winner-take-all system makes it possible for a candidate to be elected who lost the total popular vote

---

2. The number of electoral votes equals the total number of senators and representatives (535) plus three votes for the residents of Washington, D.C. Please see Amendment XXIII on page 671.

but won the electoral vote. This has happened twice—in the elections of Rutherford B. Hayes in 1876 and Benjamin Harrison in 1888. Critics of the electoral college point out that this could happen again. In 1960, John F. Kennedy, a Democrat, defeated Richard Nixon, a Republican. If only nine thousand people in Illinois and Missouri had voted for Nixon instead of Kennedy, Nixon would have won the electoral college votes in those two states. As a result, Nixon would have won the election while still losing the popular vote by a narrow margin.

The electoral system has been criticized by many as being out of date and undemocratic. Over the years, more than five hundred amendments calling for changes in the electoral system have been brought before Congress. Proposals have ranged from modifying it to throwing it out completely and electing the president by direct popular vote. All amendments on the subject have failed.

SECTION 3 REVIEW

1. How would you classify the various types of elections in the United States?
2. How does state law divide local government for election purposes?
3. What is an Australian ballot? What are the different types of Australian ballots?
4. How does the electoral college system work to elect the president?
5. **For critical analysis:** Should the electoral vote for president be replaced by a direct popular vote? Explain why or why not.

SECTION 4

The Role of the Media in Campaigns and Elections

Preview Questions
- What types of television coverage are used by candidates during campaigns?
- What is negative campaign advertising?
- What is propaganda and what are some propaganda techniques?

The media, especially television, have had a wide-ranging effect on politics in general. Their most immediate and obvious impact, however, is during campaigns and elections. Years ago, the biggest expense in a campaign budget might have been the campaign train

rental. Today, the biggest expense is unquestionably television advertising, which consumes about half of the total budget for a major campaign.

The Candidates and Television

Candidates use several types of television coverage in campaigns: debates, political advertising and news coverage.

Debates The first great television debate was in 1960 between Republican presidential candidate Richard M. Nixon and the youthful Democratic Senator John F. Kennedy from Massachusetts. Too rushed to shave before the debates, Nixon used a cosmetic product called "Lazy Shave" to hide his five o'clock shadow. As a result he looked unshaven and drawn in contrast to Kennedy's fresh appearance. In the debate itself, Nixon answered questions like the college debater he once was, while Kennedy aimed his remarks directly at the television audience. Many believe the debate turned the tide in Kennedy's favor and established the importance of good television appearance for a presidential candidate.

Since that first debate, many others have helped influence the outcome of elections. Television debates are a unique opportunity for voters to find out how candidates differ on issues, but they are also a way for candidates to capitalize on the power of television to project a positive image. They view television debates as a chance to

▼ The presidential debate between candidates Richard Nixon and John F. Kennedy, which was held in 1960, was the first great television debate. Why was this debate so important?

BUILDING SOCIAL STUDIES SKILLS
Evaluating Political Commercials

Most candidates now spend large amounts of money on television commercials. In fact, as the figure on the next page illustrates, the amount spent on political advertising rises significantly with every election year.

Television commercials do provide exposure for and information about candidates and their issues. They also provide an opportunity for candidates to speak directly to the electorate.

Many people, however, feel that the growing use of television advertising is also draining out the content of campaigns. The issues are often presented in a shortened or overstated form. As with printed ads, TV ads reduce complex issues such as balancing the federal budget, military policy, or cleaning up the environment to mere slogans. Commercials use emotional appeal, rather than facts, to persuade voters. There is also a trend toward more negative advertising, which may involve blaming other candidates for current social problems or attacking their personal lives.

Remember that political commercials, like any other commercial, are trying to sell you a product or service. In this case the "product" is a political candidate. Knowing how to evaluate television ads during an election campaign will help you learn to evaluate political candidates and issues. Start by asking yourself:

● **Which individual or group paid for the commercial?** All political advertising is required by law to identify who paid for it. Think about why the ad's sponsor is interested in electing the candidate.

● **What forms of communication are used?** Is the message conveyed through urgent music, shocking pictures, soft images, popular symbols? What is the narrator's tone of voice? What's the story line? Recognizing these elements of an ad will tell you how it is trying to make you feel.

● **Does the ad present facts or does it appeal directly to your emotions?**

● **Is the ad about the candidate being advertised, or does it only attack her or his opponent?** Does it blame another candidate for current problems? Is it negative or positive advertising?

● **Does the ad deal with issues that are appropriate to the office?** For example, a candidate for governor might take a stand on military spending. (Military spending is normally a question for the federal level and not the state level, and therefore has no real bearing on that race.)

● **Does the ad tell you anything substantial about the candidate or does it only seek to boost her or his image?** Look at the propaganda techniques listed on page 255 and 256 to find out if any are used.

Regardless of their strengths or weaknesses, it seems that political candidates, like laundry detergent and soft drinks, are destined to be sold through television commercials. As voters, it is up to each of us to sift through the advertising hype and make sound judgments regarding each candidate's qualifications and abilities.

---

improve their own image, or a chance to point out the failings of their opponent. The post-debate commentaries by news analysts also play a crucial role in what the public thinks, even when the commentaries are biased.

Political Advertising The first political commercials appeared on television in the 1952 presidential campaign, along with the first televising of party conventions. In the United States there were only about 15 million television sets at that time, a total that climbed to about 54 million in 1960, 93 million in 1970, and well over 100 million today.

Making a political commercial is just like any other type of advertising. The ad writers have thirty or sixty seconds to communicate a message that viewers will remember. Usually she or he will center the ad around the most positive personality traits of a candidate.

The phenomenon of **negative campaign advertising**, however, has somewhat changed these methods. One of the most negative campaign announcements

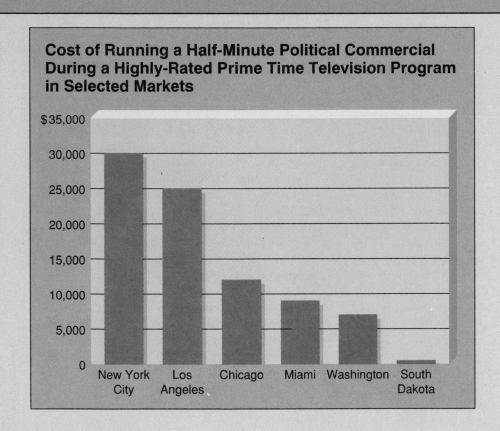

Cost of Running a Half-Minute Political Commercial During a Highly-Rated Prime Time Television Program in Selected Markets

PRACTICING YOUR SKILLS

1. Use the questions on page 250 to evaluate a political commercial on local television. If there is no current election, see if you can view footage of previous campaign ads at a local television station. If this is not possible, look at campaign ads in old editions of your local or national newspapers. Then evaluate the ads according to the guidelines presented.

2. Do you think negative advertising about a political opponent is fair? Find examples of what you feel is negative advertising to support your position. Present the ad and your opinions to the class.

appeared in President Lyndon Johnson's campaign against Barry Goldwater in 1964. In this ad, a little girl stood quietly in a field of daisies. She held a daisy and pulled off the petals, counting to herself. Suddenly, when she reached the last petal, a deep voice was heard counting, "10, 9, 8, 7, 6 . . ." When it hit zero, the unmistakable mushroom cloud of an atom bomb filled the screen. Then President Johnson's voice was heard saying, "These are the stakes: To make a world in which all of God's children can live, or to go into the dark. We must either love each other or we must die." A message then read: "Vote for President Johnson on November 3." The implication, of course, was that Goldwater would lead the country into a nuclear war. Even though the ad was removed within a few days, it remains a classic example of negative advertising.

Every election year since then has been marked by some amount of negative advertising. In 1988 a negative ad produced for the Bush campaign mentioned Michael Dukakis' support for granting Massachusetts prisoners

CITIZENSHIP SKILLS AND RESPONSIBILITIES

Talking Back to Your Television

Several groups have been successful in influencing local TV programming when they believed their local television station was not living up to its public service obligations as a free user of public air waves. Concerned citizens have objected to various problems, such as a station's hiring practices, its programming, and the percentage of time given to news and public affairs. If you want to find out about your local station's policies, go to the station's headquarters and ask to see its public file.

The public file that stations must keep available to citizens includes applications filed with the FCC, data on station ownership, employment practices, an FCC manual entitled "The Public and Broadcasting—a Procedure Manual" (if the station is commercial), letters from the audience, and a list of the ten problems needing service in that community and how the station's programming meets those needs.

There are a number of citizen-action organizations that attempt to monitor or influence television programming in various ways. If you are concerned or interested in the quality or content of what is being broadcast today, some of the following organizations might be helpful to you:

- **Accuracy in Media (AIM)** (1275 K St. NW, Washington, DC 20005) is a nonprofit educational organization dedicated to fighting what it considers distorted news reporting by the major media.

- **Action for Children's Television (ACT)** (46 Austin St., Newtonville, MA 02160) is an organization dedicated to making networks more responsive to the views of teachers and parents who are concerned with the quality of children's television programming.
- **Media Access Project** (1609 Connecticut Ave. NW, Washington, DC 20009) is a public interest law firm that represents individuals and groups trying to increase public access to the mass media. They have represented minorities, environmentalists, and consumers.
- **National Black Media Coalition** (38 New York Ave. NE, Washington, DC 20002) is made up of over seventy African-American organizations that are dedicated to eliminating racism from broadcasting.
- **National Organization for Women (NOW)** (1776 K St. NW, Washington, DC 20006). NOW's *Media Project* gives assistance to those working to promote both employment and positive images of women in broadcasting.

TAKING ACTION

1. Contact one of the above organizations and find out more about their activities. Report back to the class on what you discover.
2. Think of one way in which you could influence a local media source. Write out the steps you would use to do so.

---

brief working leaves from prison, or furloughs, while he was governor of that state. It showed a picture of a revolving door with men in striped uniforms leaving a prison gate and then cut to a picture of Willie Horton, a convicted murderer who was released on furlough and committed yet another killing while he was on official leave from the penitentiary. The ad was meant to give the impression that Dukakis was soft on crime.

The practice of negative advertising became widespread in recent campaigns, and is expected to continue. Its effectiveness is the main reason for its continued growth. Research seems to indicate that negative com-

mercials can at least temporarily create large swings in public opinion.

Critics, many of whom are politicians themselves, have stepped forth with suggestions to curtail such methods. At least five bills have been introduced in the Senate, the most far reaching of which would outlaw political commercials that refer to a candidate's opponent unless the sponsoring candidate appears personally in the ad. The measure would also require radio and television stations to offer free time for candidates to respond to ads sponsored by independent political committees— groups not affiliated with a particular candidate but that

▶ Campaigns and candidates are natural targets for media attention. How do candidates and their campaign staffs work to make the most of this attention?

try to influence the outcome of elections. (No political advertisement may contain false material, however. Laws against defamation preclude this.)

News Coverage   Candidates try to manipulate their images though advertising, but they have less control over the other face of media—the news. To take advantage of the media's interest in campaigns, whether at the presidential or congressional levels, the campaign staff tries to influence the quantity and type of coverage. Besides becoming aware of how camera angles and timing affect a candidate's appearance, the staff learns to plan its political events to accommodate the press. The staff attempts to make what its candidate is doing appear photogenic and interesting. It also knows that journalists and political reporters compete for stories, and that they can be manipulated through granting favors such as an exclusive personal interview with a candidate.

The Impact of Television

Many voters receive much of their information about politics by watching the TV news. For this reason, television has had an impact on the way people see the candidates, understand the issues, and cast their votes. Research indicates that, in general, roughly one-third of all voters decide whom to vote for before the conventions, another third during the conventions, and a final third during the fall campaign. Because television is the major information source on both conventions and campaigns, it probably plays an important role in these voting decisions, even though voters rarely attribute such influence to television itself.

Critics argue that television has made the issues seem unimportant because it focuses on the candidates' personalities and their exciting activities. They argue that in order to capture viewers, television tries to reduce campaign and election stories to thirty-second ''soundbytes'' that catch viewers' attention, but give little or no relevant information.

▼ As a former actor, Ronald Reagan was especially at home in front of the camera and has been called the television president. Why are some observers critical of television's role in modern campaigns?

GOVERNMENT IN ACTION

PROFILE

Connie Chung

The media in America have changed dramatically in terms of the ethnic, racial, and gender makeup of their participants over the last century. Connie Chung represents a prime example of this change.

Connie Chung was born on August 20, 1946 in Washington, D.C. She was the youngest child of William Ling and Margaret Chung. Of the nine other children born to her parents, five died in China during World War II. In 1944 the Ling-Chungs moved to America. Connie grew up around Washington, D.C. While in college she was a copy clerk with a television station in Washington, D.C. When she graduated in 1969 she worked as a secretary at the same television station (WTTG).

She quickly became an on-the-air reporter covering everything from anti-war demonstrations to congressional activity on Capitol Hill, to murders and airplane disasters. She went on to work at CBS's Washington bureau, continuing to take on just about any assignment.

By 1976 Ms. Chung was living in Los Angeles and working as anchorperson for the local CBS station. She appeared three times a day and boosted that station's ratings so much that in less than seven years her salary jumped from $27,000 a year to $600,000.

Her next job was with NBC where she did everything from early morning news broadcasts to co-writing and hosting prime-time documentaries. She won a host of honors and awards from her peers and from outside of the industry.

Chung has kept her interest in politics keen through all of these years. In 1988, for example, she covered the presidential elections from their primaries on. She did exit-poll analysis of many primary elections and she acted as a floor correspondent during the national nominating conventions.

In 1989 she left NBC to go back to CBS where she frequently substitutes as news anchor for Dan Rather.

THINK ABOUT IT _____

1. What motivates a television journalist to switch networks?
2. How do you think Connie Chung prepared for becoming a television journalist?

Television also dictates how a campaign is run. Almost every decision that consultants make about a candidate's activities—where to eat dinner, what to wear, and what to say about the Middle East—is calculated according to its potential media impact. Many observers see this as a new era of politics in which the slick slogan and smooth image will dominate.

Overall, television has created a new kind of political candidate—one who must be at ease with the camera. These days, no candidate can ignore this important part of campaigning. As Democratic candidate Walter Mondale commented after he lost the 1984 presidential election, "I never warmed up to television and television never warmed up to me."

▶ There are many forms of propaganda used by candidates. One form of propaganda involves getting well-known people to publicly support the candidate. Here film star Arnold Schwartzenegger lends his support to George Bush. Why might this technique be effective with some voters?

News organizations, according to the critics, believe that policy issues are of less interest to voters than the campaign game itself. The result is that news coverage is disproportionately devoted to campaign strategies, guesses about who is ahead, and poll results, rather than substantive information about the issues.

Remember that even if the evening news is not the best source of facts, good sources do exist. Public television, special network programs, magazines, and newspapers all provide more complete, in-depth coverage, so one should supplement one's television watching with these other sources. It may take more work to seek out good information, but if being an informed citizen is important, it is worth the effort.

Recognizing Propaganda Techniques

A message that is meant to influence people's ideas, opinions, or actions in a certain way is called **propaganda**. The word *propaganda* usually has a negative meaning and is associated with using lies or false information. But propaganda itself can be either positive or negative: Although it can include lies, it can also contain truthful (or mostly truthful) information. A message is called propaganda when it tells only one side of the story, distorts the truth, or appeals mostly to people's emotions. Even commercial advertising is a type of propaganda.

Sometimes political candidates and PACs make use of different kinds of propaganda. Seven of the most common propaganda techniques are discussed below. When you read or listen to political messages, ask yourself if these techniques are being used.

1. **Glittering generalities   Glittering generalities** is the technique of using vague words or ideas that sound exciting but do not really say much. The words or ideas usually stand for something that everyone believes, but have no specific meaning. For example, a candidate might say, "I stand for freedom and a strong America." Almost every American agrees with such a statement, but it says nothing about the candidate or what he or she will do if elected.

2. **Card stacking   Card stacking** is using only those facts that support a candidate's argument, while ignoring any other aspects. For example, a candidate may state that her opponent voted against raising

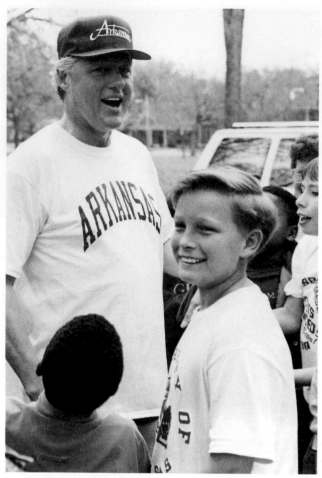

▲ Another propaganda technique is called the "plain folks" technique. How does this photograph illustrate this technique in action?

just like them. For example, candidates might have their picture taken eating a hot dog, or playing softball with children, or meeting with working citizens outside a factory or supermarket. She or he might stress her or his modest beginnings, growing up in a poor family, and so on.

6. **Bandwagon effect** The **bandwagon effect** is a method of convincing people that everyone else is joining the movement, so they should too. This method plays on the voters' fears that they are being left out of something. Thus announcing a public opinion poll that shows a candidate is ahead may be enough to convince undecided voters that this candidate will be a winner, and that they should "hop on the bandwagon."

7. **Transfer** **Transfer** is associating a person with a respected person, group, or symbol. For example, a candidate might say, "I have always said, just as Abraham Lincoln always believed, that . . ." A candidate might make a commercial of himself or herself standing before a plane with troops returning from the Persian Gulf War in 1991 and greeting the soldiers' families. The events in the background probably have nothing to do with the candidate but the setting gives the impression that they do.

Recognizing these seven propaganda techniques is just one of the tasks you must accomplish to make wise voter decisions. You must also recognize the strategies behind political advertising and the limitations of television news coverage. Wading through the flood of information both from the media and from candidates can be a tiresome chore. It is the responsibility of each of us to vote and make the best possible choices when we vote.

Social Security benefits without mentioning that he did so because the proposed increase was too small.

3. **Testimonials** Using **testimonials** involves getting a well-known person, such as a prominent government official or famous entertainer, to endorse (publicly support) a candidate or issue. People admire the endorser and therefore accept his or her judgment about the person or issue being endorsed.

4. **Name calling** **Name calling** refers to giving people or things a bad label so that they will be rejected or disliked. For example, a candidate might call his opponent a "radical," "un-American," or "liberal."

5. **Plain folks** **Plain folks** is a technique involving a candidate going out of her or his way to convince voters that she or he is an average American citizen

SECTION 4 REVIEW _____

1. What types of television coverage do candidates use during campaigns?
2. What is negative campaign advertising?
3. Define three of the seven propaganda techniques and explain how each is used.
4. **For critical analysis:** In your opinion, which propaganda techniques, if any, are more acceptable than others in political campaigns? Give reasons for your answer.

CHALLENGE TO THE AMERICAN DREAM

The Overwhelming Importance of Campaign Money

THE VOTE THAT REALLY COUNTS

By permission of Bill Mauldin and Wil-Jo Associates.

The former Speaker of the House of Representatives, Thomas P. (Tip) O'Neill once said, "There are four parts to any campaign: The candidate, the issues, ... the campaign organization, and the money. Without money you can forget the other three."

Money leads to a dilemma in politics. Many people feel that individuals and groups should be allowed to buy as much media time as they want and can afford in order to express their points of view. They argue that buying media time is just another form of constitutionally protected freedom of speech. Many people also believe that individuals and groups should be allowed to provide as much money as they want to their favorite candidates.

Other people are very uneasy when they see those with great wealth buying political media time. They believe money threatens our democratic ideal of political equality, which tells us that government should represent us all, poor and rich. Thus everyone should have equal access to government.

The public, members of Congress, and presidents have all expressed concern with the campaign finance system and the rising costs of campaigns. Several proposals for reforming the system have been offered, including complete government funding for campaigns and allowing each candidate a fixed amount of free media time.

The challenge to the American dream is finding a way to allow candidates their constitutionally guaranteed freedom of speech while preventing our representative government from representing only monied interests that can contribute heavily to election campaigns.

 ## You Decide

1. Do you think that groups and individuals should be allowed to contribute as much money as they want to whichever candidates they choose? Explain why or why not.
2. Do you feel that our political system might deter good candidates from running for office? Explain.

CHAPTER 10 REVIEW

Key Terms

Australian ballot 246
ballot 233
bandwagon effect 256
blanket primary 236
campaign manager 238
card stacking 255
caucuses 234
closed primary 235
Credentials
   Committee 238
delegates 234
direct primary 235
electoral college 247

electors 247
general election 245
glittering
   generalities 255
image building 240
keynote speaker 238
mandatory preference
   poll 237
name calling 256
negative campaign
   advertising 250
nominating
   convention 234

nomination 233
nonpartisan
   elections 236
office-group ballot 246
open primary 235
party-column
   ballot 246
petition 233
plain folks 256
plurality 236
political
   consultants 240
political machines 246

popular vote 247
preference poll 237
propaganda 255
runoff election 236
self-nomination 233
special election 245
testimonials 256
tracking polls 242
transfer 256
winner-take-all-
   system 247
write-in candidate 234

CHAPTER 10 REVIEW—Continued

Summary

1. The first step in the election process is the nomination, that is the naming or choosing of the candidates from each party who will seek office. The methods of nomination used in American politics are (1) self-nomination and petition, (2) party caucus, (3) nominating convention, and (4) direct primary. In a closed direct primary, only party members can vote to choose that party's candidates, and they may vote only in the primary of their own party. In an open direct primary voters can vote in either party primary without disclosing their party affiliation. Runoff primaries are used in states in which a candidate must receive a majority of votes. Nonpartisan primaries are used to nominate candidates for nonpartisan offices. About three-fifths of the states hold presidential primaries to choose delegates to attend the national convention, where presidential candidates are actually nominated.

2. Election campaigns must be well organized and well planned. The campaign manager coordinates and plans the campaign strategy. Some candidates hire political consultants, who are paid professionals, to devise campaign strategies and work on the candidate's public image. Campaigns have become very expensive and the connection between money and campaigns has created difficult problems in American politics. The Federal Election Campaign Act of 1974 established the Federal Election Commission (F.E.C.), provided for public financing for presidential primaries and general elections, limited presidential campaign spending, required disclosure of finances, and limited contributions. Political Action Committees (PACs) may be organized to help finance political campaigns.

3. Because most elective offices in the United States are on the state and local levels, most election laws are state laws. A general election is a regularly scheduled election at which voters cast their final votes for public officeholders. General elections are held in the even-numbered years on the first Tuesday after the first Monday in November. State law divides local units of government into precincts, within each of which voters cast their ballots at one polling place. In 1888 the Australian ballot was introduced in the United States, which had four main features: (1) it was printed by election officials at public expense; (2) it listed the names of all candidates in an election; (3) it was passed out only at the polling places to qualified voters; and (4) the actual voting was done in secret. In an office-group ballot, all candidates are listed together, regardless of party affiliation. In a party-column ballot, candidates are listed under their party label. Over half of all voters cast ballots on voting machines. In the United States, the electoral college, not the popular vote, determines our next president.

4. The media, especially television, have had a wide-ranging effect on politics in general, especially on campaigns and elections. Candidates use several types of television coverage during campaigns: debates, political advertising, and news coverage. The use of negative advertising is becoming more widespread. Television has had an impact on the way people see the candidates, understand the issues, and cast their votes. Propaganda is a message meant to influence people's ideas, opinions, or actions in certain ways.

Review Questions

1. What is the purpose of the nominating process?
2. Describe the methods by which candidates can be nominated.
3. What is a direct primary? How does a closed primary differ from an open primary?
4. What other types of primaries are there?
5. What is the purpose of national party conventions?
6. Why is the organization and planning of a campaign important?
7. How has Congress tried to regulate campaign finances?
8. Explain the purpose of PACs.
9. What is a general election?
10. What are the other types of elections in the United States and what are they called?
11. What is an Australian ballot and what forms does it take?
12. How did the electoral college system develop and how does it work today?
13. Name the three ways that candidates use television coverage in their campaigns.
14. What is propaganda? What are four commonly used techniques?
15. What is one way in which you can "talk back to your television"?

CHAPTER 10 REVIEW—Continued

Questions for Thought and Discussion

1. If you could choose a primary system for your state, which would you choose? Give reasons for your answer.
2. Why are secret ballots critical to free elections?
3. What factors do you think have led to the growth in the number of PACs? Do you think they should be further regulated? Explain.
4. How would our presidential elections change if we abolished the electoral college and used the direct popular vote instead?
5. Explain why the media and candidates are dependent on each other.
6. Should the media be required to provide equal coverage for all candidates and for all political parties? Is is fair that the two major political parties can buy or otherwise obtain greater coverage in the news than the minor parties? Explain why or why not.

Improving Your Skills
Communication Skills
Comparing and Contrasting

Comparing and contrasting is a skill you will need to fully understand and evaluate information, write and deliver oral reports, and express your opinion. To compare and contrast items means putting them side by side and looking for the similarities and differences. It may be helpful to look for the similarities first and then go on to search for differences.

Check carefully that the categories you are using to make the comparison/contrast apply to both items. For example, if you are comparing and contrasting two mayoral candidates you should be sure that your list of categories, such as experience in government, leadership abilities, voting records, positions on environmental issues, knowledge of community, and so forth, can be applied equally to both candidates.

Writing

Choose two candidates for any level of political office from a past or current election. Write a list of ten categories by which to compare and contrast the candidates.

List the similarities between the candidates with respect to your categories. Then list the differences between the candidates. Write a summary statement of similarities and of differences.

Social Studies Skills
Reading Maps

Look at the map of the United States on page 248. Answer the following questions:

1. What is the reason for showing the map?
2. How is the number of electoral votes determined for each state?
3. Which state has the most electoral votes for president?
4. What are the fewest possible electoral votes that a state can have?
5. How many states have the minimum electoral votes?
6. Will it ever be possible for a state to have fewer than 3 electoral votes?
7. A president can be elected with 270 electoral votes. Determine the minimum number of states that the candidate must win in order to obtain 270 votes and list those states.

Activities and Projects

1. Interview a candidate or a candidate's aide who has campaigned in a recent election. Ask the candidate about how the campaign was organized, planned, and financed. Report your results to the class.
2. Prepare a campaign plan for an imaginary candidate. Invent a campaign theme and decide on how the campaign should be organized. Then think of how your staff can make the best use of the media. Present your plan to the class.
3. Prepare a bulletin board display that lists all the propaganda techniques and gives examples of each one.
4. Stage a debate on the following statement: Candidates for president shall not be allowed to spend more than $25 million for their campaign, candidates for senator $5 million, and for representative no more than $3 million.

CHAPTER 11

Voters and Voting Behavior

CHAPTER OBJECTIVES

To learn and understand

- The history and expansion of the right to vote in the United States.
- What factors affect voting and nonvoting.
- The factors affecting the behavior of voters.

Keynote

Nobody will ever deprive the American people of the right to vote except the American people themselves.

——— **Franklin D. Roosevelt (1882–1945) Thirty-Second President of the United States**

INTRODUCTION

The right to vote—the **franchise**—is vital to the success of a representative democracy. After all, democracy means "rule by the people." In order to rule, the people must elect representatives to act on their behalf. Voting in elections is a method by which we as citizens can directly participate in the governing process in this country.

The struggles that many groups have waged in this country have resulted in the right to vote for all American citizens ages 18 and over. There are over 185 million people in the **electorate** (the potential voting population), yet less than 50 percent of these citizens actually vote, while turnout in several other nations often exceeds 85 percent. In fact, the United States has one of the lowest rates of voter participation of any democracy in the world.

Are Americans becoming more apathetic toward politics, more hostile toward candidates, less trustful of government, or less confident of their own abilities to make a difference in an election? If any or all of these are true, then American democracy may be in trouble, as Franklin D. Roosevelt pointed out in the opening quote of this chapter. If, in contrast, many people do not vote simply because they are content with the way things are, then there might be less reason for concern.

Many of you will have the opportunity to vote yourselves for the first time in the very near future. By looking at the history and the expansion of the right to vote in the United States, perhaps you will begin to understand why so many people have sacrificed so much to secure for themselves, and for us, the right to vote.

In this chapter we will survey the history of voting in America, as well as current patterns of voter behavior and voter turnout.

History of Voting and Current Requirements

Preview Questions
- What were the early restrictions placed on voting in America?
- How were African Americans denied the vote? What events changed this?
- How did women gain the right to vote?
- What are current voting eligibility requirements?

In America today, all citizens at least 18 years of age have the right to vote. This was not always true, however: restrictions on **suffrage**, the legal right to vote, have existed since the founding of our nation. Expanding the right to vote has been an important part of the gradual democratization of the American electoral process.

Several of the founding fathers felt that because many of the government's functions were economic in nature, it was fair and reasonable that only those people who had an interest in property should be allowed to vote. No one even thought about extending the vote to African Americans (most of whom were slaves) or to women. The notion of allowing all citizens to vote was, according to South Carolina delegate Charles Pinckney, merely "theoretical nonsense." Consistent with the first Chief Justice of the Supreme Court John Jay's statement that "the people who own the country ought to govern it," most states limited suffrage to adult white males who owned property. The logic behind this type of reasoning was challenged by Thomas Paine in his pamphlet *Common Sense:*

Here is a man who today owns a jackass, and the jackass is worth $60. Today the man is a voter and goes to the

261

George Caleb Bingham's painting *The County Election,* shown here, depicts rural voters lining up to vote in the nineteenth century. What common traits do all of the voters shown in this painting share?

polls and deposits his votes. Tomorrow the jackass dies. The next day the man comes to vote without his jackass and cannot vote at all. Now tell me, which was the voter, the man or the jackass?

Early Restrictions

The Constitution left the power to set suffrage qualifications to the individual states. Some states placed so many restrictions on the right to vote that only five to six percent of the adult population was eligible. There were numerous restrictions based on property ownership, race, sex, religious beliefs, and payment of taxes.

Religious restrictions were the first to be removed, and by 1810 they were abolished in all states. Next, with the growth of democratic sentiment and the expansion of the western frontier, property ownership and tax-payment requirements gradually began to disappear. Men without property were first given the right to vote in the Western states, and by 1850 an era of universal white male suffrage had arrived.

Women and the Right to Vote

During the era when the Constitution was written, some women argued for women's rights but were largely ignored. Beginning in the 1820s in Tennessee school board elections, women had the right to vote in some places on the local level. The first time a woman voted on the national level occurred in 1807, when the New Jersey constitution failed to explicitly prevent women from voting. The state legislature acted quickly to amend the constitution, making it clear that women were not allowed to vote.

After the Civil War in 1869, Susan B. Anthony and Elizabeth Cady Stanton organized the National Women Suffrage Association, which adopted as its goal a

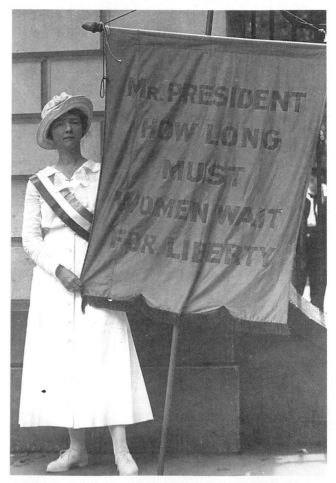

The woman shown above was one of a group of suffragettes that picketed the White House in 1917 to call the nation's attention to their cause. Was this effort effective?

262

Extension of the Right to Vote

Year	Action	Impact
1870	Fifteenth Amendment	Discrimination based on race outlawed.
1920	Nineteenth Amendment	Discrimination based on sex outlawed.
1924	Congressional Act	All Native American Indians given citizenship.
1944	Smith v. Allwright	Supreme Court prohibits white primary.
1957	Civil Rights Act of 1957	Justice Department can sue to protect voting rights in various states.
1960	Civil Rights Act of 1960	Courts authorized to appoint referees to assist voter registration procedures.
1961	Twenty-third Amendment	Residents of District of Columbia given right to vote.
1964	Twenty-fourth Amendment	Poll tax in national elections outlawed.
1965	Voting Rights Act of 1965	Literacy test prohibited; federal voter registrars authorized in seven southern states.
1970	Voting Rights Act Amendments of 1970	Voting age for federal elections reduced to 18 years; maximum 30-day residency requirement for presidential elections; state literacy test abolished.
1971	Twenty-sixth Amendment	Minimum voting age reduced to 18 for all elections.
1975	Voting Rights Act Amendments of 1975	Federal voter registrars authorized in ten more states; bilingual ballots to be printed if 5 percent or more of state population does not speak English.
1982	Voting Rights Act Amendment of 1982	Extended provisions of two previous voting rights act amendments; allows private parties to sue for violations.

▲ FIGURE 11–1 **Extension of the Right To Vote.** The table above shows the major landmarks in the effort to grant all Americans the right to vote. Which of the above landmarks reduced the minimum voting age to 18 for all elections?

women's suffrage amendment to the Constitution. They lobbied Congress and the state legislatures for women's voting rights. The first suffrage bill was introduced in Congress in 1868, and each year thereafter until 1893.

When Wyoming applied to join the union in 1889, it had already granted women the right to vote. At first, Congress tried to bar Wyoming for that reason, but surrendered when the Wyoming territorial legislature declared, ''We will remain out of the Union 100 years rather than come in without the women.''

Vigorous campaigns by women suffragists between 1910 and 1914 led seven other states, all west of the Mississippi, to give women the right to vote. Throughout the early 1900s, however, strong opposition existed, even within progressive circles, to a constitutional amendment granting women the vote. On President Wilson's inauguration day in 1913, a group of militant suffragists organized a demonstration that ended in a near riot. Other demonstrations bordered on violence and leaders were jailed and fined. In 1917, the National Women's Party organized an around-the-clock picket line at the White House. They were arrested and subsequently force fed during hunger strikes, which embarrassed the Woodrow Wilson administration and won some support for the movement. These efforts, along with women's contributions to the war effort during World War I, led Congress in 1919 to pass the Nineteenth Amendment, which granted the vote to women.

I n the early days of our country, women had none of the rights that are taken for granted today. They could not own property unless their husbands controlled it, could not sue anyone in the courts, could not be legal guardians of their own children if they divorced, and could not become involved in politics. It was believed that women did not need a formal education, and should not be treated as equals of men. Women were also not allowed to vote, which meant that over 50 percent of adult citizens in the nation had no voice in electing those who governed. As women became more educated, a few became more outspoken about their lack of legal rights. One such leader among these women was Susan B. Anthony.

Susan B. Anthony was born February 15, 1820, in Adams, Massachusetts. She was raised in a Quaker household, and from her religious upbringing developed a belief in the equality of all men and women before God. She became a teacher in her father's school and served as the head of the female department of the Canajoharie Academy in New York. Abandoning education for reform activities, she devoted her first efforts to temperance (discouraging the use of alcoholic beverages) and the abolitionist cause, being among the first to advocate black suffrage after the Civil War.

Gradually, she shifted her energies to the women's suffrage movement. She quickly became a key organizer in a series of state and national women's rights conventions. In 1869, she and Elizabeth Cady Stanton formed the National Woman Suffrage Association to fight for a women's suffrage amendment to the United States Constitution. Ridiculed by men and ignored by many women, the movement's leaders faced a long uphill fight. In 1872, Anthony was arrested when she challenged the law by voting in that year's presidential election. She was tried by a judge who refused to let her speak in her own defense.

Anthony spent the rest of her life traveling and lecturing on women's rights. She was president of the National Woman Suffrage Association between 1892 and 1900 as they continued their struggle. Although many states began to give women more rights, full equality was still years away. Anthony died on March

13, 1906, fourteen years before her dream was realized. But her seventy-plus years of effort and dedication finally met with success in 1920, when the necessary number of states ratified the Nineteenth Amendment, which declared that "The right of citizens of the United States to vote shall not be denied or abridged by the United States or by any State on account of sex."

HER WORDS

It may be delayed longer than we think; it may be here sooner than we expect; but the day will come when man will recognize woman as his peer, not only at the fireside but in the councils of the nation. Then, and not until then, will there be the perfect comradeship, the ideal union between the sexes that shall result in the highest development of the race. What this shall be we may not attempt to define, but this we know, that only good can come to the individual or to the nation through the rendering of exact justice.

Susan B. Anthony

▲ The suffragettes shown above are celebrating the ratification of the Nineteenth Amendment giving women the right to vote.

Upon voting illegally in 1872:

Friends and fellow citizens: I stand before you under indictment for the alleged crime of having voted in the last presidential election, without having a lawful right to vote. . . . I not only committed no crime, but instead simply exercised my citizen's right, guaranteed to me and all United States citizens by the National Constitution beyond the power of any state to deny.

DEVELOPING CRITICAL THINKING SKILLS

1. What did Anthony mean when she argued that women should be recognized as peers to men "not only at the fireside but in the councils of the nation"?

2. What do you think Anthony meant when she spoke of "the highest development of the race"?
3. Where in the Constitution did Anthony find support for her statement that every citizen has the right to vote, and that that power cannot be denied by any state?

FOR FURTHER READING

Dorr, Rheta C. *Susan B. Anthony, the Woman who Changed the Mind of a Nation.* New York: AMS Press Inc., 1980

Flexner, Eleanor. *Century of Struggle.* New York: Atheneum, 1974.

Hahn, Emily. *Once Upon a Pedestal.* New York: Thomas Y. Cromwell, 1974.

CHAPTER 11 REVIEW—Continued

Summary

1. In the United States today, all citizens of at least 18 years of age have the right to vote. In our nation's past, there have been many restrictions on suffrage, but today almost all legal barriers to voting have been eliminated. The Fifteenth Amendment guaranteed suffrage to African-American males in 1870, but various methods were used for the next century to restrict their ability to vote. The civil rights movement, the Civil Rights Act of 1964, and the Voting Rights Act of 1965 finally made the Fifteenth Amendment an effective part of the Constitution. The passage of the Nineteenth Amendment in 1920 prohibited voter discrimination on the basis of sex. The passage of the Twenty-sixth Amendment in 1971 gave 18-year-olds the right to vote.

2. Even though these barriers to voting have been abolished, only about half of those citizens eligible to vote practice this right. Some of the reasons include inability to vote due to illness or physical handicap, not meeting residency and registration requirements, not having a sense of political effectiveness, being "turned off" by political campaigns, the time-consuming election procedures, lack of interest, and satisfaction with the status quo. There are also a certain number who cannot vote because they are confined to mental institutions or prisons. The characteristics that influence whether or not a person votes include education, age, marital status, income and minority status, and government employment. Some people view low voter turnout as a threat to representative democracy, while others view it as a sign that people are satisfied with the way things are.

3. Several factors influence voters' choices. Party identification is the most prominent indicator of how a person will vote. Voters are also influenced by the image they have of a candidate. Policy voting occurs when people vote for candidates who reflect their own views on the issues. Voters are also influenced by socioeconomic factors such as age, sex, education, occupation and income, religion and ethnic background, and geographic region.

Review Questions

1. What were some of the early restrictions placed on the right to vote in the United States?

2. What did the passage of the Fifteenth Amendment guarantee? How did many states respond to this amendment?

3. Explain some of the early tactics used to prevent African Americans from voting.

4. What events led to the passage of the Voting Rights Act of 1965?

5. What does the Nineteenth Amendment prohibit? What events led to its passage?

6. List and explain five possible reasons for not voting.

7. What are the characteristics that make people most likely to vote?

8. What are two views about the effects of low voter turnout?

9. Do party identification, candidates' images, and policy choices affect voters' choices?

10. How do socioeconomic factors influence whether or not a person votes?

11. What are the typical voting requirements?

12. What ideas did the "Challenge to the American Dream" feature present as suggestions for getting people more involved in elections?

Questions for Thought and Discussion

1. How do you think people would respond to a compulsory voting law in the United States? How would it affect the way the electoral system works?

2. Historical struggles over the extension of suffrage have given more Americans the right to vote than ever before, yet only about half of those eligible vote. How would you explain this phenomenon? Do you think it is a problem? Why or why not?

3. Absentee ballots account for almost 8 percent of all votes cast throughout the United States in any one election year. Some commentators believe, nonetheless, that election results would not be any different even if absentee ballots were not allowed. Do you agree or disagree? Why or why not?

4. Some argue that low voter turnout is not a problem provided that those who do not go to the polls believe the government is being run correctly. Do you agree or disagree with this statement? Give reasons for your answer.

CHAPTER 11 REVIEW—Continued

Improving Your Skills
Communication Skills
Using Library Resources

Before writing a report or giving an oral report, you will need to do research in the library. Before you begin, there are several basic resources with which you should be familiar.

Card Catalog: Use the card catalog when trying to find a specific book. Every book in the library is listed on separate cards in the card catalog, which is arranged alphabetically. Books are usually listed in several ways: by author, by title, and by subject. On the front of each drawer of the card catalog is a label that will tell you what parts of the alphabet the drawer covers. Each card usually tells you the title, author, Dewey Decimal number, publisher, date, and number of pages of the book.

Library Scanner: Many libraries use a computer scanner instead of a card catalog. Just like the card catalog, every book in the library is listed on a scanning screen by title, author, and subject.

Reader's Guide to Periodical Literature: If you are not looking for a specific book, but for articles on a general subject, a good place to start is with the *Reader's Guide to Periodical Literature*. The *Reader's Guide* lists all the articles published in almost two hundred magazines, and is itself published ten times a year. Articles are listed under a general subject and the listing contains the author, the magazine, the volume of the magazine, the page number, the date it was published, and whether or not it is illustrated.

News Banks: Many libraries have a computerized system called a news bank or something similar. You choose a specific topic and the computer tells you where to look in newspapers throughout the United States. Then you have to go to the newspaper room of the library in which you will find newspapers from many major cities on microfiche machines. You can read the appropriate articles and have copies made of the ones you want. These systems are located in university libraries and major libraries throughout the country. (Remember, many university libraries allow anybody to use them, but only students and faculty can check out books.)

Writing

Think about a major topic related to politics that you would like to learn more about, such as the latest presidential campaign, the life of an important political figure, a congressional ethics scandal, or restrictions on congressional terms in office. Using the resources listed in this feature, develop a list of at least four references related to that topic that you find in your library. Write a one-paragraph summary about what is included in each reference. You can obtain a summary of the information included in each reference by reading the preface and the table of contents if it is a book, or by reading the first few paragraphs if it is a newspaper article.

Social Studies Skills
Reading Political Cartoons

Study the cartoon on page 271 and answer the following questions.

1. Who is the man slumped in the chair supposed to represent?
2. Why is wanting a king the logical progression from voter apathy?
3. What does candidate apathy mean?
4. Do you think the cartoonist is sympathetic to the feelings of the man in the chair?

Activities and Projects

1. Use library resources to gather information about voter turnout in European nations and in the United States. Compare and contrast the information you find, and prepare a report that explains the similarities and differences. Present the report to the class.
2. Interview an election official in your state to find out about registration and residency requirements. Prepare a bulletin board display that shows what the procedures are in your area.
3. Develop and produce a voter's brochure that could be used for new residents in your state. Include voter requirements and procedures for your state, and a brief write-up that tries to persuade citizens to vote.
4. Stage a debate on one of these statements: (1) The United States should enact a compulsory voting law; (2) There should be no registration or residency requirements placed on voting.

The Federal Legislative Branch

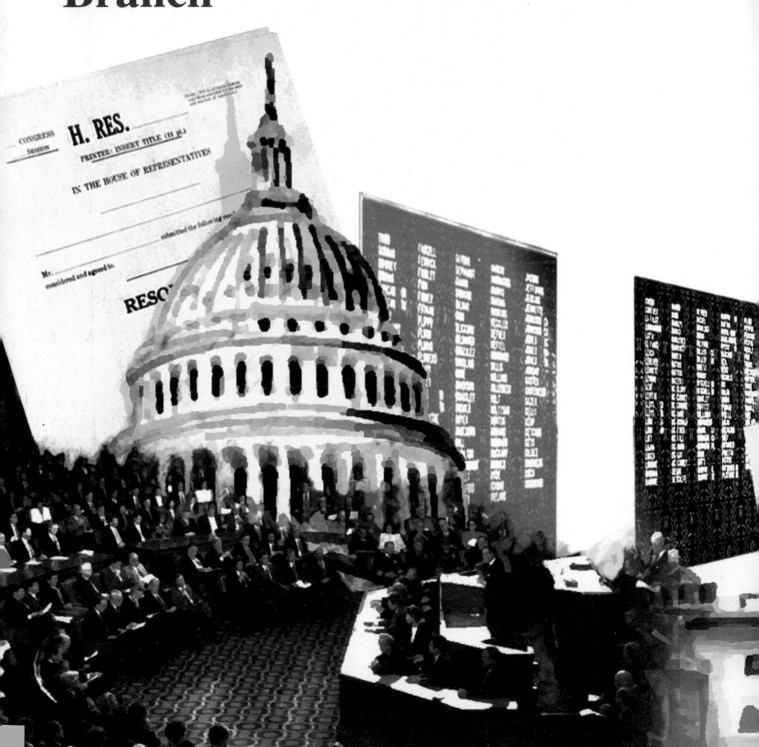

UNIT CONTENTS

- *Chapter 12* The Organization of Congress
- *Chapter 13* The Powers of Congress
- *Chapter 14* How Congress Makes Laws

281

C-SPAN 1

CHAPTER 12

The Organization of Congress

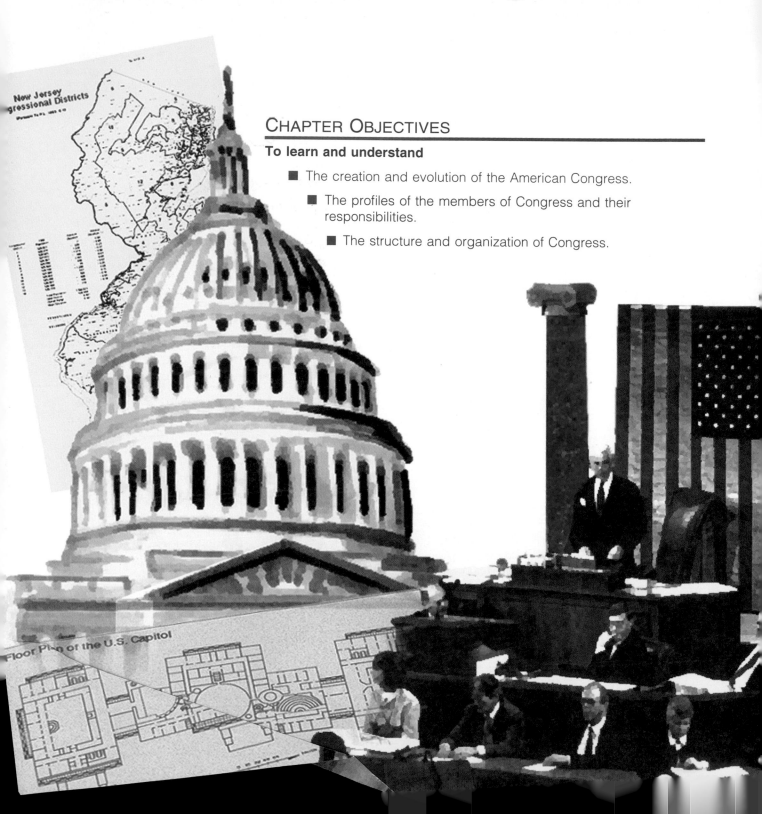

CHAPTER OBJECTIVES

To learn and understand

- The creation and evolution of the American Congress.
- The profiles of the members of Congress and their responsibilities.
- The structure and organization of Congress.

New Jersey Congressional Districts

Floor Plan of the U.S. Capitol

Keynote

"The language of the Constitution is not ambiguous or qualified. It places not some legislative powers in Congress; Article I, Section 1 says, "All legislative powers herein granted . . . ."

——— **William O. Douglas**
(1898–1980) Associate Justice
United States Supreme Court

INTRODUCTION

Congress was established as the first branch of government and is often called the federal branch closest to the people. This is because members of Congress are elected directly by the people, whereas the president and vice president are elected through the electoral college and Supreme Court members are appointed by the president with the approval of the Senate. Thus, among this nation's leaders, members of Congress are most directly accountable to its citizens. Because of this, Congress is sometimes called "the voice of the people."

The founders granted Congress the most critical function of a democracy: translating the public will into public policy. As the opening quote from William O. Douglas points out, they devoted the First Article of the Constitution to Congress, which reads:

> *All legislative powers herein granted shall be vested in a Congress of the United States, which shall consist of a Senate and House of Representatives.*

Despite the fact that Congress makes the policies that shape our lives, many Americans do not understand its myriad committees, complicated procedures, and endless debates.

Each American is represented by a congressperson and two senators. These members of Congress are elected to serve the public. As American citizens, it is important that we understand Congress and its responsibilities to ensure that this powerful institution remains the voice of the people. In this chapter, you will read about the creation and development of the United States Congress. You will also look at the men and women who make up Congress and the structure and organization of its two houses.

SECTION 1

Creation and Evolution of Congress

Preview Questions

- What is a bicameral legislature? Why did the founders create a bicameral legislature in this country?
- How is the total number of seats apportioned in the House of Representatives? How is it reapportioned every ten years?
- What are congressional districts? What methods have been used over the years to unfairly draw them?

The founders of the American republic believed that a central legislature should be responsible for the bulk of the power exercised by a national government. Their experience with King George III of England and his often dictatorial or incompetent royal governors had left them with a deep suspicion of strong executive authority. They were also aware of how ineffective the Congress had been during its brief existence under the Articles of Confederation.

As a result of these concerns, Congress is charged under the Constitution with the **legislative power**—the power to make laws. The founders intended Congress to be the central institution of American government and therefore gave it more powers than any other branch. As James Madison said, Congress is "the first branch of the government."

Bicameral Legislature

The founders of this nation did not, however, agree about the organization of Congress. In fact, one of the most serious conflicts of the Constitutional Convention

283

was a long and heated debate between the large and small states over congressional representation. After a month of struggle, the delegates finally adopted the Great Compromise, which you read about in Chapter 2.

By a narrow margin, the Convention voted for a **bicameral legislature**, a Congress of two houses—a Senate and a House of Representatives. The British Parliament, which the framers and most other Americans knew quite well, had consisted of two houses since the 1300s. Each American state, large or small, would be represented by two senators, thereby giving each state equal power in the Senate. In the House, however, representatives would be distributed according to population, so that the larger the state's population, the more representatives it would have. The Constitution requires that each state, no matter how small, have at least one representative.

Besides the needed compromise, the founders favored a bicameral legislature so that the two houses might serve as checks on each other's power and activity. The House was to represent the people as a whole—the will of the majority—by having its members apportioned by population. The Senate was to represent the states, and would protect the interests of the small states by giving them the same representation as the larger states. Because the House was to be elected directly by the people, it was to be the "common person's" chamber. The Senate, originally to be chosen by the elected representatives sitting in state legislatures, was to protect the elite interests against the tendencies of the House to protect the masses (similar to the division between the House of Commons and the House of Lords in England). The Senate was to be a safeguard against the passage of "emotional" legislation. As George Washington was said to have remarked, "We shall pour House legislation into the Senatorial saucer to cool it."

Congressional Meetings

Each Congress lasts for a meeting period, or a **term**, of two years. Each term is numbered consecutively beginning from March 4, 1789. The date for the **convening** (formal opening) of each term was reset by the Twentieth Amendment in 1933 and now begins on January 3 of an odd-numbered year unless Congress sets another date.

Each term of Congress is divided into two regular **sessions**, or meetings—one for each year. Until about 1940, Congress remained in session for only four or five months, but the complicated rush of legislation and increased demand for services from the public in recent

◄
The Congress of the United States has been called the federal branch of government closest to the people. Why is this description used?

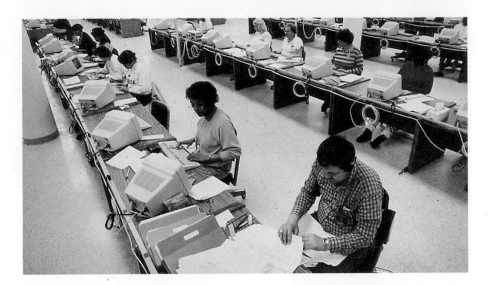

▶ Every ten years, the Census Bureau takes an official count of our population. How does this census affect Congress?

years have forced Congress to remain in session through most of each year.[1] Both houses, however, schedule short **recesses**, or breaks for holidays and vacations.

Congress remains in session until its members vote to adjourn. Neither house may adjourn a session without the consent of the other. Only the president may call Congress to meet during a scheduled recess. Such meetings are called **special sessions** and only twenty-six such sessions have ever been held. The fact that Congress is now so busy and meets nearly year-round makes the need for a special session unlikely.

Apportionment of the House of Representatives

The Constitution provides that the total number of House seats shall be **apportioned** (distributed) among the states on the basis of their respective populations. Because representation in the House is based on population, the more people a state has, the more representatives it will send to the House. California, for example, with a 1990 population of almost 30 million, has fifty-two representatives. North Carolina, with a population of 6.7 million, has twelve representatives. Wyoming, with a population of 460,000, has one representative. Each state is guaranteed at least one seat, no matter what its population. Today seven states have only one representative. The District of Columbia, American Samoa,

Guam, and the American Virgin Islands each send nonvoting delegates to the House. Puerto Rico, a self-governing possession of the United States, is represented by a nonvoting resident commissioner.

Reapportionment   The Constitution directs Congress to take a **census**, or official count of the population, every ten years. This allows Congress to increase the number of House seats according to changes in the population. The census results are then used to apportion the seats among the states.

With each census year, the number of representatives in the House has grown. By 1910, it had reached 435. In the census year of 1920, as our population swelled, House leaders and many Americans were concerned that an even larger House would get out of hand. Many thought it was growing too big for effective action. When the official census figures were revealed in 1921, the House stalled for eight years before taking any action to increase its membership.

In 1929, President Hoover called a special session of Congress to address the situation and urged it to provide apportionment guidelines for the upcoming 1930 census. As a result, Congress passed the Reapportionment Act of 1929, which established a permanent system of **reapportionment**, or redistribution, of the 435 House seats following each census. The law provides that:

1. The size of the House remains stable at 435.
2. After each census, the Census Bureau determines the number of seats each state should receive according to the census results.

---

1.   Some observers maintain that another reason Congress *can* stay in session longer is because of the invention of air conditioning. Prior to that, none of its members wanted to stay in session during the hot and sticky spring, summer, and fall months.

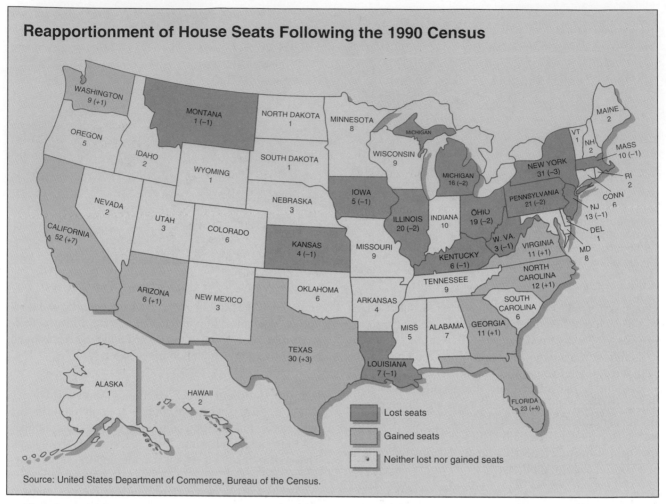

▲ | FIGURE 12–1 Reapportionment of House Seats Following the 1990 Census. The map above shows the apportionment of House seats for each state based on the population figures from the 1990 census. Based on this map, what region of the country lost the most seats?

3. The Census Bureau presents a plan to the president that shows the distribution of seats.
4. The president submits this information in a message to Congress. If Congress does not voice its opposition within sixty days, the plan goes into effect.

Thus, shifts in our nation's population greatly affect the distribution of House seats. In the last few decades, increasing numbers of Americans have moved from northeastern and midwestern states to the sunbelt states of the South and the West. The map in Figure 12–1 illustrates this trend by showing the changes made in each state's House seats after the 1990 census was taken.

Congressional Districting Senators are elected to represent all of the people in the state, while representatives

are elected by the voters of a particular area known as a **congressional district**. The 435 members of the House are chosen by the voters in 435 separate congressional districts across the country. If a state's population allows it to have only one representative, such as in the case of Wyoming and Vermont, the entire state is one congressional district. Texas, by contrast, has thirty congressional districts and hence thirty representatives. The lines of the congressional districts are chosen by state legislatures. This often means that the party with the majority in the legislature will attempt to redraw districts so as to improve that party's power.

This system was not always used. The Constitution makes no provisions for congressional districts, and in the early 1800s each state was given the right to decide whether or not to have districts at all. Most states set up **single-member districts** in which voters in each district elected one of the state's representatives. In states that chose not to have districts, representatives were chosen **at large**, from the state as a whole.

Over the years, many people became dissatisfied with this system, claiming it was unfair for a political party whose candidates won the congressional election by a slight margin to win all of the House seats for the state. In 1842 Congress responded by passing an act that required all states to send representatives to Congress from single-member districts. It gave each state legislature the responsibility of drawing its own district lines, but required that each district be made up of **contiguous** (adjoining) boundaries. Later revisions of the law required that districts contain, as nearly as possible, an equal number of people. This requirement is important because each House member would then represent approximately the same number of people, and the people would be equally represented in the House. Districts were also required to be of compact territory, which meant that states could not draw boundaries that spread one district into parts throughout the state.

The requirements of the 1842 act, however, were largely ignored by states as many state legislatures continued to seek advantages for their own political parties. They did so in two ways, which are discussed below.

● **Congressional districts of unequal population** If congressional districts are not made up of equal populations, the value of people's votes is not the same. One way that legislatures used this fact to ensure their power was to create districts with unequal populations. For example, many state legislatures traditionally were controlled by rural areas. By creating districts that were not equal in population, rural leaders hoped to block the transfer of representatives to growing urban areas. There was a point during the 1960s, for example, when there were many states in which the largest district had twice the population of the smallest district. This meant that in these states a person's vote in the largest congressional districts had only half the value of a person's vote in the smallest districts.

The Supreme Court finally addressed this issue. In *Baker* v. *Carr* (1962), the Court ruled that the Tennessee state legislature's **malapportionment** violated the constitutional requirement of equal protection under the law. Finally, in 1964 it ruled in *Wesberry* v. *Sanders* that congressional districts

must have equal population. This principle has come to be known as the "one person–one vote" rule; that is, one person's vote has to count as much as another's vote. The long-standing tendency of state legislatures to apportion in the ways that overrepresented rural voters began to be corrected.

● **Gerrymandering** Since the early 1800s, the practice of drawing district boundaries to benefit a certain party, group, or candidate has been called **gerrymandering**. Gerrymandering often results in very oddly shaped election districts. This practice took its name in "honor" of Elbridge Gerry, governor of Massachusetts. In 1812, the state legislature carved up Essex County in a way that favored his party, making the district look like a salamander. A cartoonist, observing a map that detailed the strange shape of the districts, penciled in a head, wings, and claws and commented that the map now resembled a salamander. A news editor replied, "Better say a *gerrymander*!"

Two different methods of gerrymandering have been used. One way, called "packing" by

▲ This cartoon depicts the original "gerrymander." When Elbridge Gerry had this Massachusetts district drawn to ensure the election of a Republican in 1812, a cartoonist added a head, wings, and claws so that it resembled a salamander. Thus, the gerrymander was born.

BUILDING SOCIAL STUDIES SKILLS

Using a Political Map

A good source for finding political information is a political map. A map is an illustration, drawn to scale, of an area under study. To effectively gather information from a map, follow these guidelines:

1. **Study the map's title.** The title will tell you the subject and purpose of the map, and may also give information about the time period and area that the map represents.
2. **Study the map legend, or key.** The legend, or key, contains information that explains special symbols used on the map. Before trying to interpret the map, study the legend to make sure that you know what all the colors, shadings, and lines represent.
3. **Check the map's directions.** Some maps have a compass rose or direction indicator. If not, it is always assumed that north is at the top of the map.

4. **Study the distance scales.** Maps present their scales in miles or kilometers. A scale must be used to determine the distance between two places.

Special-Purpose Maps Many types of special-purpose maps are also used to study government and politics. These maps relate specific data to a geographic area.

Study the map below and answer the following questions:

1. How many states lost population between 1980 and 1990? What was the average population loss among these states?
2. What was the average population gain in the states that gained population?
3. Is it possible to tell from this map what the population size is in any state?

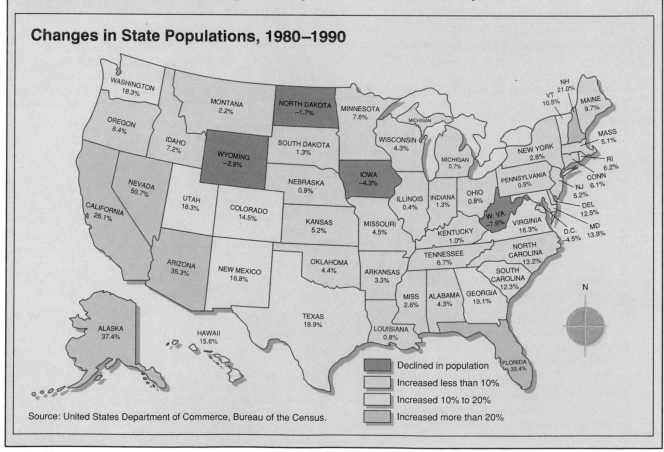

Changes in State Populations, 1980–1990

WASHINGTON 18.3%
OREGON 8.4%
MONTANA 2.2%
NORTH DAKOTA –1.7%
MINNESOTA 7.6%
MICHIGAN
NH 21.0%
VT 10.5%
MAINE 9.7%
IDAHO 7.2%
SOUTH DAKOTA 1.3%
WISCONSIN 4.3%
MICHIGAN 0.7%
NEW YORK 2.8%
MASS 5.1%
RI 6.2%
WYOMING –2.9%
NEBRASKA 0.9%
IOWA –4.3%
PENNSYLVANIA 0.5%
CONN 6.1%
NJ 5.2%
NEVADA 50.7%
CALIFORNIA 26.1%
UTAH 18.3%
COLORADO 14.5%
ILLINOIS 0.4%
INDIANA 1.3%
OHIO 0.8%
DEL 12.5%
KANSAS 5.2%
MISSOURI 4.5%
KENTUCKY 1.0%
W. VA. –7.6%
VIRGINIA 16.3%
D.C. –4.5%
MD 13.8%
ARIZONA 35.3%
NEW MEXICO 16.8%
OKLAHOMA 4.4%
ARKANSAS 3.3%
TENNESSEE 6.7%
NORTH CAROLINA 13.2%
SOUTH CAROLINA 12.3%
ALASKA 37.4%
HAWAII 15.6%
TEXAS 19.9%
LOUISIANA 0.8%
MISS 2.6%
ALABAMA 4.3%
GEORGIA 19.1%
FLORIDA 33.4%
N

Legend:
- Declined in population
- Increased less than 10%
- Increased 10% to 20%
- Increased more than 20%

Source: United States Department of Commerce, Bureau of the Census.

politicians, is drawing the congressional district lines so they include as many of the political party's voters as possible. The other method, called "cracking" by politicians, involves drawing the lines so that the opponent's strength is divided among two or more districts. In this way the opponent has a more difficult time getting enough votes to win an election.

Because gerrymandering has not been specifically outlawed, there are still instances of its use today, although with much less frequency. The Court ruled in *Wesberry* that congressional districts must be "compact and contiguous." These requirements combined with the one person–one vote ruling usually have prevented the worst forms of gerrymandering.

SECTION 1 REVIEW

1. With what basic governmental power is Congress charged?
2. Why did the founders create a bicameral legislature?
3. What is apportionment? What was the significance of the Reapportionment Act of 1929?
4. How have congressional districts been determined in the past? How are they determined today?
5. **For critical analysis:** Does the fact that a census is only taken every ten years cause problems of unfair representation for those states whose population is growing rapidly? Explain.

SECTION 2

House and Senate Organization

Preview Questions
- What are the terms of office and constitutional qualifications set forth for members of the
- House of Representatives? For members of the Senate?
- How does the Constitution allow the House and Senate to judge the conduct of their members?

House of Representatives

With its 435 members, the House of Representatives is over four times larger than the Senate, but is still referred to as the lower house of Congress.

Terms of Office   Members of the House of Representatives are elected for two-year terms. The framers believed that such a short term of office would make representatives more responsive to the people. Many people still believe this today; others argue that a two-year term is impractical because representatives spend too much time during the second year campaigning for the next election. A constitutional amendment to lengthen the term for House membership has been proposed several times, but has never been successful.

Elections are held in November of even-numbered years, and representatives begin their term of office January 3 following the November election. This means that all 435 members must run for reelection at the same time and the House begins anew following each election.

Despite the short terms of office, there is still a great deal of continuity among members of the House. In the past decade well over 90 percent of all House incumbents have been reelected. In 1990, 96 percent of the incumbents who ran were reelected. Some representatives have been reelected over a dozen times.

There are several possible explanations for the repeated successes of incumbents. One explanation, although the least likely one, is that voters know how their representatives vote on important policy issues, agree with their positions, and want to send them back to Washington. The more likely factor for their success, however, is visibility. Incumbents work very hard at making themselves known throughout their districts so that at the

▼ Members of the House of Representatives such as John Lewis (R., Georgia), who was elected in 1990, serve two-year terms. Why are House terms so short?

and House dining rooms, free recreational facilities, and research help from the Library of Congress.

Salaries of congresspeople are high in comparison to the average American family income of about $40,000, but they are low in comparison to people in the upper ranks of business, professional sports, and other professions. The presidents of some large corporations make millions of dollars per year, as do some professional athletes and entertainers. The annual salaries of many lawyers and doctors are in the hundreds of thousands. Congressional salaries are even quite low in comparison with the salaries of top officials of the interest groups that lobby Congress.

Privileges of Members

Members of Congress also have certain special constitutional privileges to protect them while carrying out their legislative duties. Article I, Section 6, commands that senators and representatives

> shall in all Cases, except Treason, Felony and Breach of the Peace, be privileged from Arrest during their Attendance at the Session of their respective Houses, and in going to, and returning from the same; . . .

Originally, this arrest immunity clause was designed to protect the legislative branch against interference by the executive branch. Before the colonies became independent, British officials often harassed colonial legislators and kept them from performing their duties. American leaders wanted to prevent this from reoccurring. The arrest immunity provision applies to arrests in civil cases, but does not protect members from criminal arrests. The provision has been of little importance in our national history.

A more important privilege set out in the Constitution is the speech and debate clause, which guarantees freedom of speech to members while they are conducting congressional business. This provision allows members to address their colleagues in open debate without fear of lawsuits for making harmful or false statements. A member may make any allegations or other statements he or she wishes in connection with official duties and not normally be sued for libel or slander, or be otherwise subject to legal action. This privilege does not cover speeches, articles, or conversations made in public apart from legislative business. This form of protection is called **congressional immunity**. The goal of this pro-

vision of the Constitution is to protect the freedom of legislative debate.

The Roles

In 1899, one senator said, "God made a day twenty-four hours long for the ordinary man. After a man becomes a United States senator, he requires a day forty-eight hours long." These words still ring true for senators as well as for representatives. Studies show that national legislators work almost sixty-hour weeks while Congress is in session. They must spend a great deal of time learning about the issues on which they will vote, reviewing bills introduced by other legislators, and getting support for their own bills. Committee and subcommittee work occupy a great deal of time. They also try to be present on the floor of the House or Senate chambers as much as possible where they listen to speeches, give speeches, and vote on bills. Every day there are dozens of people wanting to see them: a fellow member with questions about a bill, a lobbyist with arguments against a bill, a constituent visiting the Capitol. Between meetings, members prepare bills, study reports, attend party functions, and write speeches and articles.

Most hearings are held midweek, with Wednesday being the crest of the midweek wave. This phenomenon is known colloquially as "the Tuesday–Thursday Club," bespeaking Congress's desire to arrange long weekends to stay in touch with their home states and constituencies.

The 535 members of Congress have several different but closely related roles.

Policymaker The Constitution requires that policymaking be the primary role of Congress and its members. Congress is the highest elected body in the country charged with making the legal rules that govern our society. Policymaking includes conducting investigations to identify problems, researching and deciding upon bills, and voting intelligently for policies in the national interest. Policymakers decide many important matters such as establishing the rate of federal taxes and the size of the federal budget.

Representative A congressperson is also a representative, expected by "the folks back home" to represent their views in Washington. They are supposed to reflect and translate into action the interests and concerns of constituents. Some political philosophers argue that representatives should vote exactly as their constituents

▶ Members of Congress, such as Representative Dan Rostenkowski of Illinois and Senator Lloyd Bentsen of Texas shown here, have several different roles. Which of these roles do you feel is the most important?

would have them vote. They should vote the preference of the constituents as if the constituents themselves were present and voting. This is the concept of representative as *instructed delegate,* in which delegate means the agent of the people. Others argue that representatives should vote according to their own best judgment and evaluation of the issue, which is the concept of representative as *trustee*, someone who administers the affairs of another.

Constituent Servant   Representatives and senators not only represent the voting decisions of their constituents but also act as constituent servants. In this way they work as intermediaries between their constituents and the imposing and complicated federal bureaucracy. Helping constituents with problems is part of a congressperson's casework.

The average member of Congress is swamped with thousands of constituents' requests from the moment he or she takes office. These requests range from appearing in a local parade with the mayor of a city, to helping to secure an appointment to a service academy such as West Point, to helping with Social Security benefits, to helping with an immigration or passport problem. These small but time-consuming tasks take up hours of a congressperson's day, even though the routine tasks are delegated

to the staff. This is time spent away from the main responsibility of policymaking, but a constituency well served is a constituency well satisfied, especially at the next election. So important is constituency service to legislators that it has been suggested (somewhat mischievously) that they prefer to maintain the complexity of the federal bureaucracy in order to maximize the number of occasions to perform good deeds for their constituents.

Committee Members   The typical senator is a member of eleven committees and subcommittees; the average representative is a member of six. If a member is on a committee long enough, he or she will become a policy expert whose advice is sought by other members. As you will learn in the upcoming ''Government in Action'' feature on page 304, if members are able to sit on committees whose subject matter especially concerns their constituencies, they can potentially be more effective as constituent representatives.

Politician and Party Member   All of the roles members of Congress play are somehow related to their role as politician and party member. In order to continue as policymakers, constituent servants, and representatives, they must get reelected, and reelection campaigns take

CITIZENSHIP SKILLS AND RESPONSIBILITIES

How to Find Out What's Going On in Congress

Who is in Congress? If you want to find out who is in Congress or who your representatives or senators are, you can look in the *Congressional Directory*, published each year by the federal government and available in most libraries or from the U.S. Government Printing Office, Washington, DC 20402. It includes biographies of lawmakers, lists of committees and staff members, and maps of districts. The *Almanac of American Politics*, edited by Michael Barone and others and published every two years by *National Journal*, can help you learn more about your members' views. Another resource that summarizes and evaluates each member's performance and describes each district is *Politics in America: Members of Congress in Washington and at Home* (Washington, D.C.: Congressional Quarterly Press).

Your representative and senators have telephone numbers in both Washington, D.C., and in your state.

What Is Happening in Congress? If you want to know whether or not a bill has been introduced in the current session, or what the current status is of a bill in Congress, you can call the Legislative Status Office, 202-225-1772. Its computer can produce a free printout overnight. To find out whether a bill has been passed, call 202-456-2226. To learn what the current legislative program is, call 202-225-7400 for the House, or 202-224-8601 for the Senate. You can also obtain a copy of a bill from the House or Senate Document Room. Both the Democratic and Republican parties prepare tapes to provide running accounts of proceedings on the floors of both houses. To listen to these tapes call:

Senate Democratic: 202-224-8541
Senate Republican: 202-224-8601
House Democratic: 202-225-7400
House Republican: 202-225-7430

If you want to follow what happens in Congress, you can subscribe to the *Weekly Report*, published by a private Washington research organization called Congressional Quarterly (CQ). Many libraries have this publication or you can subscribe as a student for $90 a year, from CQ, 1414 22nd Street NW, Washington, DC 20037.

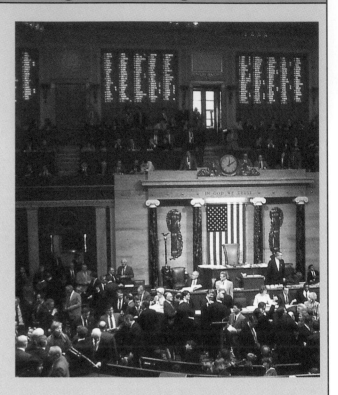

TAKING ACTION

1. Read through a local or national newspaper or a national news magazine. Find an article that mentions a proposed bill in Congress. With the information presented in the feature, determine the status of the bill in Congress. Contact the office of your senator or representative to find out his or her views on the bill. Follow the progress of the bill over the next few weeks as it passes through the houses.

2. Use one of the references listed above to help you make a profile of the representative for your district or one of the senators for your state. In the profile include what committees the member is on, how many staff members he or she has, what bills he or she has introduced recently, and what political action committees (PACs) support him or her.

time and energy. Every action they take as policymakers, representatives, and constituent servants affects votes in the next election. Even if they dislike politics, without being a politician they will not be around long enough to shape policy.

SECTION 3 REVIEW

1. How would you describe the average congressperson?
2. What are some of the benefits received by members of Congress?
3. What is the speech and debate clause?
4. Briefly describe each of the different roles that a congressperson plays.
5. **For critical analysis:** Should senators always vote the way their constituents want, or should they vote according to their own best judgment? Give reasons for your answer.

▲ Speaker of the House Thomas Foley, shown here, is the presiding officer of the House and the leader of the majority party in the House. How is the Speaker of the House selected?

SECTION 4

The Structure of Congress

Preview Questions

- How is the Speaker of the House chosen and what are his or her powers?
- Who are the other House leaders and what are their functions?
- Who presides over the Senate and what is his or her role?
- Why has the committee and subcommittee system evolved in Congress?
- What are the different types of committees?
- What are the various types of congressional support?

The organization of Congress is based on political party lines. The **majority party** in each house is the one with the greatest number of members. Being the majority party is quite important because that party chooses the major officers of each house of Congress, controls debate on the floor, selects all committee chairpersons, and has a majority on all committees.

House Leadership

Both the House and the Senate have a system of leadership. Before Congress begins work, members of each party in each house meet to choose their leaders. The Constitution provides for the presiding officers of the House and Senate; Congress may choose what other leaders it feels it needs.

Speaker of the House Chief among those leaders in the House of Representatives is the **Speaker of the House**. This office is mandated by the Constitution, to be filled by majority vote at the beginning of each congressional term. The speaker has traditionally been a long-time member of the majority party who has risen in rank and influence through years of service in the House. The candidate for Speaker is selected by the majority party caucus; all the rest of the House must do is approve the selection.

As the presiding officer of the House and the leader of the majority party, the Speaker has a great deal of power. In the early nineteenth century the Speaker had even more power and was known as the "king of the congressional mountain." Speakers known by such names as "Uncle Joe Cannon" and "Czar Reed" ruled the House with almost exclusive power. A revolt in 1910 reduced the Speaker's powers and gave them to some of the committees. Today, the Speaker still has many important powers, which include:

- Controlling substantially which bills get assigned to which committees.
- Presiding over the sessions of the House, recognizing or ignoring members who wish to speak.

CHAPTER 12 REVIEW—Continued

3. How are House seats divided among the states?
4. What is gerrymandering? What events have reduced its use?
5. Despite the fact that representatives serve short terms, why is there a great deal of continuity in the House?
6. How did the Constitution ensure that the Senate would be a continuous body?
7. How does Congress punish the misconduct of its members?
8. What are the typical characteristics of members of Congress?
9. What special privileges do members of Congress have to protect themselves while carrying out their duties?
10. List and briefly explain the five roles of a member of Congress.
11. What is the role of the Speaker of the House?
12. Who are the leaders in each political party in both Houses and what are some of their duties?
13. What purposes do committees serve in Congress?
14. Briefly describe the four types of committees and their purposes in Congress.
15. What kinds of activities are performed by a congressperson's personal staff?
16. What agencies perform support services for Congress?
17. Describe two ways to find out what is going on in Congress.
18. What are the arguments for and against limiting terms of members of Congress?

Questions for Thought and Discussion

1. Can you think of situations in which the different roles of a congressperson might come into conflict with one another? Describe three such instances and present possible ways to resolve them.
2. How would Congress be different if it were an exact cross section of the American public?
3. Do you think members of Congress are ever offered bribes or other inducements for favors? Do you think this practice is common? Give evidence to support your answer.
4. Should members of Congress vote the way they think is best for the country or should they vote the way

their constituents want them to? Give reasons for your answer.
5. Describe the ways that a member of Congress can be placed on important committees and subcommittees. What do you think is the single most important requirement for getting an important committee assignment in Congress?

Improving Your Skills
Communication Skills

Continuity in Writing: Transitional Phrases

Before writing an essay or report, it is important to know how to connect your ideas to make them more readable and clear to the reader. Continuity in writing is strengthened by using transitional phrases—bridges that carry the reader from one sentence to the next.

Compare these two paragraphs:

1.

Incumbent representatives are more visible than opponents. They are better able to keep constituents informed. They win friends by servicing constituents. They are in a better position to raise campaign funds. They get reelected over 90 percent of the time.

2.

Incumbent representatives are more visible than opponents. They are better able to keep constituents informed. They win friends by servicing constituents. They are in a better position to raise campaign funds. Consequently, they get reelected over 90 percent of the time.

The difference between the two paragraphs is the word *consequently*. Without this transitional word, the relationship of the last sentence to the preceding sentences is unclear. The transitional word or phrase links the last sentence to the list of statements supporting it.

Use the following tips to strengthen the continuity of your writing.

● *Use logic*. Organize your sentences so that ideas progress naturally and logically.
● *Use transitional words and phrases to show relationships between ideas*. Study the list below for ideas:

CHAPTER 12 REVIEW—Continued

Result: consequently, thus, as a result, therefore
Summary: in conclusion, in summary, in short
Sequence: first, second, then, finally, meanwhile
Emphasis: most importantly, especially
Addition: also, furthermore, further, moreover, including

Writing

Pick two topics from this chapter. On each topic write two separate short paragraphs. In the first one do not use any transitional words or phrases. In the second one use at least one or more of the transitional words listed above. After you have completed this assignment, write down how the transitional words and phrases make a difference in the two paragraphs for each of the topics.

Social Studies Skills

Reading Political Maps

Look at the map on page 286. It shows the reapportionment of seats in the House of Representatives for the year 1992 through 2001.

1. How is color used in this map?
2. When was the data collected to make this map?
3. How many states saw no change in their number of representatives?
4. How many states suffered a reduction in their number of representatives?
5. Of those states that gained seats, what was the size of the average gain in seats?

Activities and Projects

1. Prepare a biography of your representative or one of your senators using the resources list on page 298, your library, and information you can obtain from the congressperson's office. Present your report to the class.
2. Make a list of the committees and subcommittees that your senators have been on for the last decade. Establish whether the committees and subcommittees they have been on have been particularly important for your state or region. For example, if you live in an area where there is aerospace manufacturing, has your senator been named to a committee or subcommittee that determines spending in the area of national defense? Write a short report that summarizes your research results.
3. Describe the job of a member of the House or Senate by creating a want ad for a congressperson. In the ad include qualifications, benefits and salary, and skills needed. Also include facts that demonstrate the typical responsibilities of members.
4. Find out which select committees are currently active. Keep track of the action of one of these committees for one month. Present the results of what you learn in a two-page report, a short speech, or a bulletin board.

The Powers of Congress

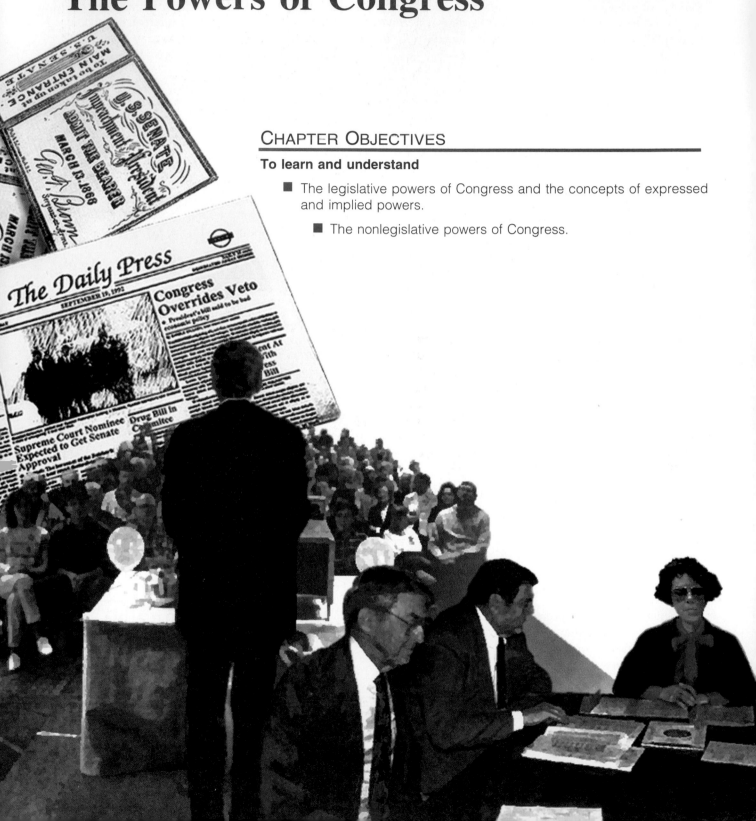

CHAPTER OBJECTIVES

To learn and understand

- The legislative powers of Congress and the concepts of expressed and implied powers.

- The nonlegislative powers of Congress.

Keynote

"The accumulation of all powers, legislative, executive, and judiciary, in the same hands, whether one, a few, or many . . . may justly be pronounced the very definition of tyranny."

———— **James Madison**
(1751–1836) Fourth President of the
United States

INTRODUCTION

The power to make laws for an entire nation is a tremendous responsibility. The founders recognized this, which is perhaps why they devoted the first and lengthiest article of the Constitution to carefully spelling out the powers of Congress. It is also why they reserved certain powers to the states, denied large areas of power to Congress, and gave other powers to the judicial and executive branches. They also stipulated that some powers would be shared. They felt, as illustrated by James Madison's statement above, that powers must be divided among the three branches of government. This sharing and division of powers is part of the system of checks and balances they created to avoid what James Madison called "the very definition of tyranny." For example, the president can veto an act of Congress and the Supreme Court has the power to declare acts of Congress unconstitutional. Although the powers of Congress are great, they are also limited.

SECTION 1

Legislative Powers

Preview Questions
- What is the concept of expressed powers?
- What powers does Congress have concerning the nation's budget and economy?
- What powers does Congress have concerning foreign affairs?
- What other expressed powers does Congress possess?
- What is the necessary and proper clause and how has it been applied?

Article I, Section 1 of the Constitution provides that all powers to make laws for the United States government shall be given to Congress. It reads:

> All legislative Powers herein granted shall be vested in a Congress of the United States, which shall consist of a Senate and House of Representatives.

That is, Congress is the only one of the three branches of the federal government that has the power to make laws. Because legislative powers are directly listed, they are referred to as the **expressed powers**. Sometimes they are also called the **delegated** or **enumerated powers**.

Expressed Powers

Although the powers of Congress are spelled out in the Constitution, the actual scope of these powers is not. The wording is brief and very general. The scope and content of these powers has been defined by how Congress has used its powers over the years, and by the interpretations handed down by the Supreme Court.

The Power to Tax and Spend   The first power listed in Article 1, Section 8, gives Congress the power to:

> [levy] and collect taxes, duties, imports, and excises, to pay the debts, and provide for the common defense and general welfare of the United States.

This clause gives Congress the power to collect and to spend money. This "power of the purse" is among the most important powers of Congress. The main purpose of the power to tax is to raise the money needed to finance the operations of government. Under the Articles of Confederation, Congress had no power of taxation; as a result the government never had enough money to function well. To remedy this, the Constitution granted Congress such power.

313

BUILDING SOCIAL STUDIES SKILLS
Cause and Effect versus Correlation

The world is full of correlations, or relationships. There seems to be a correlation, for example, between exercising and good health. But it is important to remember that correlation is not the same as causation. Causation occurs when a change in one variable *causes* a change in another. There are scientific ways to prove such causation.

There are numerous correlations that can be discovered in American politics. During election time, analysts might expect to find correlations between being African American and voting Democratic, being wealthy and voting Republican, and being young and not voting at all. Although certain demographic traits are correlated or associated with voting patterns, these are not *causal* explanations. Being under thirty does not cause people not to vote. Rather, the transient lifestyles of younger Americans and their lack of attachment to a community and family tend to keep them away from the polls.

Consider another example. Every president elected in a year ending with the number zero, from William H. Harrison in 1840 to John F. Kennedy in 1960, died in office. The correlation is between years ending in zero and presidential death. It seems quite obvious, however, that presidential death was not *caused* by the years ending in zero. Instead, this is one of those strange coincidences (called *spurious correlations* by social scientists) in American politics.

These and other correlations have nothing to do with causation. In reading and hearing about American politics it is important not to read causation into information that is simply correlational.

PRACTICING YOUR SKILLS

1. Write a brief essay describing a cause and effect relationship with which you are familiar. Explain why this is a cause and effect relationship and not merely a correlation.
2. Read an article concerning the stock market. This can be found in the business section of your local newspaper, or in a national newspaper such as the *Wall Street Journal*. Try to determine whether the writer's assessment of why the stock market went up or down involves a correlation between two events or a true cause-and-effect relationship.

Congress also has the power to acquire, manage, and dispose of various federal territories. Thus Congress has passed laws to govern territories such as the Virgin Islands, Guam, Puerto Rico, and other areas that are not states. The power also covers hundreds of military installations, national parks, dockyards, prison facilities, and other federal holdings throughout the United States.

Implied Powers

Not all of the powers of Congress are specifically listed in the Constitution. There are other powers known as **implied powers**, which are based on the last clause in Article 1, Section 8. This clause gives Congress the power:

> To make all laws which shall be necessary and proper for carrying into execution the foregoing powers, and all other powers vested by this Constitution in the Government of the United States, or in any department or office thereof.

This clause, called the **necessary and proper clause**, is also referred to as the **elastic clause** because it has allowed Congress to stretch and greatly expand its powers. Much of the adaptability of the Constitution can be traced to this provision.

Strict or Loose Interpretation? What do the words of the necessary and proper clause mean? How far can Congress stretch its powers? Almost from the time the words were written, their meaning has been under debate. The first dispute erupted in 1789 when Alexander Hamilton, as secretary of the Treasury, urged Congress to set up a federal bank.

A group opposing the idea, led by Secretary of State Thomas Jefferson, argued that the Constitution gave Congress no such power. This group was known as the **strict constructionists**, those that maintained that Congress could do only the things absolutely necessary to carry out its expressed powers.

Powers Granted to Congress by Article I, Section 8, of the Constitution

Expressed Powers

Taxation of goods Congress can set and collect taxes on goods as they are manufactured, sold, used, or imported [Clause 1].

Borrowing money Congress can borrow money on the credit of the United States [Clause 2].

Regulation of commerce Congress can regulate interstate and foreign trade [Clause 3].

Bankruptcy Congress can make laws with respect to bankruptcy [Clause 4].

Naturalization Congress can determine how aliens can become U.S. citizens [Clause 4].

Money Congress can mint coins and can print and circulate paper money [Clause 5].

Standards Congress can establish uniform weights and measures [Clause 5].

Punishment of counterfeiters Congress can punish counterfeiters of American currency [Clause 6].

Post offices and roads Congress can establish post offices and all routes over which mail is carried [Clause 7].

Copyrights and patents Congress can grant copyrights to authors and composers, and patents to inventors [Clause 8].

Lower courts Congress can set up all federal courts except the Supreme Court [Clause 9].

Punishment for certain acts in international waters Congress can prohibit acts of piracy outside U.S. territory and can punish certain other acts that all nations prohibit [Clause 10].

Declaration of war Congress can declare war and, until international law banned such action in the mid-nineteenth century, could authorize private parties to capture and destroy enemy ships in wartime [Clause 11].

The army Congress can raise and maintain an army [Clause 12].

The navy Congress can create and maintain a navy [Clause 13].

Regulation of the armed forces Congress can set rules for military forces [Clause 14].

The militia Congress can call into service the militia (known today as the National Guard) [Clause 15].

Regulation of the militia Congress can organize, arm, and discipline the militia, and can govern it when it is in the service of the United States [Clause 16].

Creation of Washington, D.C. Congress can govern Washington, D.C., and can erect such buildings there that would seem necessary for the seat of the U.S. government [Clause 17].

Implied Powers

The Elastic Clause Congress can make all laws necessary and proper for executing the foregoing expressed powers [Clause 18].

▲ **FIGURE 13–1 Powers Granted to Congress by Article I, Section 8, of the Constitution.** The table above lists both the expressed and the implied powers granted to Congress by the Constitution. How would you describe the difference between the expressed powers and the implied powers?

trips have also helped Congress make laws concerning other issues such as crime prevention, farm-price supports, and aid to African famine victims.

Congressional committees have the power to issue a **subpoena**, which is a legal order requiring a person to appear before a congressional committee (or a court of law). Sometimes dozens of witnesses are called to testify. Committees can also require witnesses to testify under oath, and prosecute witnesses for perjury (lying under oath). If a person refuses to testify or cooperate, he or she can be held in **contempt of Congress** and may be arrested and jailed.

Committees can also grant witnesses **immunity**, which is freedom from prosecution, if the witness provides certain information that helps to solve a crime. Witnesses granted immunity can give testimony about activities in which they may have been involved without fear of prosecution. The Watergate Committee for example, granted immunity to twenty-seven witnesses.

Despite these powers, a congressional committee is not a court of law. A congressional investigation, however, may result in a criminal indictment of individuals in state or federal court. It could also mean changes in a government program, loss of government contracts for businesses, or passage of new laws and regulations.

Oversight Function

The power to examine how effectively the executive branch and its officials carry out the laws passed by Congress is part of Congress' **oversight func-** **tion**, sometimes referred to as the "watchdog function."[2]

Congress has defined its oversight functions in several laws. The Legislative Reorganization Act of 1946 calls for Congress to exercise "continuous watchfulness" over executive agencies. In the Reorganization Act of 1970, Congress states that "Each standing committee shall review and study, on a continuing basis, the application, administration, and execution" of laws relating to its interests.

Methods of Oversight   Congress exercises its oversight function in several ways. One method, as you have just seen, is by holding committee hearings and investigations. A second oversight technique is to require agencies to submit reports to Congress on their activities. During one term, Congress may receive more than 1,000 such reports from various agencies.

Congress also exercises oversight by controlling the budget. The House and Senate review the budgets of all executive agencies every year. If it evaluates the agency positively, Congress may reward the agency by increasing the budget, while others may receive cuts or status quo budgets (budgets at the present level).

Lawmakers often dispatch one of the congressional support agencies such as the Government Accounting Office (GAO) to undertake a study of an executive agency's work. In fact, nearly every important piece of

---

2.   The term *oversight* can have two opposing meanings. In casual conversation, one talks about an oversight, meaning something that was inadvertently missed or ignored. In the context of this chapter, *oversight* means "carefully watched over."

PROFILE

Daniel Ken Inouye

▶ Senator Daniel Inouye (seated center) has held many important positions in the Senate, including chairman of the special Senate committee that investigated the Iran–*contra* affair in 1986.

Senator Daniel Inouye first became a congressman in Hawaii when it became a state in 1959. He was elected to the Senate in 1962 and has remained there, receiving 73 percent of the vote in the last election. Inouye was born in Honolulu on September 7, 1924. His paternal grandparents left Japan to work in the sugar plantations in Hawaii when his father, Hyotaro, was 4 years old. In March 1943, Inouye enlisted in the Army and served in Europe with a group of Japanese Americans led by white officers. Just weeks before the war ended, he lost his right arm in an attack against a German bunker in northern Italy. He received the Distinguished Service Cross, Bronze Star, Purple Heart with Cluster, Good Conduct Medal, five unit citations, and five battle stars. As he worked to graduate from the University of Hawaii and the George Washington School of Law in 1952, he took an interest in politics.

Daniel Inouye's name is not often heard outside the Senate corridors, but when it is heard, the occasion tends to be important. As senior Democratic senator, he was appointed chairman of the special Senate committee to look into the Iran-*contra* affair in 1986. He had already served on the special Senate committee that investigated the Watergate scandal. In 1976, when Congress was seeking to curb abuses by the CIA, he became the first chairman of the Senate Select Committee on Intelligence. Although he has never served as the chairman of a standing Senate committee, he has risen to the number three position among Senate Democrats, and was recommended to Walter Mondale as vice-presidential candidate in 1984.

Inouye is often cited for his loyalty to the Senate and to his friends, and he has a record of making difficult decisions. Even though some would say he lacks the political clout of some of his junior senators, when a job opens up that calls for honesty and courage, senators seem to turn to their colleague from Hawaii.

THINK ABOUT IT _____

1. While Inouye was serving in the Army during World War II, something else was happening to many Japanese Americans living on the West Coast of the United States. What was it?
2. What are some reasons that Inouye has never been a chairman of a standing Senate committee? (HINT: Could it have to do with the size of the state he represents?)

legislation passed by Congress directs the GAO to study its effects. The GAO issued 880 reports and 3,800 legal rulings in 1991, for example, and began 1,500 audits and investigations. Three-fourths of the agency's recommendations are adopted.

Limits of Oversight   For several reasons, Congress is limited in its ability to effectively perform the oversight function. The actions of the executive branch are not reviewed on a regular basis and sometimes the review hearings are not effective. Federal agency representatives often spend too much time on minor details and neglect broader problems. Members are often under a great deal of pressure because of other issues, and meetings are sometimes poorly attended.

The complexity, size, and number of federal programs also makes oversight difficult. There are dozens of executive agencies, many of which have large numbers of employees.

Political considerations also influence how seriously oversight functions will be carried out. In the 1980s, for example, it became known that some of President Reagan's staff had allowed arms to be sold to Iran in exchange for Iran's help in releasing American hostages held in the Middle East. The profits from those arms sales were then funneled to the *contra* rebels in Nicaragua. Both of these actions were in violation of U.S. law. A year before this scandal became publicized, two congressional committees had begun investigating fundraising efforts for the Nicaraguan *contras* that had been undertaken by a member of the president's staff, Colonel Oliver North. The previous investigations were dropped, however, because some key members on the congressional committees did not wish to challenge a popular president.

Limits on the Powers

There are important limits to the seemingly sweeping powers of Congress. One way Congress is limited is by the system of checks and balances. The president, as head of the executive branch, can veto proposed legislation passed by Congress. The judicial branch can declare laws passed by Congress unconstitutional.

The Constitution also explicitly places certain prohibitions on Congress. The purpose of the Bill of Rights was to limit or deny certain powers to the federal government such as prohibiting it from restricting freedom of speech. Congress is also limited by the fact that the Constitution does not delegate certain powers to Congress. Thus, Congress may not create a national school system, establish units of local government, require that all eligible persons vote on election day, or pass a national divorce law. Congress cannot do these and a great many other things because it has not been given the power to do them.

Article I, Section 9 of the Constitution lists specific limits placed on Congress. The most important of these limits protect the rights of citizens. The Constitution says that Congress shall not take away a citizen's right to a writ of habeas corpus, except in times of invasion or civil war. (As you learned in Chapter 5, a writ of habeas corpus is the paper that orders the police to bring a citizen charged with a crime before a judge. The court then decides if there is enough evidence to hold the citizen. If not, the citizen must be released.)

The Constitution also prevents Congress from passing bills of attainder. (As you learned in Chapter 5, a bill of attainder is a law that convicts a person of a crime without a trial.) In addition, Congress shall not pass ex post facto laws—laws that make a particular act a crime and then punish people who committed the act *before* the law was passed.

The Constitution also does not allow Congress to grant titles of nobility to any person, or to pass commerce laws more favorable to one state than to another.

These limits on the powers of Congress are in place so that the legislative branch does not come to exemplify James Madison's "very definition of tyranny." As you have learned, Congress still possesses the powers needed to perform its immense job. Through those powers expressed in the Constitution and those implied by the necessary and proper clause, Congress is able to act as an effective legislative body. Congress also wields nonlegislative powers in such areas as impeachment, the constitutional amendment process, investigation, and oversight.

SECTION 2 REVIEW

1. Which house of Congress has the exclusive power to impeach?
2. How may a constitutional amendment be proposed?
3. What are Congress' responsibilities concerning the election of the president?
4. Which appointments must the Senate approve?
5. What are the major methods of oversight that Congress may use?
6. **For critical analysis:** Are Congress' current powers to oversee the president's actions sufficient to prevent the president from becoming too powerful? Explain your answer.

CHALLENGE TO THE AMERICAN DREAM

Limits on the Congressional Power to Investigate

One of the more controversial powers of Congress has been its power to conduct investigations while fulfilling its legislative function. Part of the controversy stems from the fact that these investigative powers are not explicitly stated in the Constitution. Over the decades, however, the authority to conduct investigations has been viewed as essential to Congress' main functions of passing and administering legislation, informing the people of various public affairs, and protecting the integrity of the federal government.

It has been argued that without the authority to obtain factual information upon which to base its legislative decisions, Congress could not effectively exercise any of the powers bestowed upon it. In 1885 Woodrow Wilson said that, "the informing function of Congress should be preferred even to its legislative function." Just prior to his appointment to the Supreme Court in 1937, Senator Hugo Black referred to congressional investigations as a "useful and fruitful" function of Congress. Others, however, have disagreed. National columnist Walter Lippmann once characterized the congressional investigation as "that legalized atrocity in which congressmen, starved of their legitimate food for thought, go on a wild and feverish manhunt and do not stop at cannibalism."

One of the most controversial modern-day investigations by Congress occurred after World War II in the climate of growing concern about the spread of communism. During the late 1940s and into the 1950s, committees in both chambers of Congress used their investigative powers against individuals suspected of being Communist sympathizers or members of subversive organizations. The House Un-American Activities Committee (HUAC) called over three thousand witnesses during this period and questioned many of them on their political beliefs, affiliations, and actions deemed potentially dangerous to the United States government. Many suspects and witnesses invoked the Fifth Amendment protection against self-incrimination and others refused to testify, insisting that the committee's interrogation went beyond Congress's legislative function. Nearly 150 people were cited for contempt of Congress.

Senator Joseph McCarthy headed one of these investigating committees in the Senate in the 1950s. He repeatedly made unsubstantiated (unprovable) charges against public officials and private individuals suspected of political subversion. His allegations, along with those of the HUAC, resulted in a series of security investigations into the backgrounds and activities of public employees, scientists, screenwriters, movie directors, and academics. Additionally, loyalty oaths were imposed on public employees, and anti-Communist legislation was passed. Although he never had any evidence to prove or support his accusations, it was not until December of 1954 that McCarthy was censured by the Senate. This, however, did little to help the ruined reputations and lives of those whom he had destroyed. Later, there were many calls for reforming the congressional investigation process to prevent the recurrence of such abuses.

The challenge to the American dream is to allow Congress to carry out its lawful job of oversight without allowing it to violate the constitutional rights of those being investigated.

You Decide

1. In a court of law, the accused has many more rights and guarantees than individuals who come under the investigation of congressional committees. Do you think that the same rules that apply to court trials should be applied to congressional investigations? Why or why not?

2. Some have argued that many senators and representatives have started congressional investigations in order to put themselves in the public limelight. Is there any way to determine a valid congressional investigation as opposed to a publicity effort? Explain.

CHAPTER 13 REVIEW

Key Terms

appropriation 314
bankruptcy 315
contempt of
    Congress 326
copyright 317
currency power 315
delegated, expressed,
    or enumerated
    powers 313

direct tax 314
elastic clause 318
federal budget 315
government bonds 315
immunity 326
impeach 321
implied powers 318
impoundment 320
indirect tax 314

interstate
    commerce 315
loose
    constructionists 321
national debt 315
necessary and proper
    clause 318
oversight function 326

patent 317
revenue bills 314
senatorial courtesy 324
strict
    constructionists 318
subpoena 326

Summary

1. Article I Section 1 of the Constitution requires that all power to make laws shall be given to Congress. The powers that are specifically provided for—the expressed powers—include the power to tax and spend; the power to borrow and coin money and set bankruptcy laws; the commerce power; the power to approve treaties, to declare war, to create federal courts below the level of the Supreme Court; to establish post offices, copyrights, and patents; and powers of naturalization and dominion over territories. The powers known as implied powers are based on the necessary and proper clause. Early in our history the issue of whether to interpret the clause strictly or loosely was debated. In *McCulloch* v. *Maryland* (1819) the Court ruled that the necessary and proper clause gave Congress the right to make any laws necessary to carry out its other powers.

2. The Constitution also gives Congress a number of nonlegislative duties, which include the power to impeach government officials and to propose constitutional amendments. The Senate must approve presidential appointments to many important positions in the executive and judicial branches. The Senate must also give its advice and consent to ratifying treaties made by the president. Through its investigative committees, Congress also has the power to hold hearings during which it investigates important problems, such as fraud by government contractors. The power to oversee and scrutinize how effectively the executive branch and its officials carry out the laws passed by Congress is called the oversight function. Congress exercises this function by holding committee hearings and investigations, requiring

agencies to submit reports, reviewing the budgets of agencies, and dispatching one of the congressional support agencies such as the GAO to study an executive agency's work.

Review Questions

1. What are expressed powers?
2. Why is the congressional power to tax and spend important?
3. Why does the nation have a national debt?
4. Explain the commerce power of Congress and how the definition of commerce has expanded.
5. How does Congress share war powers with the president?
6. Why is the necessary and proper clause also called the elastic clause? How has this clause been used?
7. How was the main issue in *McCulloch* v. *Maryland* resolved? Why is it an important precedent?
8. What are Congress' nonlegislative powers?
9. How has Congress used its investigative powers?
10. Name four guidelines for writing a letter to a member of Congress.
11. How has the congressional power to investigate evolved and how is it limited?

Questions For Thought and Discussion

1. Do you agree with the War Powers Resolution of 1973, which limits the president's power to send troops into combat without congressional approval? Why or why not?

CHAPTER 13 REVIEW—Continued

2. How do the leadership positions in the Democratic and Republican parties affect leadership positions within Congress?

3. Originally, the framers of the Constitution wanted to ensure that Congress could not involve itself in the states' internal affairs. Nonetheless, the necessary and proper clause has been expanded so that Congress now has control over virtually all economic activities, even when they are strictly carried out within each state's borders. Do you think this is a fair exercise of congressional power? Give reasons for your answer.

Improving Your Skills
Communication Skills

Common Considerations in Writing:

Whether you are writing a letter, a report, or an essay, you must consider three common considerations: the reader, the purpose, and the subject matter.

Know Your Reader: Before you write anything, think about who the reader is. You would write a letter to your friend very differently than one to your congressperson. When you understand the needs of your reader, you will be able to write a more meaningful message.

Know Your Purpose: Before you begin writing, think about what the purpose of your writing is. Most writing is done for one of the following reasons:

- to inform
- to request
- to inquire
- to confirm
- to persuade
- to entertain

Know Your Subject: Know as much as possible about the subject of your writing. Use the research guidelines on page 279 and the interview techniques on page 97, if necessary. Think of innovative ways to learn about your subject.

Writing

1. Think of an issue about which you are concerned. Compose one letter to a friend and one letter to a congressional representative expressing your views. Compare the two letters. Describe your purpose in writing the letter. Make a list of any other information you could obtain that would improve your letters. Identify where the information could be located.

Social Studies Skills
Understanding Symbols

Many charts and graphs in your textbook have symbols to help illustrate key points and to make such diagrams easier to read and understand. Look at Figure 13-1 on page 319.

1. What is the focus of this figure?

2. Make a list of all of the symbols that are used.

3. How does the top-most symbol relate to the first power of Congress?

4. To which power does the symbol of the Statue of Liberty refer and why?

5. What is the symbol used that relates to Congress' copyright powers?

Activities and Projects

1. Divide into groups of five or six. Ask each member to collect articles from newspapers and magazines that describe congressional actions. Create a bulletin board display, grouping each article according to which type of congressional power—expressed, implied, or nonlegislative—the action falls under. Discuss how each article illustrates those powers.

2. Debate the following—Resolved: No member of Congress shall serve on any committee for more than six years.

3. Research how often the War Powers Act of 1973 has been effectively used. Write a short report detailing your findings.

CHAPTER 14

How Congress Makes Laws

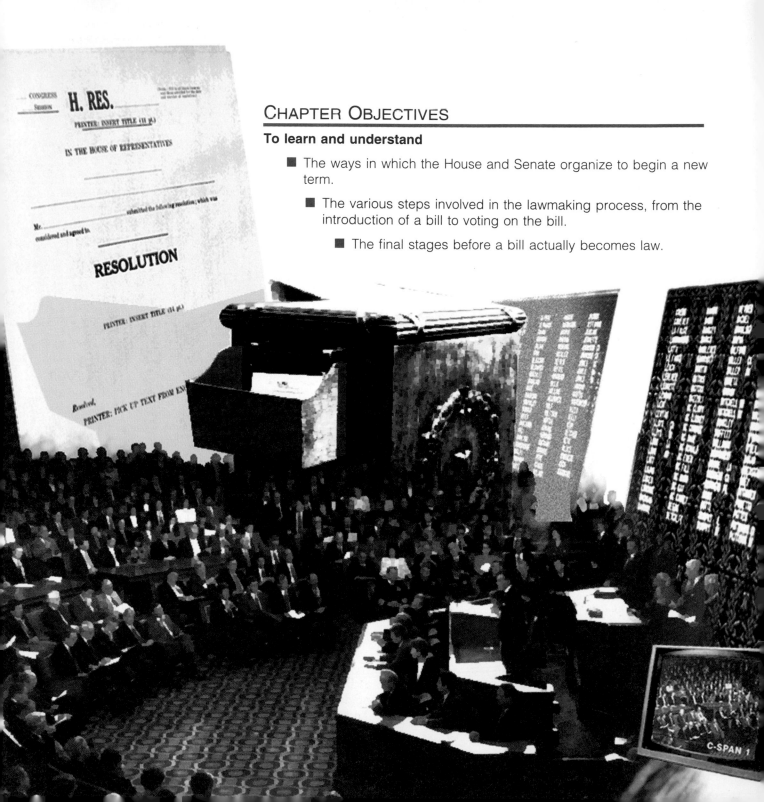

CHAPTER OBJECTIVES

To learn and understand

- The ways in which the House and Senate organize to begin a new term.

- The various steps involved in the lawmaking process, from the introduction of a bill to voting on the bill.

- The final stages before a bill actually becomes law.

H. RES.

PRINTER: INSERT TITLE (11 pt.)

IN THE HOUSE OF REPRESENTATIVES

RESOLUTION

C-SPAN 1

Keynote

"Congress in its committee rooms is Congress at work".

———— **Woodrow Wilson**
(1856–1924) Twenty-Eighth President
of the United States

INTRODUCTION

You have seen how Congress is organized to carry out its functions and you have learned about the powers of Congress. You will now take a look at how Congress performs its most important function: lawmaking. The laws of Congress have helped shape this country into the nation we have today, and those laws will continue to guide the nation in the future.

This chapter will explore how the lawmaking process actually works. First you will look at the opening of a congressional session and the different forms new legislation may take. Then you will read about the steps that a bill must go through in order to become a law. As reflected in Woodrow Wilson's quote above, while some congressional work takes place on the floor of the House and Senate, much of it takes place in committees. Still other work by Congress is done informally in political conferences. This has caused some writers to compare the operation of Congress to a great stage play in which much of the action takes place offstage.

SECTION 1

Congress Begins Its Work

Preview Questions:
- What roles do political caucuses play during the congressional term?
- How are the opening days of the House and Senate different?
- What are the different types of legislation considered each year?

As you learned already, a new term of Congress begins every two years on January 3 of every odd-numbered year. During each term, out of the thousands of bills that are introduced, few become law. The legislative process that each of these bills passes through is complicated. Consequently, Congress must organize itself so that congressional members can consider all of these bills.

This process of organization begins with the political parties with which members of Congress identify. After all, those political parties are largely responsible for getting members elected to the offices they now must fill. It is not surprising, then, that the houses of Congress are also made up of political groups that begin work even before each term begins.

Political Caucuses

Before a new term begins, Democratic and Republican members of the House and Senate meet in separate private party conferences called **caucuses**. Both the Senate and House hold two party caucuses—one for Republicans and one for Democrats. These caucuses meet in order to reach agreement among themselves about key issues so they can act as a unified force, and to plan the party's strategy for the upcoming term. They also choose the party leaders who will organize and direct party activities during the congressional term. These choices are often made on the basis of seniority.

The number of caucuses has grown in recent years. Caucuses have generally been organized on the basis of regions and special interests. Examples are the Congressional Sunbelt Council and the Congressional Steel Caucus. They have also been organized on the basis of gender and ethnicity: The Black Caucus, the Congressional Women's Caucus, and the Hispanic Caucus are other examples of such groups. The activities of these caucuses are directed toward their fellow members of Congress and toward administrative agencies such as the Federal Trade Commission (FTC) and the Federal Aviation Administration (FAA). Within Congress, they press for

◄ Opening day in the Congress focuses attention on the pressing issues to be discussed in the coming congressional term. What issues do you think the current Congress should be addressing?

committees to hold hearings, push particular legislation, and lobby for votes on bills they favor. Thus, even before the term begins, members of Congress have set the legislative process in motion.

Opening Day of Congress

On the opening day of Congress, members of each chamber meet in their own wing of the Capitol building, shown in Figure 14–1 on the next page.

Every House member is up for election every two years, so each term begins anew. All members have to be sworn in, whether it is their first term or their tenth; rules have to be made; and organization has to be decided upon. The **clerk of the House** from the previous session presides at the beginning of the first day's session. The chamber is called to order and a roll call is taken. The members then *officially* elect a Speaker of the House. This election is only a formality because the Speaker has already been chosen by the majority party caucus. The Speaker of the House is sworn in by the member of the House who has served the longest. The Speaker then swears in the rest of the representatives.

Next the House *officially* elects its nonmember, or staff, officers such as the clerk, sergeant at arms, and postmaster. Again these choices have previously been decided by the majority party caucus. Then the rules that will govern how the House proceeds throughout the term are adopted. The rules of the House have been evolving for over two hundred years and they are usually readopted with little or no change. Finally, members are appointed to permanent committees, and committee

chairpersons, also determined previously by majority party caucus, are formally selected. The opening day of the House ends with the House telling the Senate that it is ready for the president's annual message to Congress.

Opening Day in the Senate

On opening day in the Senate, only one-third of the Senate's members are beginning new terms, which makes the Senate a continuous body. This means its members have less organizational business to attend to than do members of the House. The Senate swears in its recently elected members and fills vacancies in its organizations and committees. The Senate then informs the House that it is ready for the president's annual address.

State of the Union Address

After both houses have organized, a joint committee of the two officially notifies the president that Congress is in session and ready to begin work. Within a few days, the president delivers his annual **State of the Union Address**. Members of both houses, together with the members of the Cabinet, the Supreme Court, the foreign service corps, and other dignitaries, assemble in the large chamber of the House of Representatives to hear the annual address.

The State of the Union Address was originally a long and often boring speech. Our third president, Thomas

Floor Plan of the U.S. Capitol

Rooms on Second Floor of the Capitol

House Side

H-201, 202, 203, 204, 205, 206. Speaker.
H-207. House reception room
  (Sam Rayburn Room).
H-208. Committee on Ways and Means.
H-209, 210. Speaker's Rooms.
H-211. Parliamentarian.
H-212, 213, 214. Representatives' retiring rooms.
H-216, 217, 218. Committee on Appropriations.
H-219. Minority Whip.
H-221, 223. Republican cloakrooms.
H-222, 224. Democratic cloakrooms.
H-226. House document room.
H-227, 228, 229, 230, 231, 232, 233, 236.
  Minority Leader.
H-234. Prayer room.
H-235. Congresswomen's Suite.

Senate Side

S-201, 202, 203, 204, 205, 237, 238, 239, 240, 241, 242.
  Senators' offices.
S-206. President *Pro Tempore.*
S-207. Senator's conference room (Mike Mansfield Room).
S-208, 209. Secretary of the Senate.
S-210. Secretary of the Senate (John F. Kennedy Room).
S-211. Secretary of the Senate (Lyndon B. Johnson Room).
S-212. Vice President.
S-213. Senators' reception room.
S-214. Ceremonial Office of the Vice President.
S-215. Senators' retiring room (Marble Room).
S-216. President's Room.
S-218, 219. Official Reporters of Debates.
S-220. Bill Clerk and Journal Clerk.
S-221, 222, 223, 224. Majority Leader (Robert C. Byrd Rooms).
S-225. Democratic cloakroom.
S-226. Republican cloakroom.
S-227. Executive clerk.
S-229, 243. Assistant Republican Leader.
S-230, 231, 232, 233, 234, 235, 235A, 236. Republican Leader
  (Howard H. Baker, Jr. Rooms).

▲ **FIGURE 14–1 Floor Plan of the U.S. Capitol.** The above floor plan is for the
second floor of the U.S. Capitol where both the Senate and House of
Representatives meet. According to this floor plan, which of the congressional
leaders is given the most space? Why do you think this is?

GOVERNMENT IN ACTION

PROFILE

Ileana Ros-Lehtinen

Ileana Ros-Lehtinen left Cuba as a child when her parents fled the Castro regime. In a special congressional election in Florida in 1989, Ros-Lehtinen, now a naturalized American citizen, defeated a native-born American for the seat. As a Republican, she took over a seat that had been Democratic for the past forty years and was held much of that time by one person, Claude Pepper.

Ros-Lehtinen is a conservative Republican who spent seven years in the Florida legislature before running for Congress. Her election demonstrates the political effect of growth in the number of new Americans coming from Hispanic backgrounds. It may represent a turning point in the political balance of power between Hispanic and non-Hispanic residents in Florida. A major challenge facing her in Congress will be the job of smoothing relations between the Hispanic community and other ethnic groups.

Ros-Lehtinen's Latin American heritage overshadowed most other issues during the campaign. Her opponent urged voters to keep the congressional seat "an American seat." Voting was described as "an ethnic war," sharply divided along racial and ethnic lines. The issue of Ros-Lehtinen's ethnic heritage was used by both sides in the campaign. As it turned out, her background worked to her advantage.

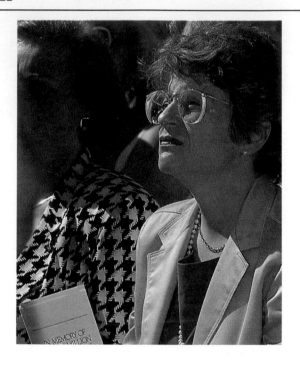

THINK ABOUT IT _____

1. Does the Constitution allow naturalized American citizens to hold all federal offices?
2. How might Ros-Lehtinen go about "smoothing relations between the Hispanic community and other ethnic groups"?

Jefferson, started a precedent when he submitted the speech in writing, claiming that speaking before Congress was too much like a British monarch's opening speech to Parliament. In 1913, Woodrow Wilson broke the precedent by personally delivering his first State of the Union Address. He used the speech as a chance to outline his administration's overall agenda and to urge the passage of certain programs.

The media, especially television, have added to the importance of the speech over the years, and today presidents use it as a ceremonial way of reporting on the "health" of the nation and its concerns, both domestic and foreign. It is also a speech in which the president lays out the administration's broad policies and makes legislative recommendations.

Bills and Resolutions

Congress considers several different kinds of legislation each year. Most pieces of legislation are in the form of bills. **Bills** are drafts of laws presented to the House and Senate for enactment.

One of the first official functions of any new Congress is to listen to the president deliver his annual State of the Union Address. How have the media changed the State of the Union Address?

Public Bills There are two kinds of bills: public and private. **Public bills** involve matters of national interest. For example, a federal tax increase, a proposal for health-care guidelines, a proposed ban on assault-style automatic weapons, a clean air bill, or an appropriation of funds for a military program would all be public bills. Public bills are often controversial, such as a civil rights bill or a gun-control bill, and may be debated for months or possibly years before they ever become law.

Private Bills **Private bills** are those bills that apply to certain persons or places rather than to the nation as a whole. For example, a private bill might pay a settlement to a woman whose car was demolished by a U.S. Postal Service truck, or a private bill might grant the right to enter the United States to a certain group of refugees.

Joint Resolutions **Joint Resolutions** (a formal declaration of opinion by vote of both houses of Congress and sent to the president for his approval) are very similar to bills: They must go through the same steps as a bill to become law, and when they are passed they have the same force of law. Joint resolutions often deal with temporary or unusual matters or correct an error in an earlier law. For example, money for a special military action overseas might be authorized by joint resolution. Joint resolutions are also used to propose constitutional amendments.

Concurrent Resolutions **Concurrent resolutions** deal with matters requiring the action of the House and Senate, but for which a law is not needed. They are measures intended to express an opinion or an official policy. For example, a concurrent resolution might ex-

press an opinion of Congress commemorating the anniversary of a successful space exploration or the welcoming of an important visitor, such as the Queen of England. A concurrent resolution may set the date for the adjournment of Congress. Concurrent resolutions must be passed by both chambers of Congress, but do not require the president's signature and do not have the force of law.

Simple Resolutions A **simple resolution** deals with matters affecting only one house of Congress and is

Senators such as Howard Metzenbaum (D., Ohio), shown above, consider several kinds of legislation each year. What is the most common form of legislation considered by members of Congress?

337

GOVERNMENT IN ACTION

CASE STUDY

Many Laws Proposed, Few Passed

In principle, Congress is for all Americans who want government to pass legislation in their favor. Business groups, farmers, labor unions, various interest groups, federal agencies, the president, and many others all look to Congress to pass laws favorable to their interests. As many as twenty thousand bills are introduced in the House and Senate during a congressional term, yet fewer than 10 percent of these bills become public laws. As President Kennedy once noted, "It is very easy to defeat a bill in Congress. It is much more difficult to pass one." Why do so few of the bills introduced become law?

One reason is that the lawmaking process is long and complex. The steps involved in passing a new law leave many opportunities for members of Congress to delay, alter, or kill a bill. These legislative hurdles give opponents of the bill numerous advantages: If their efforts to stop the bill fall short at one step along the way, they can always try again further down the line.

Bills that are opposed by important interest groups are not likely to be passed. Because members of Congress depend on interest-group money to get reelected, they are reluctant to antagonize these groups. For example, in every Congress since 1978, the House and Senate Banking Committees have tried to restructure the financial industry by attempting to overhaul a 1933 law. But reform has been hopelessly deadlocked because of the conflicting interests of big banks, small banks, insurance companies, and securities firms.

With the rise of negative campaigning, many members have concluded that it is safer to duck hard issues than to make any choices at all and risk losing favor with one side or the other. They increasingly appoint outside commissions and task forces to study any truly controversial problem, a process that often takes many months and does not produce a solution. For example, the Bipartisan Commission on Comprehensive Health Care devoted nine months and $1.5 million to propose an annual $66 billion "solution" to the health needs of the uninsured elderly. The report was immediately abandoned because feuding panelists omitted any reference to how the program was to be funded.

A plan designed to shield the elderly from the high costs of health care for major illnesses had strong bipartisan support, but was dropped when a small but vocal group of well-off seniors spoke in revolt over the plan's required tax-rate increases. "Five percent of the elderly swung us around like a dead cat," said Senator Alan Simpson, a Republican from Wyoming.

Another reason so few bills become law is that lawmakers sometimes introduce laws knowing they have no chance of passing. They may introduce such bills because they want to draw public attention to legislation in such areas as crime control or education or because they want to go on record in support of the idea. They may introduce such a bill to satisfy a group of voters from their district or an important special interest group. This can help them avoid criticism during election time because they can report they have taken "action" on the issue. They can blame committees and other lawmakers for the bill's failure to become law.

THINK ABOUT IT _____

1. Why do opponents of a bill have an advantage over supporters?
2. Should lawmakers be able to introduce bills that they know have no chance of becoming law? Why or why not?
3. Should lawmakers be able to introduce bills for the benefit of interest groups? Why or why not?

Selected Bills from the 102nd Congress

Bill	Subject
H.R. 355	Drought Assistance Relief
H.R. 525	Amending the Federal Charter for Boy's Clubs of America
H.R. 1304	Telephone Advertising Consumer Rights Act
H.R. 2100	Defense Authorization for Fiscal Year '92
H.R. 2707	Labor, Health, and Human Services Appropriations for Fiscal Year '92
H.R. 2722	Abandoned Infants Assistance Act of 1991
H.R. 2763	National Geological Mapping Act of 1991
H.R. 2790	Cave Creek Canyon Protection Act of 1991
H.R. 3245	Designating Certain National Forest System Lands in the State of Georgia as Wilderness
H.R. 3635	Preventive Health Block Grant Amendments of 1991
S. 668	Grants to Indian Tribal Governments to Regulate Environmental Quality on Indian Reservations
S. 1284	Judicial Improvements Act Technical Correction
S. 1475	Protection and Advocacy for Mentally Ill Individuals Amendments Act of 1991
S. 1568	American Legion Eligibility

▲ FIGURE 14–2 **Selected Bills from the 102nd Congress.** As you have learned, Congress considers different types of bills. What type of bills are listed above?

passed by that house alone. Simple resolutions are regularly used to adopt a new rule or procedure or to amend an existing one. Resolutions may also be used to express an opinion. For example, the Senate may pass a resolution in support of an action taken by the president toward The People's Republic of China. Like concurrent resolutions, they are not sent to the president for approval, and they do not have the force of law.

Riders   A bill or resolution usually deals with only one subject. Sometimes, however, a rider is attached to the bill. A **rider** is a provision that is unlikely to pass on its own so it is attached to an important measure that is likely to pass into law. The rider's sponsors hope it will ''ride'' through the legislative process on the strength of the measure in the bill. Riders become law if the bill to which they are attached is passed. Riders often deal

with controversial issues and sometimes have led to the defeat of the bill to which they are attached.

SECTION 1 REVIEW

1. What is the purpose of party caucuses prior to the convening of Congress?
2. How do the opening days of the House and Senate differ?
3. What does the president discuss in the State of the Union Address in modern times?
4. What types of bills are proposed in Congress? How do they differ?
5. **For critical analysis:** If the Speaker of the House, the clerk, the sergeant at arms, and other officials have already been chosen by the majority party caucus, why do you think the House continues to *officially* elect its officers on opening day?

How a Bill Becomes a Law

Preview Questions

- How is a bill introduced in Congress?
- How are bills assigned to committees? What happens within the committees?
- How does the House act on a bill? What are the different methods used for taking votes?
- What action on a bill is taken in the Senate and how is it different from that taken in the House?

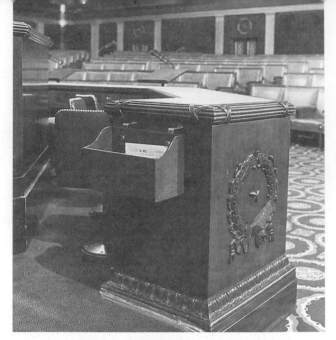

▲ To introduce a bill in the House, a representative simply drops the written proposal into the hopper, shown above. What happens to the bill next?

Introducing Legislation

Ideas for legislation originate from various sources. An idea might have been suggested by a constituent or a lobbyist, or it might have originated in a federal agency or been thought up by a member of Congress or one of his or her staff. Most bills, however, are proposed by the executive branch. Although almost anyone may suggest legislation, only a member of Congress can formally introduce it.

The Constitution states that all revenue bills must first be introduced in the House of Representatives, but any other type may begin in either house. A representative introduces a bill by simply dropping the written proposal into the **hopper**, a box near the clerk's desk. A senator introduces a bill by presenting it to the clerk at the presiding officer's desk, or formally presents the bill from the floor of the Senate. Those who draft and propose bills are called **sponsors**. Bills are then printed, distributed, and numbered according to when they are introduced. For example, H.R. 288 would be the 288th measure introduced in the House during the congressional term. Having received a number, the bill is entered in the House *Journal* and in the *Congressional Record* for the day. The House *Journal* and the *Congressional Record* are official publications of Congress.

When the number of the bill is printed in the *Congressional Record,* then the bill has been placed at *first reading.* For a bill to become law, it must have *three* readings at different stages of its progress through either house. The second reading usually occurs when floor debate begins. The third takes place after any amendments have been added to the bill and the House is ready to take a final vote.

Study by the Committee

As soon as a bill is introduced and assigned a number, it is sent to the appropriate standing committee. In the House, the Speaker assigns the bill to the appropriate standing committee. In the Senate, the presiding officer assigns bills to the proper committees. For example, a farm bill would be sent to the Agriculture Committee; a gun-control bill would be sent to the Judiciary Committee. Committee chairpersons may, in turn, send the bill on to a subcommittee. For example, a bill concerning conventional military weapons in Europe would be sent to the Senate Foreign Relations Subcommittee on European Affairs. Each committee sorts the bills it receives and considers only those it feels are important. The chairperson may decide to **pigeonhole** a bill, that is, put it aside and ignore it. Most bills that are pigeonholed die in committee.

If a bill is not pigeonholed, it is placed on the committee agenda or assigned to a subcommittee. The committee staff members go to work researching the bill and sometimes hold public hearings, during which people who support or oppose the bill may express their views. Committees also have the power to order witnesses to testify at public hearings. Witnesses may be executive agency officials, experts on the subject, or representatives of interest groups concerned about the bill. Depending on the interest in the subject, the hearings may be attended by only a few people or by a large group. For

A DAY IN THE LIFE

Senator Lloyd Bentsen

Senator Lloyd Bentsen, Democrat from Texas, was first elected to Congress in 1948 at age 27. After six years, he left Congress to begin an insurance business. In 1970, he decided to run for office again. This time he ran for the U.S. Senate, and defeated a Republican congressman from Houston named George Bush.

As chairman of the Senate Finance Committee, Bentsen was extremely influential in policy areas, such as taxes and international trade. He ran as the vice-presidential candidate of Michael Dukakis in the 1988 election. Upon taking office in 1993, President Bill Clinton named him his secretary of the Treasury. No doubt his schedule as a member of the Cabinet is different from the sample listed here, but it is certainly just as full.

	Wednesday
9:45	Senate Convenes
10:30	Meeting with Lt. Governor Brereton Jones and Wendell Ford of Kentucky

11:15	Finance Committee Executive Session, Re: Honda Audit
12:00	Meeting with John Mobley
12:30	Texas Congressional delegation— Closed luncheon
12:30	Democratic Caucus
12:30	Meeting with Senator Robert Byrd, W. Virginia
2:00	Meeting with Texas cardiologists
2:00	Finance Medicare Subcommittee
2:30	Meeting with Fruit of the Loom executives
3:00	Meeting on Pensions
3:30	Meeting with the National Governor's Association on Medicare funding
4:00	Texas Academy of Family Physicians
4:00	Reception for Leonid Kravchuk, leader of Ukraine
4:30	Meeting with Texas letter carriers
7:00	CNN's Moneyline, live interview on economic policy
8:00	Dinner honoring the president of the World Bank

THINK ABOUT IT _____

1. Aside from being an able and experienced legislator, what other attributes made Bentsen an attractive running mate for Massachusetts Governor Michael Dukakis?
2. During this day Senator Bentsen has met several times with his Texas constituents. Why do you think this is important?

GOVERNMENT IN ACTION

example, on March 20, 1991, April Glaspie, the former U.S. Ambassador to Iraq, was called to testify before the Senate Foreign Relations Committee concerning the United States diplomatic action with Iraq prior to the Persian Gulf War. The hearing was attended by a large group of senators, twenty-five photographers, a network camera pool, and three full tables of reporters. It was covered live by Cable News Network (CNN) and the Senate cable system. On the other side of Capitol Hill, a House Banking Committee hearing about overcharging in certain types of mortgage accounts was attended by only a few people.

Sometimes a subcommittee will make a trip to gather information on the bill. These trips, called **junkets**, are made to locations affected by the proposed measure. For example, if proposed legislation concerns an urban housing project, a member of the Senate Committee on Banking, Housing, and Urban Affairs may visit an inner-city area. If proposed legislation concerns wolves in a national park, the National Parks and Public Lands Subcommittee of the House Committee on Interior and Insular Affairs may visit the national park in question.

The subcommittee then meets to approve the bill as is, add new amendments, or draft a new bill. This meeting is known as the **markup session**. If members cannot agree on changes, a vote is taken. When a subcommittee completes its work on a bill it goes to full committee, which then meets for its own markup session. It may hold its own hearings, amend the subcommittee's version, or simply approve the subcommittee's recommendations.

Finally the committee will report the bill back to the full House. It can report the bill favorably, report the bill with amendments, or report a newly written bill. It can also report it unfavorably, but usually it will have been pigeonholed earlier instead. Along with the bill, the committee will send to the House or Senate a written report that explains the committee's actions, describes the bill, lists the major changes made by committee, and gives opinions on the bill.

Scheduling Legislation

Next, the bill is placed on a calendar and scheduled for debate. A **calendar** is a schedule of the order in which bills will be taken up on the floor. There are five calendars in the House, depending on the nature and subject matter of the bill. These calendars are:

1. **The Union Calendar.** Formally called The Calendar of the Committee of the Whole House on the State of the Union, all government property, revenue, and appropriations bills go on this calendar.
2. **The House Calendar.** All other public bills go on this calendar.
3. **The Private Calendar.** Formally known as The Calendar of the Committee of the Whole House, almost all private bills go on this calendar.
4. **The Consent Calendar.** This is for all bills removed from the first-two-mentioned calendars and agreed to by unanimous consent. These are typically minor bills.
5. **The Discharge Calendar.** All petitions designed to discharge bills from committees are placed on this calendar.

There is an elaborate schedule for House consideration of certain bills, but these arrangements are not always followed closely. The **House Rules Committee** plays a major role in the scheduling process. This committee, along with the House leaders, regulates the flow of the bills through the House. The Rules Committee can move bills ahead quickly, hold them back, or stop them completely. It can also set up special rules that limit the time set for debate and the number of amendments that can be suggested for the bill.

The Senate is much smaller and only a few leading members control the flow of bills to committees and to the floor. The Senate has only one calendar, the **Calendar of General Orders**, which lists all bills to be considered by the Senate. The Senate brings bills to the floor by "unanimous consent," a motion by which all members present on the floor set aside the Senate's formal rules and consider a bill from the calendar. In contrast to the procedure in the House, individual senators have the power to disrupt work on legislation.

The Constitution requires that before any action can take place on the floor, a certain number of members must be present. This number, known as a **quorum**, is a majority of the full House (218 members) or a majority of the Senate (51 members).

Action in the House

When a bill reaches the House floor, it receives its second reading as the clerk reads the bill through. After each paragraph, amendments may be offered and debate can take place. Many bills are minor and pass with little or no opposition. Because of its large size and the number of bills introduced, the House has developed several procedures to speed up the legislative process for some of the more important matters.

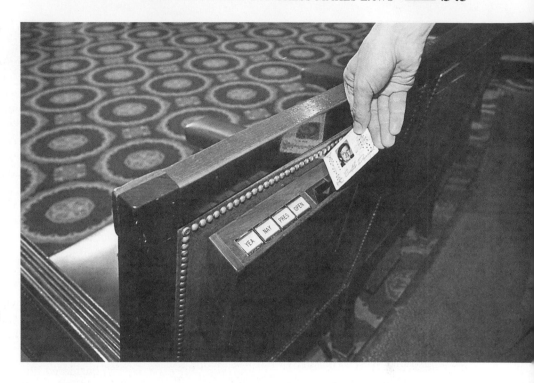

In 1973, the House of Representatives installed 48 electronic voting stations, such as the one shown here. For what type of vote are these stations used?

Committee of the Whole To speed along the passage of an important bill, the entire House may sit as a **committee of the whole**. In this committee, a temporary chairperson is appointed by the Speaker of the House and the usual formal House rules do not apply. At least 100 members must be present in order to conduct business, instead of the official quorum of 218. The measure is debated or amended, with votes on amendments as needed. The committee of the whole can approve or reject bills by a majority vote. The committee adjourns when it completes its action, and the House returns to its normal session and procedures. The Speaker presides once again, the full House hears the chairperson report the committee's recommendations, and it formally adopts them.

Debate Because of its large size, the House has severe limitations on floor debate. The Speaker recognizes those who may speak and can force any member who does not "stick to the subject" to give up the floor. Normally, the chairperson of the standing committee reporting the bill will take charge of the session during which it is debated. You can often watch such debates on C-SPAN (a cable television service that covers congressional activities, among other things).

Any member may propose an amendment to a bill during floor debate. At any time, any member may "move the previous question," which is a demand for a vote on the issue before the House. If that motion passes, only forty minutes of further debate is allowed before a vote is taken.

Vote After a House bill has been fully debated and amended, it is ready for a vote. The bill now has its third reading and a vote on the entire floor is taken. The House uses four different methods for taking floor votes:

1. Voice votes are the most common method of taking a floor vote. In a **voice vote**, the presiding officer asks those members in favor to say "Aye," and those opposed to say "No." The Speaker determines which side has the most voice votes.
2. If a member questions the results of the voice vote, a **standing vote** may be demanded. First, those in favor of the bill stand and are counted, then those opposed stand and are counted.
3. A **teller vote** may be demanded at the request of one-fifth of a quorum. The Speaker appoints two tellers, one member from each party. The members pass between them and are counted, for and against. Teller votes are rare today and have been replaced by electronic voting.
4. A **roll-call vote,** also known as a **record vote**, is recorded electronically. In 1973, the House installed a computerized voting system in which members insert a plastic card and press a button in one of forty-

CITIZENSHIP SKILLS AND RESPONSIBILITIES

Locating and Interpreting Congressional Voting Records

If you want to be an informed citizen concerning the voting records of your representatives and senators, you can obtain this information. All record or roll-call votes are printed in the *Congressional Record,* or Congressional Quarterly's *Weekly Report,* both of which are found in most large libraries. Some large newspapers such as the *Washington Post* and the *New York Times,* as well as some local papers, usually print weekly summaries of how local members voted on key issues.

Reading these final votes, however, does not give you the full picture. A member of Congress may have voted one way during committee and the other way in the final process. He or she may have wanted to go on record as voting according to public opinion in the final stage of passage. Members may also have changed their votes after the voting was completed. For example, they might have voted against the interests of their district, but when they discovered their vote was not crucial to its passage, they may have changed it to look good in the eyes of their constituents.

One way of examining a member's voting behavior throughout the process is by reading studies prepared by interest groups. Dozens of groups prepare studies and rate congressional members' voting records. (Remember, though, that these groups have their own set of standards—find out what they are.) Some of these groups include:

Consumer Federation of America
1012 14th St. NW
Washington, DC 20005

Environmental Action
1346 Connecticut Ave. NW
Washington, DC 20036

Women's Lobby, Inc.
1345 G St. SE
Washington, DC 20003

American Farm Bureau Federation
425 13th St. NW
Washington, DC 20004

TAKING ACTION

1. Write to one of the groups listed above to obtain information about its organization and its ratings of the senators and representatives in your state. Decide whether you think the group would be considered liberal, middle-of-the-road, or conservative. Then determine whether your members of Congress are considered liberal, middle-of-the-road, or conservative by the group. You might want to extend this activity by presenting your findings to your senators and representatives in the form of a letter. Ask them to respond to the group's assessment of their performance.

2. Obtain a record of one of your state's senator's voting record over the last year. Determine where on the political spectrum that senator's views lie. Compare your determination with one of the rating systems that you have already obtained from one of the groups listed above. How would you explain the differences, if there are any, between their evaluation and yours?

eight voting stations around the floor. Their votes are flashed on large display panels above the Speaker's desk, on other walls of the House, and on consoles located on the leadership tables. The board shows which members have voted as well as how they voted.

If a bill is approved by a majority, it is signed by the Speaker. A page then carries it to the Senate and places it on the vice president's (Senate president's) desk. (Congressional pages are juniors in high school who normally spend one school year living in Washington, D.C., and working for a senator or representative. There are normally about 100 of them who run errands between offices, work on the floor of the two houses, and answer phones in the cloak room.)

Action in the Senate

Although the steps in the lawmaking process are similar in both chambers, there are differences in floor

▲ During a filibuster over the passage of the Civil Rights Act in 1957, cots were set up in the old Supreme Court Chamber so that senators could rest. This filibuster by Senator Strom Thurmond of South Carolina was a record-setting 24 hours and 18 minutes long. What is the point of a filibuster?

debates. While floor debates are strictly limited in the House, debates are usually unlimited in the Senate. Generally, senators may speak on the floor for as long as they wish and there is no rule that they speak only about the measure under consideration. There is no routine motion to call for a vote. The Senate's dedication to freedom of debate is intended to encourage the fullest possible discussion of matters on the floor.

The Filibuster One way for a single senator or a group of senators to defeat a bill they oppose is to filibuster against it. To **filibuster** means to keep talking until a majority of the Senate either abandons the bill or agrees to modify its most controversial provisions. Essentially, filibustering is a tactic to delay or block action by "talking a bill to death."

All that senators need do to filibuster is stay on their feet and keep talking. After three hours, they may talk about any topic they want or even read a book aloud. In 1935, for example, Senator Huey Long (Democrat from Louisiana) spoke for more than fifteen hours and shared his recipes for southern-style cooking. Senator Strom Thurmond of South Carolina set the record for a filibuster when he spoke against the Civil Rights Act of 1957 for

twenty-four hours and eighteen minutes. Although later efforts have not equalled these, the practice on a less dramatic scale is still often used. Even the threat of a filibuster has resulted in the Senate's failure to consider a number of bills and the amending of many more.

Cloture Rule **Cloture** is a parliamentary rule by which debate is ended and an immediate vote is taken on the matter under discussion. The Senate can end filibusters by using the **cloture rule**, a procedure that limits debate by allowing a minimum of sixteen senators to move that debate be limited. If three-fifths of the entire Senate (sixty senators) approves, no senator may speak for more than one hour on the bill being considered. After that time, the bill under consideration must be brought to a vote. Obtaining a vote in favor of cloture, however, is usually difficult. Many senators hesitate to support most cloture motions because of the Senate tradition of open debate and because they themselves may want to filibuster a bill in the future.

Voting in the Senate

Voting in the Senate is very similar to voting in the House. However, there are no teller votes in the Senate.

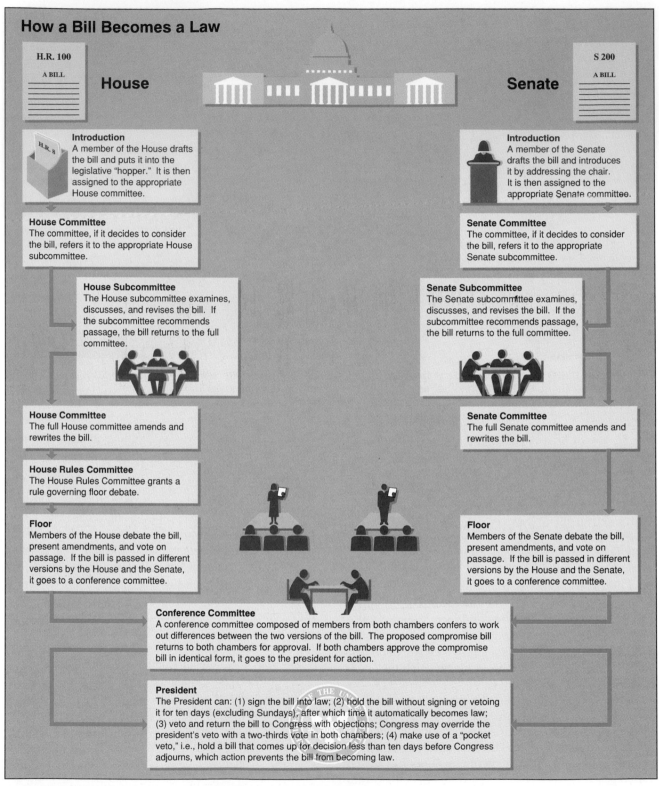

FIGURE 14–3 How a Bill Becomes a Law. The above figure maps out the steps involved in the process for enacting laws. At what stage in the process do members from both chambers work together to create a compromise bill?

SECTION 2 REVIEW

1. How are bills introduced in the House? How are they introduced in the Senate?
2. What happens during permanent committee meetings?
3. How are bills scheduled for debate?
4. What is the committee of the whole?
5. How does debate differ in the House and in the Senate?
6. **For critical analysis:** Why do you think the Senate allows unlimited debate in the form of a filibuster?

SECTION 3

The Final Stages

Preview Questions:
- When is a conference committee formed and what is its purpose?
- What options does a president have on receiving a bill passed by Congress?

Bills passed in one chamber are then sent to the other chamber where the legislative process begins again. To become law, a bill must be passed in *identical* form by both chambers of Congress. For example, in 1990 both chambers passed legislation that would revise and expand environmental laws for the first time in thirteen years. The two bills varied significantly in their prescriptions for acid rain, toxic pollutants, automobile emissions, and urban smog. What happens when the two houses pass separate versions of the same bill?

Conference Committees

When the House or the Senate will not accept the other's version of a bill, the measure is turned over to a **conference committee**—a temporary joint committee of the two houses. The conference committee members try to work out the differences between the two bills and come up with an acceptable compromise bill.

Members of the committee, called **conferees** or managers, are made up mostly of members of the standing committees that handled the bill in each house. In theory, the conference committee can only consider those points in a bill on which the two houses disagree; no proposals are allowed to be added. In reality, however, the conference committee sometimes makes important changes in the bill or adds new provisions.

Once conferees agree on the final compromise bill, a **conference report** is submitted to each house. The bill must be accepted or rejected by both houses as it was written by the committee, with no further amendments made. If the bill is approved by both houses, it is ready for action by the president.

Presidential Action

The Constitution requires that all bills passed by Congress must be submitted to the president for approval. The president has four choices in handling the bill:

1. The president may approve the legislation by signing it, at which point the bill becomes law.
2. A president who is not strongly in favor of the bill can refuse to act on it for ten days, excluding Sundays. If the president does not sign the bill while Congress is in session, the bill becomes law after the ten-day lapse. A president may use this procedure if he mostly approves of the bill but objects to some of its provisions. By letting the bill become law without his signature, the president indicates his dissatisfaction with these provisions. This procedure is rarely used.

▲ When the president signs a bill passed by Congress, it becomes law. What are the three other ways a president may deal with a bill passed by Congress?

BUILDING SOCIAL STUDIES SKILLS

Analyzing Information

A reader in any social studies subject must be able to analyze information. When you do research about any topic in government and political science, as well as in any other social studies subject, you will read books, articles, biographies, and primary source documents such as laws or constitutions.

When you analyze information, you have to break it apart and decide how much of what you are reading is cause and effect, how much is fact and opinion. After you take the information apart you have to put it back together and draw your own conclusions. Here are the steps you should follow when you analyze any information in social studies.

1. **Carefully read the material.** If you don't understand what you are reading, you cannot analyze it correctly. When you read the material, look for the main ideas and supporting details.
2. **Keep asking yourself questions.** While you read, ask yourself who is involved and why, when the main events actually occurred, and other key questions. The main question you want to keep asking yourself is ''Why?''

3. **Determine whether there is bias.** If you are reading a speech by a political candidate, the bias may be easy to find. If you are reading an analysis written by a researcher, identifying bias may be more difficult.

In your examination of bias, you need to separate fact from opinion. A fact is something that can be proven or verified; an opinion is a subjective viewpoint that cannot be confirmed.
4. **Reach a conclusion.** After you have analyzed the information in the manner presented above, you need to reach a conclusion. For example, after reading an article on your senator you might conclude that he or she supports gun control.

PRACTICING YOUR SKILLS

Look in your local daily newspaper and select an article from the first page to analyze. For the article you choose, write down a list of the facts presented in one column and a list of the opinions in another column. Then determine whether you can detect any bias in what you have read.

---

3. The President may **veto**, or refuse to sign the bill. (*Veto* is Latin for ''I forbid.'') The bill must then be returned to the house in which it originated, together with the president's objections to the bill. Congress may try to amend the bill to suit the president and repass it, or it may try to override the president's veto by a two-thirds vote of the members present in each house. Although it seldom happens, an override would pass the bill over the president's veto. The president who holds the record for the greatest number of vetoes is Franklin D. Roosevelt, who vetoed 631 bills during his thirteen years in office. Congress overrode only nine of those vetoes.
4. The president may kill a bill passed during the last ten days Congress is in session by simply refusing to act on it. This is called a **pocket veto**. The president simply does not sign the bill and because Congress in no longer in session, it does not have the opportunity to override the veto.

Each time a bill makes it through all these stages and becomes law it stands as an example of the legislative process in action. This process has continued for over two hundred years but also begins anew with each congressional term, when both the House and Senate organize for action. As the nation has evolved and become more complex, so too has this process, with committees and subcommittees playing an ever increasing role. Regardless of these changes, the legislative process remains a vital part of our representative democracy.

SECTION 3 REVIEW

1. What happens when the two chambers of Congress pass two different versions of the same bill?
2. What is the purpose of a conference committee?
3. **For critical analysis:** Do you think it is necessary for a bill to go through so many steps to become a law? Why or why not?

CHALLENGE TO THE AMERICAN DREAM

Do Members of Congress Get the Wrong Signals?

As representatives of the people, shouldn't lawmakers always base their decisions on what their constituents want? It doesn't always work this way. Many factors may influence a legislator's decision-making process.

Voters The political career of all lawmakers depends on how the voters back home feel about their decisions. Thus, a major influence on lawmakers' decisions is what they believe the voters want.

Other Lawmakers and Staff Legislators sometimes take cues from other trusted or more senior members of Congress. Because members do not have the time to study the details of all the pieces of legislation they handle, they turn to key colleagues for advice on how to vote. In addition, a legislator's personal staff can have a great deal of influence. While many staffers do routine work, others help draft legislation, meet with lobbyists, and decide what should take priority in the legislator's day. The way the staff member filters information may very well determine how that member of Congress votes.

Party Influence Both major parties generally take stands on major issues and come out in favor of or in opposition to specific legislation. In the House of Representatives, members vote with their party about two-thirds of the time. Senators are a little less likely to follow their party's position. On some issues, members of the party tend to vote together more often. When voting on labor issues, for example, Democrats tend to lean toward the side of the unions and Republicans lean toward business interests.

The President Presidents try to influence congressional members by giving or withholding favors and support. For example, in the 1960s, Senator Frank Church of Idaho was critical of President Johnson's policies regarding the Vietnam War. When he showed the president a newspaper column written by journalist Walter Lippmann to support his view, President Johnson said, ''All right, the next time you need a dam for Idaho, you go ask Walter Lippmann.''

Recent presidents have actively lobbied members of Congress who seem undecided on an issue by inviting them for a visit at the Oval Office, by calling them, and by having key aides and cabinet officers testify at hearings. Presidents can also appear on national television to try to gain support from voters who will in turn influence lawmakers.

Lobbyists and Interest Groups The main purpose of the many lobbyist and interest groups is to persuade members of Congress to vote for legislation in their interests. Lobbyists, some of them former members of Congress, can provide current legislators with crucial information and often with assurances of financial aid in the next campaign. They visit lawmakers and try to persuade them to support their positions.

The challenge to the American dream is whether members of Congress can vote on proposed legislation in a manner that is consistent with their role as representatives and trustees of the people. In particular, if they allow interest groups to overwhelmingly influence their voting decisions, then the best interest of the public may not be served. If they let an overly strong president influence their voting decisions, then only when the president's views represent the best interests of the nation will the public be best served.

You Decide

1. How do you think members of Congress should make decisions? Which factor should have the greatest influence on their decision making?
2. Which groups or individuals, if any, do you feel have too much influence on members of Congress?

CHAPTER 14 REVIEW

Key Terms

bills 336
calendar 342
Calendar of General
  Orders 342
caucuses 333
clerk of the House 334
cloture 345
cloture rule 345
committee of the
  whole 343
concurrent
  resolutions 337

conferees 347
conference
  committee 347
conference report 347
filibuster 345
hopper 340
House Rules
  Committee 342
joint resolutions 337
junkets 342
markup session 342
pigeonhole 340

pocket veto 348
private bills 337
public bills 337
quorum 342
record vote 343
rider 339
roll-call vote 343
simple resolution 337
sponsors 340
standing vote 343

State of the Union
  Address 334
teller vote 343
veto 348
voice vote 343

Summary

1. Before a new term begins, Democratic and Republican members of the House and Senate meet in separate party caucuses to reach agreement among themselves on key issues and to plan the party's strategy for the upcoming term. They also choose party leaders to organize and direct party activities during the congressional term. The House of Representatives is reorganized and begins anew every two years, while the Senate is a continuous body. After both houses are organized, the president delivers the State of the Union Address, which outlines the administration's broad policies and makes legislative recommendations. Bills are proposed laws and are either public (concerning matters of national interest) or private (concerning specific persons or places). Joint resolutions deal with temporary or unusual matters and when passed have the force of law. Concurrent resolutions are measures intended to express an opinion or a public policy and do not have the force of law. Simple resolutions deal with matters affecting only one house of Congress and are passed by that house alone. They do not have the force of law.

2. Although almost anyone may suggest legislation, only a member of Congress can formally introduce it. Bills introduced in either house are referred to standing committees. Bills that are reported out of committee may then be debated and voted on by members on the floor of the House and Senate. Debate is severely limited in the House, but is unlimited in the Senate. Filibustering is a common technique to kill a bill in the Senate.

3. To become a law, a bill must be passed in identical form by both chambers of Congress. When the two chambers do not agree, a conference committee attempts to iron out differences and produce a compromise version acceptable to both houses. The bill is then sent to the president, who has the choice of signing it, letting it become law without signing it, or vetoing it.

Review Questions

1. What are the purposes of private party caucuses?
2. What happens in the House and Senate on the opening day of Congress?
3. Briefly describe the two types of bills that may be introduced and the three types of resolutions that may be passed in Congress.
4. Who may propose legislation for Congress to consider? How is a bill formally introduced?
5. Describe what happens when a committee considers a bill.
6. What procedure has the House developed to speed up the legislative process?
7. How does debate in the Senate differ from debate in the House?
8. What is a filibuster and what is the cloture rule?
9. When is a conference committee formed and what is its purpose?
10. What options does the president have upon receiving a bill passed by both houses?

CHAPTER 14 REVIEW—Continued

Questions for Thought and Discussion

1. The sessions of the House and Senate are now broadcast on cable stations around the country. How, if at all, do you think this affects the operation of Congress and the behavior of individual congresspersons? Do you think committee sessions should be broadcast?
2. Is the process of lawmaking too complicated? Does it give too many opportunities for special interest groups to block needed legislation? Explain.
3. What, if any, reforms do you think should be made in congressional legislation-producing procedures?

Improving Your Skills
Communication Skills
Composing an Essay

An essay is a short report written on a specific topic. When writing an essay, follow these guidelines:

1. *Read the directions carefully.* Look for terms that will help you identify what information is asked for. Words such as *purpose, reasons, details* or *objectives* are examples of such terms. Look also for performance terms that will tell you what to write. Some performance clues include:

   ● **Discuss:** tell in some detail.
   ● **Describe or show:** create a picture with actions and examples.
   ● **State:** Make a complete formal statement.

2. *Make a short outline.* In order to know where you are going with your essay, you need to create an outline. The more detailed your outline, the smoother the writing of your essay will be.
3. *Write the first draft.* Using the logical flow of information you have written down in your outline, start your first draft. The more detailed your outline, the simpler this task will be. Make sure that in your first paragraph your topic, or thesis, statement appears. Be precise in your writing and stay with your topic. Include examples to support your statements.

4. *Edit your first draft.* When you edit your first draft you should ask yourself the following questions:

   ● Does my essay stay on the topic?
   ● Does it contain any unnecessary information?
   ● Is it missing any information?
   ● Is it interesting and informative?
   ● Do I support my thesis statement?

   Keep these questions in mind as you edit your draft. Make sure that you have used correct grammar and spelling. If you are writing with a word processor, you may be able to run your essay through a spelling checker and even a grammar checker.

5. *Make a polished draft.* The final draft of your essay should look like a final draft. It should not contain spelling or grammatical errors, nor should it wander from the central topic.

Writing

Following the five steps given above, write an essay on one of the following topics:

   ● Filibustering
   ● How a bill becomes law
   ● The difference between the opening days of the House and of the Senate

Social Studies Skills
Understanding Flow Charts

Examine the flow chart on page 346.

1. What differences are there, if any, between the flow on the right-hand side and the flow on the left-hand side.

Activities and Projects

1. Gather information on a problem related to a current issue. Use the guidelines presented in the previous ''Improving Your Communication Skills'' feature to write a bill that proposes a solution.
2. Stage a class debate on the following: ''Resolved—Filibustering should be eliminated from the Senate.''
3. Stage a mock committee hearing on an issue currently being debated in Congress.

The Federal Executive Branch

UNIT CONTENTS

■ *Chapter 15* The Presidency
 ■ *Chapter 16* The President at Work
  ■ *Chapter 17* The Bureaucracy in Action

353

The man who preserved the American Union during the Civil War and who proved to the world that democracy could be a lasting form of government was born on February 12, 1809 in Hardin, Kentucky, in a one-room, dirt-floor, log cabin. Whenever the young Abraham and his sister, Sarah, didn't have to help their parents, they attended school in a log schoolhouse. From the age of seven to twenty-one, however, the future president only had about a year of formal schooling. He said in his autobiography that "Of course when I came of age I did not know much. Still somehow, I could read, write, and cipher . . . ; but that was all."

In 1830, Lincoln settled in southern Illinois, where he operated a store, practiced surveying, and served as postmaster at New Salem while he studied law. In 1836, after he was admitted to the bar, he moved to Springfield where he opened a law office and quickly obtained a reputation as an outstanding jury lawyer. He also became well known for his ready wit, down-home logic, and seemingly endless supply of clever anecdotes. Lincoln was a member of the Illinois legislature from 1834 to 1842. He was nominated to run for the U.S. Senate at the Illinois Republican Convention. His acceptance speech popularized the phrase, "A house divided against itself cannot stand," a reference to the growing conflict between the North and the South. Lincoln and his opponent, incumbent Stephen A. Douglas, faced one another in a series of seven famous debates across Illinois. Although Lincoln lost the election, he had established himself as a national figure.

Lincoln was nominated for and won the presidency in 1860. By 1861, seven states had seceded from the Union, and Lincoln was thrust into the center of the Civil War. As late as August 1862, he expressed his reluctance to turn the war into a crusade to free the slaves. "My paramount object in the struggle," he declared, "is to save the Union, and it is not either to save or to destroy slavery." In September 1862, however, Lincoln issued the Emancipation Proclamation, which declared that all slaves in states or parts of states still fighting against the United States on January 1, 1863, would, from that time on, be forever free.

Lincoln was a diplomat in handling both his cabinet and generals, and after numerous military victories, easily won reelection in 1864. On April 14, 1865, in Ford's Theater in Washington D.C., John Wilkes Booth, a deranged actor sympathetic to the Southern cause, shot the president in the back of the head with a .44 single-shot derringer. He was the first chief executive to die at the hands of an assassin.

Lincoln has been called a keen and profound politician, a shrewd diplomat, a great storyteller, and a skillful judge of men. Historians and political scientists who rank presidents often rank him with the greatest.

The Battle of Gettysburg, which took place over three days in July of 1863, was the bloodiest engagement of the Civil War. The combined casualties of the Union and Confederate Armies numbered over 50,000 men. It was a decisive battle for the Union Army and marked the last time that the Confederate Army would have the strength to carry the War into Union territory. In November of that same year, President Lincoln wrote the following speech as he traveled by train to Gettysburg to dedicate a national memorial cemetery. The Gettysburg Address, which was delivered before a large crowd, is one of the most famous American political speeches.

Abraham Lincoln

Shown here is the first reading of the Emancipation Proclamation before Abraham Lincoln's cabinet in 1862; standing left to right: Chase, Smith, Blair; seated left to right: Stanton, Lincoln, Welles, Seward, Bates.

HIS WORDS

"Four score and seven years ago our fathers brought forth on this continent, a new nation, conceived in Liberty, and dedicated to the proposition that all men are created equal.

Now we are engaged in a great civil war, testing whether that nation or any nation so conceived and so dedicated, can long endure. We are met on a great battle-field of that war. We have come to dedicate a portion of that field, as a final resting place for those who here gave their lives that that nation might live. It is altogether fitting and proper that we should do this.

But, in a larger sense, we can not dedicate—we can not consecrate—we can not hallow—this ground. The brave men, living and dead, who struggled here, have consecrated it, far above our poor power to add or detract. The world will little note, nor long remember what we say here, but it can never forget what they did here. It is for us the living, rather, to be dedicated here to the unfinished work which they who fought here have thus far so nobly advanced. It is rather for us to be here dedicated to the great task remaining before us—that from these honored dead we take increased devotion to that cause for which they gave the last full measure of devotion—that we here highly resolve that these dead shall not have died in vain—that this nation, under God, shall have a new birth of freedom—and that government of the people, by the people, for the people, shall not perish from the earth."

DEVELOPING CRITICAL THINKING SKILLS

1. What did Lincoln mean when he said, "We can not consecrate . . . this ground"?
2. Lincoln made a prediction in this speech that turned out to be completely inaccurate. What was that prediction and why was it inaccurate?
3. What was the "unfinished work" that Lincoln mentioned in this speech?

FOR FURTHER READING

Sandberg, Carl. *Abraham Lincoln: The Prairie Years and the War Years.* (Six volumes.) New York: Harcourt, Brace, and World, 1926–1939.

Oates, Stephen B. *Abraham Lincoln: The Man Behind the Myths.* New York: Harper, 1984.

Charnwook, Lord. *Abraham Lincoln.* Garden City, New York: Garden City Publishing, 1917.

CHAPTER 15 REVIEW

Key Terms

balance the ticket 365
budget 370
cabinet 365
chief of staff 369
chief executive 356

Council of Economic
   Advisors (CEA) 371
Executive Office of the
   President (EOP) 369
fiscal year 370

Kitchen Cabinet 368
National Security
   Council (NSC) 371
Office of Management
   and Budget (OMB) 370

press conferences 370
press secretary 369
succession 359

Summary

1. The president of the United States holds one of the most powerful elective offices in the world. Article II of the Constitution states that the president shall hold the nation's executive power. The past two centuries have seen the office expand. The president must satisfy three constitutional qualifications: (1) being a natural-born citizen, (2) being at least thirty-five years old, (3) being a resident of the United States at least fourteen years before taking office. Other informal qualifications have also developed such as political experience and political acceptability. The president is chosen to serve a four-year term and may serve only twice. He is paid $200,000 a year and receives many other benefits. The vice president assumes the presidency should the office become vacant. The order of succession following the vice president was fixed by Congress according to the Presidential Succession Act of 1947.

2. The vice presidency has historically been seen as an insignificant position, but has become increasingly important in recent years. The vice president's constitutional duties are to preside over the Senate, to help decide whether a president is disabled, and to assume the duties of the presidency if necessary. The official qualifications for vice president are the same as those for president. The person chosen by a party to run for president usually names his own running mate. Often his choice is influenced by the need to pick someone to balance the ticket.

3. The cabinet is an advisory group chosen by the president to help accomplish the work of the executive branch. The cabinet is not mentioned in the Constitution but has evolved out of tradition. The president appoints the heads of executive departments, thereby appointing the cabinet members. In choosing cabinet members, the president takes several factors into consideration such as political party affiliation, experience in the given area, geographic background, and the desires of interest groups. The cabinet has no official power as a body, and the extent of the power and influence of the cabinet is strictly up to the individual president.

4. The Executive Office of the President (EOP) is made up of the top advisors and assistants who help the president carry out major duties. The White House Office is led by the chief of staff, who in recent years has been one of the most influential of presidential aides. Other EOP agencies include the Office of Management and Budget, the National Security Council, the Office of Policy Development, and the Council of Economic Advisors.

Review Questions

1. What qualifications must a president have, according to the Constitution?
2. According to the Twenty-second Amendment, how many terms may a president serve?
3. What did the Twenty-fifth Amendment establish?
4. What are the constitutional duties of the vice president?
5. How is the vice president selected?
6. How is the cabinet chosen?
7. How are the role and influence of the cabinet determined?
8. How is the White House Office organized?
9. What is the function of the Office of Management and Budget?
10. Who are the members of the National Security Council?
11. Why is it important to gain an understanding of your political ideology?
12. What are the arguments in favor of and what are the arguments against giving the vice president greater political responsibility during his term?

CHAPTER 15 REVIEW—Continued

Questions for Thought and Discussion

1. What qualifications or characteristics do you think a president should have? Which of the recent presidents, if any, have had these qualifications or characteristics?
2. Do you think the role of the vice president will expand or diminish in the future? What factors do you think will have a bearing on his or her role and influence?
3. Which cabinet members currently have the most influence on the president? Give evidence to support your answer.
4. Why do you think the Executive Office of the President has grown so dramatically? Do the numerous agencies and staff really assist the president in his job?

Improving Your Skills

Communication Skills

Paraphrasing

In doing homework, answering questions, and writing reports, you will sometimes be asked to **paraphrase**. Paraphrasing is restating someone else's writing or ideas in your own words. Paraphrasing will help you recognize the main idea, condense information, and organize material. Paraphrasing might be useful when answering questions such as, ''What were the president's views on the new budget?'' or ''What were the instructions for completing this assignment?''
Follow these guidelines when paraphrasing:

- Read or listen to the material carefully.
- Review the information, and while retaining the author or speaker's point or view, rewrite it in your own words. Do not include any ideas of your own.
- Include all the ideas of the original material, but reword them using your own writing style, tone, and vocabulary.

Writing

Turn to the ''Architect of the American Dream'' feature on page 360. Write an account of Lincoln's speech as if you were a newspaper reporter covering the event. You might wish to add to your story by reporting facts about the battle and the day. Use a history book to find any additional facts you may need.

Social Studies Skills

Comparing Similarities and Differences

One key social studies skill that you should master is the ability to compare similarities and differences between and among political systems, political parties, interest groups, political documents, and, of course, politicians and world leaders. In order to make such comparisons accurately you must specifically choose issues on which to base your analysis. For example, when you compare the two major political parties, decide in advance on which points you will focus, such as each party's stand on abortion, expanded health care, research funds for AIDS, and so on. The same system should be used for comparing leaders, such as current and past presidents, or political candidates.

Use the above ideas to compare the similarities and differences between one or more of the following:

1. The Republican party and the Libertarian party.
2. Direct democracy and representative democracy.
3. The two senators from your state.
4. The last two major presidential candidates.
5. President Herbert Hoover and President Franklin D. Roosevelt.
6. The National Rifle Association and the American Medical Association.
7. *The Federalist Papers* Numbers 10 and 51.

Activities and Projects

1. Choose a cabinet member and research his or her background, experience, and influence on the president. Write a biographical account of the cabinet member that includes your opinion on whether this person is qualified to head his or her particular department.
2. Conduct a class debate on the following: Resolved—The president shall hold a single term of office for six years only.

CHAPTER 16

The President at Work

CHAPTER OBJECTIVES

To learn and understand

- The powers of the president as outlined in the Constitution and as they have developed with the office.

- The many interrelated roles of the president.

- The limits placed on presidential powers.

Keynote

"The first twelve years are the hardest."

——— **Franklin D. Roosevelt
(1882–1945) Thirty-Second President
of the United States**

INTRODUCTION

As Franklin D. Roosevelt's statement reveals, serving in the nation's highest public office is never easy, even after many years. The president heads the largest organization in the nation, a government that has about 3 million civilian and 1½ million military employees. Entrusted with carrying out the laws of the land, the president is also chief architect of American foreign policy, an increasingly difficult task in our rapidly changing world. The president is head of the world's most powerful military arsenal, negotiator of treaties with other nations, chief collector of taxes, and chief persuader of public opinion. With a multitude of powers and duties that have increased greatly over time, the office of the presidency has grown to become more powerful and more complex. As President Harry S Truman once said, "The pressures and complexities of the presidency have grown to a state where they are almost too much for one man to endure."

SECTION 1

Presidential Powers

Preview Questions

- What are the constitutional powers of the president?
- What other sources are presidential powers built upon?
- How have strong presidents contributed to the growth of presidential powers?
- How have the media enhanced the power of the presidency?

The Constitution is the first place to look to find out what our presidents are supposed to do and how they are supposed to do it. Article II of the Constitution outlines the powers of the president, as shown in the list below.

The president's powers are, of course, limited by the checks and balances of the other two branches of government. But the president can use these limited powers in a variety of ways.

Constitutional Powers

Article II begins by simply stating that "the Executive Power shall be vested in the President of the United States of America."

As you have learned, the founders wanted a strong president, but had difficulty agreeing on the amount of strength and level of power the president should have. As a result, Article II grants the president broad but vaguely described powers. From the very beginning there were differing views as to what exactly the "executive power" clause enabled the president to do. Because this power is not precisely defined, its meaning can change with differing circumstances.

Sections 2 and 3 of Article II go on to list specific presidential powers. You will see what these powers mean in practice later in the chapter when the president's many roles are discussed. According to Sections 2 and 3, the president has the power:

1. to serve as commander in chief of the armed forces and the state militias;
2. to appoint heads of executive departments with Senate approval;
3. to grant reprieves and pardons, except in cases of impeachment;
4. to make treaties, with the advice and consent of the Senate;
5. to appoint ambassadors, federal court judges, justices of the Supreme Court; and other top officials, with Senate consent;

Receiving ambassadors and other representatives from foreign countries, such as Chief Buthelezi of South Africa's Zulu Tribe, is one of the president's constitutional powers. Where in the Constitution are specific presidential powers listed?

6. to deliver the annual State of the Union Address to Congress and to send other messages to Congress from time to time;
7. to call either or both houses of Congress into special sessions;
8. to receive ambassadors and other representatives from foreign countries;
9. to commission all military officers of the United States;
10. to ensure that all laws passed by Congress are carried out.

Other Sources of Power

Today the president has much more power than the Constitution alone suggests, and it comes from many sources. For example, a call from the president to a head of state, a senator, a military commander, or a television producer, rarely goes unanswered. The president can summon up a report on a foreign ruler or a recommended appointee by using intelligence sources and law enforcement agencies. For example, the president can find out just about anything he wants to know about the current head of the government in Germany. If the president wants to know anything about the current leader of an American environmentalist group, he can find it out. Such power comes from the fact that he has access to various kinds of classified information. The president has access to whomever he wishes to see; he can determine who gets certain jobs; and he can guide how federal money is spent. All these factors make people highly responsive to the president's demands.

After three years on the job, Harry Truman made this remark about the powers of the president:

The president may have a great many powers given to him in the Constitution and may have certain powers under certain laws which are given to him by the Congress of the United States; but the principal power that the president has is to bring people in and try to persuade them to do what they ought to do without persuasion. That's what the powers of the president amount to.

Besides this "persuasive" power of the office, presidents have developed other powers, derived from many sources. One important source of these powers is the actions of strong past presidents that have evolved into customs.

Strong Presidents Certain presidential powers that are today considered part of the rights of the office were simply assumed by strong presidents and then carried on by their successors. In this way, the greatest growth in presidential powers has been through what is often called inherent powers—powers that seem to be attached to the office itself. Since the birth of the republic in 1787, many presidents have strengthened the executive branch by their actions. Most experts agree that the strongest presidents have been George Washington, Thomas Jefferson, Andrew Jackson, Abraham Lincoln, Theodore Roosevelt, Woodrow Wilson, and Franklin D. Roosevelt. Each one ruled in difficult times and acted decisively, and each set a precedent for a certain activity.

For example, George Washington took the liberty of removing officials from office even though he was not given this authority in the Constitution. He also established the practice of meeting regularly with the heads of the three departments that then existed. He began the practice of submitting proposed legislation to Congress, which set a precedent of the president as chief legislator. He began the practice of vetoing legislation. As commander in chief, he used troops to put down a rebellion in Pennsylvania, and as chief diplomat, he made foreign policy without consulting Congress. This latter action took Congress by surprise and laid the groundwork for our long history of active foreign-policy making by the president.

President Lincoln, confronting the problems of the Civil War, took important actions while Congress was not in session. He suspended certain constitutional liberties, spent funds that Congress had not appropriated, blockaded Southern ports, and banned "treasonable correspondence" from the United States mails. All of these acts were done in the name of his powers as commander in chief and his responsibility to "take care that the laws be faithfully executed."

Theodore Roosevelt defined his position for a strong presidency in what he called the "stewardship theory." He said:

> My belief was that it was not only his [the president's] right but his duty to do anything that the needs of the Nation demanded unless such action was forbidden by the Constitution or by the laws. . . . I did not usurp power [seize power without legal authority], but I did greatly broaden the use of executive power. In other words, I acted for the public welfare, I acted for the common well-being of all our people, whenever and in whatever manner was necessary, unless prevented by direct constitutional or legislative prohibition.

Franklin D. Roosevelt expanded the presidential power over the economy during the Great Depression in the 1930s, and since that time Americans expect the president to be actively involved in economic matters and social programs.

Military Powers   Many presidents have exercised military powers that Congress often argues are outside the president's authority. The United States has been involved in over two hundred activities involving the armed services, while Congress has declared war only five times. In 1846, President James K. Polk provoked Mexico into a war. Before the United States entered World War II, Franklin D. Roosevelt ordered the Navy to "shoot on sight" any German submarine that appeared in the Western Hemisphere security zone. Truman ordered, without congressional approval, American armed forces into the Korean conflict between North and South

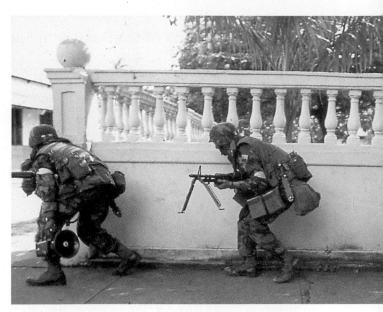

▲ As commander in chief of the nation's military forces, presidents often send troops into combat situations. Here, U.S. forces are shown during the military invasion of Panama in 1989. Why does Congress often argue with this use of presidential power?

Korea. The United States entry into the Vietnam War was done without congressional approval. No congressional vote was taken prior to President Bush sending troops into Panama in 1989 or before sending hundreds of thousands of American troops into the Middle East in 1990. (He did, however, obtain congressional approval to use American troops to expel, with the use of force, Iraq from Kuwait on January 16, 1991.)

Powers through Custom and Executive Orders
Another example of how presidential power is derived through custom is the practice of impoundment, which you learned about in Chapter 14. Also, the president has the power to issue an **executive order**, which is an order issued by the president to carry out policies described in laws that have been passed by Congress. Executive orders have the force of law. In 1941 President Franklin D. Roosevelt issued an executive order that denied defense contracts to companies that discriminated against workers because of their "race, creed, color, or national origin." In the late 1940s President Harry Truman used an executive order to end racial segregation in the nation's armed forces.

The powers that are derived from customs can be lost if they are not exercised. President Eisenhower assumed the presidency after Roosevelt and Truman, both of whom were activists—they sought much new

Media Evaluations of the Bush Administration During 1990

Subject	Good Press (Positive Evaluations)	Total News Stories Aired on ABC, CBS, and NBC
George Bush	36%	455
Total Administration	32%	1,791
Presidential Performance		
Dealing with Congress	23%	30
Diplomatic Performance	57%	96
Political Status	43%	56
Policy Issues		
Domestic Policy	17%	381
Drugs	35%	48
Taxes	19%	26
Budget	14%	64
Environment	10%	41
Civil Rights	7%	27
Savings & Loan	0%	19
Foreign Policy	39%	447
Panama	52%	29
Defense	45%	44
Persian Gulf	40%	197
Soviet Union	33%	48
China	33%	39

Source: Center for Media and Public Affairs

▲ **FIGURE 16–1 Media Evaluations of the Bush Administration During 1990.** Listed above are the number of news stories regarding the Bush administration during 1990. In which area did the Bush administration receive the greatest percentage of positive evaluations?

legislation. But Eisenhower's temperament and political philosophy led him to believe that strict limits should be placed on the exercise of presidential power. He was particularly hesitant to send in federal troops to enforce racial integration in the public schools after the 1954 Supreme Court decision declaring segregation unconstitutional.[1] His less forceful use of presidential power made it more difficult for those who came afterward to be activist presidents.

---

1. He eventually did send in the troops, however, to carry out the decision.

The Media and the Presidency

The presidency was the first institution of American government to use the vast power of the media to enhance its own power. Franklin D. Roosevelt first used the power of the media in his series of "fireside chats," during which he talked informally on the radio of the nation's problems and his ideas for solving them. Roosevelt was a skillful communicator and listeners felt he was speaking to them personally. He consequently had a powerful influence upon millions of people. Among recent presidents, Ronald Reagan, called "the great communicator," was successful in using the media to his great

BUILDING SOCIAL STUDIES SKILLS

Reading Biographies

As you study American government you will often find yourself studying people and the roles they played in shaping and influencing our nation's history. One way to learn about people who helped shape our government is through biographical accounts. A biography is the story of a person's life; information for biographies is usually derived from both primary and secondary sources. A biography usually presents the details of the person's life as well as conveys his or her beliefs, ideals, and personality. It tells of the person's accomplishments and how he or she helped to shape our country.

Use the following guidelines when reading an historical or political biography:

● Determine and track the major events in the person's life.
● Identify the personality traits, ideals, motivations, attitudes, and values that the person held. Try to determine how these traits influenced historical events surrounding the person's life.
● Try to determine what effects the person's upbringing had on his or her personal development.

● Track the person's accomplishments and assess their impact and significance on American history and government.
● Determine any author bias. Does the author or the biography generally agree or disagree with the philosophies and actions of the person he or she is writing about?

PRACTICING YOUR SKILLS

1. At your school or local library, skim through three separate biographies on one American president. Make a list of how those biographies differ. For example, one may be anecdotal, relating minor events in the president's life. Another might emphasize the president's early years. Yet another might examine only the political factors that influenced that president.
2. Read the concluding chapter in two of the biographies. Can you get a sense from your reading whether the author of the biography liked or disliked the president about whom he or she was writing? Write a short analysis of your reasoning.

---

advantage. Listeners also felt that he was talking to them personally.

President Bush, in contrast, chose to lower his television profile while increasing his access to reporters. During his first year in office, Bush attracted only a third as much coverage as Reagan had in 1981. Even excluding the surge of coverage after the assassination attempt on Reagan in 1981, Bush made less than half as much TV news coverage as his predecessor. In contrast, by April 1991, Bush had already held 76 press conferences, compared to Reagan's 48 while in office. This media-management style of lowering television visibility while increasing access to reporters was designed to minimize the extent of media criticism. Yet, as Figure 16–1 on page 380 shows, about three out of five stories on network news about President Bush were negative.

Despite the sometimes negative coverage, television gives presidents the opportunity to communicate directly to the people whenever they wish to do so. Unlike other politicians, the president can get air time whenever he wants, reaching over 70 million people. When President George Bush went on TV for the first time after he ordered American troops to bomb Iraq on January 16th, more than 100 million Americans were watching. This was the largest United States TV audience for a single program in history. Fred W. Friendly, an influential television producer, once observed that "no mighty king, no ambitious emperor, no pope or prophet, even dreamt of such awesome a pulpit, so potent a magic wand. . . . The president, in his ability to command the national attention, has diminished the power of all other politicians."

Newspapers and magazines are other powerful media sources that provide ways for presidents to bring their ideas to the public's attention. One two-year study of *Time* and *Newsweek* magazine coverage found that more

GOVERNMENT IN ACTION

A DAY IN THE LIFE OF

President George Bush

On January 20, 1989 George Herbert Walker Bush was sworn in as the 41st president of the United States. This was the culmination of a political career that began in 1964 and that included a wide variety of both elective and appointed positions.

George Bush was born on June 12, 1924 in Milton, Massachusetts, to Dorothy Walker Bush and Prescott Bush, who served as a Republican senator from Connecticut from 1952 to 1962. Following his graduation from Phillips Academy, Andover, Massachusetts, in June, 1942, Bush enlisted in the United States Navy. He received his wings and commission while only eighteen years old, making him the youngest pilot in the Navy at that time.

On active duty from August, 1942, to September, 1945, Bush flew torpedo bombers during World War II. In 1944, while making a bombing run over an island 600 miles south of Japan, Bush's plane was hit by anti-aircraft fire. Although the plane was severely damaged and on fire, he completed his mission before flying towards sea where he bailed out and was rescued by a Navy submarine. For his courageous service in the Pacific theater, Bush was awarded the Distinguished Flying Cross and three Air Medals.

In January of 1945, Bush married Barbara Pierce. Following World War II, Bush entered Yale University where he studied economics and served as captain of the varsity baseball team, graduating Phi Beta Kappa in 1948. After his graduation from Yale, George and Barbara Bush moved to Texas where he worked as an oil field supply salesman. In 1951, he co-founded a small oil field development company. Two years later, he co-founded the Zapata Petroleum Corporation and in 1954, at the age of thirty, he became co-founder and president of a third firm, Zapata Offshore, which pioneered experimental offshore drilling equipment.

In 1964, George Bush made his first attempt at elective office, losing a bid for a Senate seat. In 1966, Bush was elected to the United States House of Representatives, serving the Seventh Congressional District of Texas.

During his two terms in the House of Representatives, Bush served on the Ways and Means Committee. In 1970, Bush again unsuccessfully ran for the Senate. During the 1970s, Bush held a number of important government positions. In 1971, he was named U.S. Ambassador to the United Nations. He served in this capacity until 1973 when he left to become Chairman of the Republican National Committee. In October, 1974, Bush traveled to Beijing where he served as chief of the U.S. Liaison Office during the critical period when the United States was establishing ties with the People's Republic of China. In 1976, Bush was appointed Director of the Central Intelligence Agency.

In July, 1980, Republican presidential candidate Ronald Reagan selected George Bush to be his running mate. Four months later, Bush was elected vice president. He was sworn into office on January 20, 1981. Reagan and Bush were reelected in 1984. After eight years as vice president, George Bush ran for and received the 1988 Republican nomination for the presidency. Selecting Indiana Senator Dan Quayle as his running mate, George Bush hit the general election campaign trail in a contest against Democratic challenger Michael Dukakis. Soon, George Bush moved from the vice president's office to the Oval Office. Today, President and Mrs. Bush are the parents of five children and have twelve grandchildren.

The following is a representative day at the White House for President Bush.

8:00	Intelligence briefing. Oval Office.
8:15	National Security briefing. Oval Office.
8:45	Meeting with the Chief of Staff. Oval Office.

10:30	Presentation of National Medal of Science and Technology. Rose Garden.
11:00	Meeting with President Fujimori of Peru. Oval Office/Cabinet Room.
12:15	Luncheon with President Fujimori. Old Family Dining Room.
1:15	Departure statements with President Fujimori. South Lawn.
2:40	Teleconference with NASA students. NASA Headquarters.
3:30	Meeting with Secretary Brady. Oval Office.
4:30	Meeting with the Chief of Staff. Oval Office

THINK ABOUT IT _____

1. What effect do you think George Bush's wartime experiences have had on his political life?
2. How do you think Bush's political posts during the 1970s affect his foreign policy decisions as president? Explain.

Presidential Vetoes

Years	President	Regular Vetoes	Vetoes Overridden	Pocket Vetoes	Total Vetoes
1789-1797	Washington	2	0	0	2
1797-1801	J. Adams	0	0	0	0
1801-1809	Jefferson	0	0	0	0
1809-1817	Madison	5	0	2	7
1817-1825	Monroe	1	0	0	1
1825-1829	J.Q. Adams	0	0	0	0
1829-1837	Jackson	5	0	7	12
1837-1841	Van Buren	0	0	1	1
1841-1841	Harrison	0	0	0	0
1841-1845	Tyler	6	1	4	10
1845-1849	Polk	2	0	1	3
1849-1850	Taylor	0	0	0	0
1850-1853	Fillmore	0	0	0	0
1853-1857	Pierce	9	5	0	9
1857-1861	Buchanan	4	0	3	7
1861-1865	Lincoln	2	0	5	7
1865-1869	A. Johnson	21	15	8	29
1869-1877	Grant	45	4	48	93
1877-1881	Hayes	12	1	1	13
1881-1881	Garfield	0	0	0	0
1881-1885	Arthur	4	1	8	12

▲ FIGURE 16–2 **Presidential Vetoes.** The tables on these pages demonstrate the use of presidential vetoes by each president through 1990. Which president exercised the most vetoes? What do you know about this president that helps to explain these numbers?

by both houses of Congress is sent to the president for approval. The president's options upon receiving the bill are (1) to sign it and make it law; (2) to veto it and return it to Congress; (3) to take no action, permitting the bill to become law without signing it; or (4) if Congress is due to adjourn within ten working days, kill the bill by simply not acting on it (the so-called "pocket veto").

Veto power allows the president to act as a check on Congress. Congress has overridden a very small percentage of presidential vetoes, as can be seen in Figure 16–2 on these two pages. Sometimes just the threat of a veto will force Congress to stop a bill or to change it to fit the president's wishes.

A presidential veto is a rejection of an entire bill. The president does not have the power to do a **line-item veto**, which is the power to veto only part of a piece of legislation, as some state governors can do. At the federal level, an entire bill must be accepted or rejected.

Special Sessions   As you have learned, only the president has the power to call special sessions of Congress. Should an important issue arise while Congress is not in

Presidential Vetoes (continued)

Years	President	Regular Vetoes	Vetoes Overridden	Pocket Vetoes	Total Vetoes
1885-1889	Cleveland	304	2	110	414
1889-1893	Harrison	19	1	25	44
1893-1897	Cleveland	42	5	128	170
1897-1901	McKinley	6	0	36	42
1901-1909	T. Roosevelt	42	1	40	82
1909-1913	Taft	30	1	9	39
1913-1921	Wilson	33	6	11	44
1921-1923	Harding	5	0	1	6
1923-1929	Coolidge	20	4	30	50
1929-1933	Hoover	21	3	16	37
1933-1945	F. Roosevelt	372	9	263	635
1945-1953	Truman	180	12	70	250
1953-1961	Eisenhower	73	2	108	181
1961-1963	Kennedy	12	0	9	21
1963-1969	L. Johnson	16	0	14	30
1969-1974	Nixon	26*	7	17	43
1974-1977	Ford	48	12	18	66
1977-1981	Carter	13	2	18	31
1981-1989	Reagan	39	9	28	67
1989-1990	Bush	12	0	1	13
Total		1,431	103	952	2,383

*Two pocket vetoes, overruled in the courts, are counted here as regular vetoes.
Source: Louis Fisher, *The Politics of Shared Power; Congress and the Executive,* 2nd ed. (Washington, D.C.: Congressional Quarterly Press, 1987), p. 30; *Congressional Quarterly Weekly Report,* June 23, 1990, p. 1934.

session, the president may call a special session to deal with it. Today, such sessions are almost never needed because Congress meets throughout most of the year.

Political Party Leader and Politician

The president is also head of his political party— not by any authority of the Constitution, whose authors abhorred parties, but by tradition and practical necessity. George Washington was the only president elected without the backing of a political party. All other presidents have been elected with the help of a party, and have become the national leaders of the parties that nominated them.

As party leader the president has a number of major duties: to choose a vice president after his own nomination; to make several thousand high-government appointments, mainly to party faithfuls, (a system known as **patronage**); and to demonstrate that he is trying to fulfill the party platform. The successes of the president in these areas are recalled in the party's election campaigns, and any failures haunt the party at the polls.

GOVERNMENT IN ACTION

CASE STUDY

The Line-Item Veto

In forty-three states, governors have the power of the line-item veto—the power to reject certain items of a bill without killing the entire bill. Generally, line-item vetoes have been used with appropriations bills. U.S. presidents do not have this power. If they object to a part of the bill, they must reject the whole bill. Every president since Woodrow Wilson has favored a constitutional amendment to add the line-item veto to the president's powers. In 1984, President Ronald Reagan said that as governor of California he found the line-item veto a "powerful tool against wasteful and extravagant spending. It works in forty-three states—let's put it to work in Washington, D.C., for all the people."

Proponents of the line-item veto argue that it is needed to give the president greater control over the budget process by controlling overall congressional spending. For example, suppose an appropriations bill comes before the president to increase spending for the Department of Education. The president agrees with the major part of the bill and Congress knows that the president will not want to veto the bill even though there are several specific expenditures with which he disagrees. Without the line-item veto, the president must either accept or reject the entire bill. If he had the line-item veto power, he could veto the particular items that he felt were objectionable

or wasteful. He would not have to make the painful decision to kill the entire bill. Proponents also argue that the line-item veto would make members of Congress more reluctant to approve special projects for interest groups unless the projects could be shown to contribute to broader national goals. If such was not true, the special projects would be specifically vetoed.

Opponents of the line-item veto argue that it would grant too much power to the president and upset the delicate balance so wisely crafted by the founding fathers. They argue that it could be used as a weapon to punish or pressure the president's opponents in Congress. They also argue that it would throw the congressional schedule into chaos. Since the Congress could override the line-item vetoes, each vetoed line would have to be considered individually. This would add more debates and votes to an already overcrowded calendar.

THINK ABOUT IT

1. How might the line-item veto help the president control spending?
2. In what way might the line-item veto limit special-interest legislation?
3. Would the line-item veto upset the balance of power that the founders set up in the Constitution? Explain.

Presidents may support the party by attending party fund-raisers or by sending assistants to help elect or re-elect party members running for office as mayors, governors, or members of Congress.

As we learned in the chapters on Congress, congresspersons are politicians as well as lawmakers, always concerned about their constituencies and the next election. The president is in the same position. Like all politicians, the president wants to win elections and battles

in Congress, and wants to maintain a high level of public approval.

Other Roles

In recent years, the president has also taken on the role of being the nation's economic leader. A president's popularity, measured in the polls, often rises and falls with the nation's economic well-being. The public,

Roles of the President

Role	Description	Specific Functions
Chief of State	Performs certain ceremonial functions, as personal symbol of the nation	• Throws out first baseball of baseball season • Lights national Christmas tree • Decorates war heroes • Dedicates parks and post offices
Chief Executive	Enforces laws and federal court decisions, along with treaties signed by the United States	• Can appoint, with Senate approval, high-ranking officers of the federal government. Does not require Senate approval to dismiss presidential appointees from the executive branch. • Can grant reprieves, pardons, and amnesty
Commander in Chief	Leads the nation's armed forces	• Can commit troops for up to 90 days in response to a military threat (War Powers Act) • Can make secret agreements with other countries • Can set up military governments in conquered lands • Can end fighting by calling a cease-fire (armistice) • Can handle national emergencies during peacetime, such as riots or natural disasters
Chief Diplomat	Directs U.S. foreign policy and is the nation's most important representative in dealing with foreign countries	• Can negotiate and sign treaties with other nations, with Senate approval • Can make pacts (executive agreements) with other heads of state, without Senate approval • Can accept the legal existence of another country's government (power of recognition) • Receives foreign chiefs of state
Chief Legislator	Informs Congress about the condition of the country and recommends legislative measures	• Proposes legislative program to Congress in traditional State of Union Address • Suggests budget to Congress and submits annual economic report • Can veto a bill passed by Congress • Can call special sessions of Congress
Political Party Leader	Heads political party	• Chooses a vice president • Makes several thousand top-government appointments, often to party faithfuls (patronage) • Tries to execute the party's platform • May attend party fund-raisers • May help reelect party members running for office as mayors, governors, or members of Congress

▲ FIGURE 16–3 **Roles of the President.** The table above lists the roles of the president and cites examples of the actions and functions of each role. Can you think of any instances in which these roles might overlap?

◄ Presidents often lend their support to others from their party who are running for office. Why do you think most presidents are willing to do this?

Congress, and business and labor communities increasingly look to the president to lower unemployment, to fight inflation, to keep taxes down, and to promote economic growth. We give our presidents numerous tools with which to manage the economy, including the duty of preparing the budget, which gives the president the opportunity to determine the government's spending priorities for the coming year. The Employment Act of 1946 directed the president to submit an annual economic report to Congress and declared for the first time that the federal government had the responsibility to promote productivity, high employment, and stable purchasing power. The law created the Council of Economic Advisors (CEA) to give the president economic advice.

The office of the presidency also automatically makes its occupant the nation's chief citizen. The president is expected to be representative of all the people and to work for the public interest. ''The presidency,'' said Franklin Roosevelt, ''is not merely an administrative office. That is the least of it. It is preeminently a place of moral leadership.''

SECTION 2 REVIEW

1. What are the functions of the president as chief of state and chief executive?
2. As commander in chief, what are the president's powers?
3. What are the president's powers as chief diplomat?
4. How does the president practice the role of chief legislator?

5. Explain why the president is the leader of his political party.
6. **For critical analysis:** Do you feel the president's role as political party leader is in conflict with any of the other roles? Explain why or why not.

SECTION 3

Checks on the President's Powers

Preview Questions
● How can the Congress check presidential powers?
● How can the judiciary check presidential powers?

The framers of the Constitution were well aware of the possible abuses of an overly strong chief executive. To avoid these abuses, they built in a system of checks and balances. Both Congress and the judiciary have powers that restrict the president. The president is also checked to some degree by certain unwritten limitations.

Congressional Limitations

As you have learned, the president has the power to veto legislation, but Congress may override a president's veto. Even though it is not often done, the override remains as a powerful check by Congress on presidential

CITIZENSHIP SKILLS AND RESPONSIBILITIES
How to Contact the President

You, as an American citizen, have a right and sometimes a duty to let the president know directly about your opinion on an important public policy matter. Each president receives thousands of letters and numerous phone calls a day. Of course no president actually reads all of these letters, but many of them are read by his assistants. They tally up public opinion for and against a particular issue. When President Reagan started sending advisors and military aid to the Central American country of El Salvador in 1981, he immediately began to receive a flood of letters, which ran ten-to-one against his policy. His decisions thereafter were partly molded by such strong public opposition to militarizing that country. The opposite occurred when President Bush sent troops to the Middle East after Iraq invaded Kuwait in 1990.

Your views can, and should, be brought to the president's attention. Whenever you strongly agree with or oppose the actions taken by the president, you can contact the White House directly. Address your letter to the following:

The President of the United States
The White House
1600 Pennsylvania Ave. NW
Washington, DC 20500

You can also send a telegram to that address, or you can telephone the White House at 202-456-1414.

A less well-known, but perhaps equally effective, way to express your views to the president is by writing a letter to the editor of a major newspaper. The president's aides in the White House clip letters from newspapers across the country. These letters provide a digest of public opinion for the president and his staff to review on a regular basis.

Whether you choose to write the president directly, or to write a letter to the editor of a major newspaper, it is important to remember that your views are more likely to be given serious consideration (your letter is more likely to be printed) if your letter is well written, clearly organized, and neatly prepared. A letter that is well thought out and neatly typed can be a very effective tool for communicating your feelings to the president.

TAKING ACTION

1. As a class, choose a policy issue that concerns you today. Have each student compose a letter to the president. Send them directly to the White House.
2. Write a letter to a major newspaper editor about the same issue, remembering that it might be made part of a digest of letters given to the president by his aides.

---

powers. Since George Washington's presidency, only about 4 percent of all presidential vetoes have been overridden by Congress. The most occurred under the administration of Andrew Johnson (1865–1869) during which time there were fifteen. Both Harry Truman and Gerald Ford saw twelve of their presidential vetoes overridden.[3]

Congress also has "the power of the purse" over the president. For example, President Nixon tried to restrict government spending because of a worsening economy by cutting domestic programs while at the same time increasing some areas of military spending. Congress undermined these plans by appropriating funds for welfare programs that the president did not want and cutting appropriations for the weapons programs he favored.

The power of impeachment is considered the ultimate congressional check on the presidency. The Constitution says that Congress may impeach the president for "treason, bribery, or other high crimes or misdemeanors." Congress has only used this power once. In 1868 the House of Representatives voted to impeach President Andrew Johnson, charging that he violated the Tenure Office Act, which prohibited him from removing executive officials without consent of the Senate. The Senate, which tries cases of impeachment, found Johnson not guilty. In 1974, a House committee voted to recommend impeachment of President Nixon because of his part in

---

3. Gerald Ford wins the prize in this century, though, with the largest percentage of vetoes overridden—25 percent, or more than six times the average for all presidents.

the 1972 Watergate break-in scandal, but he resigned from the presidency before the affair reached the full House.

During the 1970s several laws limiting presidential power were passed by Congress. American involvement in Vietnam and the Watergate scandal led in 1972 to a limitation on the president's use of secret executive agreements. The 1973 War Powers Act required the president to consult with Congress before committing American troops to war. As you learned in the Government in Action case study on the budget in Chapter 13, the 1974 Budget Impoundment Control Act restrained presidential power to impound funds from executive agencies.

Other congressional checks include the Senate's approval (or lack of approval) of major appointments and treaties from the president.

Judicial Limitations

As you learned in Chapter 13 the Supreme Court case *Marbury* v. *Madison* affirmed the Supreme Court's right to review a president's actions. The president and the Supreme Court, however, are not as closely involved in the day-to-day operations of each other's affairs as are the president and Congress. In most instances, Supreme Court justices are inclined to respect the president's decisions and viewpoints.

The Supreme Court has, however, imposed some limits on the president's domestic power. In 1936, the Court declared several laws unconstitutional that had been passed by Congress as part of President Franklin Roosevelt's New Deal Program. In 1952, for example, the Court said that President Truman could not issue an executive order unless it was provided for by the Constitution or by an act of Congress. In 1975, the Court limited the power of the president to impound (withhold) money appropriated by Congress.

The Court has also set limits on a president's claim to **executive privilege**—the special right to withhold information. Presidents usually claim executive privilege based on the need for secrecy in carrying out foreign affairs or in matters of national security. George Washington first invoked the right of executive privilege when he refused to supply the House of Representatives with his own papers and documents on a matter of diplomacy on the grounds that Congress was not constitutionally entitled to them. In 1974, in the Watergate scandal, President Nixon claimed that executive privilege entitled him to keep his White House tapes and other materials from Congress, and even to prevent his officials from testi-

fying before Congress. In *United States* v. *Nixon* that same year, the Court ruled that the president could not use such a claim to withhold evidence in a criminal trial.

The fact that the Senate must approve judicial appointments made by the president limits the actions that the president may take toward shaping the Supreme Court. Usually, presidents nominate justices who are acceptable to congressional leaders and to their supporters. Also, the justices chosen for the Court are not bound to follow the president who appointed them. Because the Supreme Court is an independent body, the justices may follow their own interpretations of the law. In fact, sometimes the persons appointed to the Supreme Court disappoint the presidents who chose them by taking opposing views. For example, President Dwight D. Eisenhower appointed Earl Warren as chief justice in 1953. Warren soon moved away from Eisenhower's conservative stand on social issues, and led the Court to many liberal decisions that were disliked by the Eisenhower administration.

Political Limitations

One of the most severe restraints on the president is not legal, but political. Public opinion and media attention put pressure on the president and can greatly influence how power is exercised. Without favorable public opinion, a president cannot succeed in carrying out a political program, especially if the president would like to run for a second term of office.

Despite the congressional, judicial, and political limitations, the office of president of the United States remains one of the most powerful in all the world. This power is derived from the Constitution, from institutional sources, and from the actions of strong presidents in the past. The president uses this power to perform his many functions and fulfill his many roles. As you can see, along with these powers comes the burden of enormous responsibility.

SECTION 3 REVIEW

1. How may Congress limit the president's powers?
2. How may the Supreme Court limit the president's powers?
3. **For critical analysis:** If the Congress only overrides presidential vetoes 4 percent of the time, does this mean that the president has unlimited power to reject bills passed by the Congress? Why or why not?

CHALLENGE TO THE AMERICAN DREAM

The Abuse of Presidential Power

On June 17, 1972, the police caught five intruders inside the offices of the Democratic National Committee at the Watergate, a complex of business offices and apartment buildings in Washington, D.C. The break-in was quickly dismissed as a "third-rate burglary," and seemed destined to be forgotten. But it soon became clear that there was more to the story. First the FBI began investigating the incident, and later the Senate formed a special committee to investigate the Watergate case. The press, especially the *Washington Post,* followed up on clues. These investigations turned up the following:

- Crisp, consecutive $100 bills found on the burglars were traced to CREEP, the Committee for the Reelection of the President, a pro-Nixon campaign group. About $420,000 (taken mainly from Nixon campaign contributions), was used as "hush money" to keep the burglars quiet about who had hired them and what they were doing.
- CREEP solicited big contributions from people being investigated by government agencies, and sought illegal contributions from corporations.
- CREEP collected money from the dairy industry about the same time the president approved an increase in the federal price supports for milk.
- The president approved the formation of a Special Investigations, or "Plumbers Unit," in the White House to stop security leaks. The "Plumbers" tapped the phones of administration officials, poked through private files, and broke into private offices.
- The acting director of the FBI destroyed vital Watergate evidence at the instigation of two of the president's top assistants.

- An "enemies list" of people who opposed Nixon was compiled by the president's staff. The income-tax forms of people on the enemies list were singled out for investigation by the Internal Revenue Service.

President Nixon blocked many of the efforts by Congress and the courts to find out if the White House had ordered the Watergate break-in. He did so by invoking the doctrine of executive privilege—the special right to withhold information, usually in affairs dealing with national security and foreign affairs. The Supreme Court finally ruled that neither the president nor members of the executive branch could use executive privilege to withhold information about a crime.

Thus, the president was forced to surrender information in the form of tape recordings that had been made by concealed microphones in various White House offices and in the Executive Office Building. On the tape for June 23, 1972, Nixon was heard approving a plan to use the CIA to block the FBI investigation of the break-in.

In July 1974, the House Judiciary Committee recommended that the House of Representatives impeach President Richard Nixon on the grounds of obstructing justice, abusing presidential powers, and obstructing the impeachment process. It appeared likely that, for the first time since 1868, the president of the United States would be impeached. President Nixon resigned before the impeachment hearings and was later pardoned by his successor, President Gerald Ford.

The challenge to the American dream is to ensure that the president is never above the law. The American form of democracy is one in which laws rule rather than men and women.

You Decide

1. Do you think that President Nixon should have gone to trial for any criminal activities for which he had been responsible? Why or why not?
2. What, if anything, can Congress do to ensure that no future Watergate scandals occur?

CHAPTER 16 REVIEW

Key Terms

agenda 389
ambassador 388
amnesty 386
armistice 387
cease-fire 387
chief diplomat 387

diplomat 387
executive
  agreements 388
executive order 379
executive privilege 396
line-item veto 390

pardon 386
patronage 391
power of
  recognition 388
reprieve 386
treaty 387

veto power 389
White House Press
  Corps 382

Summary

1. There are several sources of presidential power. The Constitution grants broad powers to the president. The presidency has derived additional powers from the fact that the president has access to powerful resources, such as information on important people. Certain presidential powers that are today considered part of the rights of the office were simply assumed by strong presidents and then carried on by their successors. The media, especially television, have also enhanced the power of the president.

2. The president has many different but interrelated roles. The president serves the dual roles of chief of state and chief executive. The president is commander in chief of the armed services and, as such, has certain war powers. As chief diplomat, the president has the power to negotiate and sign treaties with other countries, but the Senate must approve the treaties by a two-thirds vote. The president also has the power to recognize other countries. As chief legislator, the president has become a major shaper of the congressional agenda. The president is also a political party leader and politician.

3. To avoid any misuse of power, the framers of the Constitution built in a system of checks and balances. Congress has the power to override the president's veto. Congress also has the ''power of the purse,'' and the ultimate power of impeachment. Finally, the Supreme Court has the right to review the president's actions.

Review Questions

1. What basic power is granted to the president in the Constitution?
2. What other sources contribute to presidential power?
3. How have strong presidents contributed to the powers of the presidency?

4. What effect have the media had on the presidency?
5. What is the president's role as chief of state?
6. What are the powers of the president as chief executive?
7. How are the war powers divided between the president and Congress? How does the War Powers Act attempt to limit the president's war powers?
8. As chief diplomat, what are the powers and duties of the president?
9. How does a treaty differ from an executive agreement?
10. How does the president recognize the legal existence of another country's government? Can the president repeal that recognition?
11. Explain the president's role as chief legislator.
12. Why is the president a political party leader?
13. How can Congress check the powers of the president?
14. How can the Supreme Court restrain the president's powers?
15. What is one way to contact the White House?
16. Briefly describe how President Nixon's actions in the Watergate scandal were abuses of presidential power.

Questions for Thought and Discussion

1. In your opinion, what is the most important role that the president plays? Why do you think that role is so important?
2. Do you think the power of the presidency has increased or decreased in recent years? What do you think accounts for this?
3. What do you think the president should do if Congress passed a law that violated his party platform?

CHAPTER 16 REVIEW—Continued

4. The roles of the president are sometimes in conflict. Name some instances when the political needs of the president may not be consistent with the needs of the nation.

5. How has television changed the relationship between the president and the American people? How has it affected his power?

Improving Your Skills
Communication Skills

Synthesizing

Synthesizing means combining two or more sources of information into a single unified whole. Learning to synthesize information will help you answer questions, make decisions, take notes, do research, and write reports. Synthesizing is necessary whenever you have to take two or more sources of information and blend the ideas in a coherent way that reflects your own writing or speaking style. When synthesizing, follow these guidelines:

- Read the materials carefully and decide on your point of view, opinion, and approach.
- Select the ideas or examples that support your ideas. Think about how your ideas and the ideas in the sources relate to each other.
- Combine these ideas into a synthesized whole.

Writing

Find three articles about a recent presidential decision or issue. Write a synthesis of the articles based on your view of how the ideas presented are interrelated.

Social Studies Skills

Evaluating a Policy Decision

As a student of American government, you must also be able to evaluate policy decisions. The following guidelines will help you evaluate decisions made by government officials at every level.

- Determine the nature of the decision and the surrounding circumstances at the time the decision had to be made.
- List what other choices and alternatives were available at the time. Remember that some alternatives that are apparent now may not have been apparent at the time.
- Determine the risks and benefits of each alternative. Each one will probably have several short- and long-term effects. Remember that some long-range effects may not be immediately evident.
- Make a decision, based on your considerations.
- Analyze the results of the decision. Determine whether or not a good decision was made, all things considered.

1. Choose a recent policy decision made in your school or community. Evaluate the policy decision by using the steps above. Report your evaluation to the class.

2. As a group, discuss and evaluate a national policy decision using the steps above.

Activities and Projects

1. Collect cartoons that refer to a current issue that the president is addressing. Paste the cartoons on a posterboard or in a booklet and write a summary of each one. In your summary, discuss whether the messages the cartoonists are trying to convey are positive or negative, and whether or not you agree with the cartoonists' depictions of the president's actions. Then try to determine the president's actual stand on the issue, and draw your own editorial cartoon in which you express your views on his stand.

2. Keep close track of the president's activities for three weeks by watching news programs and reading newspapers and magazines. Notice how closely you can or cannot keep track of his daily life. Keep track of what you learn in a president's log. Report your results to the class and explain why you think the media are so interested in what the president does.

3. Have the class debate the following statement: Resolved—The president shall be given the power to exercise a line-item veto.

4. Make a list of ten executive orders that one president made during his administration.

5. Make a list of ten executive agreements that one president made during his administration.

CHAPTER 17

The Bureaucracy in Action

CHAPTER OBJECTIVES

To learn and understand

- The nature, size, and growth of the federal bureaucracy.
- The makeup of the various executive departments.
- The purposes and functions of federal independent agencies and government corporations.
- How the civil service works.
- How bureaucrats make policy.

Keynote

"Government is not the solution to our problem; government is the problem".

——— **Ronald Reagan**
(1911–   ) Fortieth President of the
United States

INTRODUCTION

Did you eat breakfast this morning? If you did, **bureaucrats**—individuals who work in the offices of government—had a lot to do with your breakfast. If you had bacon, the meat was inspected by federal agents. If you drank milk, the price was affected by rules and regulations of the Department of Agriculture. If you looked at a cereal box, you saw fine print about minerals and vitamins, which was the result of regulations made by several other federal agencies.

Despite the negative implications of the word, a bureaucrat is simply a member of a large administrative organization—a **bureaucracy**—that carries out the policies of elected government officials. Bureaucrats deliver our mail, clean our streets, and run our national parks. Life without the government bureaucracy would be quite different.

Some critics think that the bureaucracy has grown too big, as President Ronald Reagan expressed in the opening quote above. But before we can examine the growth of the bureaucracy, we need first to look at its nature.

SECTION 1

Bureaucracy: Its Nature and Size

Preview Questions
- What is a bureaucracy and how is it organized?
- How much has the bureaucracy in our country grown?

The concept of a bureaucracy is not confined to the federal government. Any large-scale organization has to have a bureaucracy. Even small businesses operate as bureaucracies, for bureaucracy simply means an organization that is structured in a pyramid-like fashion. In each bureaucracy, everybody (except the head of the bureaucracy) reports to at least one other person. For the federal government, the head of the bureaucracy is the president of the United States.

A bureaucratic form of organization allows each person to concentrate on his or her area of knowledge and expertise. In your school, for example you do not expect the school nurse to solve the problems of the principal. You do not expect the football coach to solve the problems of the finance department.

Another key aspect of any bureaucracy is that the power to act resides in the *position* rather than in the *person*. In your school, the person who is currently vice

'Frankly, trimming the bureaucracy has me worried. . . . It just means fewer people to handle all the red tape."

Reprinted with special permission of NAS, Inc.

401

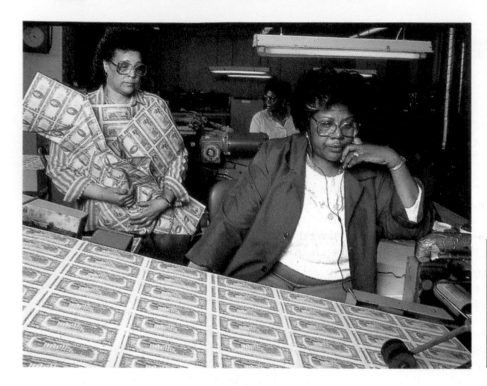

◄ The Department of the Treasury, like all government departments, has grown dramatically throughout the history of our nation. In 1789, there were only 39 employees in the Department of the Treasury. By 1992, this number had grown to 165,000. Why did this department grow so much?

principal has more or less the same authority as any other previous vice principal.

The Growth of Bureaucracy

Today the word *bureaucracy* automatically evokes a negative reaction. During election time throughout the nation there are calls from politicians to "cut big government and red tape," and "get rid of overlapping and wasteful bureaucracies." President Ronald Reagan campaigned on a platform of reducing the size of the federal bureaucracy in 1980, but it actually grew larger during his eight years as president.

No one campaigns for office on a platform calling for a bigger bureaucracy, but candidates promise to establish programs that would require many new employees—which means the bureaucracy would have to grow. Americans constantly demand more services, and with each new service comes a new group of bureaucrats.

The federal bureaucracy that was created in 1789 was small. There were only three departments with a few employees in each: (1) The Department of State (nine employees); (2) The Department of War (two employ-

ees); and (3) The Department of the Treasury (thirty-nine employees).

By 1798 the federal bureaucracy was still tiny. The secretary of state had seven clerks. His total expenditures on stationery and printing amounted to $500, or about $5,000 by today's standards. The Department of War spent a grand total of $1.4 million each year, or about $13 million in today's terms.

The times have changed. The federal bureaucracy has grown to about three million employees and spends over $1.5 trillion each year. The Executive Office of the President alone has over 1,500 employees. State governments employ another 3.5 million civilians and local governments employ nearly 10 million. (You'll find out more about state and local governments in Chapters 21 to 25.) In total, about 15 percent of the entire labor force is employed directly by federal, state, and local governments, including those in the military.

Throughout the 1980s, expenditures by all levels of government were about 35 percent of the total value of the goods and services produced in a year. Some part of this was financed by fees and borrowing. The greatest single source of goverment revenue comes from the taxes paid by the average citizen.

BUILDING SOCIAL STUDIES SKILLS

Reading an Organization Chart

Organization charts are used to illustrate the parts of both private and government organizations and how they operate. Each person, department, or segment is illustrated with a symbol or box which is usually labeled with the title of the office or its administrator. (Vertical lines between the boxes or symbols show levels of responsibility and horizontal lines show lines of authority.) In most organization charts, the person or department with the most power and authority is shown at the top.

In any formal organization chart there is a chain of command which shows how the company, club, agency, or department organizes its activities. That is what is shown in an organization chart.

Every chart will show lines of authority typically going from the person or group with the most authority down to lower and lower levels of authority. Typically, an organization has departments. For example, in the chart shown for the Santa Barbara

County Association of Governments, there is someone who is head of the planning department and someone who is head of the program development department.

Typically, each lower level must report to a higher level. Therefore, in the Santa Barbara County Association of Governments, both the deputy director of planning and the deputy director of program development would report to the executive director, who in turn reports to the board of directors.

PRACTICING YOUR SKILLS

1. Describe the flow of power and authority from the regional analyst to the executive director.
2. How are decisions arrived at in this agency? How can you tell?
3. Which positions have the same authority as executive director?

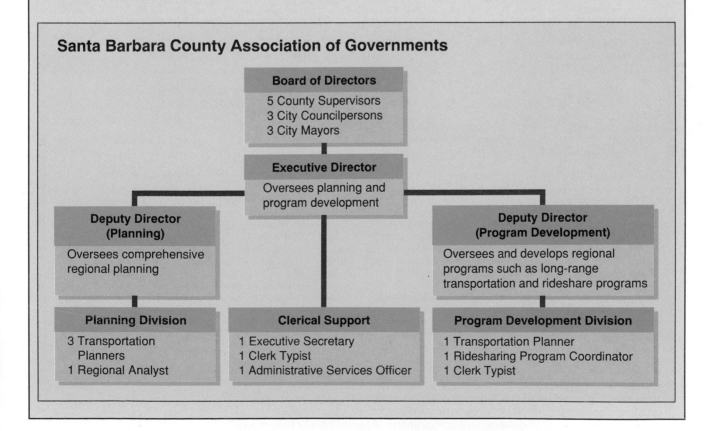

Santa Barbara County Association of Governments

Board of Directors

5 County Supervisors
3 City Councilpersons
3 City Mayors

Executive Director

Oversees planning and program development

Deputy Director (Planning)

Oversees comprehensive regional planning

Deputy Director (Program Development)

Oversees and develops regional programs such as long-range transportation and rideshare programs

Planning Division

3 Transportation Planners
1 Regional Analyst

Clerical Support

1 Executive Secretary
1 Clerk Typist
1 Administrative Services Officer

Program Development Division

1 Transportation Planner
1 Ridesharing Program Coordinator
1 Clerk Typist

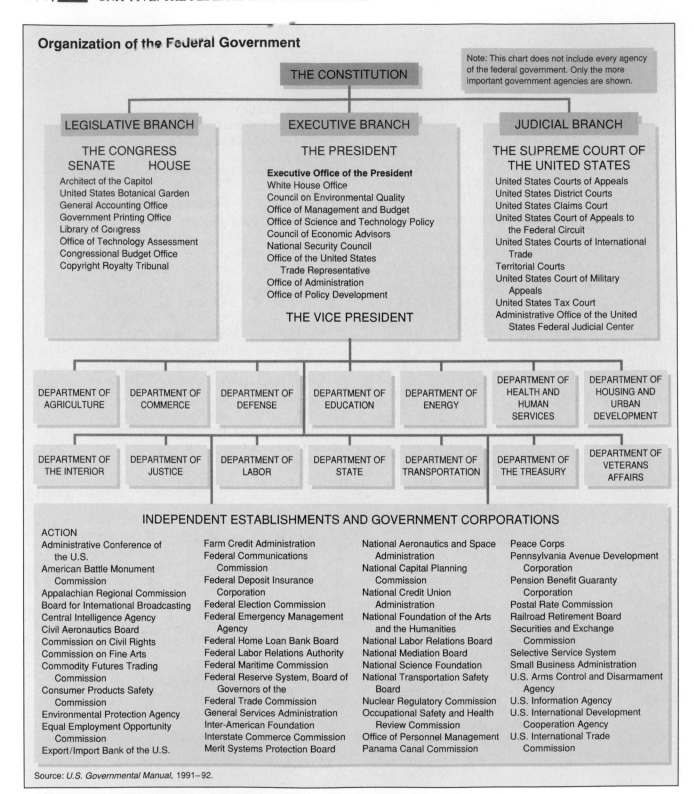

Organization of the Federal Government

THE CONSTITUTION

Note: This chart does not include every agency of the federal government. Only the more important government agencies are shown.

LEGISLATIVE BRANCH

THE CONGRESS
SENATE   HOUSE

Architect of the Capitol
United States Botanical Garden
General Accounting Office
Government Printing Office
Library of Congress
Office of Technology Assessment
Congressional Budget Office
Copyright Royalty Tribunal

EXECUTIVE BRANCH

THE PRESIDENT

Executive Office of the President
White House Office
Council on Environmental Quality
Office of Management and Budget
Office of Science and Technology Policy
Council of Economic Advisors
National Security Council
Office of the United States
  Trade Representative
Office of Administration
Office of Policy Development

THE VICE PRESIDENT

JUDICIAL BRANCH

THE SUPREME COURT OF
THE UNITED STATES

United States Courts of Appeals
United States District Courts
United States Claims Court
United States Court of Appeals to
  the Federal Circuit
United States Courts of International
  Trade
Territorial Courts
United States Court of Military
  Appeals
United States Tax Court
Administrative Office of the United
  States Federal Judicial Center

DEPARTMENT OF AGRICULTURE	DEPARTMENT OF COMMERCE	DEPARTMENT OF DEFENSE	DEPARTMENT OF EDUCATION	DEPARTMENT OF ENERGY	DEPARTMENT OF HEALTH AND HUMAN SERVICES	DEPARTMENT OF HOUSING AND URBAN DEVELOPMENT

DEPARTMENT OF THE INTERIOR	DEPARTMENT OF JUSTICE	DEPARTMENT OF LABOR	DEPARTMENT OF STATE	DEPARTMENT OF TRANSPORTATION	DEPARTMENT OF THE TREASURY	DEPARTMENT OF VETERANS AFFAIRS

INDEPENDENT ESTABLISHMENTS AND GOVERNMENT CORPORATIONS

ACTION
Administrative Conference of
  the U.S.
American Battle Monument
  Commission
Appalachian Regional Commission
Board for International Broadcasting
Central Intelligence Agency
Civil Aeronautics Board
Commission on Civil Rights
Commission on Fine Arts
Commodity Futures Trading
  Commission
Consumer Products Safety
  Commission
Environmental Protection Agency
Equal Employment Opportunity
  Commission
Export/Import Bank of the U.S.

Farm Credit Administration
Federal Communications
  Commission
Federal Deposit Insurance
  Corporation
Federal Election Commission
Federal Emergency Management
  Agency
Federal Home Loan Bank Board
Federal Labor Relations Authority
Federal Maritime Commission
Federal Reserve System, Board of
  Governors of the
Federal Trade Commission
General Services Administration
Inter-American Foundation
Interstate Commerce Commission
Merit Systems Protection Board

National Aeronautics and Space
  Administration
National Capital Planning
  Commission
National Credit Union
  Administration
National Foundation of the Arts
  and the Humanities
National Labor Relations Board
National Mediation Board
National Science Foundation
National Transportation Safety
  Board
Nuclear Regulatory Commission
Occupational Safety and Health
  Review Commission
Office of Personnel Management
Panama Canal Commission

Peace Corps
Pennsylvania Avenue Development
  Corporation
Pension Benefit Guaranty
  Corporation
Postal Rate Commission
Railroad Retirement Board
Securities and Exchange
  Commission
Selective Service System
Small Business Administration
U.S. Arms Control and Disarmament
  Agency
U.S. Information Agency
U.S. International Development
  Cooperation Agency
U.S. International Trade
  Commission

Source: *U.S. Governmental Manual,* 1991–92.

▲ **FIGURE 17–1 Organization of the Federal Government.** The table above details the organization of the federal government including the more important executive departments, independent executive agencies, independent regulatory agencies, and government corporations. Approximately how many people are employed by the federal government?

How the Federal Bureaucracy Is Organized

A complete organization chart of the federal government would be large enough to cover an entire wall. A simplified version is provided in Figure 17–1 on page 404. The executive branch consists of a number of bureaucracies that provide services to Congress, the federal courts, and to the president directly.

There are four major types of bureaucratic structures within the executive branch of the federal government:

- Executive Departments
- Independent Executive Agencies
- Independent Regulatory Agencies
- Government Corporations

Each type of bureaucratic structure has its own relationship to the president and its own internal workings.

SECTION 1 REVIEW _____

1. What is a bureaucracy?
2. Describe the growth of government bureaucracy in historical terms.
3. **For critical analysis:** Why do you think state and local bureaucracies (in total) are so much larger than the federal bureaucracy?

SECTION 2

The Executive Departments

Preview Questions:
- What are some of the major executive departments and their duties?
- Which departments primarily serve the president?
- How are the departments organized?

You have already been introduced to the various executive departments in Chapter 15 when you read about the president at work with his cabinet and other close advisors. The fourteen executive departments, called line organizations, are the major service organizations of the federal government. They are directly accountable to the president and are responsible for performing government functions, such as training troops (Department of Defense), printing money (Department of the Treasury), and enforcing federal laws setting minimum safety and health standards for workers (Department of Labor).

Each department was created by Congress as the need arose, and each manages a specific policy area. The head of each department is known as the secretary. For the Department of Justice the head is called the attorney general. Each department head is appointed by the president, and confirmed by the Senate.

Figure 17–2 on the next two pages provides an overview of each of the departments in the executive branch and their main duties.

Organization within Departments

While there are organizational differences among the departments, each generally follows a typical bureaucratic structure. For example, the organization of the Department of Agriculture provides a model for how an executive department is organized.

One aspect of the secretary of agriculture's job is to carry out the president's agricultural policies. Another aspect, however, is to promote and protect the department. The secretary will spend time ensuring that Congress allocates enough money for the department to work effectively. The secretary also makes sure that **constituents**—the people the department serves, usually owners of major farming corporations—are happy. In general, the secretary tries to maintain or improve the status of the department with respect to all the other departments and units of the federal bureaucracy.

The secretary of agriculture is assisted by a deputy secretary and several assistant secretaries, all of whom are nominated by the president and put into office with

▼ The activities of the secretary of agriculture can have a major impact on American farmers everywhere. What are the basic duties of the secretary of agriculture?

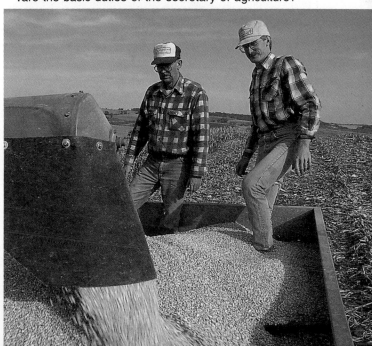

Executive Departments

Department (Year Established)	Principal Duties	Most Important Sub-Agencies
State (1789)	Negotiates treaties; develops our foreign policy; protects citizens abroad.	Passport Agency; Bureau of Diplomatic Security; Foreign Service; Bureau of Human Rights and Humanitarian Affairs; Bureau of Consular Affairs; Bureau of Intelligence and Research
Treasury (1789)	Pays all federal bills; borrows money; collects federal taxes; mints coins and prints paper currency; operates the Secret Service; supervises national banks.	Internal Revenue Service (IRS); Bureau of Alcohol, Tobacco, and Firearms; United States Secret Service; U.S. Mint; Customs Service
Interior (1849)	Supervises federally owned lands and parks; operates federal hydroelectric power facilities; supervises Native-American affairs.	United States Fish and Wildlife Service; National Park Service; Bureau of Indian Affairs; Bureau of Mines; Bureau of Land Management
Justice (1870)	Furnishes legal advice to the president; enforces federal criminal laws; supervises the federal corrections system (prisons).	Federal Bureau of Investigation (FBI); Drug Enforcement Administration (DEA); Bureau of Prisons (BOP); United States Marshals Service; Immigration and Naturalization Service (INS)
Agriculture (1889)	Provides assistance to farmers and ranchers; conducts research to improve agricultural activity and to prevent plant disease; works to protect forests from fires and disease.	Oil Conservation Service; Agricultural Research Service; Food and Safety Inspection Service; Federal Crop Insurance Corporation; Farmers Home Administration; Forest Service
Commerce (1903)	Grants patents and trademarks; conducts the national census; monitors the weather; protects the interests of businesses.	Bureau of the Census; Bureau of Economic Analysis; Minority Business Development Agency; Patent and Trademark Office; National Oceanic and Atmospheric Administration; United States Travel and Tourism Administration
Labor (1913)	Administers federal labor laws; promotes the interests of workers.	Occupational Safety and Health Administration (OSHA); Bureau of Labor Statistics; Employment Standards Administration; Office of Labor-Management Standards; Employment and Training Administration

▲ FIGURE 17–2 **Executive Departments.** The figure on this page and the next lists and describes each of the 14 executive departments, their principal duties, and most important sub-agencies. Which of these departments is responsible for the maintenance and care of federally owned lands and parks?

Executive Departments (continued)

Department (Year Established)	Principal Duties	Most Important Sub-Agencies
Defense (1947)[1]	Manages the armed forces (Army, Navy, Air Force, Marines); operates military bases; responsible for civil defense.	National Guard; Defense Investigation Service; National Security Agency; Joint Chiefs of Staff; Departments of the Air Force, Navy, Army
Health and Human Services (1953)	Administers the Social Security and Medicare programs; promotes public health; enforces pure food and drug laws; is involved in health-related research.	Social Security Administration; Family Support Administration; Office of Human Development Services; Public Health Service
Housing and Urban Development (1965)	Concerned with the nation's housing needs; develops and rehabilitates urban communities; promotes improvements in city streets and parks.	Office of Block Grant Assistance; Emergency Shelter Grants Program; Office of Urban Development Action Grants; Assistant Secretary for Fair Housing and Equal Opportunity
Transportation (1967)	Finances improvements in mass transit; develops and administers programs for highways, railroads, and aviation; involved with offshore maritime safety.	Federal Aviation Administration (FAA); Federal Highway Administration; National Highway Traffic Administration; United States Coast Guard; Urban Mass-Transit Administration
Energy (1977)	Involved in conservation of energy and resources; analyzes energy data; conducts research and development.	Energy Information Administration; Economics Regulatory Administration; Bonneville Power Administration; Office of Nuclear Energy; Energy Information Administration; Office of Conservation and Renewable Energy
Education (1979)[2]	Coordinates federal programs and policies for education; administers aid to education; promotes educational research.	Office of Special Education and Rehabilitation Services; Office of Elementary and Secondary Education; Office of Postsecondary Education; Office of Vocational and Adult Education
Veterans Affairs (1989)	Promotes the welfare of veterans of the U.S. armed forces	Health Care Service Benefit Programs; Memorial Affairs; Medical Training

[1] Formed from the Department of War (1789) and the Department of the Navy (1798).
[2] Formed from the Department of Health, Education, and Welfare (1953).

GOVERNMENT IN ACTION

PERSONAL LAW

Your Rights as an Employee

The composition of the American work-force has changed dramatically. When our nation's government was established over 200 years ago, 90 percent of American workers could be classified as farmers. Today, only a very small percentage of Americans work in agriculture. Most work in offices (32 percent), factories (15 percent), restaurants, stores, or retail outlets (13 percent), or schools or medical facilities (15 percent). As you have learned in this chapter, close to 15 percent of the American workforce is employed by the government.

To protect the rights of a civilian labor force of more than 122 million workers, government regulations and laws have been established.

Your Basic Employee Rights

Every employee is entitled to be compensated (paid) by their employer for the work which they have done. Many salespeople are paid a commission, that is, a percentage of the sales made. The federal government sets legal minimum wages that you have to be paid, typically called the *minimum wage*. There are also laws about how much you have to be paid extra if you work over a specified number of hours a week, such as 37½ hours. If you do not receive such overtime pay, you can sue for the money owed.

Every employee is entitled to safe working conditions. According to the Federal Occupational Safety and Health Act of 1970, employers must furnish a place of employment that is free from recognized hazards that may cause serious physical harm or death. Most states have similar regulations.

While you as an employee have no legal right to fringe benefits, virtually all jobs offer them to you. Fringe benefits include medical insurance, retirement plans, vacations and holidays with pay, legal-aid plans, maternity and paternity leave, and many others.

Fighting Discrimination

A major part of modern legislation protecting workers involves preventing and punishing discrimination. For example, the federal Equal Pay Act of 1963 prohibits employers from offering different wages solely on the basis of gender for jobs that require equal skill, effort, and responsibility. The Civil Rights Act of 1964 makes it unlawful for employers to "refuse to hire or discharge any individual, or otherwise discriminate against any individual, with respect to compensation, terms, conditions, or privileges of employment because of such individual's race, color, religion, sex, or national origin." In 1967, Congress passed the Age Discrimination and Employment Act which makes it unlawful for employers to discriminate against persons because of their age. In 1990, Congress passed the Americans with Disabilities Act which prohibits discrimination in employment against persons with disabilities and demands that employers make reasonable accommodations for disabled persons in the workplace, if at all possible.

Wrongful Discharge

In many states, if you think you have been fired improperly, you can sue your employer for wrongful discharge. Your employer has to prove that he or she had good cause (for example, insubordination, lack of business, bankruptcy) to let you go.

In most states, at a minimum, the following three rules have emerged:

1. Your employer cannot fire you because you refuse to follow a company order to lie or engage in an illegal action.
2. If you have a contract with your employer, even if it is only *implied,* and you have been carrying on your duties in good faith and honestly, your employer may be held

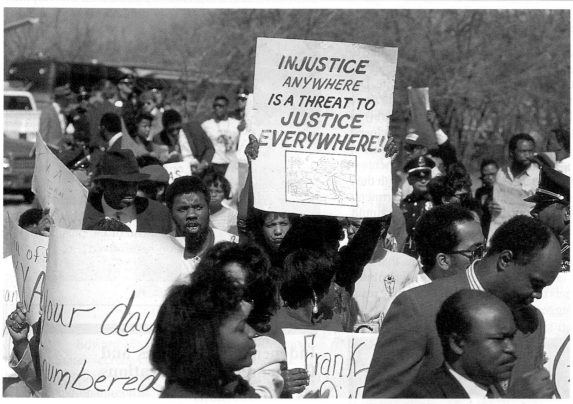

▲ Discrimination based on race or gender is still a problem in many areas of American life. The Equal Pay Act of 1963, the Civil Rights Act of 1964, and the Civil Rights Act of 1991 are all designed to eliminate such discrimination in the workplace.

liable if you are fired in violation of that contract.

3. If you have received favorable job evaluations for a long period of time, especially when accompanied by salary increases, then your employer will be held in violation of an implied *agreement of continued employment* if he or she fires you.

THINK ABOUT IT

1. Under what circumstances, if any, would it be appropriate to allow employers to hire and fire employees at will? Explain.

2. Does everyone who works have a right to a minimum amount of fringe benefits, such as health insurance? Explain.

3. The Equal Pay Act outlaws different pay based solely on gender. Nonetheless, women in America, on average, make less than men. Does this necessarily mean the Equal Pay Act continues to be violated by employers? Explain.

4. There has been a great deal of legislation designed to eliminate discrimination in the workplace. Do you think that more legislation is needed? If so, what type of legislation would you recommend?

Selected Independent Executive Agencies

Name	Date Formed	Principal Duties
Central Intelligence Agency (CIA)	1947	Gathers and analyzes political and military information about foreign countries so that the United States can improve its own political and military status; conducts activities outside the United States, with the goal of countering the work of intelligence services operated by other nations whose political philosophies are inconsistent with our own.
General Services Administration (GSA)	1949	Purchases and manages all property of the federal government; acts as the business arm of the federal government, overseeing federal government spending projects; discovers overcharges in government programs.
National Science Foundation (NSF)	1950	Promotes scientific research; provides grants to all levels of schools for instructional programs in the sciences.
Small Business Administration (SBA)	1953	Protects the interests of small businesses; provides low-cost loans and management information to small businesses.
Commission on Civil Rights	1957	Evaluates information on discrimination that is based on sex, race, national origin, religion, or physical handicap.
National Aeronautics and Space Administration (NASA)	1958	Responsible for U.S. space program, including building, testing, and operating space vehicles.
Federal Election Commission	1974	Ensures that candidates and states follow the rules established by the Federal Election Campaign Act.

▲ FIGURE 17–3 **Selected Independent Executive Agencies.** The table above lists the major independent executive agencies, the date each was formed, and the principal duties of each agency. Why are these agencies independent?

- The Citizens' Stamp Advisory Committee
- The East-West Foreign Trade Board
- The Susquehanna River Basing Commission

Independent Regulatory Agencies

Independent regulatory agencies are responsible for a specific type of public policy. Their function is to create and implement rules that regulate private activity and protect the public interest in a particular sector of the economy. They are sometimes called the "alphabet soup" of government, because most such agencies are known in Washington by their initials.

One of the earliest agencies was the Interstate Commerce Commission (ICC), established in 1887. At the time the ICC was founded, Americans were beginning to seek some form of government control over business and industries. The goal of the ICC was to make

The U.S. space program, which includes the missions of the U.S. Space Shuttle Atlantis and its crew shown here, is the responsibility of the National Aeronautics and Space Administration (NASA). What type of agency is NASA?

technical, non-political decisions about allowable rates and profits for different transportation and shipping businesses. These rates were to be for the benefit of the entire public. Changing these rates would not require congressional legislation every time a new rule was proposed because the agency had the power to make such changes.

After the ICC was formed, other agencies were created to regulate aviation (the Civil Aeronautics Board, or CAB, no longer in existence), communication (the Federal Communication Commission, or FCC), the stock market (the Securities and Exchange Commission, or SEC), and many other areas of business.

Figure 17–4 on the next page lists the major independent regulatory agencies.

Administration of Regulatory Agencies All regulatory agencies are administered independently of the executive, judicial, and executive branches of government. The regulatory agencies therefore combine some functions of all three branches of government.

They are legislative in that they make rules that have the force of law. For example, the Federal Trade Commission (FTC) enacted a three-day ''cooling-off'' rule with respect to door-to-door sales. Anytime you sign a

The Interstate Commerce Commission (ICC) was established in 1887 to help regulate transportation and shipping businesses. What type of agency is the ICC?

CHAPTER 17 REVIEW—Continued

Summary

1. A bureaucracy is an organization that is structured in a pyramid-like fashion. The federal bureaucracy is headed by the president. The government at all levels spends more than 40 percent of the nation's annual income.

2. The fourteen executive departments, called line organizations, are the major service organizations of the federal government and are directly accountable to the president. Each department was created by Congress as the need arose and each manages a specific policy area. The head of each department is known as the secretary, except for the head of the Department of Justice, who is known as the attorney general. Each department head is appointed by the president and must be confirmed by the Senate. The so-called "inner" departments—State, Defense, Justice, and Treasury—exist primarily to serve the president.

3. Independent executive agencies report directly to the president. They have a single function and were created to be independent because of the sensitive nature of their functions or to protect them from partisan politics. Independent regulatory agencies are responsible for a specific type of public policy. They implement rules to protect the public interest in their particular sector. A government corporation is a business that is owned by the government. The United States Postal Service is an example of a government corporation.

4. Most federal workers belong to the civil service. In our nation's early history, federal workers were appointed on the basis of the president's political party preferences. But because of inefficiency and corruption, many Americans called for reform. In 1883, the Civil Service Reform Act was passed, which created the Civil Service Commission and established the principle of federal employment on the basis of open competitive examinations. In 1978, the Civil Service Commission was divided into the Office of Personnel Management, in charge of hiring federal employees, and the Merit Systems Protection Board, to protect the integrity of the federal merit system.

5. Even though bureaucratic agencies are prohibited from lobbying Congress, they have developed techniques to help them gain congressional support. The so-called iron triangle is a three-way alliance among legislators, bureaucrats, and the interest groups that those bureaucrats influence. Presumably, each group helps satisfy the other groups' needs and in turn receives what it needs. An important reform in the last few years involves more protection for so-called whistle-blowers.

Review Questions

1. What is the federal bureaucracy?
2. Describe the way the federal bureaucracy has grown.
3. Name three executive agencies.
4. Which departments make up the "inner" departments?
5. Identify two reasons Congress has set up independent agencies.
6. What are independent regulatory agencies responsible for and how are they administered?
7. What is a government corporation?
8. How did the Pendleton Act change the way federal employees are chosen?
9. What rule did the Hatch Act establish?
10. What is the main function of the Office of Personnel Management and of the Merit Systems Protection Board?
11. How does the federal bureaucracy help to shape public policy?
12. How does the iron triangle work?
13. What does the Freedom of Information Act allow citizens to do?
14. Is the federal bureaucracy representative of the population in terms of race and gender? Why or why not?

Questions for Thought and Discussion

1. The bureaucracy has often been called the "fourth branch of government." Do you agree with this assessment? Why or why not?
2. What steps, if any, do you think should be taken to make the bureaucracy more open, efficient, and responsive?
3. Many administrations have sought to reduce the confusion, size, and complexity of the federal bureau-

CHAPTER 17 REVIEW—Continued

cracy. Why do you think their attempts have generally not succeeded?

4. How might the federal government make civil service a more appealing career to you and your friends?

5. You may have heard news stories of $5,000 screwdrivers and $500 nails being purchased by the Department of Defense. Who do you think is responsible for such waste and inefficiency?

Improving Your Skills
Communication Skills
Giving an Oral Report

Oral reports are a way of sharing information with your classmates. If you are well prepared and know the information, you will most likely feel more confident, because you will know what you are presenting.

Begin with a written report that you have researched and created according to earlier exercises in this text. Having researched the topic yourself, you will be prepared to elaborate on the subject or answer questions that might come up. The more you have researched the topic, the more sure of yourself you will be. Follow these suggestions:

- Reread your written report several times. Review some of your most significant sources of information.
- Write an outline from your report that covers the most important points. Include examples and details you think are particularly important and illustrative.
- Transfer your outline to index cards, which you can use while giving your oral report. Use abbreviations that will help trigger your memory. Put some type of mark, a star, or check, for instance, in places at which you want to give examples or details.
- Practice delivering your oral report as often as you can to friends and family. Ask them for criticism and helpful tips. Practice maintaining eye contact with them, which will help make your speech more interesting. Also practice in front of the mirror so you can improve your presentation. Pay close attention to your tone of voice, how loud you are

speaking, how fast you are speaking, and how convincing you sound.

Writing

Create a written report and then transform it into an oral report.

Social Studies Skills
Working with Organization Charts

Look at Figure 17–1 on page 404. Answer the following questions:

1. Does the chart show all of the federal agencies that exist today?

2. Is the U.S. Information Agency part of the judicial branch? If it is not, to what branch of government does it belong?

3. In this chart, does the fact that location of the Department of State is below that of the Department of Education mean that one has a higher ranking within the executive branch than the other?

Activities and Projects

1. Learn the details of the federal hiring process and find out how to apply for a federal job by contacting the federal job center in your state. Look under Federal Information Center in your telephone directory, or contact the Office of Public Affairs, OPM, 1900 E Street NW, Washington, DC 20415. You can also look up the OPM's regional office in your area in the *Government Annual* found in most libraries.

2. Do a research project on the Freedom of Information Act. How many of the over five hundred thousand requests received each year actually come from private citizens like yourself, as opposed to individuals making requests for businesses or attorneys?

3. Do a research project on either the U.S. Postal Service or AMTRAK. In particular, determine to what extent over the years those government corporations have been funded by the fees collected and to what extent they have been subsidized by American taxpayers.

4. Stage a class debate on the following statement: Resolved—The size of the federal bureaucracy shall be frozen at three million individuals.

The Federal
Judicial Branch

UNIT CONTENTS

■ *Chapter 18*   The Federal Courts

DISTRICT COURTS

CHAPTER 18

The Federal Courts

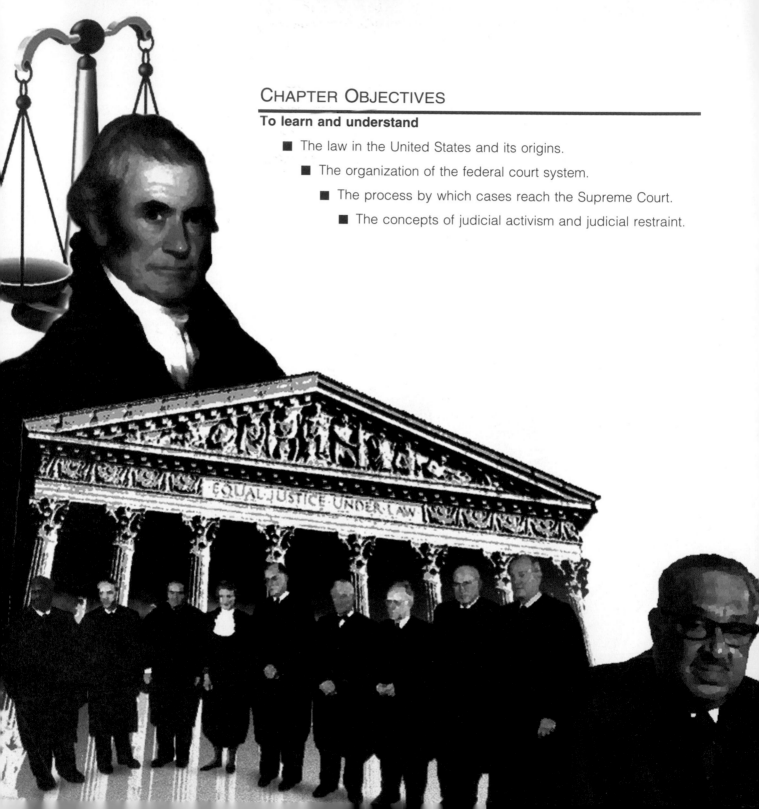

CHAPTER OBJECTIVES

To learn and understand

- The law in the United States and its origins.
- The organization of the federal court system.
- The process by which cases reach the Supreme Court.
- The concepts of judicial activism and judicial restraint.

"*The peace, the prosperity, and the very existence of the Union are nestled in the hands of . . . federal judges. Without them the Constitution would be a dead letter.*"

——— **Alexis de Tocqueville**
(1805–1859) French Political Writer

INTRODUCTION

A few years ago, William Frazee, who was unemployed, applied to Kelly Services for temporary work. When Kelly Services offered him a temporary retail position that would require him to work on Sunday, however, Frazee refused the job. He told the temporary employment company that, as a Christian, he could not work on "the Lord's day." Then Frazee applied to the Illinois Department of Employment Security for unemployment benefits. He claimed that there was good cause for his refusal to work on Sunday. But the Illinois government denied his application. Frazee appealed his case by maintaining that the denial of unemployment benefits violated his First Amendment right to the free practice of his religion. His case eventually went to several different courts in Illinois and finally reached the Supreme Court of the United States. In *Frazee* v. *Illinois Department of Employment Security* (1989) the court declared that, indeed, by denying Frazee unemployment benefits, the state of Illinois had violated the freedom of religion clause of the First Amendment.

For Mr. Frazee and countless other Americans, French political commentator Alexis de Tocqueville's opening quote could not ring any truer. It is indeed the federal judges who make certain that the Constitution is not a "dead letter."

The judges in the federal courts continue to examine and re-examine the Constitution and their own decisions so that justice and the Constitution are well served. As Supreme Court Justice Louis Brandeis pointed out, "The Court bows to the lessons of experience and the force of better reasoning, recognizing that the process of trial and error, so fruitful in the physical sciences, is appropriate also in the judicial function." Thus, through "trial and error," the Supreme Court may overrule its earlier decisions as it protects what Alexis de Tocqueville described as "the peace, the prosperity, and the very existence of the Union".

SECTION 1

Law and Where It Comes From

Preview Questions
- What is the difference between common law and statutory law?
- What is constitutional law?
- What is the difference between civil and criminal law?
- What does it mean for a court to have jurisdiction?

In 1066 the Normans conquered England, and William the Conqueror and his successors began the process of unifying the country under Norman rule. One of the means they used to do this was the establishment of the king's court, or *curia regis.* Before the Norman conquest, disputes had been settled according to local customs. The king's court sought to establish a common, or uniform, set of customs for the whole country. As the number of courts and cases increased, the most important decisions of each year were gathered together and recorded in *Year Books.*

Judges, settling disputes similar to ones that had been decided before, used the *Year Books* as the basis for their decisions. If a case was unique, judges had to create new laws, but whenever possible they based their decisions on the general principles suggested by earlier cases. The body of judicial law that developed under this system is still used today and is known as **common law**—the body of law that developed from custom and court decisions in England and the United States.

Common Law

Common law began as the ancient unwritten law of England. The **case law** of the United States since the

431

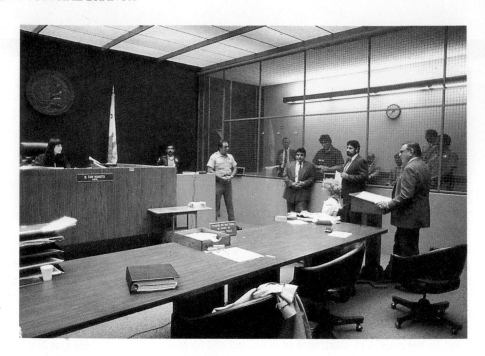

In this criminal courtroom, the suspected criminals are kept encaged behind a barrier. What is the difference between criminal law and civil law?

American Revolution is a predominant part of our common law, consisting of rules of law announced in separate court decisions. Case law includes all reported court cases that interpret statutes, regulations, and the Constitution. Such interpretations become part of the authoritative law on the subject and further serve as a **precedent**, or an example for future cases. The case involving Mr. Frazee was a precedent-setting case decided by the Supreme Court of the United States.

Constitutional Law

The federal government and the states have separate constitutions that set forth the general organization, powers, and limits of their respective governments. The U.S. Constitution is the supreme law of the land. A law in violation of the Constitution, no matter what its source, will be declared unconstitutional and will not be enforced. Similarly, unless they conflict with the U.S. Constitution, state constitutions are supreme within their respective borders. The U.S. Constitution defines the powers and limitations of the federal government. All powers not granted to the federal government are retained by the states or by the people.

Statutory Law

Statutes enacted by the U.S. Congress and the various state legislative bodies make up another source of law,

which is generally referred to as **statutory law**. The statutory law of the United States also includes laws passed by cities and counties, none of which can violate the U.S. Constitution or the relevant state constitutions. Today, legislative bodies and regulatory agencies assume an ever-increasing share of lawmaking. Much of the work of modern courts consists of interpreting what the legislators meant when the law was passed and applying it to a present set of circumstances.

Civil versus Criminal Law

Civil law spells out the duties that exist between persons or between citizens and their governments. Law concerning contracts for business transactions, for example, is part of civil law. If you sign a contract to purchase a car on credit, the law governing that transaction is civil law.

Criminal law, by contrast, has to do with wrongs committed against the public as a whole. Criminal acts are prohibited by local, state, or federal government statutes. In a criminal case, the government seeks to impose a penalty (fines and/or imprisonment) upon a person suspected of having violated a criminal law. When someone robs a convenience store, that person has committed a crime and if caught and proven guilty, will normally be in prison for some period of time.

CASE STUDY

Gideon v. Wainwright

GOVERNMENT IN ACTION

The Sixth Amendment to the U.S. Constitution provides that "in all criminal prosecutions, the accused shall enjoy the right . . . to have the assistance of counsel for his defense." By the passage of the Fourteenth Amendment in 1868, following the Civil War, this and other rights and privileges contained in the Bill of Rights were to be secured for all U.S. citizens, and no state could "deprive any person of life, liberty, or property without due process of law." Nearly a century passed, however, before the right to counsel was made available to accused persons in state criminal proceedings. As late as 1942 the Supreme Court held in *Betts* v. *Bradey* that, except in capital cases, criminal defendants were not automatically guaranteed the right to have a lawyer present when they were tried in court.

In 1963, however, the *Betts* v. *Brady* precedent was overturned by the decision in *Gideon* v. *Wainwright,* which became a landmark case in securing the right to counsel for criminal defendants.[a] The case began in 1962 when Clarence Earl Gideon sent a petition to the Supreme Court to review his most recent conviction—breaking into a pool hall and stealing money in Panama City, Florida. In his petition, Gideon claimed he could not afford to pay a lawyer to file the petition for him. He also claimed that his conviction and sentencing to a five-year prison term violated the due process clause of the Fourteenth Amendment. Gideon reported that when he asked for the assistance of a lawyer at the time of his trial, the court refused. The heart of Gideon's petition was his claim that "to try a poor man for a felony without giving him a lawyer was to deprive him of due process of law."

Gideon was successful. He had the help of the American Civil Liberties Union (ACLU) and its appointed lawyer, Abe Fortas, whom President Johnson later appointed to the Supreme Court. The Court decided in Gideon's favor, stating that persons accused of **felonies** (serious crimes) who can show they are unable to afford a lawyer must be given one at the government's expense. Represented by a court-appointed attorney, Gideon was retried and found to be innocent of the charges.

THINK ABOUT IT

1. What change in criminal procedure resulted from Clarence Earl Gideon's petition?
2. How does the Supreme Court's decision in favor of Gideon change the way state governments must spend their money?

---

a. A biography of Clarence Earl Gideon and the significance of this case is presented in Anthony Lewis, *Gideon's Trumpet* (New York: Vintage Books, 1964).

Jurisdiction

In Latin, *juris* means "law," and *diction* means "to speak." Thus, **jurisdiction** literally refers to the power "to speak the law." Jurisdiction applies either to the geographical area within which a court has the right and power to decide cases, or to the right and power of a court to decide matters concerning certain persons, property, or subject matter. Before any court can hear a case, it must have jurisdiction over the person against whom the suit is brought, the property involved in the suit, and the subject matter.

Jurisdiction over Persons and Property Generally, a court's power is limited to the geographical boundaries of the state in which it is located. Thus, a court has jurisdiction over anyone who can be served a **summons** (an order to appear in court) within those boundaries. A court normally will also have jurisdiction over residents

CITIZENSHIP SKILLS AND RESPONSIBILITIES
Serving on a Jury

▲ These jurors listen attentively while the lawyer makes her point. Why do you think serving on a jury is often referred to as jury *duty*?

If you are an American citizen of sound mind and have never committed a serious crime, you may one day be summoned by a state or federal court for **jury duty**. Names of jurors are usually chosen from tax assessor's polls, lists of registered voters, and driver's license registrations.

If your name is chosen, in most states the clerk of the court will send you a jury qualification form, which you must fill out and return. You will then receive a summons requiring you to appear in court at a particular time and place. If for some reason you cannot be there, you must explain this to the court. There are few valid reasons for being excused. The court will respond by either excusing you from jury duty or ordering you to appear. If you don't appear when so ordered, the court has the power to send a sheriff's deputy to bring you to court.

Being employed is not a valid excuse to be exempted from jury duty. The law protects you from being fired from your job or penalized in any way for the time you spend serving on a jury. (Be sure to notify your employer as soon as you have been called for jury duty.)

When you appear in court, you may be asked to wait in a room with other prospective jurors until you are called. Then you will be escorted to the courtroom. You will be asked to take an oath that you will answer questions truthfully. Lawyers on both sides will ask you questions to determine whether or not you are likely to be biased. They will ask you questions about your background, beliefs, your relationship to the people involved in the trial, and whether you have already formed an opinion about the case. If one or the other lawyers finds a reason why you may be biased in the case, you will be disqualified by the judge.

If you are accepted to serve on the jury, you will take another oath in court along with the other jurors, and will be told when you are to reappear.

Before the trial begins you will be instructed by the judge on court procedures, which include:

- Nothing you see or hear outside the courtroom can be considered in reaching your verdict.
- It is your sworn duty to decide the case by considering only the testimony and evidence you hear and see in the courtroom proceedings. Your personal prejudices or sympathies should have no bearing.
- You may not speak to anyone outside the courtroom—not even your family—about the trial.

When the trial begins, you must listen carefully to all the testimony. You may not be permitted to take notes, so you must try to remember the details of what you hear. In some cases, you might be told that the case has been settled out of court. If this happens you will be dismissed. If the case continues, both sides will be presented. Cases can last anywhere from one day to several weeks. When both sides have presented their cases, the judge will instruct you about the law to be applied. Then you and the other jurors will be asked to decide the facts of the case.

You and the other jurors will be taken to a private room. You will have the opportunity to share your views about the evidence you have heard. You must listen to the other jurors' views, and may try to persuade the others to take your position. A fellow citizen's future and your community are at stake, so you should take the responsibility seriously.

Sometimes juries take a considerable amount of time to discuss and evaluate all the evidence. If the jury cannot agree on a verdict (a situation which is called a **hung jury**), either another trial is held with a different jury or the matter is dropped.

Most juries are able to come to a unanimous decision. When all of the jurors agree on their verdict, the jury members will be ushered back into the courtroom. They will pronounce their decision. This decision is final and the trial is ended. Generally, the judge thanks the jury and dismisses it.

Serving on a jury can be interesting and educational. It is also an opportunity for you to participate in our system of equal justice under the law.

TAKING ACTION

1. Stage a mock trial in your class. Choose a prosecuting attorney, a defense attorney, a defendant, a judge, and a jury. Perhaps you can use the case of William Frazee presented in the introduction of this chapter as the fact pattern for your mock jury trial.
2. Arrange to be an observer in a jury trial in the court nearest to your house. Listen to the evidence presented and determine what your verdict would be if you were on the jury.
3. You may be excused from jury duty under special circumstances. Make a list of the reasons that you think might be serious enough to prevent you from serving on a jury.

U.S. District Courts

At the federal level, the trial court of general jurisdiction is the district court. There is at least one federal district court in every state. The number of districts can vary over time, according to population changes and the size of caseloads.

In the Federal Judgeship Act of 1984, Congress increased the total number of district court judgeships in the United States. The law now provides for 563 district court judgeships within the 96 judicial districts.

U.S. Courts of Appeals

Congress has established twelve **judicial circuits** that hear appeals from the district courts located within their respective circuits. The decisions of the courts of appeals are final in most cases, but appeal to the U.S. Supreme Court is possible. Appeals from federal administrative agencies, such as the Federal Trade Commission (FTC), are also made to the U.S. courts of appeals. See Figure 18–2 below for the geographical boundaries of U.S. district courts and U.S. courts of appeals.

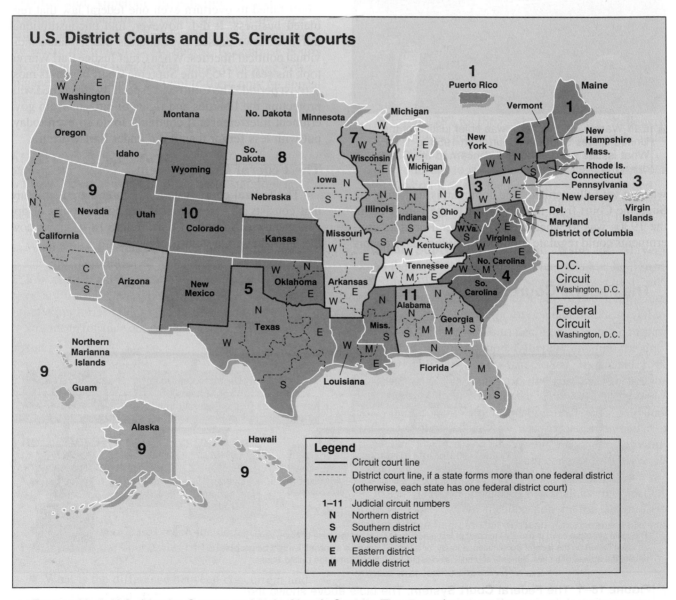

U.S. District Courts and U.S. Circuit Courts

Legend

— Circuit court line

---- District court line, if a state forms more than one federal district (otherwise, each state has one federal district court)

1–11 Judicial circuit numbers
N Northern district
S Southern district
W Western district
E Eastern district
M Middle district

▲ **FIGURE 18–2 U.S. District Courts and U.S. Circuit Courts.** The map above shows the U.S. District Courts and the U.S. Courts of Appeals, or Circuit Courts. How many judicial circuits make up the U.S. Circuit Courts?

Under the Federal Judgeship Act of 1984, there are now 168 circuit court judgeships with 13 circuits (including the federal circuit).

The Supreme Court

The Supreme Court is the highest level of the three-tiered federal court system. According to the language of Article III of the Constitution, there is only one national Supreme Court. All other courts in the federal system are considered inferior. Congress is empowered to create other inferior courts as it deems necessary, which include the U.S. courts of appeals, the district courts, and any other courts of limited jurisdiction.

The Supreme Court consists of nine justices, all of whom are nominated by the president and confirmed by the Senate. As with all federal district and appeals judges, Supreme Court justices receive lifetime appointments (since under Article III they "hold their offices during Good Behavior"). Although the Supreme Court has original jurisdiction in rare instances such as those involving ambassadors (set forth in Article III, Section 2), most of its work is as an appeals court. The Supreme Court can review any case decided by any of the federal courts of appeals, and it also has authority to review some cases decided in the state courts.

Jurisdiction of the Federal Courts and Judicial Review

Because the federal government is a government of limited powers, the jurisdiction of the federal courts is also limited. Article III of the U.S. Constitution established the boundaries of federal judicial power.

The Constitutional Boundaries of Federal Judicial Power   In line with the checks-and-balances system of the federal government, Congress has the power to control the number and kind of inferior courts in the federal system. Except in those cases in which the Constitution gives the Supreme Court original jurisdiction, Congress can regulate the jurisdiction of the Supreme Court. Although the Constitution sets the outer limits of federal judicial power, Congress can set other limits on federal jurisdiction. Furthermore, the courts themselves

▼ The nine justices of the Supreme Court, all of whom are nominated by the president and confirmed by the Senate, are pictured here. Why do you think the framers of the Constitution chose to call this court the *Supreme Court*?

J ohn Marshall has been called the architect of the American constitutional system, even though his true genius wasn't appreciated until after his death in 1835. Until John Marshall became the fourth chief justice of the Supreme Court, the Court was seen as having little power, with almost no influence over the other two branches of government. John Marshall changed all that. After he had been chief justice for a few years, the Court began to assume its place as the third equal branch of government, and in a series of brilliant decisions from 1810 to 1835, Marshall almost single-handedly gave new power to the Constitution.

John Marshall was born in a log cabin in Germantown, on the Virginia frontier, on September 24, 1755. He was the first of fifteen children born to Thomas Marshall, a descendant of Welsh immigrants, and his wife, Mary Keith Marshall, who was the daughter of a Scottish clergyman. He grew up on a farm and had only two years of formal schooling. As a young man he fought in the colonial army during the American Revolution as lieutenant and captain. Later he attended six weeks of law lectures at William and Mary College, and began to practice law in 1781. His legal library at the time consisted solely of notes he had taken while reading a borrowed copy of Francis Bacon's *Abridgement of English Law*.

Early in his legal career, Marshall was recognized as an excellent attorney and was elected to the first of four terms in the Virginia Assembly. When the Constitution was submitted to the Virginia legislature to be ratified, Marshall played a leading role in the fight to adopt it. He turned down the position of attorney general offered to him by George Washington, and also declined the post of minister to France. He won a seat in Congress in 1799, and in 1800 became secretary of state to John Adams. A year later, he was appointed chief justice of the Supreme Court.

John Marshall's thirty-four years on the bench established the prestige of the Court. In his talks and writings he argued that the nation needed an effective judiciary with the power to review the acts of the states and to decide whether the actions of the other two national branches were consistent with the principles of the Constitution. His opinion in *Marbury* v. *Madison* (1803) is regarded as the classic justification of judicial review and the fundamental premise on which the United States constitutional doctrine rests. In *McCulloch* v. *Maryland* (1819), he ruled that when state and federal powers conflict, the federal powers are stronger.

In these and other cases, Marshall established three basic principles that became the foundation of the federal union: (1) the principle of judicial review—that the Supreme Court had the power to determine when a law of Congress was unconstitutional. This idea was debated and denied, but was eventually accepted; (2) the Supreme Court had the power to set aside laws of state legislatures when these laws were contrary to the federal Constitution; (3) the Supreme Court had the power to reverse the decisions of state courts. Other significant rulings by the Marshall court in essence refused to bind the federal government to the literal limits of its expressed powers. Rather, he argued that it is necessary for those interpreting and living under the Constitution to treat it as a "living" document that can be accommodated to the changing needs of the American people.

John Marshall

"THIS, SIR, IS MY CASE! IT IS THE CASE NOT MERE-LY OF THAT HUMBLE INSTITUTION, IT IS THE CASE OF EVERY COLLEGE IN OUR LAND!...IT IS, SIR, AS I HAVE SAID, A SMALL COLLEGE. AND YET..."

▲
Daniel Webster, *standing,* argues before the Supreme Court in a twentieth-century painting by Robert Burns. Chief Justice John Marshall, *fourth from the left,* presides over the Court.

HIS WORDS

From *Marbury* v. *Madison* (1803):
"To what purpose are (congressional) powers limited, and to what purpose is that limitation committed to writing, if these limits may, at any time, be passed by those intended to be restrained? . . . It is a proposition too plain to be contested that the Constitution controls any legislative act repugnant to it. . . . A legislative act contrary to the Constitution is not law . . . it is emphatically the province and duty of the judicial department to say what the law is. . . ."

From *Gibbons* v. *Ogden* (1824):
"We are now arrived at the inquiry, What is this power? It is the power to regulate; that is, to prescribe the rule by which commerce is to be governed. This power, like all others vested in Congress, is complete in itself, may be exercised to its utmost extent, and acknowledges no limitations other than are prescribed in the Constitution."

From *McCulloch* v. *Maryland* (1819):
"Let the end be legitimate, let it be within the scope of the constitution, and all means which are appropriate, which are plainly adapted to that end, which are not prohibited, but consist with the letter and spirit of the constitution, are constitutional."

DEVELOPING YOUR CRITICAL THINKING SKILLS

1. What did Marshall mean when he said that it is the ''duty of the judicial department to say what the law is''?
2. What clause in the Constitution was Marshall referring to when he said that ''the Constitution controls . . .''?
3. Study *Marbury* v. *Madison* on page 60 and *McCulloch* v. *Maryland* on page 89. How did each of these decisions establish basic principles that have helped to strengthen the federal government?

FOR FURTHER READING

Leonard Baker, *John Marhsall: A Life in Law,* MacMillan, New York, (1974).
Albert Beveridge, *The Life of John Marshall,* Houghton Mifflin, Boston, (1916–1919).

CHAPTER 18 REVIEW—Continued

Summary

1. Common law began as the ancient unwritten law of England but today includes the laws made by legislatures and the case law background of England and of the American colonies prior to the American revolution. Statutory law is law enacted by state legislatures and the U.S. Congress. A law in violation of the Constitution, no matter what its source, will be declared unconstitutional and will not be enforced. Civil law spells out the duties that exist between persons or between citizens and their governments. Criminal law, in contrast, has to do with wrongs committed against the public as a whole. Jurisdiction refers to the geographical area within which a court has the power to decide cases.

2. The federal court system is a three-tiered structure that consists of trial courts, intermediate courts of appeals, and the Supreme Court. Congress has established twelve judicial circuits (plus the federal circuit) that hear appeals from the district courts located within their respective circuits. Article III of the Constitution established the boundaries of federal judicial power. Among the cases in which federal courts have jurisdiction are cases involving federal law and cases involving diversity of citizenship, bankruptcy, patents, and copyrights.

3. Thousands of cases are filed with the Supreme Court each year, yet on average, it hears only about two hundred. To bring a case before the Supreme Court, a party requests the Court to issue a writ of *certiorari*, which is an order issued to a lower court requiring it to send the record of the case in question. Whether the Court will issue the writ is entirely within its discretion. The Court's decisions are written in an opinion. When all justices unanimously agree on an opinion, it is written for the entire court in a unanimous opinion. When there is not a unanimous opinion, a majority opinion is written, outlining the views of the majority of justices involved in the particular case. In other than unanimous opinions, one or more dissenting opinions are usually written by those justices who did not agree with the majority. Law clerks undertake much of the research and preliminary drafting necessary for the justices to form an opinion. Each Friday during the annual term, the justices meet in conference to discuss cases under consideration and to decide which new appeals and petitions the Court will accept.

4. The power to nominate Supreme Court justices belongs solely to the president, but the nominee must be confirmed by the Senate. Ideology plays an important role in the president's choices and in the Senate's confirmation. The makeup of the federal judiciary is not typical of the American public.

5. Those advocating the practice of judicial activism believe the Court should use its power to alter the direction of the activities of Congress, state legislatures, and administrative agencies. Those advocating the practice of judicial restraint believe the Court should only rarely use its powers of judicial review. Political checks limit the extent to which courts can exercise judicial review. The legislature, the executive branch, other courts, and the public all place checks on the courts.

Review Questions

1. What is common law?
2. What is the difference between civil law and criminal law?
3. What is meant by jurisdiction?
4. Briefly describe the three-tiered structure of the federal court system.
5. What is the role of the court of appeals in the federal court system?
6. What was the significance of *Marbury* v. *Madison*?
7. How do cases reach the Supreme Court?
8. Name several situations in which the Supreme Court may issue a writ of *certiorari*.
9. Describe the four types of written opinions that can be presented by the Supreme Court.
10. Briefly describe the procedures the Supreme Court justices follow when deciding a case.
11. How are Supreme Court justices nominated? What role does the Senate play in the nomination process?
12. Name the most common characteristics of the Supreme Court justices.
13. Define the practices of judicial activism and judicial restraint.
14. What political checks limit the extent to which the courts can exercise judicial review and make activist changes?
15. What does it mean to be summoned for jury duty?

CHAPTER 18 REVIEW—Continued

Questions for Thoughts and Discussion

1. Do you think it is a good idea that Supreme Court justices are appointed for life? What are the advantages and disadvantages of such an arrangement?
2. Do you think federal judges should be popularly elected? What qualifications would you like to see in a federal judge?
3. Some analysts argue that the Supreme Court often makes the law instead of interpreting it. Do you agree or disagree with this statement? Give reasons for your answer.
4. Sometimes cases arise in which there is no precedent. How do you think a judge should decide such a case?

Improving Your Skills
Communication Skills

Conducting an Interview

Interviewing people who have worked in and around government is an excellent way of learning more about how our government works. These people can often offer insights and firsthand information that is difficult to obtain by reading newspapers and watching the news. To conduct a successful interview you will need to be well prepared and organized. Follow these guidelines:

- **Arrange the details, in person or by telephone, with the person to be interviewed.** Politely and clearly identify yourself, your school, and your teacher. Tell the person why you would like the interview. If the person agrees, suggest a few different times and dates that might be convenient for the person.
- **Decide in advance what information you want to obtain from the interview.** Decide ahead of time which questions will most likely lead to that information. Prioritize the questions, taking into consideration the amount of time you have with that person. Avoid questions that require only yes or no answers. Try to ask questions that will encourage the person to go into detail about the subject matter. Encourage the person to use examples and stories to illustrate the point.

- **Write down a formal list of questions.** If you are working in a group, decide who will ask which questions and in what order. Check the questions with your teacher.
- **Practice asking the questions to classmates.**
- **During the interview, try to make the person feel welcome and comfortable.** Do not become argumentative.
- **After the interview, thank the person.** Send a thank-you note as a final follow-up.

Writing

Suppose that you have the opportunity to interview a Supreme Court justice. Decide what information you would most like to know from this person. Create a formal list of ten questions, written down in order of priority, that you would most likely ask. Give a brief explanation of why you think each of these questions is important.

Social Studies Skills

Map Reading

Carefully examine again Figure 18–2 on page 438. What can be said about the size of the judicial districts in the East relative to the size of those in the West? How would you explain this difference?

Activities and Projects

1. Research a presidential appointee to the Supreme Court who has been rejected by the Senate. In your research, try to find out why the Senate opposed the nominee. Then decide whether you think the Senate's decision was correct. Report your findings to the class.
2. Go to the nearest courthouse in which you would be allowed to sit in on a jury trial. Sit in on a trial, taking note of what the issue is, who the accused is, and the arguments of the two different sides. Write a summary of what happened during the time you spent in the trial.
3. Stage a debate in class on the following: Resolved—The makeup of the federal judiciary should better represent the makeup of the nation in terms of gender, ethnicity, and race.

UNIT SEVEN

American Policy in a Changing World

UNIT CONTENTS

■ *Chapter 19*   Economic Policy, Poverty, and the Environment
■ *Chapter 20*   Defense and Foreign Policy

457

CHAPTER 19

Economic Policy, Poverty, and the Environment

CHAPTER OBJECTIVES

To learn and understand

- How the government exercises its power to regulate the economy through monetary and fiscal policies.

- The different kinds of taxes and systems of taxation.

- Some of the methods the government has used to fight poverty.

- The government's policies in dealing with the environment.

Keynote

"Taxes are what we pay for civilization."

——— **Oliver Wendell Holmes
(1841–1935) United States Supreme
Court Justice**

INTRODUCTION

The basic function of government is to create and carry out public policies, of which there are hundreds. There are national economic policies, such as controlling unemployment and inflation, creating jobs, and implementing systems of taxation. (As Oliver Wendell Holmes points out in the opening quote, without taxes society cannot function.) There are national social policies that strive to clean up the environment and provide needed services for the poor and elderly. And there are policies to maintain a strong national defense. In this chapter you will read about national economic policies and selected social programs. In Chapter 20, you will read about defense and foreign policy.

SECTION 1

Monetary and Fiscal Policy

Preview Questions

- What are the tools used by the government to regulate and promote the economy?
- How does monetary policy affect the economy?
- What role does the Federal Reserve System play in the nation's economy?
- What is fiscal policy and who determines it?
- What is deficit spending? How does the public debt affect the economy?

The basic tools that the federal government uses to manage the national economy are monetary policy and fiscal policy. **Monetary policy** includes regulating the amount of money in circulation. This is the responsibility of an independent agency called the **Federal Reserve System**. **Fiscal policy**, which is the responsibility of the president and Congress, involves adjusting federal taxes and spending in an attempt to improve the nation's economy.

Monetary Policy

You may have read or heard a news report in which a business executive or public official complained that money is "too tight." Or you may have run across a story about an economist warning that money is "too loose." In these cases, the terms *tight* and *loose* refer to the monetary policy of the Federal Reserve System, also known as "the Fed." Monetary policy involves monitoring and adjusting how much money is in circulation, which affects the amount of credit (money available to buy goods and services sold with promise of payment later), which consequently affects business activity in the economy.

Like any other good or service, credit has a cost. For people who want to buy items on credit, the cost is interest (the amount the creditor charges for using the loaned money). As interest rates (the cost of credit) increase, the extent to which businesses and consumers want to use it decreases. In contrast, when the cost of credit drops, the amount of credit businesses and consumers want to use rises.

If the country has a **loose monetary policy**, credit is abundant and inexpensive to use. Under such a policy, people are usually willing to borrow more. Consumers will take out loans to buy new cars, new homes, and other desired items. Businesses will borrow to expand or to start new plants and hire more workers. These workers will have more income to spend, which, in turn, will stimulate further production. If, in contrast, a country has a **tight monetary policy**, credit is expensive and in

459

Brief History of Our Nation's Banking and Monetary Policies

Year	Development in U.S. Banking and Monetary Policies
1791	In response to Alexander Hamilton's proposal, Congress established in Philadelphia the First Bank of the United States, and gave it a twenty-year charter. The bank—the largest corporation in the country—was a private business, though the government supplied one-fifth of its starting capital. It served as a depository for government funds, loaned money to the government and to private individuals and businesses, and regulated the activities of banks with state charters. It also issued bank notes backed by gold, which provided reliable currency.
1816	Following the financial confusion caused by the War of 1812, Congress established the Second Bank of the United States. Like the First Bank, it brought order to the banking system. Opposition remained, however, to a strong national bank. In 1832, President Andrew Jackson vetoed legislation to extend the Second Bank's charter; the following year he withdrew federal funds. The bank closed in 1836.
1835	Inflation increased and continued until 1837, leading to a depression from 1839 to 1843. Between 1836 and 1863, two sets of banks—private unincorporated banks and incorporated banks with charters from state governments—were allowed to co-exist. Passed in 1863, the National Banking Act required all federal banks to invest a portion of their capital in U.S. government bonds, prohibited them from making real estate loans, and required them to hold reserves in the form of gold, cash, or deposits in larger banks.
1913	To control the amount of money in circulation, Congress established the Federal Reserve System. It served as the nation's central bank and could regulate reserves in state and national banks, loan money to member banks, and control the growth of the money supply. In 1914, the system began issuing Federal Reserve Notes, which soon became the predominant form of money in circulation.
1929–1933	Stocks and other investments owned by banks lost much of their value. Bankrupt businesses and individuals were unable to repay their loans. A nationwide financial panic caused thousands of banks to collapse. When President Franklin Roosevelt took office on March 4, 1933, four-fifths of the states had stopped all banking operations. The following day, Roosevelt declared a "bank holiday," closing all banks. Each bank was allowed to reopen only after it had proven itself to be financially sound. Congress passed the Glass-Steagall Banking Act in June, establishing the Federal Deposit Insurance Corporation (FDIC). The new agency helped restore public confidence in banks by insuring funds of individual depositors against bank failure.
1960s–1970s	Congress passed a series of laws protecting consumers in dealing with banks and other depository institutions. The Truth in Lending Act of 1968, the Equal Credit Opportunity Act of 1974, and the Community Reinvestment Act of 1977 established the rights and responsibilities of banks and consumers. They also provided individuals with procedures to file complaints if treated unfairly.
1980s	As part of the general move toward deregulation of business, Congress passed the Depository Institutions Deregulation and Monetary Control Act of 1980. It gradually removed ceilings on the interest that financial institutions could pay on savings, and permitted interest payments on checking accounts. It also allowed savings and loan associations and savings banks to compete more directly with commercial banks. In addition, it gave the Federal Reserve System the power to set reserve requirements on *all* financial institutions, not just member banks in the Federal Reserve System. Savings and loans got into serious trouble. Congress passed the Thrift Bailout Act of 1989, which will cost taxpayers at least $500 billion.
1990s	Savings and loans continue to go out of business. Commercial banks also start getting into trouble.

▲ FIGURE 19–1 **Brief History of our Nation's Banking and Monetary Policies.** The figure above presents a look at our nation's banking and monetary policies over the last 200 years. Which aspect of banking and monetary policy do you think will lead to additional legislation in the coming years?

short supply. Consumers may not buy as many new cars and homes. Business executives may postpone or cancel plans for expansion. Workers who become unemployed because of the business slowdown will have less income to spend. As a result, businesses may cut back even more. A weakening of the economy and possibly a serious decline may follow.

If this is the case, why would any nation want a tight money policy? If money becomes too plentiful too quickly under a loose monetary policy, the result could be **inflation**, when all prices increase and the purchasing power of the dollar decreases. For example, during the Revolutionary War the supply of Continental currency grew so rapidly that the notes became almost worthless. An expression that came out of the era was, ''Not worth a Continental.''

The goal of monetary policy is to strike a balance between tight and loose money. It is the Federal Reserve's responsibility to ensure that money and credit are plentiful enough to allow the economy to expand. The Fed cannot, however, let the money supply become so plentiful that rapid inflation results. The time line in Figure 19–1 on page 460 gives a brief history of our nation's banking and monetary policies.

The Monetary Authority: The Federal Reserve System

Congress established our current central bank, the Federal Reserve, in 1913. It is led by a board of governors that consists of seven individuals, including the powerful chair. The Federal Reserve System is divided into geographic areas. The map below shows the twelve Federal Reserve districts and their main offices. The Fed is an

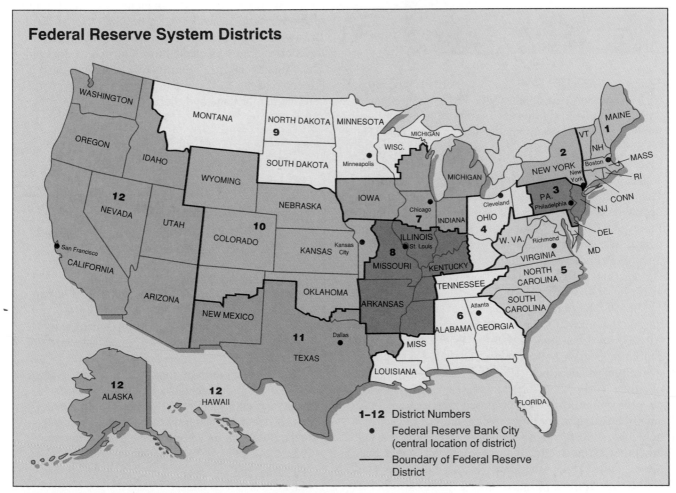

Federal Reserve System Districts

1–12 District Numbers
● Federal Reserve Bank City (central location of district)
— Boundary of Federal Reserve District

▲ FIGURE 19–2 **Federal Reserve System Districts.** This map shows the 12 Federal Reserve districts and their main offices. Under what principle is the Federal Reserve's monetary policy supposed to operate?

ARCHITECT OF
The American Dream

F ranklin Delano Roosevelt was born in Hyde Park, New York, on January 30, 1882. He graduated from Harvard and studied at Columbia University Law School, and went on to practice law in New York. He became state senator in 1911 and served as assistant secretary of the Navy from 1913 to 1920. He became James Cox's vice-presidential running mate on the Democratic ticket in 1920, but both Cox and he were defeated. In 1921 Roosevelt was stricken with polio. Paralyzed from the waist down, he fought to regain partial use of his legs and established the Warm Springs Foundation in Georgia for others so afflicted. He was elected governor of New York in 1928 and again in 1930.

In 1932 he defeated Herbert Hoover for president during the midst of the Great Depression. He campaigned on the argument that the federal government should help to provide direct relief to the needy and give direct aid to farmers. He called for a broad program of public works, such as building large dams and major government buildings. He proposed laws to protect the small-bank depositor, the stock purchaser, and the homeowner. Referring to the unemployed workers, the desperate farmers, and others, Roosevelt stated that these ''forgotten'' Americans ''at the bottom of the economic pyramid'' had to have a ''new deal.'' He

began his administration with a ringing call to the American people to face the future with courage and faith. ''The only thing we have to fear is fear itself,'' he confidently stated. His calm words helped to lift the American people from their despair and to rally them behind his new administration. The New Deal was interrupted by the United States' entry into World War II, but for five years a steady stream of New Deal measures poured out of Washington, each of which was an attempt to restore the nation's social, economic, and political health.

Roosevelt was largely responsible for U.S. aid to Great Britain after France surrendered to Hitler. He contributed notably to achieving unity among the Allies during World War II and conducted his own foreign relations rather than relying on the State Department. He was the first president to break the no-third-term tradition and he was elected to a fourth term in 1944. Three months after his fourth term had begun, and on the verge of the Allies' victory he was stricken with a cerebral hemorrhage and died.

HIS WORDS*

''This is pre-eminently the time to speak the truth, the whole truth, frankly and boldly. Nor need we shrink from honestly facing conditions in our country today. This great nation will endure as it has endured, will revive and will prosper.

So, first of all, let me assert my firm belief that the only thing we have to fear is fear itself—nameless, unreasoning, unjustified terror which paralyzes needed efforts to convert retreat into advance. . . .

Our greatest primary task is to put people to work. This is no unsolvable problem if we face it wisely and courageously. It can be accomplished in part by direct recruiting by the government itself, treating the task as we would treat the emergency

*Excerpted from the First Inaugural Address, March 4, 1933.

Franklin Delano Roosevelt

◀ This December 1943 conference in Teheran, Iran attended by Josef Stalin of the Soviet Union, President Roosevelt, and Winston Churchill of the United Kingdom, was one of five historic conferences among the Allied leaders. During the three-day conference pictured here, Roosevelt, Stalin, and Churchill devised definite plans for the defeat of Germany and Japan and the end of the Second World War.

of a war, but at the same time, through this employment, accomplishing greatly needed projects to stimulate and reorganize the use of our natural resources.

. . . Our Constitution is so simple and practical that it is possible always to meet extraordinary needs by changes in emphasis and arrangement without loss of essential form.

That is why our constitutional system has proved itself the most superbly enduring political mechanism the modern world has produced. It has met every stress of vast expansion of territory, of foreign wars, of bitter internal strife, of world relations.

It is to be hoped that the normal balance of executive and legislative authority may be wholly adequate to meet the unprecedented task before us. But it may be that an unprecedented demand and need for undelayed action may call for temporary departure from that normal balance of public procedure.

I am prepared under my constitutional duty to recommend the measures that a stricken nation in the midst of a stricken world may require.''

DEVELOPING CRITICAL THINKING SKILLS

1. When Roosevelt spoke these words, the nation was in the greatest economic depression it had ever seen. How do you think people who were unemployed at the time might have reacted to his statement, ''The only thing we have to fear is fear itself''?
2. What did Roosevelt mean when he called for a ''temporary departure from that normal balance of public procedure''?
3. To whom was Roosevelt going ''to recommend the measures'' required?

FOR FURTHER READING

Gies, Joseph, *Franklin D. Roosevelt*. Garden City, New York Doubleday, 1971

Alsop, Joseph, *FDR 1882–1945: A Centenary Remembrance*. New York, Viking, 1982

Burns, James MacGregor, *Roosevelt: The Soldier of Freedom*. New York, Harcourt Brace Jovanovich, 1972 independent commission, which means it is free from the direct political control of either Congress or the president. It has the vital responsibility for determining the nation's monetary and credit policies. All members of the Board of Governors are appointed by the president, with the appointments being approved by the Senate. Each member can serve up to fourteen years on the board.

The Fed's Record

In principle, the Federal Reserve's monetary policy is supposed to be countercyclical (acting in the opposite direction the economy is going). The economy goes through so-called **business cycles**, the extremes of which are **recessions** (and sometimes **depressions** which are very bad recessions) when unemployment is high and businesses are not working at full capacity, and boom times when unemployment is low and businesses are operating at peak capacity. Such booms often result in inflation.

In order for its policy to be countercyclical, the Federal Reserve must take actions that act counter to the trend of national business activity. Researchers who have watched the Fed since 1914 have concluded that often its policy has not been countercyclical because of the time it has taken the Fed to act. By the time the Fed started pumping money into the economy, for example, it was time to withdraw it; by the time it started reducing the rate of growth of the money supply, it was time to start increasing it.

Fiscal Policy and Employment

While monetary policy is carried out by the independent Federal Reserve System, fiscal policy is determined by Congress and the president. Traditionally, fiscal policy has involved lowering taxes during times of recession and raising them during times of inflation. Alternatively, fiscal policy can include increasing government spending during times of recession (which is generally done by borrowing money to increase the total demand in the economy) and decreasing government spending during times of inflation. But fiscal policy can also include targeting specific aspects of society that are malfunctioning. For example, public works programs such as the Civilian Conservation Corps (CCC) and the Works Progress Administration (WPA) during the Great Depression in the 1930s, and the Comprehensive Employment and Training Act (CETA) in the 1970s, were designed to use federal tax dollars directly to employ unemployed individuals.

The government formally took on the responsibility of reducing unemployment when it passed the Employment Act of 1946, which reads as follows:

> The Congress hereby declares that it is the continuing policy and responsibility of the federal government to use all practicable means consistent with its needs and obligations and other essential considerations of national policy, with assistance and cooperation of industry, agriculture, labor and state and local governments to coordinate and utilize all its plans, functions, and resources for the purpose of creating and maintaining, in a manner calculated to foster and promote free competitive enterprise and the general welfare, conditions under which there will be afforded useful employment opportunities, including self-employment, for those able, willing, and seeking to work and to promote maximum employment, production, and purchasing power.

The effect of this legislation was to require the federal government to monitor the unemployment rate and the overall state of the national economy and adjust fiscal policy as needed.

Fiscal Policy and the Federal Budgeting Process

The preceding discussion of fiscal policy might give the impression that there is some overriding policy that a single agency puts into effect for the benefit of the nation as a whole.

It is important to realize that no single governmental body designs and implements fiscal policy. The president, with the aid of the director of the Office of Management and Budget (OMB), the secretary of the treasury, and the Council of Economic Advisors, only recommends the desired mix of taxes and government expenditures. It is Congress, with the aid of its many committees (the House Ways and Means Committee, the Senate Finance Committee, and the Senate Budget Committee, to name a few), that enacts fiscal policy. The president, however, does have veto power over congressional fiscal policy. Disagreement as to proper fiscal policy might—and usually does—emerge among members of Congress or between Congress and the president. Although the procedure required for an ultimate solution is clearly spelled out in the U.S. Constitution, in practice resolving these conflicts is often a tedious and time-consuming process, during which numerous hearings may be called, and many experts may give testimonies.

In sum, our government's regulation of monetary and fiscal policies can be compared to driving a car with only an accelerator and a brake, but no steering wheel. All

CASE STUDY

Making Sense of Dollars and Cents

Every year the United States Mint produces approximately twelve *billion* new pennies, and Americans promptly lose, store, mutilate, or otherwise dispose of half of them—that's six billion pennies rattling around people's dressers, jackets, car floors, and penny jars. These days there is serious debate in Washington, D.C., over the fate of this coin.

The penny has its supporters and opponents. James Benfield, the founder and only paid employee of the Coin Coalition, an organization intent on getting rid of the penny, claims that "the penny's a nuisance." Michael Brown, in contrast, opposes abolition of the smallest U.S. currency unit, arguing that rounding off prices ($4.00 instead of $3.98) would cost U.S. consumers over half a billion dollars each year. Brown is a spokesman for Americans for Common Cents, an organization backed by the zinc industry (the penny is 97 percent zinc), the manufacturers of the blanks (which are stamped out as pennies), and U.S. coin collectors.

The controversy about pennies was stimulated by the Senate Banking Committee's "coinage reform," an effort to pinpoint needed changes in U.S. currency. This reform also brought about the movement to create a one-dollar coin and to do away with the one-dollar bill. This idea is supported by the U.S. vending machine industry (including video machine manufacturers), the American Council for the Blind, the copper industry, the convenience store industry, and mass-transit business. It is opposed by the ink and paper producers that supply these ingredients for the printing of paper currency.

Opponents of the paper dollar bill claim that handling such bills manually, including straightening and unfolding them, arranging them right side up, and counting them, is a very expensive and time-consuming process. Also, the U.S. Treasury spends over $300

million each year shredding and replacing worn-out dollar bills. The paper dollar bill is difficult for visually impaired people to identify. Dollar coins in vending machines and mass-transit turnstiles, in contrast, would be convenient and reduce both the handling of smaller coins and the need to make change. The copper industry supports a proposed copper dollar for obvious reasons.

In 1979, a one-dollar coin, called the Susan B. Anthony dollar, was introduced but failed to gain public acceptance. In response to this failure, the new strategy would involve introducing a new coin dollar and phasing out entirely the paper dollar, which would force Americans to use the coin. This was successfully done in Canada in 1987 with the Loon dollar coin. A 1991 Gallup poll, however, showed that while 62 percent of the American population opposes abolishing the penny, 85 percent opposes abolishing the dollar bill in favor of a dollar coin.

THINK ABOUT IT

1. Who do you think would lose if the penny were eliminated? Who would gain?
2. Who would lose and who would gain if the one-dollar bill were replaced with the one-dollar coin?

GOVERNMENT IN ACTION

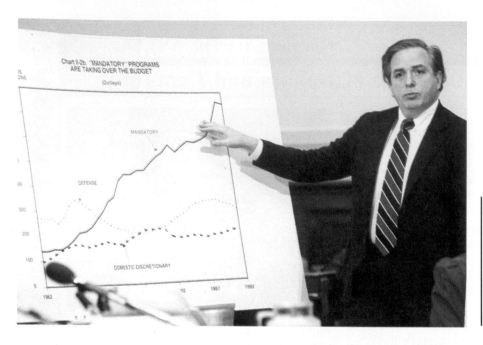

Chart II-2b. "MANDATORY" PROGRAMS ARE TAKING OVER THE BUDGET
(Outlays)

MANDATORY
DEFENSE
DOMESTIC DISCRETIONARY

1962   '82   1987   1992

Richard Darman, the Director of the Office of Management and Budget, is shown here as he discusses the president's 1992 budget proposal with the House Appropriations Committee. Which governmental body is responsible for designing and implementing fiscal policy?

the government can do is speed the economy up or slow it down. It seldom is successful at keeping it steady.

Government Spending and the Public Debt

Whenever the federal government spends more than it receives in tax revenues, it runs a **budget deficit**. The federal government has run a deficit in every year except two since 1960. As you learned in Chapter 13, the Constitution gives Congress the power to borrow money. Every time a budget deficit occurs, the federal government borrows money by issuing **U.S. Treasury bonds**. The sale of these bonds to corporations, private individuals, pension plans, foreign governments, foreign businesses, and foreign individuals adds to the **public debt** (also called the **national debt**), defined as the total amount the federal government owes to these parties. Each year there is a federal government budget deficit. The amount of that deficit is *added* to the public debt. Figure 19–3 on page 467 shows what has happened to the public debt over time. Politicians and the public alike are concerned about this problem.

Is the Public Debt a Burden to the Public?

We often hear about the burden of the public debt. Some argue that the government is eventually going to go bankrupt, but as long as the government can collect taxes to pay for interest on its public debt, that will never happen. What does happen is that when Treasury Bonds come due, they are simply "rolled over," or refinanced. That is, if a $1 million Treasury Bond comes due (gets cashed in) today, the U.S. Treasury pays it off with the money it gets from selling another $1 million bond.

As for the interest payments on these bonds, they are paid by federal taxes. Not all of the interest payments are paid to Americans. Corporations, governments, and private citizens in other countries can and do legally purchase U.S. Treasury Bonds in the open market. About 16 percent, or one in six dollars, of our national debt is owed to foreigners. Some fear that if foreigners own too large of a percentage of our national debt, they may have too much influence over our federal government.

PROGRAMS

$

© 1989 by John Trever, Albuquerque Journal.

Public Debt of the Federal Government, 1940–1993 (est.)

Year	Net Public Debt*
1940	42.7
1945	235.2
1950	219.0
1955	226.6
1960	237.2
1965	261.6
1970	284.9
1975	396.9
1980	709.3
1983	1,141.8
1986	1,736.2
1989	2,190.3
1990	2,410.3
1991	2,717.6
1992 (est.)	2,995.4
1993 (est.)	3,301.2

* In billions of current dollars.

▶ **FIGURE 19–3 Public Debt of the Federal Government 1940–1993.** By looking at this table, you can see the alarming increase in public debt. From what source does the money used to pay the interest payments on this debt come?

There is another factor to consider in this dilemma. Even though most interest payments are being paid to American citizens, the more the federal government borrows to meet these payments, the greater the percentage of its budget is committed to making these payments. This reduces the government's ability to supply money for needed community services, such as transportation, education, and housing programs. Indeed, a simple projection of the government's current spending trends would show that some time in the twenty-first century, the federal government will be spending almost 100 percent of its budget on interest payments! While this is unlikely to occur, it highlights the problem of running larger and larger deficits and borrowing more and more money to cover them.

The Difficulty of Reducing the Deficit—The Gramm-Rudman Act

In 1985 Congress passed the Gramm-Rudman-Hollings Deficit Reduction Act in an effort to require that Congress reduce the size of its budget deficits.

Gramm and Rudman are the members of Congress who originally sponsored the bill (the act is often simply referred to as ''Gramm-Rudman''). According to the act,

▶ Senator Phil Gramm

BUILDING SOCIAL STUDIES SKILLS

Reading Line Graphs

Line graphs are used to show changes in trends over a period of time. The federal deficit, a president's popularity, or a student's grades over a period of years could all easily be shown on a line graph.

To read a line graph, begin by reading the title, then read the axes. The horizontal axis usually shows time on a scale of days, months, or years. The vertical axis usually gives a scale for measuring quantities.

The graph below shows the percentage of U.S. debt that has been owned by foreigners over a thirty-five-year timespan. Study the graph and answer the questions that follow.

PRACTICING YOUR SKILLS

1. What was the lowest percentage of U.S. public debt held by foreigners?
2. What was the highest percentage of U.S. public debt held by foreigners?
3. In approximately which year was the percentage of U.S. public debt held by foreigners the highest?

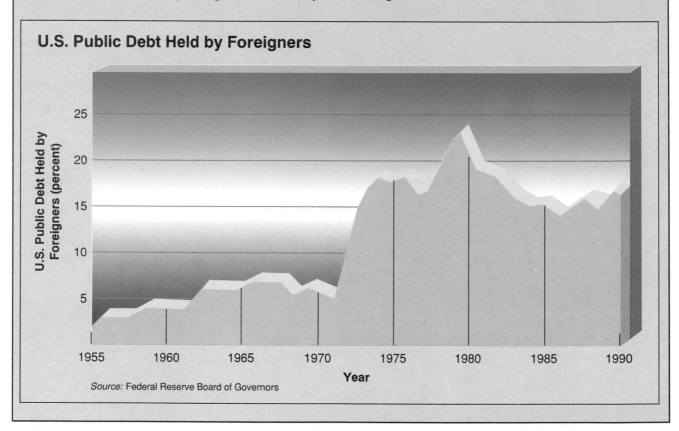

U.S. Public Debt Held by Foreigners

Source: Federal Reserve Board of Governors

the deficit was required to drop from $171.9 billion in 1986 to zero in 1991. After the first two years of failure to comply with the target deficit reductions, Congress passed a revised act requiring that the 1988 deficit be $144 billion and that it drop to zero by 1993. The first three years of the Revised Deficit Reduction Act saw Congress again fail to meet deficit reductions. In 1990, another revised of set Gramm-Rudman targets was pro-posed, allowing for a 1991 deficit of over $200 billion, excluding the cost of the savings and loan bailout. In fact, the true deficit in 1991 turned out to be closer to $300 billion and an estimated $350 billion in 1992.

Some observers believe that Congress's inability to comply with its own law indicates that our governing body can no longer be fiscally responsible. In reality, the prospect of ever balancing the budget is dim.

The federal budget deficit is probably much higher than is actually reported. Each year, in an effort to make the deficit look smaller, Congress takes more and more government expenditures out of the official budget and puts them in a category called **off-budget items**. For example, the government removed all of the operating losses of the U.S. Postal Service from the official budget. Also, numerous government-sponsored enterprises are slowly but surely building up large amounts of debt that have not shown up in the official figures. The estimate for 1993 is over $1 trillion of such debt.

Many observers of the federal government's fiscal management strategies contend that the only way to end budget deficits is to pass a constitutional amendment requiring a balanced budget. Few observers, however, believe that such an amendment will soon be passed.

SECTION 1 REVIEW

1. What is monetary policy? Who is responsible for the nation's monetary policy?
2. How does the Federal Reserve System regulate monetary policy?
3. How is fiscal policy carried out?
4. Briefly describe deficit spending.
5. **For critical analysis:** Why is it so difficult for our government to reduce the deficit?

SECTION 2

Systems of Taxation

Preview Questions
- What is the benefits-received principle of taxation?
- What is the ability-to-pay principle of taxation?
- What is the difference between progressive, regressive, and proportional tax systems?
- What are the major types of taxes?
- How do taxes direct economic activity?

Governments—federal, state, and local—have various methods of taxation at their disposal. The best known of these is the federal personal income tax system. At the state and local levels, property taxes make up the bulk of the taxes collected. In addition to these taxes, there are corporate income taxes, sales taxes, excise taxes, inheritance taxes, and gift taxes. About 85 percent of all federal, state, and local government revenues come from taxation. Figure 19–6 on page 471 lists the major

▲ Whenever we buy gasoline, we not only must pay for the gasoline, but also federal taxes on the gasoline. These taxes are used to pay for highway construction and repair. Which principle of taxation does this type of tax exemplify?

taxes that the various levels of government use to raise revenue.

Principles of Taxation

Taxes can be justified according to one of three major principles.

Benefits-Received Principle Under the **benefits-received principle**, those who use a particular government service support it with taxes in proportion to the benefits they receive. Those who do not use the service do not pay taxes for it. For example, a gasoline tax to pay for highway construction and repair is based on this principle. Those who use the highways usually buy more gasoline, and therefore pay more in gasoline taxes.

A tax based on the benefits-received principle is useful in raising money to pay for a service used only by certain individuals. Many government services, however, such as national defense, benefit everyone equally. Also, there are circumstances in which those who most need certain services, such as the elderly and the poor, are the ones least able to pay taxes for them.

Ability-to-pay Principle Under the **ability-to-pay principle**, those with higher incomes pay more in taxes

469

Proportional Tax System

Income	Proportional Rate	Tax
First $100	10%	$10
Second $100	10%	$10
Third $100	10%	$10
Total Income: $300		Total Tax: $30

◀ **FIGURE 19–4 Proportional Tax System.** This table illustrates the principle of proportional taxation. With the same proportional tax, how much tax would be paid on the total income of $650.00?

than those with lower incomes, regardless of the number of government services they use.

The Sacrifice Principle The third principle of taxation, the **sacrifice principle**, holds that the sacrifices people make to pay their taxes should be equitable. Generally, it is assumed that the sacrifices people make when paying taxes to the government become smaller as their incomes become larger. When a $100 tax is paid, a millionaire is surely sacrificing less than a person who earns $10,000 a year. The problem with this principle is determining how to make everyone's sacrifice equitable.

Forms of Taxation

There are three ways in which taxes can be classified, depending on their effects on those who are taxed.

Proportional Taxation **Proportional taxation** is a system by which taxpayers pay a fixed percentage on every dollar of income. When their incomes increase or decrease, the taxes they pay increase or decrease accordingly. If the proportional tax rate is 10 percent, you pay ten cents in taxes out of every dollar you earn. If

you earn $1,000, you pay $100 in taxes; if you earn $1 million, you pay $100,000 in taxes. Figure 19–4 above illustrates the principle of proportional taxation.

Progressive Taxation In contrast to proportional taxation, **progressive taxation** means that the actual *percentage* of taxes, or tax rate, rises as income rises. The progressive system can be described as one in which the marginal tax rate increases. The term **marginal tax rate** refers to the rate paid on *additional* amounts of income. Figure 19–5 below illustrates the principle of progressive taxation.

Regressive Taxation As you can imagine, **regressive taxation** is the opposite of progressive taxation. In a regressive tax system, the rate of taxation decreases as income rises. The marginal rate falls and is usually below the average rate. For example, imagine that all government revenues were obtained from a 50 percent tax on food. Because the percentage of income spent on food falls as the total income rises, we also know that the percentage of total income that would be paid in taxes under such a system would likewise fall as income rises. This would be a regressive taxation plan.

Progressive Tax System

Income	Marginal Rate	Tax
First $100	10%	$10
Second $100	20%	$20
Third $100	30%	$30
Total Income: $300		Total Tax: $60

◀ **FIGURE 19–5 Progressive Tax System.** This table illustrates the principle of progressive taxation. Which individuals in our society are most likely to feel that a progressive tax system is unfair?

Major Taxes

Tax	Description	Type (Progressive, Regressive, or Proportional)
Personal Income	Tax paid as a percentage of income. This is the major source of revenue for the federal government. Many states and some local governments also levy personal income taxes.	Progressive at the federal level, but sometimes proportional at the state level.
Social Insurance (Social Security)	Taxes covered by the Federal Insurance Contributions Act (FICA). This is the second largest source of federal government revenue.	Proportional up to $55,500 in 1992; regressive above that.
Corporate Income	Tax paid to the federal government as a percentage of corporate profits. Some states also levy corporate income taxes.	At the federal level, progressive up to $100,000; proportional above that.
Excise	Tax paid by the consumer on the manufacture, use, or consumption of certain goods. The major federal excise taxes are on alcohol, tobacco, and gasoline. Some states also levy excise taxes.	Generally regressive.
Estate	Federal tax on the property of someone who has died. Some states also levy an estate tax.	Progressive; percentage of tax increases with the value of the estate.
Inheritance	Tax paid by those who inherit property from someone who has died. This is a state tax only.	Varies by state.
Gift	Tax paid by the person who gives a gift. This is a federal tax only.	Progressive; percentage increases with the value of the gift.
Sales	Tax paid on purchases. Almost all states, as well as many local governments, levy a sales tax. The rate varies from state to state and within states. Items that are taxed also vary from state to state. Some states tax clothing, but many states do not.	Generally regressive.
Property	State and local taxation of the value of property. Both real property, such as buildings and land, and personal property, such as stocks, bonds, and home furnishings, may be taxed.	Proportional; percentage is set by state and local governments.
Custom duties	Tax on imports that is paid by the importer.	Proportional.

▲ FIGURE 19–6 **Major Taxes.** The table above lists and describes the major taxes in this country. Which of the above taxes are progressive in nature?

Some examples of regressive taxes are sales taxes on food and clothing, the Social Security tax, and the excise tax on gasoline.

How Our Progressive Federal Income Tax System Evolved

The Constitution in Article I, Section 8 gives Congress the authority "to lay and collect taxes, duties, imposts and excises," but no reference was made to an income tax at the time the Constitution was drafted. In 1894, however, the Wilson-Gorman Tariff Act provided for individual income taxes of 2 percent on incomes above $4,000. The country knew about income taxes from the period during the Civil War, when $4.4 million of such taxes were collected. Nonetheless, the concept of income taxation set forth by the Wilson-Gorman Tariff Act was aggressively challenged and had to be settled by a Supreme Court decision in 1895. Finally, in 1913, the Sixteenth Amendment was passed, which reads as follows:

> The Congress shall have power to lay and collect taxes on incomes, from whatever source derived, without apportionment among the several states, and without regard to any census or enumeration.

Congress responded by passing Section 2 of the Underwood-Simmons Tariff Act of 1913, which provided for a 1 percent rate on taxable income with an exemption of $3,000 plus $1,000 more to a married head of household. This concept of exempting the first several thousand dollars of income from taxes has continued to the present time, in the form of personal exemptions and standard deductions.

The Underwood-Simmons Tariff Act also provided for a surtax (an additional tax) that was levied progressively on incomes over $20,000, with a maximum total tax rate of 7 percent on incomes over $500,000. These taxes may seem paltry in comparison to today's rates, but they were considered quite large in those times. The concept of progressiveness introduced in 1913 met with considerable debate, which continued for several years thereafter.

Undoubtedly, progressiveness is here to stay, at least in principle, but the progressive nature of our personal income tax system is much less obvious than it once was. Until 1961, the maximum tax rate was a whopping 91 percent; from 1961 through 1986, it was 50 percent. Subsequent to the Tax Act of 1990, it is now 31 percent.

Federal income taxes are the largest and the most important source of federal tax revenues. See Figure 19–7.

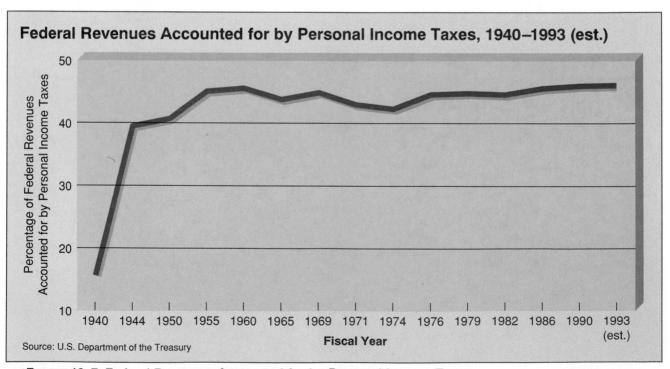

Federal Revenues Accounted for by Personal Income Taxes, 1940–1993 (est.)

Source: U.S. Department of the Treasury

▲ FIGURE 19–7 **Federal Revenues Accounted for by Personal Income Taxes, 1940–1993 (est.).** This graph shows the percentage of federal revenues that are accounted for by personal income taxes. During which period of time did this percentage show its most dramatic increase?

**Federal Revenues Accounted for by Personal In-
come Taxes** In 1940, individual income taxes accounted for 15.5 percent of federal revenues. Now, however, individual income taxes account for 46 percent of
federal revenues.

Comparing the Tax Burden
Across Countries

It may seem that the U.S. taxpayer is overburdened
with taxes. After all, the average American worker works
for the government well into the month of May before
having earned enough to pay all federal, state, and local
taxes for that year. But compared to workers in Denmark,
Sweden, the Netherlands, the United Kingdom, Finland,
Germany, and other countries, the American worker pays
less in income taxes and social insurance payments.
However, it should be noted that many of these countries
provide a greater array of expensive social services, such
as health care, child care, and higher education to all citizens. Figure 19–8 shows the tax burden of workers
throughout the industrialized world.

Taxation as a Way of
Directing Economic Activity

Taxation is more than a way for government to raise
money; it is also a way in which the government can

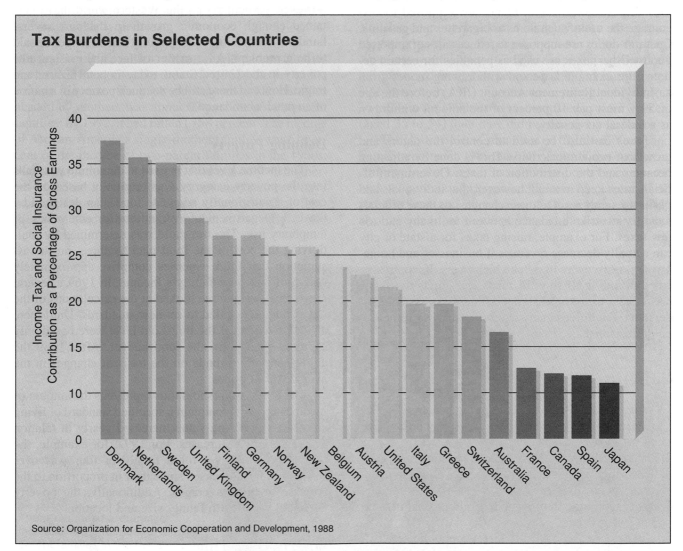

Tax Burdens in Selected Countries

Source: Organization for Economic Cooperation and Development, 1988

▲ | **FIGURE 19–8 Tax Burdens in Selected Countries.** This graph shows the
income tax and social insurance contributions of workers in selected countries
throughout the world. Why do you think the tax burdens are so much higher in
Denmark, the Netherlands, and Sweden?

PROFILE

Antonia Coello Novello

Antonia Coello Novello, as Surgeon General of the United States, holds one of the most important medical posts in the nation. For example, it is through her office that the nation is made aware of the dangers of smoking, of drinking excessive alcohol, and of AIDS. In 1990 when she was sworn in, she became the nation's first Hispanic and also first female surgeon general.

Dr. Novello was born in Puerto Rico, went to school there, and received her medical degree in pediatrics from the University of Puerto Rico's School of Medicine in 1970. While she was working toward her medical degree, she was chosen Intern of the Year. She went on to do advanced degree work in public health at Maryland's Johns Hopkins University in 1982. She became medical advisor to Senator Orrin Hatch of Utah when he served on the U.S. Senate Committee on Labor and Human Resources. She later became the Deputy Director of the National Institute of Child Health and Human Development. While working there she specialized in the ef-

fects of AIDS on newborns and young children.

She is particularly concerned about the dangers of cigarette smoking. During the first meeting of a federal committee discussing smoking, Dr. Novello urged the states to enforce laws barring cigarette sales to minors. She believes that unless something is done, about five million of the children living today will die of smoking-related diseases.

Additionally, Novello is concerned about AIDS: "AIDS is the only epidemic in the world where children will survive their parents," she said. "By the year 2000, we might have as many as ten million children who are orphans of this epidemic. We have got to do the best we can for all children." (For more about AIDS, see the Extended Case Study in the Resource Center.)

Alcohol abuse also remains high on her priorities of problems that need to be solved, particularly among the nation's youth. In interview after interview she points out that alcohol "is the only drug whose use has not been declining significantly." Alcohol-impaired driving remains one the of leading causes of death among our youth. "Kids still think that drinking is cool, and that is what frightens me so much," she said in an interview in the *Saturday Evening Post* in 1991.

In that same interview she talked about the future: "I want to be able to look back some day and say, 'I did make a difference,' whether it was to open the minds of people to think that a woman can do a good job, or whether it is the fact that so many kids out there think they could be me. Then all the headaches . . . will have been worth it."

THINK ABOUT IT

1. How much importance should be given to the declaration of the surgeon general of the United States that smoking is injurious to one's health?

SECTION 4

Cleaning Up the Environment

Preview Questions

- What are some of the more recent major federal environmental laws? What did they set out to accomplish?
- What were the major provisions of the National Environmental Policy Act of 1969?
- What are global warming and the greenhouse effect? What has been the federal government's response to these problems?

When the Exxon supertanker *Valdez* struck Bligh Reef in the pristine, frigid waters of Prince William Sound in Alaska in 1989, it spilled a quarter of a million barrels (more than 10 million gallons) of crude oil into the water, causing the worst oil spill in North American history. Within a week the oil slick covered almost 1,000 square miles, killing and maiming marine animals, fish, and migratory birds. Within four weeks the slick had grown to 1,600 square miles and threatened wildlife living hundreds of miles to the southwest of the accident site. By the end of the summer of 1989, Exxon Corporation had already spent more than $1 billion on cleanup efforts but probably recovered less than one-fourth of the crude oil that had escaped from the hold of the *Valdez*. (See the Resource Center for original source materials on this case.) Two years later, in the winter of 1991, the world saw an oil spill ten to twenty times worse than the one that occurred in Alaska. This spill, however, was not an accident. It was created during the Persian Gulf War when Iraq opened the spigot on a Kuwaiti supertanker loading platform.

Oil spill disasters in the United States and elsewhere serve as constant reminders that human actions often create unwanted side effects—the destruction of our environment and of our ecology. Human beings emit pollutants into the air and the water every day. Each year the atmosphere of our planet receives 20 million metric tons of sulfur dioxide, 18 million metric tons of ozone pollutants, and 60 million metric tons (one metric ton is about 2,200 pounds) of carbon monoxide.

How the Government Has Addressed the Pollution Problem

Our country's government has been responding to pollution problems since before the American Revolu-

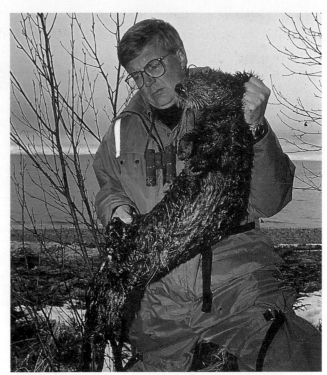

▲ This otter was one of the tragic casualties of the disaster that occurred in Alaska in 1989 when the Exxon *Valdez* spilled a quarter of a million barrels of crude oil into the water. What steps do you think our government should take to see that such disasters are averted in the future?

tion, when the Massachusetts Bay Colony issued regulations to try to stop the pollution of Boston Harbor. In the nineteenth century, states passed laws controlling water pollution after scientists and medical researchers convinced most policymakers that dumping sewage into drinking and bathing water caused disease. At the national level, the first Water Pollution Control Act in 1948 mandated research and assistance to the states, but little was done. In 1952, the first state air-pollution law was passed in Oregon. Again at the national level, the Air Pollution Control Act of 1955 gave some assistance to states and cities. Figure 19–9 on pages 480 and 481 lists the major landmarks of environmental legislation in the United States.

The National Environmental Policy Act The year 1969 marks perhaps the true start of federal government involvement in pollution controls. In that year, the conflict between oil interests and environmentalists literally erupted when a Union Oil Company's oil well exploded six miles off the coast of Santa Barbara, California,

Major Federal Environmental Legislation

Legislation	Description
1899 Refuse Act	Made it unlawful to dump refuse into navigable waters without a permit. A 1966 court decision made all industrial wastes subject to this act.
1955 Federal Water Pollution Control Act	Set standards for treatment of municipal water waste before discharge. Revisions to this act were passed in 1965 and 1967.
1963 Clean Air Act	Coordinated research and assisted state and local governments in establishing control programs.
1965 Clean Air Act Amendments	Authorized establishment of federal standards for automobile exhaust emissions, beginning with 1968 models.
1965 Solid Waste Disposal Act	Provided assistance to state and local governments for control programs and authorized research in this area.
1965 Water Quality Act	Authorized the setting of standards for discharges into waters.
1967 Air Quality Act	Established air quality regions, with acceptable regional pollution levels. Required local and state governments to implement approved control programs or be subject to federal controls.
1969 National Environmental Policy Act	Established Council for Environmental Quality for the purpose of coordinating all federal pollution control programs. Authorized the establishment of the Environmental Protection Agency to implement CEQ policies on a case-by-case basis.
1970 Clean Air Act Amendments	Authorized the Environmental Protection Agency to set national air pollution standards. Restricted the discharge of six major pollutants into the lower atmosphere. Required automobile manufacturers to reduce nitrogen oxide, hydrocarbon, and carbon monoxide emissions by 90 percent (in addition to the 1965 requirements) during the 1970s. Set aircraft emission standards. Required states to meet deadline for complying with EPA standards. Authorized legal action by private citizens to require EPA to enforce approved standards against undiscovered offenders.

▲ FIGURE 19–9 **Major Federal Environmental Legislation.** The figure above lists and describes important pieces of federal environmental legislation. When was the first of these acts passed? With what was it concerned?

releasing 235,000 gallons of crude oil. The result was an oil slick that covered an area of eight hundred square miles, washing up on the city's beaches and killing plant life, birds, and numerous fish. Hearings in Congress revealed that the Interior Department did not know which way to go in the energy-environmental trade-off—allow more oil exploration with possible damage to the ecology or save the environment at all costs.

Congress did know, however, and passed the National Environmental Policy Act in 1969. This landmark legislation established, among other things, the Council on Environmental Quality (CEQ), and mandated that an

Major Federal Environmental Legislation (continued)

Legislation	Description
1972 Federal Water Pollution Control Act Amendments	Set national water quality goal of restoring polluted waters to swimmable, fishable waters by 1983.
1972 Pesticide Control Act	Required that all pesticides used in interstate commerce be approved and certified as effective for their stated purposes. Required certification that they were harmless to humans, animal life, animal feed, and crops.
1974 Clean Water Act	Originally called the Safe Water Drinking Act, this law set (for the first time) federal standards for water suppliers serving more than twenty-five people, having more than fifteen service connections, or operating more than sixty days per year.
1976 Resource Conservation and Recovery Act	Encouraged conservation and recovery of resources. Put hazardous waste under government control. Disallowed the opening of new dumping sites. Required that all existing open dumps be closed or upgraded to sanitary landfills by 1983. Set standards for providing technical, financial, and marketing assistance to encourage solid waste management.
1977 Clean Air Act Amendments	Pushed deadline for automobile emission requirements ahead to 1981.
1980 Comprehensive Environmental Response, Compensation and Liability Act	Established a "superfund" to clean up toxic waste dumps.
1990 Clean Air Act	The most comprehensive legislation to date. This act mandated the following: the oldest coal-burning power plants must cut emissions by 40 percent to reduce acid rain; industrial emissions of 189 toxic chemicals must be reduced by 90 percent by the year 2000; production of CFCs must stop by the year 2002; controls on other factories and businesses intended to reduce smog in 96 cities to healthful levels by 2005. Utilities were granted "credits" to emit certain amounts of sulfur dioxide, and those that emit less than the maximum allowed can sell their credits to other polluters.

environmental impact statement be prepared for every recommendation, report on legislation, or major federal action that would significantly affect the quality of the environment. The act therefore gave citizens and public interest groups concerned with the environment a weapon against unnecessary and inappropriate use of our resources by government.

Clean Air Act of 1990 In 1990 a new amendment to the 1983 Clean Air Act was passed, which consisted of over one thousand pages of regulations on American industry.

One innovative aspect of this act was that Congress mandated formulas for new gasoline that will be used in cars in the smoggiest cities. Also, the act required

CITIZENSHIP SKILLS AND RESPONSIBILITIES

How to Be a Waste-Conscious Consumer

We live in what many people have called a "throwaway society." Much of what we buy is disposable—razors, plastic dishes and cups, diapers, newspapers, and even such items as cameras. Every year we throw away 25 billion styrofoam cups, over 2 billion razors, and 200 million automobile tires. Americans throw out ten times their weight in trash every year, or about a half ton (one thousand pounds) for every person. No other country in the world can match the United States' output of garbage on a per capita (per person) basis. The total amount of trash generated in the United States each day—400,000 tons—is overwhelming.

Each of us can take steps to be less wasteful. Being a waste-conscious consumer only requires awareness and a little extra effort at times. Here are some simple places to begin:

- **Recycle purchased goods packaged in recyclable materials.** Glass, aluminum, paper, and some plastics can be recycled; other kinds of plastics and styrofoam cannot. Look at the containers to see if they have been recycled and/or are recyclable.
- **Buy bulk.** Encourage your family to buy products in bulk or in family-size amounts. This reduces packaging wastes and also saves money.
- **Buy recycled paper products.** Napkins, bathroom tissue, paper towels, greeting cards, and stationery are all available now on recycled paper. If your grocers or stationers don't supply these products, ask them to start.
- **Purchase fresh fruits and vegetables.** Fresh produce is often more nutritious than packaged; it also requires less packaging.
- **Buy durable, long-lasting products.** These products won't wear out quickly, which means you'll be throwing away less often. (You get better quality and a better bargain, too—check ratings in *Consumer Reports* magazine before making a major purchase.)
- **Take care of what you own.** The better care you take, the longer your goods will last, and the less waste you will create.
- **Borrow or rent before you buy.** Don't buy something you will use only once or twice, such as special party supplies, unusual tools, or a sporting goods item that may only be a temporary interest. Borrow or rent the equipment or products to find out if you really need to own them.
- **Donate what you no longer need.** Goodwill, the Salvation Army, or a local church can find people who would be happy to make use of clothes or furniture that you no longer want or need.
- **Avoid impulse buying.** Plan your purchases so that you don't end up with things you don't really want or need. (This will also help you not to waste your income.)

TAKING ACTION

1. Make a list of ten ways that you could change your everyday activities to reduce the amount of waste you create.
2. Take a tour through a pharmacy or a supermarket and make a list of all the products that are packaged in nonrecyclable materials. Then think of ways in which those items could be packaged in a more waste-efficient manner. Summarize your findings.

that if by the year 2003 certain cities still experience dangerous levels of pollution that continue to destroy the ozone layer of our atmosphere, automobile emissions standards for cars driven in those cities will be drastically increased. Severe restrictions on potential cancer-causing air toxins were imposed, and severe restrictions on the total emissions of sulfur dioxide from electric utilities was mandated.

Global Warming

One of the most pressing concerns in the world today is the threat of **global warming**—the gradual increase in average temperature throughout the world. Not too many years ago, ironically, most environmental observers and concerned scientists were worried about a new ice age. In the June 24, 1974, issue of *Time* magazine, for example, the editor said that "the atmosphere has been growing gradually cooler for the past three decades. The trend shows no indication of reversing." Dr. Reid Bryson, a specialist in climatology, stated in 1980 that "the overall cooling trend is unmistakable, and in coming years it will profoundly affect agriculture, geopolitics, and human survival worldwide." As late as May 12, 1983, the editors of *Rolling Stone* magazine stated the following:

For years now, climatologists have foreseen a trend toward colder weather—long range, to be sure, but a trend as in-

evitable as death. . . . According to one theory, all it would take is a single cold summer to plunge the earth into a sudden apocalypse of ice.

By the 1990s, however, scientists had determined that the earth was getting too warm. According to the National Academy of Sciences, "global environmental change [global warming] may well be the most pressing international issue of the next century . . . the future welfare of human society is . . . at risk."

Some observers believe there is a silver lining in the cloud of global warming. James R. Udall, a frequent contributor to *Audubon, National Wildlife,* and *Sierra* magazines, wrote:

A century from now historians may conclude that the threat of global warming was the best thing that ever happened to the environment. Humanity has an enormous investment in a stable climate, and global warming gives us a compelling, selfish, economic incentive to change patterns of energy use that have proved so harmful to the environment.

The Greenhouse Effect and Global Warming

The **greenhouse effect** is the trapping of heat inside the earth's atmosphere, which is the result of pollution caused largely by the burning of fossil fuels and the emission of carbon dioxide (CO_2).

Scientists still deeply disagree over the extent and nature of global warming and the greenhouse effect. It may take another ten years before objective and completely convincing evidence is available that the earth is indeed warming.

Nevertheless, some of the most complex computer models of the world's climate, such as one at the National Center for Atmospheric Research, suggest that if the current rate of the greenhouse effect continues, by the year 2050 the earth's temperature will rise by three to nine degrees Fahrenheit. This would be an enormous change in temperature and would cause ecological changes that would result in dramatic social, economic, and political upheavals: The ice caps on mountain peaks would melt; coastal water levels would rise, which would flood many cities; forests would die; and farmland and crops would be severely stressed.

Most experts now agree that the greenhouse effect and the resulting global warming may well pose one of the most serious challenges to U.S. and world leaders in the coming decades. Scientists and policymakers agree that the problem must be addressed on a global scale. The discovery of severe environmental problems in Eastern Europe, plus China and India's continued reliance on coal as a major energy source, make the issue urgent. And because the United States, with only 5 percent of the world's population, produces 23 percent of the world's carbon dioxide, the responsibility for Americans is quite clear.

Perhaps most daunting is the fact that only drastic reductions in the use of fossil fuels and the increasing use of alternative energy sources will slow down, stop, and perhaps reverse the damage already done. Those energy sources (such as nuclear energy) are not currently cost-effective or safe, and new clean-energy sources and technologies have yet to be devised, much less put on line for use.

Depletion of the Ozone Layer

The ozone layer shields the earth from excessive ultraviolet radiation from the sun. In high doses, this radiation causes skin cancer, cataracts, and suppression of the human immune system as well as harming crops and wildlife.

In 1990 scientists discovered that the ozone layer is being destroyed much faster than was previously thought—there has been a 10 percent reduction since 1987 over Europe and North America. Over the polar regions, especially in Antarctica, 50 percent of the ozone layer has been lost, which has caused the so-called "holes" in the ozone shield. Industrial chemicals that contain chlorine—chloroflurocarbons (CFCs), halons, carbon tetrachloride, and methyl chloroform—are among the principal culprits in destroying the ozone molecules.

In 1987 fifty-six nations signed a treaty in Montreal, Canada, that requires them to cut the production and use of CFCs in half by the year 2000. The new data mentioned above, however, have increased pressure for a more rapid rate of elimination of this and other ozone-depleting chemicals. The United States, Japan, and several other countries support the complete elimination of chloroflurocarbons by the end of this century.

Stiffer federal laws in the U.S. now require special disposal and handling of equipment containing ozone-reducing chemicals that might leak into the atmosphere. They also call for the reduction of CFCs in widely used consumer products such as aerosol cans.

A related issue involves destruction of the rain forests of South America, Indonesia, Hawaii, and the northwestern United States. Concerned ecologists, politicians, and ordinary citizens have joined forces throughout the world to reduce the destruction of these forests, the greatest concentration of which is in Brazil. It has been argued that because green vegetation helps produce the right mix of gases in the air that we breathe, if we continue to destroy the rain forests we will suffer in the future. To date there has been little indication that the U.S. is willing to offer the Brazilian government economic incentives for reducing rain forest destruction.

SECTION 4 REVIEW _____

1. What did the National Environmental Policy Act of 1969 establish?
2. What were the major provisions of the Clean Air Act of 1990?
3. **For critical analysis:** Can we expect poor countries to have the same environmental concerns that the United States has? Explain.

CHALLENGE TO THE AMERICAN DREAM

Can the Government Save Our Banking System?

The savings and loan industry has been in continual crisis since the mid 1980s and the banking industry in general is not in good shape. Federal policymakers, however, weren't aware of an impending savings and loan (S&L) crisis prior to 1980. After all, for the past forty years, very few savings and loan associations—called *thrifts* in the banking industry—had failed. All this changed in 1980, when 35 thrifts failed. The number of failures tripled the following year and continued to increase until about 500 thrifts were failing every year. Public concern increased with the number of failures.

Senators and representatives began worrying that massive failures in the savings and loan industry might lead to a banking panic in the entire United States and might even threaten our international banking connections. The result was the 1987 Competitive Banking and Quality Act, which provided for $10.8 billion over three years to help the beleaguered Federal Savings and Loan Insurance Corporation (FSLIC).

That money turned out to be a drop in the bucket. Lobbyists for the thrift industry argued that much, much more was needed. One of the first national problems that the Bush administration had to deal with in 1989 was the potential rescue of depositors in failed savings and loans. With the backing of the administration, the Financial Institution Reform, Recovery, and Enforcement Act of 1989 (Thrift Bailout Act) was passed.

The Causes of the S & L Crisis

The government in effect insures most deposits today in the United States up to $100,000 through the Federal Deposit Insurance Corporation (FDIC). Thrifts and banks pay a small amount to the government for this insurance. Each bank pays the same amount, no matter how risky the investments they undertake. As a result of having such a good insurance deal, some savings and loan associations and banks decide to·make risky, but potentially high-paying, investments. If those risky, high-paying investments do not pan out, the thrift or bank is vulnerable to trouble. But the depositors do not have to worry because of federal deposit insurance.

In effect, the managers of thrifts and banks who do this pay little of the costs if those high-risk, high-yielding investments go bad, but reap substantial rewards if they turn out well. Because most of them have gone bad, we have had numerous failures in the thrift and banking industries.

Because the Thrift Bailout Act of 1989 basically did not change the incentives facing the managers and owners of thrifts and banks, more trouble can be predicted for the future. Unless the cost of deposit insurance is higher when riskier investments are undertaken by thrifts and banks, many of them will continue to act recklessly. Be prepared for future bailout bills similar to the one that cost every man, woman, and child in the United States $2,000 in 1989. In other words, because the same incentive structure faces other types of American financial institutions, we can expect similar problems to arise and similar bailout bills to be passed by Congress.

The challenge to the American dream is to protect savers while at the same time removing the incentive for managers of financial institutions to take unnecessary risks simply because they know that the federal government will bail them out.

You Decide

1. Who is responsible for the increasing number of failed thrifts?
2. Most Americans have bank deposits of less than $20,000. Therefore, insuring deposits up to $100,000 benefits only a small percentage of Americans. Do you approve of the $100,000 ceiling on federally insured deposits? Why or why not?

CHAPTER 19 REVIEW

Key Terms

ability-to-pay
  principle 469
Aid to Families with
  Dependent Children
  (AFDC) 477
benefits-received
  principle 469
budget deficit 466
business cycles 464
depressions 464
environmental impact
  statement 481

Federal Reserve
  System 459
fiscal policy 459
food stamps 477
global warming 483
greenhouse effect 483
in-kind subsidies 475
income transfer 477
inflation 461
loose monetary
  policy 459
marginal tax rate 470

monetary policy 459
national debt 466
off-budget items 469
progressive
  taxation 470
proportional
  taxation 470
public debt 466
recessions 464

regressive taxation 470
sacrifice principle 470
Social Security 476
Supplemental Security
  Income (SSI) 477
tight monetary
  policy 459
U.S. Treasury
  bonds 466

Summary

1. The basic tools that the federal government uses to manage the national economy are monetary policy and fiscal policy. Monetary policy, which is the responsibility of the Federal Reserve System, involves regulating the amount of money in circulation. The Federal Reserve is governed by a board of governors and is divided into geographic areas. In principle, Federal Reserve monetary policy is supposed to be countercyclical, which means it creates policies that run counter to the current business cycle. Fiscal policy, which is the responsibility of the president and Congress, consists of adjusting federal taxes and spending to affect the rate of growth of the total demand for goods and services in the economy. When the government spends more money than it receives in revenues, it runs a budget deficit. The total amount of money owed by the federal government is the public debt. In 1985 Congress passed the Gramm-Rudman-Hollings Deficit Reduction Act in an effort to require that Congress reduce and eventually eliminate the budget deficit. Despite two sets of revisions to this act, Congress has failed to meet its deficit reductions.

2. Eighty-five percent of all government revenues are raised by taxation. There are three principles to justify different levels of taxation: benefits received, ability to pay, and sacrifice. The three ways in which taxes can be imposed are according to proportional, progressive, or regressive systems. The federal personal income tax system is a progressive tax. A comparison of tax percentages among other countries in the world shows that the United

States' tax rates are about in the middle range. Governments sometimes use taxes to direct economic activity. For example, excise taxes on cigarettes and alcohol can discourage their purchase and use.

3. The official poverty level is an absolute measure of income needed to maintain a specified standard of living as of 1963, with the value increased yearly in relation to general price increases. Traditionally, the poorer segments of our population have been minorities, the elderly, and women. Poverty rates among single-parent families, youths, and single elderly people are increasing. The 1990s has brought a new awareness of the plight of the homeless in our country. The major income-maintenance programs of the federal government are Social Security, Supplemental Security Income (SSI), Aid to Families with Dependent Children (AFDC), and food stamps.

4. The government has formal policies that deal with pollution in the environment. The National Environmental Policy Act of 1969 established the Council for Environmental Quality (CEQ) and mandated that environmental impact statements be prepared for every recommendation, report on legislation, or major federal action that would significantly affect the quality of the environment. One of the most pressing concerns in the world today is the threat of global warming. The greenhouse effect is the trapping of heat inside the earth's atmosphere, which is the result of pollution caused largely by the burning of fossil fuels and the emission of carbon dioxide. There are still deep disagreements among scientists over the extent and nature of global warming caused by the greenhouse effect. The destruc-

CHAPTER 19 REVIEW—Continued

tion of the ozone layer due to pollutants is another major threat to our environment.

Review Questions

1. What is monetary policy? What is the difference between a tight and a loose monetary policy?
2. Briefly describe the Federal Reserve System and how it functions.
3. What is fiscal policy?
4. How does the government accumulate a public debt?
5. What are the three principles of taxation?
6. What are the three types of tax systems and how do they differ?
7. What is the most important source of federal government revenues?
8. Which groups in society typically have the highest poverty rates?
9. What are the major income-maintenance programs designed by the government to help the poor and how do they work?
10. Briefly describe the major efforts on the part of the federal government to help solve the pollution problem.

Questions for Thought And Discussion

1. Our government has in the past provided loans to large businesses to save them from bankruptcy, which keeps them operating and saves thousands of jobs. What do you think are the pros and cons of such a policy?
2. Do you think the federal government should be required to have a balanced budget? Why or why not?
3. In your opinion, who should be held responsible for cleaning up the environment: businesses, the state governments, or federal taxpayers? Give reasons for your answer.

Improving Your Skills
Communication Skills

Recognizing Your Own Value Judgments
Students of government are often called upon to ex-

press their opinions on numerous subjects. Throughout this book, you have been learning how to think critically before expressing an opinion. Underlying this need to think critically is the need to recognize your own value judgments. Whether we are aware of it or not, each of us has a set of values and therefore a set of value judgments about everything that we consider. Our values are influenced by our parents, peers, schools, books we read, movies we see, religious beliefs, and countless other variables. Even though you may not be able to pinpoint or change these past influences, you can learn to be aware of them so they don't cloud your thinking about a certain issue. Not recognizing your own value judgments can close your mind to facts and reasoning.

The next time you find yourself reacting very positively or very negatively to an issue about which you do not have all the facts, stop and examine your value judgments. Ask yourself if they are clouding your judgment.

Writing
Re-read the section on the new poor on pages 475 through 476. Make a list of your value judgments concerning this issue.

Social Studies Skills
Working with Percentages and Averages
Look at Figure 19–4 and Figure 19–5 on page 470. Answer the following questions:

1. In Figure 19–4, what is the difference between the percentage income tax rate paid on the first $100 earned and on the third $100 earned?
2. In Figure 19–5, answer the same question as above.
3. What is the average rate of taxation for $300 of income earned in Figure 19–5?

Activities and Projects

1. Research the Clean Air Act of 1990. In your research, find the various estimates of the annual cost Americans will pay to conform to the act's requirements.
2. Research the latest scientific findings about global warming. Write a summary of your results.

CHAPTER 20

Defense and Foreign Policy

CHAPTER OBJECTIVES

To learn and understand

- The development of American foreign policy.

- The involvement of the president and Congress in making foreign and defense policy and the processes by which they are made.

- The structure and functions of the departments of defense and state.

- The goals of American foreign policy and the methods used to achieve them.

- The organization and functions of the United Nations.

Keynote

"The intent of American foreign policy is to promote, together with our allies, the strength and ideals of freedom in a turbulent world."

——— **Henry Kissinger**
(1923–   ) Former Secretary of
State

INTRODUCTION

Why are we as Americans concerned with what Henry Kissinger, national security advisor and secretary of state under President Nixon, called the turbulent world? Should we not be strictly concerned with our own internal affairs? For much of our nation's early history, America was relatively isolated from the rest of the world, but this is no longer true. Mass communication, transportation, world trade, and technology have entangled our everyday lives with the lives of other people around the world. Decisions about war, peace, and international trade are made jointly by many nations. Events happening in one corner of the world may affect the interests of all Americans. For example, when the country of Iraq invaded Kuwait in 1990, the war that resulted touched the lives of almost every American.

As Americans, we cannot ignore what is happening in the rest of the world. And as citizens of the world, we must learn more about international issues, and about how United States foreign policy affects this country's interests and influences global affairs.

SECTION 1

The Development of Our Foreign Policy

Preview Questions
- What is isolationism? Why was this policy abandoned by the United States?
- What was the Cold War?
- What have been some of the historical approaches of American foreign policy? How were these approaches developed?

Every nation has a **foreign policy**—some systematic and general plan that guides a country's attitudes and actions toward the rest of the world. Foreign policy includes all the economic, military, commercial, and diplomatic positions and actions a nation takes in its relationships with other countries. American foreign policy has been shaped by events and attitudes that have developed over a long period of time.

The History of American Foreign Policy

The basic purpose of American foreign policy has always been to protect the national security of the United States. **National security** means protecting the nation's freedom and independence from unwanted interference, threat, or takeover from other nations. Over the years our nation has worked to preserve national security in many ways. A brief look at the history of American foreign policy will help to explain how several approaches to foreign policy have evolved.

The Formative Years   The nation's founders and our early presidents believed that **isolationism**—avoiding political involvement with other nations—was the best way to protect American interests. The young United States tried to stay out of other nations' conflicts, particularly European wars. The reason for this policy was not because America was uninterested in the fate of Europe. Rather, there was so much to be done here at home in building a new nation. We had many problems of our own, a huge continent to explore and settle, and two oceans separating us from most of the world. Also, the colonies were not yet strong enough to directly influence European developments. Our young nation instead set an example for a new political system that was so attractive it might naturally lead Europe to political reform.

489

CHAPTER 20 REVIEW—Continued

and that the U.N. not interfere in the internal affairs of member nations. The most important principal organs of the United Nations are the General Assembly, which is a deliberative body, and the Security Council, which is responsible for maintaining international peace.

Review Questions

1. What is the basic purpose of American foreign policy?
2. Describe the original policy of isolationism and why it was abandoned.
3. Briefly describe the United States' increasing involvement in world affairs since 1898.
4. Briefly describe the Cold War.
5. What are the president's foreign policy-making powers as granted by the Constitution? Who assists him in this area?
6. What are the constitutional powers given to Congress in the area of foreign policy?
7. What responsibilities do the Department of State and the Department of Defense have in foreign policy? What other agencies are involved in foreign policy decisions?
8. What two methods have been used to recruit citizens to serve in the armed forces?
9. What are the main foreign policy goals of the United States?
10. What is diplomacy?
11. Why has the United States provided foreign aid to other nations?
12. How are alliances used to achieve American foreign policy goals?
13. How are trade measures used to achieve foreign policy goals?
14. Why was the United Nations formed?
15. What are the seven principles of the United Nations as listed in the charter?
16. What are the two most important bodies within the United Nations?
17. Who are the members of the Security Council of the United Nations?
18. Name two ways in which you can attempt to influence American foreign policy.
19. Name two examples of terrorism.

Questions for Thought and Discussion

1. Think of at least one foreign policy issue for which the president and Congress might hold different views. Which branch do you think would be most influential in determining policy for that particular issue? Why?
2. Do you think the president or Congress should have a more dominant role in foreign policy affairs? Give reasons for your answer.
3. What do you think would be the consequences for the rest of the world if the United States returned to the policy of isolationism and withdrew from world affairs?
4. Do you think international trade measures and economic policy should be used to serve foreign policy goals? Why or why not?
5. It has been said that the United States is the only superpower left in the world. Explain your reasons for agreeing or disagreeing with this statement.
6. During the war in the Persian Gulf, anti-war demonstrators argued that the United States had too many pressing problems at home—inadequate health care for the poor, a failing educational system, and urban deterioration—to be spending billions of dollars to bomb another country. Do you believe that this is a valid argument against U.S. military involvement elsewhere? Explain why or why not.

Improving Your Skills
Communication Skills

Determining Fallacies in Reasoning

Students of government must often analyze or evaluate statements and viewpoints. Part of this skill involves recognizing fallacies in reasoning. A *fallacy* is a false idea or error, which can take the form of an unsound or unsupported argument, an error in facts, or an inaccurate conclusion.

When analyzing a statement or viewpoint for fallacies, follow these guidelines:

● **Read or listen to the statement carefully.** Try to pinpoint the main idea and the conclusion.

CHAPTER 20 REVIEW—Continued

- **Ask yourself how the conclusion was reached.** The following list describes some of the most common fallacies to look for.

1. No real connection between the information presented and the conclusion.
2. Only one cause is identified when there are many.
3. Correlation is mistaken for causation. (See page 318).
4. The evidence used is irrelevant or only vaguely connected to the information presented.
5. More information is needed to support the conclusion.
6. The conclusion is not based on facts but on the argument that "everyone thinks so."

Writing

Read the statements below. Using the list above, write a short description of which fallacies apply to each of the statements.

- It is wrong for the United States to intervene in the affairs of troubled countries. We have too many problems with crime, education, and poverty in our own country.
- Public opinion overwhelmingly opposed the president's actions in Nicaragua. This proves that he was ill advised by his foreign policy team.
- The reason for intervention in the Persian Gulf in 1990 and 1991 was because of the danger that the world price of oil would be controlled by Iraq.

Social Studies Skills

Sequencing Data and Information

Part of understanding the world around you requires that you be able to put data and information in some kind of logical order. This is called *sequencing*. For example, if you read three articles on the AIDS epidemic, each one treating a different aspect of the problem, you would need to sequence the information from the three sources in order to make sense of it. When dealing with numbers—data—you have to be able to sequence such information in a way that tells you something. Often this is done for you in the form of a graph, such as Figure 20–1, which shows you how defense spending, expressed as a percentage of total federal government outlays, has changed throughout the years. These data have been sequenced for you in *chronological order*, starting from 1940 on. Data can be sequenced in many different ways. Assume that you have a table with data on average household income for each of the fifty states. One way to sequence the data is by state in alphabetical order.

1. What are at least two other ways the data could be sequenced?

Now look at Figure 20–2 on page 507 and answer these questions:

2. In what way is the data sequenced for you on the graph?
3. Would the sequencing change if the horizontal axis showed only five-year intervals?

Now skim through Section 1 in this chapter (pages 489 to 495):

1. How is the information on the history of foreign policy sequenced?
2. What other way could this information be sequenced?

Activities and Projects

1. Choose one of the last five presidents and write a report on his major foreign policy accomplishments and mistakes. Include a list and brief description of each of his closest foreign policy advisors.
2. Prepare a poster of pictures and articles that illustrate the nation working toward one of its major foreign policy goals.
3. Write a list of all the qualifications you think an ambassador to a Middle Eastern country should have. Prepare a script of all the questions you would ask the individual if you were the president considering his or her appointment.
4. Stage a debate on one of the following statements: (1) Women should be allowed to serve in combat roles in the military; (2) The president should not be allowed to order military action without prior congressional approval; (3) The Cold War is over.
5. Choose a goal of U.S. foreign policy and show with historical evidence what the U.S. has done in the last twenty years to achieve that goal.

UNIT EIGHT

State and Local Governments

UNIT CONTENTS

- *Chapter 21*   State Constitutions and Legislative Processes
  - *Chapter 22*   Governors and State Administrators
    - *Chapter 23*   The State Courts
      - *Chapter 24*   Local Government
        - *Chapter 25*   Paying for State and Local Government

519

CHAPTER 21

State Constitutions and Legislative Processes

CHAPTER OBJECTIVES

To learn and understand

- The nature of state constitutions.

- The state legislative structure and process.

- The organization of state legislatures.

- How a bill becomes a law at the state level.

- State forms of direct democracy: the initiative, the referendum, and the recall.

Keynote

"Yesterday, the greatest question was decided which ever was debated in America, and the greater perhaps never was, nor will ever be decided among men. A resolution was passed without one dissenting colony, "that these United Colonies are, and of right ought to be, free and independent States."

——— **John Adams**
(1735–1826) Second President of the United States

Introduction

In the opening quote, John Adams used key words from the Resolution of Independence passed on July 3, 1776. His reference to independent states was extremely accurate, for the fifty states in this nation are in many ways independent. Each has its own constitution, its own judiciary, and its own legislature. In this chapter you will see the elements of those constitutions and legislative processes.

In 1787, the federal government was created according to a deliberate plan. The thirteen states obviously had to be included in the system. So, too, did the large number of local units of governments that existed at that time. After 1787, however, the remaining states, cities, and other local forms of government were not created so systematically. The process has not yet ended; new local governmental units are still being created all the time.

The system as it exists today with more than eighty thousand separate government units in the United States has been called **hyperpluralism**, a word that simply means our government is so fragmented that it is difficult to make decisions and to take action. Now, of course, many things do get done. The government provides roads, hospitals, schools, social programs, and police protection, among many other things. In fact, each of you comes into contact with state and local government workers almost every day of your life.

Not surprisingly, the number of civilian employees in state and local governments has been increasing. By 1998, it is estimated that almost 15 million Americans will work directly for state and local governments. A knowledge of how these governments operate is relevant for you and every other citizen, for these are the governments with which you will have the most direct contact during your life.

SECTION 1

The U.S. Constitution and the State Constitutions

Preview Questions
- What are the powers that the U.S. Constitution gives to state governments?
- Why are state constitutions typically long and detailed compared to the U.S. Constitution?
- What major elements do state constitutions contain?
- How can a state constitution be revised?

We live in a federal system in which there are fifty separate state governments and one federal government. The U.S. Constitution gives a broad range of powers to state governments; it also prohibits state governments from engaging in certain activities. The U.S. Constitution never explicitly defines the powers of the states; rather, state powers were simply reserved, which means that states may do anything that the Constitution does not prohibit them from doing, or that is not expressly delegated to the federal government.

The major reserved powers of the states include the power to spend and regulate **intrastate commerce**, that is, commerce within a given state. The states also have general **police power**, meaning they can protect their citizens by passing and enforcing laws in the areas of public safety (through traffic laws, for example), health and welfare (through immunization and child-abuse

521

▲ General police power is one of the major powers reserved to the states in the United States Constitution. Why do you think the founding fathers chose to give this power to the states rather than to the national government?

laws), and morality (laws against pornography). The police power of the states should not be confused with the protective functions performed by police departments. The regulation of public safety is only one of the many police powers of the states, which include regulating sanitation in restaurants, setting the minimum legal age for smoking, etc.

Restrictions on state and local governmental activity are implied by the Constitution in Article VI, Paragraph 2:

> This Constitution, and the Laws of the United States, which shall be made in Pursuance thereof; and all Treaties made, or which shall be made, under the Authority of the United States, shall be the Supreme Law of the Land; and the Judges in every State shall be bound thereby, any Thing in the Constitution or Laws of any State to the Contrary notwithstanding.

The paragraph states that the Constitution is the supreme law of the land, and no state or local law can conflict with the Constitution, with laws made by the United States Congress, or with treaties entered into by the federal government. Judicially, the U.S. Supreme Court has been the final judge of conflicts arising between the federal and state governments.

State Constitutions

The United States Constitution is a model of brevity. State constitutions, in contrast, are typically models of excessive length and detail. For over two hundred years, the U.S. Constitution has endured as a binding body of law, with only twenty-seven amendments thus far. Such is not the case with state constitutions. Texas has had five constitutions; Louisiana has had eleven; Georgia has had nine; South Carolina has had seven; and Alabama, Florida, and Virginia have had six each. Many have been amended numerous times. In Texas, for example, 487 amendments have been submitted to the voters and 339 of those amendments have been adopted. The number of amendments that voters may be asked to approve in one election sometimes numbers in the hundreds. Over an 84-year period ending in 1985, the citizens of Alabama, for example, were asked to approve 656 amendments—of which they adopted 452.

Figure 21–1 on pages 524–25 provides general information on the constitutions of the various states.

Why State Constitutions Are Long The length and mass of detail of many state constitutions reflect the loss of popular confidence in state legislatures between the end of the Civil War and the early 1900s. During that period, forty-two states adopted or revised their constitutions. Constitutions that were adopted before or after that period are shorter and contain fewer restrictions on the powers of state legislatures.

An equally important reason for the length and detail of state constitutions is that the constitution framers at the state level had a difficult time distinguishing between constitutional law and statutory law. (Remember from Chapter 18 that statutory law is law made by legislatures such as the Congress of the United States or the legislatures of the various states.) Many laws that are clearly statutory have been put into state constitutions. For example, South Dakota has in its state constitution the authorization for a cordage and twine plant at the state penitentiary. The Texas constitution includes a pay schedule for state legislators. When legislators want a raise, the constitution must be amended. The Alabama constitution includes a thirteen-and-a-half-page amendment establishing the ''Alabama Heritage Trust Fund.'' An article of the California constitution discusses the tax-exempt status of the Huntington Library and Art Gallery. Obviously, the U.S. Constitution contains no such details. It leaves to the Congress the nuts-and-bolts activity of making specific statutory laws.

Typical Form and Content

State constitutions are similar in terms of their overall structure to the U.S. Constitution. They include the following:

1. A preamble.
2. A bill of rights.
3. An outline of the framework of government.
4. A listing of state powers and responsibilities.
5. A provision for local government.
6. An amending clause that details the methods of formal constitutional change.

The Preamble Most state constitutional preambles are similar to the one in the U.S. Constitution, in that they begin with ''We, the people . . . do ordain and establish. . . .'' The majority of states refer to some principle of divine guidance, something that the U.S. Constitution does not do.

Bill of Rights Often called a declaration of rights, every state has a section that spells out the civil liberties and rights of its citizens. The majority of state constitutions were adopted prior to the ratification of the Fourteenth Amendment to the U.S. Constitution, which protects individuals' rights against overbearing state governments. Consequently, while there was good reason for extensive bills of rights in state constitutions prior to July 9, 1868, today most of them add little to their citizens' civil liberties and rights beyond those in the U.S. Constitution. Some, however, do offer specific protections such as a ban against discrimination based on sex, or the right to organize labor unions.

Framework of Government A typical state constitution establishes the structure for the legislative, executive, and judicial branches of government. Through what is known as a distribution-of-powers clause, about 50 percent of the states provide for the separation of powers. In the remaining states, the separation of powers is implied from the constitution as a whole, similar to the way such separation of powers is implied in the U.S. Constitution.

Governmental Functions Some state constitutions specify in precise detail what the state government's activities may be; other states are more loose in their delegation of government duties. Most state constitutions restrict the state government's powers over taxation and finance. Most also make public education a state responsibility.

Local Governments The majority of state constitutions explain in detail the structure and power of local governments. (Local governments are under the authority of state governments.) In certain states, however, some cities and counties are allowed to conduct their affairs without state interference. (See Chapter 25 for more details on local government.)

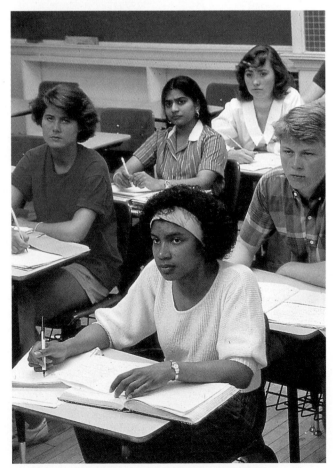

▲ Public education is spelled out as a state responsibility in most state constitutions. What other levels of government also are responsible for public education?

General Information on State Constitutions

State or Other Jurisdiction	Number of Consti- tutions*	Dates of Adoption	Effective Date of Present Constitution	Estimated Length (number of words)	Number of Amendments Submitted to Voters	Adopted
Alabama	6	1819, 1861, 1865, 1868, 1875, 1901	Nov. 28, 1901	174,000	656	452
Alaska	1	1956	Jan. 3, 1959	13,000	28	20
Arizona	1	1911	Feb. 14, 1912	28,876 (a)	187	104
Arkansas	5	1836, 1861, 1864, 1868, 1874	Oct. 30, 1874	40,720 (a)	156	71 (b)
California	2	1849, 1879	July 4, 1879	33,350	756	449
Colorado	1	1876	Aug. 1, 1876	45,679	227	108
Connecticut	4	1818(c), 1965	Dec. 30, 1965	9,564	24	23
Delaware	4	1776, 1792, 1831, 1897	June 10, 1897	19,000	(d)	115
Florida	6	1839, 1861, 1865, 1868, 1886, 1968	Jan. 7, 1969	25,100	63	41
Georgia	10	1777, 1789, 1798, 1861, 1865, 1868, 1877, 1945, 1976, 1982	July 1, 1983	25,000 (a)	11 (e)	10
Hawaii	1 (f)	1950	Aug. 21, 1959	17,453 (a)	85	77
Idaho	1	1889	July 3, 1890	21,500	183	103
Illinois	4	1818, 1848, 1870, 1970	July 1, 1971	13,200	7	3
Indiana	2	1816, 1851	Nov. 1, 1851	9,377 (a)	65	36
Iowa	2	1846, 1857	Sept. 3, 1857	12,500	48	45 (g)
Kansas	1	1859	Jan 29, 1861	11,865	107	80 (g)
Kentucky	4	1792, 1799, 1850, 1891	Sept. 28, 1891	23,500	54	2
Louisiana	11	1812, 1845, 1852, 1861, 1864, 1868, 1879, 1898, 1913, 1921, 1974	Jan 1, 1975	36,146 (a)	24	15
Maine	1	1819	March 15, 1820	13,500	181	153 (h)
Maryland	4	1776, 1851, 1864, 1867	Oct. 5, 1867	41,134	227	195
Massachusetts	1	1780	Oct. 25, 1780	36,690 (a, i)	141	116
Michigan	4	1835, 1850, 1908, 1963	Jan. 1, 1964	20,000	41	15
Minnesota	1	1857	May 11, 1858	9,500	203	109
Mississippi	4	1817, 1832, 1869, 1890	Nov. 1, 1890	23,500	124	54
Missouri	4	1820, 1865, 1875, 1945	March 30, 1945	42,000	100	62
Montana	2	1889, 1972	July 1, 1973	11,866 (a)	17	10

*The constitutions referred to in this table include those Civil War documents customarily listed by the individual states.
(a) Actual word count.
(b) Eight of the approved amendments have been superseded and are not printed in the current edition of the constitution. The total adopted does not include five amendments that were invalidated.
(c) Colonial charters with some alterations served as the first constitutions in Connecticut (1638, 1662) and in Rhode Island (1663).
(d) Proposed amendments are not submitted to the voters in Delaware.
(e) Estimated length of the printed constitution, which includes only provisions of statewide applicability. Local amendments comprise most of the total constitution.
(f) As a kingdom and a republic, Hawaii had five constitutions.
(g) The figure given includes amendments approved by the voters and later nullified by the state supreme court in Iowa (three), Kansas (one), Nevada (six), and Wisconsin (two).
(h) The figure does not include one amendment approved by the voters in 1967 that is inoperative until implemented by legislation.

▲ FIGURE 21–1 General Information on State Constitutions. As you can see from looking at the table on these pages, most state constitutions are quite wordy and many have a large number of amendments. Why are state constitutions so long?

General Information on State Constitutions (continued)

State or Other Jurisdiction	Number of Consti- tutions*	Dates of Adoption	Effective Date of Present Constitution	Estimated Length (number of words)	Number of Amendments	
					Submitted to Voters	Adopted
Nebraska	2	1866, 1875	Oct. 12, 1875	20,048 (a)	276	183
Nevada	1	1864	Oct. 31, 1864	20,770	165	100 (g)
New Hampshire	2	1776, 1784	June 2, 1784	9,200	271 (j)	141 (j)
New Jersey	3	1776, 1844, 1947	Jan. 1, 1948	17,086	48	36
New Mexico	1	1911	Jan. 6, 1912	27,200	213	104
New York	4	1777, 1822, 1846, 1894	Jan 1, 1895	80,000	270	203
North Carolina	3	1776, 1868, 1970	July 1, 1971	11,000	30	24
North Dakota	1	1889	Nov. 2, 1889	31,000	208 (k)	119 (k)
Ohio	2	1802, 1851	Sept. 1, 1851	36,900	241	142
Oklahoma	1	1907	Nov. 16, 1907	68,800	254 (l)	114 (l)
Oregon	1	1857	Feb. 14, 1859	25,965	347	174
Pennsylvania	5	1776, 1790, 1838, 1873, 1968(m)	1968(m)	21,675	24 (m)	19 (m)
Rhode Island	2	1842(c)	May 2, 1843	19,026 (a, i)	84	44
South Carolina	7	1776, 1778, 1790, 1861, 1865, 1868, 1895	Jan 1, 1896	22,500 (n)	628 (o)	454 (o)
South Dakota	1	1889	Nov. 2, 1889	23,300	178	92
Tennessee	3	1796, 1835, 1870	Feb. 23, 1870	15,300	55	32
Texas	5	1845, 1861, 1866, 1869, 1876	Feb. 15, 1876	62,000	487	339
Utah	1	1895	Jan. 4, 1896	17,500	121	73
Vermont	3	1777, 1786, 1793	July 9, 1793	6,600	206	49
Virginia	6	1776, 1830, 1851, 1869, 1902, 1970	July 1, 1971	18,500	19	16
Washington	1	1889	Nov. 11, 1889	29,400	139	76
West Virginia	2	1863, 1872	April 9, 1872	25,600	96	59
Wisconsin	1	1848	May 29, 1848	13,500	161	118 (g)
Wyoming	1	1889	July 10, 1890	31,800	90	51
American Samoa	2	1960, 1967	July 1, 1967	6,000	13	7
No. Mariana Islands	1	1977	Oct. 24, 1977	—	—	—
Puerto Rico	1	1952	July 25, 1952	9,281 (a)	6	6

(i) The printed constitution includes many provisions that have been annulled. The length of effective provisions is an estimated 24,122 words (12,490 annulled) in Massachusetts and 11,399 words (7,627 annulled) in Rhode Island.

(j) The constitution of 1784 was extensively revised in 1792. Figures show proposals and adoptions since 1793, when the revised constitution became effective.

(k) The figures do not include submission and approval of the constitution of 1889 itself and of Article XX; these are constitutional questions included in some counts of constitutional amendments and would add two to the figure in each column.

(l) The figures include one amendment submitted to and approved by the voters and subsequently ruled by the supreme count to have been illegally submitted.

(m) Certain sections of the constitution were revised by the limited constitutional convention of 1967. Eighteen amendments have been proposed and adopted since 1968.

(n) Of the estimated length, approximately two-thirds is of general statewide effect; the remainder is local amendments.

(o) Of the 628 proposed amendments submitted to the voters, 130 were of general statewide effect and 496 were local; the voters rejected 83 (12 statewide, 71 local). Of the remaining 543, the General Assembly refused to approve 100 (22 statewide, 78 local), and 443 (96 statewide, 347 local) were finally added to the constitution.

Source: *Book of the States,* 1988–89 (Lexington, Kentucky: Council of State Governments, 1990).

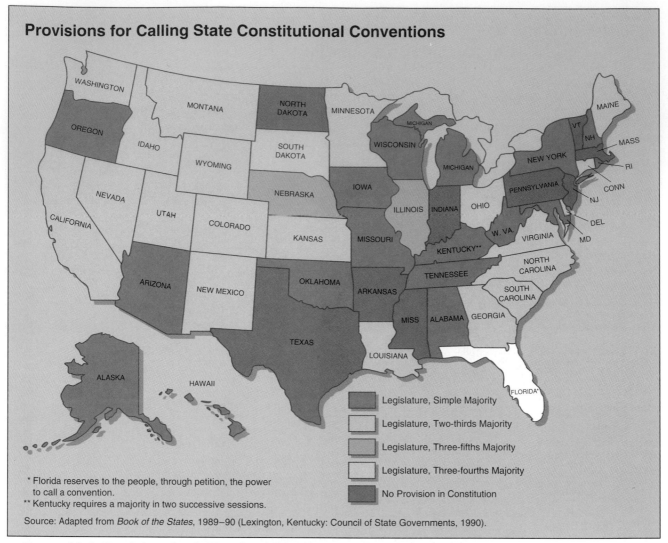

Provisions for Calling State Constitutional Conventions

Legislature, Simple Majority

Legislature, Two-thirds Majority

Legislature, Three-fifths Majority

Legislature, Three-fourths Majority

No Provision in Constitution

* Florida reserves to the people, through petition, the power to call a convention.

** Kentucky requires a majority in two successive sessions.

Source: Adapted from *Book of the States*, 1989–90 (Lexington, Kentucky: Council of State Governments, 1990).

▲ **FIGURE 21–2 Provisions for Calling State Constitutional Conventions.** As you can see from the map above, there are a variety of methods used among the states for calling state constitutional conventions. What is the most common method? Which method does your state employ?

Amending State Constitutions

There are three ways for proposing amendments that are included in the fifty state constitutions: by constitutional convention, by legislative activity, or by popular demand. The most commonly used method has been by convention.

State Constitutional Conventions By the beginning of the 1990s, almost 250 state constitutional conventions had been used to write an entirely new constitution, or to attempt to amend an existing one. This is not surprising, because four-fifths of all state constitutions ex-

pressly allow for such conventions. Some states, such as Illinois, New York, Ohio, and Michigan, require that such conventions be called periodically to consider whether changes are needed, and if so to propose them. Figure 21–2 above shows how a constitutional convention must be called in each of the states.

Proposing Amendments Amendments to state constitutions are made in two ways: by the legislature and by initiative petition.

● **By the legislature** All states authorize legislatures to propose constitutional amendments. Usu-

BUILDING SOCIAL STUDIES SKILLS

Reading Maps for Economic Information

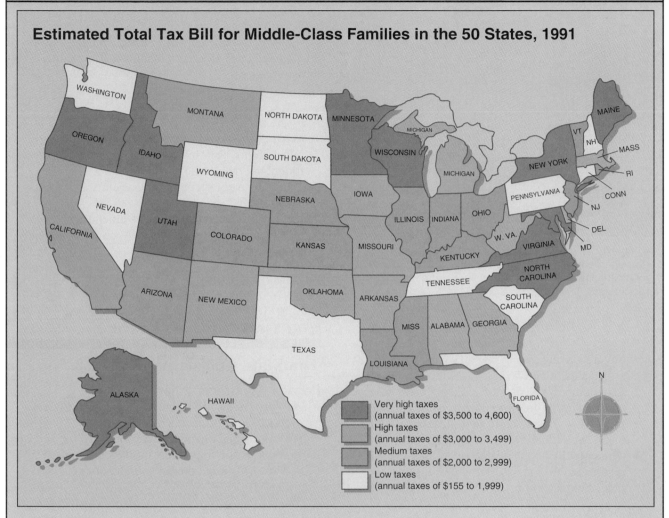

Estimated Total Tax Bill for Middle-Class Families in the 50 States, 1991

Very high taxes
(annual taxes of $3,500 to 4,600)

High taxes
(annual taxes of $3,000 to 3,499)

Medium taxes
(annual taxes of $2,000 to 2,999)

Low taxes
(annual taxes of $155 to 1,999)

Economic information comprises a wide variety of subjects: international trade, distribution of resources, business, transportation, agriculture, manufacturing. It can also include information about unemployment rates, rates of economic growth, and costs of living.

One method of finding economic information is by reading and interpreting special-purpose maps such as economic maps, which communicate specific sets of economic data.

To accurately read an economic map, use the map reading skills you learned on page 290. Then determine the kind of economic information on the

map you are studying, and use these data to help you draw conclusions about the information presented.

PRACTICING YOUR SKILLS

Study the map above.

1. What percentage of states qualify as having "low taxes"?
2. What percentage of states qualify as having "very high taxes"?
3. Is there any geographic pattern to where the low-tax states are concentrated?

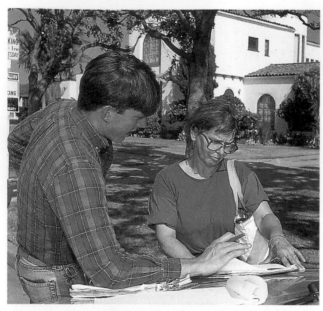

Citizens can propose constitutional amendments through petitions in 17 states including California. Are constitutional initiatives examples of representative democracy or direct democracy?

Ratification No matter which method of proposal is used, all states except Delaware require an amendment to be ratified by a majority of the voters in the general election. (In Delaware, a constitutional amendment must receive a two-thirds vote by the state legislature in two consecutive sessions.) In the states in which voter approval is required, proposals coming from the legislature are adopted far more often than those that originated by initiative.

SECTION 1 REVIEW

1. What are some powers reserved to the states?
2. What are the differences between the U.S. Constitution and most state constitutions?
3. What six major elements does each state constitution contain?
4. How can state constitutions be amended?
5. **For critical analysis:** Why do you think so many state constitutions contain what is obviously statutory law, which might better be dealt with directly by the state legislatures?

SECTION 2

The State Legislative Process

Preview Questions
- Why have state legislatures followed the national lead of bicameralism?
- Why is bicameralism criticized?
- What is the importance of the decisions in *Baker* v. *Carr* and *Reynolds* v. *Sims*?

ally an **extraordinary majority** of votes, which will typically be two-thirds or three-fifths of the total number of legislators, is required to propose an amendment. In some states a proposed amendment has to be passed in two successive sessions of the legislature.
- **The constitutional initiative** Among the states, seventeen (Arizona, Arkansas, California, Colorado, Florida, Illinois, Massachusetts, Michigan, Missouri, Montana, Nebraska, Nevada, North Dakota, Ohio, Oklahoma, Oregon, and South Dakota) have a unique feature in their constitutions called the **constitutional initiative**. This is a process that allows citizens to propose a constitutional amendment through petitions signed by a required number of registered voters. This initiative allows citizens to place a proposed amendment on the ballot without calling a whole constitutional convention. The number of signatures required to get a constitutional initiative on the ballot varies from state to state, usually between 5 and 10 percent of the total number of votes cast in the last gubernatorial election. The states that have used the initiative process most often are California and Oregon.

During the early years of the American republic, the legislative branch was clearly more important than the executive and judicial branches of state government. Most state constitutions mention the legislative branch first. It was initially regarded as the primary method for putting state constitutional law into action. Today, however, the state legislature has lost much of its glow. Governors—the states' chief executives—have emerged as the leaders of the people in legislative affairs. Nonetheless, state legislatures are important forces in state politics and state governmental decision making. The task of these assemblies is to develop and pass laws on such matters as taxes, business and commerce regulation, and funding for school systems and welfare payments. Allocation of state funds and program priorities are vital issues to residents and communities in every state.

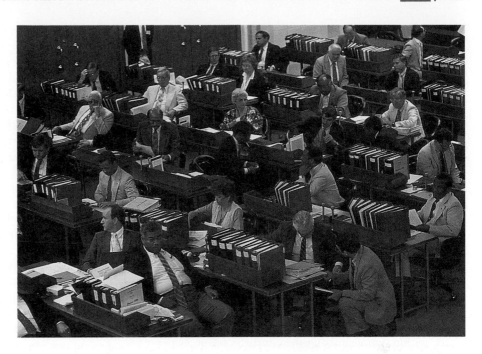

▶ Most state legislatures, such as the North Carolina legislature shown here, are bicameral. What do critics of bicameral legislatures point to as problems with this system?

Bicameral Systems

Bicameralism—a legislative system made up of two houses—exists in all state legislatures except Nebraska, which instituted a unicameral (one house) plan in 1937. Unicameral legislatures did exist in Pennsylvania (1776 to 1790), Georgia (1777 to 1789), and Vermont (1777 to 1836).

There are many reasons why bicameral legislatures prevail: they add to the checks and balances on the exercise of governmental power; they are consistent with the idea of limited government (discussed in Chapter 2); and they follow the pattern of the federal government as laid out in the U.S. Constitution. This desire to be "just like Washington, D.C." was a major reason that Pennsylvania and Georgia abandoned their single-house legislatures.

Criticisms of Bicameralism Even though bicameralism is clearly the rule in state legislatures, many experts criticize the system. Under a bicameral plan, "passing the buck" for legislative failures is easy; placing the blame is difficult. Additionally, interest groups can more easily kill proposed legislation in a bicameral system; all they have to do is squelch it in one of the two houses. As with the federal government, a bicameral state legislature requires a conference committee (discussed in Chapter 14) to resolve differences in proposed legislation. Some experts argue that these conference committees constitute a "third house" that occasionally operates irresponsibly.

By contrast, those who support unicameralism argue that a single-house legislature would be more responsible for its actions, and that a unicameral body would increase the prestige (and salaries) of state legislators. They would also be able to give more full-time service to their respective states. The experience in Nebraska since 1937 appears to confirm this. According to some studies, a typical legislator in Nebraska seems to be of higher caliber, and has become more responsive to her or his constituents than legislators under the old bicameral system.

In spite of the arguments, however, tradition remains on the side of bicameralism. The general public's lack of interest in the issue of unicameralism gives it little chance to come up for a vote.

The Sizes of the Two Houses The size of state legislatures varies dramatically. In the lower houses of representatives, 40 members sit in Alaska, 41 in Delaware, and 42 in Nevada; but 203 sit in Pennsylvania and 400 sit in New Hampshire.[1] There is less diversity in the

---

1. New Hampshire developed a strong dislike of government beyond its towns' borders when it was ruled directly from England as a royal colony. Its house of representatives has at least one member for each town regardless of population. It is the third-largest legislature in the English-speaking world, topped only by Congress and the British House of Commons.

states' upper houses. These vary from 20 seats in Alaska to 67 in Minnesota.

Apportionment

Apportioning Seats **Apportionment** is the system by which seats are distributed among the districts in a state. Each state's constitution provides for apportionment—some on the basis of districts with equal populations, some on the basis of geographical area, and some on the basis of other economic factors. In almost all cases, however, population is at least one of the major bases for distributing legislative seats. As with the federal government, state legislators have often attempted to use **reapportionment** as a way to guarantee that one district remains in Republican party hands or one district remains in Democratic party hands. Reapportionment occurs when population increases, decreases, or shifts within a state. Usually reapportionment has to occur every ten years, within two years after the census is taken, as outlined in the U.S. Constitution.

Baker* v. *Carr For years rural areas were able to dominate state legislatures because geography instead of population was used as the primary means of setting districts. This meant that areas with few citizens had as much power as areas with many more citizens. This practice came to an end in 1962, when the Supreme Court ruled in *Baker* v. *Carr* that federal courts could properly hear cases in which citizens claimed that the pattern of legislative apportionment in their state denied them equal protection of the law under the Fourteenth Amendment.

Reynolds* v. *Sims In a landmark case in 1964, *Reynolds* v. *Sims,* the U.S. Supreme Court changed the rules governing the election of state legislators even further. The Court said that every state electoral district for both houses of the state legislatures had to be drawn with equal populations. Until 1964, state legislatures were controlled by rural, less populated sections of each state, causing rural overrepresentation and therefore urban underrepresentation. But as the Court said in 1964:

> Legislators represent people, not trees or acres. [They] are elected by voters, not farms or cities. . . . [T]he seats in both houses of a bicameral state legislature must be apportioned on a population basis.

For the first time after *Reynolds* v. *Sims,* urban, minority, and suburban populations were able to influence state legislatures in a way that had never been possible. Not surprisingly, the new reapportioned legislatures often drafted and adopted completely new state constitutions. In other states, numerous constitutional amendments were passed to streamline and modernize many parts of the state government. An important aspect of this modernization was the trend toward full-time professional legislators, as well as the hiring of expert legislative assistants.

Creative Map Making

Gerrymandering (discussed in Chapter 12) is an example of creative map making, where legislative districts are drawn in order to guarantee that one political party maintains control of a particular voting district. Figure

The Supreme Court ruling in *Reynolds* v. *Sims* that all electoral districts had to be drawn with equal populations led to increased representation for urban, suburban, and minority populations. This change is reflected in the growing number of minority legislators such as these. What other reforms in state legislatures were prompted by the *Reynolds* v. *Sims* decision?

CITIZENSHIP SKILLS AND RESPONSIBILITIES
Witnessing a Crime

▲ Helping law enforcement officials is one of the responsibilities each of us as citizens share. Why do you think many people seek to avoid this responsibility?

Witnessing a crime can be a frightening and intimidating experience. The first reaction is often to run away and forget about it. As a citizen, however, you have a responsibility to help enforce law and order in your community, which in this case may involve identifying yourself as a witness to a crime. If you run away from this responsibility, it may be more difficult to prosecute the criminal, leaving him or her free to commit more crimes and harm more victims in your community. Offering your account as a witness can help make your community and neighborhood a safer place to live.

If you witness a crime, find the nearest phone and call the police immediately, which you can usually do by dialing 911. If the victim needs medical attention, call an ambulance first (also usually by dialing 911). Give the time, place, and the nature of the crime. While you wait for the police or ambulance to arrive, try to remember as many specific details as possible about the crime, the perpetrator (the person who committed the crime), and any vehicle involved. When the police arrive, answer all their

questions in as much detail as you can. Do not leave out any details, even if you think they are not important. Also, do not exaggerate or add any personal commentary. If you are asked to sign a testimony, be sure to read what the officer has written and check it for accuracy before you sign.

Chances are you will not be contacted again. You may, however, be called to testify in court. Again, answer the questions as completely and honestly as possible. Do not leave out details and do not exaggerate. The attorney for the defendant will probably cross-examine you. Remember that you are not on trial and do not need to defend yourself. She or he may ask you questions that sound confusing or accusatory, but remember that she or he is only trying to do a job, and is probably trying to bring out any inconsistencies or weaknesses in your testimony. If you answer honestly, directly, briefly, and to the point, you should have no problem. You will have fulfilled your responsibility as a citizen. Remember that crime affects all of us and that each of us is responsible for doing what we can to help keep our communities safe.

TAKING ACTION

1. See if there is a "crime alert" program in your neighborhood. If there is, obtain information on how it works and how you and your household can participate.
2. Many newspapers have a local section that lists the reported crimes in your area. If your newspaper has this regular section, read it for several weeks in a row. Note what percentage of the crimes reported were actually witnessed by someone.
3. The next time you attend a school sporting event with a friend, have each of you spend ten minutes observing what is happening in the crowd around you. The following morning, write down what you observed. Compare your observations with those of your friend. Try to determine why differences might exist in your observations.

Proposed Sixty-Ninth Assembly District in California

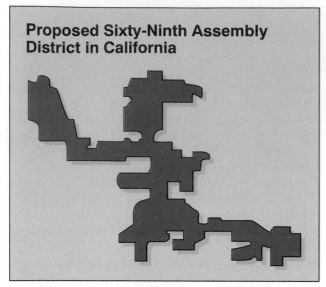

▲ **FIGURE 21–3 Proposed 69th Assembly District in California.** Although the proposed assembly district above does not exactly resemble a salamander, as did the original gerrymander, it has obviously been drawn for political purposes. Why is such gerrymandering attempted?

21–3 shows how a proposed district was gerrymandered in California. This particular example of gerrymandering was done in an unsuccessful attempt to create a Democratic district in Orange and Los Angeles counties in California.

In spite of continuing attempts to gerrymander, in most states (with the exception of a few rural states) the state legislatures fairly represent the population. Most of the real political power in state politics has moved from the countryside to the cities and suburbs. This shift in political power throughout the states was reflected during the early 1990s when state legislatures in California, Texas, Florida, and other states had to redraw congressional districts for the U.S. House of Representatives in Washington, D.C.

SECTION 2 REVIEW

1. Why have all states but one adopted bicameral legislatures?
2. Which population groups within the states have benefited most from the Supreme Court's decisions in *Baker* v. *Carr* and *Reynolds* v. *Simms*?
3. How have *Baker* v. *Carr* and *Reynolds* v. *Simms* changed the way states are apportioned?
4. **For critical analysis:** Do you think it is possible for a state house of representatives with hundreds of members in it, such as in New Hampshire, to be an effective legislative body? Why or why not?

SECTION 3

State Legislators

Preview Questions
● What are the typical terms of office of state legislators?
● What is the difference between a partisan and nonpartisan election?

State legislators have been criticized as being less professional and less qualified than those in the U.S. Congress. The reality is that most state legislators are paid relatively little and given relatively fewer resources to work with. In almost twenty states legislators are paid less than $10,000 per year. Figure 21–4 on pages 534–35 shows how well your state legislators are paid.

The low salaries for state legislators are partially explained by the fact that, while members of the U.S. Congress have regular, year-round jobs as congressmen or congresswomen, state legislators by contrast, serve actively for erratic periods—full time for a few months and at odd times for the remainder of their terms. This means that state legislators often have other jobs and look upon their legislative duties as a sideline. In some states, such as California and New York, however, there is a trend toward making the job of legislator a full-time and adequately paying job, as well as increasing funding for legislative staff and providing research assistants.

About 40 percent of all state legislators are lawyers or farmers; many others are business executives. Most state legislators move on to other jobs in government

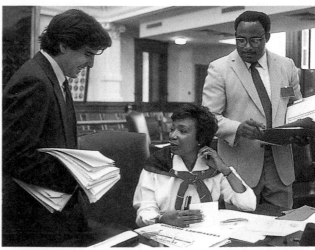

▲ Eddie Bernice Johnson is a member of the Texas State Senate. On average, are state legislators paid like their federal counterparts?

CASE STUDY

The "Congressionalization" of State Legislatures

In the past decade there has been an explosion of lobbyists at the state level, both in numbers and in the range of types. For example, the number of registered lobbyists in Iowa more than doubled between 1984 and 1992.

There are many reasons for this surge in state lobbyists. Deregulation by the federal government has given states a greater role in the regulation of business, banking, consumer affairs, and the environment, which means lobbyists will exert more influence on state legislators to support their causes. For example, the prospect that the state might institute new regulations on automobile rentals in Florida prompted car-rental companies to hire more than forty lobbyists in Tallahassee in 1990. Another reason for greater state lobbying is the drying up of federal funds. With funding for many programs now in the hands

of the states, lobbyists have even more reason to seek support in state legislatures.

Some observers believe this proliferation of lobbyists at the state level is fundamentally altering the character of state legislatures, which for a long time were regarded as unsophisticated citizen assemblies. Some believe that candidates for state offices will increasingly turn to lobbyists for money, which will lead to some of the campaign finance problems seen on the national level.

THINK ABOUT IT

1. Is there anything wrong with having more lobbyists working in state governments? Explain.
2. How could the increase in state lobbyists alter the character of state legislatures?

and the private sector after serving their term. In other words, there is a higher rate of turnover among state legislators, compared to the lengthy careers of members of the U.S. Congress.

Terms of State Legislators

You can see in Figure 21–4 that legislators serve either two-year or four-year terms. As with the U.S. Congress, state senators are often elected for longer terms than are state representatives. In all but four states—Alabama, Louisiana, Maryland, and Mississippi—representatives are chosen for two-year terms. In any given year, more than 25 percent of the 7,500 state legislators in the country are serving their first term in office.

The Election Process

In every state, legislators are chosen by popular vote. Typically, candidates for the state legislature are nominated in party primaries (discussed in Chapter 10). The general election is typically partisan—held along political party lines—pitting a Democratic party candidate for representative or senator against a Republican party

candidate. In a few states, including Delaware, legislative candidates are chosen in conventions. (In Nebraska's unicameral system, candidates are nominated in nonpartisan primaries in which no party affiliation is used for candidates.)

Most states have elections for state legislators in November in even-numbered years. The exceptions are Louisiana, Mississippi, New Jersey, and Virginia, in which elections are held in odd-numbered years. In Louisiana elections are held in October of odd-numbered years. In those four states, the goal has been to separate state and local issues from national politics. One result has been relatively lower voter turnout for elections in those four states than in the other forty-six states, in which both national and state elections are held at the same time.

When the Legislature Meets

Most states have annual legislative sessions. You can see from Figure 21–4, however, that there are some exceptions. Texas is the largest state whose legislature still meets **biennially** (every two years). In the 1990s

Characteristics of State Legislatures

	Seats in Senate	Length of Term	Seats in House	Length of Term	Years Sessions Are Held	Salary[1]
Alabama	35	4	105	4	annual	$ 10 (d)
Alaska	20	4	40	2	annual	22,140
Arizona	30	2	60	2	annual	15,000
Arkansas	35	4	100	2	odd	7,500 [2]
California	40	4	80	2	even	40,816
Colorado	35	4	65	2	annual	17,500
Connecticut	36	2	151	2	annual	16,760
Delaware	21	4	41	2	annual	23,282
Florida	40	4	120	2	annual	21,684
Georgia	56	2	180	2	annual	10,000
Hawaii	25	4	51	2	annual	27,000
Idaho	42	2	84	2	annual	30 (d)
Illinois	59	—[3]	118	2	annual	35,661
Indiana	50	4	100	2	annual	11,600
Iowa	50	4	100	2	annual	16,600
Kansas	40	4	125	2	annual	52 (d)
Kentucky	38	4	100	2	even	100 (d)
Louisiana	39	4	105	4	annual	16,800 [2]
Maine	35	2	151	2	even	7,500 [4]
Maryland	47	4	141	4	annual	25,000
Massachusetts	40	2	160	2	annual	30,000
Michigan	38	4	110	2	annual	45,450
Minnesota	67	4	134	2	odd	26,395
Mississippi	52	4	122	4	annual	10,000
Missouri	34	4	163	2	annual	22,414

[1] Salaries annual unless otherwise noted as (d), per day, or (b), biennium (per two-year period).
[2] Plus per day.
[3] Terms vary from two to four years.
[4] For odd year, $4,000 for even year.
[5] Unicameral legislation.

▲ FIGURE 21–4 **Characteristics of State Legislatures.** This table examines state legislatures. Which state has the most seats in its legislature?

Characteristics of State Legislatures (continued)

	Seats in Senate	Length of Term	Seats in House	Length of Term	Years Sessions Are Held	Salary[1]
Montana	50	—[3]	100	2	odd	52,13 (d)
Nebraska[5]	49	4	—	—	annual	12,000
Nevada	21	4	42	2	odd	104 (d)
New Hampshire	24	2	400	2	annual	200 (b)
New Jersey	40	—[3]	80	2	annual	35,000
New Mexico	42	4	70	2	annual	75 (d)
New York	61	4	150	2	annual	57,500
North Carolina	50	4	120	2	odd	11,124
North Dakota	53	2	100	2	odd	90 (d)
Ohio	33	4	99	2	annual	31,659
Oklahoma	48	4	101	2	annual	32,000
Oregon	30	2	60	2	odd	11,868
Pennsylvania	50	4	203	2	annual	47,000
Rhode Island	50	2	100	2	annual	5 (d)
South Carolina	46	4	124	2	annual	10,000
South Dakota	35	2	70	2	annual	4,267
Tennessee	33	4	99	2	odd	16,500
Texas	31	4	150	2	odd	7,200 [2]
Utah	29	4	75	2	annual	65 (d)
Vermont	30	2	150	2	odd	6,750
Virginia	40	4	100	2	annual	18,000
Washington	49	4	98	2	annual	17,900
West Virginia	34	4	100	2	annual	6,500
Wisconsin	33	4	99	2	annual	32,239
Wyoming	30	4	64	2	annual	75 (d)

[1] Salaries annual unless otherwise noted as (d), per day, or (b), biennium (per two-year period).
[2] Plus per day.
[3] Terms vary from two to four years.
[4] For odd year, $4,000 for even year.
[5] Unicameral legislation.
Source: Adapted from Book of the States, 1989-90 (Lexington, Kentucky: Council of State Governments, 1990)

Kentucky, Minnesota, Montana, Nevada, North Carolina, North Dakota, Oregon, Tennessee, and Vermont also began meeting on a biennial basis. In California the legislature runs a continuous two-year session.

Over three-fourths of the states have limited their regular sessions to a specific number of days, ranging from 20 to 180. Other states effectively limit the length of sessions by paying legislators in such a way that their payment expires after a stated period.

In addition to regular sessions, the governors of most states may call legislators into a **special session**, which allows the state legislature to take up urgent matters such as revising the budget or eliminating a special tax.

Eight states allow a type of special session called a **veto session** to be held soon after each regular session. In Connecticut, Hawaii, Louisiana, Missouri, New Jersey, Utah, Virginia, and Washington, legislators can reconsider bills vetoed by the governor and attempt to override the governor's veto, if enough popular support within the legislature exists. (See Chapter 23 for more information on the governor's veto power.)

SECTION 3 REVIEW

1. When do most states hold their general elections?
2. How often do the legislatures in most states meet?
3. **For critical analysis:** Do you think the legislators in your state are being paid too little? Too much? What difference do you think it would make if their salaries were changed? Give reasons for your answers.

SECTION 4

How the Legislature Is Organized

Preview Questions
- Who are the leaders in a state legislature?
- What types of committees are used by state legislatures? Why are they important?

Most state legislatures are organized in a manner similar to the U.S. Congress. They use presiding officers, committee systems, and legislative aides.

The Officers

Normally, those who preside over the sessions of state legislative chambers are powerful political figures.

In all states except Nebraska, the lower house of the legislature elects its own presiding officer, known as the **speaker**. In the majority of states the popularly elected **lieutenant governor** is the president of the senate. (There are fifteen states in which the lieutenant governor does not double as the president of the senate. In these states the senators choose their own presiding officers.)

The powers of the presiding officers are basically the same in all states. Speakers appoint committees, as do most presidents of the senates. Presiding officers in most states have the ability to control the business in that chamber. They decide to which committee a bill will go, and which bills will be considered on the floor. They enforce the rules during debate, and control who speaks in debates. Typically, because the speaker of the house is a political leader, he or she has more weight than the president of the senate. This is because the president of the senate is usually a lieutenant governor who has been chosen by the people rather than by the members of the senate.

The Committee System

There are three types of committees used in state legislatures: standing, joint, and interim.

Standing Committees Most of the work of state legislatures is done through **standing committees** in each house, also referred to as permanent committees. Standing committees sort out the bills that should reach the floor for debate, and inform each chamber's members what business has been carried on within the committees. Standing committees are normally organized around areas such as education, local government, highways, and the environment. The number of standing committees varies from nine in Alaska to over thirty in other states. The number of members per committee varies from ten to forty, with the average being about twelve.

It is in standing committees that proposed bills are given the closest attention. A committee may amend or rewrite a bill, or ignore it altogether (which is the usual procedure, because 500 to several thousand bills are typically introduced in state legislatures).

Because standing committees do the most important work of the legislature, a good committee assignment is quite desirable. Legislators wage political battle in order to be assigned to a good committee. Seniority and political influence are the major factors in determining assignments, which are usually made by the speaker of the house or the president of the senate. Speakers may use committee appointments to repay political debts incurred

▶ Most state legislatures are organized in a manner similar to the United States Congress with presiding officers, committee systems, and legislative staffs. Why do you think these similarities exist?

during campaigns for the speakership. Special interest groups may lobby hard to get a favorite legislator assigned to an important committee that affects their clients.

Joint Committees **Joint committees** are another form of standing committees, but these are made up of members of both chambers of the legislature. Massachusetts, Maine, and Connecticut have used joint committees effectively for years. (Maine and Connecticut use *only* joint committees.) Over 50 percent of state legislatures have one or more joint committees. Joint committees in all bicameral legislatures have to be set up to deal with the problems of administering certain legis-

lative details, such as reconciling and making identical the two versions of the same bill before it is sent to the governor to be signed.

Interim Committees Because state legislatures are not continuously in session, the use of **interim committees** has become more popular. Interim committees study particular problems while the state legislature is out of session, and report their findings and recommendations to the next session. Some states have emergency boards that are similar to interim committees. Oregon, for example, has an emergency board that has specific power over state budget matters when the legislature is not in session.

Legislative Assistance

As mentioned before, an important aspect of most state legislatures is the use of legislative aides. In an attempt to help legislators understand the complexity of the legislation needed, legislative councils were used from 1930 to 1965. These councils were made up of experts who provided research for the legislators. Their role has been that of fact finders.

Since 1965, however, individual legislators have increased their staff size. Legislative aides now regularly do the research and analytical services that were once provided by legislative councils.

Additionally, most state legislatures have bill-drafting services, which attempt to prevent loopholes in proposed legislation. They also attempt to change bills so as to avoid future potential trouble in the courts. Bill-drafting agencies typically operate between state legislative sessions.

SECTION 4 REVIEW _____

1. What officer normally presides over a state lower house? Upper house?
2. What types of committees are used by state legislatures? Why are they important?
3. **For critical analysis:** Why do you think state legislatures gradually stopped using legislative councils in favor of their own legislative aides?

SECTION 5

How a State Bill Becomes Law

Preview Questions
- What are the necessary steps for a bill to become law in a state legislature?
- Which groups of people suggest bills to state legislators?
- How many bills are introduced each year at the state level?

Legislatures exist to make laws. The lawmaking machinery in the state legislatures is similar to that used in Congress. Figure 21–5 shows how an idea becomes first a bill and eventually a law in one state. (This procedure is similar to the one discussed in Chapter 14.)

As you can see, a bill becomes a law at the state level after going through an elaborate process, just as happens with bills in the U.S. Congress. A bill must pass first to a house committee and then to the whole house for a vote. Next it normally goes to a senate committee and then is voted on by the full senate. Finally, if it has survived thus far, it lands on the governor's desk for signature. But just as in the U.S. Congress, few bills make it through this process very easily. Most do not reach the finish line.

During any legislative session, thousands of bills are introduced. It has been estimated that approximately one hundred thousand bills are introduced in the fifty state legislatures in any one calendar year. But the number of bills introduced in any one state varies dramatically. New York might have twenty-five times more bills introduced than a state such as Utah.

When the governor signs a bill, it becomes a law in that state. In all states except North Carolina, the governor may also choose to veto a bill. When this happens, legislators can attempt to override the veto by passing the bill again with a majority vote in each house, but in most cases the governor's veto normally holds. Less than 5 percent of all vetoed bills are overridden in state legislatures.

Where State Bills Come From

At the national level, the source of bills in either house of Congress is congressional members themselves. The same is true with state legislators. Thus, with both legislative bodies, legislators are the source of legislation. Only a legislator may actually introduce a bill in the house or senate of a state legislature. In reality, however, it is the lobbyists who will often suggest to legislators that certain bills be introduced. Additionally, the governor, similar to the president of the United States, is another major source of ideas for potential bills. Finally, administrators in state and local government agencies may suggest various bills to legislators.

SECTION 5 REVIEW _____

1. Who may introduce a bill in a state legislature?
2. Who are the people who suggest bills to state legislators?
3. How many bills are introduced at the state level each year?
4. What percentage of vetoed bills are overridden by state legislators?
5. **For critical analysis:** How do you think our system of democracy would be affected if citizens could directly introduce bills at the state level?

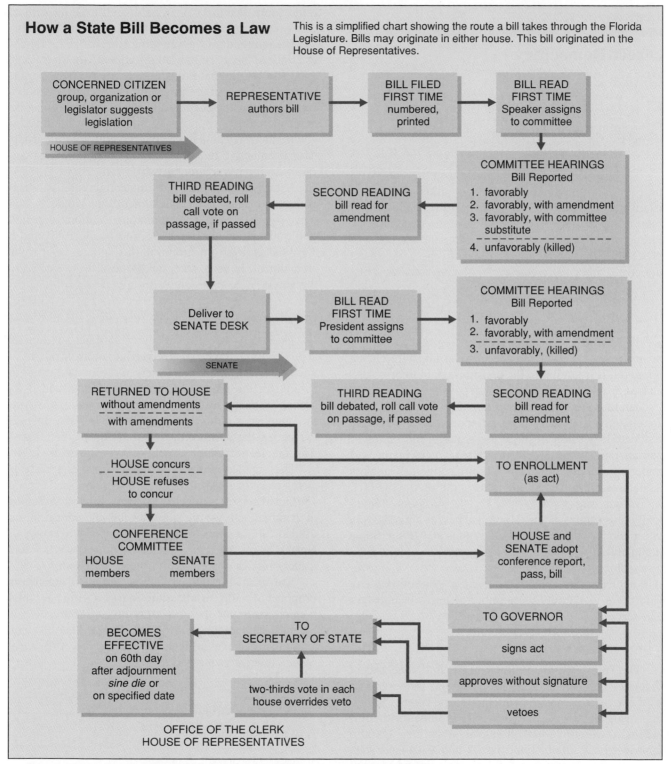

How a State Bill Becomes a Law

This is a simplified chart showing the route a bill takes through the Florida Legislature. Bills may originate in either house. This bill originated in the House of Representatives.

CONCERNED CITIZEN group, organization or legislator suggests legislation

REPRESENTATIVE authors bill

BILL FILED FIRST TIME numbered, printed

BILL READ FIRST TIME Speaker assigns to committee

HOUSE OF REPRESENTATIVES

COMMITTEE HEARINGS Bill Reported
1. favorably
2. favorably, with amendment
3. favorably, with committee substitute
4. unfavorably (killed)

THIRD READING bill debated, roll call vote on passage, if passed

SECOND READING bill read for amendment

Deliver to **SENATE DESK**

BILL READ FIRST TIME President assigns to committee

COMMITTEE HEARINGS Bill Reported
1. favorably
2. favorably, with amendment
3. unfavorably, (killed)

SENATE

RETURNED TO HOUSE without amendments
with amendments

THIRD READING bill debated, roll call vote on passage, if passed

SECOND READING bill read for amendment

HOUSE concurs
HOUSE refuses to concur

TO ENROLLMENT (as act)

CONFERENCE COMMITTEE
HOUSE members   SENATE members

HOUSE and SENATE adopt conference report, pass, bill

TO GOVERNOR

BECOMES EFFECTIVE on 60th day after adjournment *sine die* or on specified date

TO SECRETARY OF STATE

signs act

approves without signature

two-thirds vote in each house overrides veto

vetoes

OFFICE OF THE CLERK
HOUSE OF REPRESENTATIVES

▲ **FIGURE 21–5 How a State Bill Becomes a Law.** The flow chart above describes the general process through which a state bill becomes a law. As you can see, this chart has been modeled on the process in the Florida legislature. What is the function of the conference committee in this process?

SECTION 6

Direct Democracy

Preview Questions
- What is the initiative?
- What is the referendum? How is it different from the initiative?
- For what purpose is the recall used?

There is a major difference between the legislative process as outlined in the U.S. Constitution and the legislative process as outlined in the various state constitutions. Many states exercise a type of direct democracy through the initiative, the referendum, and the recall—procedures that allow voters to control the government directly. Direct democracy at the state level was first started in Oregon before the 1920s.

The Initiative

The **initiative** lets citizens bypass legislatures by proposing new statutes or changes in government for citizen approval. It is similar to the constitutional initiative discussed on page 528, but is used for new laws, as opposed to changing the state constitution. Most states that allow for citizen initiatives require that the initiative's backers circulate a petition to place the issue on the ballot. A certain percentage of the registered voters in the last gubernatorial election must sign the petition. If enough signatures are obtained, the issue is put on the ballot.

Twenty-one states use the legislative initiative, typically those states in which political parties are relatively weak and in which nonpartisan groups are strong. Some major initiatives that have been passed include a 1982 Massachusetts requirement that voters approve any future nuclear plant construction; and a 1990 initiative in California that limits the number of terms a legislator can serve.

The Referendum

The **referendum** is similar to the initiative, except that the issue (or constitutional change) is proposed first by the legislature and then directed to the voters for their approval. Thirty-six states currently provide for the referendum, which is most often used at the local level to approve local school bond issues and to amend state constitutions. In a number of states that provide for the referendum, a bill passed by the legislature may be "put on hold" by obtaining petitions with the required number of signatures from voters who oppose it. A statewide referendum election is then held, and if the majority of the voters disapprove of the bill, it is no longer valid.

The referendum was not initially intended for regular use. Indeed, it has been used infrequently in the past. Its opponents argue that it is an unnecessary check on representative government and that it weakens legislative responsibility. In recent years, the referendum has become increasingly popular as citizens have attempted to control their state and local governments. Interest groups have been active in sponsoring the petition drives necessary to force a referendum.

A fairly regular focus of state referenda has been various versions of an amendment that would bestow equal rights on women. Referendum elections were held in Florida and Nevada in 1978, in Iowa in 1980, and in Vermont in 1986 on proposals for a state equal rights amendment. In each state, the proposal was rejected by the voters.

The Recall

The **recall**—a vote to dismiss an official—is directed at public officials who are deemed incompetent or grossly unethical in their conduct. Voters may circulate a petition calling for the removal of such an official, and if the petition obtains a sufficient number of signatures (usually that number is quite high—it may be, for example, 25 percent of the number of votes cast in the last gubernatorial election), then a recall election is held.

The recall is authorized mainly in western states. Being placed on a recall ballot does not necessarily mean an elected person is guilty of anything, although charges of criminal activity are often a reason for recalling an official. So far, only former governor Lynn Frazier of North Dakota has been recalled from office, in 1922. (Later, Frazier was elected to the U.S. Senate.)

The recall is often used as a threat to legislators. Proponents of the recall in the fourteen states in which it exists argue that the possibility of recall prevents outrageously inappropriate official behavior. Its opponents argue that it makes officeholders prey to well-financed special interest groups.

SECTION 6 REVIEW

1. What is the initiative?
2. What is the referendum?
3. When is a recall used?
4. **For critical analysis:** How do you think the existence of the initiative, the referendum, and the recall affects the political behavior of state officials?

CHALLENGE TO THE AMERICAN DREAM

Limiting Lengthy Stays in the State Legislature

In the United States Congress, incumbents are re-elected more than 90 percent of the time, leading to very lengthy stays in the federal legislature. The situation is not exactly the same in state legislatures. Those who do not hold leadership positions in state legislatures generally leave within ten years and move on to another career. Those who hold leadership positions—party leaders and committee chairpersons—often keep their seats for twenty years or more.

The voters in California struck at the heart of the professional state legislature by approving with a 52 percent majority Proposition 140 in 1990. That initiative sets strict limits on the number of years any state officeholder, from governor to superintendent of education, can serve. Anyone whose office calls for a four-year term (including all forty state senators) will be allowed to serve only two terms. The eighty state assemblypersons who are elected for two-year terms can hold office for three terms only. Once a state officeholder has finished his or her time, he or she will not be allowed to return to the same office.

Those who supported Proposition 140 claimed that it would clean up the "old-boy network" that dominated the California state legislature. They were right. Immediately after Proposition 140 was passed, the majority floor leader of the lower body, Tom Hannighan, announced his retirement. The assembly speaker *pro tem,* Michael Roos, indicated he was considering retirement. The speaker of the assembly, Willie Brown, estimated that 40 percent of his colleagues would retire when their terms were up. In addition, approximately 700 of the legislature's 2500 staff members were expected to retire.

Lobbyists responded to the proposition immediately, claiming that they were losing their "investments"—long-time incumbents with whom they had developed working relationships and who understood their particular interests.

Those against Proposition 140 argued that the success of the initiative would help rather than hinder special interests and their lobbyists. Skillful lobbyists will now be able to exploit the inexperience of novice politicians, of which there will be many due to the term limitations. Others argue that term limitations will upset the balance of power between the governor and the legislature. According to this argument, only an experienced legislator aided by a savvy research staff can offset the tremendous power that the governor holds. Still others point out that legislators who have a limited time in office may waste more of the public's money because they don't have to worry about future consequences.

California was not the first state to have its citizens approve term limitation for its legislators. Oklahoma and Colorado had already done the same. The trend may be strengthened by the national debate over term limitation for representatives and senators in Washington, D.C.

With or without term limits, it is apparent that citizens are looking to take steps to ensure that elected representatives do indeed reflect the wishes and attitudes of their constituents. As you've learned in this chapter, term limits is only one of the steps currently being considered around the country. You read in Section 3 of this chapter that there is also a trend toward making the job of state legislator a full-time, adequately compensated position. The challenge to the American dream is to have experienced but dedicated state legislators run each government with the public good in mind at all times.

You Decide

1. What are the arguments in favor of term limitation?
2. What are the arguments against term limitation?
3. Do you think the same arguments can apply at the state and national levels?
4. Do you think there should be term limitation for every elected government official at all levels—local, state, and federal? Why or why not?

CHAPTER 21 REVIEW

Key Terms

apportionment 530
biennially 533
constitutional
    initiative 528
extraordinary
    majority 528
hyperpluralism 521

initiative 540
interim
    committees 537
intrastate
    commerce 521
joint committees 537
lieutenant

governor 536
police power 521
reapportionment 530
recall 540
referendum 540
speaker 536
special session 536

standing
    committees 536
veto session 536

Summary

1. The U.S. Constitution reserves powers to the state, which means states may do anything that the Constitution does not prohibit them from doing, or that is not expressly reserved for the federal government. No state or local law may be in conflict with the U.S. Constitution, with laws made by the United States Congress, or with treaties entered into by the federal government. State constitutions are typically lengthy and detailed. They usually include a preamble, a bill of rights, an outline of the framework of government, a listing of the state's powers and responsibilities, a provision for local government, and an amending clause that details the methods of formal constitutional change.

2. Bicameralism exists in all state legislatures except Nebraska, which has a unicameral legislature. The size of state legislatures varies dramatically. Each state's constitution provides for a system of apportionment—how seats are distributed among the districts of a state. A long-standing pattern of rural overrepresentation ended with the Supreme Court decision *Baker* v. *Carr* (1962). Since that case, the Court has consistently held that the Fourteenth Amendment's equal protection clause requires that electoral districts in each state contain equal numbers of persons.

3. Most state legislators are paid relatively little and are given few resources with which to work. They serve either two-year or four-year terms. In every state, legislators are chosen by popular vote. Most states have annual legislative sessions, but some meet biennially.

4. Most state legislatures are organized in a manner similar to the U.S. Congress. In all states except Nebraska, the lower house of the legislature elects its own presiding officer, known as the speaker. In a majority of states, the popularly elected lieutenant governor is president of the senate. As in Congress, a major share of the legislature's work is done in committees.

5. The lawmaking machinery in the state legislatures is similar to that used in Congress.

6. Many states exercise direct democracy through several methods. The initiative technique lets citizens bypass legislatures by proposing new statutes or changes in government for citizen approval. The referendum is an issue that is first proposed by the legislature and then directed to the voters for their approval. The recall is a petition by the citizens calling for the removal of a public official deemed incompetent or grossly unethical in conduct.

Review Questions

1. What are the major powers reserved to the states?
2. Why are most state constitutions long and detailed?
3. Which basic elements are included in each state's constitution?
4. What are the three ways in which a state constitution may be amended?
5. Why are all but one of the fifty state legislatures bicameral?
6. What are the criticisms of bicameralism?
7. How was the imbalance between urban and rural representation in state districts resolved?
8. What are the terms and salaries of your state legislators?
9. Who are the presiding officers in the state legislatures? What are their chief powers?
10. Briefly describe the functions and importance of the three types of committees used in state legislatures.

CHAPTER 21 REVIEW—Continued

11. What functions do the initiative, the referendum, and the recall serve?
12. What are the main actions you should take if you witness a crime?
13. What are the arguments for and against limitations of terms in the state legislature?

Questions for Thought and Discussion

1. Do you think every state needs its own constitution? Why or why not?
2. What qualifications do you think are important for a state legislator? To what issues and problems do you think a legislator in your state should pay particular attention?
3. The turnover rate of state legislators is fairly high due to the low salary and part-time nature of their work. What might be some other reasons for this high turnover rate? How might this problem be solved?
4. Does your state use the legislative initiative? If so, how often and for what purposes has it been used? What have been some of the more recent initiatives? Do you think that the initiative process is truly a form of direct democracy?

Improving Your Skills
Communication Skills

Seeing Both Sides of an Issue

Whether you are doing research, writing a report, debating a question, or discussing a problem, it is often important to see both sides of an issue. It is easy to become blind to other points of view after you have firmly made up your mind. If you have ever been in a position in which you felt as though someone refused to listen to your side of the story, then you know how counterproductive this can be. Sometimes it is difficult to admit, even to ourselves, that there is another side to an issue. Usually, however, there is at least one other side to the story, and it never hurts to find out as much as you can about it. You have nothing to lose by listening to your opponent; doing so will either cause you to change your position, help to strengthen your own ar-

guments, or allow you to understand the other side more clearly.

Writing

Choose an issue on which you have taken a strong position. That issue may be gun control, capital punishment, abortion, or a state or local issue that is currently in the news. Research an opposing view of the issue as thoroughly as possible and write a report on that position. When you have finished, evaluate how you now feel about the issue. Does your position remain unchanged? Do you feel even more strongly than before that your position is correct? Or do your feelings remain the same but you now have a clearer understanding of the other side? Include your impressions in your report.

Social Studies Skills
Comparing Similarities and Differences

Look at the political map on page 526. Examine the states on the left half of the map (that is, including Texas, Oklahoma, Kansas, Nebraska, South Dakota, and North Dakota, plus those states to their left.) What is the main similarity among them that you can glean from reading the map, if any?

Now look at the economic map on page 527. Examine the other states on the right side of this map. Is there any way to easily describe their differences or similarities using the information provided on the map? Explain your answer.

Activities and Projects

1. Write a brief description of your state constitution, including its main principles and its history.
2. Think of a state-sponsored program that is important to you. Imagine that funds for the program are going to be cut, and you are a lobbyist who must convince a state legislator to oppose the funding cut for that program. Write a script that spells out your argument as if you were presenting it to the legislator.
3. Prepare a bulletin board display in the form of an organization chart that shows the different members and committees of your state legislature.

CHAPTER 22

Governors and State Administrators

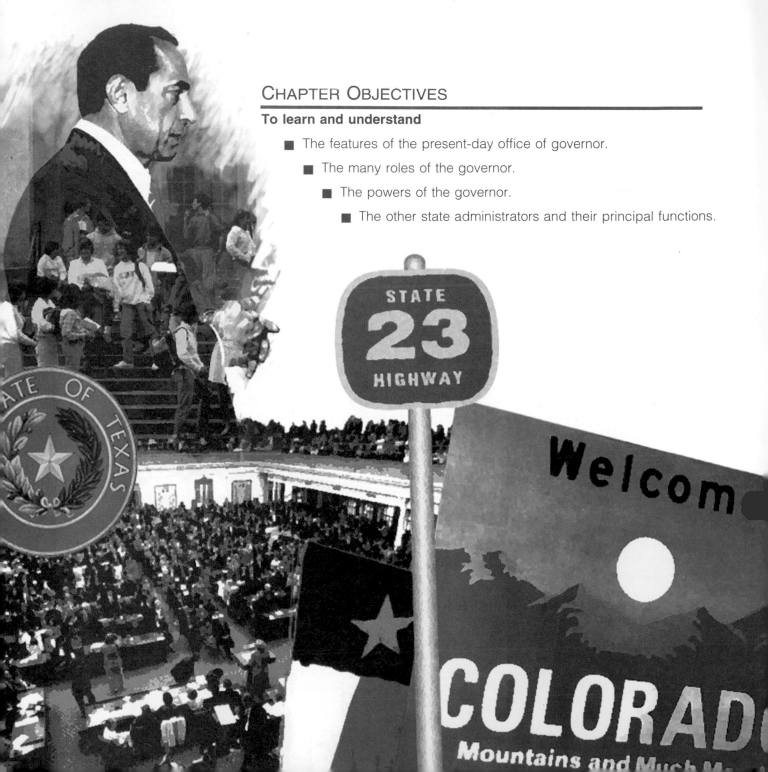

CHAPTER OBJECTIVES

To learn and understand

- The features of the present-day office of governor.

- The many roles of the governor.

- The powers of the governor.

- The other state administrators and their principal functions.

Keynote

"I have nothing but contempt for the kind of governor who is afraid, for whatever reason, to follow the course that he knows is best for the state; and as for the man who sets private friendship above the public welfare—I have no use for him either."

———— **Sophocles**
(495–406 B.C.) Greek Playwright

INTRODUCTION

When the Greek dramatist Sophocles wrote the above statement more than 2000 years ago, he expressed a sentiment that remains with us today. Whoever takes over the governorship of a state must do what is best for that state and seek the highest level of public welfare for its citizens. State governors have not always had the ability to do so, however, as one political observer found out in the 1800s.

In 1831 the French political writer Alexis de Tocqueville was interviewing an American politician. The American told de Tocqueville that "the governor counts for absolutely nothing and is paid only $1,200."[1] Clearly the office of the governor has changed since the 1830s. Indeed, just about every period of social reform in American history is associated with politicians who were governors. The policies of Governor Al Smith of New York helped pave the way for the New Deal that President Franklin D. Roosevelt put into effect during the Great Depression of the 1930s. Governor Terry Sanford of North Carolina became a civil rights moderate in a Southern state during this country's modern civil rights movement. During the 1970s, Governor Jerry Brown of California took stands on consumerism, women's rights, and the environment that made him a symbol of that era.

The governorship often serves as a stepping stone to the U.S. Senate or even to the presidency—former Governor Jimmy Carter of Georgia became president (1977–1981) as did former Governor Ronald Reagan of California (1981–1989). In all, six of our nation's presidents in this century have been former governors.

---

1. As quoted in *State Government* (52), Summer 1979, p. 95.

The reason that the political writer, Alexis de Tocqueville, said that governors counted for absolutely nothing in 1831 was because, at that time, governors were just one of a large number of elected state officials. Most states had been following the tradition of President Andrew Jackson, which held that the more state officials people elected, the more direct and more representative government would be.

But even before Jackson, there was no great love of state governors. The colonists had suffered under the royal governors, and the memories of this experience could be seen in the first state constitutions. No authority was given to the chief state executive. The governor was not even elected by the people. In every state except Massachusetts and New York, the legislature appointed the governor, and then only for a one-year term.

SECTION 1

The Modern Governor

Preview Questions
- What are the formal and informal qualifications for being a governor?
- What is the selection process and length of service for governors?
- How may a governor be removed from office?

Today a governor is the chief executive officer in each of the fifty states. The most populous states have given their governors great control over the state executive branch. Even a few less populated states, such as Alaska and Hawaii, have made provisions for strong governors.

545

Qualifications

The formal qualifications for the governor of most states are simple. He or she has to be an American citizen and has to be of a certain age, usually no younger than 25 or 30. Most states require that the governor has lived in the state for at least five years. Finally, a candidate for governor must be a qualified voter (satisfied the state's age and length of residency requirements).

These formal qualifications for governor do not even exist in Kansas and Ohio. In some states, such as California, Massachusetts, Ohio, and Wisconsin, one can become governor at the age of 18.

Because millions of men and women satisfy the formal requirements to become governor, the *informal* requirements are what truly determine who will be elected. No handbook is available to outline such qualifications, but they certainly include name familiarity, political experience, skill in relating to the media, and voter appeal, in terms of personal demeanor and personality.

To become governor, a person must first win a major party's nomination and then follow through by winning the majority of votes in the general election. The combination of personal characteristics that allows such events to occur can be summed up as the informal qualifications for governor.

The Selection Process

Today every state selects its governor by popular vote. In forty-six states a **plurality** (at least one more vote than that received by any other candidate, which may or may not be a majority of the total vote) is all that is needed for a candidate to be elected. In Arizona, Georgia, and Louisiana, if no candidate obtains a majority of votes (more than 50 percent), there is a run-off election between the two candidates with the most votes. In the absence of a majority in Mississippi, the winner is chosen by the lower chamber of the legislature. Finally, in Vermont in a similar situation the choice is made by both chambers.

Major party candidates are usually nominated in primaries, although conventions are sometimes used. In Washington state, nominees are chosen by caucus and then a primary is used to determine the final candidates.[2]

The Length of Service

Gone are the one-year terms of office that were so popular in the early days of this nation. Forty-seven states now have the governor serve for a minimum of four years. New Hampshire, Rhode Island, Arkansas, and Vermont have two-year terms.

Many states place limits on the number of terms that a governor may serve. Kentucky, New Mexico, and Virginia, for example, essentially prevent a second full term; they allow the governor to serve additional terms, but not consecutively. In twenty-seven states, governors may

---

2. Only three states—Connecticut, Utah, and Virginia—still use the convention method for nominating gubernatorial candidates.

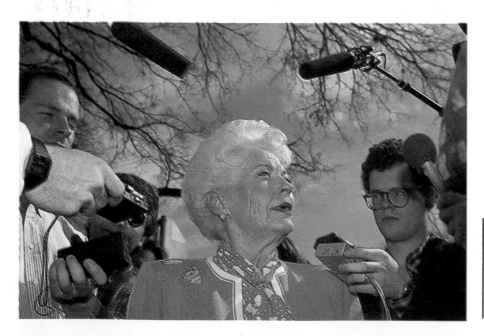

◄ Media skills are an important informal qualification for the office of governor. Here, Governor Ann Richards of Texas is shown speaking with reporters on the campaign trail. Why do you think media skills are so important?

serve two consecutive terms. Nineteen states have a two-term limit. Governors who choose to run for a second term almost always win. The power of incumbency is great at virtually all levels of government.

The all-time record for gubernatorial service is held by Governor George Clinton of New York, who held office from 1777 to 1795 and from 1801 to 1804. He did this by winning seven three-year terms. The modern record goes to Orval Faubus who was governor of Arkansas from 1955 to 1967—six consecutive two-year terms.

In the Event of Death or Removal

The governorship may become vacant because of the death or incapacity of the governor. Also governors may resign in order to take over an important cabinet position at the request of the president, or to become a U.S. senator. Some governors have been removed legally by either impeachment or recall.

Every state's constitution provides for a successor if the governorship becomes vacant. In forty-three states, the second in command—the lieutenant governor—takes over. In a few states, such as Maine, New Hampshire, New Jersey, and West Virginia, the president of the state senate takes over. In three states—Arizona, Oregon, and Wyoming—the state secretary of state becomes governor.

Impeachment As with impeachment proceedings at the national level, removing the governor in this manner usually requires an indictment by the lower chamber, a trial by the upper chamber (in which the senators are the jury members and the state supreme court justices are the judges), and conviction. Often the chief justice of the state supreme court presides at the trial.

Only Oregon does not allow the removal of the governor by impeachment. Impeachment is not impossible, but it is infrequent. Governor Evan Mecham of Arizona was impeached and removed from office in 1988 when he was convicted on criminal charges of campaign finance mishandling and lending $80,000 of state money to his car dealership. (He was later acquitted of felony charges.) In the twentieth century only four other governors have been removed in such a manner.[3]

The Recall About 25 percent of the states provide for removal of the governor by recall. By signing petitions,

▲ Evan Mecham is one of only 5 governors to have been impeached in the 20th century. How does impeachment of the chief executive at the state level compare with impeachment of the president?

voters in these states can require a special election to determine whether or not the governor (or other state officials) can be removed before the term expires. Only one governor—Lynn J. Frazier of North Dakota—has been removed in this manner, in 1921.

The Question of Pay

The annual salaries that are paid to governors range from a low of $35,000 in Arkansas to a high of $130,000 in New York, but a governor's salary is not his or her only compensation.

Governors in all states except Arizona, Massachusetts, Rhode Island, and Vermont are provided with an official residence. Additionally, all governors are given extremely generous expense accounts so that in fact most of their daily expenditures are paid for by state taxpayers.

Dollars and cents, however, are not what lure great Americans to the office of governor. Honor, prestige, and a sense of public duty are what propel some of the nation's greatest leaders into the governorship.

---

3. William Salzer of New York in 1913; James E. Ferguson of Texas in 1917; J. C. Walton of Oklahoma in 1923; and Henry S. Johnston of Oklahoma in 1929.

Like the president, governors spend time performing ceremonial functions. Here Governor Mario Cuomo of New York congratulates five Special Olympics participants. Are a governor's ceremonial functions important?

persuasion, and working through their own political parties.

Power of the Purse   In the early years of this nation, governors had virtually no budgetary powers. In most states today, in contrast, planning and carrying out the budget is a significant responsibility for the governor. Just as the president of the United States prepares an annual budget, so too do many governors prepare annual or biannual budgets. After the governor finishes the budget, it is sent to the legislature for approval.

The governor's budget can be seen as a political plan of action. She or he clearly emphasizes which programs have high priority by the amount of money that is allocated to those programs. Whenever the governor and the majority in the legislature are of different political parties, disputes will often arise about the governor's proposed budget.

Many astute governors can use their budget-making powers to effectively control state administration. Imagine, for example, that a governor is having trouble with the head of the department of public instruction. That department head has been popularly elected and is from the other political party. The governor certainly cannot fire that person, nor can she or he control that person very easily. But, the governor can use the budget-making power of the office to reduce the amount of money going to that department. The "power of the purse" often has profound effects on a department head's attitude.

Once a budget is authorized by the legislature, most governors possess the power to control the pattern of expenditures through executive agencies and departments. Governors often have the power to decide which expenditures will be made in a particular year. A governor may withhold the funding for a particular project if she or he is not satisfied with the way the project is progressing.

Power Over the Militia   The governor is the commander in chief of the armed forces of the state, which used to be called the state militia. Legislation at the close of World War I created the National Guard, which is made up of state units under the control of the governor. Whenever there is a national emergency or a war, the president of the United States can "nationalize" the National Guard and put it under the power of the United States Armed Forces. President Bush did this in August, 1990, in Operation Desert Shield, when Iraq invaded Kuwait.

Except in times of national emergency, the governor commissions officers in the National Guard. He or she can call them out to suppress riots or to help in emergencies such as floods, earthquakes, and natural disasters. The National Guard was called to help when Mount St. Helens erupted in Washington state in 1980, in Alaska when the *Exxon Valdez* oil tanker spilled oil in 1989, during the San Francisco Bay Area earthquake in California in 1989, and again in response to the Los Angeles riots in 1992.

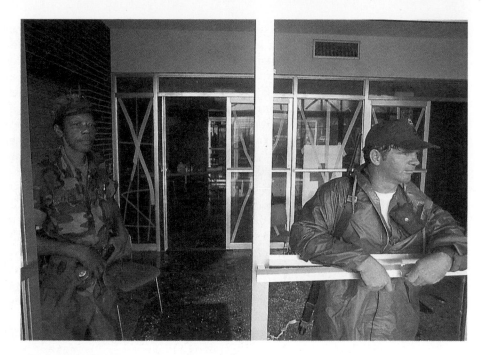

▶ The governor is commander in chief of his or her state's National Guard units. How can this power be superseded by the president?

Most governors delegate military matters to an adjunct general, and place little importance on their role as commander in chief. Sometimes governors have filled the National Guard units with officers selected on a political basis. As long as those selected are trained, no harm is necessarily done, but if they are untrained, some National Guard units may be ineffective during state emergencies.

In some states, the state police report directly to the governor.

Legislative Powers

In the role of chief state legislator, the governor has specific legislative powers that include the ability to call special legislative sessions, the power to veto legislation, and the power to recommend legislation, which you have already read about.

Calling Special Legislative Sessions   In the 1990s a number of governors had to call special sessions to solve large state budget deficit problems. In calling the special legislative sessions, the governors were exercising one of their legislative powers.

Every state gives the governor the power to call a special session of the legislature. This power is usually exclusively held by the governor. In those rare states that allow the legislature to call itself into special session, the power is rarely exercised.

About 50 percent of the states allow the governor to specify the matters that may be taken up by the legislature at the special session. In some states, constitutions do not allow the legislature to consider any other matters except those for which the session was called.

Power to Veto Legislation   The veto power of the president of the United States gives him immense leverage. The simple threat of a presidential veto often means the legislation will not be passed by Congress. The threat of a governor's veto is not necessarily as effective. Every state except North Carolina has given the governor the power to veto legislation. In some states, however, the time after the legislature passes a bill and when the governor must veto it is short. It is three days in Iowa, Minnesota, New Mexico, North Dakota, and Wyoming. In a number of other states it is only six or seven days. If the governor does not veto a measure during the designated period, it normally becomes law.

● **Pocket veto** The president of the United States has a **pocket veto**. If he refuses to sign a bill and Congress adjourns within ten working days after the bill has been submitted, the bill is killed for that session of Congress. In most states the opposite is true—bills that the governor neither signs nor vetoes after the legislature has adjourned become law without her or his signature. Thirteen states do have some form of pocket veto, however.

The time periods are usually longer than the ten days given to the president. In Oklahoma it is a 15-day period; in Florida it is a 15-day period, and in Michigan it is 14 days.

- **Line-item veto** In forty-three states, the governor has some provision for a **line-item veto**, which allows the governor to veto a particular item in a bill with which he or she disagrees, while signing the rest of the bill into law. A bill may therefore be passed with parts of it vetoed by the governor. This power is not available to the president of the United States, although presidential line-item veto has been requested (albeit unsuccessfully) by both President Reagan and President Bush.

In most states, the line-item veto is restricted to items in **appropriation bills**, which determine how much should be spent in various categories. This bill appropriates sums of money to be spent in specific areas of government, such as on public housing and highways. In twelve states the governor can reduce the amount of the appropriation, but not completely. Nineteen states give the governor the ability to use the line-item veto on more than just appropriations.

Line-item vetoes are typically used to reduce extravagant appropriations. They also can be used by a governor who wishes to punish lawmakers who have opposed his or her programs.

No governor has absolute veto power. In all states (except those thirteen in which there is some form of a pocket veto), a governor's veto can be overridden by the legislature, usually with a two-thirds vote of the full membership of each chamber. About 5 percent of all state bills are vetoed by governors. Less than 10 percent of such vetoes are overridden.

Judicial Powers

The governor's judicial powers are usually restricted to **clemency proceedings**, which involve the showing of mercy toward those convicted of a crime. In this area there are three actions that most governors can take: pardons, reprieves, and paroles.

Pardon The governors of the royal colonies also acted as **chancellors**, that is, triers of fact who decided judicial problems on the basis of the concept of fairness rather than specific laws. This role of the royal colonial governor has evolved into the present-day governor's ju-

dicial power to grant pardons. A **pardon** is the release from the penalty for a criminal offense.

Today's busy governors rarely examine more than the most notorious criminal cases. When he or she believes that a conviction is wrong or a penalty too harsh, the governor may grant a full or conditional pardon. Some states require that the governor work with a state pardon board. Others require that a governor's pardon be ratified by a council or by the state senate. Even in states in which the governor has sole pardoning power, there are state advisory pardon boards that investigate the cases and make recommendations.

The record for the highest number of pardons is held by Governor Miriam "Ma" Ferguson of Texas, who during her term from 1925 to 1927 pardoned almost four thousand convicted felons—about five a day!

Similar to the pardon is the governor's power to **commute**, or reduce, the sentence imposed by a court. Governors have commuted many death sentences to the lesser sentence of life imprisonment.

Reprieve A **reprieve** is a postponement of the carrying out of a criminal sentence, and is typically given for a specified short period of time. Criminals sentenced to die can often obtain a governor's reprieve to allow their lawyers more time to appeal their case because, for example, new evidence that may prove their innocence has been discovered. In 1991, for example, Governor L. Douglas

▲ During her term during the 1920s, Governor Miriam Ferguson of Texas pardoned almost 4000 convicted felons. What other judicial powers do most governors have?

BUILDING SOCIAL STUDIES SKILLS

Improving Your Memory

- **Search for the organization of ideas.** Use summaries, headings, and categories to synthesize and group ideas.
- **Learn what you read or hear.** Try to accurately learn and understand the material.
- **Personalize the information.** Try to relate it to something in your life.
- **Quiz yourself.** Recite the material from memory immediately after reading or hearing it, or else simply ask yourself about what you just read or heard.
- **Reinforce learning and remembering.** Use note-taking, discussing with friends, drawing, and reciting out loud to help you remember what you just learned.
- **Study in twenty- to forty-minute intervals.** Take short breaks between study periods. This helps keep comprehension and memory at peak levels.
- **Learn mnemonics.** Special memorizing systems called mnemonics (pronounced ni-'män-iks) can help you memorize long lists. For example, if you needed to memorize a list of the following four states—Florida, Arizona, California, and Texas—you could create your own mnemonic by using the first letters of the states to spell FACT. Just remembering FACT can help you remember the names of those states.

The ability to remember facts, dates, and comments accurately is important for success in school and for success in most careers. It is important to understand that you can improve your memory, much as you can improve any skill. Whether you are speaking, writing, taking a test, or studying, improving your memory is beneficial. The following guidelines can help you remember better:

- **Arouse your interest in the material.** Keep an open mind about the material. You are more likely to forget what you don't agree with. Tell yourself that you will remember what you are learning and feel confident that you will remember.

PRACTICING YOUR SKILLS _____

1. During two successive weekends, watch the same political talk show on TV. During the first week just watch the program the way you normally would. The next day write a paragraph of what the show was about.
2. During the following week's show, use the tips provided above as you watch the show. The next day again write a summarizing paragraph.
3. Compare the two paragraphs. Which is a more accurate representation of the information?

Wilder of Virginia spared the life of Joseph M. Giar-ratano Jr., a Norfolk fisherman convicted and sentenced to death for the murder of a woman and her daughter. Governor Wilder gave Giarratano a chance for a second trial after the United States Supreme Court rejected the convicted murderer's final appeal the previous year.

Parole If a governor believes that a convicted felon has served enough prison time, that governor may request early parole. **Parole** is the release of a prisoner prior to the end of his or her court-determined sentence.

Few governors enjoy exercising their clemency powers. Applications for pardons, reprieves, and paroles are numerous. In recent years, a governor who exercises such powers may be accused of ''being soft on crime.'' This is exactly what happened to Massachusetts Governor Michael Dukakis when he ran for president against George Bush in 1988. Dukakis had allowed some convicted criminals to leave jail on weekends for the purpose of getting work experience. One of them committed murder. In publicity campaigns, Bush exploited the image of Dukakis being too lenient on convicted criminals. It is not surprising that most states have full-time boards or staffs to handle these problems, instead of directly involving the governor in each one of them.

SECTION 3 REVIEW

1. What are the executive powers of the governor?
2. What are the legislative powers of the governor?
3. What are the judicial powers of the governor?
4. **For critical analysis:** What do you think are the advantages and disadvantages of having a governor and lieutenant governor from different political parties?

SECTION 4

Other State Administrators

Preview Questions
* What are the major executive officers found in most states?
* How are these officers selected and what are their primary responsibilities?

The governor in most states shares his or her executive powers with a number of other state administrators.

Only in Maine, New Jersey, and Tennessee is the governor the only popularly elected executive branch officer. It is difficult to accurately list which of the other state officers are the most important. Not only do the powers of each of the other executive officers differ from state to state, but they differ depending upon the administration within each state. One governor may give his or her lieutenant governor many responsibilities; the next may not use the lieutenant governor at all.

The Lieutenant Governor

Forty-three states have a **lieutenant governor**. This is a position similar to the vice president of the United States, although many lieutenant governors have more real power than does the vice president. In only one of those forty-three states is the lieutenant governor not elected by the people. In Tennessee the speaker of the senate is also the lieutenant governor.

As mentioned previously in this chapter, the lieutenant governor normally succeeds the governor whenever he or she dies, is incapacitated, resigns, or is impeached and convicted. In many states, the lieutenant governor presides over the state senate.

▲ Joanell Dyrstad is lieutenant governor for the state of Minnesota. Do all states have a lieutenant governor?

Individuals who seek the position of lieutenant governor often regard it as a stepping stone to the governorship. After all, no one wants to become a career lieutenant governor because of the few responsibilities that the position carries. In thirty-eight states the lieutenant governor is not even a member of the governor's cabinet. The most a lieutenant governor usually can expect to do is to serve on boards and commissions and to take over when the governor is physically absent from the state. In a few states, however, the lieutenant governor does have quite a bit of power. For example, many observers of Texas politics believe that the lieutenant governor and the speaker of the Texas House have more power than does the governor.[4]

The Attorney General

Forty-three states have popularly elected attorney generals. In Alaska, Hawaii, New Hampshire, New Jersey, and Wyoming the governor appoints the attorney general. In Tennessee, the state supreme court makes the appointment, and in Maine the attorney general is appointed by the legislature. The **attorney general** is the legal advisor to the governor, to all other executive officers, and to all legislators. (Occasionally, a state attorney general will give legal advice to local officials.) Each state attorney general acts as the chief state prosecutor in criminal proceedings and as the state defender whenever the state finds itself defending a lawsuit.

Much of the work of a state attorney general involves writing opinions that have to do with the interpretation of the state constitution and of laws passed by the legislature. When the governor's office or legislature asks for a written opinion from the attorney general's office, it may want to know whether its actions are constitutionally legal. The attorney general's opinions often have the force of law unless they are successfully challenged in court.

In the last several decades, some individuals have used the office of the attorney general as a stepping stone to the governorship. They have undertaken widely publicized campaigns against organized crime, big business, organized labor, or consumer fraud in order to impress state political party officials. The publicity these attorney generals obtain often improves their chances of being selected to run in the next gubernatorial election.

▲ In 43 states including Colorado, where Gayle Norton (shown above) is the attorney general, the attorney general is elected. What does an attorney general do?

The Secretary of State

All states except Alaska, Hawaii, and Utah have an office of the secretary of state. In Delaware, Maryland, New Jersey, New York, Oklahoma, Pennsylvania, Texas, and Virginia the governor appoints the secretary of state. In Maine, New Hampshire, and Tennessee the post is filled by the legislature. In the rest of the states, the post is elected by the voters.

The secretary of state's job is mostly routine. He or she is the official custodian of records, the keeper of the "great seal" of the state, and supervisor of all elections. State law guides most of the actions of the secretary of state. He or she can seldom affect policy, but in some states the secretary does have certain policy-making powers. For example, in Illinois the secretary of state has much legislative say in the area of drinking and driving. Additionally, in some states the secretary of state is next in the order of succession if the governor cannot fulfill his or her term of office.

---

4. It is interesting to note that although Warren G. Harding was lieutenant governor of Ohio, he ran unsuccessfully for governor. Nonetheless, he was still elected president of the United States in 1920 by the largest number of popular votes up to that time.

The Treasurer

The office of the treasurer exists in forty-seven states. From this office the financial matters of the government are carried out. In thirty-eight states, the treasurer is popularly elected. In Alaska, Michigan, New Jersey, New York, and Virginia the governor appoints the treasurer. The legislature appoints the treasurer in Maine, Maryland, New Hampshire, and Tennessee. In the remaining three states the duties of the treasurer are taken care of by another department, and the head of that department is appointed by the governor. The state treasurer's main responsibility is to make payments for payrolls and other state expenses. In some states the treasurer also collects taxes.

Many states find themselves with surplus monies during certain times of the year, particularly just after state income taxes are due. The state treasurer's job in this situation is to invest the surplus monies in order to make sure that the state obtains interest on these extra funds. In this capacity, the state treasurer becomes a money manager. He or she usually invests the surplus funds in bonds issued by the federal government and sometimes in bonds issued by local governments and even by private corporations.

The Auditor

Most states have an office of the **auditor**, sometimes called the office of the state **controller**, or the state **comptroller**. Because states' constitutions do not allow the spending of state money without legislative authorization, some state official has to verify that the legislature has actually approved each amount spent. Thus the state auditor possesses the power to authorize those payments that are provided by law. In some cases, the auditor must certify that a state expenditure is legal before the state treasurer can release the funds. In other states, the state auditor must also examine what happens after the expenditures are made. In other words, the state auditor will make sure that the spending was in accord with the law.

The Superintendent of Public Instruction

Every state has a chief school administrator, or a superintendent of public instruction, who oversees all public school instruction. Sometimes this person is known as the commissioner of education, and often shares authority with the state board of education.

558

▲ Every state has a superintendent of public instruction, or chief school administrator, who is responsible for overseeing public schools within the state. Does a superintendent of public instruction have any legislative authority?

The powers of the state head of public education vary dramatically. In some states such as Texas, the office of the superintendent of public instruction has great control over which textbooks are used in the state schools. In other states, there is relatively no control over textbooks. Some of the other powers of the superintendent of public instruction are:

- To implement all education programs instituted by law and the state legislature.
- To propose legislation for education programs.
- To mandate a course of study for public instruction and conduct and supervise state competency testing.
- To coordinate technical assistance to all school districts.
- To enforce and audit all programs in education set by the legislature, such as minimum days and special education requirements.
- To control state-financed programs in higher education.
- To inform the public on the quality of public education in the state, including both weaknesses and strengths.
- To work with the federal government in the area of special education grants.

Other Officers and Agencies

The offices previously discussed are the most significant ones in the state administration. There are hundreds of other offices, however; many were created by state constitutions, others were created by the legislatures. The list below gives a sample of the many state offices that now exist.

- Department of Health
- Department of Natural Resources
- Department of Revenue
- Department of Motor Vehicles
- Department of Consumer Services
- Department of Highway Safety
- Department of Labor and Employment Security
- Department of Professional Regulation

- Department of Water Management
- Department of Transportation
- Board of Prisons and Parole
- Board of Agriculture
- Board of Medical Examiners

SECTION 4 REVIEW _____

1. What are the major executive officers found in most states?
2. How are these officers normally selected?
3. What are the primary duties of these officers?
4. **For critical analysis:** Almost half the states now require that governors and lieutenant governors run for office as a team. Why do you think these states have adopted this requirement? Explain.

CHALLENGE TO THE AMERICAN DREAM

Off-Year Election of Governors

Increasingly, state elected officials, including the governor, are isolating themselves from national politics. This isolation results from electing their governors and other executive officials in off–presidential election years. For example, in 1920, a presidential election year, only twelve states did not have gubernatorial elections. In 1988, also a presidential election year, thirty-six states did not have gubernatorial elections.

The purpose behind this shift has been to weaken the influence of national politics over state politics. For example, if a Democratic candidate is running for governor during a presidential election year when the Democratic candidate for president is obviously going to achieve a landslide victory, the Democratic gubernatorial candidate will have a much better chance of winning. This is called the **coattail effect**. But if the governor's race is

two years later, the presidential election will have little influence.

Some argue that state politics should be isolated from national politics. In a system of federalism, state governments are as important as the federal government. Therefore, state officials should be elected on their own merits, not on the popularity of a presidential candidate.

This is a valid argument, but a major problem with separating gubernatorial elections from presidential elections is less voter participation. On average, only 75 percent of the voters who vote during the presidential election years vote during off–presidential election years.

You Decide

1. Do you think it is more important to have gubernatorial elections isolated from presidential elections at the expense of voter participation, or is it more important to increase voter participation in state elections by having the governor and the president elected during the same year? Explain your answer.
2. Why would citizens voting at the state level be influenced by who is running for president?

CHAPTER 22 REVIEW

Key Terms

appropriation bills 554
attorney general 557
auditor 558
coattail effect 559
chancellors 554

clemency
 proceedings 554
commute 554
comptroller
 controller 558

lieutenant
 governor 556
line-item veto 554
pardon 554
parole 556

plurality 546
pocket veto 553
reprieve 554

Summary

1. The governor is the chief executive officer in each of the fifty states. Most states have given their governors a great deal of control. Every state selects its governor by popular vote. Most governors serve four-year terms, while a few still serve two-year terms. In forty-three states, succession falls first to the lieutenant governor, in four states to the president of the senate, and in three to the secretary of state. The governor may be removed by impeachment in every state but Oregon and by recall in about 25 percent of the states.

2. A governor's roles in office include that of chief executive, chief legislator and policymaker, chief political party leader, and chief spokesperson.

3. In most states, executive power is shared among several officers. Important executive powers of the governor include appointing and removing officials, administering laws, planning and carrying out the budget, and commanding the National Guard. The specific legislative powers of the governor include the ability to call special legislative sessions, the power to veto legislation, and the power to recommend legislation. The governor's judicial powers are restricted to those of clemency proceedings.

4. There are several other major executive offices in every state. The leaders of these offices are usually popularly elected. They include the lieutenant governor, attorney general, secretary of state, treasurer, auditor, and superintendent of public instruction.

Review Questions

1. How do governors assume their office?
2. What is the normal length of term for a governor?

3. In most states, who succeeds the governor if he or she dies or cannot fulfill his or her term of office?
4. What is the difference between impeachment and recall?
5. Briefly describe each of the roles performed by a governor.
6. What are the governor's executive powers?
7. Why are the governor's powers of appointment and removal important?
8. Briefly describe the legislative and judicial powers of the governor.
9. What other major executive offices are found in most states today?
10. If you believe that a traffic ticket was improperly given to you, what should you do?
11. Why have most states chosen to hold gubernatorial elections during years when there is no presidential election?

Questions for Thought and Discussion

1. The governorship is considered by many to be an excellent preparation for the presidency. In what ways do you think it would prepare someone for the presidency? In what ways do you think it would not?
2. What are the advantages and disadvantages of the line-item veto? Do you think the president should have this power? Why or why not?
3. What formal qualifications must a candidate meet to run for governor in your state? What additional qualifications would you recommend?
4. What are the possible advantages of having the governor and lieutenant governor be from different parties? What are the disadvantages?

CHAPTER 22 REVIEW—Continued

Improving Your Skills
Communication Skills
Using an Almanac
Knowing where to look for information can save you hours of searching. If you are looking for up-to-date information about people, places, or events that is contained in a single volume, an almanac is often a good place to start.

An almanac is published yearly, and contains facts about states, towns, counties, cities, government agencies, population, major events, and many other subjects. There are also specialized almanacs such as state almanacs or almanacs of statistics.

Writing
Using an almanac, find out the following information about your state government and write a brief report:

1. The names of the governor and lieutenant governor.
2. When the state constitution was ratified.
3. The number of years in the governor's term.
4. The annual salary of the governor.
5. The number of members in the upper legislative house.
6. The number of members in the lower legislative house.
7. The salaries of your state legislators.
8. The number of members on the state supreme court.
9. The annual salaries of the state supreme court justices.

Social Studies Skills
Decision Making and Predicting the Consequences of Decisions
Policymakers, government officials, and indeed all types of bureaucrats must make decisions, the consequences of which may be important for many individuals. At the national level, decision makers must decide issues with consequences that might affect millions of people in many countries. Before you can make proper decisions yourself, you should be aware of the steps in decision making:

1. Define what you need or want or must do.
2. Examine all of the resources you have available to help you make the decision.
3. Identify the choices you actually have.
4. Gather as much information as you can effectively use.
5. Evaluate and compare your decision options.
6. Make your decision.

Evaluation of the consequences of your own decisions is often quite easy. If you choose to study more for one course than for another, you'll be able to see if the extra studying pays off. But policymakers in government can not so easily determine the consequences of many of their decisions. In the following examples, write down how you would evaluate the consequences of the following decisions:

1. The U.S. Postal Service decides to raise the price of sending a first-class letter by 50 percent.
2. The governor of your state asks the state legislature to cut 15 percent of all state spending by next year.
3. The lieutenant governor starts publicly criticizing the governor.

Activities and Projects

1. From a reference book in your library that deals with your state government, find an organizational chart and a budget chart for your state. Determine from the chart and your readings which agencies and commissions overlap in their responsibilities.
2. Write to a current or former state executive asking for a response to a question on a current issue. Report the executive's response back to the class.
3. Interview a current or former executive in your state. Find out about his or her office and experiences. Report on the interview for the class.
4. Prepare an organizational chart of your state's elected officials. Describe their terms, responsibilities, and relationships to each other.
5. Prepare a biography of your governor that tells his or her life history, political background, and accomplishments in office.

CHAPTER 23

The State Courts

CHAPTER OBJECTIVES

To learn and understand

- The organization of state court systems.

- The various methods by which judges are selected.

- The ways in which state criminal laws are passed and enforced.

- The prosecution and sentencing of those charged with and convicted of crimes.

Keynote

"Justice, I think, is the tolerable accommodation of the conflicting interests of society".

——— **Learned Hand**
(1872–1961) American Jurist

INTRODUCTION

Judge Learned Hand talked about justice in this chapter's opening quote. He realized that the people in any society will have conflicts with each other. They will then seek justice. Justice is dispensed in the court system that has existed since the beginning of this country.

In Chapter 18 you learned about the federal court system. The overwhelming majority of judicial disputes, however, are settled in state courts. There are fifty state court systems, none of which is exactly like another. All have the same purpose, however: to decide disputes between individuals, or between individuals and government, or to determine the guilt or innocence of those accused of committing a crime.

SECTION 1

A Typical State Court System

Preview Questions
- How are state court systems organized?
- What are the different types of state courts?
- What types of cases does each one hear?

Every state has a different court system, but most systems are organized around three levels of courts. Any person who is involved in a lawsuit typically has the opportunity to plead the case before a **trial court**. That is the first level. If that person loses the case, he or she usually has the opportunity to appeal the decision to two other levels of courts, called **appellate courts** (also called **review courts**). Appellate courts only listen to cases and reconsider decisions of trial courts. In most states a case proceeds first through a trial court with an automatic right to review by the state's appellate court;

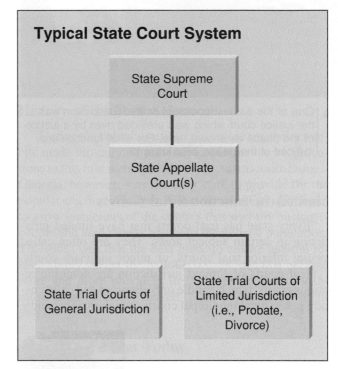

▲ **FIGURE 23–1 Typical State Court System.** As you can see from the organizational chart above, a typical state court system is similar to the federal court system discussed in chapter 18. What is meant by the term *jurisdiction* as it is used in this figure?

then, if necessary, the case goes to the state's highest review court.

Figure 23–1 above shows the three tiers of a typical state court system.

Each court has certain powers of **jurisdiction**, which, if you remember from Chapter 18, means that each court has a certain amount of power to decide cases. Courts with **limited jurisdiction** can only hear particular types of cases; courts with **general jurisdiction** can hear virtually all cases.

563

CITIZENSHIP SKILLS AND RESPONSIBILITIES

The Small Claims Court

Someday you may think you were cheated by your former landlord because you didn't get your security deposit returned when you moved out. Or perhaps a dry cleaner may ruin your best clothes and not want to pay you for the damages. Or someone may owe you money and refuse to repay you. Rather than paying for a lawyer, you may be able to take advantage of a small claims court to remedy these situations. In most states today you have the right to use the services of small claims courts when the amount in dispute is less than $5,000.

How These Courts Work

The first thing you do is ask the clerk of the small claims court in your area whether the court can handle your case. Make sure that the court has jurisdiction over the person or business you wish to sue, and that you have the correct business name and address of the company or individual being sued. Usually, the defendant must live, work, or do business within the area of the court's jurisdiction.

Remember that courts often require strict accuracy; if you cannot provide exact information, the suit will be thrown out. Also, the small claims court is not a collection agency. If you are filing suit against a firm that no longer is in business, you may have a very difficult time collecting.

While you are at the courthouse, it might prove helpful to sit in on a few proceedings. This will give you an idea of what to expect when your day in court arrives.

Once you file suit, a summons goes out to the defending party. When a company receives the summons, it may decide to resolve the issue out of court. About one-fourth of all cases for which summonses are issued are settled out of court.

Preparing for Trial

When you attend the trial, you should have on hand all necessary and pertinent receipts, canceled checks, written estimates, contracts, and any other form of documented evidence that you can show the judge. Explain the entire story in chronological order (the order in which events occurred) with supporting evidence to show the judge exactly what happened. Make sure that your dates are accurate (remember that inaccuracies can discredit your case). Also, make sure you have a copy of your "demand letter," which should be no more than two double-spaced, typewritten pages, and should clearly summarize both the facts of the case and your demands of the other party. It is important that you hand this letter to the judge on trial day. It will not only present your version of the story, but also will demonstrate that you are taking a reasonable approach to the situation.

What Happens in Court

The judge generally will let you present your case in simple language without the help of a lawyer. In fact, in some states neither the plaintiff nor the defendant is allowed to have a lawyer present. You may receive the judge's decision immediately or by notice within a few weeks.

If your opponent tries to settle the case out of court, make sure his or her proposed offer is written down so that it can be upheld if the offer is withdrawn. You should sign these written documents and file them with the court so that the agreement can be legally enforced. It is best to have your opponent appear with you before the judge to outline the settlement terms. Generally, if you win or if you settle out of court, you should be able to get your opponent to pay for the court costs, which vary greatly depending on the state.

The table on the following page provides information on small claims courts.

TAKING ACTION

1. Go to your local small claims court and obtain the necessary forms for filing suit.
2. Listen to at least one small claims court proceeding and answer the following questions:

   ● How much money was sought for damages?
   ● Was the judge understanding of the plaintiff's problems? Was the judge understanding of the defendant's position?
   ● Did you agree with the judge's rulings?

Characteristics of Small Claims Courts in Selected States

State	Maximum Amount of Suit	Lawyers Allowed?	Who Can Appeal? Plaintiff	Defendant	Initial Cost*
Alabama	$5,000	yes	yes	yes	$0–$1,000, $26; $1,001–$5,000, $44
Arizona	$1,000	no	yes	yes	$3
California	$2,000	no	no	yes	$6
Colorado	$2,000	no	yes	yes	$17
Connecticut	$1,500	yes	no	no	$20
District of Columbia	$2,000	yes	yes	yes	$1 + serving fee
Florida	$2,500	yes	yes	yes	$0–$100,$41; $101–$2,500, $50
Georgia	$3,000	yes	yes	yes	$0–$300, $38; $301–$3,000, $38
Illinois	$15,000	no	yes	yes	$0–$250, $20; $251–$500, $30; $501–$2,500, $40; $2,501–$15,000, $85
Indiana	$3,000	yes	yes	yes	$29
Iowa	$2,000	yes	yes	yes	$17 + serving fees
Kansas	$1,000	no	yes	yes	$0–$500, $10; $501–$1,000, $30
Kentucky	$1,500	yes	yes	yes	$22.85
Louisiana	$2,000	yes	no	no	$43.50
Maine	$1,400	yes	yes	yes	$20 per defendant
Maryland	$2,500	yes	yes	yes	$5 + serving fee
Massachusetts	$1,500	yes	no	yes	$0–$500, $16.25; $500–$1,500, $21.25
Michigan	$1,500	no	no	no	$0–$600, $10 + serving fee; $601–$1,500, $20 + serving fee
Minnesota	$2,000	yes	yes	yes	$500–$999.99, $19 + recording fee of $15; $1,000–$2,000, $24 + recording fee of $15
Mississippi	$1,000	yes	yes	yes	1 party, $32; 2 parties, $40
Missouri	$1,000	yes	yes	yes	$0–$99.99, $5 + fees; $100–$1,000, $10 + serving fees
New Jersey	$1,000	yes	yes	yes	$4.10
New York	$2,000	yes	judge; yes arbitrator, no	yes no	$19
North Carolina	$1,500	yes	yes	yes	$19 + serving fees
Ohio	$1,000	yes	yes	yes	$17
Oklahoma	$1,500	yes	yes	yes	$37 + serving fees
Pennsylvania	$5,000	yes	yes	yes	$1–$500, $16, $501–$2,000, $22; $2,001–$5,000, $42
South Carolina	$1,000	yes	yes	yes	$30
Tennessee	$10,000	yes	yes	yes	$42.75
Texas	$5,000	yes	yes	yes	$45
Virginia	$7,000	yes	yes	yes	$12
Wisconsin	$1,000	yes	yes	yes	$18 + serving fees
Wyoming	$750	yes	yes	yes	$13

*In some states, the initial cost will vary, depending on the amount of the claim. In Alabama, for example, if the claim in dispute is between $0 and $1,000, the initial cost (for filing fees, etc.) will be $26; if the claim is between $1,000 and $5,000, the initial cost will be $44.

Popular Election—Pros and Cons

Over three-fourths of all judges sitting in state and municipal courts today are popularly elected. In Alabama, Michigan, Mississippi, Oregon, Texas, Washington, and Wisconsin, for example, all judges are popularly elected, except for municipal court judges, who are usually appointed by their respective city councils.

The Pros Advocates of popular election claim that these judges are just as competent as those chosen by any other method. Presumably, elected judges also make decisions that are more in line with popular desires and interests than appointed judges. Finally, the popular election of judges prevents governors or the dominant party in the legislature from building up a ''party machine'' by rewarding loyal followers with judgeships.

The Cons Those who oppose the popular election of judges in partisan races point out that political bosses and party machines control the nominations and elections. Virtually the only way for a judge to be truly popularly elected is for that person to be a political activist and a strong partisan; otherwise, he or she will not get the endorsement of the local party. During the heat of an election, voters may not give sufficient consideration to the legal expertise of a particular judicial candidate. Additionally, highly qualified individuals who find playing politics distasteful may never seek a judicial office. Finally, elected judges may make decisions with an eye to reelection rather than on the merits of each case.

As the debate goes on, what is sure is that all moves to abandon the current system of popular election have failed. Political party organizations, state bar associations, lawyers' groups, and special interest groups have all vigorously supported the popular election of judges. For political parties, such elections offer an opportunity to reward faithful party loyalists. For special interest groups, they offer an opportunity to influence election results through campaign contributions. State bar associations and other lawyers' groups support popular elections because they can attempt to control elections by controlling candidate nominations.

The Missouri Plan—An Alternative?

Is it possible to combine the appointment and election processes to select judges? Yes, say the American Bar Association and the President's Commission on Law Enforcement and Administration of Justice. The American Bar Association recommends that judges (other than magistrates) be nominated by a special judicial nominating committee and appointed by the governor. Once this is done, appointees are approved or rejected at a general election after serving an initial term of three years and subsequent terms every ten years.

◄ In New Hampshire, the governor appoints all judges including those for the supreme court. This is an example of gubernatorial appointment powers. What are the two other major methods of selection for state judges?

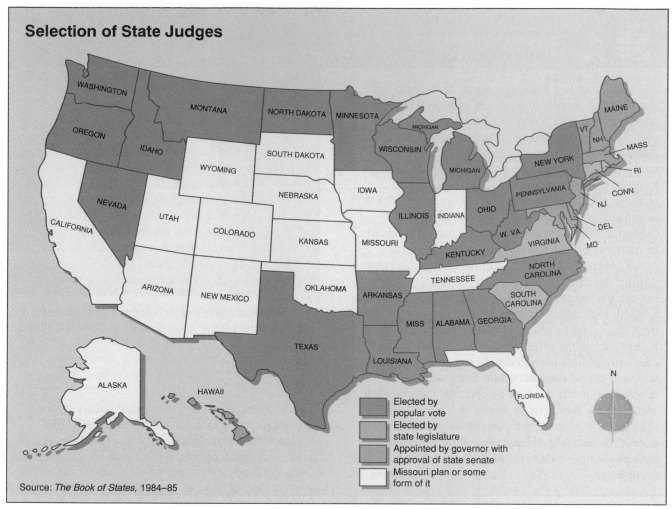

Selection of State Judges

Legend:
- Elected by popular vote
- Elected by state legislature
- Appointed by governor with approval of state senate
- Missouri plan or some form of it

Source: *The Book of States,* 1984–85

▲ **FIGURE 23–2 Selection of State Judges.** By looking at the map above, you can see which method for the selection of state judges is used in your state. Which of the methods shown on the map is recommended by the American Bar Association and the President's Commission on Law Enforcement and Administration of Justice?

This plan has been offered for over seventy years by the American Bar Association. A version of the plan was used in California in 1934. Missouri has followed the plan since adopting its new constitution in 1947. It has therefore been labeled the **Missouri Plan.**

In Missouri the governor appoints all seven justices of the state's supreme court, and the thirty-two judges of the state court of appeals.[2] Certain other trial court judges, such as those sitting in the Kansas City metropolitan area, are also appointed. The governor is required to make these appointments from a list of names rec-

ommended by a judicial nominating commission made up of members of the state bar association, private citizens, and at least one sitting judge.[3]

After the appointed jurist is in office at least one year, she or he must have her or his name appear on the next general election ballot. The voters decide whether or not the judge should be kept. If the voters say yea, the judge serves a regular term and then seeks further terms in later general elections. If the voters say nay, the governor makes a new appointment in the same manner as before.

---

2. Often the term *judge* is used to refer to those who preside over trial courts and the term *justice* for those who preside over appellate courts.

3. The term *sitting* judge distinguishes judges who are currently active in the judicial system, as opposed to those who are not. Most retired judges retain their title as judge for the rest of their lives even though they are not sitting judges.

CHAPTER 23 REVIEW—Continued

Summary

1. Every state has a different court system, but most systems are organized around three levels of courts: the trial courts of general and limited jurisdiction, the courts of appeals, and the supreme court. Limited jurisdiction means that courts can hear only certain types of cases. General jurisdiction means that courts can hear virtually all cases. Every state has at least one court of review, or appellate court.

2. State judges are selected by the governor, by the legislature, or by the people. The Missouri Plan is a selection process that combines the processes of executive appointment and popular election. Judges are normally elected for a fixed term. During their terms in office, judges may be impeached and, if convicted, removed from office.

3. Crimes are defined by state statutes, which are laws enacted by state legislatures. A number of legislatures have introduced mandatory sentencing, which fixes sentencing for certain crimes. Some states provide for victim compensation. Most criminal laws are enforced by municipal police departments. All states except Hawaii have a state police system.

4. Every state has an attorney general who presides over some type of department of justice. The prosecution of criminal suspects is normally handled by a local prosecuting attorney. Typically, criminal proceedings begin with arrest, followed by indictment, arraignment, and a trial.

5. Most criminal cases are settled by a plea bargaining arrangement in which the defendant agrees to plead guilty, usually to a lesser charge than the prosecutor originally brought. A sentence is the penalty imposed on anyone convicted of a crime. Probation is an alternative to a jail sentence, which involves subjecting the violator to certain rules and placing him or her under the supervision of a probation officer. Parole occurs when prisoners are allowed to leave prison before the end of their prison sentence and are placed under supervision.

Review Questions

1. What are the three tiers of the state court system?
2. What is meant by limited jurisdiction?
3. What is meant by general jurisdiction?
4. What are the methods by which judges are selected?
5. What are the arguments for and against the popular election of judges?
6. Briefly describe the Missouri Plan.
7. What is mandatory sentencing?
8. What are victim compensation laws?
9. What is the job of a prosecuting attorney?
10. Briefly describe the steps in a typical criminal proceeding.
11. What is plea bargaining? Why is it used so often?
12. What types of sentences can be imposed on those convicted of crimes?
13. What is the difference between probation and parole?
14. Who may use a small claims court and for what purpose?
15. What are the arguments for and against capital punishment?

Questions for Thought and Discussion

1. Do you think plea bargaining is a good way to remedy the problem of crowded courts and prisons? Why or why not?
2. Why is the right to appeal a case important?
3. Should appeals be restricted? If so, to what extent?
4. How are judges selected in your state? How do you think judges should be selected in your state?
5. What qualifications do you think are important in a state judge?
6. Should criminals be given alternatives to prison sentences? If so, what type of criminals should be offered this and what should the alternatives be?

Improving Your Skills
Communication Skills

Determining the Reliability of Information

Learning to judge the reliability of information is important to your lifelong learning, both in school and out. Information that is reliable is clear and accurate. When trying to assess the reliability of written or spoken information, ask yourself the following questions:

CHAPTER 23 REVIEW—Continued

- What is the background or qualifications of the person presenting the information? Is he or she an expert in a particular area?
- What are the biases or value judgments of the writer or speaker?
- Is the information based on primary or secondary sources?
- Which fallacies, if any, are present in the line of reasoning?
- Is the person confusing correlation ` with causation?
- What evidence is presented to support the argument? Are there alternative explanations that are being ignored? Is the information oversimplified?

Writing

Read the following excerpted article and answer each of the above questions when possible.

Energy Piracy
Forbes, October 14, 1991 p. 235.

Energy markets have been relatively trouble-free since President Reagan decontrolled oil prices in 1981, letting markets work their magic. But trouble looms as hungry lobbyists circle around a fat new package of energy pork, which is thinly justified by the quaint notion that energy is the one industry best left to Soviet-style Central planning.

The federal government is contemplating requiring Detroit to produce more electric cars, ostensibly to help the "greenhouse effect." But electric cars require electric power plants, which already account for one-third of all hydrocarbon emissions, while cars account for only one-fourth. And those costly car batteries end up as tons of toxic waste. The principal beneficiaries of a forced switch to electric cars would be the electric utility lobby.

Proponents of a federal energy policy also argue that we need to reduce our vulnerability to a disturbance in world oil supplies. But it is impossible to escape global shocks to world trade, whether a country imports oil or not. In both 1980 and 1990, Britain, which is self-sufficient in oil, sank into deep recession; Japan, which imports virtually all nonnuclear power, was unscathed.

There is no more justification for central planning in the energy market than there is in the copper market. World oil reserves are larger than ever, and

vast areas of the globe may soon open to exploration. In a world of rapidly improving technology, the worst thing we could do would be to stifle innovation and flexibility with rigid rules, and their inevitable political favoritism.

So, next time someone tells you that this country badly needs a federally supported and mandated energy policy, ask him or her: Who would be the real beneficiary?

Source: © *Forbes,* October 14, 1991 p. 235. Reprinted with permission.

Social Studies Skills

Working with Flow Charts

Look at the flow chart on page 573.

1. What process is being depicted?
2. What are the three immediate possibilities that exist after the intake screening?
3. What can happen to the arrested minor just prior to adjudication (i.e., prior to going before a juvenile court judge for a hearing, judgment, and sentencing)?

Activities and Projects

1. Research the state prisons in your state to find out about problems such as poor facilities, overcrowding, or lack of funds. Devise a plan that would solve these problems. Write a letter to the governor that tells how you see the problems and offers your proposed solutions.
2. Interview a prosecutor, judge, or defense attorney about the court system in your state. Find out about how the courts are organized and the kinds of cases each court handles. Report the results of the interview back to the class.
3. Prepare a bulletin board display of the state court system in your state.
4. Stage a debate on one of the following statements: (1) Capital punishment should be abolished. (2) Poverty causes crime. (3) Gun control laws would reduce crime. (4) Prisons should be dehumanizing. (5) Crime victims should participate in sentencing.
5. Interview a state or local police officer to find out what he or she thinks is the most pressing criminal problem today and how the problem could be solved. Present your findings to the class.

CHAPTER 24

Local Government

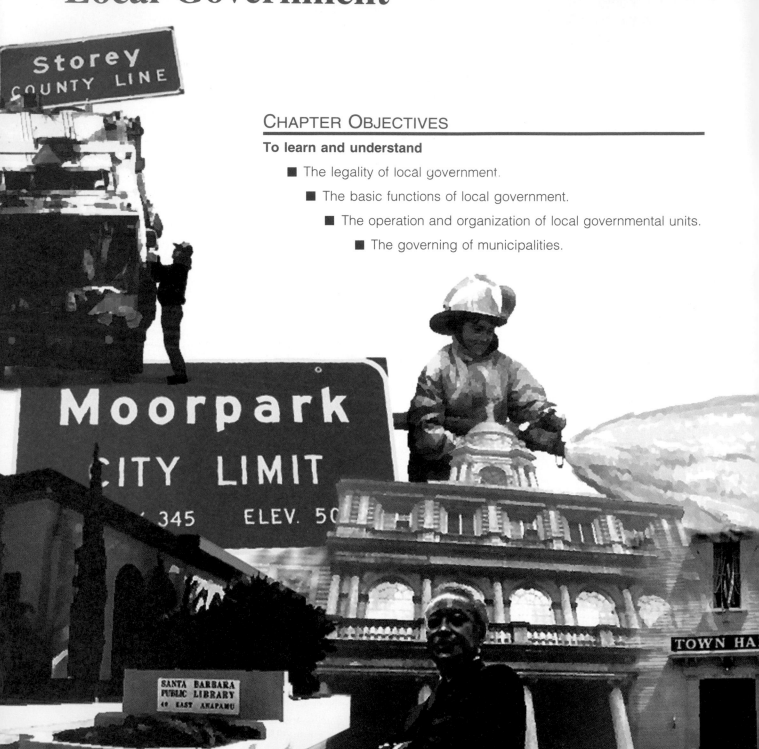

CHAPTER OBJECTIVES

To learn and understand

- ■ The legality of local government.
- ■ The basic functions of local government.
- ■ The operation and organization of local governmental units.
- ■ The governing of municipalities.

Keynote

"That is the best government which desires to make the people happy, and knows how to make them happy."

—— Lord Thomas Babington Macaulay (1800–1859) English Historian and Politician

INTRODUCTION

According to the English historian Lord Macaulay in the opening quote, the best governments are ones that work to make the people happy. For most individuals, the best government is the government closest to home, which is their local government.

Some of the oldest governments in our country are local governments. Long before the states were formed, cities and towns provided government services to their residents. Then, after each state adopted its own constitution, certain powers and responsibilities were formally granted to local government units.

For most individuals, local governments play a personal role in the American political system. Local governments provide water, sewage, garbage collection, and police and fire protection services to residents in cities, towns, and rural areas. For this reason, many people have contact with local governments on a continual basis.

SECTION 1

The Legality and Functions of Local Government

Preview Questions
- What is the relationship between state and local governments?
- What are the major functions of local government?
- What is the largest expense for most local governments?

The U.S. Constitution does not mention local governments. Thus, states have full authority in establishing local governments and in defining their powers and responsibilities. Consequently, every local government is a creation of its parent state. The state can create a local government and the state can terminate the right of a local government to exist. Indeed, states have often abolished entire counties, school districts, cities, and special districts. Since World War II, almost 20,000 school districts have gone out of existence or were consolidated with other school districts.

Dillon's Rule

Because local governments are legal creations of the state, for many years it seemed that the state government could dictate everything the local governments did. The narrowest possible view of the legal status of local governments follows **Dillon's rule**, outlined by John F. Dillon in his *Commentaries on the Law of Municipal Corporations* in 1811. He stated that municipal corporations—called **municipalities**—possess only those powers that the states expressly grant to them. Cities governed under Dillon's rule have thus been dominated by the state legislature. Those cities wishing to obtain the status of a municipal corporation have simply petitioned the state legislature for a charter, which typically has been extremely narrow. That is, the city has limited powers to tax and make laws.

The Home-Rule Movement

In a revolt against state legislative power over municipalities, the home-rule movement began. The movement was based on **Cooley's rule**, derived from an 1871 decision (*People* v. *Hurlbut*) by Michigan Judge Thomas Cooley, who stated that cities should be able to rule from home, or to govern themselves. Since 1900, about four-

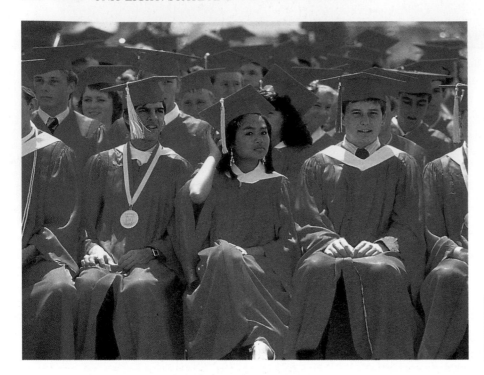

◄
Education is the single largest expense of most local governments. Who provides the funding for public education?

fifths of all states have allowed **municipal home rule**, but only on issues in which no state interests are involved.

A municipality must choose to become a **home-rule city**; otherwise, it operates as a **general-law city**. In the latter case, the state passes certain general laws relating to cities of different sizes, which are designated as first-class cities, second-class cities, or towns. Once a city, by virtue of its population, receives such a ranking, it follows the general law put down by the state for that city size. Only if it chooses to be a home-rule city can it avoid such state government restrictions. In most states, only cities with populations of 2,500 or more can choose home rule.

Take a ride through your local community. As you look around, think about how much of what you see is provided by your local government. You will pass schools, police cars, fire stations, libraries, parks, golf courses, parking lots, sports arenas, garbage trucks, hospitals, and other facilities that are maintained and operated by your city. The services that cities and counties provide are so extensive that it is difficult to catalog all of them.

Education

Schools are one service provided by local government with which you've probably become quite familiar. Education is the single largest expense of most local governments. About 45 percent of local government budgets goes toward funding for public schools.[1]

You've probably heard people in your community talking about problems or issues in the schools. Maybe you even have some concerns and opinions of your own about how your local government runs the school system. Many local citizens are concerned about public schools because the schools affect the whole community. The school system is responsible for educating young people who will one day work in the community and become its leaders. Usually, state and federal taxes pay some educational costs, but local taxpayers often provide most of the money and make the key decisions regarding the operation of the public schools.

Police and Fire Protection

Police protection is the second largest expense of most American cities, and fire protection is third. Most local communities are very concerned about how crime is being controlled by the local police force. Local governments must decide how many police officers a community needs, how these officers will be armed, and which areas they will patrol.

---

1. Education is becoming more of a state issue, however, given that states on average now expend about 25 percent of their budgets on elementary and secondary education expenditures.

Fire protection varies with the size of the community. If you live in a small town, your fire department may be staffed by volunteers. If you live in a large city, your fire department is probably staffed by full-time professionals.

Public Welfare

Although federal and state governments pay part of the cost of public welfare, the share that local governments pay continues to rise. Public welfare includes payments to the poor and needy. For the big cities, public welfare is one of the largest expenditures. New York City, for example, has 4 percent of the nation's population but 17 percent of the nation's low-income population, which means that more people in New York City need assistance than in other parts of the country.

One obstacle to local government funding of public-welfare programs is that city expenditures are growing faster than revenues, which means that the cities are spending more money than they take in. Cities are finding that they have more needy to take care of at ever higher costs.

City Planning and Zoning

Without planning, cities would probably develop haphazardly. Potential results could be industrial plants built downtown, railroads running through the heart of a city, skyscrapers shutting out sunlight on narrow streets, main roads built too far apart or too close together, and public buildings inaccessible to those who need them. Maybe you live in a city, or have visited one, that seems disorganized, run-down, or in which it is impossible to find your way around. For these reasons, most cities have seen the need to create order out of random growth, and have established planning agencies or commissions to plan how cities will grow.

Washington, D.C., is one of the few cities that began as and has remained a planned city. In 1790 Congress decided to build the nation's capital along the Potomac River. President Washington assigned the job of laying out the city to a French engineer named Major Pierre-Charles L'Enfant (1754–1825). He designed the city in a grid with streets running east to west named according to the alphabet, and streets running north to south named by number. He also planned for wide streets, scenic parks, graceful turning circles, and large areas to be reserved for public buildings. At first, both L'Enfant and his plan were dismissed as being too extravagant, but later his original plan was restudied and has been followed fairly closely through the years. Today, the National Capital Planning Commission guides the development of our nation's capital city.

In certain areas of almost any community there are only residential houses of a particular kind or areas that are only retail stores. Signs and billboards are normally only in certain areas and are similar in size. These aspects

▶ The cost of fire protection is the third largest expense for most American cities. What is the second largest expense?

Washington, D.C., The Nation's Capital

▲ **FIGURE 24–1 Map of Washington, D.C.** Washington, D.C. was planned by a French engineer named Major Pierre-Charles L'Enfant, who designed the city in a grid with streets running east to west named according to the alphabet and streets running north to south named by number. Washington, D.C. remains a planned city. Who guides the development of Washington, D.C. today?

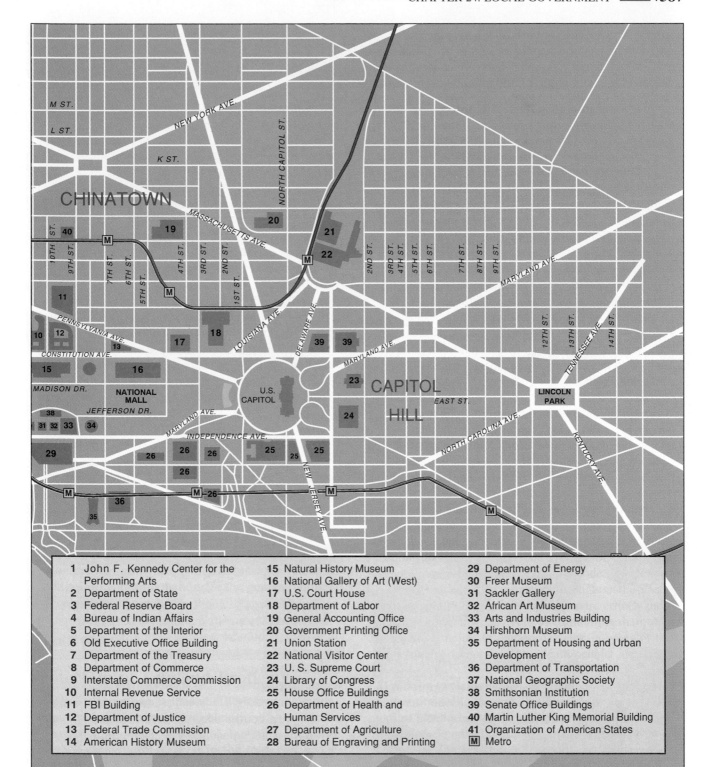

1 John F. Kennedy Center for the Performing Arts	**15** Natural History Museum	**29** Department of Energy
2 Department of State	**16** National Gallery of Art (West)	**30** Freer Museum
3 Federal Reserve Board	**17** U.S. Court House	**31** Sackler Gallery
4 Bureau of Indian Affairs	**18** Department of Labor	**32** African Art Museum
5 Department of the Interior	**19** General Accounting Office	**33** Arts and Industries Building
6 Old Executive Office Building	**20** Government Printing Office	**34** Hirshhorn Museum
7 Department of the Treasury	**21** Union Station	**35** Department of Housing and Urban Development
8 Department of Commerce	**22** National Visitor Center	**36** Department of Transportation
9 Interstate Commerce Commission	**23** U. S. Supreme Court	**37** National Geographic Society
10 Internal Revenue Service	**24** Library of Congress	**38** Smithsonian Institution
11 FBI Building	**25** House Office Buildings	**39** Senate Office Buildings
12 Department of Justice	**26** Department of Health and Human Services	**40** Martin Luther King Memorial Building
13 Federal Trade Commission	**27** Department of Agriculture	**41** Organization of American States
14 American History Museum	**28** Bureau of Engraving and Printing	Ⓜ Metro

CITIZENSHIP SKILLS AND RESPONSIBILITIES
Recycling in Your Community

We are fast becoming a nation of city dwellers. As people move to the cities, they bring their garbage with them. The amount of waste generated by U.S. residences and businesses increased by two and a half times between 1960 and 1992, from about 82 million tons to over 200 million tons. This places a demanding and costly burden on city and town governments.

Most cities have chosen to bury or burn their garbage, but landfill space is becoming more expensive, and rising costs are straining municipal budgets. While most Americans believe that proper waste disposal is crucial to a clean, safe environment, many people have a "not-in-my-backyard" attitude about dealing with waste. They do not want landfills near their homes because they worry about odors, contamination of water and soil, rodents, and other environmental problems.

One option that local governments have turned to is recycling—the re-processing of waste—such as newspapers, aluminum, and glass, into usable materials. Some experts believe that recycling could reduce the amount of our nation's trash by at least 30 percent.

One good way of promoting recycling in your community is by starting a "curbside recycling" program. In Marin County, California, a woman ral-

lied volunteers in her community, met with local garbage collectors, and started a curbside program. As a result of her efforts, Gloria Duncan began a program in which homeowners set out buckets of sorted recyclable material along with the garbage.

If you want to start a recycling program in your areas, here are some guidelines that Duncan used:

1. **Find your allies.** You will need to look for volunteers and experts in your community who are willing to help you in your efforts. These people could include municipal waste disposal administrators, environmentalists, business people, senior citizens, and legal professionals.
2. **Let the media know.** Contact newspapers, radio stations, television stations, and city magazines. Be sure the public knows your concerns and what you are trying to accomplish. To raise awareness of recycling issues, Duncan and her Solid Waste Management Committee put on an elaborate gourmet dinner, the "Garbage Gala," for four hundred people at the recycling center. All decorations used for the event were made from recycled materials.
3. **Be professional.** Be businesslike with the people you talk to. Reach out to as many people as you

Recycling is one way all of us can help protect and preserve our environment.

CITIZENSHIP SKILLS AND RESPONSIBILITIES

Recycling in Your Community (Continued)

can, but remember that they will take you more seriously if you have a professional attitude.
4. **Go to City Hall.** Consult with local political leaders. Explain your goals and ask for advice on how to achieve them. Come up with a plan and present it. Be thorough and persistent. Duncan's group was turned down at first, settled for partial funding for a study the second time, and on the third try received the support it wanted.

For help in starting a recycling program, call the National Recycling Coalition at 202-659-6883, the Environmental Protection Agency Hotline at 800-424-9346, or the Environmental Defense Fund recycling number 800-CALL-EDF.

TAKING ACTION

1. Divide your class into groups. Have each group devise steps to start recycling in your town.

of the community are often regulated by zoning boards or planning agencies. **Zoning** is the method that cities use to regulate the way property, such as land and buildings, are used. Through zoning practices, a city strives for order.

Generally, a zoning ordinance classifies each portion of land in the city as part of one of three zones: residential, commercial, or industrial. Each of these is divided into subzones. For example, one residential zone might be designated for single-family homes (houses), while another would allow apartment houses. Zoning ordinances also place limits on the height and area of structures, the distances they must be set back from other property lines, and other restrictions on land use. Nearly every major city in the United States is zoned today. (One notable exception is Houston, Texas, which only has privately contracted deed restrictions. Some critics of zoning point out that Houston is nonetheless no different than any other large city that has zoning.)

Recreational and Cultural Activities

As Americans, our leisure time has increased (compared to the 19th century) and cities have responded with recreational and cultural programs. Local governments offer community programs such as football, baseball, swimming, ice skating, and dancing. They also maintain city zoos and museums, and help build arenas, sports facilities, and convention centers.

► Cities and local governments also provide recreational facilities such as this beautiful public garden in downtown Boston. What other types of recreational facilities and programs are sponsored and maintained by local governments and cities?

County sheriff's officers answer to an elected county sheriff. What are the responsibilities of an elected county sheriff?

Elected Officials   Most boards share their powers and responsibilities with other elected officials. These officials and their duties include:

- *Sheriff*—maintains the jail and serves as the police official in unincorporated areas of the county.
- *District Attorney*—prosecutes criminal cases on behalf of the state and county.
- *Superintendent of Schools*—chief administrator for the county's elementary and secondary schools. (In some states superintendents are appointed by a school board.)
- *County Clerk*—registers and records documents such as deeds, mortgages, birth and death certificates, and divorce decrees.
- *Auditor*—keeps financial records and authorizes payments to meet county obligations.
- *Treasurer*—keeps county funds and authorizes payments from these funds.
- *Assessor*—sets value on taxable property in the county.
- *Coroner*—investigates violent deaths and those not witnessed by a doctor.

Special Boards and Commissions   In some counties, special boards may be elected or appointed to perform specific tasks. They commonly include the school board,

the board of health, the hospital board, the library board, and the planning board.

Changing County Government

Counties have developed in diverse ways throughout our nation's history. Some of their unusual characteristics have come to be perceived as problems. Some politicians and citizens believe that county governments are outmoded, and point out the need for change. According to these people, several problem areas are in need of reform.

Leadership   One of the biggest problems is the absence of real executive leadership. The confusing mass of elected county officials makes it impossible for the average citizen to learn which county official is responsible for what. Inefficiency, waste, inaction, and an unresponsive government are often the result.

- **The county-manager plan** In an effort to provide more effective leadership, some larger counties have reorganized themselves and now have a county manager, county executive, or chief administrator. Under the **county-manager plan**, the elected county board remains the legislative, policy-making arm of county government. The county manager, who is hired by and responsible to the county board, is the board's chief executive. The board makes legislation and decides policy, while the manager administers these laws and executes these policies. More than 50 counties around the country have adopted this plan.

- **The chief administrator plan** The **chief administrator plan** is a limited version of the county manager plan. The chief administrative officer (CAO) differs from the county manager because he or she shares responsibilities in certain key areas with the county board or with other individuals. In some areas, such as budgets and appointments, the CAO has little or no power. Perhaps because it is a less radical change, this plan has become more popular, and over 500 counties currently use it.
- **Elected chief executive plan** Another variation on the county manager plan is the **elected chief executive plan**. The executive officer is elected directly by the voters and works with the county board. Nearly sixty counties today have this kind of system.

The Weakness of the Counties The relative weakness of the counties in relation to the states is another problem. Most state constitutions severely restrict the powers of county boards. County officials often cannot respond effectively to modern problems because they have limited abilities to tax, spend, and legislate.

Recognizing the need for more local independence, over half the states have now provided for home rule. This means that states allow the counties to decide the details of their own governmental structures, subject to the approval of the local voters. This step toward reform has been offered to some 1,500 counties in the nation, but only about 100 have taken advantage of it.

Municipalities

When the first census was taken in 1790, only 5.1 percent of the 3,929,214 people living in the United States lived in **urban areas**, or areas that are highly populated. In the early 1800s, with the advent of large-scale manufacturing and the invention of farming machines that reduced the need for manual labor, people began to move to the new urban industrial and transportation centers. Cities grew rapidly. By 1860, the urban population had multiplied thirty times. By 1900, 39.7 percent of the population lived in cities. In 1990, this figure reached 77 percent and is still rising.

This shift from rural to urban society in the United States has meant dramatic changes in government. If you have ever lived or stayed on a farm or in the country, you know that you cannot always depend on government services to pick up your garbage, send snow plows when you need them, or put a stop sign on your corner. But in the city, the relationships between people living in close proximity are far more complex than those among people living on neighboring farms. Urban residents place more demands on government to provide services and protection. The larger the population, the greater the need and expenses of services.

Urban areas with their own units of government are called municipalities. Depending on local custom or state laws, municipalities are known as cities, towns, boroughs, or villages. Each municipality is created by the state, which has complete authority and control over all local government within the municipal borders. State constitutions and statutes contain a large number of provisions relating to municipal government.

Incorporation Cities and towns develop local governments when they are granted special legal status by the state legislature through **incorporation**. When a city becomes incorporated, it actually becomes a legal municipal corporation. Each state sets out in its constitution

▲ Urban residents place demands on government to provide services such as keeping the streets cleared of snow. What are urban areas with their own units of government called?

GOVERNMENT IN ACTION

CASE STUDY

Waging the War on Drugs

The problem of illegal drugs is widespread in the United States. While federal legislation and money spent on the war against illegal drugs get all the headlines, however, most of the costs associated with the war on drugs are faced at the local level. It is local police forces that are involved in upholding state laws against illegal drugs.

The number of robberies, violent acts, and murders associated with illegal drugs are hard to estimate. In some major cities, authorities estimate that over half of all homicides are drug-related, typically due to "turf" wars and drug deals gone awry. In many cities, drug users steal and commit assaults in order to obtain money to satisfy their expensive drug habits.

Current attempts at stopping drug sales and use have resulted in over 1.1 million drug-related arrests per year. The courts have also found themselves increasingly burdened by the increased police activity with respect to illegal drugs. Court calendars are overflowing. Because of speedy-trial statutes for criminal cases, virtually all drug cases get on the docket (court agenda) before civil cases. Civil lawsuits—those involving private parties rather than the state—often take two, three, four, and sometimes five years to get to court.

There are basically three major views of how the United States should regulate illegal drugs. The most liberal view argues for complete legalization. The most conservative view is that even harsher penalties and a higher degree of law enforcement are needed to eliminate illegal drug use. The middle view advocates increased education and regulation, and perhaps decriminalizing certain "soft" drugs such as marijuana. Currently ten states have decriminalized the possession of small amounts of marijuana for personal use.

While evidence does not indicate that the current drug war has reduced the amount of

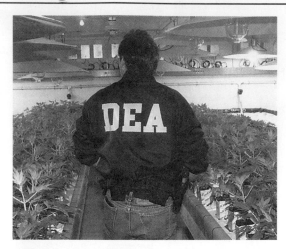

criminal activity associated with illegal drugs, there is some evidence that the casual use of illegal drugs has declined. For several years in a row, the government has reported that the use of cocaine among high school students has decreased. Certainly the use of all mind-altering drugs, including alcohol and nicotine, is currently on a downward trend. Americans seemed to be realizing more and more that the human body was not meant to consume many, if any, mind-altering drugs and still remain healthy. The amount of alcohol consumed per person in the United States has continued to decline since 1985.

(For more information, see the Extended Case Studies in the Resource Center at the end of this book.)

THINK ABOUT IT _____

1. What are the difficulties always faced by any government that attempts to make certain activities or goods illegal?
2. What kind of advice would you give to a new mayor in your city with respect to the war on drugs?

Special districts may also be referred to as authorities, boards, or corporations. Figure 24–2 on page 595 shows the different kinds of districts.

One important feature of special districts is that they cut across geographical and governmental boundaries. Sometimes special districts cut across state lines, such as the Port of New York Authority, which was established by an interstate compact between New Jersey and New York. A mosquito-control district may cut across both municipal lines and county lines. A metropolitan transit district may provide bus service to dozens of municipalities and to several counties.

Except for school districts, the typical citizen is not very aware of most special districts. Indeed, most citizens do not know what governmental unit provides their weed control, mosquito control, water supplies, or sewage services. Part of the reason for the low profile of special districts is that most administrators are appointed, not elected, and therefore receive little public attention.

Section 2 Review

1. How are the functions of county governments determined? What do county governments typically do?
2. What are some problems with county governments?
3. What are municipalities? What does incorporation mean?
4. What are special districts?
5. **For critical analysis:** What do you think would be the advantages and disadvantages of incorporation for a city?

SECTION 3

How Municipalities Are Governed

Preview Questions
- What are the major forms of municipal government?
- What are the important features of each municipal government plan?

Of the many types of municipal representative governments, most operate according to four basic systems: the commission plan, the council-manager plan, the mayor-administrator plan, and the mayor-council plan.

The Commission Plan

The **commission plan** of municipal government consists of a commission of three to nine members who have both legislative and executive powers. A commission government is organized as follows:

1. Executive and legislative powers are concentrated in a small group of individuals, who are elected at-large on a (normally) nonpartisan ballot.
2. Each commissioner is individually responsible for heading a particular municipal department, such as the department of public safety.
3. The commission is collectively responsible for passing ordinances and controlling spending.
4. The mayor is selected from the members of the commission (the mayoral position is only ceremonial).

Figure 24–3 on page 598 shows a typical commission plan. The commission plan originated in Galveston, Texas, in 1901, and had its greatest popularity during the first twenty years of this century. It appealed to municipal government reformers, who looked upon it as a type of business organization that would eliminate what they saw as built-in problems in long ballots and partisan municipal politics. Unfortunately, giving both legislative and executive power to a small group of individuals means that there are no checks and balances on administration and spending. Also, since the mayoral office is ceremonial, there is no provision for strong leadership. Not surprisingly, only about one hundred cities today use the commission plan: Tulsa, Salt Lake City, Mobile, Topeka, and Atlantic City are a few of them.

The Council-Manager Plan

In the **council-manager plan** of municipal government, an elected city council appoints a professional manager who acts as the chief executive. He or she is typically called the **city manager**. In principle, the manager is simply there to see that the general directions of the city council are carried out. In practice, he or she often makes many decisions and policies. The important features of the council-manager plan are as follows:

1. The council or commission consists of five to seven members, elected at-large on a nonpartisan ballot.
2. A professionally trained manager can hire and fire subordinates and is responsible to the council.
3. The mayor may be chosen from within the council or from outside, but he or she has no executive

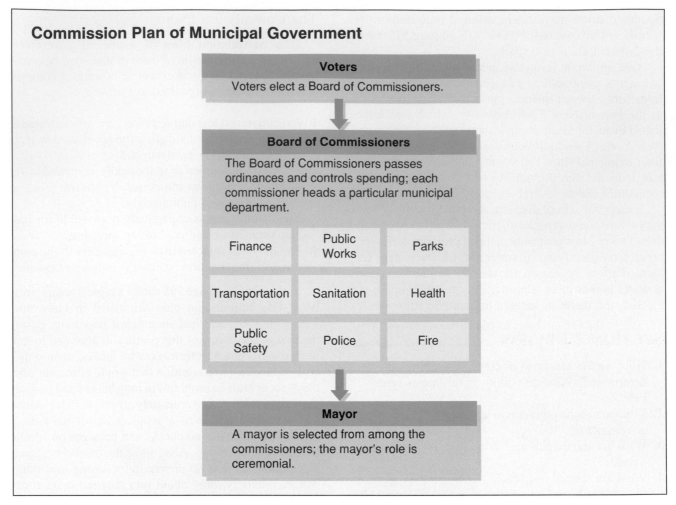

Commission Plan of Municipal Government

Voters

Voters elect a Board of Commissioners.

Board of Commissioners

The Board of Commissioners passes ordinances and controls spending; each commissioner heads a particular municipal department.

Finance	Public Works	Parks
Transportation	Sanitation	Health
Public Safety	Police	Fire

Mayor

A mayor is selected from among the commissioners; the mayor's role is ceremonial.

▲ FIGURE 24–3 **Commission Plan of Municipal Government.** The figure above shows the organization of a municipal government according to the commission plan. According to this plan, what type of role does the mayor assume?

function. As with the commission plan, the mayor's position is largely ceremonial. The city manager works for the council and not the mayor (unless, of course, the mayor is part of the council).

Figure 24–4 on the next page shows the council-manager plan of government.

Today about two thousand cities use the council-manager plan. About one-third of the cities with populations above 5,000 and about one-half of the cities with populations above 25,000 operate with this type of plan. Only four large cities of more than 500,000 people—Cincinnati, Dallas, San Antonio, and San Diego—have adopted the plan.

The major defect of the council-manager plan, as with the commission plan, is that there is no strong ex-

ecutive leadership. It is therefore not surprising that large cities rarely use such a plan. The council-manager plan is also considered undemocratic because the executive—the city manager—is not elected by the people, but rather is appointed by the council.

The Mayor-Administrator Plan

The **mayor-administrator plan** is often used in large cities where there is a strong mayor. It is similar to the council-manager plan, except that the mayor is an elected chief executive and as such has powers of political leadership. The mayor appoints an administrative officer whose function is to free the mayor from routine administrative tasks, such as personnel direction and budget supervision.

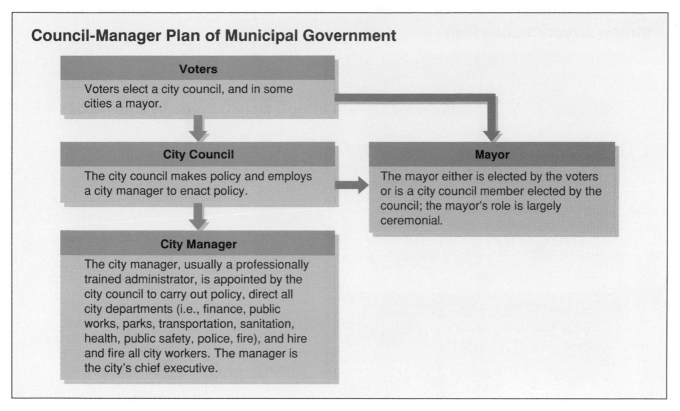

Council-Manager Plan of Municipal Government

Voters
Voters elect a city council, and in some cities a mayor.

City Council
The city council makes policy and employs a city manager to enact policy.

Mayor
The mayor either is elected by the voters or is a city council member elected by the council; the mayor's role is largely ceremonial.

City Manager
The city manager, usually a professionally trained administrator, is appointed by the city council to carry out policy, direct all city departments (i.e., finance, public works, parks, transportation, sanitation, health, public safety, police, fire), and hire and fire all city workers. The manager is the city's chief executive.

▲ FIGURE 24–4 **Council-Manager Plan of Municipal Government.** The figure above outlines the council-manager plan. Under this plan, who is responsible for carrying out policy?

The Mayor-Council Plan

The **mayor-council plan** of municipal government is the oldest and most widely used. The mayor is an elected chief executive and the council is the legislative body. Virtually all councils are unicameral (except in Everett, Massachusetts). A council typically has five to

▲ David Dinkins, shown here, is the mayor of New York City. What type of mayor-council plan is used in New York City?

nine members, except in very large cities such as Chicago, which has fifty members. Council members are popularly elected for four- to six-year terms.

Within the mayor-council plan, there are subplans known as the strong-mayor type or the weak-mayor type.

The Strong Mayor-Council Plan In the **strong mayor-council plan**, the mayor is the chief executive and has almost complete control over hiring and firing employees and preparing the budget. The mayor plays a strong role in the formation of city policies, and usually serves a four-year term. The strong-mayor system is most often found in large cities such as New York and San Francisco.

The Weak Mayor-Council Plan The **weak mayor-council plan** completely separates executive and legislative functions. The mayor is elected as chief executive officer; the council is elected as the legislative body. This traditional separation of powers allows for checks and balances on spending and administration. The mayor has only limited powers and little control over staffing and budget, and is often elected for a two-year term. This

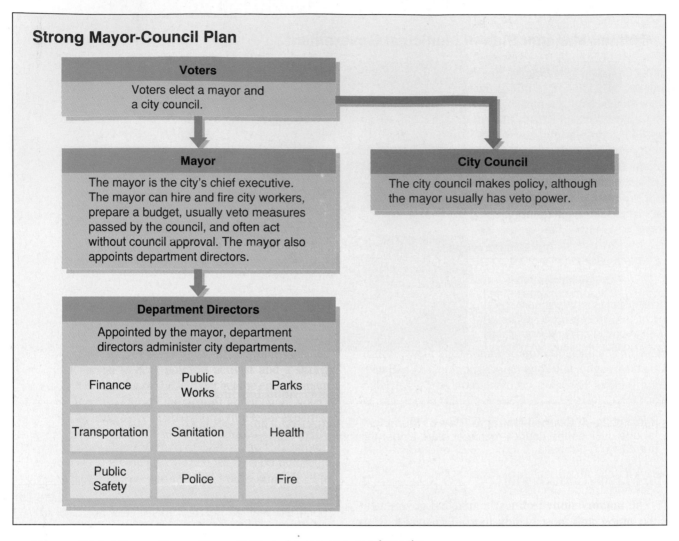

▲ |FIGURE 24–5 **Strong Mayor-Council Plan.** As you can see from the
organization chart above, under the strong mayor-council plan, the voters elect
both the mayor and the city council. In what type of city is the strong mayor-
council system most often found?

plan is often found in small or medium-sized cities; in some small cities, in fact, the office of mayor is only a part-time position.

About 50 percent of all American cities use some form of the mayor-council plan. Most recently the mayor-council plan has lost ground to the council-manager plan in small and medium-sized cities.

Figure 24–5 above, and 24–6 on page 602 show the two forms of the mayor-council plan.

A Question of Patronage— Or City Machines?

In the late nineteenth and early twentieth centuries, many major cities were run by "the machine." This was a political organization in which each city block within the municipality had an organizer, each neighborhood had a political club, and each district had a leader. All of these parts of the machine had a boss—such as Richard Daley in Chicago, Edward Crump in Memphis, or Tom Pendergast in Kansas City.

The machine emerged in the 1840s, when the first waves of European immigrants came to the United States to work in urban factories. When those individuals, who often lacked the ability to communicate in English, needed help, the machine was there to help them. The urban machine forged a strong political institution by relying on the support of the dominant ethnic groups. In this way, the machine could keep its boss (usually the mayor) in office year after year.

BUILDING SOCIAL STUDIES SKILLS

Figuring and Using Percentages

Throughout any text on American government, you are presented with many statistics, the most important of which are percentages. Percentages are often used to indicate how much of the American population is living in poverty, or how many people voted for a particular candidate.

Percentages indicate a certain number of parts per hundred. Certain expenses, such as tax rates, are determined in percentages. For example, when you buy a $20 book with a 7 percent sales tax, you have to add 7 cents in tax for every dollar you pay for the book. The calculation for this would be .07 × $20 = $1.40, which makes the total cost of the book $21.40.

Percentages can either be expressed as percentages, using the percent sign (%), or as decimals. In the calculation above, 7% was changed to .07, both of which mean 7 parts out of 100. The decimal equivalent of a percent is found by moving the decimal point two places to the left and dropping the percent sign. To change decimals to percentages, move the decimal point two places to the right and add the percent sign.

Percentages are used to figure out certain portions of a number. Say you are told, for example, that of the 400 people who voted in a recent local election, 300 voted for the Democratic candidate. You can calculate the percentage of people who voted for the Democrat in the following way: divide the number of those who voted Democrat by the total number of those who voted. The calculation would be 300 ÷ 400 = .75, or 75 percent.

In the same example, if you were told that 75 percent of the voters voted for the Democratic candidate, you can determine how many votes that candidate got if you know the total number who voted. In this case you would multiply .75 by 400 to get 300.

Remember that there is a difference between changes in *percent* and changes in *actual numbers*. For instance, a doubling of a percentage is not equivalent to increasing the total number twofold. When you are reading statistics, it's best to know whether you are actually reading about changes in percentages or changes in the actual number.

PRACTICING YOUR SKILLS

The table below gives the values of stolen property and the amounts recovered in a recent year. On a separate sheet of paper, calculate the percentages of the total amounts that were recovered. Then answer the questions below.

1. Which category of stolen property had the highest recovery rate?
2. Which category had the lowest?
3. How much greater is the highest recovery rate than the lowest recovery rate?

Property Stolen and Recovered

Type of Property	Value Stolen	Amount Recovered	Percentage Recovered
Motor Vehicles	$6 billion	$4 billion	
Firearms	$100 million	$10 million	
Currency	$1 billion	$40 million	
Televisions and Stereos	$1 billion	$50 million	

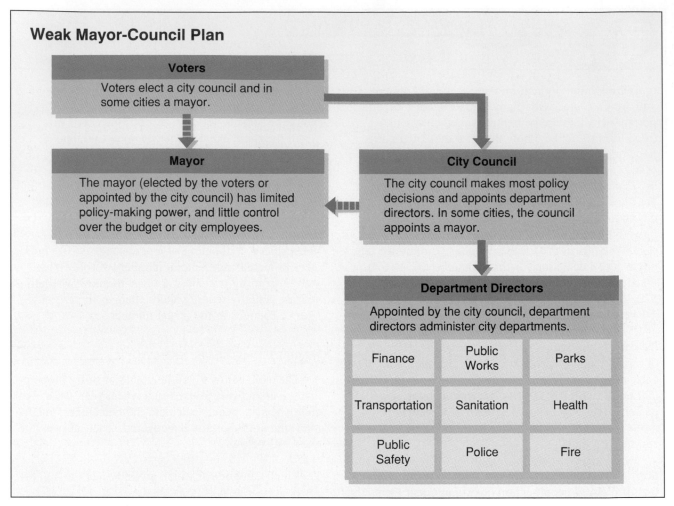

Weak Mayor-Council Plan

Voters

Voters elect a city council and in some cities a mayor.

Mayor

The mayor (elected by the voters or appointed by the city council) has limited policy-making power, and little control over the budget or city employees.

City Council

The city council makes most policy decisions and appoints department directors. In some cities, the council appoints a mayor.

Department Directors

Appointed by the city council, department directors administer city departments.

Finance	Public Works	Parks
Transportation	Sanitation	Health
Public Safety	Police	Fire

▲ FIGURE 24–6 **Weak Mayor-Council Plan.** The organization chart above is for the weak mayor-council plan. Under the weak mayor-council system, who is responsible for appointing department directors?

The machine was oiled by patronage. The party in power was often referred to as the patronage party. Loyal voters were rewarded with deliveries of Thanksgiving turkeys or coal at Christmas in return for their continued support for machine candidates. The power of the machine lay in its ability to control votes, and the votes of new urban immigrants from Europe or from rural America were especially crucial.

When the last of the big-city bosses, Mayor Richard Daley of Chicago, died in December 1976, an era that had lasted well over one hundred years died with him. The big-city machine had already begun to be in serious trouble in the 1960s, when community activists organized to work for municipal government. Soon a government of administrators began to appear. Fewer offices were elective, and more were appointive—presumably filled by professionals who had no political axes to grind, payoffs to make, or patrons to please.

SECTION 3 REVIEW

1. What are the major types of municipal representative governments?
2. Which types of city government are most common and why?
3. What is patronage? How did the machine use patronage in city politics?
4. **For critical analysis:** If you lived in a large city with serious social and economic problems, which plan of municipal government do you think would be most effective in dealing with these problems? Explain your answer.

CHALLENGE TO THE AMERICAN DREAM

Can Overlapping Governmental Units Be Avoided?

There are over eighty thousand separate and often overlapping governmental units within the United States. For example, there may be a division of the *county* government that concerns itself with water and sewage. Within that county there may be multiple *municipalities* that also concern themselves with water and sewage. This type of overlap exists throughout most of the United States. Consequently, it would seem that any attempt to reduce this confusion must involve some type of consolidation.

Consolidation

Consolidation is defined as the joining of two or more governmental units to form a single unit. Typically, a state constitution or a state statute will designate consolidation procedures.

Consolidation is often recommended for metropolitan-area problems, but to date few consolidations have actually been put into practice. The most successful consolidations have been **functional consolidations**—particularly of the police, health, and welfare departments of a city and a county. Functional consolidations group agencies according to the main job, or function, they perform. In some cases, functional consolidation is a satisfactory alternative to the complete consolidation of governmental units. The most successful form of functional consolidation was started in 1957 in Dade County, Florida. The county, now called Metro in government circles, is a union of twenty-six municipalities, each of which has its own governmental entity. The county government that oversees the municipalities operates under a home-rule charter. The county, or Metro, has authority to furnish water, planning, mass transit, and police ser-

vices, and to set minimum standards of performance by all agencies. The governing body of Metro is an elected thirteen-member board of county commissioners, which appoints a county manager and a county attorney.

Councils of Governments (COGs)

Another type of consolidation is **councils of governments** (COGs), voluntary organizations of counties and municipalities that attempt to tackle areawide problems. COGs are an alternative means of treating major regional problems that various communities are unwilling to tackle on a consolidated basis either by full consolidation or functional consolidation of governmental units. More than two hundred COGs have been established since 1966. The impetus for their establishment was and continues to be federal government grants.

Generally the power of COGs is advisory only. Each member unit simply selects its council representatives, who report back to the unit after COG meetings. Nonetheless, today there are several COGs that have begun to have considerable influence on regional policy. These include the Metropolitan Washington Council of Governments, the Supervisors' Inter-County Commission in Detroit, and the Association of Bay Area Governments in San Francisco.

The challenge to the American dream is to continue to increase the amount of consolidation at the county and local levels in order to make local government more efficient.

You Decide

1. How do you think the United States ended up with so many governmental units?
2. Who among those in government do you think would be most likely to initiate consolidation?
3. Functional consolidation seems like a good idea, yet very few governments have agreed to use it. What political forces do you think might oppose functional consolidation of city and county departments?

CHAPTER 24 REVIEW

Key Terms

boroughs 590
chief administrator
   plan 593
city manager 597
commission plan 597
consolidation 603
Cooley's rule 583
council-manager
   plan 597
councils of
   government 603
counties 590

county board 591
county-manager
   plan 592
Dillon's rule 583
elected chief executive
   plan 593
functional
   consolidations 603
general-law city 584
home-rule city 584
incorporation 593

mayor-administrator
   plan 598
mayor-council
   plan 599
municipal home
   rule 584
municipalities 583
New England town 594
parishes 590
selectmen 594
strong mayor-council
   plan 599

town manager
   system 594
town meeting 594
townships 594
unincorporated
   areas 595
urban areas 593
weak-mayor council
   plan 599
zoning 589

Summary

1. The Constitution makes no mention of local governments; consequently, every local government is a creation of the state. Since 1900, about four-fifths of all states have allowed municipal home rule.

2. Local governments provide many important services, including education, police and fire protection, public welfare, city planning and zoning, and recreational and cultural activities.

3. Every state except Connecticut and Rhode Island is divided into counties. Counties vary widely in size, population, and importance. The responsibilities and functions of a county are usually determined by the state constitution and state laws. Most counties are governed by a county board. Most boards share their powers and responsibilities with other elected officials. Many people believe that county governments are outmoded and point out the need for reform. Urban areas with their own units of government are called municipalities. Cities and towns develop local governments when they are granted special legal status by the state legislature through incorporation. Townships perform the same functions as a county. Special districts are units of government created to deal with a special function of government such as garbage collection.

4. The major forms of municipal representative government are the commission plan, the council-manager plan, the mayor-administrator plan, and the mayor-council

plan. There have been a number of attempts at reducing the confusion and overlap of governmental units. Consolidation is the union of two or more governmental units to form a single unit, and is often recommended for metropolitan-area problems. The most successful consolidations have been functional consolidations—particularly of city and county police, health, and welfare departments. Councils of government are voluntary organizations of counties and municipalities that attempt to tackle areawide problems.

Review Questions

1. What is the difference between Dillon's rule and Cooley's rule?
2. What are the major functions of local government?
3. What is zoning? Why is it important to a city?
4. Name several functions of counties.
5. What are some problems with county governments? How have some counties attempted to deal with these problems?
6. How is a municipality formed? From where does the authority to form a municipality come?
7. How do the towns of New England differ from the townships in other parts of the country?
8. Why are special districts created?
9. Briefly describe the types of municipal governments. What are the disadvantages and advantages of each?
10. What is machine politics?

CHAPTER 24 REVIEW—Continued

11. List four guidelines that you can use to start a recycling program in your community.
12. What function do councils of government provide?

Questions for Thought and Discussion

1. What is an important issue in your community that you would like to bring before the city council for action? What kind of action would you recommend that the council take?
2. Do you think the New England style of direct democracy would work in your community? Why or why not?
3. How do you think that reducing the size of local governments would affect those governments' abilities to serve the people?
4. Which plan of government does your city or town use? How well do you think that plan works? If you do not think it works well, which other plan would you recommend?
5. Compare and contrast the different types of municipal governments outlined in this chapter. Choose the one you believe most effective and explain your choice.
6. Which functions of government do you think would be easiest to consolidate?

Improving Your Skills
Communication Skills

Working in Groups

You have been or probably will be in many situations in which you will work with a group of other people. You may join a group working together to fight pollution in your community, serve on a student council or government board, or collaborate with others on a group project for school. Keep the following tips in mind when you join a group:

- Remember that you are only one member of the group. Do not dominate, but do not be afraid to contribute your opinion.
- Listen to everything others have to say. Distinguish in your mind between fact and opinion and between the important and unimportant. Ask questions if you do not understand or need more information.
- Stay focused on the goal or goals of the group.
- When it is your turn to speak, speak clearly, with proper enunciation, pronunciation, and grammar. Do not speak too quickly or too slowly.
- If people do not seem to understand each other, it may be because words sometimes mean different things to different people. It could also be that people are perceiving the situation differently. Be sure to clarify for everyone what the issue under discussion is exactly.

Writing

Write a script about a group working together who ignore all of the above tips. Role play the script with other members of your class.

Social Studies Skills
Working with Charts and Percentages

Look at the chart in Figure 24–2 on page 595. Answer these questions:

1. What percentage of the total number of special districts does the number of school districts represent?
2. What percentage of the total number of special districts does the number of fire protection districts represent?

Activities and Projects

1. Imagine that you are in charge of developing a form of government for a city of 25,000 people. Prepare a plan that tells which form of government you would use, and the responsibilities that would be given to each government official. Present the plan to the class.
2. Choose an issue in your community about which you are concerned, such as aid to the homeless. Research the issue and write a letter to a top city official addressing the issue.
3. Attend a city or county council meeting. Take notes on the procedures and report back to the class.
4. Attend a school board meeting. Write an outline of the major issues in your school district.
5. Invite a city official to your class to speak about his or her responsibilities and roles in the community.

CHAPTER 25

Paying for State and Local Government

CHAPTER OBJECTIVES

To learn and understand

- The limitations of state and local powers of taxation.

- How the federal government contributes financially to state and local governments.

- The priorities and patterns of state and local spending.

"We don't have New Federalism, we have New Feudalism, where every community fends for itself with a hodgepodge of responsibilities and taxing powers."

———— **George Sternlieb**
(1923–   ) Urban Specialist and
Professor Emeritus of Public Policy at
Rutgers University

INTRODUCTION

George Sternlieb's quote above echoes the frustrations many state and local officials have felt in recent years as the federal government has shifted a heavier financial burden and responsibility to the cities and states. At the same time, public demands for better city and state services have become enormous.

State and local governments spend over one trillion dollars per year. The money for such budgets has to come from somewhere. State governments have a large number of sources of revenue, while local governments have fewer. One of the most important of these sources is the taxes all of us pay in one form or another. There are limitations, however, on the types of taxes that state and local governments can use.

SECTION 1

Limitations on State and Local Taxation

Preview Questions
- What limits does the Constitution place upon the taxing powers of state and local governments?
- What other limitations are placed on state and local taxing power?

There are basically two types of limitations on state and local powers of taxation—those that come from the federal government and those that come from the state

governments themselves. Of course, no state or local government can exceed the taxing power given to the federal government by the U.S. Constitution. Additionally, because local governments obtain their taxing power from state governments, their taxing powers are limited by not only state constitutions, but also by laws passed by state legislatures.

U.S. Constitutional Limitations

Within the U.S. Constitution only a few limitations are placed on state and local taxing powers. These limitations apply to agencies of the federal government, interstate commerce, and due process.

Agencies of the Federal Government U.S. Supreme Court Chief Justice John Marshall said that "the power to tax involves the power to destroy." In his famous 1819 decision, *McCulloch* v. *Maryland* (discussed in detail in Chapter 4), Marshall put to rest any hope of state governments being able to tax an agency of the federal government. That Supreme Court decision still stands today and prevents states from taxing the operations, land, buildings, or any other aspect of the federal government.

Interstate Commerce Article I, Section 10, Clause 2 of the Constitution states that "no State shall . . . lay any Imposts [taxes] or Duties on Imports or Exports. . . ." Furthermore, Clause 3 states that "no State shall . . . lay any Duty of Tonnage. . . ." Clause 2 prevents the states from taxing both imports into the United States and exports to other countries. Clause 3 prevents the states from taxing ships according to their cargo capacity.

The Supreme Court has said that the U.S. Constitution gives Congress, not the states, the power to regulate interstate and foreign trade. Therefore, the states

607

▲ The Supreme Court decision in *McCullough* v. *Maryland* forbids states from taxing the operations, land, buildings, or any other aspect of the federal government. Why do you think the Supreme Court felt it was necessary to deny states this power?

cannot pass laws that prevent imports from being brought into their respective states. The states cannot tax such imports either.

Due Process   The due process clause of the Fourteenth Amendment to the U.S. Constitution can be used to limit the power of state and local governments to impose taxes. Under the due process clause, taxes must be imposed and administered fairly and not be so great as to be the equivalent of seizing property. For example, your local government could not pass a property tax that was so high that only a few people could afford to pay it and the rest would therefore have to forfeit their property.

The due process clause also forbids unreasonable classifications for the purpose of collecting taxes. It is reasonable to collect a tax on smokers by taxing cigarettes. It is reasonable to collect a tax on the users of automobiles by taxing gasoline. It is unreasonable, how-

ever, to make only blond-haired citizens pay a state income tax and to let everyone else live tax free.

State Constitutional Limitations

Each state has constitutional limitations on the taxing power of that state. Additionally, each state constitution puts limits on the taxing power of local governments. Virtually all state constitutions indicate that all taxes must be uniformly applied, and applied for public purposes only.

All states normally exempt religious organizations, museums, operas, and cemeteries from taxation. (This means that these organizations do not have to pay state and local taxes.) Some state constitutions set maximum rates for different taxes such as those on cigarettes. Others prohibit certain kinds of taxes such as a tax on any personal income.

SECTION 1 REVIEW

1. What are the two basic limitations on state and local taxation powers?
2. What restrictions does the federal Constitution place on state and local taxing powers?
3. **For critical analysis:** What did John Marshall mean when he said "the power to tax involves the power to destroy?" Explain your answer.

SECTION 2

Sources of State and Local Revenues

Preview Questions

- What are the major types of taxes used at the state and local levels?
- Which tax produces the largest amount of revenue in most states?
- Which tax produces the largest amount of revenue for local governments?
- From which principal nontax sources do state and local governments draw revenues?

There are three sources of state and local revenues: taxes, nontax revenues, and intergovernmental transfers.

Types of Taxes

There is a large variety of taxes that are assessed at all levels of government. In Chapter 19 you learned about some of these taxes, which include the following:

- Personal income tax
- Corporate income tax
- Excise tax
- Estate tax
- Inheritance tax
- Sales tax
- Property tax

Personal Income Tax These are taxes paid on personal income each year. Seven states have no personal income tax system: Florida, Nevada, South Dakota, Texas, Washington, Wyoming, and Alaska. The other 43 states have assessed taxes on personal income at rates from as low as .4 percent in Iowa to as high as 12 percent in Massachusetts.

Corporate Income Tax Corporations pay taxes on their profits in all but five states—Nevada, South Dakota, Texas, Washington, and Wyoming. In the other 45 states they pay rates from as low as one percent in Alaska and Arkansas to as high as 10.5 percent in North Dakota and 12.25 percent in Pennsylvania.

Excise Tax When there are special taxes paid by the consumer for the use and consumption of certain goods they are called **excise taxes**. A number of states collect excise taxes on cigarettes, gasoline, alcoholic beverages, and telephone use. There is very little uniformity in how much each state collects in excise taxes on cigarettes and gasoline.

Cigarette taxes per pack of 20 are the lowest in tobacco-growing states—North Carolina (5 cents), South Carolina (7 cents), Virginia (2.5 cents), and Kentucky (3 cents). The high cigarette-tax states are California, Connecticut, Illinois, Iowa, Minnesota, Nevada, New Jersey, New York, North Dakota, Washington, and Wisconsin.

Estate and Inheritance Taxes When someone dies, some states levy a tax on the value of the property (estate) that the deceased leaves behind. Some states, either in addition or instead of the estate tax, assess a tax on those who inherit property from someone who has died. The inheritance tax does not exist at the federal level, but the estate tax does. All such taxes are called **death taxes**.

Sales Tax There is no sales tax at the federal level. Only five states have no general sales tax: Alaska, Delaware, Montana, New Hampshire, and Oregon. Sales taxes in other states range from a low of 3 percent in Colorado and North Carolina to a high of 8.25 percent in parts of California. Local sales taxes are tacked on to state sales taxes in many cities. In New York City, for example, the local sales tax adds another 4.25 percent to the 4 percent state sales tax, bringing total sales tax on each dollar spent in New York City to 8.25 cents.

Property Tax The majority of states impose a tax on the value of property. Virtually every municipality uses the property tax to raise the majority of its revenues. The most well-known property tax is that levied on the value of real estate—land and the houses or buildings on it. A number of states collect taxes on personal property, such

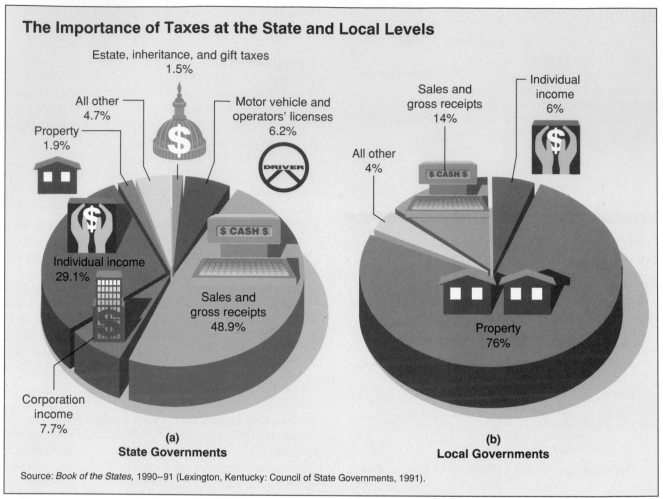

The Importance of Taxes at the State and Local Levels

Estate, inheritance, and gift taxes
1.5%

All other
4.7%

Property
1.9%

Motor vehicle and
operators' licenses
6.2%

Individual income
29.1%

Sales and
gross receipts
48.9%

Corporation
income
7.7%

(a)
State Governments

Sales and
gross receipts
14%

Individual
income
6%

All other
4%

Property
76%

(b)
Local Governments

Source: *Book of the States,* 1990–91 (Lexington, Kentucky: Council of State Governments, 1991).

▲ **FIGURE 25–1 The Importance of Taxes at the State and Local Levels.** The graphs above show the importance of each type of tax for both state and local governments. How important are property taxes to each of these levels of government?

as motor vehicles, business machines, boats, trailers, and trucks.[1]

The Importance of Each Tax

The pie charts above in Figure 25–1 show the percentages of the various kinds of taxes raised by state and local governments.

By far the most important tax for most states is the general sales tax, which is a tax levied as a proportion of the retail price of any good when it is sold. The most important tax at the local level is the property tax, which accounts for over three-fourths of all local taxes raised.

Whereas the federal government obtains more than 44 percent of its total revenues from personal income taxes, states obtain less than 15 percent from this type of tax. There is tremendous variation in the amounts of state and local taxes collected.

The highest taxes are paid by residents in Connecticut, District of Columbia, Massachusetts, and New Jersey. The lowest taxes are paid by residents of Mississippi and Utah.

State Nontax Revenues

Some state and local governments operate businesses from which they receive revenues. Like the federal government, states also borrow.

---

1. Personal property consists of things that can be moved; real property is immovable.

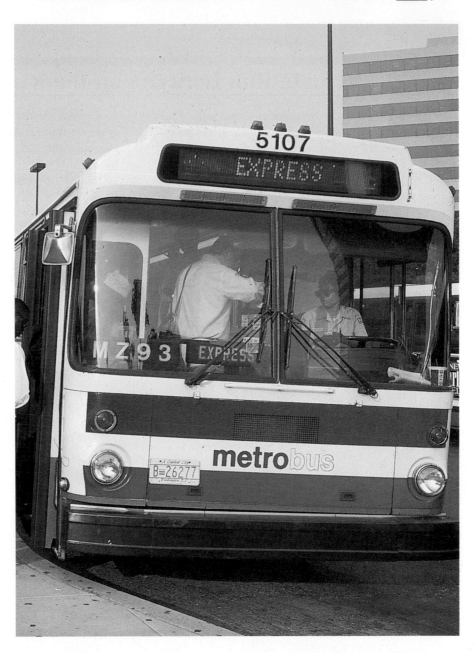

▶ A number of cities own and operate their own bus systems. Does your city own and operate its own bus system?

Government-Operated Businesses State and local governments operate toll bridges and toll roads. Some states, particularly Washington, operate ferries. Alaska has had numerous businesses including a slaughterhouse and a phone company. The state of North Dakota markets Dakota-made flour. The state of California operates a railroad line in San Francisco. Eighteen states, including Idaho, Maine, Utah, West Virginia, and Montana operate liquor stores.

A number of cities own and operate their own water systems, bus systems, and electric power companies. A number of cities operate warehouses, office buildings, and wharfs. Whenever these government-operated businesses make a profit, the profits constitute a source of revenue that can be used for other state and local expenditures.

Less important nontax sources of revenues include fines accessed in state and local courts, as well as interest on investments.

Borrowing Sometimes states and cities find that they cannot pay for all of their expenditures, and are forced

GOVERNMENT IN ACTION

CASE STUDY

State-Run Lotteries on the Rise

In 1964, the first modern state lottery was started in New Hampshire. From 1984 to 1992, thirty-two states, as well as the District of Columbia, had taken in a total of almost $100 billion in state lottery revenues. In 1992 alone, the estimate was almost $22 billion in lottery revenues. In 1975 the per-person ticket sales in the states that had lotteries was only $23; by 1992 it had jumped to $129 per person. The chart below shows how lottery sales increased over a period of fifteen years.

Sometimes states hold super lotteries that generate tremendous revenues. In 1991, for example, the state of New York held a super lottery that had a $90 million jackpot. Ticket sellers sold 61 million tickets in ten days—more than 21,000 a minute in the period just prior to the drawing. When a Florida lottery jackpot reached $106 million, the rate of ticket sales toward the end reached 44,000 tickets a minute and lottery officials were pleading on TV for the public to remain calm.

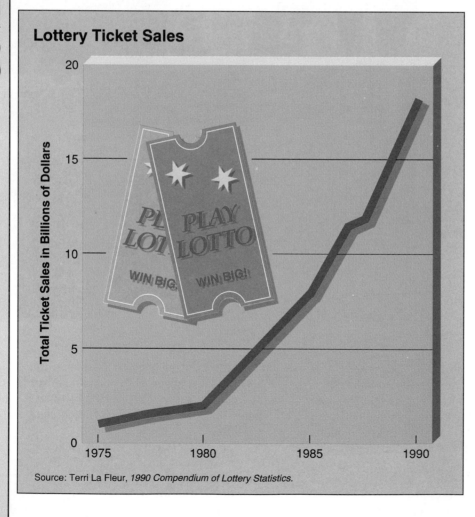

Lottery Ticket Sales

Total Ticket Sales in Billions of Dollars

Source: Terri La Fleur, *1990 Compendium of Lottery Statistics.*

It might be surprising that so many people invest so much in a game that offers such a small chance of winning. Chances of winning a big jackpot are about 13 million to 1 (compare these odds with the chances of being killed by lightning during a thunderstorm, which are about 400,000 to 1).

Some argue that state lotteries, even though voluntary, represent a regressive tax system. (Remember from Chapter 19, that in a regressive tax system, the percentage of income tax paid decreases as income increases.) The reason it is called regressive is that poorer families spend a higher percentage of their income on lottery tickets than richer families. According to one study, the true tax rate on lottery purchases is higher than the total tax on cigarettes or alcohol. In other words, the average lottery expenditure seems to be about the same, no matter what a person's income is. That means that the tax on those expenditures, expressed as a percentage of income, falls as income increases. In California, for example, average yearly lottery expenditures fall from 1.5 percent of income in the lowest-income class (under $10,000) to less than .01 percent of income in the $50,000 to $60,000 class.

Nonetheless, lotteries probably will be around for a long time because they are an attractive way to obtain needed revenues. They represent a revenue source that was not used prior to 1964. Most observers believe that virtually every state in the nation will have a lottery by the year 2010.

In addition to the lottery, more and more states are seeking revenues from allowing other forms of legalized gambling. The video lottery terminal (VLT) looks and sounds like other video arcade games. Instead of playing a video game, however, participants play poker, blackjack, and bingo. If participants win, they do not get their money immediately, but rather the VLT prints out a receipt that allows them to collect the money elsewhere. South Dakota first started operating these machines under the state lottery system in 1989. In the first nine months of legalization, South Dakota VLTs took in $127 million from 3,800 machines, which is about $180 per person in the state, or four times the revenues they were receiving from the state lottery. In Oregon, there is legalized betting on professional football. People bet on their favorite team to beat or tie the "point spread," or number of points by which the favored team is expected to win.

In 1975 the federal government lifted its ban against advertising lotteries on TV and radio. Every state that currently has a lottery is using increasingly clever advertising to sell it. In Michigan, for example, a TV ad shows a man in a convenience store who says he would never play the lottery because he would have a better chance of being struck by lightning. At that instant he is struck by a bolt out of the blue. He then says, "One ticket, please."

Although the rate of increase in lottery ticket sales slowed in 1991 and 1992, lotteries remain a popular way for states to generate revenue. It appears that what is for citizens a 13-million-to-1 long shot has become for many states a sure thing.

THINK ABOUT IT

1. There are laws against gambling in almost every state in the nation. Why, then, do states have legal lotteries? In other words, what might be the difference between gambling in a state-run lottery and any other type of gambling?
2. If lottery ticket sales represent a form of regressive taxes, what are the benefits that the poor receive from these implicit taxes?

Organizing for Community Action

Every week decisions are made in your community that directly affect your local environment and daily life. Getting involved in local government is a good way to learn where you stand politically, and a good place to develop skills for community action. Suppose you read in the newspaper that the city planning board has decided to demolish the oldest neighborhood in town, where your grandparents' Victorian-style apartment building still stands, to make room for a fish cannery. Suppose you hear that the city plans to cut down all the trees lining your street to widen the road. Suppose you see on the news that the police department has decided to reduce police patrols in your neighborhood, even though burglaries and violent crimes have risen dramatically and you feel unsafe.

Some decisions may be difficult to fight because of the many demands placed on local government, but if enough citizens are in opposition, government officials can be persuaded. After all, in a democracy, government officials are responsible to everyone. Here are some steps you can take to influence the decisions of your local government.

1. **Organize a group.** Gather together the people in your community who also oppose the government action. Start with your friends and plan a meeting. Tell them to talk with their friends and neighbors and invite them all to come. Also invite anyone who can speak knowledgeably about your cause.

Conduct the meeting as an open forum and let everyone express their opinion.

2. **Attend public hearings.** Urge all the members of your group to attend. Present your opinions in a clear, straightforward manner.

3. **Decide on your exact goals.** Having decided on your goals, come up with a plan of action. Give your group a name and appoint a leader. Announce the purpose of your group to public officials involved. Organize activities to express your views.

4. **Attract attention.** Write press releases and send them to local TV stations, radio stations, and newspapers. Be direct and give good reasons for your opinions. Be sure to emphasize the importance of your cause to the community.

5. **Start a petition drive.** Circulate petitions around your neighborhood through your group members and get as many signatures as possible. Submit the petitions to the appropriate public officials.

TAKING ACTION

1. Choose a local problem in which you have a strong interest. Follow newspaper reports on this problem for two weeks. Then write down the way you would organize community action to solve this problem.
2. Put at least one of your steps into action.

to borrow by issuing state and municipal bonds. State and local governments choose to sell bonds in order to complete many large projects. The building of highways, bridges, dams, schools, and government buildings are often paid for through this kind of borrowing.

Many states have found that they have had to borrow on a grand scale as their expenditures have greatly exceeded their revenues. For example, in 1991 California found itself with a projected budget shortfall—a negative difference between projected spending and estimated revenues—of almost $13 billion. Other states that have run into fiscal trouble in the 1990s include Connecticut,

Florida, Michigan, Maryland, Massachusetts, New Jersey, Pennsylvania, and Virginia.

Often state and local governments can easily sell bonds to cover their deficits because the interest earned by the purchasers is exempt from federal income taxes.

Intergovernmental Transfers

An increasingly important source of revenue for state and local governments is the receipt of funds from the federal government. In the next section you will read

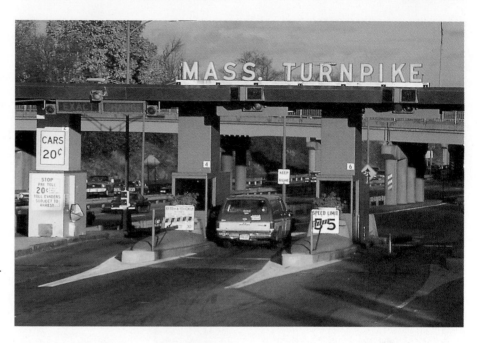

▶ This turnpike in Massachusetts is just one example of a government-operated business. What other types of government-operated businesses exist around the nation?

about how the federal government gives money back to the states.

SECTION 2 REVIEW

1. What are the major taxes used at the state and local levels?
2. Which tax produces the largest amount of revenue for the states? For the local governments?
3. What are the major sources of nontax revenues?
4. **For critical analysis:** Some people argue that some items such as food and prescription drugs should be exempt from sales tax because they are necessities. Others argue that sales taxes from such items are important sources of revenue, and that everyone should contribute to the government's revenue base. Which side do you agree with? Give reasons for your answer.

SECTION 3

Money from Uncle Sam

Preview Questions
- What are the methods by which the federal government distributes federal tax dollars to state and local governments?
- How do these methods differ?

Today, the federal government collects over 60 percent of all tax dollars. As part of our system of coop-

erative federalism, the federal government gives a significant amount of the funds collected from these taxes back to the states (which give to the local governments). In fiscal year 1992, the federal government distributed almost $110 billion, although this amount represents a decline over earlier years. Figure 25–2 on the next page shows the pattern of federal contributions over a period of thirty years.

There are basically three separate methods by which the federal government returns federal tax dollars to state and local governments: categorical grants-in-aid, block grants, and general grants-in-aid (also called general revenue sharing).

Categorical Grants

The concept of a federal government grant-in-aid was derived from a 1902 law providing that revenues from the sale of federally owned lands were to be shared with certain states and territories for irrigation and land reclamation. Such grants are tied to specific categories of government spending. They are therefore called **categorical grants**. Others include the establishment of agricultural extension programs, highway construction, vocational education, and maternal and child health. During Roosevelt's first two terms in office, categorical grants increased from $200 million to $3 billion per year.

The number and scope of the categorical grants expanded further as part of the Great Society program of President Lyndon Johnson during the 1960s. Grants became available in the fields of education, pollution control, conservation, recreation, and highway construction

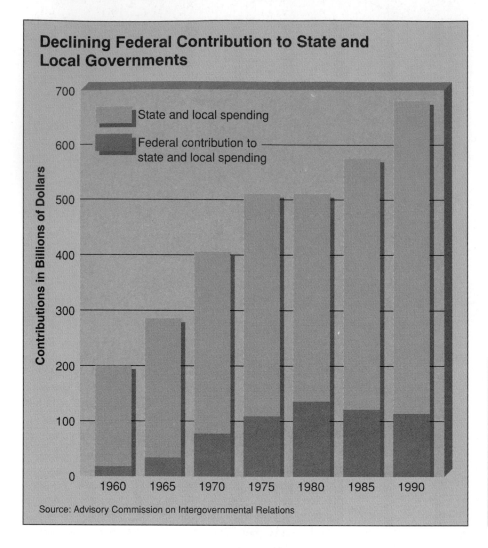

Declining Federal Contribution to State and Local Governments

State and local spending

Federal contribution to state and local spending

Contributions in Billions of Dollars

1960 1965 1970 1975 1980 1985 1990

Source: Advisory Commission on Intergovernmental Relations

◄
FIGURE 25–2 Declining Federal Contribution to State and Local Governments. As you can see from looking at this bar graph, state and local governments are having to spend an increasing amount of money to fund their programs. According to this chart, in what year was the federal contribution to state and local spending at its highest?

and maintenance. For some of the categorical grant programs, the state and local governments must contribute the same amount of money offered by the federal government, which is called **matching funds**. For other types of programs, the funds are awarded according to a formula that takes into account the relative wealth of the state. This is a process known as **equalization**.

Although all state and local officials, as well as their congressional representatives, enjoy taking credit for the results of projects funded by categorical grants, many would prefer to get the money with fewer restrictions. Local officials argue, for example, that the materials specified as suitable for a federally subsidized highway project in the South are not the best ones for roads in the North. It can be argued, however, that these specifications are necessary to raise local standards and practices to a uniform level. In general, categorical grants

have remained under fairly tight control by Congress.

In a move to bypass the states, Congress established the **project grant** approach, which allows state and local agencies to apply directly for assistance to local offices that administer federal funds. In this way, the funds can be directly placed where—in the eyes of Congress—they are most needed.

Block Grants

Although they did not originate with him, **block grants** were an important part of President Ronald Reagan's "new federalism" program, which he outlined in his first State of the Union Address in 1982. Block grants are federal funds that are transferred to state and local governments to provide broad support in areas such as health care and criminal justice.

Reagan supported block grants as an alternative to categorical grants, partly because it is politically easier to reduce block grants than it is to reduce categorical grants. A categorical grant affects one particular group. That group is often willing to spend considerable effort and resources to prevent a budget cut from affecting its funds. A block grant, however, affects many programs in one general area. For the grant recipients, then, it is politically more difficult to muster the necessary opposition to prevent a budget cut.

Supporters of block grants argue that they are necessary to reduce the kind of waste that has occurred under categorical grants. Opponents argue that block grants reduce overall federal aid, that state and local officials are not as capable of administering programs as are federal officials, and that state and local officials do not have sufficient information about, or interest in, the people who are supposed to benefit from the programs. In addition, critics say, a block-grant approach to federalism contributes to increasing inequality among the states and is potentially harmful to the poor, because state legislatures are less likely than the federal government to spend funds on social welfare programs.

General Grants-in-Aid, or Revenue Sharing

In an effort to move away from the federal government's involvement with categorical grants, the Nixon administration in 1972 asked Congress to remit to state and local governments a certain percentage of federal tax revenues each year, on a more or less automatic basis, with few strings attached. Under this arrangement, one-third of the funds went to the states and two-thirds were sent directly to local governments. It is clear that the major impetus behind revenue sharing was President Nixon's desire to reduce the role of the federal government while increasing that of state and local governments. Revenue sharing grew for several years and then started to decline. One reason for the decline of revenue sharing relative to other types of assistance was the exclusion of state governments from the program in 1980. Although some argue that revenue-sharing funds were wasted on unimportant problems, many mayors and county officials saw the funds as a way to pay for needed facilities and to reduce the local tax burden. The budget crisis confronting the federal government in the mid-1980s led Congress to abolish revenue sharing to local governments at the end of 1986. There has been some talk during the 1990s, however, of reviving the revenue-sharing program.

Federal Grants Carry Strings Attached

The federal government rarely gives federal grants without imposing more regulations on state and local affairs. For example, it forced all states to lower the speed limit on their roads to 55 miles per hour by enacting the Emergency Highway Conservation Act of 1974. This act prohibited federal funding for highway construction in states that had a speed limit greater than 55. (Congress then passed a law in 1987 that allowed states to raise highway speed limits to 65 miles per hour on most rural interstate highways.) The federal government used a similar tactic in 1984 to impose a nationwide minimum

▲ Although all state and local officials need and appreciate the federal funding they receive for projects such as the bridge construction shown here, these funds do not come without strings attached. How is the 55 m.p.h. speed limit an example of the type of strings that are often attached to federal funds?

BUILDING SOCIAL STUDIES SKILLS

Reading Statistical Tables

Statistics are numerical data. Tables help organize large amounts of data so that they can be analyzed more easily. It makes it easier to make comparisons and see relationships. Reading statistical tables involves scanning groups of numbers in rows and columns. Follow these guidelines:

- Read the title and subtitle and any other labels to identify what types of data are being presented.
- Check to see in what quantities each category of statistics is presented. Values may vary, so look closely. Often, a note in parentheses will indicate whether numbers are meant to indicate thousands, millions, tons, dollars, or other units.
- Examine the statistics in each row and column and look for comparisons and relationships. Note differences and similarities.
- Read footnotes, if any are presented. They will sometimes explain any deviations in the presentation of data or any recording procedures that have changed. A blank space usually means that no figures were available or no activity took place.

PRACTICING YOUR SKILLS

Study the table below and answer the following questions:

1. What does *conterminous* mean? (Check your dictionary.) What does "balance of conterminous U.S." mean?
2. What was the total increase of population living within fifty miles of the coastal shoreline in the United States from 1940 to 1990? What percentage change did that represent?
3. When you add the total population in coastal areas and the "balance of conterminous U.S.," what is the result?

Population in Coastal Areas, 1940–1990

Year	Population of the Conterminous United States (in Millions)	Total Population Within 50 Miles of U.S. Coasts (in Millions)	Resident Populations of Counties Within 50 Miles of U.S. Shorelines (in Millions)				Population of the Balance of the Conterminous United States (in Millions)
			Atlantic Ocean	Pacific Ocean	Great Lakes	Gulf of Mexico	
1940	131.7	60.5	29.9	7.5	18.9	4.2	71.2
1950	150.7	73.5	34.6	11.5	21.8	5.6	77.2
1960	178.5	92.7	41.7	16.8	26.4	7.8	85.7
1970	202.3	108.5	48.2	21.5	29.3	9.5	93.8
1980	225.2	118.5	50.7	25.4	29.8	12.6	106.7
1990	250.4	132.5	56.4	30.7	30.3	15.1	117.9

Source: *Statistical Abstract of the United States.* Washington, D.C.: U.S. Government Printing Office, 1991.

drinking age of 21. Congress passed a law that withheld up to 15 percent of federal highway funding from any state that did not raise its drinking age to 21 by the end of 1987.

SECTION 3 REVIEW

1. By what methods does the federal government return federal tax dollars to state and local governments?
2. Briefly describe each of these methods.
3. **For critical analysis:** How do you think the loss of federal revenues since 1986 has affected your city or town, if at all?

SECTION 4

State and Local Government Spending

Preview Questions

- What are the largest three categories of state expenditures?
- What are the largest three categories of local expenditures?
- What are two important growth areas in state and local budgets?

Figure 25–3 on the right shows state expenditures for the latest year for which data are available. Figure 25–4 on the next page shows the same data for local governments. If you look at the tables carefully, you will notice a clear pattern. Both state and city expenditures are concentrated in the areas of education, public welfare, highways, and health and hospitals. Education is the biggest category of expenditure, particularly at the local level. This expenditure pattern stands in sharp contrast to the spending of the federal government, which allocates only about four percent of its budget to education.

Several areas of spending have become a cause for growing concern in state budgets. Among these areas are prisons and education.

The High Cost of Prisons

State and local governments are almost entirely responsible for housing our prison population (over one million Americans). The estimated total prison budget

State Expenditures (in Percentages)

Spending Category	Percentage of Total Spending
Education	26.66
Public welfare	21.04
Highways	15.51
Health and hospitals	10.28
Interest on general debt	4.32
Natural resources	3.80
Corrections	2.46
Financial administration	2.03
General control	1.67
Social insurance administration	1.63
Police	1.48
General public building	.59
Air transportation	.30
Housing and urban renewal	.28
Water transport and terminals	.24
Libraries	.10
Other	7.61

Source: The Tax Foundation, *Facts and Figures on Government Finance,* 1990.

▲ **FIGURE 25–3 State Expenditures.** The table above shows the major categories of state expenditures. What percentage of state funds are expended for highways?

for 1992 is $25 billion, of which the federal government is providing less than $2 billion. While prison maintenance represents an average of only four percent of state spending, some states such as Michigan spend over seven percent of its budget on prisons. On the whole, spending on prisons has grown between 13 and 15 percent per year since 1986.

Even though the number of reported crimes is actually declining, public opinion on how criminals should be treated is shifting away from rehabilitation and toward punishment, which means longer prison terms. In addition to the one million inmates already in prison across the nation, over 2,500 new inmates are introduced every week. In one year alone, this number is enough to fill five average-sized prisons. Prison expansion is

Local Expenditures (in Percentages)

Spending Category	Percentage of Total Spending
Education	44.88
Public welfare	7.06
Health and hospitals	6.78
Highways	5.66
Police	5.08
Interest on general debt	3.84
Sewerage	3.72
General control	2.58
Fire protection	2.44
Parks and recreation	2.42
Housing and urban renewal	1.80
Sanitation (other than sewerage)	1.44
Financial administration	1.26
General public building	1.25
Corrections	.89
Air transportation	.76
Libraries	.72
Natural resources	.64
Water transport and terminals	.30
Parking facilities	.21
Other	6.27

Source: The Tax Foundation, *Facts and Figures on Government Finance*, 1990.

▲| **FIGURE 25–4 Local Expenditures.** The table above shows the major categories for local expenditures. What percentage of total local spending is devoted to police? How does this compare with state expenditures?

expensive—housing each inmate in new prisons costs up to $25,000 per year.

Education

One of the biggest items in every state and local budget is education. During the 1980s and 1990s, there has been a big emphasis on improving education, particularly in low-income districts. Consequently, state and

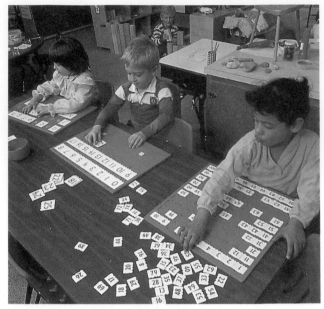

▲| One of the biggest expenses faced by state and local governments is the cost of education. How have education costs grown?

local spending on elementary and secondary schools doubled in the 1980s from less than $100 billion to almost $200 billion per year.

In the past, local governments have borne the brunt of all the costs of public schooling. Since the 1970s, however, state governments have taken on a greater share of total spending. The states now account for up to half of all public school spending. This occurs through aid to local districts.

SECTION 4 REVIEW _____

1. List five major spending categories at the state level.
2. List three major spending categories at the local level.
3. What has happened to state and local spending on prisons in the past decade?
4. **For critical analysis:** While the state governments have had to take on increasing responsibility for financing local public schools, the federal government has actually reduced such aid. Why do you think the federal government has reduced its assistance to education?

CHALLENGE TO THE AMERICAN DREAM

Cities and States in Need

All across the United States, state and local governments have been stricken with financial crises. The immediate cause of the problems seemed to begin with the nation's economic downturn in the late 1980s, but conditions have been worsening over the past decade. What state and city public officials are now facing is the combined effect of several long-term trends:

- Beginning with President Carter's administration and accelerating under President Reagan's "new federalism," the federal government has shifted a heavier financial burden to the states and cities, cutting or eliminating federal grants for housing, education, mass transportation, and public works projects. In the late 1970s, the federal government provided 25 percent of state and local budgets. It now provides less than 17 percent.
- The public is increasingly resistant to new or higher taxes, partly because it believes government is not spending money wisely. Several states have passed initiatives to limit or roll back taxes, and several other states have ousted officials who raised taxes.
- The pressures to spend are enormous. Much of the pressure comes from the public's increasing demand for better schools, harsher punishment of criminals, and better care for the increasing numbers of elderly people. Other pressures come from the growing number of federal rules and regulations that often place new responsibilities on states and cities without giving them sufficient money to carry out the rules. Still other pressures come from the courts, which have forced states to build new prisons to ease overcrowding, or to make changes in education programs.

Unlike the federal government, which can and does operate at a deficit, all states except Vermont are legally bound to have balanced budgets. This leaves states with options of limiting spending or raising taxes, although recently states have often violated the law by running deficits. In the early 1990s, governors of northeastern states such as New York, Massachusetts, and Rhode Island called for severe cutbacks in education, health, and other services and the layoff of thousands of state workers to reduce those states' mounting deficits.

The search for additional revenue sources continues at all levels of government. As pointed out in this chapter, many states have instituted lotteries in order to obtain more revenues. One state has even instituted something called the **value-added tax**, or VAT, which is a tax on the value increase of a company's product. A VAT is a tax on the difference between the costs that go into producing a product and the revenues received from selling the product.

No matter what additional taxes are used in various states and municipalities, a fiscal crisis will be a problem for the United States for many years to come. The number of state employees almost everywhere has increased much faster than the population. In the decade of the 1980s, for example, state and local government employment increased over ten times faster than the population increased in the state of New York. There is no way that such increases in government employment can be handled without taxpayers paying a larger percentage of their income to the government.

The challenge to the American dream is to supply and improve state and local government services wherever such improvement is needed, and to pay for these improvements in a way that does not overburden voters and cause them to revolt.

You Decide

1. Should states be allowed to operate with a deficit? Why or why not?
2. Do you think states and cities will be forced to raise taxes? Why or why not?

CHAPTER 25 REVIEW

Key Terms

block grants 616
categorical grants 615

death taxes 609
equalization 616

excise taxes 609
matching funds 616

project grant 616
value-added tax 621

Summary

1. The federal government and the state governments place limitations on state and local powers of taxation. The U.S. Constitution prevents states from taxing the operations, land, buildings, or any other aspect of the federal government. It prohibits states from regulating and taxing interstate and foreign trade, and the due process clause requires state and local governments to impose and administer taxes fairly. It also forbids unreasonable classifications for the purpose of collecting taxes. Each state also has constitutional limitations on the taxing power of that state and its local governments.

2. Major state and local taxes include the personal income tax, corporate income tax, excise tax, estate tax, inheritance tax, sales tax, and property tax. The most important tax at the state level is sales tax. The most important tax at the local level is property tax. Some state and local governments operate businesses from which they receive revenues. States and cities also borrow by issuing state and municipal bonds.

3. The federal government returns federal tax dollars to state and local governments in three ways. Categorical grants-in-aid are funds for specific purposes or programs. Block grants transfer federal funds to state and local governments to provide broad support in areas such as health care and criminal justice. Revenue sharing occured when a certain percentage of tax income each year was remitted to state and local governments.

4. A breakdown of state government expenditures shows that spending on education, public welfare, highways, and health and hospitals uses about 75 percent of the entire state government budget. At the local level, education uses about 45 percent of local budgets. Public welfare, health and hospitals, highways, and police use up another 25 percent of local budgets. Two areas of growing concern in state and local spending are the increased spending levels on prisons and on education.

Review Questions

1. What limits does the U.S. Constitution place on the taxing abilities of state and local governments?
2. Which are the two major taxes used at the state level?
3. What is the most important tax used at the local level?
4. What types of nontax revenues do state and local governments receive?
5. What are the methods by which the federal government returns federal tax dollars to the states?
6. What is the largest single category of government spending at the state level?
7. What is the largest single category of government spending at the local level?
8. What steps can you take to persuade others that action about a certain issue should be taken in your community?
9. Why have states and cities developed fiscal crises?

Questions for Thought and Discussion

1. It is argued by some that revenue sharing is better than grants-in-aid because grants-in-aid give too much power to the federal government. Others favor them, fearing that revenue sharing encourages waste, corruption, and inefficiency. Give reasons for both arguments.
2. Many people argue that schools are in dire need of improvement and that the nation's future is at risk because schools are performing poorly. If state fiscal conditions worsen in the years ahead, school budgets are unlikely to escape without cutbacks. How do you think this conflict can be solved? What do you think are some of the causes for the breakdown in the school system?
3. In which areas, if any, do you think your local government spends too much money? Too little money? Give reasons for your answers.

CHAPTER 25 REVIEW—Continued

4. Do you think state and local governments should depend on the federal government for a major share of their revenues? Why or why not?
5. Why do you think states rely so heavily on sales taxes? Why do you think cities rely so heavily on property taxes? What kinds of alternatives would you propose to reduce heavy reliance on these taxes?
6. Do you think state and local governments should be allowed to raise money through business enterprises? Why or why not?

Improving Your Skills
Communication Skills

Using Context Clues to Determine Word Meanings

In your reading and studies, you will occasionally come across words you do not recognize. If you do not know the meaning of a word, you may not fully understand the passage you are reading. One way to find the meaning of unfamiliar words is to look them up in the dictionary. Another way is to carefully examine the way the word is used in context. A careful reader may find many clues to the meaning of a word in surrounding words and sentences, and in the main idea of the writing.

Writing

Read the following sentences. Use context clues to determine the meanings of the underlined words. Then write your own definition of each of the words. Check your definitions against the dictionary for accuracy.

The conventional view is that the burgeoning of the American nation-state occurred hand in hand with the shrinkage in the role and power of the individual American states. Certainly from the 1930s to the 1960s state governments declined in relative importance. Governors and state legislatures wallowed in mediocrity. Social and economic problems seemed to be susceptible only to national solutions. The states came to be widely regarded as historical anomalies, of no particular significance in a new, thoroughly nationalized society.

Social Studies Skills

Working with Sequencing Data and Statistical Tables

Statistical tables are one of the many ways to sequence data and information. The way that the data are sequenced is often up to the person who is presenting the data. For example, the data on state and local expenditures presented in Figure 25–3 on page 619 and Figure 25–4 on page 620 are sequenced in *decreasing* order of expenditures (except for the last, catch-all category of "Other"). The data could have also been presented in *increasing* order of expenditures.

1. What is at least one other way the data could have been presented? (Hint: Look at the other figures in this chapter.)
2. Once you have chosen another way of presenting the same data, sketch out how this other presentation would look.
3. Do you have choices in how you order the data with this other way of presentation?
4. If your answer to question 3 above is yes, give reasons why you would want the data presented in one order rather than another.

Activities and Projects

1. Imagine that you are a lobbyist for a particular program whose funds have been cut. Develop an oral argument to present to the legislature that will convince your state legislators to restore the program's funding.
2. Obtain a copy of your state budget. Analyze the budget to determine the items on which your state spends the most money. Write a paragraph on each of the top three items that tells why you think your state spends the most money in these areas.
3. If your state has a lottery, get the statistics showing the growth in revenues collected since the lottery began. Then find out what percentage of these revenues has gone to finance public education. Is this percentage increasing or decreasing?
4. Write a paragraph or two summarizing how your state compares to other states with respect to the amount of state and local taxes collected and the manner in which those taxes are collected.

UNIT NINE

Other Nations

Unit Contents

■ *Chapter 26*   Comparing Governments and Economic Systems

625

CHAPTER 26

Comparing Governments and Economic Systems

CHAPTER OBJECTIVES

To learn and understand

■ The nature of the constitutional monarchy in Great Britain.

■ The French system of government.

■ The Japanese system of government.

■ The different types of economic systems.

■ The main characteristics of the American economy.

■ The main characteristics of Marxian economics and the converging of the world's political systems.

The Daily Press

Trade Gap Widens

Keynote

"Economic freedom is . . . an indispensable means toward the achievement of political freedom."

——— **Milton Friedman**
(1912–   ) American Economist

INTRODUCTION

One glimpse at a news broadcast reveals that there are massive and mystifying differences among governments around the world. Custom, religion, tradition, dress, and language all seem to differ greatly from culture to culture. The titles and powers of those in office vary from nation to nation. The lawmaking bodies have various forms and the economic systems are often very different. The people in other countries have widely differing ideas of what government should do.

Not all governments would agree with Milton Friedman's opening quote. The extent to which other peoples have true economic and political freedom varies dramatically from country to country throughout the world. The downfall in the late 1980s and early 1990s of the political and economic systems that have greatly restricted political freedom has certainly driven this point home to the rest of the world.

As you learned in Chapter 4, governments can be grouped into several distinct types such as unitary, federal, and confederal. You also learned the difference between parliamentary and presidential systems, and the differences between dictatorial and democratic rule. This chapter will present a more specific examination of several other governments in the world: Great Britain, France, and Japan.

This chapter takes a comparative approach in discussing other governments and economic systems. By comparing these governments and economic systems with our own, you should gain an insight into the complexities involved in our political and economic dealings with these countries.

Additionally in this chapter, we will look at the role technology plays in shaping a new world order. Because news and information can be almost instantaneously transmitted throughout the world, political leaders are subject now, more than ever, to the influence of world public opinion.

SECTION 1

Great Britain

Preview Questions
- What are the main characteristics of the British political system?
- What are the similarities and differences between the British and American political systems?
- What is the function of the monarchy in Great Britain today?
- How does the British Parliament operate?

Many principles of the political system in the United States originated in England. For this reason, Americans are inclined to think that the government of Great Britain is similar to our own. While both the United States and Great Britain are democracies, there are fundamental differences between the two.

Constitutional Monarchy

The United States is a republic, a country in which the sovereign power is held by the voters and is exercised by elected representatives who are responsible to the people. Great Britain, in contrast, is a monarchy, in which sovereignty lies with the **hereditary ruler**, someone who rules because he or she was the son or daughter of a previous ruler. The monarchy falls to the oldest son or daughter of the current monarch. The new monarch then holds the title of King or Queen.

The laws and customs that define the powers of the monarch have evolved throughout history. English monarchs once ruled with absolute power, but since the 1800s, the powers of the monarch have decreased significantly. The Queen's duties today as head of state are mainly ceremonial, such as "opening" the sessions of

627

The president of France is the only nationally elected official in the country and serves a seven-year term (which may soon become five years). The constitution gives the president the power to appoint the prime minister and other high officials, as well as the power to negotiate treaties and act as commander in chief of the military.

Two other significant constitutional powers are available to the French president that do not exist in the British or American systems. One gives the president the power to bypass Parliament completely. He or she may call for a national referendum. The other power gives the president the right to take complete control of the government in times of grave emergency. Basically, he or she can then undertake virtually any necessary action to suit the gravity of the national emergency.

Whenever the French president does not like the way his or her legislative program is being treated in the lower house—called the **National Assembly**—he or she can ask for new elections. This is known as dissolving the Parliament.

The Government:
The Prime Minister and Cabinet

The president and the prime minister and his or her cabinet are often referred to as ''the government,'' as is done in Britain. Both the prime minister and his or her cabinet are allowed to have executive and legislative powers simultaneously. The French president picks the prime minister, in contrast to the way the legislature does in Britain. Then the prime minister picks his or her own cabinet members. These individuals head various executive departments such as foreign affairs and finance. They are called ministers, just as in Britain. Cabinet members can be chosen from the Parliament (and then must resign), but usually are from the business, legal, or cultural worlds outside of politics. Many are career civil servants who have specialized in the area in which they are appointed, such as agriculture or the arts.

In spite of the fact that cabinet members are not members of Parliament, they still control the course of bills as they are taken through the legislature. In other words, the prime minister and cabinet determine the legislative agenda. They introduce bills and sit in the National Assembly. In fact, all taxing and spending bills must originate from the cabinet. When the president is not happy with the popularity of his or her prime minister, the president can fire the person and put someone else in place who may do a job that is better accepted by the French electorate.

The Legislature

Parliament has two houses, the National Assembly and the Senate. As in the U.S., the Senate is considered the upper house. The Assembly consists of 491 deputies; the Senate has 305 senators.

The French Parliament is limited in its lawmaking powers by the constitution, which specifically outlines

◄ The lower house of the French legislature is called the National Assembly. What type of powers does the French president have over the National Assembly?

the subjects that may be legislated. These areas include education, criminal justice, social welfare, civil rights, and administration of local communities. The subjects *not* listed are the sole area for which the government is able to enact laws by decree, that is, without approval of the Parliament.

Parliament has little authority over the budget and may not reduce revenues or raise expenditures.

Similar to the American system, all bills must be approved by both houses in France and then signed by the president. Also similar to the U.S. system, there are permanent, or standing, committees in both houses, all with a number of subcommittees. In the U.S., all such subcommittees are highly specialized. But in France, they are closer to the British subcommittees, which are responsible for general areas. If the Assembly and the Senate pass different versions of a bill, the prime minister appoints a joint committee to resolve the differences. (The somewhat similar process occurs in the U.S. system.) If this appointed committee cannot resolve the issues in dispute, the prime minister can ask the Assembly to vote on the bill. If it does so and the president signs the bill, it becomes law.

Elections and Political Parties

All parties can nominate candidates for the presidency. To be elected, a candidate must win a majority vote. If no candidate wins a clear majority, a second runoff election is held two weeks later. In this election, only the two candidates with the most votes run, and the winner is named president. There is no limit on the number of terms a president may serve.

Since the formation of the Fifth Republic in 1958, there have been four presidents, the first one being World War II hero General Charles de Gaulle. He remained in power until 1969. Then Georges Pompidou was elected and died in office in 1974. Valery Giscard d'Estaing was elected that year and stayed until 1981, when François Mitterand took over.

Members of the Assembly are popularly elected from single-member districts for five-year terms, unless new elections are called sooner. Senate members are chosen by a body composed mostly of elected officials in the country's ninety-six geographical governmental divisions called **departments**. Senators serve nine-year terms, and one-third of the seats are up for election every three years.

As with all democracies, France has many political parties. For many years, the most important party was the Rally for the Republic, popularly known as the

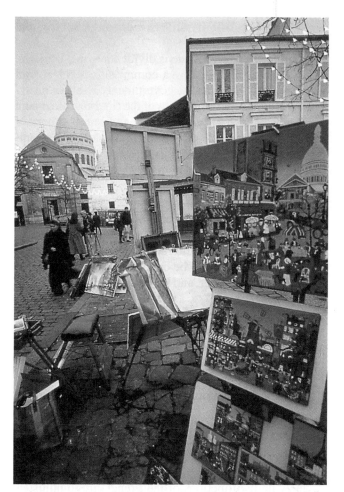

France has a unitary form of government. What does this mean for the people in the cities and towns of France?

Gaullists. The Socialist Party became the most important in the 1980s and early 1990s. This is the party to which Mitterand belongs. The National Front, an extreme right-wing party, began capturing more support in the 1990s. It is headed by Jean LePen, who believes in severely restricting immigration. Except for supporters of the Communist Party, the French do not tend to identify strongly with political parties and voters may shift parties from election to election. Different parties, however, do attract broad groups of people. For example, the Socialist Party consists mainly of salaried workers and government bureaucrats.

Local Government

The central government in Paris has long controlled all local government with an iron fist. This has been possible because France has a unitary system of govmally they do not vote. The reality is that most of the legislation proposed by the government's party ends up, in one form or another, becoming law.

The Prime Minister and His Cabinet

As stated before, the prime minister is chosen by the Diet and is a member of the Diet. Of the eighteen members of his or her cabinet, at least half must be from the Diet. In reality, virtually all members of the Japanese government's cabinet are also legislators. Sometimes an important member of the bureaucracy is chosen by the prime minister to become part of the cabinet. As with the U.S. cabinet, the Japanese cabinet includes the heads of various ministries (executive departments) such as agriculture and forestry, education, labor, health and welfare, justice, and foreign affairs. Much of the job of the cabinet involves pushing government-sponsored legislation through the Diet. If the prime minister is not satisfied with the progress of the legislation that his or her government has proposed, he or she may dissolve the House of Representatives. Then new elections are called. Consequently, not all members of the House of Representatives are allowed to serve a full four-year term.

In keeping with the consensus tradition, virtually no dissent is allowed within the cabinet. That is to say, if a cabinet member disagrees with what the prime minister is doing, that cabinet member must resign.

The All-Powerful Bureaucracy

While the bureaucracy is sometimes considered the fourth branch of government in the United States, in Japan it can truly be said to have taken on a much more serious and important role. The federal bureaucracy in America has relatively little to do with making government policy. Not so in Japan. Some students of Japanese politics even argue that bureaucrats are an important ruling force in the country.

Some of the best and the brightest of those who complete college in Japan decide to enter the bureaucracy. They are not attracted by the pay, for the pay scale in the government in Japan (as in virtually all other developed countries) is relatively low. In other words, top-ranked college graduates in Japan can almost always earn higher incomes if they go into private business. But a Japanese government bureaucrat is highly regarded in that society. Such jobs carry prestige, which overcomes the relatively low salary scale.

To show how much confidence legislators have in the bureaucracy, they write legislation in a very general way. They leave it up to the bureaucracy to fill in the details of rulemaking and implementation. Some bureaucracies make important policy decisions with respect to interest rates and the availability of credit. Other powerful bureaucracies decide which industries to help and which not to help.

In America, the head of a government agency may meet infrequently, if at all, with the Congress. Just the opposite situation exists in the Japanese system. There, politicians have frequent meetings with the heads of different agencies. Although career bureaucrats in Japan do not particularly like politicians who interfere, the bureaucrats accept the need to justify their actions to the legislators.

◄ In recent years, Japan has become an economic power, exporting many products, including these automobiles. What role do you think the bureaucracy plays in Japan's economic success?

CITIZENSHIP SKILLS AND RESPONSIBILITIES

How to Support Human Rights

There are still many places in the world where men, women, and children are being illegally imprisoned and tortured. These people aren't guilty of any crime except being born a different color, practicing a different religion, speaking a different language, or having different political views from the people who are torturing them. If you are interested in learning more about struggles for human rights around the world, a good place to start is with Amnesty International.

Amnesty International was founded in 1961 to organize the world to take a stand against human rights injustices. In 1977 it won the Nobel Peace Prize for "defending human dignity against violence and subjugation." In 1986 Amnesty International enlisted the support of rock musicians to bring the human rights message to American youth; their "Conspiracy of Hope" tour boosted national action. Each year it has enlisted more people to support its cause.

Today, Amnesty International has grown into a worldwide network of over 700,000 people with branches in many countries and more than 100 researchers who compile the latest information on torture and state-supported abuses of human rights. As

of 1992, Amnesty International had taken on more than 31,000 individual cases and was a key factor in the release of almost 2,000 political prisoners. Other goals are to ensure prompt and fair trials for political prisoners and to end torture and executions. It attempts to achieve these goals through publicity, lobbying, legal aid, and letter-writing campaigns that focus on the cases of specific individuals.

To become a member, send whatever donation you can. The suggested membership fees are $25, or $15 for students and senior citizens. If you are interested, write to Amnesty International USA, 322 Eighth Avenue, New York, NY 10001, or telephone 212-807-8400.

TAKING ACTION

1. Do further research on three specific cases in which Amnesty International has recently been involved. Report back to the class on your findings and your assessment of the organization.
2. Research human rights violations in a particular country in which you are interested.
3. Research the history of apartheid in South Africa.

In June of 1989, a popular movement for democracy in the People's Republic of China was openly crushed by government tanks and soldiers. How long has the People's Republic of China been under communist rule?

in its satellite countries for a little over 40 years. For most researchers, that is a sufficient time period during which to determine whether the "experiment" worked. It did not.

All of the former communist countries in Eastern Europe and in what was the Soviet Union are now attempting in various ways to revitalize their economies and democratize their political systems. While the future of the Commonwealth of Independent States within the former Soviet Union is unknown (and in fact that loose confederation of nations may not even exist when you read this), one thing is certain: the challenges that face the people and political representatives are enormous. New political and economic structures will surely emerge. Some forms of central command and socialism will undoubtedly remain, but certainly not very much. Former Prime Minister Winston Churchill of Britain was once rumored to have said that democracy was the worst system known to civilization, but the best of all the alternatives. The same could probably be said about capitalism as an economic system.

What About China?

While command socialism fell apart in the former Soviet Union and Eastern Europe, it continued in force in the People's Republic of China.

After the communists emerged victorious in China's Civil War following World War II, they instituted an economic system similar in nature to the one in the former Soviet Union. Central planning from the capital, Beijing, occurred not only with respect to deciding all

economic questions but also in deciding all political questions. The Communist Party has ruled since 1949. From that time until his death in 1976, Chairman Mao ruled with an iron fist. In 1978 a new leader, Deng Xiaoping, took over power. On the economic front, Deng did decentralize Chinese industry to some extent. He also allowed some foreign investment. The result has been an increase in Chinese living standards.

Politically, though, there has been relatively little movement towards democracy.

The Results of Centralized Control   An interesting comparison can be made between the more open, market-oriented economies in Taiwan and Hong Kong and the centralized, command economy in mainland China. In 1950 the average income per person of China and Taiwan was about the same. Hong Kong had a little more. By 1992, the average income in Taiwan was 30 times that of mainland China and in Hong Kong 35 times more.

Creating Special Economic Zones   The Chinese leadership was aware of this great difference in income between its centrally planned command socialist economy and the market economies just next door. In 1979, Deng Xiaoping designated fourteen cities along China's coast as "coastal open cities," with extra freedoms and tax breaks for foreign trade and investment. Additionally, five "special economic zones" were created with even more free market privileges.

The result has been a boom in the coastal arc stretching from Hainan Island in the southwest through Guangdong Province, adjacent to Hong Kong, and on to Fujian

CHALLENGE TO THE AMERICAN DREAM

Can We Ever Solve the World's Problems?

After reading this text, you may get the impression that the world's problems are insurmountable. After all, the AIDS epidemic seems to be increasing worldwide; the drug and crime problem in the United States is getting worse, not better; and war is definitely not something in the past for it has happened as recently as 1991 (and maybe even more recently by the time you read this book). Moreover, throughout the previous pages in this text, you have read about many other problems in the United States and throughout the world.

There is another side to all this negativity, however. Just look at what has happened in the United States in only two hundred years. We went from being an almost purely agricultural society to one in which agriculture occupies less than 3 percent of the population. At the same time, the standard of living of the average American has skyrocketed. Indeed, what well-to-do people had available at the beginning of this nation's history would be considered a relatively low standard of living today.

Even though we read about epidemics, health problems, pollution, and cancer-causing food additives and toxins, the average life expectancy in the United States continues to rise.

Even though we continue to read about increasing crime rates in the United States, the average American is actually safer than he or she was in the major cities of the world several hundred years ago.

Even though we read about horrible plane crashes, the average flyer on an airplane is over one hundred times safer than someone driving the same distance in a car, and three or four times safer than the average airplane passenger was thirty years ago.

While it is true that the AIDS epidemic is a horrible scourge on humanity, it has only been around for little more than a decade and medical science has already started to find potential cures.

While it is true that some indicators of educational achievement are not very heartwarming, the average American today is many times more educated than he or she was several hundred years ago or even fifty years ago. Indeed, so many Americans are becoming educated that four years of college has become accepted as an educational standard.

Even though environmental problems continue to grow, more Americans than ever before have begun to make changes in the way they live, in what they buy, and in how they view the environment. This *greening* of America reflects a positive trend for saving the environment.

Think about how much leisure time Americans have today compared to the past. The average work week is 37.5 hours in the United States. Several hundred years ago it exceeded 60 hours a week.

Nonetheless, do not go too far in looking at the positive side of everything. There are numerous challenges to the American dream just as there are numerous challenges to the dream of worldwide peace, prosperity, and equality for all. Concerned, educated, and dedicated Americans will always be needed to understand and help solve the many challenges that exist now and the many new ones that will exist in the future.

◢ You Decide

1. On the whole, do you think that the benefits of economic progress in the United States have outweighed the costs? Why or why not?
2. Of all the challenges that face our society today, which ones do you think need the most urgent attention? Why?
3. Some people say bad news sells and good news does not. Therefore, all we hear about are problems. Do you agree? Why or why not? Is it possible that this philosophy affects textbooks also?

Province, which is opposite Taiwan. Fujian Province, for example, with 30 million people was one of China's poorest provinces in the 1970s. Yet industrial output has increased seven times from 1990 to 1992.

SECTION 6 REVIEW

1. What were some of the socialist ideas introduced by Karl Marx?

2. What event occurred in the last few years that changed many people's view of communism?
3. How has mainland China fared economically compared to Taiwan and Hong Kong?
4. **For critical analysis:** Can the failure of command socialism and communism in the former Soviet Union be equated to the triumph of capitalism?

CHAPTER 26 REVIEW

Key Terms

administrative councils 631	county boroughs 631	law lords 629	opposition 630
capital 638	departments 633	market 639	Parliament 628
capitalism 639	economic system 638	market economic system 639	prime minister 629
command economic system 638	free enterprise system 642	Members of Parliament 628	private property 643
communism 638	hereditary ruler 627	ministers 629	profit incentive 644
competition 644	heredity peers 629	mixed economy 640	unitary government 630
constitutional monarch 628	House of Commons 628	National Assembly 632	vote of confidence 630
	House of Lords 629	National Diet 635	

Summary

1. Great Britain is a democratic constitutional monarchy. It has no constitution in our sense of the word but rather has a whole body of agreements, some written and some unwritten. Since the 1800s the monarch has served mainly a ceremonial function. The British Parliament is a bicameral legislature made up of the House of Commons, which has most of the power, and the House of Lords. The majority party in the House of Commons elects one of its members as the prime minister, who in turn selects other members to form the cabinet. Great Britain has a unitary form of government, which means powers are centralized at the national level.

2. The French democratic government operates under a written constitution that was adopted in 1958 and that created a mixed parliamentary/presidential system. The president is the most powerful governmental figure and is the only nationally elected official. The French Parliament consists of the National Assembly and the Sen-

ate. The president chooses the prime minister, who in turn appoints cabinet members. The French government is unitary and highly centralized.

3. Japan's constitution was set down by the occupying American forces and went into effect in 1947. Japan's legislature has a parliament of two houses, called the National Diet, in which the upper house is the House of Councilers, and the lower house is the House of Representatives. The House of Representatives has the most power. It consists of more than five hundred members chosen from 130 election districts. The upper house has 252 members. Legislation is normally introduced by the bureaucracy or the government in power rather than by the legislators themselves. The prime minister is a member of the Diet; he or she selects the cabinet, half of whose members must be from the Diet. Japan has a multiparty system with one dominant party, the Liberal Democratic Party (LDP).

4. An economic system is the way in which a nation uses its resources to satisfy its people's needs and wants.

CHAPTER 26 REVIEW—Continued

In a command economic system, the government controls the means of production and the individual has very little influence over how the economy functions. In a market economic system, government does not intervene: Individuals own the means of production and make decisions based on the trends of the market. Today, almost all economic systems are mixed economies; some contain more characteristics of a command economy and some more closely resemble a market economy.

5. A pure market economic system has six major characteristics: little or no government control, freedom of enterprise, freedom of choice, private property, profit incentive, and competition. In the United States, the government's role in the economy is much greater than it would be if it were a pure market system. Capitalism is defined as an economic system in which private individuals own the means of production.

6. Many of the former centrally planned socialist and communist countries in Eastern Europe and the former Soviet Union (and the People's Republic of China) based their economic theories on the works of Karl Marx, whose most important book was *Das Kapital,* written in 1867. Marx outlined his labor theory of value and talked about capitalists exploiting the surplus value of the workers. He predicted the eventual failure of capitalism. He believed that socialism and communism would ultimately prevail. The break-up of the former Soviet Union and its satellite countries has proven Marx to be incorrect. China remains a socialist country; but is gradually opening up larger and larger parts to capitalism.

Review Questions

1. What is the difference between the United States Constitution and the British Constitution?
2. How does the British Parliament differ from the United States Congress?
3. What is meant by the term *government* in Great Britain?
4. What are the powers of the French president?
5. Why is the French parliamentary system unique?
6. What limits the French Parliament's lawmaking powers?
7. What is the difference between American, British, and French political parties?

8. What is the similarity between the French and British local governments?
9. What are the key aspects of the Japanese constitution?
10. How is the Japanese legislature formed?
11. Who performs the executive functions of government in Japan and are they separate from the legislative branch?
12. Briefly describe the command and market economic systems.
13. Why are most economies considered mixed?
14. List the six major characteristics of a pure market economic system.
15. Briefly describe Adam Smith's idea of competition and how he viewed the role of government in the economy.
16. Why is the United States called a free enterprise system?
17. What role does profit play in capitalism?
18. What were some of the predictions that Marx made?
19. What happened to most of the world's communist countries between 1989 and 1991?
20. How is China governed?
21. Describe the goals of Amnesty International.

Questions for Thought and Discussion

1. Why do you think Great Britain continues to have a monarch even though his or her role is now mainly ceremonial? How do you think most American people would react to a monarch in this country?
2. What, if any, features of other nations' governments do you think should be incorporated into our government? Give reasons for your answer.
3. Some people think that the United States' government should play no role in the economy and that we should work toward a pure free-enterprise economy. What do you think the benefits of such an arrangement would be? What would be the problems?

Improving Your Skills
Communication Skills
Determining the Strength of an Argument

Whether you are doing research, debating an issue, or listening to the argument of a friend, teacher, or sales-

CHAPTER 26 REVIEW—Continued

person, it is important to be able to determine the strength of an argument. It is sometimes easy to be persuaded by an overbearing writer or speaker, by flowery language, or by the manner in which the argument is presented. To assess the strength of an argument, you must look past these elements to examine the evidence and the reasons that the argument uses as a basis.

This skill is also critical when you are presenting an argument. Just presenting an opinion is not enough. You also must support your argument with evidence and sound reasoning. Ask these questions to determine the strength of your own or another's arguments:

- Is the argument stated in the clearest and most understandable way?
- What evidence, if any, is used to support the argument? Is the evidence relevant and accurate?
- What reasons are presented for making the argument? Do they directly relate to the issue?
- Are there enough reasons and evidence to support the argument, or are more needed?
- Has important evidence been left out that would weaken or disprove the argument?
- Would an unbiased person hearing the argument, evidence, and reasons be convinced?

Writing Exercise

Listen to a speech or debate, taking notes on what you hear. After the event, review your notes and write out answers to the questions above. Then write a paragraph explaining your opinion on the strengths of the arguments presented.

Social Studies Skills

Comparing Similarities and Differences

In your study of other governments and economic systems, you cannot help but make comparisons of both the similarities and differences. Also, it is natural to compare what is new and different with what you already know. Specifically, you might automatically compare the parliamentary system of Britain with the way the United States political system operates. When you read about command socialism in China, you might automatically compare it to the more-or-less decentralized capitalist system in the United States.

Consider the British and the French political systems. Reread the sections on them before you answer the following questions.

1. In what ways is the selection of the prime minister the same or different?
2. What are the similarities between the French Senate and the British House of Lords? What are the differences?
3. Does the prime minister in each country have about the same amount of power? If the answer is no, explain your answer.
4. Explain the similarities and differences between the way in which a national law becomes effective in each country.
5. The two systems are both called parliamentary. Does that mean they are the same? If your answer is no, explain your answer.

Activities and Projects

1. Create a bulletin board display that compares the main features of the governments discussed in this chapter.
2. Research the political system of a country not discussed in this chapter, such as Mexico, South Africa, or India. Write a report comparing the government of the country to that of the United States.
3. Find a person in your community who is originally from another country. Interview that person to get his or her impressions on the differences and similarities between the governmental and economic systems in his or her native country and in the United States. Find out his or her opinions about which systems work better, and what kinds of experiences he or she has had with either government.

THE RESOURCE CENTER

CONTENTS

Original Source Documents 654
   Constitution of the United States of America 654
   The Bill of Rights 665
   The Magna Carta (1215) 672
   Mayflower Compact (1620) 674
   Declaration of Independence (1776) 675
   Articles of Confederation (1781–1789) 677
   Federalist Papers #10 and #51 (1787/1788) 681
   Anti-Federalist Writings (1787–1788) 687
   Monroe Doctrine (1823) 687
   Seneca Falls Declaration (1848) 689
   Emancipation Proclamation (1862) 689
   Pledge of Allegiance (1892) 690
   The American's Creed (1917) 691
   Brown v. Board of Education of Topeka (1954) 691
   The Preamble to the Charter of the United Nations 692
Annotated Table of Legal Cases 692
   How to Read Legal Case Citations and Find Court Decisions 692
   Table of Court Cases 693
Extended Case Studies 701
   Immigration Reform and Control Act of 1986 and Amnesty 701
   The AIDS Epidemic 703
   The War on Drugs 705
   Exxon Valdez 707
Presidents and Vice Presidents of the United States 710
Supreme Court Chief Justices and Associate Justices Since 1789 721
State Atlas 726
U.S. and World Maps 737
   Map of the United States 738
   Map of the World 740

Constitution of the United States of America*

The Preamble

We the People of the United States, in Order to form a more perfect Union, establish Justice, insure domestic Tranquility, provide for the common defence, promote the general Welfare, and secure the Blessings of Liberty to ourselves and our Posterity, do ordain and establish this Constitution for the United States of America.

The Preamble declares that ''We the People'' are the authority for the Constitution (unlike the Articles of Confederation, which derived their authority from the states). The Preamble also sets out the purposes of the Constitution.

Article I. (Legislative Branch)

The first part of the Constitution is called Article 1; it deals with the organization and powers of the lawmaking branch of the national government, the Congress.

Section 1. Legislative Powers

All legislative Powers herein granted shall be vested in a Congress of the United States, which shall consist of a Senate and House of Representatives.

Section 2. House of Representatives

Clause 1: Composition and Election of Members. The House of Representatives shall be composed of Members chosen every second Year by the People of the several States, and the Electors in each State shall have the Qualifications requisite for Electors of the most numerous Branch of the State Legislature.

Each state has the power to decide who may vote for members of Congress. Within each state, those who may vote for state legislators may also vote for members of the House of Representatives (and, under the Seventeenth Amendment, for U.S. senators). When the Constitution was written, nearly all states limited voting rights to white male property owners or taxpayers at least twenty-one years old. Subsequent amendments granted voting power to African-American men, all women, and eighteen-year-olds.

Clause 2: Qualifications. No Person shall be a Representative who shall not have attained to the Age of twenty five Years, and been seven Years a Citizen of the United States, and who shall not, when elected, be an Inhabitant of that State in which he shall be chosen.

Each member of the House must (1) be at least twenty-five years old, (2) have been a U.S. citizen for at least seven years, and (3) be a resident of the state in which she or he is elected.

Clause 3: Apportionment of Representatives and Direct Taxes. Representatives [and direct Taxes][1] shall be apportioned among the several States which may be included within this Union, according to their respective Numbers [which shall be determined by adding to the whole Number of free Persons, including those bound to Service for a Term of Years, and excluding Indians not taxed, three fifths of all other Persons].[2] The actual Enumeration shall be made within three Years after the first Meeting of the Congress of the United States, and within every subsequent Term of ten Years, in such Manner as they shall by Law direct. The Number of Representatives shall not exceed one for every thirty Thousand, but each State shall have at Least one Representative; and until such enumeration shall be made, the State of New Hampshire shall be entitled to chuse three, Massachusetts eight, Rhode Island and Providence Plantations one, Connecticut five, New York six, New Jersey four, Pennsylvania eight, Delaware one, Maryland six, Virginia ten, North Carolina five, South Carolina five, and Georgia three.

---

*The spelling, capitalization, and punctuation of the original have been retained here. Brackets indicate passages that have been altered by amendments to the Constitution.

[1]Modified by the Sixteenth Amendment.
[2]Modified by the Fourteenth Amendment.

A state's representation in the House is based on the size of its population. Population is counted in each decade's census, after which Congress reapportions House seats. Since early in this century, the number of seats has been limited to 435.

Clause 4: Vacancies. When vacancies happen in the Representation from any State, the Executive Authority thereof shall issue Writs of Election to fill such Vacancies.

The ''Executive Authority'' is the state's governor. When a vacancy occurs in the House, the governor calls a special election to fill it.

Clause 5: Officers and Impeachment. The House of Representatives shall chuse their Speaker and other Officers; and shall have the sole Power of Impeachment.

The power to impeach is the power to accuse. In this case, it is the power to accuse members of the executive or judicial branch of wrongdoing or abuse of power. Once a bill of impeachment is issued, the Senate holds the trial.

Section 3. The Senate
Clause 1: Term and Number of Members. The Senate of the United States shall be composed of two Senators from each State [chosen by the Legislature thereof],[3] for six Years; and each Senator shall have one Vote.

Every state has two senators, each of whom serves for six years, and has one vote in the upper chamber. Since the Seventeenth Amendment in 1913, all senators are elected directly by voters of the state during the regular election.

Clause 2: Classification of Senators. Immediately after they shall be assembled in Consequence of the first Election, they shall be divided as equally as may be into three Classes. The Seats of the Senators of the first Class shall be vacated at the Expiration of the second Year, of the second Class at the Expiration of the fourth Year, and of the third Class at the Expiration of the sixth Year, so that one third may be chosen every second Year; [and if Vacancies happen by Resignation, or otherwise, during the Recess of the Legislature of any State, the Executive thereof may make temporary Appointments until the next Meeting of the Legislature, which shall then fill such Vacancies].[4]

One-third of the Senate's seats are open to election every two years (unlike the House, all of whose members are elected simultaneously).

[3]Repealed by the Seventeenth Amendment.
[4]Modified by the Seventeenth Amendment.

Clause 3: Qualifications. No Person shall be a Senator who shall not have attained to the Age of thirty Years, and been nine Years a Citizen of the United States, and who shall not, when elected, be an Inhabitant of that State for which he shall be chosen.

Every senator must be at least thirty years old, a citizen of the United States for a minimum of nine years, and a resident of the state in which he or she is elected.

Clause 4: The Role of the Vice President. The Vice President of the United States shall be President of the Senate, but shall have no Vote, unless they be equally divided.

The vice-president presides over meetings of the Senate but cannot vote unless there is a tie. The Constitution gives no other official duties to the vice-president.

Clause 5: Other Officers. The Senate shall chuse their other Officers, and also a President pro tempore, in the Absence of the Vice President, or when he shall exercise the Office of President of the United States.

When the vice-president is absent, the Senate votes for one of its members to preside; this person is usually called the president pro tempore because of the temporary situation of the position.

Clause 6: Impeachment Trials. The Senate shall have the sole Power to try all Impeachments. When sitting for that Purpose, they shall be on Oath or Affirmation. When the President of the United States is tried, the Chief Justice shall preside: And no Person shall be convicted without the Concurrence of two thirds of the Members present.

The Senate conducts trials of officials that the House impeaches. The Senate sits as a jury, with the vice-president presiding if the president is not on trial.

Clause 7: Penalties for Conviction. Judgment in Cases of Impeachment shall not extend further than to removal from Office, and disqualification to hold and enjoy any Office of honor, Trust, or Profit under the United States: but the Party convicted shall nevertheless be liable and subject to Indictment, Trial, Judgment, and Punishment, according to Law.

On conviction on impeachment charges, the Senate can only force an official to leave office and prevent him or her from holding another office in the federal government. The individual, however, can still be tried in a regular court.

Section 4. Congressional Elections: Times, Manner, and Places

Clause 1: Elections.   The Times, Places and Manner of holding Elections for Senators and Representatives, shall be prescribed in each State by the Legislature thereof; but the Congress may at any time by Law make or alter such Regulations, except as to the Places of chusing Senators.

Congress set the Tuesday after the first Monday in November in even-numbered years as the date for congressional elections. In states with more than one seat in the House, Congress requires that representatives be elected from districts within each state. Under the Seventeenth Amendment, senators are elected at the same places as other officials.

Clause 2: Sessions of Congress.   [The Congress shall assemble at least once in every Year, and such Meeting shall be on the first Monday in December, unless they shall by Law appoint a different Day.]⁵

Congress has to meet every year at least once. The regular session now begins at noon on January 3 of each year, subsequent to the Twentieth Amendment, unless Congress passes a law to fix a different date. Congress stays in session until its members vote to adjourn. Additionally, the president may call a special session.

Section 5. Powers and Duties of the Houses

Clause 1: Admitting Members and Quorum.   Each House shall be the Judge of the Elections, Returns, and Qualifications of its own Members, and a Majority of each shall constitute a Quorum to do Business; but a smaller Number may adjourn from day to day, and may be authorized to compel the Attendance of absent Members, in such Manner, and under such Penalties as each House may provide.

Each chamber may exclude or refuse to seat a member-elect.
     The quorum rule requires that 218 members of the House and 51 members of the Senate be present in order to conduct business. This rule is normally not enforced in the handling of routine matters.

Clause 2: Rules and Discipline of Members.   Each House may determine the Rules of its Proceedings, punish

---

⁵Changed by the Twentieth Amendment.

its Members for disorderly Behaviour, and, with the Concurrence of two thirds, expel a Member.

The House and the Senate may adopt their own rules to guide their proceedings. Each may also discipline its members for conduct that is deemed unacceptable. No member may be expelled without a two-thirds majority.

Clause 3: Keeping a Record.   Each House shall keep a Journal of its Proceedings, and from time to time publish the same, excepting such Parts as may in their Judgment require Secrecy; and the Yeas and Nays of the Members of either House on any question shall, at the Desire of one fifth of those Present, be entered on the Journal.

The journals of the two houses are published at the end of each session of Congress.

Clause 4: Adjournment.   Neither House, during the Session of Congress, shall, without the Consent of the other, adjourn for more than three days, nor to any other Place than that in which the two Houses shall be sitting.

Congress has the power to determine when and where to meet, provided, however, that both houses meet in the same city. Neither house may recess in excess of three days without the consent of the other.

Section 6. Rights of Members

Clause 1: Compensation and Privileges.   The Senators and Representatives shall receive a Compensation for their services, to be ascertained by Law, and paid out of the Treasury of the United States. They shall in all Cases, except Treason, Felony and Breach of the Peace, be privileged from Arrest during their Attendance at the Session of their respective Houses, and in going to and returning from the same; and for any Speech or Debate in either House, they shall not be questioned in any other Place.

Congressional salaries are to be paid by the U.S. Treasury rather than by the members' respective states. The original salaries were $6 per day; in 1857 they were $3,000 per year. Both representatives and senators currently are paid $125,100 each year.

Members cannot be arrested for things they say during speeches and debates in Congress. This immunity applies to the Capitol Building itself and not to their private lives.
     Treason is defined in Article III, Section 3. A felony is any serious crime. A breach of the peace is any indictable

offense less than treason or a felony. Members cannot be arrested for anything they say in speeches or debates in Congress.

Clause 2: Restrictions. No Senator or Representative shall, during the Time for which he was elected, be appointed to any civil Office under the Authority of the United States, which shall have been created, or the Emoluments whereof shall have been encreased during such time; and no Person holding any Office under the United States, shall be a Member of either House during his Continuance in Office.

During the term for which a member was elected, he or she cannot concurrently accept another federal government position.

Section 7. Legislative Powers: Bills and Resolutions
Clause 1: Revenue Bills. All Bills for raising Revenue shall originate in the House of Representatives; but the Senate may propose or concur with Amendments as on other Bills.

All tax and appropriation bills for raising money have to originate in the House of Representatives. The Senate, though, often amends such bills and may even substitute an entirely different bill.

Clause 2: The Presidential Veto. Every Bill which shall have passed the House of Representatives and the Senate, shall, before it becomes a Law, be presented to the President of the United States; If he approve he shall sign it, but if not he shall return it, with his Objections to the House in which it shall have originated, who shall enter the Objections at large on their Journal, and proceed to reconsider it. If after such Reconsideration two thirds of that House shall agree to pass the Bill, it shall be sent together with the Objections, to the other House, by which it shall likewise be reconsidered, and if approved by two thirds of that House, it shall become a Law. But in all such Cases the Votes of both Houses shall be determined by Yeas and Nays, and the Names of the Persons voting for and against the Bill shall be entered on the Journal of each House respectively. If any Bill shall not be returned by the President within ten Days (Sundays excepted) after it shall have been presented to him, the Same shall be a Law, in like Manner as if he had signed it, unless the Congress by their Adjournment prevent its Return in which Case it shall not be a Law.

When Congress sends the president a bill, he or she can sign it (in which case it becomes law) or send it back to

the house in which it originated. If it is sent back, a two-thirds majority of each house must pass it again for it to become law. If the president neither signs it nor sends it back within ten days, it becomes law anyway, unless Congress adjourns in the meantime.

Clause 3: Actions on Other Matters. Every Order, Resolution, or Vote to which the Concurrence of the Senate and House of Representatives may be necessary (except on a question of Adjournment) shall be presented to the President of the United States; and before the Same shall take Effect, shall be approved by him, or being disapproved by him, shall be repassed by two thirds of the Senate and House of Representatives, according to the Rules and Limitations prescribed in the Case of a Bill.

The president must either sign or veto everything that Congress passes, except votes to adjourn and resolutions not having the force of law.

Section 8. The Powers of Congress
Clause 1: Taxing. The Congress shall have Power To lay and collect Taxes, Duties, Imposts and Excises, to pay the Debts and provide for the common Defence and general Welfare of the United States; but all Duties, Imposts and Excises shall be uniform throughout the United States;

Duties are taxes on imports and exports. Impost is a generic term for tax. Excises are taxes on the manufacture, sale, or use of goods.

Clause 2: Borrowing. To borrow Money on the credit of the United States;

Congress has the power to borrow money, which is normally carried out through the sale of U.S. treasury bonds on which interest is paid. Note that the Constitution places no limit on the amount of government borrowing.

Clause 3: Regulation of Commerce. To regulate Commerce with foreign Nations, and among the several States, and with the Indian Tribes;

This is the Commerce Clause, which gives to the Congress the power to regulate interstate and foreign trade. Much of the activity of Congress is based on this clause.

Clause 4: Naturalization and Bankruptcy. To establish a uniform Rule of Naturalization, and uniform Laws on the subject of Bankruptcies throughout the United States;

Only Congress may determine how aliens can become citizens of the United States. Congress may make laws with respect to bankruptcy.

Clause 5: Money and Standards.   To coin Money, regulate the Value thereof, and of foreign Coin, and fix the Standard of Weights and Measures;

Congress mints coins and prints and circulates paper money. Congress can establish uniform measures of time, distance, weight, etc. In 1838 Congress adopted the English system of weights and measurements as our national standard.

Clause 6: Punishing Counterfeiters.   To provide for the Punishment of counterfeiting the Securities and current Coin of the United States;

Congress has the power to punish those who copy American money and pass it off as real. Currently, the fine is up to $5,000 and/or imprisonment for up to fifteen years.

Clause 7: Roads and Post Offices.   To establish Post Offices and post Roads;

Post roads include all routes over which mail is carried—highways, railways, waterways, and airways.

Clause 8: Patents and Copyrights.   To promote the Progress of Science and useful Arts, by securing for limited Times to Authors and Inventors the exclusive Right to their respective Writings and Discoveries;

Authors' and composers' works are protected by copyrights established by copyright law, which currently is the 1978 Copyright Act. Copyrights are valid for the life of the author or composer plus fifty years. Inventors' works are protected by patents, which vary in length of protection from three and a half to seventeen years. A patent gives a person the exclusive right to control the manufacture or sale of her or his invention.

Clause 9: Lower Courts.   To constitute Tribunals inferior to the supreme Court;

Congress has the authority to set up all federal courts, except the Supreme Court, and to decide what cases those courts will hear.

Clause 10: Punishment for Piracy.   To define and punish Piracies and Felonies committed on the high Seas, and Offences against the Law of Nations;

Congress has the authority to prohibit the commission of certain acts outside U.S. territory and to punish certain violations of international law.

Clause 11: Declaration of War.   To declare War, grant Letters of Marque and Reprisal, and make Rules concerning Captures on Land and Water;

Only Congress can declare war, although the president, as commander in chief, can make war without Congress's formal declaration. Letters of marque and reprisal authorized private parties to capture and destroy enemy ships in wartime. Since the mid-nineteenth century, international law has prohibited letters of marque and reprisal, and the United States has honored the ban.

Clause 12: The Army.   To raise and support Armies, but no Appropriation of Money to that Use shall be for a longer Term than two Years;

Congress has the power to create an army; the money used to pay for it must be appropriated for no more than two-year intervals. This latter restriction gives ultimate control of the army to civilians.

Clause 13: Creation of a Navy.   To provide and maintain a Navy;

This clause allows for the maintenance of a navy. In 1947 Congress created the air force.

Clause 14: Regulation of the Armed Forces.   To make Rules for the Government and Regulation of the land and naval Forces;

Congress sets the rules for the military mainly by way of the Uniform Code of Military Justice, which was enacted in 1950 by Congress.

Clause 15: The Militia.   To provide for calling forth the Militia to execute the Laws of the Union, suppress Insurrections and repel Invasions;

The militia is known today as the National Guard. Both Congress and the president have the authority to call the National Guard into federal service.

Clause 16: How the Militia is Organized.   To provide for organizing, arming, and disciplining the Militia, and for governing such Part of them as may be employed in the Service of the United States, reserving to the States respectively, the Appointment of the Officers, and the Authority of training the Militia according to the discipline prescribed by Congress;

This clause gives Congress the power to "federalize" state militia (National Guard). When called into such service, the National Guard is subject to the same rules that Congress has set forth for the regular armed services.

Clause 17: Creation of the District of Columbia. To exercise exclusive Legislation in all Cases whatsoever, over such District (not exceeding ten Miles square) as may, by Cession of particular States, and the Acceptance of Congress, become the Seat of the Government of the United States, and to exercise like Authority over all Places purchased by the Consent of the Legislature of the State in which the Same shall be, for the Erection of Forts, Magazines, Arsenals, dock-Yards, and other needful Buildings;—And

Congress established the District of Columbia as the national capital in 1791. Virginia and Maryland had granted land for the District, but Virginia's grant was returned because it was believed it would not be needed. Today, the District is sixty-nine miles square.

Clause 18: The Elastic Clause. To make all Laws which shall be necessary and proper for carrying into Execution the foregoing Powers, and all other Powers vested by this Constitution in the Government of the United States, or in any Department or Officer thereof.

This clause—the Necessary and Proper Clause, or the Elastic Clause—grants no specific powers, and thus it can be stretched to fit different circumstances. It has allowed Congress to adapt the government to changing needs and times.

Section 9. The Powers Denied to Congress

Clause 1: Question of Slavery. The Migration or Importation of such Persons as any of the States now existing shall think proper to admit, shall not be prohibited by the Congress prior to the Year one thousand eight hundred and eight, but a Tax or duty may be imposed on such Importation, not exceeding ten dollars for each Person.

"Persons" referred to slaves. Congress outlawed the slave trade in 1808.

Clause 2: Habeas Corpus. The privilege of the Writ of Habeas Corpus shall not be suspended, unless when in Cases of Rebellion or Invasion the public Safety may require it.

A writ of habeas corpus is a court order directing a sheriff or other public officer who is detaining another person to "produce the body" of the detainee so the court can assess the legality of the detention.

Clause 3: Special Bills. No Bill of Attainder or ex post facto Law shall be passed.

A bill of attainder is a law that inflicts punishment without a trial. An ex post facto law is a law that inflicts punishment for an act that was not illegal when it was committed.

Clause 4: Direct Taxes. [No Capitation, or other direct, Tax shall be laid, unless in Proportion to the Census or Enumeration herein before directed to be taken.][6]

A capitation is a tax on a person. A direct tax is a tax paid directly to the government, such as a property tax. This clause was intended to prevent Congress from levying a tax on slaves per person and thereby taxing slavery out of existence.

Clause 5: Export Taxes. No Tax or Duty shall be laid on Articles exported from any State.

Congress may not tax any goods sold from one state to another or from one state to a foreign country. (Congress does have the power to tax goods that are bought from other countries, however.)

Clause 6: Interstate Commerce. No Preference shall be given by any Regulation of Commerce or Revenue to the Ports of one State over those of another: nor shall Vessels bound to, or from, one State, be obliged to enter, clear, or pay Duties in another.

Congress may not treat different ports within the United States differently in terms of taxing and commerce powers. Congress may not tax goods sent from one state to another. Finally, Congress may not give one state's port a legal advantage over those of another state.

Clause 7: Treasury Withdrawals. No Money shall be drawn from the Treasury, but in Consequence of Appropriations made by Law; and a regular Statement and Account of the Receipts and Expenditures of all public Money shall be published from time to time.

Federal funds can be spent only as Congress authorizes. This is a significant check on the president's power.

---

[6]Modified by the Sixteenth Amendment.

Clause 8: Titles of Nobility. No Title of Nobility shall be granted by the United States: And no Person holding any Office of Profit or Trust under them, shall, without the Consent of the Congress, accept of any present, Emolument, Office, or Title, of any kind whatever, from any King, Prince, or foreign State.

No person in the United States may be bestowed a title of nobility such as a duke or duchess. This clause also discourages bribery of American officials by foreign governments.

Section 10. Those Powers Denied to the States
Clause 1: Treaties and Coinage. No State shall enter into any Treaty, Alliance, or Confederation; grant Letters of Marque and Reprisal; coin Money; emit Bills of Credit; make any Thing but gold and silver Coin a Tender in Payment of Debts; pass any Bill of Attainder, ex post facto Law, or Law impairing the Obligation of Contracts, or grant any Title of Nobility.

Prohibiting state laws "impairing the Obligation of Contracts" was intended to protect creditors. (Shays's Rebellion—an attempt to prevent courts from giving effect to creditors' legal actions against debtors—occurred only one year before the Constitution was written.)

Clause 2: Duties and Imposts. No State shall, without the Consent of the Congress, lay any Imports or Duties on Imports or Exports, except what may be absolutely necessary for executing its inspection Laws; and the net Produce of all Duties and Imposts, laid by any State on Imports or Exports, shall be for the Use of the Treasury of the United States; and all such Laws shall be subject to the Revision and Controul of the Congress.

Only Congress can tax imports. Further, the states cannot tax exports.

Clause 3: War. No State shall, without the Consent of Congress, lay any Duty of Tonnage, keep Troops, or Ships of War in time of Peace, enter into any Agreement or Compact with another State, or with a foreign Power or engage in War, unless actually invaded, or in such imminent Danger as will not admit of delay.

A duty of tonnage is a tax on ships according to their cargo capacity. No states may effectively tax ships according to their cargo unless Congress agrees. Additionally, this clause forbids any state to keep troops or warships during peacetime or to make a compact with another state or foreign nation unless Congress so agrees. States can, in contrast, maintain a militia, but its use has to be limited to internal disorders that occur within a state—unless, of course, the militia is called into federal service.

Article II. (Executive Branch)

Section 1. The Nature and Scope of Presidential Power
Clause 1: Four-Year Term. The executive Power shall be vested in a President of the United States of America. He shall hold his Office during the Term of four Years, and, together with the Vice President, chosen for the same Term, be elected, as follows.

The president has the power to carry out laws made by Congress, called the executive power. He or she serves in office for a four-year term after election. The Twenty-second Amendment limits the number of times a person may be elected president.

Clause 2: Choosing Electors From Each State. Each State shall appoint, in such Manner as the Legislature thereof may direct, a Number of Electors, equal to the whole Number of Senators and Representatives to which the State may be entitled in the Congress; but no Senator or Representative, or Person holding an Office of Trust or Profit under the United States, shall be appointed an Elector.

The "Electors" are more commonly known as the "electoral college." The president is elected by electors—that is, representatives chosen by the people—rather than by the people directly.

Clause 3: The Former System of Elections. [The Electors shall meet in their respective States, and vote by Ballot for two Persons, of whom one at least shall not be an Inhabitant of the same State with themselves. And they shall make a List of all the Persons voted for, and of the Number of Votes for each; which List they shall sign and certify, and transmit sealed to the Seat of the Government of the United States, directed to the President of the Senate. The President of the Senate shall, in the Presence of the Senate and House of Representatives, open all the Certificates, and the Votes shall then be counted. The Person having the greatest Number of Votes shall be the President, if such Number be a Majority of the whole Number of Electors appointed; and if there be more than one who have such Majority, and have an equal Number of Votes, then the

House of Representatives shall immediately chuse by Ballot one of them for President; and if no Person have a Majority, then from the five highest on the List the said House shall in like Manner chuse the President. But in chusing the President, the Votes shall be taken by States, the Representation from each State having one Vote; A quorum for this Purpose shall consist of a Member or Members from two thirds of the States, and a Majority of all the States shall be necessary to a Choice. In every Case, after the Choice of the President, the Person having the greater Number of Votes of the Electors shall be the Vice President. But if there should remain two or more who have equal Votes, the Senate shall chuse from them by Ballot the Vice President.][7]

The original method of selecting the president and vice-president was replaced by the Twelfth Amendment. Apparently, the framers did not anticipate the rise of political parties and the development of primaries and conventions.

Clause 4: The Time of Elections. The Congress may determine the Time of chusing the Electors, and the Day on which they shall give their Votes; which Day shall be the same throughout the United States.

Congress set the Tuesday after the first Monday in November every fourth year as the date for choosing electors. The electors cast their votes on the Monday after the second Wednesday in December of that year.

Clause 5: Qualifications for President. No person except a natural born Citizen, or a Citizen of the United States, at the time of the Adoption of this Constitution, shall be eligible to the Office of President; neither shall any Person be eligible to that Office who shall not have attained to the Age of thirty five Years, and been fourteen Years a Resident within the United States.

The president must be a natural-born citizen, be at least thirty-five years of age when taking office, and have been a resident within the United States for at least fourteen years.

Clause 6: Succession of the Vice President. [In Case of the Removal of the President from Office, or of his Death, Resignation or Inability to discharge the Powers and Duties of the said Office, the same shall devolve on the Vice President, and the Congress may by Law provide for the Case of Removal, Death, Resignation or Inability, both of the President and Vice President, declaring what Officer shall

then act as President, and such Officer shall act accordingly, until the Disability be removed, or a President shall be elected.][8]

This former provision provided for the method by which the vice-president was to succeed to the presidency, but its wording is ambiguous. It was replaced by the Twenty-fifth Amendment.

Clause 7: The President's Salary. The President shall, at stated Times, receive for his Services, a Compensation, which shall neither be encreased nor diminished during the Period for which he shall have been elected, and he shall not receive within that Period any other Emolument from the United States, or any of them.

The president maintains the same salary during each four-year term. Moreover, she or he may not receive additional cash payments from the government. Originally set at $25,000 per year, it is currently $200,000 a year plus a $50,000 taxable expense account.

Clause 8: The Oath of Office. Before he enter on the Execution of his Office, he shall take the following Oath or Affirmation: "I do solemnly swear (or affirm) that I will faithfully execute the Office of President of the United States, and will to the best of my Ability, preserve, protect and defend the Constitution of the United States."

The president is "sworn in" prior to beginning the duties of the office. Currently, the taking of the oath of office occurs on January 20, following the November election. The ceremony is called the inauguration. The oath of office is administered by the chief justice of the United States Supreme Court.

Section 2. Powers of the President
Clause 1: Commander in Chief. The President shall be Commander in Chief of the Army and Navy of the United States, and of the Militia of the several States, when called into the actual Service of the United States; he may require the Opinion, in writing, of the principal Officer in each of the executive Departments, upon any Subject relating to the Duties of their respective Offices, and he shall have Power to grant Reprieves and Pardons for Offences against the United States, except in Cases of Impeachment.

The armed forces are placed under civilian control because the president is a civilian, but still commander in chief of the military. The president may ask for the help

---

[7]Changed by the Twelfth Amendment.

[8]Modified by the Twenty-fifth Amendment.

of the heads of each of the executive departments (thereby creating the Cabinet). The Cabinet members are chosen by the president with the consent of the Senate, but they can be removed without Senate approval.

The president's clemency powers extend only to federal cases. In those cases, he or she may grant a full or conditional pardon, or reduce a prison term or fine.

Clause 2: Treaties and Appointment. He shall have Power, by and with the Advice and Consent of the Senate, to make Treaties, provided two thirds of the Senators present concur; and he shall nominate, and by and with the Advice and Consent of the Senate, shall appoint Ambassadors, other public Ministers and Consuls, Judges of the supreme Court, and all other Officers of the United States, whose Appointments are not herein otherwise provided for, and which shall be established by Law; but the Congress may by Law vest the Appointment of such inferior Officers, as they think proper, in the President alone, in the Courts of Law, or in the Heads of Departments.

Many of the major powers of the president are identified in this clause, including the power to make treaties with foreign governments (with the approval of the Senate by a two-thirds vote) and the power to appoint ambassadors, Supreme Court justices, and other government officials. Most such appointments require Senate approval.

Clause 3: Vacancies. The President shall have Power to fill up all Vacancies that may happen during the Recess of the Senate, by granting Commissions which shall expire at the end of their next Session.

The president has the power to appoint temporary officials to fill vacant federal offices without Senate approval if the Congress is not in session. Such appointments expire automatically at the end of Congress's next term.

Section 3. Duties of the President

He shall from time to time give to the Congress Information of the State of the Union, and recommend to their Consideration such Measures as he shall judge necessary and expedient; he may, on extraordinary Occasions, convene both Houses, or either of them, and in Case of Disagreement between them, with Respect to the Time of Adjournment, he may adjourn them to such Time as he shall think proper; he shall receive Ambassadors and other public Ministers; he shall take Care that the Laws be faithfully executed, and shall Commission all the Officers of the United States.

Annually, the president reports on the state of the union to Congress, recommends legislative measures, and pro-

poses a federal budget. The State of the Union speech is a statement not only to Congress but also to the American people. After it is given, the president proposes a federal budget and presents an economic report. At any time he or she so chooses, the president may send special messages to Congress while it is in session. The president has the power to call special sessions, to adjourn Congress when its two houses do not agree for that purpose, to receive diplomatic representatives of other governments, and to ensure the proper execution of all federal laws. The president further has the ability to empower federal officers to hold their positions and to perform their duties.

Section 4. Impeachment

The President, Vice President and all civil Officers of the United States, shall be removed from Office on Impeachment for, and Conviction of, Treason, Bribery, or other high Crimes and Misdemeanors.

Treason denotes giving aid to the nation's enemies. The definition of high crimes and misdemeanors is usually given as serious abuses of political power. In either case, the president or vice-president may be accused by the House (called an impeachment) and then removed from office if convicted by the Senate. (Note that impeachment does not mean removal, but rather the state of being accused of treason or high crimes and misdemeanors.)

Article III. (Judicial Branch)

Section 1. Judicial Powers, Courts, and Judges

The judicial Power of the United States, shall be vested in one supreme Court, and in such inferior Courts as the Congress may from time to time ordain and establish. The Judges, both of the supreme and inferior Courts, shall hold their Offices during good Behaviour, and shall, at stated Times, receive for their Services a Compensation, which shall not be diminished during their Continuance in Office.

The Supreme Court is vested with judicial power, as are the lower federal courts that Congress creates. Federal judges serve in their offices for life unless they are impeached and convicted by Congress. The payment of federal judges may not be reduced during their time in office.

Section 2. Jurisdiction

Clause 1: Cases Under Federal Jurisdiction. The judicial Power shall extend to all Cases, in Law and Equity, arising under this Constitution, the Laws of the United States, and Treaties made, or which shall be made, under their Authority;—to all Cases affecting Ambassadors, other public Ministers and Consuls;—to all Cases of admiralty and maritime Jurisdiction;—to Controversies to which the United States shall be a Party;—to Controversies between two or more States; [—between a State and Citizens of another State;—]⁹ between Citizens of different States;—between Citizens of the same State claiming Lands under Grants of different States, [and between a State, or the Citizens thereof, and foreign States, Citizens or Subjects.]¹⁰

The federal courts take on cases that concern the meaning of the U.S. Constitution, all federal laws, and treaties. They also can take on cases involving citizens of different states and citizens of foreign nations.

Clause 2: Cases for the Supreme Court. In all Cases affecting Ambassadors, other public Ministers and Consuls, and those in which a State shall be a Party, the supreme Court shall have original Jurisdiction. In all the other Cases before mentioned, the supreme Court shall have appellate Jurisdiction, both as to Law and Fact, with such Exceptions, and under such Regulations as the Congress shall make.

In a limited number of situations, the Supreme Court acts as a trial court and has original jurisdiction. These cases involve a representative from another country or involve a state. In all other situations, the cases must first be tried in the lower courts and then can be appealed to the Supreme Court. Congress may, however, make exceptions. Today the Supreme Court acts as a trial court of first instance on rare occasions.

Clause 3: The Conduct of Trials. The Trial of all Crimes, except in Cases of Impeachment, shall be by Jury; and such Trial shall be held in the State where the said Crimes shall have been committed; but when not committed within any State, the Trial shall be at such Place or Places as the Congress may by Law have directed.

Any person accused of a federal crime is granted the right to a trial by jury in a federal court in that state in which the crime was committed. Trials of impeachment are an exception.

Section 3. Treason
Clause 1: The Definition of Treason. Treason against the United States, shall consist only in levying War against them, or, in adhering to their Enemies, giving them Aid and Comfort. No Person shall be convicted of Treason unless on the Testimony of two Witnesses to the same overt Act, or on Confession in open Court.

---

⁹Modified by the Eleventh Amendment.
¹⁰Modified by the Eleventh Amendment.

Treason is the making of war against the United States or giving aid to its enemies.

Clause 2: Punishment. The Congress shall have Power to declare the Punishment of Treason, but no Attainder of Treason shall work Corruption of Blood, or Forfeiture except during the Life of the Person attainted.

Congress has provided that the punishment for treason range from a minimum of five years in prison and/or a $10,000 fine to a maximum of death. ''No Attainder of Treason shall work Corruption of Blood'' prohibits punishment of the traitor's heirs.

Article IV. (Relations Among the States)

Section 1. Full Faith and Credit
Full Faith and Credit shall be given in each State to the public Acts, Records, and judicial Proceedings of every other State. And the Congress may by general Laws prescribe the Manner in which such Acts, Records and Proceedings shall be proved, and the Effect thereof.

All states are required to respect one another's laws, records, and lawful decisions. There are exceptions, however. A state does not have to enforce another state's criminal code. Nor does it have to recognize another state's grant of a divorce if the person obtaining the divorce did not establish legal residence in the state in which it was given.

Section 2. Treatment of Citizens
Clause 1: Privileges and Immunities. The Citizens of each State shall be entitled to all Privileges and Immunities of Citizens in the several States.

A citizen of a state has the same rights and privileges as the citizens of another state in which he or she happens to be.

Clause 2: Extradition. A Person charged in any State with Treason, Felony, or other Crime, who shall flee from Justice, and be found in another State, shall on Demand of the executive Authority of the State from which he fled, be delivered up, to be removed to the State having Jurisdiction of the Crime.

Any person accused of a crime who flees to another state must be returned to the state in which the crime occurred.

Clause 3: Fugitive Slaves. [No Person held to Service or Labour in one State, under the Laws thereof, escaping into another, shall, in Consequence of any Law or Regulation therein, be discharged from such Service or Labour, but shall be delivered up on Claim of the Party to whom such Service or Labour may be due.][11]

This clause was struck down by the Thirteenth Amendment, which abolished slavery in 1865.

Section 3. Admission of States
Clause 1: The Process. New States may be admitted by the Congress into this Union; but no new State shall be formed or erected within the Jurisdiction of any other State; nor any State be formed by the Junction of two or more States, or Parts of States, without the Consent of the Legislatures of the States concerned as well as of the Congress.

Only Congress has the power to admit new states to the union. No state may be created by taking territory from an existing state unless the state's legislature so consents.

Clause 2: Public Land. The Congress shall have Power to dispose of and make all needful Rules and Regulations respecting the Territory or other Property belonging to the United States; and nothing in this Constitution shall be so construed as to Prejudice any Claims of the United States, or of any particular State.

The federal government has the exclusive right to administer federal government public lands.

Section 4. Republican Form of Government
The United States shall guarantee to every State in this Union a Republican Form of Government, and shall protect each of them against Invasion; and on Application of the Legislature, or of the Executive (when the Legislature cannot be convened) against domestic Violence.

Each state is promised a form of government in which the people elect their representatives, called a republican form. The federal government is bound to protect states against any attack by foreigners or during times of trouble within a state.

Article V. (Methods of Amendment)
The Congress, whenever two thirds of both Houses shall deem it necessary, shall propose Amendments to this Constitution, or on the Application of the Legislatures of two thirds of the several States, shall call a Convention for pro-

posing Amendments, which, in either Case, shall be valid to all Intents and Purposes, as Part of this Constitution, when ratified by the Legislatures of three fourths of the several States, or by Conventions in three fourths thereof, as the one or the other Mode of Ratification may be proposed by the Congress; Provided that no Amendment which may be made prior to the Year One thousand eight hundred and eight shall in any Manner affect the first and fourth Clauses in the Ninth Section of the First Article; and that no State, without its Consent, shall be deprived of its equal Suffrage in the Senate.

Constitutional Amendments may be proposed by either of two ways: a two-thirds vote of each house (Congress) or by majority vote at a convention called by Congress at the request of two-thirds of the states. Ratification of amendments may be carried out in two ways: by the legislatures of three-fourths of the states or by the voters in three-fourths of the states. No state may be denied equal representation in the Senate.

Article VI. (National Supremacy)
Clause 1: Existing Obligations. All Debts contracted and Engagements entered into, before the Adoption of this Constitution shall be as valid against the United States under this Constitution, as under the Confederation.

During the Revolutionary War and the years of the Confederation, Congress borrowed large sums. This clause pledged that the new federal government would assume those financial obligations.

Clause 2: Supreme Law of the Land. This Constitution, and the Laws of the United States which shall be made in Pursuance thereof; and all Treaties made, or which shall be made, under the Authority of the United States, shall be the supreme Law of the Land; and the Judges in every State shall be bound thereby, any Thing in the Constitution or Laws of any State to the Contrary notwithstanding.

This is typically called the Supremacy Clause; it declares that federal law takes precedence over all forms of state law. No government, at the local or state level, may make or enforce any law that conflicts with any provision of the Constitution, acts of Congress, treaties, or other rules and regulations issued by the president and his or her subordinates in the executive branch of the federal government.

Clause 3: Oath of Office. The Senators and Representatives before mentioned, and the Members of the several

---

[11]Repealed by the Thirteenth Amendment.

State Legislatures, and all executive and judicial Officers, both of the United States and of the several States, shall be bound by Oath or Affirmation, to support this Constitution; but no religious Test shall ever be required as a Qualification to any Office or public Trust under the United States.

Every federal and state official must take an oath of office promising to support the U.S. Constitution. Religion may not be used as a qualification to serve in any federal office.

Article VII. (Ratification)

The Ratificaut of the Conventions of nine States shall, be sufficient for the Establishment of this Constitution between the States so ratifying the Same.

Nine states were required to ratify the Constitution. Delaware was the first and New Hampshire the ninth.

Done in Convention by the Unanimous Consent of the States present the Seventeenth Day of September in the Year of our Lord one thousand seven hundred and Eighty seven and of the Independence of the United States of America the Twelfth. In witness whereof we have hereunto subscribed our Names,

Go. WASHINGTON
Presid't. and deputy from Virginia

Attest
WILLIAM JACKSON
Secretary

DELAWARE
Geo. Read
Gunning Bedfordjun
John Dickinson
Richard Basset
Jaco. Broom

MASSACHUSETTS
Nathaniel Gorham
Rufus King

CONNECTICUT
Wm. Saml. Johnson
Roger Sherman

NEW YORK
Alexander Hamilton

NEW JERSEY
Wh. Livingston
David Brearley.
Wm. Paterson.
Jona. Dayton

PENNSYLVANIA
B. Franklin
Thomas Mifflin
Robt. Morris
Geo. Clymer
Thos. FitzSimons
Jared Ingersoll
James Wilson.
Gouv. Morris

NEW HAMPSHIRE
John Langdon
Nicholas Gilman

MARYLAND
James McHenry
Dan of St. Thos. Jenifer
Danl. Carroll.

VIRGINIA
John Blair
James Madison Jr.

NORTH CAROLINA
Wm. Blount
Richd. Dobbs Spaight.
Hu. Williamson

SOUTH CAROLINA
J. Rutledge
Charles Cotesworth
Pinckney
Charles Pinckney
Pierce Butler.

GEORGIA
William Few
Abr. Baldwin

Articles in addition to, and amendment of the Constitution of the United States of America, proposed by Congress and ratified by the Legislatures of the several states, pursuant to the Fifth Article of the original Constitution.

Amendments to the Constitution of the United States

The Bill of Rights[12]

Amendment I.
Religion, Speech, Assembly, and Politics

Congress shall make no law respecting an establishment of religion, or prohibiting the free exercise thereof; or abridging the freedom of speech, or of the press; or the right of the people peaceably to assembly, and to petition the Government for a redress of grievances.

Congress may not create an official church or enact laws limiting the freedom of religion, speech, the press, assembly, and petition. These guarantees, like the others in the Bill of Rights (the first ten amendments), are not absolute—each may be exercised only with regard to the rights of other persons.

Amendment II.
Militia and the Right to Bear Arms

A well regulated Militia, being necessary to the security of a free State, the right of the people to keep and bear Arms, shall not be infringed.

---

[12]On September 25, 1789, Congress transmitted to the state legislatures twelve proposed amendments, two of which, having to do with Congressional representation and Congressional pay, were not adopted. The remaining ten amendments became the Bill of Rights.

To protect itself, each state has the right to maintain a volunteer armed force. States and the federal government regulate the possession and use of firearms by individuals.

Amendment III.
The Quartering of Soldiers

No Soldier shall, in time of peace be quartered in any house, without the consent of the Owner, nor in time of war, but in a manner to be prescribed by law.

Before the Revolutionary War, it had been common British practice to quarter soldiers in colonists' homes. Military troops do not have the power to take over private houses during peacetime.

Amendment IV.
Searches and Seizures

The right of the people to be secure in their persons, houses, papers, and effects, against unreasonable searches and seizures, shall not be violated, and no Warrants shall issue, but upon probable cause, supported by Oath or affirmation, and particularly describing the place to be searched, and the persons or things to be seized.

Here the word warrant *means "justification" and refers to a document issued by a magistrate or judge indicating the name, address, and possible offense committed. Anyone asking for the warrant, such as a police officer, must be able to convince the magistrate or judge that an offense probably has been committed.*

Amendment V.
Grand Juries, Self-incrimination, Double Jeopardy, Due Process, and Eminent Domain

No person shall be held to answer for a capital, or otherwise infamous crime, unless on a presentment or indictment of a Grand Jury, except in cases arising in the land or naval forces, or in the Militia, when in actual service in time of War or public danger; nor shall any person be subject for the same offence to be twice put in jeopardy of life or limb; nor shall be compelled in any criminal case to be a witness against himself, nor be deprived of life, liberty, or property, without due process of law; nor shall private property be taken for public use, without just compensation.

There are two types of juries. A grand jury considers physical evidence and the testimony of witnesses, and decides whether there is sufficient reason to bring a case to trial. A petit jury hears the case at trial and decides it.

"For the same offence to be twice put in jeopardy of life or limb" means to be tried twice for the same crime. A person may not be tried for the same crime twice or forced to give evidence against herself or himself. No person's right to life, liberty, or property may be taken away except by lawful means, called the due process of law. Private property taken for use in public purposes must be paid for by the government.

Amendment VI.
Criminal Court Procedures

In all criminal prosecutions, the accused shall enjoy the right to a speedy and public trial, by an impartial jury of the State and district wherein the crime shall have been committed, which district shall have been previously ascertained by law, and to be informed of the nature and cause of the accusation; to be confronted with the witnesses against him; to have compulsory process for obtaining witnesses in his favor, and to have the assistance of counsel for his defence.

Any person accused of a crime has the right to a fair and public trial by a jury in the state in which the crime took place. The charges against that person must be so indicated. Any accused person has the right to a lawyer to defend him or her and to question those who testify against him or her, as well as the right to call people to speak in his or her favor at trial.

Amendment VII.
Trial by Jury in Civil Cases

In Suits at common law, where the value in controversy shall exceed twenty dollars, the right of trial by jury shall be preserved, and no fact tried by jury, shall be otherwise re-examined in any Court of the United States, than according to the rules of the common law.

A jury trial may be requested by either party in a dispute in any case involving more than $20. If both parties agree to a trial by a judge without a jury, the right to a jury trial may be put aside.

Amendment VIII.
Bail, Cruel and Unusual Punishment

Excessive bail shall not be required, nor excessive fines imposed, nor cruel and unusual punishments inflicted.

Bail is that amount of money that a person accused of a crime may be required to deposit with the court as a guar-

antee that she or he will appear in court when requested. The amount of bail required or the fine imposed as punishment for a crime must be reasonable compared with the seriousness of the crime involved. Any punishment judged to be too harsh or too severe for a crime shall be prohibited.

Amendment IX.
The Rights Retained by the People

The enumeration in the Constitution, of certain rights, shall not be construed to deny or disparage others retained by the people.

Many civil rights that are not explicitly enumerated in the Constitution are still hailed by the people.

Amendment X.
Reserved Powers of the States

The powers not delegated to the United States by the Constitution, nor prohibited by it to the States, are reserved to the States respectively, or to the people.

Those powers not delegated by the Constitution to the federal government or expressly denied to the states belong to the states and to the people. This clause in essence allows the states to pass laws under its "police powers."

Amendment XI
(Ratified on February 7, 1795).
Suits Against States

The Judicial power of the United States shall not be construed to extend to any suit in law or equity, commenced or prosecuted against one of the United States by Citizens of another State, or by Citizens or Subjects of any Foreign State.

This amendment has been interpreted to mean that a state cannot be sued in federal court by one of its citizens, by a citizen of another state, or by a foreign country.

Amendment XII
(Ratified on June 15, 1804).
Election of the President

The Electors shall meet in their respective states, and vote by ballot for President and Vice-President, one of whom, at least, shall not be an inhabitant of the same State with themselves; they shall name in their ballots the person voted for as President, and in distinct ballots the person voted for as Vice-President, and they shall make distinct lists of all persons voted for as President, and of all persons voted for as Vice-President, and of the number of votes for each, which lists they shall sign and certify, and transmit sealed to the seat of the government of the United States, directed to the President of the Senate;—The President of the Senate shall, in the presence of the Senate and House of Representatives, open all the certificates and the votes shall then be counted;—The person having the greatest number of votes for President, shall be the President, if such number be a majority of the whole number of Electors appointed; and if no person have such majority, then from the persons having the highest numbers not exceeding three on the list of those voted for as President, the House of Representatives shall choose immediately, by ballot, the President. But in choosing the President, the votes shall be taken by States, the representation from each State having one vote; a quorum for this purpose shall consist of a member or members from two-thirds of the States, and a majority of all States shall be necessary to a choice. [And if the House of Representatives shall not choose a President whenever the right of choice shall devolve upon them, before the fourth day of March next following, then the Vice-President shall act as President, as in the case of the death or other constitutional disability of the President.][13]—The person having the greatest number of votes as Vice-President, shall be the Vice-President, if such number be a majority of the whole number of Electors appointed, and if no person have a majority, then from the two highest numbers on the list, the Senate shall choose the Vice President; a quorum for the purpose shall consist of two-thirds of the whole number of Senators, and a majority of the whole number shall be necessary to a choice. But no person constitutionally ineligible to the office of President shall be eligible to that of Vice-President of the United States.

The original procedure set out for the election of president and vice-president in Article II, Section 1, resulted in a tie in 1800 between Thomas Jefferson and Aaron Burr. It was not until the next year that the House of Representatives chose Jefferson to be president. This amendment changed the procedure by providing for separate ballots for president and vice-president.

Amendment XIII
(Ratified on December 6, 1865).
Prohibition of Slavery

Section 1.
Neither slavery nor involuntary servitude, except as a punishment for crime whereof the party shall have been duly

[13]Changed by the Twentieth Amendment.

convicted, shall exist within the United States, or any place subject to their jurisdiction.

Some slaves had been freed during the Civil War. This amendment freed the others and abolished slavery.

Section 2.

Congress shall have power to enforce this article by appropriate legislation.

Amendment XIV
(Ratified on July 9, 1868).
Citizenship, Due Process, and
Equal Protection of the Laws

Section 1.

All persons born or naturalized in the United States, and subject to the jurisdiction thereof, are citizens of the United States and of the State wherein they reside. No State shall make or enforce any law which shall abridge the privileges or immunities of citizens of the United States; nor shall any State deprive any person of life, liberty, or property, without due process of law; nor deny to any person within its jurisdiction the equal protection of the laws.

Under this provision, states cannot make or enforce laws that take away rights given to all citizens by the federal government. States cannot act unfairly or arbitrarily toward, or discriminate against, any person.

Section 2.

Representatives shall be apportioned among the several States according to their respective numbers, counting the whole number of persons in each State, excluding Indians not taxed. But when the right to vote at any election for the choice of electors for President and Vice President of the United States, Representatives in Congress, the Executive and Judicial officers of a State, or the members of the Legislature thereof, is denied to any of the male inhabitants of such State, being [twenty-one][14] years of age, and citizens of the United States, or in any way abridged, except for participation in rebellion, or other crime, the basis of representation therein shall be reduced in the proportion which the number of such male citizens shall bear to the whole number of male citizens twenty-one years of age in such State.

Section 3.

No person shall be a Senator or Representative in Congress, or elector of President and Vice President, or hold any

---
[14]Changed by the Twenty-sixth Amendment.

office, civil or military, under the United States, or under any State, who having previously taken an oath, as a member of Congress, or as an officer of the United States, or as a member of any State legislature, or as an executive or judicial officer of any State, to support the Constitution of the United States, shall have engaged in insurrection or rebellion against the same, or given aid or comfort to the enemies thereof. But Congress may by a vote of two-thirds of each House, remove such disability.

This provision forbade former state or federal government officials who had acted in support of the Confederacy during the Civil War to hold office again. It limited the president's power to pardon those persons. Congress removed this "disability" in 1898.

Section 4.

The validity of the public debt of the United States, authorized by law, including debts incurred for payment of pensions and bounties for services in suppressing insurrection or rebellion, shall not be questioned. But neither the United States nor any State shall assume or pay any debt or obligation incurred in aid of insurrection or rebellion against the United States, or any claim for the loss or emancipation of any slave, but all such debts, obligations and claims shall be held illegal and void.

Section 5.

The Congress shall have power to enforce, by appropriate legislation, the provisions of this article.

Amendment XV
(Ratified on February 3, 1870).
The Right to Vote

Section 1.

The right of citizens of the United States to vote shall not be denied or abridged by the United States or by any State on account of race, color, or previous condition of servitude.

No citizen can be refused the right to vote simply because of race or color or because that person was once a slave.

Section 2.

The Congress shall have power to enforce this article by appropriate legislation.

Amendment XVI
(Ratified on February 3, 1913).
Income Taxes

The Congress shall have power to lay and collect taxes on incomes, from whatever source derived, without apportionment among the several States, and without regard to any census or enumeration.

This amendment allows Congress to tax income without sharing the revenue so obtained with the states according to their population.

Amendment XVII
(Ratified on April 8, 1913).
The Popular Election of Senators

The Senate of the United States shall be composed of two Senators from each State, elected by the people thereof, for six years; and each Senator shall have one vote. The electors in each State shall have the qualifications requisite for electors of the most numerous branch of the State legislatures.

When vacancies happen in the representation of any State in the Senate, the executive authority of such State shall issue writs of election to fill such vacancies: *Provided,* That the legislature of any State may empower the executive thereof to make temporary appointments until the people fill the vacancies by election as the legislature may direct.

This amendment shall not be so construed as to affect the election or term of any Senator chosen before it becomes valid as part of the Constitution.

This amendment modified portions of Article I, Section 3, that related to election of senators. Senators are now elected by the voters in each state directly. When a vacancy occurs, either the state may fill the vacancy by a special election, or the governor of the state involved may appoint someone to fill the seat until the next election.

Amendment XVIII
(Ratified on January 16, 1919).
Prohibition.

Section 1.
After one year from the ratification of this article the manufacture, sale, or transportation of intoxicating liquors within, the importation thereof into, or the exportation thereof from the United States and all territory subject to the jurisdiction thereof for beverage purposes is hereby prohibited.

Section 2.
The Congress and the several States shall have concurrent power to enforce this article by appropriate legislation.

Section 3.
This article shall be inoperative unless it shall have been ratified as an amendment to the Constitution by the legislatures of the several States, as provided in the Constitution, within seven years from the date of the submission hereof to the States by the Congress.[15]

This amendment made it illegal to manufacture, sell, and transport alcoholic beverages in the United States. It was ended by the Twenty-first Amendment.

Amendment XIX
(Ratified on August 18, 1920).
Women's Right to Vote.

The right of citizens of the United States to vote shall not be denied or abridged by the United States or by any State on account of sex.

Congress shall have power to enforce this article by appropriate legislation.

Women were given the right to vote by this amendment, and Congress was given the power to enforce this right.

Amendment XX
(Ratified on January 23, 1933).
The Lame Duck Amendment

Section 1.
The terms of the President and Vice President shall end at noon on the 20th day of January, and the terms of Senators and Representatives at noon on the 3d day of January, of the years in which such terms would have ended if this article had not been ratified; and the terms of their successors shall then begin.

This amendment modified Article I, Section 4, Clause 2, and other provisions relating to the president in the Twelfth Amendment. The taking of the Oath of Office was moved from March 4 to January 20.

[15]The Eighteenth Amendment was repealed by the Twenty-first Amendment.

Section 2.

The Congress shall assemble at least once in every year, and such meeting shall begin at noon on the 3d day of January, unless they shall by law appoint a different day.

Congress changed the beginning of its term to January 3. The reason the Twentieth Amendment is called the Lame Duck Amendment is because it shortens the time between when a member of Congress is defeated for reelection and when he or she leaves office.

Section 3.

If, at the time fixed for the beginning of the term of the President, the President elect shall have died, the Vice President elect shall become President. If a President shall not have been chosen before the time fixed for the beginning of his term, or if the President elect shall have failed to qualify, then the Vice President elect shall act as President until a President shall have qualified; and the Congress may by law provide for the case wherein neither a President elect nor a Vice President elect shall have qualified, declaring who shall then act as President, or the manner in which one who is to act shall be selected, and such person shall act accordingly until a President or Vice President shall have qualified.

This part of the amendment deals with problem areas left ambiguous by Article II and the Twelfth Amendment. If the president dies before January 20 or fails to qualify for office, the presidency is to be filled in the order given in this section.

Section 4.

The Congress may by law provide for the case of the death of any of the persons from whom the House of Representatives may choose a President whenever the rights of choice shall have devolved upon them, and for the case of the death of any of the persons from whom the Senate may choose a Vice President whenever the right of choice shall have devolved upon them.

Congress has never created legislation subsequent to this section.

Section 5.

Sections 1 and 2 shall take effect on the 15th day of October following the ratification of this article.

Section 6.

This article shall be inoperative unless it shall have been ratified as an amendment to the Constitution by the legislatures of three-fourths of the several States within seven years from the date of its submission.

Amendment XXI
(Ratified on December 5, 1933).
The Repeal of Prohibition.

Section 1.

The eighteenth article of amendment to the Constitution of the United States is hereby repealed.

Section 2.

The transportation or importation into any State, Territory, or possession of the United States for delivery or use therein of intoxicating liquors, in violation of the laws thereof, is hereby prohibited.

Section 3.

This article shall be inoperative unless it shall have been ratified as an amendment to the Constitution by conventions in the several States, as provided in the Constitution, within seven years from the date of the submission hereof to the States by the Congress.

The amendment repealed the Eighteenth Amendment but did not make alcoholic beverages legal everywhere. Rather, they remained illegal in any state that so designated them. Many such "dry" states existed for a number of years after 1933. Today, there are still "dry" counties within the United States, in which alcoholic beverages are illegal.

Amendment XXII
(Ratified on February 27, 1951).
Limitation of Presidential Terms.

Section 1.

No person shall be elected to the office of the President more than twice, and no person who has held the office of President, or acted as President, for more than two years of a term to which some other person was elected President shall be elected to the office of President more than once. But this Article shall not apply to any person holding the office of President when this Article was proposed by the Congress, and shall not prevent any person who may be holding the office of President, or acting as President, during the term within which this Article becomes operative from holding the office of President or acting as President during the remainder of such term.

Section 2.
This article shall be inoperative unless it shall have been ratified as an amendment to the Constitution by the legislatures of three-fourths of the several States within seven years from the date of its submission to the States by the Congress.

No president may serve more than two elected terms. If, however, a president has succeeded to the office after the halfway point of a term in which another president was originally elected, then that president may serve for more than eight years, but not to exceed ten years.

Amendment XXIII
(Ratified on March 29, 1961).
Presidential Electors for
the District of Columbia.

Section 1.
The District constituting the seat of Government of the United States shall appoint in such manner as the Congress may direct:

A number of electors of President and Vice President equal to the whole number of Senators and Representatives in Congress to which the District would be entitled if it were a State, but in no event more than the least populous State; they shall be in addition to those appointed by the States, but they shall be considered, for the purposes of the election of President and Vice President, to be electors appointed by a State; and they shall meet in the District and perform such duties as provided by the twelfth article of amendment.

Section 2.
The Congress shall have power to enforce this article by appropriate legislation.

Citizens living in the District of Columbia have the right to vote in elections for president and vice-president. The District of Columbia has three presidential electors, whereas before this amendment it had none.

Amendment XXIV
(Ratified on January 23, 1964).
The Anti-Poll Tax Amendment.

Section 1.
The right of citizens of the United States to vote in any primary or other election for President or Vice President,

for electors for President or Vice President, or for Senator or Representative in Congress, shall not be denied or abridged by the United States, or any State by reason of failure to pay any poll tax or other tax.

Section 2.
The Congress shall have power to enforce this article by appropriate legislation.

No government shall require a person to pay a poll tax in order to vote in any federal election.

Amendment XXV
(Ratified on February 10, 1967).
A Presidential Disability and Vice
Presidential Vacancies.

Section 1.
In case of the removal of the President from office or of his death or resignation, the Vice President shall become President.

Whenever a president dies or resigns from office, the vice-president becomes president.

Section 2.
Whenever there is a vacancy in the office of the Vice President, the President shall nominate a Vice President who shall take office upon confirmation by a majority vote of both Houses of Congress.

Whenever the office of the vice-presidency becomes vacant, the president may appoint someone to fill this office, provided Congress consents.

Section 3.
Whenever the President transmits to the President pro tempore of the Senate and the Speaker of the House of Representatives his written declaration that he is unable to discharge the powers and duties of his office, and until he transmits to them a written declaration to the contrary, such powers and duties shall be discharged by the Vice President as Acting President.

Whenever the president believes she or he is unable to carry out the duties of the office, she or he shall so indicate to Congress in writing. The vice-president then acts as president until the president declares that she or he is again able to properly carry out the duties of the office.

Section 4.

Whenever the Vice President and a majority of either the principal officers of the executive departments or of such other body as Congress may by law provide, transmit to the President pro tempore of the Senate and the Speaker of the House of Representatives their written declaration that the President is unable to discharge the powers and duties of his office, the Vice President shall immediately assume the powers and duties of the office as Acting President.

Thereafter, when the President transmits to the President pro tempore of the Senate and the Speaker of the House of Representatives his written declaration that no inability exists, he shall resume the powers and duties of his office unless the Vice President and a majority of either the principal officers of the executive department or of such other body as Congress may by law provide, transmit within four days to the President pro tempore of the Senate and the Speaker of the House of Representatives their written declaration that the President is unable to discharge the powers and duties of his office. Thereupon Congress shall decide the issue, assembling within forty-eight hours for that purpose if not in session. If the Congress, within twenty-one days after receipt of the latter written declaration, or, if Congress is not in session, within twenty-one days after Congress is required to assemble, determines by two-thirds vote of both Houses that the President is unable to discharge the powers and duties of his office, the Vice President shall continue to discharge the same as Acting President; otherwise, the President shall resume the powers and duties of his office.

Whenever the vice president and a majority of the members of the Cabinet believe that the president cannot carry out his or her duties, they shall so indicate in writing to Congress. The vice president shall then act as president. When the president believes that she or he is able to carry out her or his duties again, she or he shall so indicate to the Congress. If, though, the vice president and a majority of the Cabinet do not agree, Congress must decide by a

two-thirds vote within three weeks who shall act as president.

Amendment XXVI
(Ratified on July 1, 1971).
The Eighteen Year Old Vote.

Section 1.

The right of citizens of the United States, who are eighteen years of age or older, to vote shall not be denied or abridged by the United States or by any State on account of age.

No one over eighteen years of age can be denied the right to vote in federal or state elections by virtue of age.

Section 2.

The Congress shall have power to enforce this article by appropriate legislation.

Amendment XXVII
(Ratified on May 7, 1992).
Congressional Compensation Changes.

No law, varying the compensation for the services of the Senators and Representatives, shall take effect, until an election of Representatives shall have intervened.

An intervening congressional election is required before any changes in congressional compensation may be instituted.

The Magna Carta (1215)

The Magna Carta is the "great charter" of English civil liberties. King John signed it at Runnymede on June 15, 1215. His barons forced him to do so. The document, which is excerpted below, consists of sixty-three clauses,

which protect the rights of the church, the feudal lords, the lords' subtenants, and the merchants. Royal privileges, the administration of justice, and the behavior of royal officials are also covered in the document.

John, by the grace of God, king of England, lord of Ireland, duke of Normandy and Aquitaine, count of Anjou, to all his archbishops, bishops, abbots, earls, barons, justiciars, foresters, sheriffs, stewards, servants, and all bailiffs and faithful men, health. * * *

Chapter 1

First, we grant to God, and by this our present charter we confirm, for us and our heirs forever, that the English church be free, and have its rights whole and its liberties unimpaired; * * * We have granted to all free men of our realm, for ourself and our heirs forever, all these under-written liberties to have and to hold, for themselves and their heirs, from us and our heirs.

Chapter 20

A free man shall not be amerced for a small offense unless according to the measure of the offense, and for a great offense he shall be amerced according to the greatness of the offense, saving his tenement, and the merchant in the same manner, saving his merchandise, and the villein shall be amerced in the same manner, saving his tools of husbandry, if they fall into our mercy, and none of the aforenamed mercies shall be imposed except by the oath of reputable men of the vicinage.

Chapter 21

Earls and barons shall not be amerced but by their equals, and only according to the measure of the offense.

Chapter 28

No constable, or other bailiff of ours, shall take the corn or chattels of anyone, unless he forthwith pays money for them, or can have any respite by the good will of the seller.

Chapter 30

No sheriff or bailiff of ours, or any other, shall take horses and carts of any free man for carrying, except by the will of the free man.[1]

_____

1. In 1216 the chapter was modified to say that the horses and carts should not be taken unless the owner received a specified amount of money. In 1217 a chapter was inserted that prohibited bailiffs from taking carts from the demesne of a cleric, a knight, or a lady. In 1225 chapters 30 and 31 from the Charter of 1215 and the new chapter were combined into a single chapter.

Chapter 31

Neither we nor our bailiffs will take any wood for our castles, or other of our works, except by consent of the man whose wood it is.

Chapter 32

We will not hold the lands of those who are convict of felony, except for one year and one day, and then the lands shall be returned to the lords of the fees.

Chapter 38

No bailiff in future shall put anyone to law by his mere word, without trustworthy witnesses brought forward for it.

Chapter 39

No free man shall be seized, or imprisoned, or disseised, or outlawed, or exiled, or injured in any way, nor will we enter on him or send against him except by the lawful judgment of his peers, or by the law of the land.

Chapter 40

We will sell to no one, or deny to no one, or put off right or justice.

Chapter 41

All merchants shall have safe conduct and security to go out of England or come into England, and to stay in, and go through England, both by land and water, for buying or selling, without any evil tolls, by old and right customs, except in time of war; and if they be of the land at war against us, and if such shall be found in our land, at the beginning of war, they shall be attached without loss of person or property, until it be known by us or our chief justiciar how the merchants of our land are treated who are found then in the land at war with us; and if ours be safe there, others shall be safe here.[2]

Chapter 46

All barons who have founded abbeys, whence they have charters of the kings of England, or ancient tenure, shall have their custody while vacant, as they ought to have it.

_____

2. In 1216 the words ''unless formerly they have been publicly prohibited'' were inserted after ''All merchants.''

Chapter 53

We will have the same respite, and in the same way, about exhibiting justice of deforesting or maintaining the forests, which Henry our father, or Richard our brother afforested, and of the wardship of the lands which are of another's fee, of which thing we have hitherto had the wardship, by reason of the fee, because someone held of us by military service, and of the abbeys which were founded on the fee of another than our own, in which the lord of the fee says he has the right; and when we return, or if we stay from our journey, we will afford full justice to those who complain of these things.

Chapter 54

No one shall be seized or imprisoned for the appeal of a woman about the death of any other man but her husband.

Chapter 60

All these aforesaid customs and liberties which we have granted to be held in our realm, as far as belongs to us, towards our own, all in our realm, both clergy and lay, shall observe, as far as belongs to them, towards their own.

Chapter 63

Wherefore we will and firmly order that the English church should be free, and that the men of our realm should have and hold all the aforenamed liberties, rights, and grants, well and in peace, freely and quietly, fully and completely, for them and their heirs, from us and our heirs, in all things and places, forever, as is aforesaid. It is sworn both by us, and on the part of the barons, that all these aforesaid shall be kept in good faith and without ill meaning. Witnesses, the abovenamed and many others. Given by our hand, in the meadow which is called Runnymede, between Windsor and Staines, on the fifteenth day of June, in the seventeenth year of our reign.

Source: William Stubbs, ed., *A Translation of Such Documents as Are Unpublished in Dr. Stubbs' Select Charters* (n.d.), pp. 187–197.

Mayflower Compact (1620)

The Mayflower Compact was entered into by the adult male Pilgrims in the cabin of the Mayflower *on November 11, 1620. The forty-one men who signed it agreed to establish a preliminary government. The compact bound the signers to a government by majority rule during the time they knew they had to wait for a royal charter. Many view this compact as the first step in the development of democracy in America.*

In the name of God, Amen. We, whose names are underwritten, the loyal subjects of our dread sovereign lord King James, by the grace of God, of Great Britain, France, and Ireland, king, defender of the faith, &c. Having undertaken for the glory of God, and advancement of the Christian faith, and the honor of our king and country, a voyage to plant the first colony in the northern parts of Virginia, do by these presents, solemnly and mutually, in the presence of God and one another, covenant and combine ourselves together into a civil body politic, for our better ordering and preservation and furtherance of the ends aforesaid; and by virtue hereof do enact, constitute, and frame such just and equal laws, ordinances, acts, constitutions, and officers, from time to time, as shall be thought most meet and convenient for the general good of the colony; unto which we promise all due submission and obedience. In witness whereof we have hereunto subscribed our names at Cape Cod the eleventh of November, in the reign of our sovereign lord King James, of England, France, and Ireland, the eighteenth, and of Scotland, the fifty-fourth, anno Domini, 1620.

Mr. John Carver	Digery Priest
Mr. William Bradford	Thomas Williams
Mr. Edward Winslow	Gilbert Winslow
Mr. William Brewster	Edmund Margesson
Isaac Allerton	Peter Brown
Miles Standish	Richard Bitteridge
John Alden	George Soule
John Turner	Edward Tilly
Francis Eaton	John Tilly
James Chilton	Francis Cooke
John Craxton	Thomas Rogers
John Billington	Thomas Tinker
Joses Fletcher	John Ridgdale
John Goodman	Edward Fuller
Mr. Samuel Fuller	Richard Clark
Mr. Christopher Martin	Richard Gardiner
Mr. William Mullins	Mr. John Allerton
Mr. William White	Thomas English
Mr. Richard Warren	Edward Doten
John Howland	Edward Liester
Mr. Steven Hopkins	

Source: Ben Perley Poore, ed., *The Federal and State Constitutions, Colonial Charters, and Other Organic Laws of the United States,* vol. 1 (1878), p. 931.

Declaration of Independence (1776)

The Declaration of Independence was adopted by the Second Continental Congress on July 4, 1776. It was the formal mechanism by which the thirteen American colonies justified their separation from Britain. The formal signing of the declaration took place on August 2, 1776.

IN CONGRESS, JULY 4, 1776
THE UNANIMOUS DECLARATION of the thirteen united STATES OF AMERICA

WHEN in the Course of human events, it becomes necessary for one people to dissolve the political bands which have connected them with another, and to assume among the powers of the earth, the separate and equal station to which the Laws of Nature and of Nature's God entitle them, a decent respect to the opinions of mankind requires that they should declare the causes which impel them to the separation.

We hold these truths to be self-evident, that all men are created equal, that they are endowed by their Creator with certain unalienable Rights, that among these are Life, Liberty and the pursuit of Happiness. That to secure these rights, Governments are instituted among Men, deriving their just powers from the consent of the governed; That whenever any Form of Government becomes destructive of these ends, it is the Right of the People to alter or to abolish it, and to institute new Government, laying its foundation on such principles and organizing its powers in such form, as to them shall seem most likely to effect their Safety and Happiness. Prudence, indeed, will dictate that Governments long established should not be changed for light and transient causes; and accordingly all experience hath shown, that mankind are more disposed to suffer, while evils are sufferable, than to right themselves by abolishing the forms to which they are accustomed. But when a long train of abuses and usurpations, pursuing invariably the same Object evinces a design to reduce them under absolute Despotism, it is their right, it is their duty, to throw off such Government, and to provide new Guards for their future security.

Such has been the patient sufferance of these Colonies; and such is now the necessity which constrains them to alter their former Systems of Government. The history of the present King of Great Britain is a history of repeated injuries and usurpations, all having in direct object the establishment of an absolute Tyranny over these States. To prove this, let Facts be submitted to a candid world.

He has refused his Assent to Laws, the most wholesome and necessary for the public good.

He has forbidden his Governors to pass Laws of immediate and pressing importance, unless suspended in their operation till his Assent should be obtained; and when so suspended, he has utterly neglected to attend to them.

He has refused to pass other Laws for the accommodation of large districts of people, unless those people would relinquish the right of Representation in the Legislature, a right inestimable to them and formidable to tyrants only.

He has called together legislative bodies at places unusual, uncomfortable, and distant from the depository or their public records, for the sole purpose of fatiguing them into compliance with his measures.

He has dissolved Representative Houses repeatedly, for opposing with manly firmness his invasions on the rights of the people.

He has refused for a long time, after such dissolutions, to cause others to be elected; whereby the Legislative powers, incapable of Annihilation, have returned to the People at large for their exercise; the State remaining in the mean time exposed to all the dangers of invasion from without, and convulsions within.

He has endeavored to prevent the population of these States; for that purpose obstructing the Laws for Naturalization of Foreigners; refusing to pass others to encourage their migration hither, and raising the conditions of new Appropriations of Lands.

He has obstructed the Administration of Justice, by refusing his Assent to Laws for establishing Judiciary powers.

He has made Judges dependent on his Will alone, for the tenure of their offices, and the amount and payment of their salaries.

He has erected a multitude of New Offices, and sent hither swarms of Officers to harrass our people, and eat out their substance.

He has kept among us, in times of peace, Standing Armies, without the Consent of our legislatures.

He has affected to render the Military independent of and superior to the Civil power.

He has combined with others to subject us to a jurisdiction foreign to our constitution, and unacknowledged by our laws; giving his Assent to their Acts of pretended Legislation:

For quartering large bodies of armed troops among us;

For protecting them, by a mock Trial, from punishment for any Murders which they should commit on the Inhabitants of these States;

For cutting off our Trade with all parts of the world;

For imposing Taxes on us without our Consent;

For depriving us in many cases, of the benefits of Trial by Jury;

For transporting us beyond Seas to be tried for pretended offences;

For abolishing the free System of English Laws in a neighbouring Province, establishing therein an Arbitrary government, and enlarging its Boundaries so as to render it at once an example and fit instrument for introducing the same absolute rule into these Colonies;

For taking away our Charters, abolishing our most valuable Laws, and altering fundamentally the Forms of our Governments;

For suspending our own Legislatures, and declaring themselves invested with power to legislate for us in all cases whatsoever.

He has abdicated Government here, by declaring us out of his Protection and waging War against us.

He has plundered our seas, ravaged our Coasts, burnt our towns, and destroyed the lives of our people.

He is at this time transporting large Armies of foreign Mercenaries to complete the works of death, desolation and tyranny, already begun with circumstances of Cruelty and perfidy scarcely paralleled in the most barbarous ages, and totally unworthy the Head of a civilized nation.

He has constrained our fellow Citizens taken Captive on the high Seas to bear Arms against their Country, to become the executioners of their friends and Brethren, or to fall themselves by their Hands.

He has excited domestic insurrections amongst us, and has endeavored to bring on the inhabitants of our frontiers, the merciless Indian Savages, whose known rule of warfare, is an undistinguished destruction of all ages, sexes and conditions.

In every state of these Oppressions We have Petitioned for Redress in the most humble terms. Our repeated Petitions have been answered only by repeated injury. A Prince, whose character is thus marked by every act which may define a Tyrant, is unfit to be the ruler of a free people.

Nor have We been wanting in attentions to our British brethren. We have warned them from time to time of attempts by their legislature to extend an unwarrantable jurisdiction over us. We have reminded them of the circumstances of our emigration and settlement here. We have appealed to their native justice and magnanimity, and we have conjured them by the ties of our common kindred to disavow these usurpations, which would inevitably interrupt our connections and correspondence. They too have been deaf to the voice of justice and consanguinity. We must, therefore, acquiesce in the necessity, which denounces our Separation, and hold them, as we hold the rest of mankind, Enemies in War, in Peace Friends.—

WE, THEREFORE, the REPRESENTATIVES of the UNITED STATES OF AMERICA, in General Congress, Assembled, appealing to the Supreme Judge of the world for the rectitude of our intentions, do, in the Name, and by Authority of the good People of these Colonies, solemnly publish and declare, That these United Colonies are, and of Right ought to be FREE AND INDEPENDENT STATES; that they are Absolved from all Allegiance to the British Crown, and that all political connection between them and the State of Great Britain, is and ought to be totally disolved; and that as Free and Independent States, they have full Power to levy War, conclude Peace, contract Alliances, establish Commerce, and to do all other Acts and Things which Independent States may of right do. And for the support of this Declaration, with a firm reliance on the protection of Divine Providence, we mutually pledge to each other our Lives, our Fortunes and our sacred Honor.

John Hancock	Benj. Franklin
Button Gwinnett	John Morton
Lyman Hall	Geo. Clymer
Geo. Walton	Jas. Smith
Benj. Harrison	Geo. Taylor
Thos. Nelson, Jr.	James Wilson
Francis Lightfoot Lee	Geo. Ross
Carter Braxton	Caesar Rodney
Lewis Morris	Geo. Read
Richd. Stockton	Tho. M: Kean
Jno. Witherspoon	Wm. Floyd
Fras. Hopkinson	Phil. Livingston
Wm. Hooper	Frans. Lewis
Joseph Hewes	John Hart
John Penn	Abra. Clark
Edward Rutledge	Josiah Bartlett
Thos. Heyward, Jr.	Wm. Whipple
Thomas Lynch, Jr.	Saml. Adams
Arthur Middleton	John Adams
Samuel Chase	Robt. Treat Paine
Wm. Paca	Elbridge Gerry
Thos. Stone	Step. Hopkins
Charles Carroll of	William Ellery
Carrollton	Roger Sherman
George Wythe	Sam. Huntington
Richard Henry Lee	Wm. Williams
Th. Jefferson	Oliver Wolcott
Robt. Morris	Matthew Thornton
Benjamin Rush	

Articles of Confederation (1781–1789)

The Articles of Confederation were in effect the first constitution of the United States, formally joining all the colonies under a centralized government. They were submitted to the Continental Congress in 1776, adopted the next year, but not ratified by all the states until 1781. They remained in force until the ratification of the U.S. Constitution in 1788.

To all to whom these Presents shall come, we the undersigned Delegates of the States affixed to our Names send greeting

Whereas the Delegates of the United States of America in Congress assembled did on the fifteenth day of November in the Year of our Lord One Thousand Seven Hundred and Seventy-seven, and in the Second Year of the Independence of America agree to certain articles of Confederation and perpetual Union between the States of Newhampshire, Massachusetts-bay, Rhode-island, and Providence Plantations, Connecticut, New York, New Jersey, Pennsylvania, Delaware, Maryland, Virginia, North-Carolina, South-Carolina and Georgia in the Words following, viz.

Articles of Confederation and perpetual Union between the States of Newhampshire, Massachusetts-bay, Rhodeisland and Providence Plantations, Connecticut, New-York, New-Jersey, Pennsylvania, Delaware, Maryland, Virginia, North-Carolina, South-Carolina and Georgia.

Article I

The stile of this confederacy shall be ''The United States of America.''

Article II

Each State retains its sovereignty, freedom and independence, and every power, jurisdiction and right, which is not by this confederation expressly delegated to the United States, in Congress assembled.

Article III

The said States hereby severally enter into a firm league of friendship with each other, for their common defense, the security of their liberties, and their mutual and general welfare, binding themselves to assist each other, against all force offered to, or attacks made upon them, or any of them, on account of religion, sovereignty trade or any other pretence whatever.

Article IV

The better to secure and perpetuate mutual friendship and intercourse among the people of the different States in this Union, the free inhabitants of each of these States, paupers, vagabonds and fugitives from justice excepted, shall be entitled to all privileges and immunities of free citizens in the several States; and the people of each State shall have free ingress and regress to and from any other State, and shall enjoy therein all the privileges of trade and commerce, subject to the same duties, impositions and restrictions as the inhabitants thereof respectively, provided that such restrictions shall not exceed so far as to prevent the removal of property imported into any State, to any other State of which the owner is an inhabitant; provided also that no imposition, duties or restriction shall be laid by any State, on the property of the United States, or either of them.

If any person guilty of, or charged with treason, felony, or other high misdemeanor in any State, shall flee from justice, and be found in any of the United States, he shall upon demand of the Governor or Executive power, of the State from which he fled, be delivered up and removed to the State having jurisdiction of his offense.

Full faith and credit shall be given in each of these States to the records, acts and judicial proceedings to the courts and magistrates of every other State.

Article V

For the more convenient management of the general interests of the United States, delegates shall be annually appointed in such manner as the legislature of each State shall direct, to meet in Congress on the first Monday in November, in every year, with a power reserved to each State, to recall its delegates, or any of them, at any time within the year, and to send others in their stead, for the remainder of the year.

No State shall be represented in Congress by less than two, nor by more than seven members; and no person shall be capable of being a delegate for more than three years in any term of six years; nor shall any person, being a delegate, be capable of holding any office under the United States, for which he, or another for his benefit receives any salary, fees or emolument of any kind.

Each state shall maintain its own delegates in a meeting of the States, and while they act as members of the committee of the States.

In determining questions in the United States, in Congress assembled, each State shall have one vote.

Freedom of speech and debate in Congress shall not be impeached or questioned in any court, or place out of Congress, and the members of Congress shall be protected in their persons from arrests and imprisonments, during the time of their going to and from, and attendance on Congress, except for treason, felony, or breach of the peace.

Article VI

No State without the consent of the United States in Congress assembled, shall send any embassy to, or receive any embassy from, or enter into any conference, agreement, alliance or treaty with any king, prince or state; nor shall any person holding any office or profit or trust under the United States, or any of them, accept of any present, emolument, office or title of any kind whatever from any king, prince or foreign state; nor shall the United States in Congress assembled or any of them, grant any title of nobility.

No two or more States shall enter into any treaty, confederation or alliance whatever between them, without the consent of the United States in Congress assembled, specifying accurately the purposes for which the same is to be entered into, and how long it shall continue.

No State shall lay any imposts or duties, which may interfere with any stipulations in treaties, entered into by the United States in Congress assembled, with any king, prince or state, in pursuance of any treaties already proposed by Congress, to the courts of France and Spain.

No vessels of war shall be kept up in time of peace by any State, except such number only, as shall be deemed necessary by the United States in Congress assembled, for the defence of such State, or its trade; nor shall any body of forces be kept up by any State, in time of peace, except such number only, as in the judgement of the United States, in Congress assembled, shall be deemed requisite to garrison the forts necessary for the defence of such State; but every State shall always keep up a well regulated and disciplined militia, sufficiently armed and accoutered, and shall provide and constantly have ready for use, in public stores, a due number of field pieces and tents, and a proper quantity of arms, ammunition and camp equipage.

No State shall engage in any way without the consent of the United States in Congress assembled, unless such State be actually invaded by enemies, or shall have received certain advice of a resolution being formed by some nation of Indians to invade such State, and the danger is so imminent as not to admit of a delay, till the United States in Congress assembled can be consulted: nor shall any State grant commissions to any ships or vessels of war, nor letters of marque or reprisal, except it be after a declaration of war by the United States in Congress assembled, and then only

against the kingdom or state and the subject thereof, against which war has been so declared and under such regulations as shall be established by the United States in Congress assembled, unless such State be infested by pirates, in which case vessels of war may be fitted out for that occasion, and kept so long as the danger shall continue, or until the United States in Congress assembled shall determine otherwise.

Article VII

When land-forces are raised by any State for the common defence, all officers of or under the rank of colonel, shall be appointed by the Legislature of each State respectively by whom such forces shall be raised, or in such manner as such State shall direct, and all vacancies shall be filled up by the State which first made the appointment.

Article VIII

All charges of war, and all other expenses that shall be incurred for the common defence or general welfare, and allowed by the United States in Congress assembled, shall be defrayed out of a common treasury, which shall be supplied by the several States, in proportion to the value of all land within each State, granted to or surveyed for any person, as such land and the buildings and improvements thereon shall be estimated according to such mode as the United States in Congress assembled, shall from time to time direct and appoint.

The taxes for paying that proportion shall be laid and levied by the authority and direction of the Legislatures of the several States within the time agreed upon by the United States in Congress Assembled.

Article IX

The United States in Congress assembled, shall have the sole and exclusive right and power of determining on peace and war, except in the cases mentioned in the sixth article— of sending and receiving ambassadors—entering into treaties and alliances, provided that no treaty of commerce shall be made whereby the legislative power of the respective States shall be restrained from imposing such imposts and duties on foreigners, as their own people are subjected to, or from prohibiting the exportation or importation of any species of goods or commodities whatsoever—of establishing rules for deciding in all cases, what captures on land or water shall be legal, and in what manner prizes taken by land or naval forces in the service of the United States shall be divided or appropriated—of granting letters of marque and reprisal in times of peace—appointing courts for trial of piracies and felonies committed on the high seas and establishing courts for receiving and determining finally appeals in all cases of captures, provided that no member of Congress shall be appointed a judge of any of the said courts.

The United States in Congress assembled shall also be the last resort on appeal in all disputes and differences now subsisting or that hereafter may arise between two or more States concerning boundary, jurisdiction or any other cause whatever; which authority shall always be exercised in the manner following. Whenever the legislative or executive authority or lawful agent of any State in controversy with another shall present a petition to Congress, stating the matter in question and praying for a hearing, notice thereof shall be given by order of Congress to the legislative or executive authority of the other State in controversy, and a day assigned for the appearance of the parties by their lawful agents, who shall then be directed to appoint by joint consent, commissioners or judges to constitute a court for hearing and determining the matter in question: but if they cannot agree, Congress shall name three persons out of each of the United States, and from the list of such persons each party shall alternately strike out one, the petitioners beginning, until the number shall be reduced to thirteen; and from that number not less than seven, nor more than nine names as Congress shall direct, shall, in the presence of Congress be drawn out by lot, and the persons whose names shall be so drawn or any five of them, shall be commissioners or judges, to hear and finally determine the controversy, so always as a major part of the judges who shall hear the cause shall agree in the determination: and if either party shall neglect to attend at the day appointed, without showing reasons, which Congress shall judge sufficient, or being present shall refuse to strike, the Congress shall proceed to nominate three persons out of each State, and the Secretary of Congress shall strike in behalf of such party absent or refusing; and the judgment and sentence of the court to be appointed, in the manner before prescribed, shall be final and conclusive; and if any of the parties shall refuse to submit to the authority of such court, or to appear or defend their claim or cause, the court shall nevertheless proceed to pronounce sentence, or judgment, which shall in like manner be final and decisive, the judgment or sentence and other proceedings being in either case transmitted to Congress, and lodged among the acts of Congress for the security of the parties concerned: provided that every commissioner, before he sits in judgment, shall take an oath to be administered by one of the judges of the supreme court of the State where the cause shall be tried, ''well and truly to hear and determine the matter in question, according to the best of his judgment, without favour, affection or hope of re-

ward:'' provided also that no State shall be deprived of territory for the benefit of the United States.

All controversies concerning the private right of soil claimed under different grants of two or more States, whose jurisdiction as they may respect such lands, and the States which passed such grants are adjusted, the said grants or either of them being at the same time claimed to have originated antecedent to such settlement of jurisdiction, shall on the petition of either party to the Congress of the United States, be finally determined as near as may be in the same manner as is before prescribed for deciding disputes respecting territorial jurisdiction between different States.

The United States in Congress assembled shall also have the sole and exclusive right and power of regulating the alloy and value of coin struck by their own authority, or by that of the respective States.—fixing the standard of weights and measures throughout the United States.—regulating the trade and managing all affairs with the Indians, not members of any of the States, provided that the legislative right of any State within its own limits be not infringed or violated—establishing and regulating post-offices from one State to another, throughout all the United States, and exacting such postage on the papers passing thro' the same as may be requisite to defray the expenses of the said office—appointing all officers of the land forces, in the service of the United States, excepting regimental officers—appointing all the officers of the naval forces, and commissioning all officers whatever in the service of the United States—making rules for the government and regulation of the said land and naval forces, and directing their operations.

The United States in Congress assembled shall have authority to appoint a committee, to sit in the recess of Congress, to be denominated ''a Committee of the States,'' and to consist of one delegate from each State; and to appoint such other committees and civil officers as may be necessary for managing the general affairs of the United States under their direction—to appoint one of their number to preside, provided that no person be allowed to serve in the office of president more than one year in any term of three years; to ascertain the necessary sums of money to be raised for the service of the United States, and to appropriate and apply the same for defraying the public expenses—to borrow money or emit bills on the credit of the United States transmitting every half year to the respective States an account of the sums of money so borrowed or emitted,—to build and equip a navy—to agree upon the number of land forces, and to make requisitions from each State for its quota, in proportion to the number of white inhabitants in such State; which requisition shall be binding, and thereupon the Legislature of each State shall appoint the regimental officers, raise the men and cloath, arm and equip them in a soldier like manner, at the expense of the United States; and the officers and men so cloathed, armed and equipped shall march to the place appointed, and within the time agreed on by the United States in Congress assembled; but if the United States in Congress assembled shall, on consideration of circumstances judge proper that any State should not raise men, or should raise a smaller number than its quota, and that any other State should raise a greater number of men than the quota thereof, such extra number shall be raised, officered, cloathed, armed and equipped in the same manner as the quota of such State, unless the legislature of such State shall judge that such extra number cannot be safely spared out of the same, in which case they shall raise officer, cloath, arm and equip as many of such extra number as they judge can be safely spared. And the officers and men so cloathed, armed, and equipped, shall march to the place appointed, and within the time agreed on by the United States in Congress assembled.

The United States in Congress assembled shall never engage in a war, nor grant letters of marque and reprisal in time of peace, nor enter into any treaties or alliances, nor coin money, nor regulate the value thereof, nor ascertain the sums and expenses necessary for the defence and welfare of the United States, or any of them, nor emit bills, nor borrow money on the credit of the United States, nor appropriate money, nor agree upon the number of vessels of war, to be built or purchased, or the number of land or sea forces to be raised, nor appoint a commander in chief of the army or navy, unless nine States assent to the same: nor shall a question on any other point, except for adjourning from day to day be determined, unless by the votes of a majority of the United States in Congress assembled.

The Congress of the United States shall have power to adjourn to any time within the year, and to any place within the United States, so that no period of adjournment be for a longer duration than the space of six months, and shall publish the journal of their proceedings monthly, except such parts thereof relating to treaties, alliances or military operations, as in their judgment require secresy; and the yeas and nays of the delegates of each State on any question shall be entered on the journal, when it is desired by any delegate; and the delegates of a State, or any of them, at his or her request shall be furnished with a transcript of the said Journal, except such parts as are above excepted, to lay before the Legislatures of the several States.

Article X

The committee of the States, or any nine of them, shall be authorized to execute in the recess of Congress, such of the powers of Congress as the United States in Congress assembled, by the consent of nine States, shall from time to time think expedient to vest them with; provided that no power be delegated to the said committee, for the exercise of which, by the articles of confederation, the voice of nine States in the Congress of the United States assembled is requisite.

Article XI

Canada acceding to this confederation, and joining in the measures of the United States, shall be admitted into, and entitled to all the advantages of this Union: but no other colony shall be admitted into the same, unless such admission be agreed to by nine States.

Article XII

All bills of credit emitted, monies borrowed and debts contracted by, or under the authority of Congress, before the assembling of the United States, in pursuance of the present confederation, shall be deemed and considered as a charge against the United States, for payment and satisfaction whereof the said United States, and the public faith are hereby solemnly pledged.

Article XIII

Every State shall abide by the determinations of the United States in Congress assembled, on all questions which by this confederation are submitted to them. And the articles of this confederation shall be inviolably observed by every State, and the Union shall be perpetual; nor shall any alteration at any time hereafter be made in any of them; unless such alteration be agreed to in a Congress of the United States, and be afterwards confirmed by the Legislatures of every State.

And whereas it has pleased the Great Governor of the world to incline the hearts of the Legislatures we respectively represent in Congress, to approve of, and to authorize us to ratify the said articles of confederation and perpetual union. Know ye that we the undersigned delegates, by virtue of the power and authority to us given for that purpose, do by these presents, in the name and in behalf of our respective constituents, fully and entirely ratify and confirm each and every of the said articles of confederation and perpetual union, and all and singular the matters and things therein contained: and we do further solemnly plight and engage the faith of our respective constituents, that they shall abide by the determinations of the United States in Congress assembled, on all questions, which by the said confederation are submitted to them. And that the articles thereof shall be inviolably observed by the States we re[s]pectively represent, and that the Union shall be perpetual.

In witness whereof we have hereunto set our hands in Congress.

Done at Philadelphia in the State of Pennsylvania the ninth day of July in the year of our Lord one thousand seven hundred and seventy-eight, and in the third year of the independence of America.

On the part and behalf of the State of New Hampshire

| JOSIAH BARTLETT, | JOHN WENTWORTH, Junr., August 8th, 1778. |

On the part and behalf of the State of Massachusetts Bay

JOHN HANCOCK,	FRANCIS DANA,
SAMUEL ADAMS,	JAMES LOVELL,
ELBRIDGE GERRY,	SAMUEL HOLTEN.

On the part and behalf of the State of Rhode Island and Providence Plantations

| WILLIAM ELLERY, | JOHN COLLINS. |
| HENRY MARCHANT, | |

On the part and behalf of the State of Connecticut

ROGER SHERMAN,	TITUS HOSMER,
SAMUEL HUNTINGTON,	ANDREW ADAMS.
OLIVER WOLCOTT,	

On the part and behalf of the State of New York

| JAS. DUANE, | WM. DUER, |
| FRA. LEWIS, | GOUV. MORRIS. |

On the part and in behalf of the State of New Jersey, Novr. 26, 1778

| JNO. WITHERSPOON, | NATHL. SCUDDER. |

On the part and behalf of the State of Pennsylvania

ROBT. MORRIS,	WILLIAM CLINGAN,
DANIEL ROBERDEAU,	JOSEPH REED,
JONA. BAYARD SMITH,	22d July, 1778.

On the part & behalf of the State of Delaware

| THO. M'KEAN, Feby. 12, 1779. | NICHOLAS VAN DYKE. |
| JOHN DICKINSON, May 5th, 1779 | |

On the part and behalf of the State of Maryland

| JOHN HANSON, March 1, 1781. | DANIEL CARROLL, Mar. 1, 1781. |

On the part and behalf of the State of Virginia

RICHARD HENRY LEE,	JNO. HARVIE,
JOHN BANISTER,	FRANCIS LIGHTFOOT LEE.
THOMAS ADAMS,	

On the part and behalf of the State of No. Carolina

| JOHN PENN, July 21st, 1778. | JNO. WILLIAMS. |
| CORNS. HARNETT, | |

On the part & behalf of the State of South Carolina

HENRY LAURENS,	RICHD. HUTSON,
WILLIAM HENRY DRAYTON,	THOS. HEYWARD, Junr.
JNO. MATHEWS,	

On the part & behalf of the State of Georgia

| JNO. WALTON, 24th July, 1778. | EDWD. LANGWORTHY. |
| EDWD. TELFAIR, | |

Federalist Papers No. 10 and No. 51 (1787/1788)

During the battle over ratification of the U.S. Constitution in 1787 and 1788, Alexander Hamilton, James Madison, and John Jay wrote a series of eighty-five political essays favoring the adoption of the document. James Madison wrote, among others, two of the most famous—Number 10 and Number 51. Number 10, considered a classic in political theory, deals with the nature of groups, or factions, as he called them. His view, favoring a large republic, is presented in Number 51.

The Federalist No. 10
James Madison, November 22, 1787
TO THE PEOPLE OF THE STATE OF NEW YORK.
Among the numerous advantages promised by a well con-

structed Union, none deserves to be more accurately developed than its tendency to break and control the violence of faction. The friend of popular governments, never finds himself so much alarmed for their character and fate, as when he contemplates their propensity to this dangerous vice. He will not fail therefore to set a due value on any plan which, without violating the principles to which he is attached, provides a proper cure for it. The instability, injustice and confusion introduced into the public councils, have in truth been the mortal diseases under which popular governments have every where perished; as they continue to be the favorite and fruitful topics from which the adversaries to liberty derive their most specious declamations. The valuable improvements made by the American Constitutions on the popular models, both ancient and modern, cannot certainly be too much admired; but it would be an unwarrantable partiality, to contend that they have as effectually obviated the danger on this side as was wished and expected. Complaints are every where heard from our most considerate and virtuous citizens, equally the friends of public and private faith, and of public and personal liberty; that our governments are too unstable; that the public good is disregarded in the conflicts of rival parties; and that measures are too often decided, not according to the rules of justice, and the rights of the minor party; but by the superior force of an interested and over-bearing majority. However anxiously we may wish that these complaints had no foundation, the evidence of known facts will not permit us to deny that they are in some degree true. It will be found indeed, on a candid review of our situation, that some of the distresses under which we labor, have been erroneously charged on the operation of our governments; but it will be found, at the same time, that other causes will not alone account for many of our heaviest misfortunes; and particularly, for that prevailing and increasing distrust of public engagements, and alarm for private rights, which are echoed from one end of the continent to the other. These must be chiefly, if not wholly, effects of the unsteadiness and injustice, with which a factious spirit has tainted our public administrations.

By a faction I understand a number of citizens, whether amounting to a majority or minority of the whole, who are united and actuated by some common impulse of passion, or of interest, adverse to the rights of other citizens, or to the permanent and aggregate interests of the community.

There are two methods of curing the mischiefs of faction: the one, by removing its causes; the other, by controlling its effects.

There are again two methods of removing the causes of faction: the one by destroying the liberty which is essential to its existence; the other, by giving to every citizen the same opinions, the same passions, and the same interests.

It could never be more truly said than of the first remedy, that it is worse than the disease. Liberty is to faction, what air is to fire, an aliment without which it instantly expires. But it could not be a less folly to abolish liberty, which is essential to political life, because it nourishes faction, than it would be to wish the annihilation of air, which is essential to animal life, because it imparts to fire its destructive agency.

The second expedient is as impracticable, as the first would be unwise. As long as the reason of man continues fallible, and he is at liberty to exercise it, different opinions will be formed. As long as the connection subsists between his reason and his self-love, his opinions and his passions will have a reciprocal influence on each other; and the former will be objects to which the latter will attach themselves. The diversity in the faculties of men from which the rights of property originate, is not less an insuperable obstacle to a uniformity of interests. The protection of these faculties is the first object of Government. From the protection of different and unequal faculties of acquiring property, the possession of different degrees and kinds of property immediately results: and from the influence of these on the sentiments and views of the respective proprietors, ensues a division of the society into different interests and parties.

The latent causes of faction are thus sown in the nature of man; and we see them every where brought into different degrees of activity, according to the different circumstances of civil society. A zeal for different opinions concerning religion, concerning Government and many other points, as well of speculation as of practice; an attachment to different leaders ambitiously contending for pre-eminence and power; or to persons of other descriptions whose fortunes have been interesting to the human passions, have in turn divided mankind into parties, inflamed them with mutual animosity, and rendered them much more disposed to vex and oppress each other, than to co-operate for their common good. So strong is this propensity of mankind to fall into mutual animosities, that where no substantial occasion presents itself, the most frivolous and fanciful distinctions have been sufficient to kindle their unfriendly passions, and excite their most violent conflicts. But the most common and durable source of factions, has been the various and unequal distribution of property. Those who hold, and those who are without property, have ever formed distinct interests in society. Those who are creditors, and those who are debtors, fall under a like discrimination. A landed interest, a manufacturing interest, a mercantile interest, a monied interest, with many lesser interests, grow up of necessity in civilized nations, and divide them into different classes, actuated by different sentiments and views. The regulation of these various and interfering interests forms the principal task of modern Legislation, and involves the spirit of party and faction in the necessary and ordinary operations of Government.

No man is allowed to be a judge in his own cause; because his interest would certainly bias his judgment, and, not improbably, corrupt his integrity. With equal, nay with greater reason, a body of men, are unfit to be both judges and parties, at the same time; yet, what are many of the most important acts of legislation, but so many judicial determinations, not indeed concerning the rights of single persons, but concerning the rights of large bodies of citizens, and what are the different classes of legislators, but advocates and parties to the causes which they determine? Is a law proposed concerning private debts? It is a question to which the creditors are parties on one side, and the debtors on the other. Justice ought to hold the balance between them. Yet the parties are and must be themselves the judges; and the most numerous party, or, in other words, the most powerful faction must be expected to prevail. Shall domestic manufactures be encouraged, and in what degree, by restrictions on foreign manufactures? are questions which would be differently decided by the landed and the manufacturing classes; and probably by neither, with a sole regard to justice and the public good. The apportionment of taxes on the various descriptions of property, is an act which seems to require the most exact impartiality; yet, there is perhaps no legislative act in which greater opportunity and temptation are given to a predominant party, to trample on the rules of justice. Every shilling with which they over-burden the inferior number, is a shilling saved to their own pockets.

It is in vain to say, that enlightened statesmen will be able to adjust these clashing interests, and render them all subservient to the public good. Enlightened statesmen will not always be at the helm: Nor, in many cases, can such an adjustment be made at all, without taking into view indirect and remote considerations, which will rarely prevail over the immediate interest which one party may find in disregarding the rights of another, or the good of the whole.

The inference to which we are brought, is, that the *causes* of faction cannot be removed; and that relief is only to be sought in the means of controlling its *effects*.

If a faction consists of less than a majority, relief is supplied by the republican principle, which enables the majority to defeat its sinister views by regular vote: It may clog the administration, it may convulse the society; but it

will be unable to execute and mask its violence under the forms of the Constitution. When a majority is included in a faction, the form of popular government on the other hand enables it to sacrifice to its ruling passion or interest, both the public good and the rights of other citizens. To secure the public good, and private rights, against the danger of such a faction, and at the same time to preserve the spirit and the form of popular government, is then the great object to which our enquiries are directed: Let me add that it is the great desideratum, by which alone this form of government can be rescued from the opprobrium under which it has so long labored, and be recommended to the esteem and adoption of mankind.

By what means is this object attainable? Evidently by one of two only. Either the existence of the same passion or interest in a majority at the same time, must be prevented; or the majority, having such co-existent passion or interest, must be rendered, by their number and local situation, unable to concert and carry into effect schemes of oppression. If the impulse and the opportunity be suffered to coincide, we well know that neither moral nor religious motives can be relied on as an adequate control. They are not found to be such on the injustice and violence of individuals, and lose their efficacy in proportion to the number combined together; that is, in proportion as their efficacy becomes needful.

From this view of the subject, it may be concluded, that a pure Democracy, by which I mean, a Society, consisting of a small number of citizens, who assemble and administer the Government in person, can admit of no cure for the mischiefs of faction. A common passion or interest will, in almost every case, be felt by a majority of the whole; a communication and concert results from the form of Government itself; and there is nothing to check the inducements to sacrifice the weaker party, or an obnoxious individual. Hence it is, that such Democracies have ever been spectacles of turbulence and contention; have ever been found incompatible with personal security, or the rights of property; and have in general been as short in their lives, as they have been violent in their deaths. Theoretic politicians, who have patronized this species of Government, have erroneously supposed, that by reducing mankind to a perfect equality in their political rights, they would, at the same time, be perfectly equalized and assimilated in their possessions, their opinions, and their passions.

A republic, by which I mean a government in which the scheme of representation takes place, opens a different prospect, and promises the cure for which we are seeking. Let us examine the points in which it varies from pure democracy, and we shall comprehend both the nature of the cure and the efficacy which it must derive from the union.

The two great points of difference, between a democracy and a republic, are, first, the delegation of the government, in the latter, to a small number of citizens, elected by the rest; secondly, the greater number of citizens, and greater sphere of country, over which the latter may be extended.

The effect of the first difference is, on the one hand, to refine and enlarge the public views, by passing them through the medium of a chosen body of citizens, whose wisdom may best discern the true interest of their country, and whose patriotism and love of justice, will be least likely to sacrifice it to temporary or partial considerations. Under such a regulation, it may well happen, that the public voice, pronounced by the representatives of the people, will be more consonant to the public good, than if pronounced by the people themselves, convened for the purpose. On the other hand the effect may be inverted. Men of factious tempers, of local prejudices, or of sinister designs, may by intrigue, by corruption, or by other means, first obtain the suffrages, and then betray the interest of the people. The question resulting is, whether small or extensive republics are most favorable to the election of proper guardians of the public weal, and it is clearly decided in favor of the latter by two obvious considerations.

In the first place, it is to be remarked that, however small the republic may be, the representatives must be raised to a certain number, in order to guard against the cabals of a few; and that however large it may be, they must be limited to a certain number, in order to guard against the confusion of a multitude. Hence, the number of representatives in the two cases not being in proportion to that of the constituents, and being proportionally greatest in the small republic, it follows, that if the proportion of fit characters be not less in the large than in the small republic, the former will present a greater option, and consequently a greater probability of a fit choice.

In the next place, as each Representative will be chosen by a greater number of citizens in the large than in the small Republic, it will be more difficult for unworthy candidates to practise with success the vicious arts, by which elections are too often carried; and the suffrages of the people being more free, will be more likely to center on men who possess the most attractive merit, and the most diffusive and established characters.

It must be confessed, that in this, as in most other cases, there is a mean, on both sides of which inconveniences will be found to lie. By enlarging too much the number of electors, you render the representative too little acquainted with all their local circumstances and lesser interests; as by reducing it too much, you render him unduly attached to these, and too little fit to comprehend and pursue great and national objects. The Federal Constitution forms a happy combination in this respect; the great and aggregate interests being referred to the national, the local and particular, to the state legislatures.

The other point of difference is, the greater number of citizens and extent of territory which may be brought within the compass of Republican, than of Democratic Government; and it is this circumstance principally which renders factious combinations less to be dreaded in the former, than in the latter. The smaller the society, the fewer probably will be the distinct parties and interests composing it; the fewer the distinct parties and interests, the more frequently will a majority be found of the same party; and the smaller the number of individuals composing a majority, and the smaller the compass within which they are placed, the more easily will they concert and execute their plans of oppression. Extend the sphere, and you take in a greater variety of parties and interests; you make it less probable that a majority of the whole will have a common motive to invade the rights of other citizens; or if such a common motive exists, it will be more difficult for all who feel it to discover their own strength, and to act in unison with each other. Besides other impediments, it may be remarked, that where there is a consciousness of unjust or dishonorable purposes, communication is always checked by distrust, in proportion to the number whose concurrence is necessary.

Hence it clearly appears, that the same advantage, which a Republic has over a Democracy, in controlling the effects of faction, is enjoyed by a large over a small Republic—is enjoyed by the Union over the States composing it. Does this advantage consist in the substitution of Representatives, whose enlightened views and virtuous sentiments render them superior to local prejudices, and to schemes of injustice? It will not be denied, that the Representation of the Union will be most likely to possess these requisite endowments. Does it consist in the greater security afforded by a greater variety of parties, against the event of any one party being able to outnumber and oppress the rest? In an equal degree does the increased variety of parties, comprised within the Union, increase this security? Does it, in fine, consist in the greater obstacles opposed to the concert and accomplishment of the secret wishes of an unjust and interested majority? Here, again, the extent of the Union gives it the most palpable advantage.

The influence of factious leaders may kindle a flame within their particular States, but will be unable to spread a general conflagration through the other States: a religious sect, may degenerate into a political faction in a part of the Confederacy but the variety of sects dispersed over the entire face of it, must secure the national Councils against any danger from that source: a rage for paper money, for an abolition of debts, for an equal division of property, or for any other improper or wicked project, will be less apt to pervade the whole body of the Union, than a particular member of it; in the same proportion as such a malady is more likely to taint a particular county or district, than an entire State.

In the extent and proper structure of the Union, therefore, we behold a Republican remedy for the diseases most incident to Republican Government. And according to the degree of pleasure and pride, we feel in being Republicans, ought to be our zeal in cherishing the spirit, and supporting the character of Federalists.

Publius

The Federalist No. 51

James Madison, February 6, 1788

TO THE PEOPLE OF THE STATE OF NEW YORK.

To what expedient then shall we finally resort for maintaining in practice the necessary partition of power among the several departments, as laid down in the constitution? The only answer that can be given is, that as all these exterior provisions are found to be inadequate, the defect must be supplied, by so contriving the interior structure of the government, as that its several constituent parts may, by their mutual relations, be the means of keeping each other in their proper places. Without presuming to undertake a full development of this important idea, I will hazard a few general observations, which may perhaps place it in a clearer light, and enable us to form a more correct judgment of the principles and structure of the government planned by the convention.

In order to lay a due foundation for that separate and distinct exercise of the different powers of government, which to a certain extent, is admitted on all hands to be essential to the preservation of liberty, it is evident that each department should have a will of its own; and consequently should be so constituted, that the members of each should have as little agency as possible in the appointment of the members of the others. Were this principle rigorously adhered to, it would require that all the appointments for the supreme executive, legislative, and judiciary magistracies, should be drawn from the same fountain of authority, the people, through channels, having no communication whatever with one another. Perhaps such a plan of constructing the several departments would be less difficult in practice than it may in contemplation appear. Some difficulties however, and some additional expense, would attend the execution of it. Some deviations therefore from the principle must be admitted. In the constitution of the judiciary department in particular, it might be inexpedient to insist rigorously on the principle; first, because peculiar qualifications being essential in the members, the primary consideration ought to be to select that mode of choice, which best secures these qualifications; secondly, because the permanent tenure by which the appointments are held in that department, must soon destroy all sense of dependence on the authority conferring them.

It is equally evident that the members of each department should be as little dependent as possible on those of the others, for the emoluments annexed to their offices. Were the executive magistrate, or the judges, not independent of the legislature in this particular, their independence in every other would be merely nominal.

But the great security against a gradual concentration of the several powers in the same department, consists in giving to those who administer each department, the necessary constitutional means, and personal motives, to resist encroachments of the others. The provision for defense must in this, as in all other cases, be made commensurate to the danger of attack. Ambition must be made to counteract ambition. The interest of the man must be connected with the constitutional rights of the place. It may be a reflection on human nature, that such devices should be necessary to control the abuses of government. But what is government itself but the greatest of all reflections on human nature? If men were angels, no government would be necessary. If angels were to govern men, neither external nor internal controls on government would be necessary. In framing a government which is to be administered by men over men, the great difficulty lies in this: You must first enable the government to control the governed; and in the next place oblige it to control itself. A dependence on the people is no doubt the primary control on the government; but experience has taught mankind the necessity of auxiliary precautions.

This policy of supplying by opposite and rival interests, the defect of better motives, might be traced through the whole system of human affairs, private as well as public. We see it particularly displayed in all the subordinate distributions of power; where the constant aim is to divide and arrange the several offices in such a manner as that each may be a check on the other; that the private interest of every individual, may be a sentinel over the public rights. These inventions of prudence cannot be less requisite in the distribution of the supreme powers of the state.

But it is not possible to give to each department an equal power of self defense. In republican government the legislative authority, necessarily, predominates. The remedy for this inconveniency is, to divide the legislature into different branches; and to render them by different modes of election, and different principles of action, as little connected with each other, as the nature of their common functions, and their common dependence on the society, will admit. It may even be necessary to guard against dangerous encroachments by still further precautions. As the weight of the legislative authority requires that it should be thus divided, the weakness of the executive may require, on the other hand, that it should be fortified. An absolute negative, on the legislature, appears at first view to be the natural defense with which the executive magistrate should be armed. But perhaps it would be neither altogether safe, nor alone sufficient. On ordinary occasions, it might not be exerted with the requisite firmness; and on extraordinary occasions, it might be prefidiously abused. May not this defect of an absolute negative be supplied, by some qualified connection between this weaker department, and the weaker branch of the stronger department, by which the latter may be led to support the constitutional rights of the former, without being too much detached from the rights of its own department?

If the principles on which these observations are founded be just, as I persuade myself they are, and they be applied as a criterion, to the several state constitutions, and to the federal constitution, it will be found, that if the latter does not perfectly correspond with them, the former are infinitely less able to bear such a test.

There are moreover two considerations particularly applicable to the federal system of America, which place that system in a very interesting point of view.

First. In a single republic, all the power surrendered by the people, is submitted to the administration of a single government; and usurpations are guarded against by a division of the government into distinct and separate departments. In the compound republic of America, the power surrendered by the people, is first divided between two distinct governments, and then the portion allotted to each, subdivided among distinct and separate departments. Hence a double security rises to the rights of the people. The different governments will control each other; at the same time that each will be controlled by itself.

Second. It is of great importance in a republic, not only to guard the society against the oppression of its rulers; but to guard one part of the society against the injustice of the other part. Different interests necessarily exist in different classes of citizens. If a majority be united by a common interest, the rights of the minority will be insecure. There are but two methods of providing against this evil: The one by creating a will in the community independent of the majority, that is, of the society itself, the other by comprehending in the society so many separate descriptions of citizens, as will render an unjust combination of a majority of the whole, very improbable, if not impracticable. The first method prevails in all governments possessing an hereditary or self appointed authority. This at best is but a precarious security; because a power independent of the society may as well espouse the unjust views of the major, as the rightful interests, of the minor party, and may possibly be turned against both parties. The second method will be exemplified in the federal republic of the United States. While all authority in it will be derived from and dependent on the society, the society itself will be broken into so many parts, interests and classes of citizens, that the rights of individuals or of the minority, will be in little danger from interested combinations of the majority. In a free government, the security for civil rights must be the same as for religious rights. It consists in the one case in the multiplicity of interests, and in the other, in the multiplicity of sects. The degree of security in both cases will depend on the number of interests and sects; and this may be presumed to depend on the extent of country and number of people comprehended under the same government. This view of the subject must particularly recommend a proper federal system to all the sincere and considerate friends of republican government: Since it shows that in exact proportion as the territory of the union may be formed into more circumscribed confederacies or states, oppressive combinations of a majority will be facilitated, the best security under the republican form, for the rights of every class of citizens, will be diminished; and consequently, the stability and independence of some member of the government, the only other security, must be proportionally increased. Justice is the end of government. It is the end of civil society. It ever has been, and ever will be pursued, until it be obtained, or until liberty be lost in the pursuit. In a society under the forms of which the stronger faction can readily unite and oppress the weaker, anarchy may as truly be said to reign, as in a state of nature where the weaker individual is not secured against the violence of the stronger: And as in the latter state even the stronger individuals are prompted by the uncertainty of their condition, to submit to a government which may protect the weak as well as themselves: So in the former state, will the more powerful factions or parties be gradually induced by a like motive, to wish for a government which will protect all parties, the weaker as well as the more powerful. It can be little doubted, that if the state of Rhode Island was separated from the confederacy, and left to itself, the insecurity of rights under the popular form of government within such narrow limits, would be displayed by such reiterated oppressions of factious majorities, that some power altogether independent of the people would soon be called for by the voice of the very factions whose misrule had proved the necessity of it. In the extended republic of the United States, and among the great variety of interests, parties and sects which it embraces, a coalition of a majority of the whole society could seldom take place on any other principles than those of justice and the general good; and there being thus less danger to a minor from the will of the major party, there must be less pretext also, to provide for the security of the former, by introducing into the government a will not dependent on the latter; or in other words, a will independent of the society itself. It is

no less certain than it is important, notwithstanding the contrary opinions which have been entertained, that the larger the society, provided it lie within a practicable sphere, the more duly capable it will be of self government. And happily for the *republican cause,* the practicable sphere may be carried to a very great extent, by a judicious modification and mixture of the *federal principle.*

Publius

Anti-Federalist Writings (1787–1788)

Those who opposed the ratification of the United States Constitution were called the Anti-Federalists to show their opposition to the Federalists, who were in favor of the Constitution's ratification. Many of the Anti-Federalists' writings were published under pen names, just as were some of the writings of the Federalists.

Because the original Constitution (without its amendments) did not contain a bill of rights, many Anti-Federalist writers were opposed to ratification as is evidenced by the excerpt below, written by an unknown Anti-Federalist.

The truth is, that the rights of individuals are frequently opposed to the apparent interests of the majority—For this reason the greater the portion of political freedom in a form of government the greater the necessity of a bill of rights— Often the natural rights of an individual are opposed to the presumed interests or heated passions of a large majority of democratic government; if these rights are not clearly and expressly ascertained, the individual must be lost; and for the truth of this I appeal to every man who has borne a part in the legislative councils of America. In such government the tyranny of the legislative is most to be dreaded.

—A (Maryland) Farmer in the Maryland Gazette, *April 1788.*

Because the United States was so large a territory, many Anti-Federalists did not believe that it could be governed by one national government. They believed that it would not be a government by the will of the people and, therefore, it would become arbitrary. Robert Yates of New York, using the pen name Brutus, presented these ideas in the following excerpt:

In every free government, the people must give their assent to the laws by which they are governed. This is the true criterion between a free government and an arbitrary one. The former are ruled by the will of the whole [the people], expressed in any manner they may agree upon; the latter by the will of one, or a few. If the people are to give their assent to the laws, by persons chosen and appointed by them, the manner of the choice and the number chosen must be such, as to possess, be disposed, and consequently qualified to declare the sentiments of the people; for if they do not know, or are not disposed to speak the sentiments of the people, the people do not govern, but the sovereignty is in a few. Now, in a large-extended country, it is impossible to have a representation, possessing the sentiments, and of integrity, to declare the minds of the people . . . .

—Brutus, October 1787

Monroe Doctrine (1823)

The Monroe Doctrine is a statement about U.S. foreign policy prepared by John Quincy Adams, and presented by President James Monroe to the Congress on December 2,

1823. The goal of the doctrine was to prevent European involvement in Latin America's new republics.

Fellow citizens of the Senate and House of Representatives:

Many important subjects will claim your attention during the present session, of which I shall endeavor to give, in aid of your deliberations, a just idea in this communication. I undertake this duty with diffidence, from the vast extent of the interests on which I have to treat and of their great importance to every portion of our Union. I enter on it with zeal from a thorough conviction that there never was a period since the establishment of our revolution when, regarding the condition of the civilized world and its bearing on us, there was greater necessity for devotion in the public servants to their respective duties, or for virtue, patriotism, and union in our constituents.

Meeting in you a new Congress, I deem it proper to present this view of public affairs in greater detail than might otherwise be necessary. I do it, however, with peculiar satisfaction, from a knowledge that in this respect I shall comply more fully with the sound principles of our government. The people being with us exclusively the sovereign, it is indispensable that full information be laid before them on all important subjects, to enable them to exercise that high power with complete effect. If kept in the dark, they must be incompetent to it. We are all liable to error, and those who are engaged in the management of public affairs are more subject to excitement and to be led astray by their particular interests and passions than the great body of our constituents, who, living at home in the pursuit of their ordinary avocations, are calm but deeply interested spectators of events and of the conduct of those who are parties to them. To the people every department of the government and every individual in each are responsible, and the more full their information the better they can judge of the wisdom of the policy pursued and of the conduct of each in regard to it. From their dispassionate judgment much aid may always be obtained, while their approbation will form the greatest incentive and most gratifying reward for virtuous actions and the dread of their censure the best security against the abuse of their confidence. Their interests in all vital questions are the same, and the bond, by sentiment as well as by interest, will be proportionably strengthened as they are better informed of the real state of public affairs, especially in difficult conjunctures. It is by such knowledge that local prejudices and jealousies are surmounted, and that a national policy, extending its fostering care and protection to all the great interests of our Union, is formed and steadily adhered to. . . .

At the proposal of the Russian imperial government, made through the minister of the emperor residing here, a full power and instructions have been transmitted to the minister of the United States at St. Petersburg to arrange by amicable negotiation the respective rights and interests of the two nations on the northwest coast of this continent.

A similar proposal had been made by his imperial Majesty to the government of Great Britain, which has likewise been acceded to. The government of the United States has been desirous by this friendly proceeding of manifesting the great value which they have invariably attached to the friendship of the emperor and their solicitude to cultivate the best understanding with his government. In the discussions to which this interest has given rise and in the arrangements by which they may terminate the occasion has been judged proper for asserting, as a principle in which the rights and interests of the United States are involved, that the American continents, by the free and independent condition which they have assumed and maintain, are henceforth not to be considered as subjects for future colonization by any European powers. . . .

It was stated at the commencement of the last session that a great effort was then making in Spain and Portugal to improve the condition of the people of those countries, and that it appeared to be conducted with extraordinary moderation. It need scarcely be remarked that the result has been so far very different from what was then anticipated. Of events in that quarter of the globe, with which we have so much intercourse and from which we derive our origin, we have always been anxious and interested spectators. The citizens of the United States cherish sentiments the most friendly in favor of the liberty and happiness of their fellow men on that side of the Atlantic. In the wars of the European powers in matters relating to themselves, we have never taken any part, nor does it comport with our policy so to do. It is only when our rights are invaded or seriously menaced that we resent injuries or make preparation for our defense. With the movements in this hemisphere we are of necessity more immediately connected, and by causes which must be obvious to all enlightened and impartial observers. The political system of the allied powers is essentially different in this respect from that of America. This difference proceeds from that which exists in their respective governments; and to the defense of our own, which has been achieved by the loss of so much blood and treasure, and matured by the wisdom of their most enlightened citizens, and under which we have enjoyed unexampled felicity, this whole nation is devoted. We owe it, therefore, to candor and to the amicable relations existing between the United States and those powers to declare that we should consider any attempt on their part to extend their system to any portion of this hemisphere as dangerous to our peace and safety. With the existing colonies or dependencies of any European power, we have not interfered and shall not interfere. But with the governments who have declared their independence and maintained it, and whose independence we have, on great consideration and on just principles, acknowledged, we could not view any interposition for the purpose of oppressing them, or controlling in any other manner their destiny, by any European power in any other light than as the manifestation of an unfriendly disposition toward the United States. In the war between those new governments and Spain, we declared our neutrality at the time of their recognition, and to this we have adhered, and shall continue to adhere, provided no change shall occur which, in the judgment of the competent authorities of this government, shall make a corresponding change on the part of the United States indispensable to their security.

The late events in Spain and Portugal show that Europe is still unsettled. Of this important fact no stronger proof can be adduced than that the allied powers should have thought it proper, on any principle satisfactory to themselves, to have interposed by force in the internal concerns of Spain. To what extent such interposition may be carried, on the same principle, is a question in which all independent powers whose governments differ from theirs are interested, even those most remote, and surely none more so than the United States. Our policy in regard to Europe, which was adopted at an early stage of the wars which have so long agitated that quarter of the globe, nevertheless remains the same, which is, not to interfere in the internal concerns of any of its powers; to consider the government *de facto* as the legitimate government for us; to cultivate friendly relations with it, and to preserve those relations by a frank, firm, and manly policy, meeting in all instances the just claims of every power, submitting to injuries from none. But in regard to those continents, circumstances are eminently and conspicuously different. It is impossible that the allied powers should extend their political system to any portion of either continent without endangering our peace and happiness; nor can anyone believe that our southern brethren, if left to themselves, would adopt it of their own accord. It is equally impossible, therefore, that we should behold such interposition in any form with indifference. If we look to the comparative strength and resources of Spain and those new governments, and their distance from each other, it must be obvious that she can never subdue them. It is still the true policy of the United States to leave the parties to themselves in the hope that other powers will pursue the same course.

Seneca Falls Declaration (1848)

The Seneca Falls Declaration, a "declaration of sentiments," was issued at an important women's rights convention held at Seneca Falls, New York in July, 1848. The convention was organized by Elizabeth Cady Stanton and Lucretia Mott.

We hold these truths to be self-evident; that all men and women are created equal; that they are endowed by their Creator with certain inalienable rights; that among these are life, liberty, and the pursuit of happiness; that to secure these rights governments are instituted, deriving their just powers from the consent of the governed. . . .

Now, in view of this entire disfranchisement of one-half the people of this country, their social and religious degradation, in view of the unjust laws above mentioned, and because women do feel themselves aggrieved, oppressed, and fraudulently deprived of their most sacred rights, we insist that they have immediate admission to all the rights and privileges which belong to them as citizens of the United States.

[*Excerpt*]

Emancipation Proclamation (1862)

President Abraham Lincoln issued the Emancipation Proclamation on September 23, 1862, in order to gain world support for the Union cause. The document stated that after January 1, 1863, all slaves in the rebel states would be free. The proclamation did not apply to the border states of Delaware, Kentucky, Maryland, and Missouri, nor to that part of the Confederacy already occupied by Northern troops, such as Tennessee and parts of Virginia and Louisiana.

By the President of the United States of America:
A PROCLAMATION

Whereas, on the twenty-second day of September, in the year of our Lord one thousand eight hundred and sixty-two, a proclamation was issued by the president of the United States, containing, among other things, the following, to wit:

"That on the first day of January, in the year of our Lord one thousand eight hundred and sixty-three, all persons held as slaves within any state or designated part of a state, the people whereof shall then be in rebellion against the United States, shall be then, thenceforward and forever, free; and the executive government of the United States, including the military and naval authority thereof, will recognize and maintain the freedom of such persons and will do no act or acts to repress such persons, or any of them, in any efforts they may make for their actual freedom.

"That the executive will, on the first day of January aforesaid, by proclamation, designate the states and parts of states, if any, in which the people thereof, respectively, shall then be in rebellion against the United States; and the fact that any state, or the people thereof, shall on that day be in good faith represented in the Congress of the United States, by members chosen thereto at elections wherein a majority of the qualified voters of such states shall have participated, shall, in the absence of strong countervailing testimony, be deemed conclusive evidence that such state, and the people thereof, are not then in rebellion against the United States."

Now, therefore, I, Abraham Lincoln, president of the United States, by virtue of the power in me vested as commander in chief of the army and navy of the United States, in time of actual armed rebellion against the authority and government of the United States, and as a fit and necessary war measure for suppressing said rebellion, do, on this first day of January, in the year of our Lord one thousand eight hundred and sixty-three, and in accordance with my purpose so to do, publicly proclaimed for the full period of one hundred days from the day first above mentioned, order and designate as the states and parts of states wherein the people thereof, respectively, are this day in rebellion against the United States, the following, to wit:

Arkansas, Texas, Louisiana (except the parishes of St. Bernard, Plaquemines, Jefferson, St. John, St. Charles, St. James, Ascension, Assumption, Terre Bonne, Lafourche, St. Mary, St. Martin, and Orleans, including the city of New Orleans), Mississippi, Alabama, Florida, Georgia, South Carolina, North Carolina, and Virginia (except the forty-eight counties designated as West Virginia, and also the counties of Berkeley, Accomac, Northampton, Elizabeth City, York, Princess Ann, and Norfolk, including the cities of Norfolk and Portsmouth), and which excepted parts are for the present left precisely as if this proclamation were not issued.

And by virtue of the power and for the purpose aforesaid, I do order and declare that all persons held as slaves within said designated states and parts of states are, and henceforward shall be, free; and that the executive government of the United States, including the military and naval authorities thereof, will recognize and maintain the freedom of said persons.

And I hereby enjoin upon the people so declared to be free to abstain from all violence, unless in necessary self-defense; and I recommend to them that, in all cases when allowed, they labor faithfully for reasonable wages.

And I further declare and make known that such persons, of suitable condition will be received into the armed service of the United States to garrison forts, positions, stations, and other places and to man vessels of all sorts in said service.

And upon this act, sincerely believed to be an act of justice, warranted by the Constitution upon military necessity, I invoke the considerate judgment of mankind and the gracious favor of Almighty God.

In witness whereof, I have hereunto set my hand and caused the seal of the United States to be affixed.

Done at the city of Washington this first day of January, in the year of our Lord one thousand eight hundred and sixty-three, and of the independence of the United States of America the eighty-seventh.

By the President:
William H. Seward,   Abraham Lincoln
Secretary of State.

Pledge of Allegiance (1892)

The Pledge of Allegiance, a solemn oath of allegiance to the United States, has been attributed to Francis Bellamy, a Baptist minister.

I pledge allegiance to the Flag of the United States of America and to the Republic for which it stands, one Nation under God,* indivisible, with liberty and justice for all.

---

*The words "under God" were added in 1954.

The American's Creed (1917)

The American's Creed, composed by William Tyler Page in 1917, is a statement of our common political values. It is a set of beliefs about the proper role of government and the dignity of the individual. It attempts to show the consensus of Americans' values and beliefs. The values expressed are individualistic, democratic, and egalitarian.

Composed in 1917 by William Tyler Page (1868–1942).

"I believe in the United States of America as a government of the people, by the people, for the people; whose just powers are derived from the consent of the governed; a democracy in a Republic; a sovereign Nation of many sovereign States; a perfect Union, one and inseparable; established upon those principles of freedom, equality, justice, and humanity for which American patriots sacrificed their lives and fortunes.

"I therefore believe it is my duty to my country to love it; to support its Constitution; to obey its laws; to respect its flag; and to defend it against all enemies."

Brown v. Board of Education of Topeka (1954)

The landmark Supreme Court case Brown v. Board of Education of Topeka overturned the "separate but equal doctrine" established by the 1896 case of Plessy v. Ferguson. At the time of this decision, the Supreme Court was led by Chief Justice Earl Warren.

In approaching this problem, [w]e must consider public education in the light of its full development and its present place in American life throughout the Nation. Only in this way can it be determined if segregation in public schools deprives these plaintiffs of the equal protection of the laws.

Today, education is perhaps the most important function of state and local governments. Compulsory school attendance laws and the great expenditures for education both demonstrate our recognition of the importance of education to our democratic society. It is required in the performance of our most basic public responsibilities, even service in the armed forces. It is the very foundation of good citizenship. Today it is a principal instrument in awakening the child to cultural values, in preparing him for later professional training, and in helping him to adjust normally to his environment. In these days, it is doubtful that any child may reasonably be expected to succeed in life if he is denied the opportunity of an education. Such an opportunity, where the state has undertaken to provide it, is a right which must be made available to all on equal terms.

We come then to the question presented: Does segregation of children in public schools solely on the basis of race, even though the physical facilities and other 'tangible' factors may be equal, deprive the children of the minority group of equal educational opportunities? We believe that it does.

To separate [African Americans] from others of similar age and qualifications solely because of their race generates a feeling of inferiority as to their status in the community that may affect their hearts and minds in a way unlikely ever to be undone.

We conclude that in the field of public education the doctrine of 'separate but equal' has no place. Separate educational facilities are inherently unequal. Therefore, we hold that the plaintiffs and others similarly situated for whom the actions have been brought are, by reason of the segregation complained of, deprived of the equal protection of the laws guaranteed by the Fourteenth Amendment. This disposition makes unnecessary any discussion whether such segregation also violates the Due Process Clause of the Fourteenth Amendment.

Because these are class actions, because of the wide applicability of this decision, and because of the great variety of local conditions, the formulation of decrees in these cases presents problems of considerable complexity. On reargument, the consideration of appropriate relief was necessarily subordinated to the primary question—the constitutionality of segregation in public education. We have now announced that such segregation is a denial of the equal protection of the laws.

[Excerpts]

The Preamble to the Charter of the United Nations

Just as the United States is governed by the rules set forth in the Constitution, so too is the United Nations governed by the rules set forth in the Charter of the United Nations drafted and put into force in 1945. The U.N. Charter, like the Constitution, begins with a preamble that expresses the spirit of the organization.

We the peoples of the United Nations determined

to save succeeding generations from the scourge of war, which twice in our lifetime has brought untold sorrow to mankind, and

to reaffirm faith in fundamental human rights, in the dignity and worth of the human person, in the equal rights of men and women and of nations large and small, and

to establish conditions under which justice and respect for the obligations arising from treaties and other sources of international law can be maintained, and

to promote social progress and better standards of life in larger freedom,

and for these ends

to practice tolerance and live together in peace with one another as good neighbors, and

to unite our strength to maintain international peace and security, and

to ensure, by the acceptance of principles and the institution of methods, that armed force shall not be used, save in the common interest, and

to employ international machinery for the promotion of the economic and social advancement of all peoples,

have resolved to combine our efforts to accomplish these aims.

Accordingly, our respective governments, through representatives assembled in the city of San Francisco, who have exhibited their full powers found to be in good and due form, have agreed to the present Charter of the United Nations and do hereby establish an international organization to be known as the United Nations.

ANNOTATED TABLE OF LEGAL CASES

How to Read Legal Case Citations and Find Court Decisions

Court decisions are recorded and published in various places. When a court case is mentioned, the notation used to refer to, or to cite, it denotes where the published decision can be found.

State courts of appeal decisions are usually published in two places, the state reports of that particular state and the more widely used *National Reporter System* published

by West Publishing Company. Some states no longer publish their own reports. The *National Reporter System* divides the states into the following geographic areas: Atlantic (A. or A.2d, where 2d refers to second series), South Eastern (S.E. or S.E.2d), South Western (S.W. or S.W.2d), North Western (N.W. or N.W.2d), North Eastern (N.E. or N.E.2d), Southern (So. or So.2d), and Pacific (P. or P.2d).

Federal trial court decisions are published unofficially in West's *Federal Supplement* (F.Supp.), and opinions from the circuit courts of appeal are reported unofficially in West's *Federal Reporter* (F. or F.2d). Opinions from the United States Supreme Court are reported in the *United States Reports* (U.S.), the *Lawyer's Edition of the Supreme Court Reports* (L.Ed.), West's *Supreme Court Reporter* (S. Ct.), and other publications. The *United States Reports* is the official edition of the United States Supreme Court decisions published by the federal government. Many early decisions are missing from these volumes. An unofficial and more complete edition of Supreme Court decisions, the *Lawyer's Edition of the Supreme Court Reports,* is pub-

lished by the Lawyers Cooperative Publishing Company of Rochester, New York. West's *Supreme Court Reporter* is an unofficial edition of decisions dating from October 1882. These volumes contain headnotes and brief editorial statements of the law involved in the case.

State courts of appeal decisions are cited by giving the name of the case; the volume, name, and page number of the state's official report (if the state publishes its own reports); the volume, unit, and page number of the *National Reporter;* and the volume, name, and page number of any other selected reporter. Federal court citations are also listed by giving the name of the case and the volume, name, and page number of the reports.

Table of Court Cases

■ *Afroyim* v. *Rusk* (1967)	A civil rights/citizenship case in which the Court ruled that all citizens have "a constitutional right to remain a citizen in a free country unless [they] voluntarily relinquish that citizenship." Part of the Nationality Act of 1940 was declared unconstitutional because it provided for the automatic expatriation of any American citizen who voted in a foreign election.
■ *Baker* v. *Carr* (1962)	A Fourteenth Amendment/apportionment case in which the Court ruled that state legislatures had to be apportioned to provide equal protection under the law.
■ *Barron* v. *Mayor of Baltimore* (1833)	A civil rights/Bill of Rights case in which the Court ruled that the Bill of Rights applied only to the national government, not to the state governments.
■ *Betts* v. *Brady* (1942)	A rights of the accused/right to an attorney case in which the Court held that criminal defendants were not automatically guaranteed the right to have a lawyer present when they were tried in court, except in capital cases (overturned in *Gideon* v. *Wainright*).
■ *Bigelow* v. *Virginia* (1975)	A freedom of speech/advertising case involving so-called commercial speech in which the Court held that the state cannot prohibit newspaper advertising of abortion services.
■ *Board of Education of Westside Community Schools* v. *Mergens* (1990)	A separation of church and state case in which the Court ruled in favor of a Christian Bible club that wanted to meet on school grounds after regular school hours in Omaha, Nebraska.
■ *Brandenburg* v. *Ohio* (1969)	A free speech/national security decision in which the Court narrowed its definition of seditious speech so that advocating the use of force is legal unless such advocacy "is directed to inciting or producing imminent lawless action and is likely to produce such action."

Table of Court Cases—*Continued*

■ *Branzburg* v. *Hayes* (1972)	A freedom of speech/confidentiality case in which the Court held that the First Amendment grants no special privileges to reporters. They must therefore respond to questioning during a valid criminal trial or investigation.
■ *Brown* v. *Board of Education* (1955)	A civil rights case in which the Court asked for rearguments concerning the way in which the states should implement civil rights decisions including its 1954 decision *Brown* v. *Board of Education of Topeka.* The Court indicated that the lower courts must ensure that African Americans be admitted to schools on a nondiscriminatory basis "with all deliberate speed."
■ *Brown* v. *Board of Education of Topeka* (1954)	A civil rights case that established that public schools' segregation of races violated the equal protection clause of the Fourteenth Amendment.
■ *Burstyn* v. *Wilson* (1952)	A freedom of press case involving the motion picture industry in which the Court held that "liberty of expression by means of motion pictures is guaranteed by the First and Fourteenth Amendments." Nonetheless, the Court held that prior censorship of films by local and state authorities may be constitutional under certain circumstances, usually involving obscenity.
■ *Cox* v. *New Hampshire* (1941)	A freedom of assembly case in which the Court ruled that sixty-eight Jehovah's Witnesses had violated the statute prohibiting parading without a permit and further upheld the right of a municipality to control its public streets.
■ *De Jonge* v. *Oregon* (1937)	A freedom of assembly case involving a man convicted for holding a public meeting that was sponsored by the Communist Party. The Court overturned his conviction, ruling that the Oregon law restricted too much the rights of free speech and assembly. This case put the right of assembly on equal footing with the rights of free speech and press.
■ *Dennis* v. *United States* (1951)	A free speech and national security case in which the Court ruled that the Smith Act—a law against seditious speech—could be applied to members of the Communist Party.
■ *Dillon* v. *Gloss* (1921)	A case ruling that allows Congress to place a "reasonable time limit" on the ratification process for amendments to the United States Constitution.
■ *Dred Scott* v. *Sandford* (1857)	A civil rights/citizenship case in which the Court declared that slaves were not citizens of any state or of the United States. (The Court also declared unconstitutional the Missouri Compromise because it deprived a person of his property [his slave] without due process of law.)
■ *Engel* v. *Vitale* (1962)	The so-called Regents' Prayer Case, in which the Court outlawed even the voluntary saying of a nondenominational prayer written by the New York State Board of Regents. An important separation of church and state case.

Table of Court Cases—*Continued*

■ *Escobedo* v. *Illinois* (1964)	A rights of the accused/right to counsel case in which the Court overturned the conviction of Danny Escobedo, who had been arrested by Chicago police in connection with the murder of his brother-in-law. Escobedo's request to see his lawyer had been refused even though the lawyer was in the police station trying to see Escobedo during his questioning.
■ *Everson* v. *Board of Education* (1947)	A First Amendment/establishment clause case in which the Court ruled in favor of tax-supported busing of students who attended parochial schools.
■ *Feiner* v. *New York* (1951)	A freedom of assembly case in which the Court upheld a conviction for unlawful assembly because the police had acted to preserve public order. Feiner, during a speech in Syracuse, New York, verbally attacked President Harry S Truman and the mayor of Syracuse. When the police were called, the crowd was on the verge of attempting to stop Feiner from speaking.
■ *Ford* v. *Wainwright* (1986)	An Eighth Amendment/capital punishment case in which the Court ruled that the U.S. Constitution bars states from executing convicted killers who have become insane while waiting on death row.
■ *Frontiero* v. *Richardson* (1973)	A civil liberties/gender classification case in which the Court ruled against any sex discrimination based on "romantic paternalism."
■ *Furman* v. *Georgia* (1972)	An Eighth Amendment/capital punishment case in which the Court struck down Georgia's laws allowing the death penalty because the laws gave too much discretion to juries and judges in deciding whether capital punishment should be imposed.
■ *Gannet Company* v. *De Pasquale* (1979)	A freedom of press/gag order case in which the Court held that if a judge found a reasonable probability that news publicity would harm a defendant's right to a fair trial, the court could impose a gag rule: "Members of the public have no constitutional right under the Sixth and Fourteenth Amendments to attend criminal trials."
■ *Gibbons* v. *Ogden* (1824)	For the first time, the national government's power over commerce was defined in an expansive way. In effect, the power of the national government to regulate commerce has no limitations other than those specifically found in the Constitution.
■ *Gideon* v. *Wainwright* (1963)	A rights of the accused/right to counsel case in which the Court said that persons who can demonstrate that they are unable to afford to have a lawyer present and are accused of felonies must be given a lawyer at the expense of the government.
■ *Gitlow* v. *New York* (1925)	A free speech/bad-tendency rule case that allows First Amendment freedoms to be curtailed if there is a possibility that such expression might lead to some evil. In this case, a member of a left-wing group was convicted of violating New York State's criminal anarchy statute when he published and distributed materials urging the violent overthrow of the U.S. government.

Table of Court Cases—*Continued*

■ *Gregg* v. *Georgia* (1976)	An Eighth Amendment/capital punishment case in which the Court indicated for the first time that the death penalty does not "invariably violate the Constitution."
■ *Griswold* v. *Connecticut* (1965)	A civil liberties/right to privacy case in which the Court overthrew a Connecticut law that effectively prohibited the distribution of contraceptives. In the case Justice William O. Douglas claimed that the First, Third, Fourth, Fifth, and Ninth Amendments created "penumbras, formed by emanations from those guarantees that help give them life and substance," and went on to talk about zones for privacy that are guaranteed by these rights.
■ *Hazelwood School District* v. *Cathy Kuhlmeier* (1988)	A First Amendment/freedom of speech and press case in which the Court held that school officials may impose reasonable restrictions on the speeches of students, teachers, and other members of the school community.
■ *Hoyt* v. *Florida* (1961)	A civil rights/gender classification case in which the Court ruled as constitutional a law that required men to serve on juries, but allowed women to choose whether or not they wished to serve.
■ *Kaiser Aluminum and Chemical Co. (United Steelworkers of America)* v. *Weber* (1979)	A civil rights/reverse discrimination case in which a union apprenticeship program that used a racial quota was deemed legal even if it violated the words of the Civil Rights Act of 1964 because it did not violate the spirit. Essentially, any form of reverse discrimination—even explicit quotas—is permissible provided that it is the result of legislative, executive, or judicial findings of past discrimination.
■ *Katz* v. *United States* (1967)	A Fourth Amendment/wiretapping case in which the Court overturned Katz's conviction for transmitting betting information across state lines from a public phone booth in Los Angeles. The FBI had placed recording devices outside the booth without a warrant.
■ *Klopfer* v. *North Carolina* (1967)	A Sixth Amendment/right to a speedy trial case in which the Court first held that the Sixth Amendment's guarantee applies to the states because of the Fourteenth Amendment.
■ *Lemon* v. *Kurtzman* (1971)	An excessive entanglement case in which the Court held that the establishment clause was designed to prevent sponsorship, financial support, and active involvement of the government in religious activity. The Court did not allow a Pennsylvania law that provided for financial payments to private schools to cover their costs for textbooks, some teachers' salaries, and other teaching materials for nonreligious courses only.
■ *Louisiana* v. *Resweber* (1947)	An Eighth Amendment cruel and unusual punishment case in which the Court held that a convicted murderer could be subjected to a second electrocution after the first one failed to work properly.

Table of Court Cases—*Continued*

■ *Lynch* v. *Donnelly* (1984)	A separation of church and state case in which the Court said that the city of Pawtucket, Rhode Island, could include a nativity scene in its holiday display because the scene formed part of an ensemble with Santa's sleigh and reindeer and a Christmas tree.
■ *Mapp* v. *Ohio* (1961)	A rights of the accused/exclusionary rule case in which the Court overturned the conviction of Dollree Mapp for possession of obscene materials because police had found pornographic books in her apartment after searching it without a warrant despite her verbal refusal to let them in.
■ *Marbury* v. *Madison* (1803)	The Court ruled for the first time an act of Congress unconstitutional, thereby establishing the principle of judicial review.
■ *McCollum* v. *Board of Education* (1948)	A "release time" program case in which the Court would not allow such a program in Champaign, Illinois, because school classrooms were being used for religious purposes.
■ *McCulloch* v. *Maryland* (1819)	The Court's ruling upheld the constitutionality of a creation of the Bank of the United States and denied to the states the power to tax it because "the power to tax involves the power to destroy." The ruling clarified the doctrine of implied powers of the national government.
■ *Miller* v. *California* (1973)	A freedom of speech/obscenity case in which the Court created a formal list of requirements as a legal test of obscenity. They are that (1) the average person finds that it violates contemporary community standards; (2) the work taken as a whole appeals to prurient interest in sex; (3) the work shows patently offensive sexual conduct; and (4) the work lacks serious redeeming literary, artistic, political, or scientific merit.
■ *Minersville School District* v. *Gobitis* (1940)	A free exercise of religion/flag salute case in which the Court held that because the flag was a symbol of national unity, requiring that it be saluted was not an infringement on the free exercise of religion.
■ *Miranda* v. *Arizona* (1966)	A rights of the accused/right to remain silent case in which a mentally disturbed suspect, Ernesto Miranda, had been arrested, questioned for two hours, and confessed to the crime of kidnapping and rape. His conviction was reversed by the Court on the basis of the Fifth and Sixth Amendments. Now people are read their rights, including the right to remain silent.
■ *Mueller* v. *Allen* (1983)	An excessive entanglement case in which the Court upheld a Minnesota tax law giving parents a state income-tax deduction for the cost of textbooks, transportation for elementary and secondary schoolchildren, and tuition whether the children go to private or public schools.
■ *Murray* v. *Giarratano* (1989)	An Eighth Amendment/capital punishment case in which the Court held that indigent death-row inmates have no constitutional right to a lawyer for a second round of state court appeals.

Table of Court Cases—*Continued*

▪ *Myers* v. *United States* (1926)	The presidential removal power case in which the Court held unconstitutional an 1876 law that required Senate consent before the president could dismiss a postmaster.
▪ *Near* v. *Minnesota* (1931)	A freedom of press/prior restraint case in which a Minnesota law prohibiting the publication of malicious and scandalous newspapers or magazines was held to be invalid because it constituted unconstitutional prior restraint in violation of the First and Fourteenth Amendments.
▪ *New York Times* v. *United States* (1971)	A freedom of press/prior restraint case involving the publication of sensitive government documents relating to the government's policy in Vietnam from 1945 to 1967. The U.S. government attempted to suspend the publication of the so-called *Pentagon Papers,* but the Court held that the government could only prosecute after publication, not before.
▪ *In re Oliver* (1948)	A Sixth Amendment/right to a public trial case in which the Court ruled that not only must a trial be speedy, but it also must be held in public.
▪ *Penry* v. *Lynaugh* (1989)	An Eighth Amendment/capital punishment case in which the Court held that mentally retarded persons may be executed for murder.
▪ *Plessy* v. *Ferguson* (1896)	A civil rights case in which the Court ruled that state laws enforcing segregation by race were constitutional when accommodations were equal as well as separate. (Subsequently overturned by *Brown* v. *Board of Education of Topeka.*)
▪ *Powell* v. *Alabama* (1932)	A Sixth Amendment right to counsel case in which the Court ruled that the accused has a right to a lawyer in capital punishment cases.
▪ *Powell* v. *McCormack* (1969)	A congressional qualifications case in which the Court ruled that the House of Representatives could not exclude any elected member who met the Constitution's requirements for citizenship, residence, and age.
▪ *Reed* v. *Reed* (1971)	A civil rights/gender classification case in which the Court ruled against an Idaho law that gave fathers preferences over mothers in taking care of their children's estates.
▪ *Regents of the University of California* v. *Bakke* (1978)	A civil rights/reverse discrimination case in which the Court allowed the University of California, Davis Campus, School of Medicine to admit students on the basis of race if the school's aim is to combat the effects of past discriminations. The Court held, nonetheless, that Bakke must be admitted to the medical school because its admissions policy had used race as the *sole* criterion for a limited number of "minority" positions.
▪ *Reynolds* v. *Sims* (1964)	A congressional reapportionment case in which the Court ruled that both chambers of a state legislature must be apportioned with equal populations in each district. This "one-person, one-vote" principle had already been applied to congressional districts in *Wesberry* v. *Sanders.*

Table of Court Cases—*Continued*

■ *Reynolds* v. *United States* (1879)	A free exercise of religion case in which the Court held that Reynolds, a Mormon living in Utah who had been convicted of polygamy, had violated federal law. The Court ruled that polygamy was a crime and therefore could not be excused as religious practice. Hence, people are free to believe and worship as they wish so long as their conduct does not violate laws that protect the safety, health, or morals of the community.
■ *Richmond* v. *Croson* (1989)	A civil rights/reverse discrimination case in which the Court ruled that any program that favors blacks over whites has to be judged by the same constitutional test applicable to any law that favors whites over blacks.
■ *Richmond Newspapers, Inc.* v. *Virginia* (1980)	A freedom of press/gag order case in which the Court ruled that actual trials must be opened to the public except under unusual circumstances.
■ *Robinson* v. *California* (1962)	A Eighth Amendment/no cruel and unusual punishment case in which the Court ruled that the Fourteenth Amendment extends the Eighth Amendment to the states. Here the Court struck down a California law that defines drug addiction as a crime to be punished rather than an illness to be treated.
■ *Rochin* v. *California* (1952)	A due process of law/procedural due process case, sometimes referred to as "the stomach pumping case," in which a suspected illegal drug user was taken to a hospital and administered a liquid that forced him to vomit. Morphine capsules thereby recovered were used to convict him of violating the state's narcotics laws. The Court overruled the conviction, holding that it violated the Fourteenth Amendment's guarantee of procedural due process.
■ *Roe* v. *Wade* (1973)	A privacy case in which the Court ruled that state antiabortion laws were unconstitutional except when they applied to the last three months of pregnancy.
■ *Rostker* v. *Goldberg* (1981)	A civil rights/gender classification case in which the Court upheld the U.S. government selective service law that requires only men to register for the draft.
■ *Schenck* v. *United States* (1919)	A free speech case involving the clear and present danger test in which the Court upheld the Espionage Act of 1917, which made it a crime to encourage resistance to the military draft. The Court said that a person who encourages draft resistance during a war is a "clear and present danger."
■ *Smith* v. *Allwright* (1944)	A voting rights case in which the Court declared that the white primary was a violation of the Fifteenth Amendment. The Court reasoned that the political party was actually performing a state function in holding a primary election and therefore not acting as a private group.
■ *South Carolina* v. *Katzenback* (1966)	A voting rights case in which the Court held that Congress had acted correctly by passing the Voting Rights Act as a way to implement the Fifteenth Amendment guarantee of the right to vote to every citizen of the United States regardless of race, color, or previous condition of servitude.

Table of Court Cases—*Continued*

■ *Stone* v. *Graham* (1980)	A separation of church and state case in which the Court would not allow a Kentucky law that required the Ten Commandments to be posted in all public classrooms.
■ *Teitel Film Corporation* v. *Cusack* (1968)	A freedom of press/motion picture case in which the Court held that the government can ban a film if at a judicial hearing it is proven to be obscene.
■ *Thornhill* v. *Alabama* (1940)	A freedom of speech/picketing case in which the Court held that picketing was a form of expression protected by the First and Fourteenth Amendments. Nonetheless, picketing may be prevented if it is set in a background of violence, and even peaceful picketing may be controlled if it is being done for an illegal purpose.
■ *United States* v. *Nixon* (1974)	A presidential executive privilege case in which the Court ruled that President Nixon had to hand over secret tapes containing his Oval Office conversations while in the White House. The Court ruled that executive privilege could not be used to prevent evidence from being heard in criminal proceedings.
■ *Walz* v. *New York City Tax Commission* (1970)	A separation of church and state case in which the Court ruled that tax exemptions for churches do not violate the First Amendment, but rather show the state's "benevolent neutrality" toward religion.
■ *Wesberry* v. *Sanders* (1964)	A Fourteenth Amendment/congressional districting case in which the Court ruled that the state of Georgia's formation of congressional districts created such huge population differences that they violated the Constitution. This case was the basis of the Court's ruling later requiring one person, one vote.
■ *West Virginia Board of Education* v. *Barnette* (1943)	A free exercise of religion/flag salute case in which the Court held that laws requiring a flag salute were an unconstitutional interference with the free exercise of religion.
■ *Wilkinson* v. *Jones* (1987)	A freedom of speech and press/cable TV case in which the Court held that state government cannot regulate independent cable programming. The case involved a Utah law prohibiting the cable broadcast of indecent material between 7 A.M. and midnight.
■ *Yates* v. *United States* (1957)	A free speech and national security case in which the Court said that merely advocating the overthrow of a government is not illegal, because such speech only addresses people's belief as opposed to causing them to undertake actions against the government.
■ *Zorach* v. *Clauson* (1952)	A "release time" case in which the Court upheld a New York City program because that program required religious classes to be held in private places and not on school campuses.

EXTENDED CASE STUDIES

Immigration Reform and Control Act of 1986 and Amnesty

Introduction

In 1986 Congress passed the first major revision of the nation's immigration policy in twenty years. The Immigration Reform and Control Act of that year contained several controversial provisions. One provided amnesty and legal status for illegal aliens who could prove they had lived continuously in the U.S. since at least January 1, 1982. Another provision granted amnesty to agricultural workers who were employed for 90 days in the twelve-month period preceding May 1, 1986. A third section made it illegal for all U.S. employers to hire illegal aliens knowingly. Penalties were stiff, ranging from $250 to $10,000 for each alien on the payroll.

A Source Document:

Excerpts from the Immigration and Control Act of 1986

§ 1255a. Adjustment of status of certain entrants before Jan. 1, 1982, to that of person admitted for lawful residence

(a) Temporary resident status. The Attorney General shall adjust the status of an alien to that of an alien lawfully admitted for temporary residence if the alien meets the following requirements:

(1) Timely application. (A) During application period. Except as provided in subparagraph (B), the alien must apply for such adjustment during the 12-month period beginning on a date (not later than 180 days after the date of enactment of this section [enacted Nov. 6, 1986]) designated by the Attorney General.

* * * *

(C) Information included in application. Each application under this subsection shall contain such information as the Attorney General may require, including information on living relatives of the applicant with respect to whom a petition for preference or other status may be filed by the applicant at any later date under section 204(a) [8 USCS § 1154(a)].

(2) Continuous unlawful residence since 1982. (A) In general. The alien must establish that he entered the United States before January 1, 1982, and that he has resided continuously in the United States in an unlawful status since such date and through the date the application is filed under this subsection. (B) Nonimmigrants. In the case of an alien who entered the United States as a nonimmigrant before January 1, 1982, the alien must establish that the alien's period of authorized stay as a nonimmigrant expired before such date through the passage of time or the alien's unlawful status was known to the Government as of such date.

* * * *

(3) Continuous physical presence since enactment. (A) In general. The alien must establish that the alien has been continuously physically present in the United States since the date of the enactment of this section [enacted Nov. 6, 1986]. (B) Treatment of brief, casual, and innocent absences. An alien shall not be considered to have failed to maintain continuous physical presence in the United States for purposes of subparagraph (A) by virtue of brief, casual, and innocent absences from the United States. (C) Admissions. Nothing in this section shall be construed as authorizing an alien to apply for admission to, or to be admitted to, the United States in order to apply for adjustment of status under this subsection.

Media Reports

The bill will go down in history as the largest amnesty program for illegal aliens in modern history—also the longest and one of the more generous. But was it a success? That is still a lingering question in the minds of many. No one argues that it was perfect, not even Senator Alan Simpson of Wyoming, co-sponsor of the bill. ''There will never be a perfect bill, any more than there are perfect children, perfect marriages, or perfect crimes,'' he said. Below is a sample of some of the media articles at the time.

U.S. Border Control: Holes in the Policy?
Los Angeles Times, *February 10, 1992.*

In the last several days, news stories in San Diego and Los Angeles came together, quite coincidentally, to remind us how difficult—perhaps even impossible—it is to stop the flow of illegal migrant workers from Mexico into this country. All of the stories involve what is arguably the federal government's most unappreciated agency, the U.S. Immigration and Naturalization Service. It is surely the most underfunded and overworked.

Of course the U.S.-Mexican border has been open so long to the flow of people and goods that it can never be completely closed. Nor should it be— for the only long-term solution to illegal migration is free and open trade that eventually equalizes economic opportunity in the two countries. But meanwhile the flow of people across the line must be better regulated so it is not the chaotic, and often dangerous, free-for-all it is now.

Source: Copyright, 1992, *Los Angeles Times.* Reprinted by permission.

Why Amnesty Failed
by Jason DeParle
The Washington Monthly, *April 1988, p. 11.*

Eva has a problem. She's lived in Chicago for eight years as an illegal immigrant. The new immigration law that took effect last May gives her the chance to shed that illegal status for a work permit and eventual citizenship. But Eva lacks the paper trail she needs to prove her history of U.S. residence. She lacks the hundreds of dollars it would cost her to apply. And she lacks the faith that immigration authorities won't deport her children, who didn't begin arriving from Mexico until 1984, two years after the amnesty cut-off date. "If I give them the names of my children," she says, "they'll take them."

As the year-long legalization program draws to a close, there are hundreds of thousands of Evas:

illegal immigrants too poor, confused, or afraid to capitalize on its one-time offer. When the program kicked off last May, immigration officials predicted that between 2 million and 3.9 million people would register. But as March began only a million had come forward, and head-counters have consistently deflated their final prediction, which has now sagged to only 1.35 million. To spur a last-minute surge, sombrero-topped immigration officials have been Texas two-stepping from one photo op to another, broadcasting Spanish jingles and attending burrito bakes. They've even begun placing flyers in the bags of tortillas sold in grocery stores, urging people to apply. But all the salsa in San Diego won't coax forth the number of illegals the law was intended to help.

Source: Reprinted by permission from *The Washington Monthly.* Copyright by The Washington Monthly Company, 1611 Connecticut Avenue, NW, Washington D.C., 20009. (202) 462-0128.

As the end of the year approached and the legalization program drew to a close, some wanted to buy more time and asked Congress to extend the deadline for a year.

Slamming the Golden Door
Newsweek, *May 9, 1988, p. 18.*

A last-minute push to extend the amnesty program for six months died in the Senate last week when amnesty's original sponsor, Wyoming Republican Alan Simpson, jumped ship to join Texas's Phil Gramm in leading the fight against it. The bill's backers wanted the extension to reach more aliens who were still afraid to apply, but then accepted the INS argument that the law was sufficiently understood. "This is it," said Simpson. "It's a one-time shot. If you want to live the dream, you have to do it by midnight, May 4. It will never come again." The rush to register, which had been speeding up for months, was expected to become a stampede this week. Even so, the slow pace in the early months of the program meant the final total of aliens registered would be well below the original INS prediction of 2 million or more.

Nobody knows how many illegal residents there are; estimates of the underground population run from 4.5 million to 7 million or more. Immigrant activists worried that many aliens, particularly in Asian communities, still didn't understand the law and hadn't applied. And from now on, warns Leonel Castillo, a former INS commissioner still active in immigration affairs in Houston, "those who did not qualify for amnesty are going to have to hide much more cleverly and do much more dangerous things to stay out of reach."

Conclusion

The amnesty program passed by Congress in 1986 remains as one of Congress's most obvious admissions that America is indeed a land of immigrants. Undoubtedly there will be other amnesty programs as the Congress attempts to deal with similar problems in the future.

Analysis Questions

1. What does the heading of the section of the Act reproduced above mean when it states "adjustment of status of certain entrants"?
2. Why does the Act require "continuous unlawful residence since 1982"?
3. In the quote from the article in the *Washington Monthly,* did the author, Jason DeParle, believe the program was working? Why or why not?
4. Why was there an attempt to extend the time period during which the amnesty program was to remain in effect?

The AIDS Epidemic

Introduction

One of the most serious medical, social, and economic problems facing the United States and the world today involves the disease called acquired immune deficiency syndrome (AIDS). AIDS has become a worldwide epidemic. Experts estimate that by the year 2000, 40 million individuals will be infected with the human immunodeficiency virus (HIV) that normally causes AIDS. Further, it is estimated that in America several million individuals will be infected by HIV by the same year. Already, well over 100,000 Americans have died from AIDS.

Media Reports

The following article was taken from a domestic media source.

The AIDS Disaster
by Steven Findlaw
U.S. News & World Report, *June 17, 1991, p 22.*

How many will die? Will a cure or vaccine be found? Will the health-care system become overwhelmed? These questions have no precise answers. Science and modern medicine may eventually triumph over AIDS, but the best guess of most scientists is that neither a cure nor a vaccine will be found by the end of the century. In the meantime, it is clear that the last thing America should treat AIDS with is complacency. In all likelihood, the spread of HIV and the death toll will rise steeply in the decade ahead, tempered only by the effectiveness of local responses, including education and prevention efforts. By the year 2000, the World Health Organization projects that 40 million people worldwide will be infected with HIV, including an appalling 10 million children. Five to 10 million people could die of the disease, including a projected 500,000 in the United States. San Francisco might lose 4 percent of its population in the 1990s to AIDS; New York, 2 to 3 percent. Some cities in East and Central Africa could lose 15 percent.

At the same time, more and more of the faces of AIDS in the United States will be black or brown, many poor and disenfranchised. In a few years, minorities will account for much more than half of all new cases. "Nowhere do I see any planning for the future of what will be a complex and expensive disease to treat," says William Haseltine of Harvard's Dana-Farber Cancer Institute.

If, by most standards, the AIDS epidemic will become harder to combat in the decade ahead, it could become easier in one respect: More at-risk groups may support testing for HIV. When the AIDS antibody test became available in 1985, gay groups and many public-health officials counseled people to avoid it lest they invite discrimination. The discouragement proved remarkably effective: The Centers for Disease Control estimates that 75 percent of the 1 million to 1.5 million HIV-infected persons in the United States do not know they are infected. But beginning in 1989, some gay leaders and public-health experts—despite the persistence of

HIV-based discrimination—started changing their minds about routine testing, particularly for groups like hospital patients, clients at sexual-disease clinics, health-care workers, newborns and pregnant women.

Source: Copyright, June 17, 1991, _U.S. News & World Report._

A Foreign Media Source

Sometimes a different "slant" on a problem can be gleaned from reading the foreign media. Specifically, it is easy for Americans to get magazines and newspapers published in Britain and other English-speaking countries. In the example below, _The Economist_ magazine, published in London, talks about the problem of AIDS in Africa.

An African Example
The Economist
September 21, 1991, p. 24.

For a small, poor country like Uganda, AIDS causes troubles that existing medical and social services cannot cope with. Uganda was the first African country openly to acknowledge that it had an AIDS epidemic. Just how big an epidemic is still unknown, but certainly it is vast. One estimate puts the number of people infected with HIV at 1m [million], 11% of the adult population. Some projections based on such figures suggest that Uganda will have 22m people in 2015, one-third of whom will be infected; without AIDS, the population might have been around 37m.

The effects of AIDS on village life are devastating. Young couples may die within a few years or even months of each other, leaving behind orphans and parents whom normally they would care for. Instead, the elderly find themselves forced to care for their sick children and grandchildren. Foreign aid workers and local charities alike are straining their resources to build orphanages and old peoples' homes. The traditional family structure may begin to break up.

The economic consequences of the epidemic are considerable. Beside the direct loss of hard-working young adults, many people have to stay away from work to care for relatives. A less obvious burden is that of funerals, which professionals in Kampala worry about constantly. Ugandans are buried in their traditional villages, and it is customary for all the dead person's colleagues to attend the funeral. This can mean that entire government departments are absent for days at a time, attending funerals in far-flung parts.

Efforts to prevent AIDS run up against a basic problem: it is hard in Uganda, as anywhere else, to make people believe that what they do now will have consequences in several years' time, especially when they receive conflicting advice. Witch-doctors, often trusted more than modern doctors, may explain AIDS as the result of curses. Phoney cures abound. A year ago President Daniel arap Moi of Kenya claimed Kemron, a type of interferon created by a Kenyan-Japanese-American research team, as a miracle cure. Many people in Africa still believe him, though there is no proof that it works.

Educators have more than ignorance to contend with. Women may refuse to listen to advice at all if it involves talking about sex. Men, who may consider venereal disease almost a mark of pride, see the use of condoms as unmasculine. There is also apathy. Uganda has undergone 20 years of war, looting and terror. It suffers from terrible endemic diseases, which in some areas still kill more people than AIDS. Many do not see why they should change sexual habits just because of another disease; arguments that would be compelling elsewhere can be weak in a society inured to death.

The spread of information too is difficult. Newspapers are few, and nearly 60% of Ugandans are illiterate anyway. Noreen Kaleeba, director of the AIDS Support Organisation (TASO) in Kampala, believes that the only effective way of teaching people how to avoid AIDS is one-to-one counselling, with a special African twist. TASO goes to villages to find local story-tellers responsible for recounting village history and brings them to Kampala, where they are trained about AIDS, and sent back to incorporate their new knowledge into their tales. The result may not be undiluted scientific truth— embellishment is a traditional part of African story-telling—but success, measured in questionnaires showing how many people now use condoms, is much higher than it was in the past.

For all its difficulties, the fact that Uganda does anything at all is testimony to the qualities of its president, Yoweri Museveni. Halting the spread of AIDS requires a willingness to admit that the problem exists. Many other African governments, notably Kenya's, have refused to acknowledge its extent. In

Uganda, honesty about AIDS was possible in the atmosphere of political openness and press freedom that followed the end of a civil war. Other countries may require political upheavals before they too acknowledge their plight.

Source: © 1991 The Economist Newspaper Ltd. Reprinted with permission.

Conclusion
AIDS is one of the most momentous problems we face today. There is hope that a vaccine soon will be developed. In the meantime, the United States and the world will have to pay the price of this deadly disease. That price includes illness, tragedy, and enormous medical and social costs.

The War on Drugs

Introduction
America's fight against the sale and use of illegal drugs takes on greater proportions every year. It has been estimated that federal, state, and local spending on the war on drugs exceeds $30 million annually. Some argue that the war against illegal drugs should only be a part of the war against all harmful drugs, including alcohol and nicotine, two of this country's most significant causes of death and illness.

The Federal Government's Response
For many years the federal government has been deeply involved in the war on drugs. As part of President Bush's campaign against the war on drugs he commissioned a National Drug Control Strategy. The following is the letter that he wrote to the Speaker of the House when he submitted the National Drug Control Strategy in 1989.

The White House
Washington, September 5, 1989

Dear Mr. Speaker:

Consistent with section 1005 of the Anti-Drug Abuse Act of 1988 (21 U.S.C. 1504), I am today pleased to transmit my Administration's 1989 National Drug Control Strategy for congressional consideration and action.

This report is the product of an unprecedented national effort over many months. America's fight against epidemic illegal drug use cannot be won on any single front alone; it must be waged *everywhere*—at every level of Federal, State, and local government and by every citizen in every community across the country. Accordingly, we have conducted a thorough, intensive, and unflinching review of Federal anti-drug efforts to date. And we have solicited advice and recommendations from hundreds of interested and involved anti-drug leaders outside the Federal Government. The result is a comprehensive blueprint for new direction and effort—and for success in the near- and long-term future.

I am especially grateful for the valuable contributions made during this process by Members of Congress, with whom we consulted broadly as our strategy was being conceived and formulated these past 6 months. I ask that this spirit of bipartisan cooperation now be extended to the difficult but necessary work that lies ahead: full swift funding and implementation of the many proposals and initiatives contained in this report. On behalf of those Americans most directly suffering from the scourge of drugs—and all the many more who must be further protected from it—I ask for your help and support.

Sincerely,
George Bush

The Honorable Thomas S. Foley
Speaker of the House of Representatives
Washington, D.C. 20515

Analysis Questions
1. In your reading of the excerpt from the *U.S. News and World Report* article, do you get the impression that the author thinks AIDS will be cured in the near future? Explain your answer.
2. About how many Americans who are HIV infected know they are so infected?
3. What are some of the problems that African countries have in solving the AIDS problem?
4. Why is the spread of information difficult in Uganda and in other African countries?

Media Reports

In any one week, countless newspapers, magazines, and other media sources run articles on the war on drugs. In the following excerpt you can read how effective the president's war on drug abuse has been.

Cocaine Use Jumps Despite Bush's War Against Drug Abuse
The Greenville News
December 19, 1991, p. 17.

WASHINGTON (AP)—After three years of the Bush administration's war against drugs, cocaine use increased this year and drug-related visits to hospital emergency rooms jumped, according to studies made available Wednesday.

Administration drug policy officials pointed to some good news in the statistics: Younger people seem to be turning against drugs, so the drug-use figures should decline in the future.

But for now, "The problem seems to be collapsing into groups within our society who can least afford the problems caused by their addiction: older and inner city addicts," said Bob Martinez, director of the Office of National Drug Control Policy.

* * * *

Overall, the household survey found that current use of any illicit drug—at least once in the previous month—has fallen steadily, from 14.5 million in 1988 to 12.6 million this year.

For cocaine, however, past month use rose from 1.6 million last year to 1.9 million this year. That still remained far below the 2.9 million who said they had used cocaine within the previous month in 1988.

The overwhelming bulk of the increase this year was among people age 35 and older, while monthly cocaine use among people 12–34 has dropped steadily from 2.5 million in 1988 to 1.37 million this year, the survey found.

That, the finding that past-month use of any illicit drug by people under age 35 declined steadily from 12.2 million in 1988 to 9.2 million this year and that the decline has been pronounced among adolescents is "very good news," said Martinez.

"It means that we are shutting down the pipeline into drug addiction, especially among young Americans," he said.

At the same time, Americans 35 and older increased their use of all illicit drugs, especially cocaine and marijuana.

"This dramatically points out one of the sad lessons of the drug war—once you start to use drugs, it's very hard to get off and stay off," Martinez said.

The findings prompted criticism from Rep. Charles B. Rangel, D-N.Y. and the chairman of the House Select Committee on Narcotics, who said the findings were incomplete, but said they "indicate that we are not turning the corner on the drug problem, as the administration has been saying for the last year."

Source: Reprinted with the permission of Associated Press.

Media Reports—A Different View

Not everyone believes that "getting tough" on drugs is the way to solve the problem. Indeed, there are some who argue for legalization of certain drugs that are now illegal. One of them is a U.S. federal judge.

U.S. Judge: Legalize Drugs
By David Lyons
The Miami Herald, *Thursday, November 28, 1991, p. 2B.*

Reflecting the frustration of fellow judges inundated by cocaine and marijuana cases, a South Florida federal judge has publicly called for the legalization of drugs.

U.S. District Judge James C. Paine made the stunning statement last week during a luncheon meeting of the Federal Bar Association in Miami.

"I know there are a lot of people who do not agree," Paine said Wednesday in an interview from his West Palm Beach office. "I just think it's kind of inevitable."

Paine, 67, is regarded widely as a conservative in South Florida legal circles. But after 12 years on the bench, presiding over an unabated flood of drug cases in his courtroom, he said it is time to find other ways to combat the drug problem.

"I'd say I've held this viewpoint for three or four years," Paine said. "I'd been thinking about it for quite a long time."

Before a shocked audience of about 50 people, Judge Paine made these points:

■ Federal courts were not designed—and cannot accommodate—"every case involving crack cocaine or all of the drug-related cases in which local police make an arrest on every day of each week."

- Criminal caseloads in the federal courts have exploded.
- The prohibition of alcohol—sold to the public as "an economic and moral bonanza"—was a failure. As with the war on alcohol in the 1920s, the war on drugs benefited smugglers and "the forces of big government."
- Illegal drugs breed more crime, stronger drugs and the abuse of civil liberties.

Paine isn't the first judge to urge legalization. Two years ago, U.S. District Judge Robert W. Sweet of New York made similar remarks.

Source: Reprinted with the permission of *The Miami Herald.*

Conclusion

The human and economic costs of drug abuse continue to plague American society. The reality, though, is that most Americans do not abuse drugs of any kind, even alcohol and nicotine. Indeed, alcohol consumption per capita has been declining since 1985. Tobacco addiction has decreased even more dramatically: Back in the 1950s, fully 60 percent of American adults were smokers. Today that number is less than 29 percent. Also, it appears that casual use of cocaine and marijuana declined somewhat in the late 1980s and early 1990s. Some observers believe that educational programs against abuse of all drugs have started to have an effect in America.

Analysis Questions

1. When you compare the first newspaper article with George Bush's hopes expressed in his letter, what conclusions can you reach? Explain your answer.
2. What are the arguments that counter the federal judge's call for legalizing drugs?
3. What steps do you think you can take to help in the war on drugs?

Exxon Valdez

Introduction

The fate of the oil tanker *Exxon Valdez* begins, perhaps, when a captain with too much alcohol in his blood turns over the command of his tanker to an unqualified third mate. The mate sends contradictory orders to the engine room and the vessel is impaled on Bligh Reef, causing millions of gallons of oil to gush from the mangled hull. The supposedly impossible has happened. And it couldn't have happened at a worse time in a worse place, threatening and eventually killing thousands of birds, eagles, sea otters, and other marine life teeming along the jagged coast of Prince William Sound in Alaska. By the middle of the week, Exxon, owner of the wounded tanker, admits that the largest oil spill in U.S. history is spreading out of control.

Media Reports

The *Exxon Valdez* disaster dominated news stories for many weeks following the spill. The following excerpts present a timely view of this environmental tragedy and its aftermath.

Alaska Oil Spill May Be Largest in U.S. Waters
By Maura Dolan and Ronald B. Taylor
Los Angeles Times, *March 25, 1989, p. 1.*

A Long Beach-bound Exxon oil tanker ran aground on a reef Friday and spilled up to 12 million gallons of crude oil into Alaska's Prince William Sound, a pristine Pacific waterway rich in wildlife, fisheries and tourist attractions. It is shaping up as the nation's largest oil spill ever.

The *Exxon Valdez,* a 987-foot tanker owned by Exxon Shipping Co., rammed the Bligh Reef about 25 miles from the city of Valdez, the northernmost ice-free port in the United States at, 12:30 a.m.

"This is the largest oil spill in U.S. history, and it unfortunately took place in an enclosed water body with numerous islands, channels, bays and fiords," Richard Golob, publisher of the Golob Oil Pollution Bulletin, told the Associated Press.

Source: Copyright 1989, *Los Angeles Times.* Reprinted by permission.

It's Nature's Turn to Repair the Damage
Newsweek, *September 18, 1989, p. 50.*

The slick is gone from the gray-green waters of Alaska's southern coast, the place that has become known to millions of Americans as Pristine Prince

William Sound. The 11 million-gallon sea of petroleum that came boiling up from the tanks of the *Exxon Valdez* has long since broken up into floating ponds; the ponds reduced to puddles; the puddles in turn eroded into sticky, amorphous globs of tar or whipped by waves into the frothy emulsion known as mousse. Some has evaporated; 2.6 million gallons have been recovered and returned to their owner, Exxon; and a substantial fraction has washed ashore. The slick is gone—and by the end of this week the army of out-of-work fishermen, volunteer housewives and fortune seekers that Exxon mobilized for the fantastic task of scrubbing more than 1,000 miles of rocks will be gone, too, departing just ahead of the storms of the early Alaskan autumn. Exxon, a billion dollars poorer and, it is to be hoped, a little wiser, is going home; and what it leaves behind, it leaves to the lonely wind, the rippling tide and the slow but inexorable processes of tort law.

Drop by Drop: A Box Score

Oil spilled: **10,836,000 gallons**

Shoreline contaminated by oil: **1,090 miles**

Shoreline treated by Exxon: **1,087 miles**

Shoreline still needing cleaning, according to the state: **At least 1,000 miles**

Number of dead birds: **33,126**
of dead eagles: **138**
of dead otters: **980**

Cost of cleanup to Exxon: **$1.28 billion (after-tax cost; insurance companies will reimburse Exxon $400 million)**

People involved in cleanup: **12,000**

Vessels and planes used in cleanup: **1,385**

Oil recovered: **2,604,000 gallons (est.)**

Waste from oil cleanup: **24,000 tons**

Lawsuits filed against Exxon: **145**

Sources: Exxon, U.S. Fish and Wildlife Service, Alaska Department of Environmental Conservation

Source: From *Newsweek*, September 18, 1989. © 1989 Newsweek, Inc. All rights reserved. Reprinted by permission.

Secret Studies Put Spill Damage at $15 Billion
By Michael Parrish
Los Angeles Times, *October 8, 1991, p. A1.*

Unpublished studies by state and federal researchers contend that the true cost of environmental damage from the *Exxon Valdez* oil spill in Alaska could be as high as $15 billion, according to experts familiar with the secret reports.

The figure stands in dramatic contrast to the $1.125-billion settlement that Exxon Corp. agreed to last week to settle criminal and civil complaints brought by the state of Alaska and the federal government.

Nobel laureate economists connected with the studies include Robert M. Solow of MIT on the Alaska team, James Tobin of Yale University on the federal team and Kenneth J. Arrow of Stanford University and George Stigler of the University of Chicago, both doing research for Exxon.

The state team's estimates range from $3 billion to as high as $15 billion for damages to Prince William Sound, though there are some indications that they have begun to focus on a much narrower range. Federal researchers apparently see a range of $4 billion to $10 billion. Exxon spokesman Lance Lamberton declined comment on anything having to do with Exxon's studies.

Source: Copyright, 1991, *Los Angeles Times.* Reprinted by permission.

Other Source Materials

Even while Exxon and other groups were cleaning up in the aftermath of this tremendous oil spill, the courts and government agencies were investigating the captain and the company. A transcript of the marine radio discussion between the man in charge of the ship, Captain Joseph Hazelwood, and the head of the Coast Guard for the area encompassing Valdez Harbor, Commander Steve McCall, was widely broadcast. The following is part of that conversation reproduced in Art Davidson's *In the Wake of the Exxon Valdez* (Sierra Club Books, San Francisco, 1990, pp. 19–20.)

McCALL: *Exxon Valdez,* this is the captain of the port, Commander McCall. Do you have any more of an estimate as to your situation at this time? Over.

HAZELWOOD: Oh, not at the present, Steve . . . but we are working our way off the reef . . . the vessel has been holed. Right now we're trying to steer off the reef. And we'll get back to you as soon as we can.

McCALL: Roger on that. You know, we've got all our planned mechanisms in place to give you what assistance we can. . . . Take it, take it slow and easy and, you know, I'm telling you the obvious, but . . . take it slow and easy and we are getting help out as fast as we can.

HAZELWOOD: Okay. We're in pretty good shape right now stabilitywise. We're just trying to extract her off the shoal here and you can probably see me on your radar. And once I get underway I'll let you know.

McCALL: Roger. Yeah. Another thing, now again, before you make any drastic attempt to get underway you make sure you don't . . . start doing any ripping. You got a rising tide. You got another about an hour and a half worth of tide in your favor. Once you hit the max I wouldn't recommend doing much wiggling. Over.

HAZELWOOD: Okay. Yeah, I think . . . the major damage has kind of been done. We've kind of . . . rolled over it and we're just kind of hung up in the stern here. We'll just drift over it and I'll get back to you. We'll be standing by. *Exxon Valdez,* clear.

Conclusion

On September 30, 1991, a settlement among Exxon, the State of Alaska, and the U.S. Department of Justice was announced. The settlement called for Exxon to pay $900 million in civil damages and an additional $100 million, if needed, for environmental cleanup. Exxon further had to pay $25 million in criminal penalties and $100 million in criminal restitution. This settlement was approved by the U.S. District Court on October 8, 1991.

Captain Hazelwood was acquitted of criminal charges. Some say the polluted area will never be the same.

Analysis Questions

1. How much money did the Exxon Corporation spend on cleaning up the oil spill? (Note that there are two estimates in the source materials. Make sure you indicate from which source your estimate comes.)
2. One of the sources claims that 145 law suits were filed against Exxon. Write down a list of the people, companies, and groups that might have sued Exxon and the reasons they would have done so.
3. Reread the marine radio conversation between Captain Hazelwood and Commander McCall. How would you characterize the tone of their conversation in light of the enormity of the event?

PRESIDENTS AND VICE PRESIDENTS OF THE UNITED STATES

1 GEORGE WASHINGTON

Born: February 22, 1732
Died: December 14, 1799
Dates in office: 1789–1797
Profession before presidency:
   Planter
Political party: None
State of birth: Virginia

George Washington took his oath of office as the first president of the United States on the balcony of Federal Hall on Wall Street in New York City. Understanding the precedent-setting role of his position, Washington acted cautiously as president, working to flesh out the framework of government that was described in the Constitution.

Vice president: **John Adams**
(see John Adams's listing under Presidents)

2 JOHN ADAMS

Born: October 30, 1735
Died: July 4, 1826
Dates in office: 1797–1801
Profession before presidency:
   Lawyer
Political party: Federalist
State: Massachusetts

On at least two occasions, John Adams went against popular public opinion. As a lawyer, Adams defended the British soldiers who killed three Americans at the Boston Massacre in 1770, feeling a mob mentality was taking over the colony. As president, Adams ignored public sentiment for war with France and instead coaxed France to accept neutrality rights at sea with the United States in exchange for most-favored-nation status.

Vice president: **Thomas Jefferson**
(see Jefferson's listing under Presidents)

3 THOMAS JEFFERSON

Born: April 13, 1743
Died: July 4, 1826
Dates in office: 1801–1809
Profession before presidency:
   Planter
Political party: Democratic-Republican
Home state: Virginia

Not known for his eloquence, Thomas Jefferson was the "silent member" of the Continental Congress. He used his writing skills to draft the Declaration of Independence at age 33. During Jefferson's first term as president, he approved the purchase of the vast Louisiana Territory for a paltry $15 million dollars. However, he had originally sent his negotiators to buy only West Florida and New Orleans.

Vice president: **Aaron Burr**
Home state: New Jersey
Political party: Democratic-Republican
Profession: Lawyer

Vice president: **George Clinton**
Home state: New York
Political party: Democratic-Republican
Profession: Lawyer

4 JAMES MADISON

Born: March 16, 1751
Died: June 28, 1836
Dates in office: 1809–1817
Profession before presidency:
   Lawyer
Political party: Democratic-Republican
Home state: Virginia

The shortest and slightest president, James Madison stood about 5 feet 4 inches and weighed just 100 pounds.

Madison contributed to the ratification of the Constitution with his co-authored *Federalist* essays. According to Daniel Webster, ''Madison had as much to do as any man in framing the Constitution, and as much to do as any man in administering it.''

Vice president: **George Clinton**
Home state: New York
Political party: Democratic-Republican
Profession: Lawyer

Vice president: **Elbridge Gerry**
Home state: Massachusetts
Political party: Democratic-Republican
Profession: Importer and shipper

5 JAMES MONROE

Born: April 28, 1758
Died: July 4, 1831
Dates in office: 1817–1825
Profession before presidency: Lawyer
Political party: Democratic-Republican
Home state: Virginia

James Monroe faced a nation's fears that Spain might attempt to retake its former colonies in Latin America and that Russia might extend its claims in Alaska to the Oregon Territory. He consequently declared to Congress in 1823 a warning to European nations about intervention in the Western Hemisphere. The message came to bear his name: the Monroe Doctrine.

Vice president: **Daniel D. Tompkins**
Home state: New York
Political party: Democratic-Republican
Profession: Lawyer

6 JOHN QUINCY ADAMS

Born: July 11, 1767
Died: February 23, 1848
Dates in office: 1825–1829
Profession before presidency: Lawyer
Political party: Democratic-Republican
Home state: Massachusetts

John Quincy Adams was the only president who was the son of a president. Adams ambitiously proposed a strong program sponsored by the federal government to link the sections of the nation with highways and canals, to create a national university, and to build an astronomical observatory. The programs were largely passed over by Congress, however. Adams obtained only the extension of the Cumberland Road into Ohio and the construction of the Chesapeake and Ohio Canal.

Vice president: **John C. Calhoun**
Home state: South Carolina
Political party: Democratic-Republican
Profession: Lawyer

7 ANDREW JACKSON

Born: March 15, 1767
Died: June 8, 1845
Dates in office: 1829–1837
Profession before presidency: Lawyer
Political party: Democratic
Home state: South Carolina

As a major general in the War of 1812, Andrew Jackson became a national hero due to his victory over the British at New Orleans. More than any president who came before him, Jackson was elected by the popular vote of common citizens. Later, as president, he recommended eliminating the electoral college.

Vice president: **John C. Calhoun**
Home state: South Carolina
Political party: Democratic-Republican
Profession: Lawyer

Vice president: **Martin Van Buren**
(see Van Buren's listing under Presidents)

8 MARTIN VAN BUREN

Born: December 5, 1782
Died: July 24, 1862
Dates in office: 1837–1841
Profession before presidency: Lawyer
Political party: Democratic
Home state: New York

Only about 5 feet 6 inches tall, Martin Van Buren, the "Little Magician," was elected vice president on Andrew Jackson's ticket in 1832. He won the presidency in 1836. A severe economic slump plagued Van Buren's term. Over nine hundred banks closed across the country. Many of Van Buren's deflationary measures contributed to the prolonged depression.

Vice president: **Richard M. Johnson**
Home state: Kentucky
Political party: Democratic
Profession: Lawyer

9 WILLIAM H. HARRISON

Born: February 9, 1773
Died: April 4, 1841
Dates in office: 1841
Profession before presidency:
 Lawyer
Political party: Whig
Home state: Virginia

William H. Harrison was the last president born a British subject. His presidency lasted exactly one month. He caught a cold, which turned into pneumonia, while delivering his inaugural address. Shortly before he died, he spoke his last words: "I wish you to understand the true principles of the government. I wish them carried out. I ask nothing more."

Vice president: **John Tyler**
(see Tyler's listing under Presidents)

10 JOHN TYLER

Born: March 29, 1790
Died: January 18, 1862
Dates in office: 1841–1845
Profession before presidency:
 Soldier
Political party: Whig
Home state: Virginia

As vice president, John Tyler took the office of president upon the death of William H. Harrison. He became known as "a president without a party" after the Whigs expelled him for failing to go along with them on their plan to establish a national bank. Nevertheless, Tyler was able to

enact much positive legislation. For example, his "Log Cabin" Bill allowed settlers to claim and later purchase 160 acres of land before it was put on the public market.

11 JAMES K. POLK

Born: November 2, 1795
Died: June 15, 1849
Dates in office: 1845–1849
Profession before presidency:
 Lawyer
Political party: Democratic
Home state: North Carolina

James K. Polk was a candidate committed to the nation's "Manifest Destiny," the belief that the United States was divinely destined to rule from sea to sea. He urged reannexation of Texas and reoccupation of Oregon. He also favored acquiring California. These views plunged Polk and the United States into, among other things, the Mexican War. This conflict lasted from 1846 to 1848, when the border between the two countries was fixed at the Rio Grande.

Vice president: **George M. Dallas**
Home state: Pennsylvania
Political party: Democratic
Profession: Lawyer

12 ZACHARY TAYLOR

Born: November 24, 1784
Died: July 9, 1850
Dates in office: 1849–1850
Profession before presidency:
 Soldier
Political party: Whig
Home state: Virginia

Zachary Taylor was nicknamed "Old Rough and Ready" from his days as a general in the Mexican War. President Taylor was a former slave owner who told the Southern states that threatened secession that he would personally lead the Union army against them if any of them tried to secede. Taylor's only son, Richard, served in the Civil War as a general in the Confederate army.

Vice president: **Millard Fillmore**
(see Fillmore's listing under Presidents)

13 MILLARD FILLMORE

Born: January 7, 1800
Died: March 8, 1874
Dates in office: 1850–1853
Profession before presidency:
   Lawyer
Political party: Whig
Home state: New York

Millard Fillmore embraced the compromise between slave and free states that Zachary Taylor had opposed. Called the Compromise of 1850, it included bills that admitted California as a free state; settled the Texas boundary; granted territorial status to New Mexico; approved the controversial Fugitive Slave Act, which required the federal government to assist in returning escaped slaves to their masters; and abolished slave trade in the District of Columbia.

14 FRANKLIN PIERCE

Born: November 23, 1804
Died: October 8, 1869
Dates in office: 1853–1857
Profession before presidency:
   Lawyer
Political party: Democratic
Home state: New Hampshire

Franklin Pierce entered the presidency on the heels of tragedy. Just two months before he took office, he and his wife saw their eleven-year-old son killed in a train wreck. Then the tranquility of the years after the Compromise of 1850 ended when Senator Stephen Douglas proposed the Kansas-Nebraska Act, which said in part that the residents of the new territories could decide the slavery question themselves. The result was a rush into Kansas, where southerners and northerners battled in a prelude to the Civil War.

Vice president: **William R. King**
Home state: North Carolina
Political party: Democratic
Profession: Lawyer

15 JAMES BUCHANAN

Born: April 23, 1791
Died: June 1, 1868
Dates in office: 1857–1861
Profession before presidency:
   Lawyer
Political party: Democratic
Home state: Pennsylvania

James Buchanan was the only president who never married. He served at a frightful time for the fast-dividing nation. Buchanan misread the political realities of his time. He thought that the problems between North and South could be solved constitutionally through the Supreme Court. In his inaugural address, he said that the Supreme Court was about to settle the situation "speedily and finally."

Vice president: **John C. Breckinridge**
Home state: Kentucky
Political party: Democratic
Profession: Lawyer

16 ABRAHAM LINCOLN

Born: February 12, 1809
Died: April 15, 1865
Dates in office: 1861–1865
Profession before presidency:
   Lawyer
Political party: Republican
Home state: Kentucky

Abraham Lincoln constantly reminded the world that the issues of the Civil War involved more than North versus South, slave versus free. At Gettysburg, he proclaimed "that this nation, under God, shall have a new birth of freedom—and that government of the people, by the people, for the people shall not perish from the earth." On January 1, 1863, Lincoln issued the Emancipation Proclamation, which declared slaves free within states controlled by the Confederacy. He was assassinated on Good Friday, April 14, 1865, by John Wilkes Booth at Ford's Theatre in Washington, D.C.

Vice president: **Hannibal Hamlin**
Home state: Maine
Political party: Republican
Profession: Lawyer

Vice president: **Andrew Johnson**
(see Andrew Johnson's listing under Presidents)

17 ANDREW JOHNSON

Born: December 29, 1808
Died: July 31, 1875
Dates in office: 1865–1869
Profession before presidency:
   Tailor
Political party: National
   Union
Home state: North Carolina

To Andrew Johnson fell the task of reconstructing the nation after the Civil War and Abraham Lincoln's death. Johnson restored legal rights to the Southern states swiftly, since in his view they had never technically left the Union (because the Union was indissoluble). Johnson faced impeachment by the House when he allegedly violated the Tenure of Office Act by wrongly dismissing the secretary of war. He was tried by the Senate and acquitted by one vote.

18 ULYSSES S. GRANT

Born: April 27, 1822
Died: July 23, 1885
Dates in office: 1869–1877
Profession before presidency:
   Soldier
Political party: Republican
Home state: Ohio

Ulysses S. Grant became commander of all Union armies in March 1864. Robert E. Lee formally surrendered to Grant at Appomattox, Virginia, on April 9, 1865. As president, Grant clashed with speculators, whose attempt to corner the gold market greatly disrupted American business. Grant realized his shortcomings as president. He said, "It was my fortune, or misfortune, to be called to the office of Chief Executive without any previous political training."

Vice president: **Schuyler Colfax**
Home state: New York
Political party: Republican
Profession: Deputy auditor

Vice president: **Henry Wilson**
Home state: New Hampshire
Political party: Republican
Profession: Shoe factory owner

19 RUTHERFORD B. HAYES

Born: October 4, 1822
Died: January 17, 1893
Dates in office: 1877–1881
Profession before presidency:
   Lawyer
Political party: Republican
Home state: Ohio

Rutherford B. Hayes won the most disputed election in American history. Hayes's election depended upon disputed electoral votes in Louisiana, South Carolina, and Florida. He needed every electoral vote from those states to win; a panel established by Congress determined that Hayes did indeed win the election: 185 electoral votes to 184 over Governor Samuel J. Tilden of New York.

Vice president: **William A. Wheeler**
Home state: New York
Political party: Republican
Profession: Lawyer

20 JAMES A. GARFIELD

Born: November 19, 1831
Died: September 19, 1881
Dates in office: 1881
Profession before presidency:
   Lawyer
Political party: Republican
Home state: Ohio

On July 2, 1881, James A. Garfield was strolling in a Washington, D.C., railroad station. He was shot in the back by Charles Guiteau, a man who had been rebuffed by the president for an appointment to a diplomatic post following the election. Garfield lay wounded in the White House for weeks. Alexander Graham Bell, the inventor of the telephone, designed an electrical device in an attempt to find the bullet still lodged in the president. On September 6, Garfield, seemingly recuperating, was taken to a New Jersey resort. He died there on September 19.

Vice president: Chester A. Arthur
(See Arthur's listing under Presidents)

21 CHESTER A. ARTHUR

Born: October 5, 1829
Died: November 18, 1886
Dates in office: 1881–1885
Profession before presidency:
Lawyer
Political party: Republican
Home state: Vermont

Chester A. Arthur was appointed by President Grant as collector of the port of New York in 1871. He was responsible for collection of about 75 percent of the nation's duties from ships that landed within his jurisdiction. The customhouse was riddled with scandal, including the proven charge that employees were expected to kick back part of their salaries to the Republican Party. As president, Arthur sought to rid himself of machine politics. In 1883, Congress passed the Pendleton Act, which protected employees against removal from their jobs for political reasons.

22 GROVER CLEVELAND

Born: March 18, 1837
Died: June 24, 1908
Dates in office: 1885–1889;
1893–1897
Profession before presidency:
Lawyer
Political party: Democratic
Home state: New Jersey

Grover Cleveland was the only president to leave the White House and return for a second term four years later. After his defeat by Benjamin Harrison in 1888, Cleveland returned to his law practice in New York City, seemingly retired from active political life. In his second term, the nation faced a great depression. When railroad workers went on strike in Chicago, Cleveland said, "If it takes the entire army and navy of the United States to deliver a postcard in Chicago, that card will be delivered."

Vice president: Thomas A. Hendricks
Home state: Ohio
Political party: Democratic
Profession: Lawyer

23 BENJAMIN HARRISON

Born: August 20, 1833
Died: March 13, 1901
Dates in office: 1889–1893
Profession before presidency:
Lawyer
Political party: Republican
Home state: Ohio

Benjamin Harrison was the grandson of William H. Harrison, the nation's ninth president. Benjamin Harrison signed the Sherman Anti-Trust Act in 1890, the first of the antitrust laws to curb the abuse of monopolies that conspired to restrict trade. Harrison was defeated for reelection in 1892 by Grover Cleveland, the man he had triumphed over four years earlier.

Vice president: Levi P. Morton
Home state: Vermont
Political party: Republican
Profession: Businessman and banker

(See earlier entry)

24 GROVER CLEVELAND

Vice president: Adlai E. Stevenson
Home state: Kentucky
Political party: Democratic
Profession: Lawyer

25 WILLIAM McKINLEY

Born: January 29, 1843
Died: September 14, 1901
Dates in office: 1897–1901
Profession before presidency:
Lawyer
Political party: Republican
Home state: Ohio

During William McKinley's term, the United States intervened in the Spanish-American War and destroyed the Spanish fleet outside Santiago harbor in Cuba, captured Manila, in the Philippines, and occupied Puerto Rico. McKinley followed public opinion in annexing the acquired territories (except Cuba). McKinley was assassinated in 1901. He was shot while standing in a receiving line at a Pan American Exposition in Buffalo, New York.

Vice president: **Garret A. Hobart**
Home state: New Jersey
Political party: Republican
Profession: Lawyer

Vice president: **Theodore Roosevelt**
(see Theodore Roosevelt's listing under Presidents)

26 THEODORE ROOSEVELT

Born: October 27, 1858
Died: January 6, 1919
Dates in office: 1901–1909
Profession before presidency:
  Author
Political party: Republican
Home state: New York

Theodore Roosevelt was not quite forty-three years old when he took over as president for the slain William McKinley. Roosevelt was a charismatic man who led the American people and Congress toward progressive reforms and a strong foreign policy. Roosevelt staunchly defended the right by the United States to use military force, if necessary, to defend the principles of the Monroe Doctrine. His famous words were "Speak softly and carry a big stick; you will go far."

Vice president: **Charles W. Fairbanks**
Home state: Ohio
Political party: Republican
Profession: Lawyer

27 WILLIAM H. TAFT

Born: September 15, 1857
Died: March 8, 1930
Dates in office: 1909–1913
Profession before presidency:
  Lawyer
Political party: Republican
Home state: Ohio

William H. Taft was appointed a federal circuit judge at thirty-four years old. He always would prefer law to politics. Nevertheless, he rose politically through presidential appointments and was nominated as Theodore Roosevelt's Republican successor in 1908. Taft was uncomfortable as president. After he was defeated for reelection, he was appointed chief justice of the Supreme Court of the United States by President Warren G. Harding. He considered the appointment his greatest honor. "I don't even remember being President," he said.

Vice president: **James S. Sherman**
Home state: New York
Political party: Republican
Profession: Lawyer

28 WOODROW WILSON

Born: December 29, 1856
Died: February 3, 1924
Dates in office: 1913–1921
Profession before presidency:
  Educator
Political party: Democratic
Home state: Virginia

Woodrow Wilson's campaign slogan for reelection in 1916 was "He kept us out of war." But after his election, Wilson knew that the United States could not remain neutral in the world war. On April 2, 1917, he asked Congress to declare war on Germany. Early the next year, Wilson set forth his famous Fourteen Points, the only basis, he insisted, on which lasting peace could be made. The armistice was signed on November 11, 1918.

Vice president: **Thomas R. Marshall**
Home state: Indiana
Political party: Democratic
Profession: Lawyer

29 WARREN G. HARDING

Born: November 2, 1865
Died: August 2, 1923
Dates in office: 1921–1923
Profession before presidency:
  Editor
Political party: Republican
Home state: Ohio

Warren G. Harding was a master of the great phrase, and this, combined with his handsome looks, won him a landslide election in 1920. Harding appeared to be on his way to carrying out his campaign promise of ''less government in business and more business in government'' when word got to him that some of his friends were using their official positions for their own gain. Harding said, ''My friends, they're the ones keeping me walking the floor nights.'' Harding died in office of a heart attack while in San Francisco in 1923. A historians' poll in 1962 ranked him, along with Ulysses S. Grant, as the worst of the presidents.

Vice president: **Calvin Coolidge**
(see Coolidge's listing under Presidents)

30 CALVIN COOLIDGE

Born: July 4, 1872
Died: January 5, 1933
Dates in office: 1923–1929
Profession before presidency:
 Lawyer
Political party: Republican
Home state: Vermont

Calvin Coolidge's father, a notary public, administered his son the oath of office at their family home upon learning of the death of President Warren G. Harding. Coolidge quickly became a popular president, known for his dry wit. Once, a woman sitting next to him at a dinner party confided that she had bet that she could get at least three words from him in conversation. ''You lose,'' he quietly responded.

Vice president: **Charles G. Dawes**
Home state: Ohio
Political party: Republican
Profession: Lawyer

31 HERBERT C. HOOVER

Born: August 10, 1874
Died: October 20, 1964
Dates in office: 1929–1933
Profession before presidency:
 Engineer
Political party: Republican
Home state: Iowa

Herbert C. Hoover gained international attention during World War I by leading the distribution of food and supplies to war-torn Europe. He was the secretary of commerce under Presidents Harding and Coolidge before being nominated for president in 1928. Hoover became a scapegoat for the depression that plagued the nation after the stock market crash of 1929. Under the later Truman and Eisenhower administrations, Hoover was appointed to head the commissions that reorganized the executive departments.

Vice president: **Charles Curtis**
Home state: Kansas
Political party: Republican
Profession: Lawyer

32 FRANKLIN D. ROOSEVELT

Born: January 30, 1882
Died: April 12, 1945
Dates in office: 1933–1945
Profession before presidency:
 Lawyer
Political party: Democratic
Home state: New York

Franklin D. Roosevelt became president in the midst of the Great Depression. He declared in his inaugural address, ''The only thing we have to fear is fear itself.'' He pledged that his primary task was to put people back to work. By 1935, the nation's economy had recovered somewhat, but Roosevelt's New Deal policies were being criticized increasingly by American businessmen and bankers. Roosevelt was elected to three more terms, the most for any president. After the bombing of Pearl Harbor, Roosevelt directed the United States into World War II.

Vice president: **John N. Garner**
Home state: Texas
Political party: Democratic
Profession: Lawyer

Vice president: **Henry A. Wallace**
Home state: Iowa
Political party: Democratic
Profession: Writer and editor

Vice president: **Harry S Truman**
(see Truman's listing under Presidents)

33 | HARRY S TRUMAN

Born: May 8, 1884
Died: December 26, 1972
Dates in office: 1945–1953
Profession before presidency:
  Businessman
Political party: Democratic
Home state: Missouri

Harry S Truman was only vice president for a few weeks when President Franklin D. Roosevelt died on April 12, 1945. As president, Truman made some of the most important decisions in history. He ordered the atomic bomb to be dropped on two cities in Japan at the close of World War II. In June 1945, he witnessed the signing of the Charter of the United Nations. Truman won a close election in 1948 over Republican Thomas Dewey and proudly displayed an early edition of the *Chicago Tribune* that proclaimed otherwise: "Dewey Defeats Truman."

***Vice president:* Alben W. Barkley**
Home state: Kentucky
Political party: Democratic
Profession: Lawyer

34 | DWIGHT D. EISENHOWER

Born: October 14, 1890
Died: March 28, 1969
Dates in office: 1953–1961
Profession before presidency:
  Soldier
Political party: Republican
Home state: Texas

Dwight D. Eisenhower was the commanding general for the Allied forces in Europe in World War II. As president, he concentrated on maintaining world peace. Eisenhower sent federal troops to Little Rock, Arkansas, to ensure compliance with the federal court order to desegregate the schools. He pointed to peace as his administration's legacy. "The United States never lost a soldier or a foot of ground in my administration. We kept the peace," he said.

***Vice president:* Richard M. Nixon**
(see Nixon's listing under Presidents)

35 | JOHN F. KENNEDY

Born: May 29, 1917
Died: November 22, 1963
Dates in office: 1961–1963
Profession before presidency:
  Author
Political party: Democratic
Home state: Massachusetts

John F. Kennedy was the youngest president to die. He was assassinated in Dallas, Texas, in November 1963. Kennedy won a close election over Richard M. Nixon, due in part to Kennedy's performance in a series of televised debates. He was the first Roman Catholic president. At his inauguration, he declared, "Ask not what your country can do for you—ask what you can do for your country."

***Vice president:* Lyndon B. Johnson**
(see Lyndon B. Johnson's listing under Presidents)

36 | LYNDON B. JOHNSON

Born: August 27, 1908
Died: January 22, 1973
Dates in office: 1963–1969
Profession before presidency:
  Teacher
Political party: Democratic
Home state: Texas

Lyndon B. Johnson's "Great Society" program became the agenda for his administration. Aid to education, attack on disease, Medicare, urban renewal, war on poverty, and the removal of obstacles to the right to vote were many of the recommendations that Johnson sent to Congress. The escalating Vietnam War was Johnson's downfall; controversy over the war fueled protests at home. Johnson declined to seek reelection in 1968.

***Vice president:* Hubert H. Humphrey**
Home state: South Dakota
Political party: Democratic
Profession: Pharmacist, teacher

37 RICHARD M. NIXON

Born: January 9, 1913
Dates in office: 1969–1974
Profession before presidency:
  Lawyer
Political party: Republican
Home state: California

Richard M. Nixon succeeded in bringing an end to the Vietnam War and improving relations with the Soviet Union and China. His election in 1968 was a political comeback. He had been defeated for the presidency in 1960 and for governor of California in 1962. Nixon's presidency ended in the Watergate scandal, in which a break-in of the Democratic headquarters during the 1972 reelection campaign was tied to his administration. Faced with the prospect of impeachment, Nixon resigned on August 9, 1974. He was the only president to resign the office.

Vice president: **Spiro T. Agnew**
Home state: Maryland
Political party: Republican
Profession: Lawyer

Vice president: **Gerald R. Ford**
(see Ford's listing under Presidents)

38 GERALD R. FORD

Born: July 14, 1913
Dates in office: 1974–1977
Profession before presidency:
  Lawyer
Political party: Republican
Home state: Nebraska

In September 1974, Gerald R. Ford granted former president Nixon "a full, free and absolute pardon for all offenses against the United States which he has committed or may have committed or taken part in" during his term in office. Gradually, Ford chose a presidential cabinet of his own. Ford won the Republican nomination for president in 1976 but lost the election to Jimmy Carter. At his inauguration, President Carter began: "For myself and for our nation, I want to thank my predecessor for all he has done to heal our land."

Vice president: **Nelson A. Rockefeller**
Home state: Maine
Political party: Republican
Profession: Businessman

39 JAMES E. CARTER, JR.

Born: October 1, 1924
Dates in office: 1977–1981
Profession before presidency:
  Businessman
Political party: Democratic
Home state: Georgia

James E. ("Jimmy") Carter, Jr., began campaigning for the presidency in December 1974. His two-year campaign gained momentum, and he was a first-ballot nominee of the Democratic Party. Carter established a national energy program during his administration and sought to improve the environment. His greatest foreign policy accomplishment was the Camp David agreement of 1978 between Egypt and Israel.

Vice president: **Walter F. Mondale**
Home state: Minnesota
Political party: Democratic
Profession: Lawyer

40 RONALD W. REAGAN

Born: February 6, 1911
Dates in office: 1981–1989
Profession before presidency:
  Actor
Political party: Republican
Home state: Illinois

As president of the Screen Actors Guild, Ronald W. Reagan became tangled in disputes involving communism. His political views subsequently changed from liberal to conservative. As president, Reagan obtained legislation to stimulate economic growth, curb inflation, increase employment, and strengthen national defense. His "peace through strength" foreign policy is credited as one of the reasons for the collapse of the Communist bloc shortly after his second term.

Vice president: **George H. W. Bush**
(see Bush's listing under Presidents)

41 GEORGE H. W. BUSH

Born: June 12, 1924
Dates in office: 1989–1993
Profession before presidency:
    Businessman
Political party: Republican
Home state: Massachusetts

George H. W. Bush pledged a return to traditional American values and aimed to make America "a kinder and gentler nation." Bush's handling of the brief Persian Gulf War in 1991 increased his popularity. One of Bush's primary domestic goals was to put an end to "the scourge of drugs" that racked the nation.

Vice president: **J. Danforth Quayle**
Home state: Indiana
Political party: Republican
Profession: Lawyer

42 WILLIAM J. B. CLINTON

Born: August 19, 1946
Dates in office: 1993–
Profession before presidency:
    Governor of Arkansas
Political Party: Democrat
Home State: Arkansas

Running a campaign that focused on change, William Jefferson Blythe Clinton was swept into the presidency in an election that saw the first upturn in voter turnout since the election of John F. Kennedy. On election night he spoke at a victory rally in Little Rock, Arkansas and said, "My fellow Americans, with high hopes and brave hearts, in massive numbers, the American people have voted to make a new beginning."

Vice president: **Albert Gore, Jr.**
Home state: Tennessee
Political Party: Democrat
Profession: Journalist

SUPREME COURT CHIEF JUSTICES AND ASSOCIATE JUSTICES SINCE 1789

*Each justice is listed along with a notation of the president who nominated him or her and the home state of the justice. (** indicates chief justices)*

Robert H. Harrison, 1789–1790
George Washington
Maryland

James Iredell, 1790–1799
George Washington
North Carolina

Thomas Johnson, 1791–1793
George Washington
Maryland

William Paterson, 1793–1806
George Washington
New Jersey

Chief Justice John Jay

**John Jay, 1789–1795
George Washington
New York

John Rutledge, 1789–1791
George Washington
South Carolina

William Cushing, 1789–1810
George Washington
Massachusetts

James Wilson, 1789–1798
George Washington
Pennsylvania

John Blair, 1789–1796
George Washington
Virginia

Chief Justice John Rutledge

**John Rutledge, 1795[a]
George Washington
South Carolina

Samuel Chase, 1796–1811
George Washington
Maryland

---

[a]John Rutledge served as Chief Justice from August, 1795, until he was rejected in December of the same year.

Chief Justice Oliver Ellsworth

**Oliver Ellsworth, 1796–1799
George Washington
Connecticut

Bushrod Washington, 1798–1829
John Adams
Virginia

Alfred Moore, 1799–1804
John Adams
North Carolina

Chief Justice John Marshall

**John Marshall, 1801–1835
John Adams
Virginia

William Johnson, 1804–1834
Thomas Jefferson
South Carolina

Henry Brockholst Livingston, 1806–1823
Thomas Jefferson
New York

Thomas Todd, 1807–1826
Thomas Jefferson
Kentucky

Joseph Story, 1811–1845
James Madison
Massachusetts

Gabriel Duval, 1812–1835
James Madison
Maryland

Smith Thompson, 1823–1843
James Monroe
New York

Robert Trimble, 1826–1828
John Quincy Adams
Kentucky

John McLean, 1829–1861
Andrew Jackson
Ohio

Henry Baldwin, 1830–1844
Andrew Jackson
Pennsylvania

James M. Wayne, 1835–1867
Andrew Jackson
Georgia

Chief Justice Roger B. Taney

**Roger B. Taney, 1836–1864
Andrew Jackson
Maryland

Philip P. Barbour, 1836–1841
Andrew Jackson
Virginia

John Catron, 1837–1865
Andrew Jackson
Tennessee

John McKinley, 1837–1852
Martin Van Buren
Alabama

Peter V. Daniel, 1841–1860
Martin Van Buren
Virginia

Samuel Nelson, 1845–1872
John Tyler
New York

Levi Woodbury, 1845–1851
James K. Polk
New Hampshire

Robert C. Grier, 1846–1870
James K. Polk
Pennsylvania

Benjamin R. Curtis, 1851–1857
Millard Fillmore
Massachusetts

John A. Campbell, 1853–1861
Franklin Pierce
Alabama

Nathan Clifford, 1858–1881
James Buchanan
Maine

Noah H. Swayne, 1862–1881
Abraham Lincoln
Ohio

Samuel F. Miller, 1862–1890
Abraham Lincoln
Iowa

David Davis, 1862–1877
Abraham Lincoln
Illinois

Stephen J. Field, 1863–1897
Abraham Lincoln
California

Chief Justice Salmon P. Chase

**Salmon P. Chase, 1864–1873
Abraham Lincoln
Ohio

William Strong, 1870–1880
Ulysses S. Grant
Pennsylvania

Joseph P. Bradley, 1870–1892
Ulysses S. Grant
New Jersey

Ward Hunt, 1872–1882
Ulysses S. Grant
New York

Chief Justice Morrison R. Waite

**Morrison R. Waite, 1874–1888
Ulysses S. Grant
Ohio

John M. Harlan, 1877–1911
Rutherford B. Hayes
Kentucky

William B. Woods, 1880–1887
Rutherford B. Hayes
Georgia

Stanley Matthews, 1881–1889
James A. Garfield
Ohio

Samuel Blatchford, 1881–1893
Chester A. Arthur
New York

Horace Gray, 1882–1902
Chester A. Arthur
Massachusetts

Lucius Q. C. Lamar, 1888–1893
Grover Cleveland
Mississippi

Chief Justice Melville W. Fuller

**Melville W. Fuller, 1888–1910
Grover Cleveland
Illinois

David J. Brewer, 1889–1910
Benjamin Harrison
Kansas

Henry B. Brown, 1890–1906
Benjamin Harrison
Michigan

George Shiras, Jr., 1892–1903
Benjamin Harrison
Pennsylvania

Howell E. Jackson, 1893–1895
Benjamin Harrison
Tennessee

Edward D. White, 1894–1910
Grover Cleveland
Louisiana

Rufus W. Peckham, 1895–1909
Grover Cleveland
New York

Joseph McKenna, 1898–1925
William McKinley
California

Oliver W. Holmes, 1902–1932
Theodore Roosevelt
Massachusetts

William R. Day, 1903–1922
Theodore Roosevelt
Ohio

William H. Moody, 1906–1910
Theodore Roosevelt
Massachusetts

Horace H. Lurton, 1909–1914
William H. Taft
Tennessee

Charles E. Hughes, 1910–1916
William H. Taft
New York

Chief Justice Edward D. White

**Edward D. White, 1910–1921
William H. Taft
Louisiana

William Van Devanter, 1911–1937
William H. Taft
Wyoming

Joseph R. Lamar, 1911–1916
William H. Taft
Georgia

Mahlon Pitney, 1912–1922
William H. Taft
New Jersey

James C. McReynolds, 1914–1941
Woodrow Wilson
Tennessee

John H. Clarke, 1916–1922
Woodrow Wilson
Ohio

Louis D. Brandeis, 1916–1939
Woodrow Wilson
Massachusetts

Chief Justice William H. Taft

**William H. Taft, 1921–1930
Warren G. Harding
Connecticut

George Sutherland, 1922–1938
Warren G. Harding
Utah

Pierce Butler, 1922–1939
Warren G. Harding
Minnesota

Edward T. Sanford, 1923–1930
Warren G. Harding
Tennessee

Harlan F. Stone, 1925–1941
Calvin Coolidge
New York

Chief Justice Charles E. Hughes

**Charles E. Hughes, 1930–1941
Herbert C. Hoover
New York

Owen J. Roberts, 1930–1945
Herbert C. Hoover
Pennsylvania

Benjamin N. Cardozo, 1932–1938
Herbert C. Hoover
New York

Hugo L. Black, 1937–1971
Franklin D. Roosevelt
Alabama

Stanley F. Reed, 1938–1957
Franklin D. Roosevelt
Kentucky

Felix Frankfurter, 1939–1962
Franklin D. Roosevelt
Massachusetts

William O. Douglas, 1939–1975
Franklin D. Roosevelt
Connecticut

Frank Murphy, 1940–1949
Franklin D. Roosevelt
Michigan

Chief Justice Harlan F. Stone

**Harlan F. Stone, 1941–1946
Franklin D. Roosevelt
New York

James F. Byrnes, 1941–1942
Franklin D. Roosevelt
South Carolina

Robert H. Jackson, 1941–1954
Franklin D. Roosevelt
New York

Wiley B. Rutledge, 1943–1949
Franklin D. Roosevelt
Iowa

Harold H. Burton, 1945–1958
Harry S Truman
Ohio

Chief Justice Frederick M. Vinson

**Frederick M. Vinson, 1946–1953
Harry S Truman
Kentucky

Tom C. Clark, 1949–1967
Harry S Truman
Texas

Sherman Minton, 1949–1956
Harry S Truman
Indiana

Chief Justice Earl Warren

**Earl Warren, 1953–1969
Dwight D. Eisenhower
California

John M. Harlan, 1955–1971
Dwight D. Eisenhower
New York

William J. Brennan, Jr., 1956–1990
Dwight D. Eisenhower
New Jersey

Charles E. Whittaker, 1957–1962
Dwight D. Eisenhower
Missouri

Potter Stewart, 1958–1981
Dwight D. Eisenhower
Ohio

Byron R. White, 1962–
John F. Kennedy
Colorado

Arthur J. Goldberg, 1962–1965
John F. Kennedy
Illinois

Abe Fortas, 1965–1969
Lyndon B. Johnson
Tennessee

Thurgood Marshall, 1967–1991
Lyndon B. Johnson
New York

Chief Justice Warren E. Burger

**Warren E. Burger, 1969–1986
Richard M. Nixon
Minnesota

Harry A. Blackmun, 1970–
Richard M. Nixon
Minnesota

Lewis F. Powell, Jr., 1972–1987
Richard M. Nixon
Virginia

Chief Justice William H. Rehnquist

**William H. Rehnquist, 1972–
Richard M. Nixon
Arizona

John Paul Stevens, 1975–
Gerald R. Ford
Illinois

Sandra Day O'Connor, 1981–
Ronald W. Reagan
Arizona

Antonin Scalia, 1986–
Ronald W. Reagan
Virginia

Anthony M. Kennedy, 1988–
Ronald W. Reagan
California

David H. Souter, 1990–
George H. W. Bush
Maine

Clarence Thomas, 1991–
George H. W. Bush
Mississippi

ALABAMA

Originally the name for "tribal town," the territory of Alabama was later the home of the Alabama, or Alibamon, Indians of the Creek confederacy.

Capital: Montgomery
Size: 51,705 sq. mi. (132,365 sq. km)
Population: 4,062,608
Order admitted: 22
Date admitted: December 14, 1819
Number of U.S. Congressional Districts: 7
Number of Registered Voters: 2,375,444
   No party registration

ALASKA

The Russians adopted the word meaning "great lands" or "land that is not an island" from the Aleutian word alakshak.

Capital: Juneau
Size: 591,004 sq. mi. (1,512,970 sq. km)
Population: 551,947
Order admitted: 49
Date admitted: January 3, 1959
Number of U.S. Congressional Districts: 1 At Large
Number of Registered Voters: 306,264
   Number of Democrats: 58,913 (19%)
   Number of Republicans: 64,622 (21%)
   Number of unaffiliated and minor parties: 182,729
    (60%)

ARIZONA

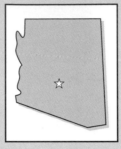

The Spanish coined the name either from the Pima Indian word meaning "little spring place" or from the Aztec ari-zuma, *meaning "silver-bearing."*

Capital: Phoenix
Size: 114,000 sq. mi. (291,840 sq. km)
Population: 3,667,985
Order admitted: 48
Date admitted: February 14, 1912
Number of U.S. Congressional Districts: 6
Number of Registered Voters: 1,863,418
   Number of Democrats: 779,351 (42%)
   Number of Republicans: 871,073 (47%)
   Number of unaffiliated and minor parties: 212,994
    (11%)

ARKANSAS

Once the territory of the Siouan Quapaw (downstream people), Arkansas is the French derivative of this Indian name.

Capital: Little Rock
Size: 53,187 sq. mi. (136,159 sq. km)
Population: 2,362,239
Order admitted: 25
Date admitted: June 15, 1836
Number of U.S. Congressional Districts: 4
Number of Registered Voters: 1,150,414
   No party registration

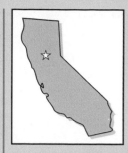

CALIFORNIA

The name of a fictitious earthly paradise in Las Serges de Esplandian, *a sixteenth-century Spanish romance. It is believed that Spanish conquistadors named this state.*

Capital: Sacramento
Size: 158,706 sq. mi. (406,287 sq. km)
Population: 29,839,250
Order admitted: 31
Date admitted: September 9, 1850
Number of U.S. Congressional Districts: 52
Number of Registered Voters: 13,478,027
  Number of Democrats: 6,671,747 (50%)
  Number of Republicans: 5,290,202 (39%)
  Number of unaffiliated and minor parties: 1,516,078 (11%)

COLORADO

A Spanish word for "red." The name Colorado *first referred to the Colorado River.*

Capital: Denver
Size: 104,091 sq. mi. (266,473 sq. km)
Population: 3,307,912
Order admitted: 38
Date admitted: August 1, 1876
Number of U.S. Congressional Districts: 6
Number of Registered Voters: 1,921,653
  Number of Democrats: 598,041 (31%)
  Number of Republicans: 653,464 (34%)
  Number of unaffiliated and minor parties: 670,148 (35%)

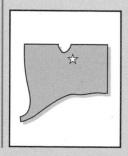

CONNECTICUT

The Algonquin and Mohican Indian word for "long river place."

Capital: Hartford
Size: 5,018 sq. mi. (12,846 sq. km)
Population: 3,295,669
Order admitted: 5
Date admitted: January 9, 1788
Number of U.S. Congressional Districts: 6
Number of Registered Voters: 1,700,871
  Number of Democrats: 667,523 (39%)
  Number of Republicans: 461,374 (27%)
  Number of unaffiliated and minor parties: 534,595 (34%)

DELAWARE

This version of the name of Lord De La Warr, a governor of Virginia, was first used to name the Delaware River and later adopted by the Europeans to rename the local Indians, originally called the Lenni-Lenape.

Capital: Dover
Size: 2,044 sq. mi. (5,233 sq. km)
Population: 668,696
Order admitted: 1
Date admitted: December 7, 1787
Number of U.S. Congressional Districts: 1 At Large
Number of Registered Voters: 298,246
  Number of Democrats: 127,197 (42%)
  Number of Republicans: 112,524 (37%)
  Number of unaffiliated and minor parties: 58,525 (20%)

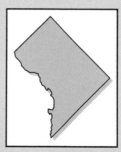

DISTRICT OF COLUMBIA

Named for Christopher Columbus in 1791.

The city of Washington is coextensive with the District of Columbia.
Size: 69 sq. mi. (177 sq. km)
Population: 604,000
Became seat of the federal government: June 10, 1800
Number of U.S. Congressional Districts: 1 At Large
Number of Registered Voters: 308,105

DISTRICT OF COLUMBIA,
Continued
Number of Democrats: 233,313 (76%)
Number of Republicans: 26,677 (9%)
Number of unaffiliated and minor parties: 48,115 (16%)

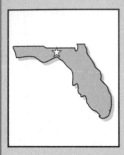

FLORIDA

In his search for the "Fountain of Youth," Ponce de Leon named this region "flowery Easter" or "feast of flowers" on Easter Sunday, 1513.

Capital: Tallahassee
Size: 58,644 sq. mi. (150,180 sq. km)
Population: 13,003,362
Order admitted: 27
Date admitted: March 3, 1845
Number of U.S. Congressional Districts: 23
Number of Registered Voters: 6,031,161
Number of Democrats: 3,149,747 (52%)
Number of Republicans: 2,448,488 (41%)
Number of unaffiliated and minor parties: 432,926 (7%)

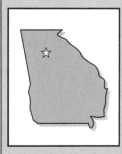

GEORGIA

Named for King George II of England, who granted James Oglethorpe a charter to found the colony of Georgia in 1732.

Capital: Atlanta
Size: 58,910 sq. mi. (150,810 sq. km)
Population: 6,508,419
Order admitted: 4
Date admitted: January 2, 1788
Number of U.S. Congressional Districts: 11
Number of Registered Voters: 2,772,816
No party registration

HAWAII

Commonly believed to be an English adaptation of the native word for "homeland," hawaiki or owhyhee.

Capital: Honolulu
Size: 6,471 sq. mi. (16,566 sq. km)
Population: 1,115,274
Order admitted: 50
Date admitted: August 21, 1959
Number of U.S. Congressional Districts: 2
Number of Registered Voters: 453,389
No party registration

IDAHO

A named coined by the state meaning "gem of the mountains" or "light on the mountains." Originally the name Idaho was to be used for the Pike's Peak mining territory in Colorado, and later for the mining territory of the Pacific Northwest. Others believe the name derives from the Kiowa Apache word for the Comanche.

Capital: Boise
Size: 83,564 sq. mi. (213,924 sq. km)
Population: 1,011,986
Order admitted: 43
Date admitted: July 3, 1890
Number of U.S. Congressional Districts: 2
Number of Registered Voters: 540,247
No party registration

ILLINOIS

From the French version of the Algonquin word meaning "men" or "soldiers," Illini.

Capital: Springfield
Size: 57,871 sq. mi. (148,150 sq. km)
Population: 11,466,682
Order admitted: 21
Date admitted: December 3, 1818
Number of U.S. Congressional Districts: 20
Number of Registered Voters: 6,031,858
  No party registration

INDIANA

English-speaking settlers named the territory to mean "land of the Indians."

Capital: Indianapolis
Size: 36,413 sq. mi. (93,217 sq. km)
Population: 5,564,228
Order admitted: 19
Date admitted: December 11, 1816
Number of U.S. Congressional Districts: 10
Number of Registered Voters: 2,764,768
  No party registration

IOWA

The Sioux word for "one who puts to sleep" or "beautiful land."

Capital: Des Moines
Size: 56,275 sq. mi. (144,064 sq. km)
Population: 2,787,424
Order admitted: 29
Date admitted: December 28, 1846
Number of U.S. Congressional Districts: 5
Number of Registered Voters: 1,580,160
  Number of Democrats: 599,704 (38%)

Number of Republicans: 496,193 (31%)
Number of unaffiliated and minor parties: 484,263
  (31%)

KANSAS

Derived from the Sioux word for those who lived south (the "south wind people") of their territory, which was mainly Wisconsin, Iowa, Minnesota, and North and South Dakota.

Capital: Topeka
Size: 82,277 sq. mi. (210,629 sq. km)
Population: 2,485,600
Order admitted: 34
Date admitted: January 29, 1861
Number of U.S. Congressional Districts: 4
Number of Registered Voters: 1,204,574
  Number of Democrats: 358,331 (30%)
  Number of Republicans: 530,628 (44%)
  Number of unaffiliated and minor parties: 315,615
  (26%)

KENTUCKY

Originally the term for the Kentucky Plains in Clark County, Kentucky is believed to derive from the Indian word meaning "dark and bloody ground," "meadow land," or "land of tomorrow."

Capital: Frankfort
Size: 40,409 sq. mi. (103,447 sq. km)
Population: 3,698,969
Order admitted: 15
Date admitted: June 1, 1792
Number of U.S. Congressional Districts: 6
Number of Registered Voters: 1,854,315
  Number of Democrats: 1,249,312 (67%)
  Number of Republicans: 547,932 (30%)
  Number of unaffiliated and minor parties: 57,071
  (3%)

LOUISIANA

Present-day Louisiana is just a fraction of the territory that was named for the French King Louis XIV by Sieur de La Salle.

Capital: Baton Rouge
Size: 47,752 sq. mi. (122,245 sq. km)
Population: 4,238,216
Order admitted: 18
Date admitted: April 30, 1812
Number of U.S. Congressional Districts: 7
Number of Registered Voters: 2,169,099
  Number of Democrats: 1,605,967 (74%)
  Number of Republicans: 385,422 (18%)
  Number of unaffiliated and minor parties: 177,710
   (8%)

MAINE

Originally a French territory, Maine was the ancient French word for "province." It is also believed that it refers to the mainland, as distinct from the many islands off the state's coast.

Capital: Augusta
Size: 33,265 sq. mi. (85,158 sq. km)
Population: 1,233,223
Order admitted: 23
Date admitted: March 15, 1820
Number of U.S. Congressional Districts: 2
Number of Registered Voters: 824,658
  Number of Democrats: 272,089 (33%)
  Number of Republicans: 246,277 (30%)
  Number of unaffiliated and minor parties: 306,292
   (37%)

MARYLAND

Named for Queen Henrietta Maria, wife of Charles I of England.

Capital: Annapolis
Size: 10,460 sq. mi. (26,778 sq. km)
Population: 4,798,622
Order admitted: 7
Date admitted: April 28, 1788
Number of U.S. Congressional Districts: 8
Number of Registered Voters: 2,123,209
  Number of Democrats: 1,341,857 (63%)
  Number of Republicans: 613,714 (29%)
  Number of unaffiliated and minor parties: 167,638
   (8%)

MASSACHUSETTS

The name of the Indian tribe that lived near Milton, Massachusetts, meaning "large hill place."

Capital: Boston
Size: 8,284 sq. mi. (21,207 sq. km)
Population: 6,029,051
Order admitted: 6
Date admitted: February 6, 1788
Number of U.S. Congressional Districts: 10
Number of Registered Voters: 3,213,763
  Number of Democrats: 1,342,239 (42%)
  Number of Republicans: 441,982 (14%)
  Number of unaffiliated and minor parties: 1,429,582
   (44%)

MICHIGAN

Believed to be from the Chippewa word micigama, *meaning "great water," after Lake Michigan, although Alouet defined it in 1672 as designating a clearing.*

Capital: Lansing
Size: 58,527 sq. mi. (151,584 sq. km)
Population: 9,328,784
Order admitted: 26
Date admitted: January 26, 1837
Number of U.S. Congressional Districts: 16
Number of Registered Voters: 5,892,001
  No party registration

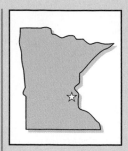

MINNESOTA

*Named from the Sioux descrip-
tion of the Minnesota River,
"sky-tinted water" or "muddy
water."*

Capital: Saint Paul
Size: 86,614 sq. mi. (221,732 sq. km)
Population: 4,387,029
Order admitted: 32
Date admitted: May 11, 1858
Number of U.S. Congressional Districts: 8
Number of Registered Voters: 2,830,649
   No party registration

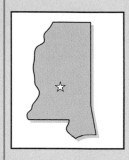

MISSISSIPPI

*Most likely derived from the
Chippewa words* mici *(great)
and* zibi *(river), it was first written by La Salle's lieutenant
Henri de Tonti as "Michi Sepe."*

Capital: Jackson
Size: 47,689 sq. mi. (122,084 sq. km)
Population: 2,586,443
Order admitted: 20
Date admitted: December 10, 1817
Number of U.S. Congressional Districts: 5
Number of Registered Voters: 1,592,992
   No party registration

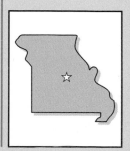

MISSOURI

*Meaning "muddy water," this
state is named after an Algonquin Indian tribe.*

Capital: Jefferson City
Size: 69,697 sq. mi. (178,424 sq. km)
Population: 5,137,804
Order admitted: 24
Date admitted: August 10, 1821
Number of U.S. Congressional Districts: 9
Number of Registered Voters: 2,747,000
   No party registration

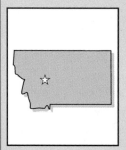

MONTANA

*Derived from the Latin word
meaning "mountainous."*

Capital: Helena
Size: 147,046 sq. mi. (376,438 sq. km)
Population: 803,655
Order admitted: 41
Date admitted: November 8, 1889
Number of U.S. Congressional Districts: 1
Number of Registered Voters: 435,900
   No party registration

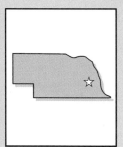

NEBRASKA

Descriptive of the Platte River,
Nebraska *is from the Omaha or
Otos Indian word for "broad
water" or "flat river."*

Capital: Lincoln
Size: 77,355 sq. mi. (198,029 sq. km)
Population: 1,584,617
Order admitted: 37
Date admitted: March 1, 1867
Number of U.S. Congressional Districts: 3
Number of Registered Voters: 890,579
   Number of Democrats: 374,023 (42%)
   Number of Republicans: 449,335 (50%)
   Number of unaffiliated and minor parties: 67,221
      (8%)

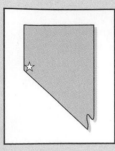

NEVADA

Spanish word meaning "snow-clad."

Capital: Carson City
Size: 110,561 sq. mi. (283,036 sq. km)
Population: 1,206,152
Order admitted: 36
Date admitted: October 31, 1864
Number of U.S. Congressional Districts: 2
Number of Registered Voters: 364,965
  Number of Democrats: 166,497 (46%)
  Number of Republicans: 160,930 (44%)
  Number of unaffiliated and minor parties: 37,537
   (10%)

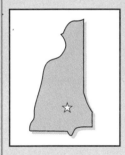

NEW HAMPSHIRE

Captain John Mason named this colony for his home county in England in 1629.

Capital: Concord
Size: 9,279 sq. mi. (23,754 sq. km)
Population: 1,113,915
Order admitted: 9
Date admitted: June 21, 1788
Number of U.S. Congressional Districts: 2
Number of Registered Voters: 658,716
  Number of Democrats: 192,217 (29%)
  Number of Republicans: 253,972 (39%)
  Number of unaffiliated and minor parties: 202,527
   (31%)

NEW JERSEY

Named after the Isle of Jersey in England by John Berkeley and Sir George Carteret.

Capital: Trenton
Size: 7,787 sq. mi. (19,935 sq. km)
Population: 7,748,634
Order admitted: 3
Date admitted: December 18, 1787
Number of U.S. Congressional Districts: 13
Number of Registered Voters: 3,705,175
  Number of Democrats: 1,199,098 (32%)
  Number of Republicans: 787,822 (21%)
  Number of unaffiliated and minor parties: 1,718,255
   (46%)

NEW MEXICO

Named by the Spanish for the territory north and west of the Rio Grande.

Capital: Santa Fe
Size: 121,593 sq. mi. (311,278 sq. km)
Population: 1,521,779
Order admitted: 47
Date admitted: January 6, 1912
Number of U.S. Congressional Districts: 3
Number of Registered Voters: 658,374
  Number of Democrats: 387,441 (59%)
  Number of Republicans: 233,616 (35%)
  Number of unaffiliated and minor parties: 37,317
   (6%)

NEW YORK

Originally named New Netherland, New York was later named after the Duke of York and Albany, who received a patent to the region from his brother Charles II of England and captured it from the Dutch in 1664.

Capital: Albany
Size: 52,735 sq. mi. (135,002 sq. km)
Population: 18,044,505
Order admitted: 11
Date admitted: July 26, 1788
Number of U.S. Congressional Districts: 31
Number of Registered Voters: 8,201,532

Number of Democrats: 3,884,984 (47%)
Number of Republicans: 2,620,288 (32%)
Number of unaffiliated and minor parties: 1,696,260
   (21%)

NORTH CAROLINA

From the Latin name Carolus,
*meaning "Charles." The colony
was originally given to Sir
Robert Heath by Charles I and
was to be called Province of
Carolana. Carolana was divided
into North and South Carolina
in 1710.*

Capital: Raleigh
Size: 52,669 sq. mi. (134,833 sq. km)
Population: 6,657,630
Order admitted: 12
Date admitted: November 21, 1789
Number of U.S. Congressional Districts: 12
Number of Registered Voters: 3,347,635
   Number of Democrats: 2,132,379 (64%)
   Number of Republicans: 1,029,892 (31%)
   Number of unaffiliated and minor parties: 185,364
      (6%)

NORTH DAKOTA

*From the Sioux word meaning
"friend" or "ally."*

Capital: Bismarck
Size: 70,702 sq. mi. (180,997 sq. km)
Population: 641,364
Order admitted: 39
Date admitted: November 2, 1889
Number of U.S. Congressional Districts: 1 At Large
Number of Registered Voters: No state voter
   registration

OHIO

*From an Iroquois Indian word
variously meaning "great,"
"fine," or "good river."*

Capital: Columbus
Size: 44,787 sq. mi. (114,655 sq. km)
Population: 10,887,325
Order admitted: 17
Date admitted: March 1, 1803
Number of U.S. Congressional Districts: 19
Number of Registered Voters: 5,833,653
   Number of Democrats: 1,879,405 (32%)
   Number of Republicans: 1,270,446 (22%)
   Number of unaffiliated and minor parties: 2,683,802
      (46%)

OKLAHOMA

*The Choctaw Indian word mean-
ing "red man," which was
coined by the Reverend Allen
Wright, a Choctaw-speaking
Indian.*

Capital: Oklahoma City
Size: 69,956 sq. mi. (179,087 sq. km)
Population: 3,157,604
Order admitted: 46
Date admitted: November 16, 1907
Number of U.S. Congressional Districts: 6
Number of Registered Voters: 2,010,684
   Number of Democrats: 1,305,291 (65%)
   Number of Republicans: 656,714 (33%)
   Number of unaffiliated and minor parties: 48,697
      (2%)

OREGON

*One theory maintains that it may
have been a variation on the
name of the Wisconsin River,
called* Ouaricon-sint *on a French
map dated 1715. Later, Major*

OREGON, *Continued*

Robert Rogers named a river "called by the Indians Ouragon" in his request to seek a Northwest Passage. Another theory derives the word from the Algonquin wauregan, *meaning "beautiful water."*

Capital: Salem
Size: 97,073 sq. mi. (248,507 sq. km)
Population: 2,853,733
Order admitted: 33
Date admitted: February 14, 1859
Number of U.S. Congressional Districts: 5
Number of Registered Voters: 1,476,500
   Number of Democrats: 692,100 (47%)
   Number of Republicans: 570,933 (39%)
   Number of unaffiliated and minor parties: 213,467
      (14%)

PENNSYLVANIA

Named after the colony's founder, the Quaker William Penn. The literal translation is "Penn's woods."

Capital: Harrisburg
Size: 46,043 sq. mi. (118, 870 sq. km)
Population: 11,924,710
Order admitted: 2
Date admitted: December 12, 1787
Number of U.S. Congressional Districts: 21
Number of Registered Voters: 5,659,189
   Number of Democrats: 2,907,156 (51%)
   Number of Republicans: 2,476,222 (44%)
   Number of unaffiliated and minor parties: 275,811
      (5%)

RHODE ISLAND

Possibly named by Giovanni de Verrazano, who charted an island about the size of an island of the same name in the Mediterranean. Another theory suggests Rhode Island was named Roode Eylandt by Dutch explorer Adrian Block because of its red clay.

Capital: Providence
Size: 1,212 sq. mi. (3,103 sq. km)
Population: 1,005,984
Order admitted: 13
Date admitted: May 29, 1790
Number of U.S. Congressional Districts: 2
Number of Registered Voters: 536,773
   No party registration

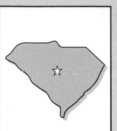

SOUTH CAROLINA

See *North Carolina.*

Capital: Columbia
Size: 31,113 sq. mi. (79,649 sq. km)
Population: 3,505,707
Order admitted: 8
Date admitted: May 23, 1788
Number of U.S. Congressional Districts: 6
Number of Registered Voters: 1,360,082
   No party registration

SOUTH DAKOTA

See *North Dakota.*

Capital: Pierre
Size: 77,116 sq. mi. (197,417 sq. km)
Population: 699,999
Order admitted: 40
Date admitted: November 2, 1889
Number of U.S. Congressional Districts: 1 At Large
Number of Registered Voters: 420,351
   Number of Democrats: 180,181 (43%)
   Number of Republicans: 207,036 (49%)
   Number of unaffiliated and minor parties: 33,134
      (8%)

TENNESSEE

The state of Franklin, or Frankland, from 1784 to 1788, it was finally named after the Cherokee villages called tanasi *on the Little Tennessee River.*

Capital: Nashville
Size: 42,144 sq. mi. (107,889 sq. km)
Population: 4,896,641
Order admitted: 16
Date admitted: June 1, 1796
Number of U.S. Congressional Districts: 9 At Large
Number of Registered Voters: 2,460,968
   No party registration

TEXAS

Also written texias, tejas, *and* teysas, Texas *is a variation on the Caddo Indian word for "friend" or "ally."*

Capital: Austin
Size: 266,807 sq. mi. (691,030 sq. km)
Population: 17,059,805
Order admitted: 28
Date admitted: December 29, 1845
Number of U.S. Congressional Districts: 30
Number of Registered Voters: 7,701,499
   No party registration

UTAH

Meaning "upper" or "higher." Utah *is derived from a name used by the Navajos (Utes) to designate a Shoshone tribe.*

Capital: Salt Lake City
Size: 84,899 sq. mi. (217,341 sq. km)

Population: 1,727,784
Order admitted: 45
Date admitted: January 4, 1896
Number of U.S. Congressional Districts: 3
Number of Registered Voters: 780,555
   No party registration

VERMONT

It is believed Samuel de Champlain coined the name from the French words vert *(green) and* mont *(mountain). Later, Dr. Thomas Young proposed this name when the state was formed in 1777.*

Capital: Montpelier
Size: 9,614 sq. mi. (24,612 sq. km)
Population: 564,964
Order admitted: 14
Date admitted: March 4, 1791
Number of U.S. Congressional Districts: 1 At Large
Number of Registered Voters: 350,349
   No party registration

VIRGINIA

Named for the Virgin Queen of England, Queen Elizabeth I, by Sir Walter Raleigh, who first visited its shores in 1584.

Capital: Richmond
Size: 40,767 sq. mi. (104,364 sq. km)
Population: 6,216,568
Order admitted: 10
Date admitted: June 25, 1788
Number of U.S. Congressional Districts: 11
Number of Registered Voters: 2,735,339
   No party registration

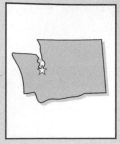

WASHINGTON

Originally named the Territory of Columbia, it was changed to Washington in honor of the first U.S. President because of the already existing District of Columbia.

Capital: Olympia
Size: 68,139 sq. mi. (174,436 sq. km)
Population: 4,887,941
Order admitted: 42
Date admitted: November 11, 1889
Number of U.S. Congressional Districts: 9
Number of Registered Voters: 2,225,101
   No party registration

WEST VIRGINIA

Named when this area refused to secede from the Union in 1863.

Capital: Charleston
Size: 24,231 sq. mi. (62,031 sq. km)
Population: 1,801,625
Order admitted: 35
Date admitted: June 20, 1863
Number of U.S. Congressional Districts: 3
Number of Registered Voters: 884,839
   Number of Democrats: 585,755 (66%)
   Number of Republicans: 275,556 (31%)
   Number of unaffiliated and minor parties: 23,528
     (3%)

WISCONSIN

A Chippewa word that was spelled Ouisconsin and Mesconsing by early explorers. Wisconsin was formally named by Congress when it became a state.

Capital: Madison
Size: 56,153 sq. mi. (145,436 sq. km)
Population: 4,906,745
Order admitted: 30
Date admitted: May 29, 1848
Number of U.S. Congressional Districts: 9
Number of Registered Voters: No state voter
   registration

WYOMING

The Algonquin word meaning "large prairie place," the name was adopted from Wyoming Valley, Pennsylvania, the site of an Indian massacre. It was widely known from Thomas Campbell's poem "Gertrude of Wyoming."

Capital: Cheyenne
Size: 97,809 sq. mi. (250,391 sq. km)
Population: 455,975
Order admitted: 44
Date admitted: July 10, 1890
Number of U.S. Congressional Districts: 1 At Large
Number of Registered Voters: 222,331
   Number of Democrats: 77,140 (35%)
   Number of Republicans: 125,900 (57%)
   Number of unaffiliated and minor parties: 19,291
     (9%)

MAP OF THE UNITED STATES

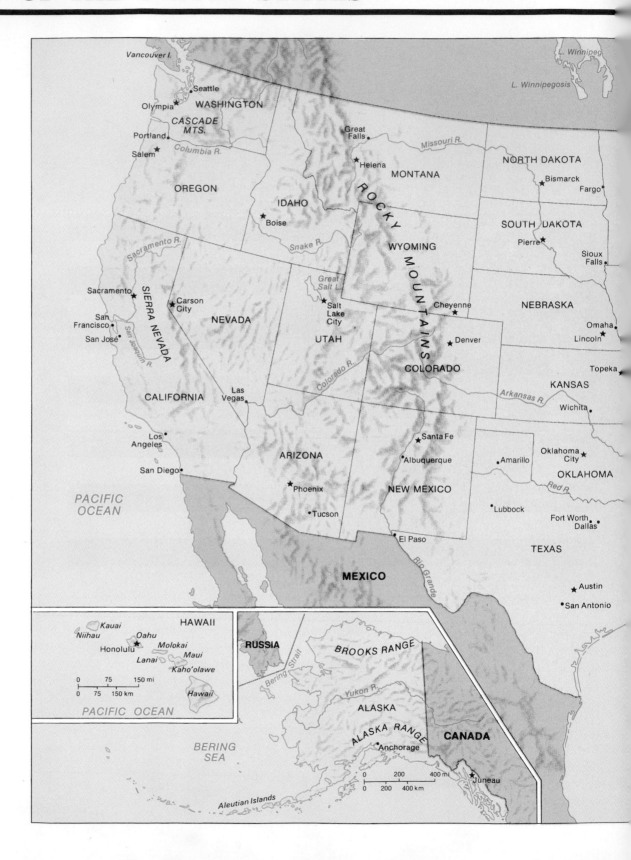

Vancouver I.

L. Winnipeg

L. Winnipegosis

Seattle

Olympia ★

WASHINGTON

CASCADE MTS.

Great Falls

Missouri R.

Portland

Columbia R.

Salem ★

Helena

MONTANA

NORTH DAKOTA

Bismarck ★

Fargo

OREGON

IDAHO

Boise ★

ROCKY

SOUTH DAKOTA

Pierre ★

Sioux Falls

Snake R.

WYOMING

Sacramento ★

SIERRA NEVADA

Carson City ★

NEVADA

Great Salt L.

Salt Lake City ★

MOUNTAINS

Cheyenne ★

NEBRASKA

San Francisco

UTAH

Denver

Omaha

Lincoln

San José

San Joaquin R.

COLORADO

Topeka ★

CALIFORNIA

Las Vegas

Colorado R.

Arkansas R.

KANSAS

Wichita

Los Angeles

Santa Fe ★

Oklahoma City ★

San Diego

ARIZONA

Albuquerque

NEW MEXICO

Amarillo

OKLAHOMA

PACIFIC OCEAN

Phoenix ★

Lubbock

Red R.

Fort Worth

Dallas

Tucson

MEXICO

El Paso

Rio Grande

TEXAS

Austin ★

San Antonio

HAWAII

Kauai

Niihau

Oahu

Honolulu ★

Molokai

Maui

Lanai

Kaho'olawe

RUSSIA

BROOKS RANGE

Bering Strait

Yukon R.

0   75   150 mi

0   75   150 km

Hawaii

ALASKA

PACIFIC OCEAN

ALASKA RANGE

CANADA

BERING SEA

Anchorage

0   200   400 mi

0   200   400 km

Juneau

Aleutian Islands

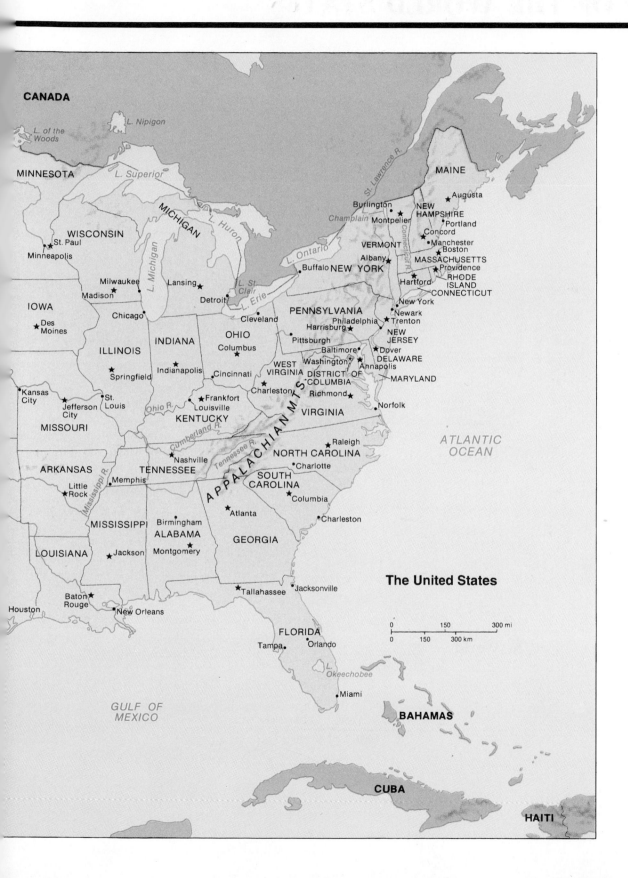

The United States

CANADA

MINNESOTA

L. of the
Woods

L. Nipigon

L. Superior

WISCONSIN

St. Paul

Minneapolis

MICHIGAN

L. Huron

L. Michigan

MAINE

Augusta

Burlington

Montpelier

NEW
HAMPSHIRE

Portland

Concord

Champlain

VERMONT

Manchester

Boston

MASSACHUSETTS

Albany

Providence

RHODE
ISLAND

L. Ontario

Buffalo

NEW YORK

Hartford

CONNECTICUT

IOWA

Des
Moines

Milwaukee

Madison

Lansing

Detroit

L. St.
Clair

L. Erie

Cleveland

PENNSYLVANIA

New York

Newark

Trenton

Chicago

ILLINOIS

INDIANA

OHIO

Columbus

Harrisburg

Philadelphia

Pittsburgh

NEW
JERSEY

Springfield

Indianapolis

Cincinnati

Baltimore

Dover

DELAWARE

Washington

Annapolis

Kansas
City

Jefferson
City

St.
Louis

Frankfort

Louisville

Ohio R.

WEST
VIRGINIA

DISTRICT OF
COLUMBIA

Richmond

MARYLAND

MISSOURI

KENTUCKY

Charleston

VIRGINIA

Norfolk

Cumberland R.

Tennessee R.

Raleigh

ATLANTIC
OCEAN

ARKANSAS

Nashville

TENNESSEE

NORTH CAROLINA

Charlotte

Mississippi R.

Little
Rock

Memphis

SOUTH
CAROLINA

Columbia

APPALACHIAN MTS.

Atlanta

Charleston

MISSISSIPPI

Birmingham

ALABAMA

GEORGIA

LOUISIANA

Jackson

Montgomery

Houston

Baton
Rouge

New Orleans

Tallahassee

Jacksonville

The United States

FLORIDA

Tampa

Orlando

0   150   300 mi

0   150   300 km

L.
Okeechobee

GULF OF
MEXICO

Miami

BAHAMAS

CUBA

HAITI

MAP OF THE WORLD

The World

0   1,000   2,000 Miles

0   1,000   2,000 Kilometers

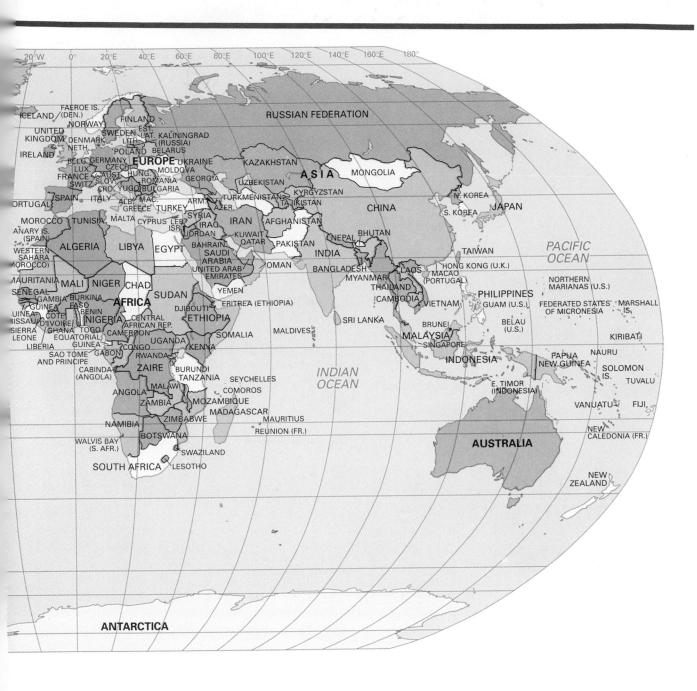

ALB.	–ALBANIA	EST.	–ESTONIA	SLOV. –SLOVENIA
ARM.	–ARMENIA	ISR.	–ISRAEL	(S. AFR.) –SOUTH AFRICAN
AUST.	–AUSTRIA	LAT.	–LATVIA	SWITZ. –SWITZERLAND
AZER.	–AZERBAIJAN	LEB.	–LEBANON	(U.K.) –BRITISH
BELG.	–BELGIUM	LITH.	–LITHUANIA	YUGO. –YUGOSLAVIA
CRO.	–CROATIA	LUX.	–LUXEMBOURG	
CZECH.	–CZECHOSLOVAKIA	MAC.	–MACEDONIA	
(DEN.)	–DANISH	NETH.	–NETHERLANDS	

GLOSSARY

ability-to-pay principle A taxation principle under which those with higher incomes pay more in taxes than those with lower incomes, regardless of the number of government services they use.

abridging Depriving or diminishing.

absentee ballot A vote that is mailed in by the voter, rather than cast at the polls.

absolute monarchs Monarchs who have complete and unlimited power. (Compare with *constitutional monarchs*.)

absolute monarchy A government in which rulers hold complete and unlimited power.

acid rain Rain that contains a high concentration of acid-forming chemicals, usually caused by pollution from industrial smokestacks being released into the atmosphere and combining with water vapor.

acquittal The delivery of a defendant from a criminal charge usually by a verdict of not guilty.

act of admissions A bill passed by Congress that admits a state into the Union.

administrative assistant A person hired to manage a lawmaker's office, supervise his or her schedule, and give advice. (Administrative assistants also work for other types of professionals.)

administrative councils Local government units in Great Britain.

affirmative action Job hiring policies that allow special considerations for traditionally disadvantaged groups (such as women or racial minorities) in an effort to overcome the present effects of past discrimination.

agenda A list or program of goals to be accomplished. In government, agenda setting usually involves deciding which public policy questions will be debated, considered, or carried out.

agents of political socialization Groups of people who influence the political opinions of others.

Aid to Families with Dependent Children (AFDC) A social program, funded in part by the federal government and administered by the state, that provides financial assistance to impoverished families with children.

alien One who is not a citizen of the state or nation in which she or he lives.

allegiance Loyalty and service to one's country and government.

alliance Association of two or more nations joined together for mutual benefit.

ambassador A diplomat of high rank who represents his or her government to a foreign country.

amendments Written changes or additions to a law or body of laws, such as the United States Constitution.

American's Creed The principles set forth in the Declaration of Independence, which include natural rights, limited government, equality under the law, and government by consent of the governed.

amnesty A governmental grant of pardon to a large group of individuals.

Anti-Federalists A political group that opposed the adoption of the Constitution because of the document's centralist tendencies and that attacked the framers of the Constitution for failing to include a bill of rights.

appellate courts Courts that review decisions reached by lower (usually trial) courts.

appellate jurisdiction Authority of a court to review decisions reached by lower courts.

apportionment Distribution and assignment of seats in a legislative body among electoral districts; the assignment, based on state population, of the 435 seats of the U.S. House of Representatives.

appropriation The authorization of money for a specific purpose; money approved by the legislature as funding for the activities of another branch of government.

appropriation bill A bill that formally sets aside money for a specific purpose.

armistice A temporary agreement between opponents to stop fighting (also called a *cease-fire*).

arraignment A preliminary court proceeding in which the defendant hears the charges and enters his or her plea.

assembly A gathering of people for a common purpose.

at large The election of an official by the voters of an entire governmental unit such as a state or county, rather than by voters of a subdivision of that area.

attaché Member of an embassy staff who serves in a particular capacity.

attorney general Head of the Department of Justice who is appointed by the president and is a member of the president's cabinet.

auditor One who examines records or accounts to check their accuracy.

Australian ballot A secret ballot that is prepared, distributed, and tabulated by government officials at public expense. The method was introduced to the United States from Australia in 1888 and replaced an open ballot.

authoritarian A concentration of power in a leader who is not constitutionally responsible to the people.

authority The power to influence thought, opinion, and behavior. (Legal authority can be defined as the power to make and enforce laws.)

autocracy A government in which the power and authority is in the hands of a single person.

bad-tendency rule The doctrine holding that speech, religious practice, or other First Amendment freedoms may be permissibly curtailed if such expressions might lead to some "evil."

bail Money that a prisoner may be required to deposit with a court to obtain his or her release and to guarantee that he or she will appear in court at a designated time.

balance the ticket A method by which a presidential candidate chooses a vice presidential candidate who possesses complementary characteristics and thus improves the chances of winning an election.

ballot A printed voting form.

bandwagon effect A propaganda technique that attempts to persuade people to support a candidate or issue because large numbers of other people are supposedly doing so.

bankruptcy The state of being legally unable to pay debts.

bench trial A trial before a judge, without a jury.

benefits-received principle A system of taxation in which those who use a particular government service support it with taxes in proportion to the benefits they receive from it.

biased sample A polling sample that does not accurately represent the population.

bicameral legislature A legislature made up of two chambers or parts. The United States has a bicameral legislature, composed of the House of Representatives and the Senate. (Compare with *unicameral legislature.*)

biennially An event that occurs once every two years.

bills Proposed laws.

bills of attainder Legislative acts that inflict punishment on particular persons or groups without granting them the right to a trial.

blanket primary A primary in which all candidates' names are printed on the same ballot, regardless of party affiliation. In a blanket primary, voters may choose candidates from more than one party.

block grants A type of funding program in which the federal government gives money to state and local governments to use in broadly defined areas of public policy, such as criminal justice or mental health.

boroughs Administrative subunits of a city. In Alaska, a borough is the equivalent of a county.

boycott An organized refusal by consumers to buy specific goods, usually in protest against certain conditions of production or manufacturing.

budget Spending plan for government submitted by the president to Congress in January of each year.

budget deficit When the federal government spends more than it receives.

burden of proof The obligation that rests with the prosecution to prove whether a defendant is guilty of a crime.

bureaucracy A large organization that is structured hierarchically to carry out specific functions.

bureaucrats Those employed by bureaucracies.

business cycle A cycle of economic activity consisting of recession, recovery, growth, and decline.

busing (for integration) A system of transporting public school students from the neighborhoods where they live to schools in other areas. The aim of busing is to eliminate school segregation based on residential patterns.

cabinet An advisory group selected by the president to assist with decision making. A cabinet is traditionally composed of the heads of the executive departments and other officers whom the president may choose to appoint.

calendar A schedule of the order in which bills will be taken up by committee or on the floor.

Calendar of General Orders A schedule that lists bills to be considered by a legislative body, such as the Senate.

campaign manager An individual hired by a candidate to be in charge of the candidate's election campaign.

canvasses The door-to-door solicitations of votes or survey of public opinion throughout a specific area.

capital Any kind of property (such as machines, buildings, tools, or money) used to produce other goods and services.

capital cases Criminal cases in which the sentence might involve the death penalty.

capitalism An economic system in which the individuals own the factors of production and have the right to use those resources in any way they choose within the limits of the law (also called a *market system* or a *free enterprise system*).

card stacking A propaganda technique that emphasizes all the favorable arguments supporting an issue or candidate but does not address the negative arguments.

case law A history of cases that, when taken together, form precedents for later judicial decisions.

casework A form of social work in which members of Congress directly involve themselves in the problems and needs of individual citizens.

caseworkers Members of congressional staffs who manage the numerous requests for help from constituents.

categorical grants Federal grants-in-aid to states or local governments for use on very specific programs or projects.

caucuses Closed meetings of party leaders to select party candidates or decide on policy.

cease-fire See *armistice.*

censorship The suppression of material (such as books, plays, music, and so on) deemed objectionable on moral, political, or other grounds.

censure An official reprimand of a legislator by his or her peers.

census An official count of the population of a city, state, or nation. A census is performed for the whole United States every ten years.

chancellors Judges in colonial times who resolved judicial disputes on the basis of fairness rather than on specific laws.

chargé d'affaires Member of an embassy who ranks below the ambassador and who may temporarily assume the duties of the ambassador.

charter A document issued by a government that grants rights to a person, group of persons, or a corporation to carry on a certain activity.

checks and balances A major principle of American government in which each of the three branches is given the means to check (to restrain or balance) the actions of the others.

chief administrator plan A plan for county government in which a chief administrative officer shares responsibilities in certain key areas with the county board or with other individuals.

chief diplomat The role of the president in recognizing and interacting with foreign governments.

chief executive Head of the executive branch of government.

chief of staff The person who directs the president's office in the White House and serves as presidential adviser.

city manager An official appointed by an elected city council to administer city government.

civil disobedience The activity of nonviolent protest used to draw attention to certain laws and issues.

civil law The body of laws that regulate disputes between private citizens over noncriminal matters, such as contractual agreements, domestic relations, and business practices.

civil liberties Individual rights protected by the Constitution against the powers of the government.

civil rights Constitutionally guaranteed rights and freedoms of Americans.

civil rights movement A political and social movement that began in the 1950s and organized blacks, whites, and people of other races to end the policies of segregation. It sought to establish equal opportunities in the political and economic sectors and to end policies that erected barriers against people because of race.

civil service The term used for the system governing the civilian employees of the government and generally for those who obtained employment through the merit system.

Civil Service Commission The central personnel agency of the federal government.

civil service examination An employment examination given as part of the civil service system to ensure that government jobs go only to qualified people.

clear and present danger The rule or test, first proposed by Justice Oliver Wendell Holmes, which holds that free speech cannot be limited unless it clearly endangers the society the government is designed to protect.

clemency proceedings Proceedings in which a governor may grant a pardon or reprieve for those convicted of a crime.

clerk of the House A non-member staff officer of the House of Representatives.

closed primaries The most widely used primary system, in which voters may only nominate candidates from the party with which they are registered.

cloture A limiting of debate by a legislature in order to get an immediate vote on the question being discussed.

cloture rule A Senate rule that imposes a one-hour limit on the amount of time a senator may speak about a bill or issue.

coalitions Alliances of political groups that cooperate to gain a majority vote.

coattail effect The influence a popular or unpopular candidate for top office can have on voter support of other candidates of the same party.

Cold War The ideological, political, and economic impasse that existed between the United States and the Soviet Union after World War II.

collective security The policy of forming international defense alliances to increase the security of each member nation.

colonial empire A group of colonized nations held under the rule of a single imperial power.

command economic system An economic system in which the government controls the factors of production and makes all decisions about their use.

commerce clause The section of the Constitution that grants Congress the power to regulate trade among the states and with foreign countries.

commercial speech Advertising statements that describe products; have some degree of First Amendment protection.

commission plan A plan for municipal government that consists of a commission of three to nine members who have both legislative and executive powers.

committee of the whole A procedure that the House of Representatives uses to expedite its business by creating itself into one large committee.

common law A body of law that originated in England in which individual judges decided cases in accordance with prevailing customs. As similar decisions were applied to similar cases, a legal standard developed for the nation. Common law forms the basis of the American legal system.

common law marriage When a man and a woman continuously live together as husband and wife for a certain period of time, such as seven years, they are considered to have entered into a common law marriage which is treated the same as all other marriages.

communism Economic and political system based on the theories of Karl Marx. In such a system, the entire economy is based on collective ownership and government control of property and the means of production. Individuals are expected to contribute to the economy according to their ability and are given income according to their needs. Also an economic and political system implemented in countries such as China and, until recently, the Soviet Union, in which the state controls the production and distribution of goods and the government is directed by a single authoritarian leader or party.

Communist bloc A group of countries that fell under Soviet rule after World War II.

commute To reduce a criminal sentence imposed by a court of law.

competition Rivalry among producers or sellers of similar goods to increase sales and profits.

comptroller (also controller) An officer who audits accounts and supervises the financial affairs of a corporation or governmental body.

concurrent jurisdiction A sharing of legal authority between federal and state courts.

concurrent majority A principle advanced by John C. Calhoun that states that democratic decisions should be made only with the agreement of all segments of society affected by the decision. Without their agreement, a decision should not be binding on those whose interests it violates.

concurrent powers Powers held by both the federal and state governments in a federal system.

concurrent resolutions Congressional measures that deal with matters requiring the action of the House and Senate, but for which a law is not needed. They are intended to express an opinion or an official policy. Concurrent resolutions must be passed by both chambers of Congress, but do not require the president's signature and do not have the force of law.

concurring opinion A statement written by a justice who agrees (concurs) with the court's decision, but for reasons different from the majority opinion.

confederal system A league of independent sovereign states, joined together by a central government that has only limited powers over them.

confederation A league of independent states that are united only for the purpose of achieving common goals.

conferees Members of a conference committee.

conference committee A special joint committee appointed to reconcile differences when a bill passes the two houses of Congress in different forms.

conference report A report submitted by a conference committee after it has drafted a single version of a bill.

congressional district The geographic area within a state that is served by one representative in Congress.

congressional immunity A privilege set out in the Constitution that guarantees freedom of speech to members while they are conducting congressional business. Protects the freedom of legislative debate.

conscription Compulsory enrollment in the armed services.

consensus General agreement among the citizenry on an issue.

consent Permission and agreement of the governed.

consent of the governed The principle that government is based on the will of the people and as such can be abolished by the people.

conservatives Those with a set of political beliefs that includes a limited role for government, support for traditional values, and preference for the status quo.

consideration That which each party receives of value when signing a contract.

consolidation The joining of two or more governmental units to form one unit.

constituents The voters in a legislator's home district.

constitutional initiative A process that allows citizens to propose a constitutional amendment through petitions signed by a required number of registered voters.

constitutional monarchy A government in which kings or queens share governmental power with elected lawmakers.

consul A member of the American consulate whose job is to promote American business interests in foreign cities.

consulate Office of the consul.

containment A U.S. diplomatic policy first adopted by the Truman administration to keep communist power contained within its existing boundaries and thus "build situations of strength" around the globe.

contempt Disrespect for or willful disobedience of the rules or orders of a court or legislative body.

contempt of Congress Disrespect for or willful disobedience of Congress.

contiguous Adjoining.

controller See *comptroller*.

convening The formal opening of each term of Congress. The Twentieth Amendment of the Constitution reset the date at January 3 of each odd-numbered year unless Congress sets another date.

Cooley's rule Derived from an 1871 decision by Michigan Judge Thomas Cooley, who stated that cities should be able "to rule from the home," that is, to govern themselves instead of being governed by the state government.

cooperative federalism The theory that the states and the federal government should cooperate in solving problems.

copyright The exclusive legal right of a person to publish, reproduce, or sell his or her own literary, musical, or artistic creations.

council-manager plan A plan for municipal government in which an elected city council appoints a professional manager who acts as the chief executive.

Council of Economic Advisors A staff agency in the executive office that advises the president on measures to maintain stability in the nation's economy. The council helps the president prepare an annual economic report for Congress and develops economic plans and budget recommendations for maintaining employment, production, and purchasing power.

councils of governments Voluntary political organizations of counties and municipalities concerned with areawide problems, formed to coordinate multiple governmental units.

counties Governmental units set up by the state to administer state law and business at the local level. Counties are drawn up by area, rather than by rural or urban criteria.

county board The governing body of a county, elected by voters to carry out county business.

county boroughs A local governmental unit in Great Britain.

county-manager plan Plan for county government in which policies are made by an elected body and are carried out by a manager hired by and responsible to that body.

Credentials Committee A committee that convenes at each political party's national convention to inspect the claims of prospective delegates and determine which may participate.

criminal law A body of law that defines crimes and determines punishment for committing them. The government is the prosecutor in criminal cases since crimes are against the public order.

currency power The power granted to Congress by the Constitution to coin money and regulate its value.

death taxes Estate and inheritance taxes levied by the state.

decentralization The shifting of power from the federal government to state and local governments.

de facto **segregation** Racial segregation that occurs not as a result of deliberate intentions but because of previous social and economic conditions and residential patterns.

de jure **segregation** Racial segregation that occurs because of laws or administrative decisions by public agencies.

delegated, expressed, or enumerated powers Those powers directly granted to the federal government by the Constitution as stated in Article I, Section 8.

delegates People who are authorized to speak, vote, or otherwise act on behalf of others. (Representatives from state political parties to a national party convention serve as *delegates* to that convention.)

deliberative organ Deliberates, discusses, and decides important issues.

democracy A system of government in which the people have ultimate political authority. The word is derived from the Greek *demos* (people) and *kratia* (authority).

denaturalization The loss of citizenship through due process of law. Often used for those who used fraud or deception in the naturalization process or for those who are thought to be obstructing the functions of government.

Dennison Rule An 1861 ruling by the U.S. Supreme Court that upheld the right of the governor of Ohio to refuse an extradition request by the governor of Kentucky for a "free man of color" on charges that he had helped a slave escape to freedom.

departments A French term for geographic divisions for the purpose of establishing local governments.

deportation Legal process by which a nation returns aliens to their country of origin.

depressions Major slowdowns of economic activity characterized by high unemployment and business downturns and failures.

détente A French word used to refer to the relaxation of tensions between the United States and the Soviet Union under the administration of President Richard Nixon.

deterrence The United States policy adopted after World War II of using the threat of massive retaliation to discourage aggression by its enemies.

dictatorship A form of government in which absolute power is exercised by a single person who has usually obtained his or her power by the use of force.

Dillon's rule A principle outlined by John F. Dillon's *Commentaries on the Law of Municipal Corporations* (1911), which states that municipal corporations possess only those powers that the states expressly grant to them.

diplomacy The process by which states establish and maintain political relations with each other through such means as treaties, agreements, and alliances.

diplomat A person who carries out the means of diplomacy on behalf of his or her native country.

direct democracy A system of government in which political decisions are made by the people themselves rather than by elected representatives. This form of government was widely practiced in ancient Greece.

direct primary An election within a party in which the voters select the candidates who will run on the party ticket in the subsequent general election.

direct tax A tax that must be paid by the person on whom it is levied.

disenfranchise To deprive voters of the ability to vote.

dissenting opinion A statement written by a justice in which he or she dissents from the conclusion reached by the majority of the court. The justice expounds his or her own views about the case.

district attorney An attorney who initiates and conducts legal action on behalf of the state, especially in criminal proceedings.

diversity of citizenship A legal concept that applies to cases arising between citizens of different states, or between a foreign country and citizens of a state or of different states.

divine right theory A theory that the right to rule by a king or a queen was derived directly from God rather than from the consent of the people.

division of powers A basic principle of federalism provided in the U.S. Constitution, by which powers are divided between units of government (such as the federal and state governments), on a geographic basis.

doctrine A particular position, policy, or principle.

doubling time The rate at which a population will double, e.g., every five years or every thirty years.

draft Compulsory service in the military.

draft registration The process by which 18-year-old males are required to present themselves as available for the draft should a draft be enacted.

dual citizenship The condition of being a citizen of two sovereign nations or of both a state and a nation.

dual federalism A system of government in which both the federal and state governments maintain diverse but sovereign powers.

due process clause The constitutional guarantees set out in the Fifth and Fourteenth Amendments to the Constitution that government will not illegally or arbitrarily deprive a person of life, liberty, or property. (Also called **due process of law**.)

economic sanctions Refusal to trade with a foreign nation as a means of expressing disapproval of that nation's political or economic policies.

economic system The way in which a nation uses its resources to satisfy people's needs and wants.

elastic clause Article I, Section 8 of the Constitution, which gives Congress the power to make all laws "necessary and proper" to carry out its functions.

elected chief executive plan A plan for county government in which the executive officer, such as a mayor, is elected directly by the voters and works with the county board.

electoral college The group of electors who are selected by the voters in each state to officially elect the president and vice president. The number of electors in each state is equal to the number of each state's representatives in both houses of Congress.

electoral college system A unique American institution, created by the Constitution, providing for the selection of the president by electors chosen by the state parties, subject to the laws of each state.

electorate All the citizens entitled to vote in a given election.

electors Those individuals chosen early in the presidential election year by state laws and political party apparatus. The electors cast ballots for the president and vice president in order to make the formal selection of president and vice president.

embassy The official residence and offices of an ambassador.

enabling act A law passed by Congress that allows a territory to draw up a constitution and become eligible for statehood.

enemy aliens Citizens of those nations with which the United States is at war.

enumerated powers See *delegated, expressed, or enumerated powers.*

environmental impact statement A statement mandated by the Environmental Policy Act that must show the costs and benefits of federal actions that could significantly affect the quality of the environment.

equal employment opportunity A goal of the 1964 Civil Rights Act to end discrimination based on race, color, religion, sex, or national origin in conditions of employment and to promote employers to foster equal job opportunities.

equalization A method for adjusting the amount of money that a state must supply to receive federal funds, which takes into account the wealth of the state and its ability to tax its citizens.

equal protection clause Clause in the Fourteenth Amendment that forbids any state to deny to any person within its jurisdiction the equal protection of the laws. This is the major constitutional restraint on the power of governments to discriminate against persons because of race, national origin, or sex.

espionage The practice of spying to obtain information about the plans and activities of a foreign power.

establishment clause A part of the First Amendment that prohibits the establishment of a church officially supported by the federal government. It has been applied to prevent government aid to religious schools, prayer in public schools, and the teaching of religious fundamentalist theories of creation (as opposed to scientific theories of evolution).

evolutionary theory A theory that holds that government evolved over time as families first joined together into clans and then into tribes: Out of the tribes a leader emerged, which eventually gave rise to the gradual establishment of government.

excessive entanglement theory A rule applied by the Supreme Court to maintain the separation of church and state. To be constitutional, government aid to religious school groups must meet three requirements: (1) the purpose must be clearly secular; (2) it must neither advance nor inhibit religion; and (3) it must avoid excessive entanglement of government and religion.

excise taxes A tax levied on certain actions, such as the manufacture or sale of certain commodities such as tobacco or liquor within a country.

exclusionary rule The rule that any illegally obtained evidence cannot be used at the court trial of the person from whom the evidence was seized. The rule is based upon the Supreme Court interpretation of the Fourth and Fourteenth Amendments.

exclusive jurisdiction A court's authority to hear cases that fall outside the legal scope of other courts.

executive agreements Binding international agreements made between chiefs of state that do not require legislative sanction.

executive authority A person with strong and wide-reaching administrative powers who oversees the executive branch of a system.

Executive Office of the President (EOP) Nine staff agencies that assist the president in carrying out major duties. Established by President Franklin D. Roosevelt by executive order under the Reorganization Act of 1939.

executive order A rule or regulation issued by a chief executive (such as a president or governor) that has the effect of law.

executive privilege The right of the president (or other officials named by the president) to refuse to appear before, or to withhold information from, a legislative committee on the grounds that revealing the information in question may threaten national security.

expatriation The act of voluntarily renouncing (giving up) citizenship in one's nation of origin.

exports Goods that a nation produces and sells to other nations.

ex post facto Criminal laws that made certain acts a crime and then punished people for committing the acts before the laws were passed. Ex post facto laws are prohibited by the Constitution.

expressed powers See *delegated, expressed, or enumerated powers.*

expulsion The forced removal of a member of Congress for misconduct.

extradition A process by which fugitive suspected criminals are returned to the jurisdiction of the prosecuting state.

extraordinary majority A majority that is greater than 50 percent plus one. The U.S. Constitution, for example, requires extraordinary majorities of two-thirds of the House and Senate for Congress to propose a Constitutional Amendment.

factions Groups or cliques within a larger group.

federal budget The federal government's itemized plan for the expenditure of funds over a certain period of time.

federal government A term that refers to the central or national government, particularly in the United States.

federal question Arises whenever the cause of action of a plaintiff is based at least in part on the United States Constitution, a treaty, or a federal law. Federal questions can be addressed only by the federal judiciary.

Federal Reserve System The central bank of the United States. "The Fed" was established in 1913 and is led by a board of governors.

federal system A form of government in which a written constitution provides for a separation of powers between a central government and several regional governments. This separation is established by an authority superior to both the central and regional governments, such as a written document. In the United States, the division of powers between the federal government and the fifty states is explained by the Constitution.

Federalists Those who favored a strong central government and the new Constitution.

felonies Serious criminal offenses punishable by imprisonment. The penalties range from one year in prison to death.

"fighting words" Words that when uttered by a public speaker are so inflammatory that they could provoke the average listener to violence.

filibuster Unlimited debate to halt action in the Senate.

First Continental Congress The first gathering of delegates from twelve of the thirteen colonies for the purpose of drafting a federal constitution. The Congress was held in Philadelphia in 1774.

fiscal policy The discretionary adjustments of government expenditures and/or taxes in order to achieve national economic goals, such as high employment and price stability.

fiscal year The twelve-month period that is determined for bookkeeping or accounting purposes. The government's fiscal year runs from October 1 through September 30.

food stamps Government-issued coupons that can be used to purchase food.

force theory A theory of the origins of government that holds that when strong persons or groups conquered territories, they forced everyone living in those territories to submit to their will.

foreign policy A nation's political and economic goals with respect to other nations; the techniques and strategies used to achieve those goals.

foreign service The cadre of officials in the State Department who serve in foreign countries.

franchise The legal right to vote. The franchise was extended to African Americans by the Fifteenth Amendment, to women by the Nineteenth Amendment, and to all citizens ages eighteen and over by the Twenty-Sixth Amendment.

franking privilege A privilege that allows members of Congress to send material through the mail by substituting their facsimile signature (frank) for postage.

free enterprise system See *capitalism*.

free exercise clause The provision of the First Amendment that guarantees the free exercise of religion.

fugitive An individual wanted for committing a crime who has fled from prosecution.

full faith and credit clause Article VI, Section I of the Constitution, which requires states to recognize one another's laws and court decisions. It ensures that rights established under deeds, wills, contracts, and other civil documents in one state will be honored by other states.

functional consolidations The cooperation of two or more units of local government in providing services to their inhabitants.

Fundamental Orders of Connecticut America's first written constitution which called for a representative assembly, made up of elected representatives from each town to serve in that assembly and to make laws. It also called for the popular election of a governor and judges.

fundamental rights Those basic rights necessary for the concept of an ordered liberty such as voting and freedom of religion.

fund-raisers Events paid for by candidates staged in order to raise funds for campaign costs.

gag orders Orders issued by judges that restrict publication of news about a trial in progress or a pretrial hearing in order to protect the accused's rights to a fair trial.

gender gap The difference in political opinions between men and women. A term used to describe the difference in the percentages of votes cast for a particular candidate by women and by men. The term was widely used after the 1980 election and brought up again before the 1992 election.

general election Regularly scheduled statewide elections at which voters make the final selection for public office-holders.

general jurisdiction The authority of a court to decide all matters that come before it.

generalization An oversimplification that doesn't hold true in every specific case.

general-law city A city operating under state laws that apply to all local government units of a similar type.

gerrymandering The practice of redrawing legislative district boundary lines to obtain voting advantages for a political party or group.

glittering generalities A propaganda method that uses broad, sweeping statements that sound impressive but have little real meaning.

global warming The gradual increase in average climatic temperatures throughout the world.

government The institutions and processes through which public policies are made for a society.

government bonds Certificates bought by individuals and companies as a means of loaning money to the government. In exchange for borrowing the money, the government promises to repay buyers the full amount of the loan, plus interest, at a later time.

government corporation An agency of government that is run as a business enterprise. Such an agency is established when the activity is primarily commercial, produces revenue, and requires greater flexibility than permitted in most government agencies.

grand jury A jury, consisting of six to twenty-three persons, that hears criminal charges against individuals and determines whether there is enough evidence to justify holding a trial.

grandfather clause A method used by Southern states to exempt whites from state taxes and literacy laws as a means of denying the franchise to black voters. The clause allowed anyone who could prove that his grandfather had voted before 1867 to vote in current elections.

green vote A vote from those who favor stronger laws to protect and preserve the environment.

greenhouse effect The trapping of heat inside the earth's atmosphere, which is a result of pollution caused largely by the burning of fossil fuels and the emission of carbon dioxide.

grievances Complaints.

habeas corpus An order designed to prevent illegal arrests and imprisonments; it demands that a prisoner be brought before the court and that the detaining officer show why the prisoner should not be released.

hereditary peers Members of the British nobility who become so by birth. There are over 700 hereditary peers with titles such as baron, viscount, earl, and duke. These are all members of the House of Lords.

hereditary ruler Someone who rules because he or she is the son or daughter of a previous ruler.

home-rule city A city with a charter that allows local voters to frame, adopt, and amend their own charter.

hopper The wooden box in the House of Representatives into which new bills are dropped.

horizontal federalism The rules laid out in the Constitution that prevent any one state from setting itself apart from the others by, for example, creating its own foreign policy.

House of Commons The lower and more powerful house of Parliament in Great Britain.

House of Lords The upper chamber of Parliament in Great Britain.

House Rules Committee A permanent committee of the House of Representatives that provides the rules under which bills can be considered, debated, and amended.

human rights Term referring to the rights and privileges of all human beings. These rights are stated in the Declaration of Independence as life, liberty, and the pursuit of happiness. They are guaranteed and protected by the Bill of Rights.

hung jury A jury that cannot agree unanimously on a verdict.

hyperpluralism A form of pluralism in which government is so decentralized and authority so fragmented that nothing is accomplished.

ideologues A term applied to individuals whose political opinions are very strong, either at the liberal or conservative extremes.

ideology A set of beliefs about the nature of people and the institutions of government.

illegal aliens Individuals who enter the United States without a legal permit or who enter as tourists and stay longer than their tourist status allows.

image building A process of molding a candidate's image to meet the particular needs of the campaign by using public and private opinion polls and other media-related devices.

immigrants People who move to a new country for the purpose of establishing permanent residency and becoming citizens.

immunity Protection against being brought to trial for certain actions.

impeachment A formal charge brought against a public official for misconduct or wrongdoing in office.

implied powers The powers of the federal government that are implied by the expressed powers in the Constitution, particularly in Article I, Section 8.

impoundment The process by which the president can refuse to spend money that Congress has appropriated for a certain purpose.

incarceration Imprisonment.

income transfer The transfer of income from one group to another, as with the farm program, and the transfer from one generation to another, as occurs in the social security program.

incorporation The process of setting up a city through the granting of a charter by the state.

incorporation theory The view that most of the protections of the Bill of Rights are incorporated into the Fourteenth Amendment's protection against infringement from state governments.

incumbent An official who is presently holding office.

independent executive agencies Federal agencies with a specific function that report directly to the president.

independent regulatory agencies Responsible for a specific type of public policy. Their function is to create and implement rules that regulate private activity and protect the public interest in a particular sector of the economy.

independents Voters who do not regularly identify themselves with a political party or support candidates of a particular party.

indictment A formal finding by a grand jury that there is sufficient evidence against a particular person to warrant a criminal trial.

indirect democracy See *representative democracy.*

indirect tax A tax levied on an individual or business but passed on to another party for payment.

inflation A general increase in prices.

information A statement issued by a prosecutor that there is enough evidence to bring the accused person to trial, without the use of a grand jury.

inherent powers The powers of the federal government which, although not expressly granted by the Constitution, belong to it by virtue of its role as the government of a sovereign state.

initiative A procedure by which voters can propose a change in state and local laws by means of gathering signatures on a petition and submitting it to the legislature for approval.

in-kind subsidies Assistance that is given in forms other than cash, such as food stamps.

institutions Organizations and establishments in a society that are devoted to the promotion of a particular cause. Some of the institutions in our government are the legal system, Congress, and the social welfare system.

intelligence Information gathered about the capabilities and intentions of foreign governments.

interdependence The condition of individuals, organizations, and nations being dependent upon one another.

interest group An organized group of individuals sharing common objectives who actively attempt to influence policy through lobbying, the publication of public opinion polls, and other methods.

interim committees Legislative committees that function between legislative sessions. Such committees study particular issues and report their findings in the next legislative session.

interstate commerce Trade between two or more states.

interstate compact An agreement between two or more states to cooperate on a policy or problem. Minor compacts are made without congressional approval, but any compact that tends to increase the power of the contracting states relative to other states or relative to the federal government generally requires the consent of Congress.

interventionism A political policy of changing or preserving the internal political affairs of foreign nations.

intrastate commerce Trade among different regions in the same state.

iron curtain Described the political boundaries between the democratic countries in Europe and the Soviet-controlled communist countries in Eastern Europe.

iron triangle Term used for a three-way alliance between legislators, bureaucrats, and interest groups to make or preserve policies that benefit their respective individual interests.

isolationism A political policy of noninvolvement in world affairs.

joint committees Legislative committees composed of members from both houses of Congress.

joint resolutions Legal measures, similar to bills, passed by Congress and signed by the president that have the force of law.

judicial activism A doctrine that advocates an active role for the Supreme Court in enforcing the Constitution and in using judicial review. An activist court takes a broad view of the Constitution and involves itself in legislative and executive matters.

judicial circuits The twelve courts that hear appeals from district courts located within their respective circuits.

judicial implementation The process by which court decisions are translated into policy.

judicial restraint A doctrine that holds that the Supreme Court should rarely use its power of judicial review or otherwise intervene in the political process.

judicial review The power of the courts to determine the constitutionality of the actions of the executive, legislative, and judicial branches of government. First established in *Marbury v. Madison* (1803).

junkets Trips by members of Congress to gather information about proposed legislation, such as a new trade bill.

jurisdiction The power of a court to try and decide certain cases.

jury duty The responsibility of all citizens, if called, to serve on a jury for a criminal trial.

jus sanguinis The "law of the blood," as grounds for American citizenship, states that a child born on foreign soil becomes an American citizen at birth if at least one of the parents is a U.S. citizen, and if that citizen has lived in the United States for at least ten years after the age of 14.

jus soli The "law of the soil," as grounds for American citizenship, states that all persons born in the United States are American citizens.

justice court A local court that hears minor civil and criminal cases, performs marriages, and legalizes documents.

justice of the peace A local judicial official who presides over the activities of the justice court.

keynote speaker A person of national renown chosen to speak and rouse enthusiasm at a political party's national convention.

Kitchen Cabinet The name given to a president's unofficial advisors who help him with policy and decisions. The name was coined during Andrew Jackson's presidency.

labor force All individuals over 16 who are working or who are actively looking for a job.

law clerk Recent law school graduates who work for justices by performing much of the research and preliminary drafting necessary for the justices to form an opinion.

law lords Nine members of the House of Lords in Great Britain. They are the equivalent of a British Supreme Court.

legal tender Legitimate currency for trade or purchasing.

legislative assistants Aides to lawmakers who make sure that the lawmakers are well informed about the bills they must deal with.

legislative correspondents Aides to lawmakers who handle their correspondence.

legislative director Aide to lawmakers who directs and manages the lawmaker's staff.

legislative power The authority to make laws.

legislature A government body primarily responsible for the making of laws.

legitimacy The legal authority of the officials, acts, and institutions of government, conferred by the people on the grounds that the government's actions are an appropriate use of power and that the government is a legally constituted authority.

libel Defamation of character in writing.

liberalism A political ideology whose advocates prefer an active government in dealing with human needs, support individual rights and liberties, and place a priority on social needs over military needs.

liberals Those who hold a set of political beliefs that includes the advocacy of active government intervention to improve the welfare of individuals, support for civil rights, and political change.

lieutenant governor A state official who acts as governor should the governor be absent from the state, become disabled, or die. He or she may act as president of the state senate.

life expectancy How many years a certain group of people is expected to live.

limited government A form of government based on the principle that government should perform only the functions that the people have given it the power to perform.

limited jurisdiction The authority of a court to hear only specific kinds of cases.

line-item veto A power used by an executive branch to veto one or more provisions of a bill while allowing the remainder of the bill to become law.

line organizations Government or corporate groups that provide direct services or products for the public.

literacy tests A voting requirement once used by Southern states that demanded that citizens prove they could read in order to qualify to vote. Primarily used to deny African Americans the right to vote, literacy tests are now outlawed.

lobbying All the efforts by individuals or organizations to affect the passage, defeat, or contents of legislation. The term comes from the lobby of the legislature itself, where petitioners used to corner legislators and speak about their concerns.

lobbyist A person who usually acts as an agent for a group that seeks to bring about the passage or defeat of legislative bills, to influence their content, or to influence administrative actions.

loose constructionists Those who believe that the Constitution should be interpreted loosely and who give broad definitions to the powers of the federal government.

loose monetary policy A policy designed to stimulate the economy by making credit inexpensive and widely available.

Madisonian Model The model of government devised by James Madison in which the powers of the government are separated into three branches: executive, legislative, and judicial.

magistrate A local judicial official with limited jurisdiction.

magistrate court A lower court in a small town or city.

Magna Carta The great charter that King John of England was forced to sign in 1215 as protection against the absolute powers of the monarchy. It included such fundamental rights as trial by jury and due process of law.

majority floor leader The chief spokesperson of the majority party in the Senate who directs the legislative program and sets the party strategy.

majority leader The leader of the majority party in the House. The majority leader of the House is elected by the caucus of party members to act as spokesperson for the party and to keep the party together.

majority opinion The written statement of the views of the majority of judges in support of a decision made by the court on which they preside.

majority party The party that holds over half the seats in the legislature.

majority rule A political system in which a majority determines the outcome of elections. A simple majority requires 50 percent plus one of the vote, whereas an extraordinary majority requires more than 50 percent plus one of the vote.

malapportionment A condition that results when, based on population and representation, the voting power of citizens in one district becomes more influential than the voting power of citizens in another district.

mandatory preference poll A type of primary election in which delegates are required to vote for the candidate chosen by the voters at the national convention.

mandatory sentencing A system by which specific crimes carry fixed terms of imprisonment.

marginal tax rate The percentage of additional dollars that must be paid in income taxes. The marginal tax rate is applied to the highest tax bracket only.

market The activity of buying and selling goods and services.

market economic system The opposite of a command economic system; otherwise known as capitalism.

markup sessions Meetings in which congressional conference committee members decide which changes, if any, should be made on a bill.

Marshall Plan A massive program of economic recovery for the nations of Europe after World War II. Named after former Secretary of State George C. Marshall, Jr., who had that post from 1947 to 1949.

mass media The technical means of communication (especially radio, newspapers, and television) designed to reach, inform, and often influence large numbers of people.

matching funds The funds a state must pay (or "match") when issued many categorical grants. Some programs require states to raise only 10 percent of the funds; others require an even share.

Mayflower Compact A document that stated that laws were to be made for the general good of the people, drawn up by Pilgrim leaders in 1620 on the voyage of the *Mayflower*.

mayor-administrator plan A plan for city government used in large urban areas in which the mayor plays a prominent political role. The mayor appoints a chief administrative officer whose function is to free the mayor from routine administrative tasks.

mayor-council plan A plan for city government in which the mayor is an elected chief executive and the council is the legislative body.

Members of Parliament Normally the elected officials of the House of Commons in Great Britain, but may also include the appointed members of the House of Lords.

merit The standard qualifications and performance criteria used to hire and promote government employees.

merit system The system used to select, promote, and retain government employees based on competitive exams and performance reviews.

minimum wage The minimum hourly wage that workers must be paid as determined by the federal government.

ministers Cabinet members in a parliamentary government.

minor party A political party that is less widely supported in a governmental system. In the United States any party other than one of the two major parties (Republican and Democratic) is considered a minor party.

minority floor leader The party officer in the Senate who commands the minority party's policies and directs its legislative program and strategy.

minority leader The leader of the minority party in the House.

minority party The party with fewer members in each house of Congress.

Miranda Rules The 1966 Supreme Court ruling that criminal suspects must be informed of their constitutional rights at the time of arrest.

Missouri Plan A method of selecting judges in which judges are first nominated by a special committee and then appointed by the governor. After serving an initial term, the judicial appointment is either confirmed or rejected at the general election.

mistrial A trial that is canceled because the judge believes it has not been fair in some way.

mixed economy An economic system that contains characteristics of both a command economy and a pure market economy. The mix may vary so that any economic system may lean more toward one pure type than another.

moderates People with political views that are in the middle ground between liberal and conservative.

monarchy A system of government ruled by a hereditary monarch (a king or a queen).

monetary policy Changes in the rate of growth of the money supply and in the availability of credit.

monopoly An industry or company that has total control over the sale of a product or service and does not face competition.

Monroe Doctrine The policy statement included in President Monroe's 1823 annual message to Congress, which set out three principles: (1) European nations should not establish new colonies in the Western Hemisphere; (2) European nations should not intervene in the affairs of independent nations of the Western Hemisphere; and (3) the United States should not interfere in the affairs of European nations.

multilateral treaties Treaties among three or more nations.

multiparty system An electoral system in which three or more political parties compete for public offices.

municipal home rule The power vested in a local unit of government to draft or change its own charter and to manage its own affairs.

municipalities Local units of government that have the authority to govern urban or city areas.

mutual-assured destruction (MAD) A theory that held that as long as the United States and the Soviet Union both had nuclear forces that were large, invulnerable, and somewhat equal, then neither nation would take the chance of waging war with the other.

mutual defense alliance An agreement among allied nations to support one another in case of an attack by enemy forces.

name calling A propaganda method that attaches a negative or unpopular label to a person to discredit that person's public image.

nation An area within a particular geographic boundary within which an organized government makes and enforces laws without the approval of a higher authority.

National Assembly The lower house of the French legislature.

national convention The meeting held by each major party every four years to select presidential and vice presidential candidates, to choose a national committee, to write a party platform, and to conduct party business.

national debt The total amount of money the national government owes as a result of borrowing and interest on borrowing. This occurs when the government exceeds its budget and spends more funds than it collects.

National Diet Through its constitution, Japan has a Parliament that is called the National Diet. It consists of two houses—the House of Councilors and the House of Representatives.

national party chairperson Individual who directs the work of the party national committee.

national party committee The political party leaders who direct party business during the time between the national party conventions. The group leads the party's national organization.

national security The nation's protection from unwanted interference, threat, or takeover from other nations. A sense of freedom and independence for the nation.

National Security Council (NSC) A council that advises the president on domestic and foreign matters concerning the safety and defense of the nation. This staff agency of the Executive Office was established by the National Security Act of 1947.

nationalists Individuals who feel strong loyalty and devotion to their nation.

nationality Membership in a particular nation or country.

natural aristocracy Officials whom President Thomas Jefferson placed in the executive bureaucracy.

natural rights Rights that do not come from governments but are inherent within every single man, woman, and child by virtue of the fact that he or she has been born and is a human being.

naturalization The legal process by which an individual born a citizen of one country becomes a citizen of another.

naturalized citizens Citizens from other countries who legally become American citizens. The naturalization process involves meeting certain requirements of residency, literacy, and acceptance of the principles of American government.

Navigation Acts Restrictions placed on colonial activity from 1651 to 1750 by Great Britain, which include the condition that only English ships could be used for trade within the British Empire.

necessary and proper clause Article I, Section 8, of the Constitution, which gives Congress the power to make all laws ''necessary and proper'' for the federal government to carry out its responsibilities.

negative campaign advertising Advertising in a political campaign aimed at discrediting and damaging the opposing candidate.

neutral competency Federal bureaucrats are expected to exhibit neutral competency, which means that they are supposed to apply their technical skills to their jobs without regard to political issues.

neutrality A position of not being aligned with either side in a dispute or conflict, such as a war.

New Deal A program ushered in by the Roosevelt administration in 1933 designed to help the United States out of the Great Depression. It included many government spending and public assistance programs, in addition to thousands of regulations of economic activity.

New England town A governmental unit in the New England states that combines the roles of city and county governments. ''Town'' includes a central village and surrounding rural areas, and practices direct democracy.

new federalism A plan to limit the federal government's role in regulating state governments, in order to give the states increased power to decide how they should spend all government revenues.

no contest A plea in a criminal case in which the defendant neither admits or denies the charges. The principal difference between a plea of guilty and a plea of no contest is that the latter may not be used against the defendant in a civil action.

nominating convention An official meeting of a political party to choose its candidates and select delegates.

nomination A party's naming and endorsing of a particular person as a candidate for public office.

nonpartisan elections Elections held without the participation of political parties to fill certain offices, such as judicial, city, or school board positions.

nonresident aliens Aliens who expect to stay in a foreign country for a short, specified time.

Northwest Ordinance A 1787 congressional act that established a basic pattern for how states should govern new territories north of the Ohio River.

obscenity A form of speech that is not protected under the First Amendment. A work that taken as a whole appeals to a prurient interest in sex by depicting sexual conduct as specifically defined by legislation or judicial interpretation in a patently offensive way, and that lacks serious literary, artistic, political, or scientific value.

off-budget items A category outside an official budget.

office-group ballot A ballot on which candidates are listed according to the office for which they are running.

Office of Management and Budget (OMB) Assists the president in preparing the proposed annual budget, which the president must submit to Congress in January of each year.

old-age pensions Retirement plans giving people money after they stop working.

one-party system An electoral system in which only one political party exists, is legal, or has any chance of winning elections.

open primary A direct primary in which voters may cast ballots without having to declare their party orientation.

opinion The statement of a court or judge concerning the decision reached in a case. It expounds the law as applied to the case and details the reasons on which the judgment was based.

opposition The next largest party in a parliamentary government, next to the ruling party. Leaders of the opposition appoint their own potential cabinet members, who ''shadow'' particular members of the ruling cabinet, and hope to some day replace them.

oral arguments The verbal arguments presented by opposing counsel.

original jurisdiction The legal authority of a court to hear the first presentation of a case.

oversight function The power of Congress to follow up on laws it has passed to ensure that they are being properly enforced and administered.

pardon The act of granting a prisoner release from punishment. A pardon can be granted by a president or a governor before or after a criminal conviction.

parishes A term used in Louisiana to describe administrative units of local government.

Parliament The name of the national legislative body in countries governed by a parliamentary system, as in England and France.

parliamentary democracy A form of democracy in which the executive leadership (which usually consists of a prime minister and his or her cabinet) is chosen by and responsible to a democratically elected parliament.

parole The release of a prisoner before the completion of his or her prison sentence.

partisan elections Elections in which candidates running for office are identified by their political parties.

partisan politics Politics in support of a particular party's ideology.

partisan preference The preference of one party over another by voters or legislators.

party identification Linking oneself to a particular party.

party platform The document drawn up by each party at the national convention that outlines the policies and positions of the party. The platform is submitted to the entire convention for approval.

party ticket A list of candidates for various offices that belong to one political party.

party-column ballot A form of ballot used in general elections in which candidates are listed in one column under their respective party names. This ballot emphasizes voting along party lines rather than for particular individuals.

passports Government-issued certificates that identify a person as a citizen of that government's country and authorize the person to travel abroad.

patent A license granted to an inventor that gives exclusive rights to manufacture and sell the invention for a specified period of time.

patronage A system of rewarding party faithfuls and workers with government employment and contracts.

peer group A group of people who share relevant social characteristics such as age and economic status. Peer groups play an important role in shaping individual attitudes and beliefs.

peers Individuals who are one's equals.

petit jury A group of up to twelve persons who hear the facts of a civil or criminal case in a court of law and give a verdict; also called *trial jury*.

petition A request that individuals submit to government officials. The petition may involve government policy or it may be a request to become a citizen.

picketing A form of protest in which workers on strike publicly march in an attempt to raise public awareness of a certain controversy and to persuade consumers not to deal with the employer until the strike is settled.

pigeonhole Filing a bill away or putting it aside for no further action. The term is borrowed from the old-time desks in committee rooms of Congress that had small compartments or ''pigeonholes'' for filing papers.

plain folks A method of propaganda that attempts to attract people to a political figure by portraying him or her as just an average American.

plaintiff A person who files suit in a court of law.

planks Issues or beliefs that make up a political party's platform.

plea bargaining Agreements between a prosecutor and a defense attorney whereby a defendant pleads guilty to a lesser charge in exchange for a lighter sentence. The prosecutor is willing to plea bargain in order to move the case through an extremely crowded court and to be ensured that the case will result in a guilty plea.

plurality A situation in which a candidate wins an election by receiving more votes than the others but does not necessarily win a majority. Most federal, state, and local laws allow for elections to be won by a plurality vote.

pocket veto A special veto power used by the chief executive after the legislature has adjourned. Bills that are not signed by the chief executive die after a specified period of time and must be reintroduced if Congress wishes to reconsider them.

police power The authority of the states to legislate for the protection of the health, safety, and welfare of the people.

policy voting When people vote for candidates who share their stand on certain key issues.

political action committee (PAC) A committee that is established by and represents the interests of corporations, labor unions, or special interest groups. PACs raise money and give donations to campaigns on behalf of the groups they represent.

political consultants Professionals hired by a political candidate to devise strategy, create campaign themes, and manage the image building of a candidate's political campaign.

political machines Organizations within a political party that control elections by granting favors in exchange for votes or money.

political participation The ways in which individuals can participate in the political process, such as by voting, serving on juries, helping with political campaigns, and running for a political office.

political party A group of organized citizens with a broad set of common beliefs who join together to elect candidates to public office and determine public policy.

political patronage A system of appointing people to political positions on the basis of service to the party rather than on any qualifications or merits.

political philosophy A set of notions or ideas about how people should be governed.

political socialization The process by which individuals develop political beliefs and form opinions about political issues. Important forces in this process include the family and the educational system.

politics The authoritative allocation of resources for a society;

the process of deciding who gets what, when, and how in a society.

poll tax A special tax that had to be paid before voting. The Twenty-Fourth Amendment outlawed the poll tax in federal elections, and in 1966 the Supreme Court declared it unconstitutional in all elections.

popular vote A vote cast by someone other than an elector; the number of actual votes cast in an election.

porkbarrel Appropriations for local projects that improve legislators' popularity in their own districts.

power The possession of control, authority, or influence over others.

power of recognition The power of the executive branch to accept the legal existence of another country's government.

preamble An introductory statement to an official document that usually explains the document's goals and purposes.

precedent A court rule that sets a standard for subsequent legal decisions in similar cases.

precincts The smallest voting districts at the local level.

preference poll A type of primary election in which voters may cast separate votes for candidates and for convention delegates.

preferred-position doctrine A Supreme Court test that requires that limitations be applied to the First Amendment only to avoid imminent, serious, and important evils.

preliminary hearing A court hearing at which evidence is submitted and testimony heard to determine whether there is enough reason to continue with court proceedings.

president of the Senate The role given by the Constitution to the vice president of the United States. As presiding officer, he or she may call on members to speak, put questions to a vote, and may cast a vote only in the event of a tie.

president *pro tempore* The temporary presiding officer of the Senate in the absence of the vice president.

presidential democracy A democracy in which the people elect both the president and the legislature. (Compare with *parliamentary democracy.*)

press conferences Scheduled interviews with the media.

press secretary A member of the White House staff who holds press conferences for reporters and lets people know what the president thinks about current national and international issues.

pressure groups Private organizations that use persuasion and pressure to see that laws are passed in favor of their interests.

preventive detention Holding accused felons without bail if judges feel that the suspect, if released, will commit another crime.

primaries Elections held before a general election in which candidates from the same party compete for the party nomination.

prime minister The chief executive in a parliamentary system who is elected by the legislature from among its own members.

principle of federalism A system of government in which

the power to govern is shared by a central (or federal) government and state governments, as outlined in a written constitution.

prior restraint The restraining of an action before it has actually occurred. Government censorship of documents or broadcasts before they are published or aired is an example of prior restraint.

private bills A legislative measure that applies only to certain persons or places, rather than to the nation as a whole.

private property Goods owned by individuals or groups rather than by government.

privileges and immunities clause A section of the Constitution that requires states not to discriminate against one another's citizens in such areas as legal protection, access to the courts, freedom to travel, and property rights.

probable cause Sufficient evidence to believe that a crime has been committed. Reasonable grounds for issuing a search warrant against an individual, his or her home, or personal possessions.

probation The suspension of a criminal sentence by a judge on the grounds that the individual maintain good behavior and be supervised by a probation officer for a specified period of time.

procedural due process A provision in the Constitution that states that the law must be carried out in a fair and orderly manner.

processes Procedures.

profit The amount of money left over after all the expenses of running a business have been paid.

profit incentive The desire to make money that motivates people to produce, buy, and sell goods and services.

progressive taxation A system of taxation in which individuals pay a higher percentage of additional tax dollars as income rises. In this way, the marginal tax rate exceeds the average tax rate.

Prohibition The fourteen-year era (from 1920 to 1933) during which it was illegal in the United States to manufacture, transport, or consume intoxicating beverages. Prohibition began with the Eighteenth Amendment and was repealed by the Twenty-First Amendment.

project grants Assistance grants that state and local agencies can apply for directly, so that funds can be allocated to where they are needed.

propaganda The spreading of ideas, information, or rumor for the purpose of helping or injuring an institution, a cause, or a person.

proportional taxation A system of taxation in which the tax *rate* remains constant regardless of a person's income.

proportionality A concept of the "just war theory," which states that the good that might be achieved by winning a war must clearly outweigh the harm that may be done.

prosecuting attorney The official who represents the government and initiates and carries out legal proceedings.

prototype A model.

psychoactives A term that applies to all drugs that affect the mind such as alcohol, nicotine, caffeine, marijuana, opiates, and cocaine.

public bills A legislative measure that applies to the nation as a whole.

public debt See *national debt.*

public defender The attorney appointed to represent a defendant in a criminal case should the defendant be unable to hire an attorney.

public-interest groups Groups that are formed with the broad goal of working for the ''public good.''

public opinion Opinions and attitudes shared by significant numbers of people on social and political issues.

public opinion poll A random survey to discover popular views on matters of public importance.

public policies Policies that affect the public at large. Public policies are typically carried out by the legislative and executive branches of local, state, and federal government.

pure speech The freely voiced, peaceful expression of thoughts, ideas, or opinions, at home or in public.

quorum The minimum number of legislators who must be present for a legislative body to conduct business.

quota A rule enforced by the government that states that a certain number of jobs, promotions, or other types of selections must be given to members of certain groups.

radical left Persons on the extreme left side of the political spectrum who do not believe in working within the established political processes to achieve their goals and who often want to destroy the established governmental system.

random sample A cross-section of a population that has been polled on a specific issue.

ratification Formal approval or final consent of a constitution, constitutional amendment, or treaty.

ratings system A system by which interest groups evaluate (rate) the performance of legislators based on how the legislators have served the interest groups.

rational-basis test A method used by the Supreme Court to ensure equal legal protection to all individuals. It applies to suspected discrimination situations that affect diverse individuals.

reactionaries People who resist change much more strongly than do either moderates or conservatives. Reactionaries not only do not want society to change, they are willing to actively fight against social change.

realigning election An election in which the electorate turns away from the dominant party and replaces it with a new dominant party.

reapportionment The redrawing of legislative district lines, usually after a census is taken, in accordance with population changes indicated by the census.

recall A procedure that allows voters to dismiss an elected official from a state or local office before the official's term is expired.

recall election An election that gives citizens the power to remove an elected official from office before the end of his or her term.

recesses Periods of time during which a legislative or judicial body is not in session.

recessions Periods of time in which the rate of economic growth is consistently lower than usual.

record vote (also **roll-call vote**) A method of voting in a legislature in which legislators call out their votes on an issue. A computer records each vote electronically and display boards show how each member has voted.

referendum A form of direct democracy in which legislative or constitutional measures are first decided upon by the legislature and then presented to the voters for approval.

refugees People who must flee from danger in their native countries and find residence outside their homeland.

registration Entering one's name onto a list of eligible voters. Registration requires meeting certain age, residency, and citizenship requirements.

regressive taxation A system of taxation in which individuals pay a lower percentage of tax dollars as income rises. In this way, the marginal tax rate is less than the average tax rate.

released time The time students are given away from regular public school classes to attend religious instruction sessions.

repeal To rescind or do away with legislation.

representative assembly A law-making body that is composed of individuals who represent the population.

representative democracy (also **indirect democracy**) A system of democracy in which the people elect representatives who work within government on behalf of the people. (Compare with *direct democracy.*)

representative government A government in which the people, by whatever means, choose a limited number of individuals to determine policy for all citizens.

representatives Officials who are elected to a legislative office for a specific time for the purpose of determining policy for all citizens.

reprieve A postponement of a criminal sentence imposed by a court of law. The president or governor has the power to grant reprieves and usually does so for humanitarian reasons.

reprimand An official reproach used by Congress for a member guilty of misconduct.

republic The name given to a nation in which the supreme power rests in those who are entitled to vote and is exercised by elected representatives who are responsible to voters and who govern according to law. (Compare with *representative democracy.*)

republican form of government A system of government in which the supreme power rests with the voters, who elect representatives to operate the government for them.

reserved powers Powers that are neither granted to the federal government nor expressly forbidden to the states and are therefore retained by the states or by the people.

residency A requirement that a person live within a state for a specified period of time in order to qualify to vote.

resident aliens People who have immigrated to the United States to establish permanent residence.

resulting powers The accumulation of several expressed powers that results in a certain power of the federal government.

revenue bills Bills that involve the raising of money for the government. According to the Constitution, revenue bills must originate in the House of Representatives.

revenue-sharing program A program in which the federal government allocated funds to states and cities with virtually no strings attached. Recipient governments could use the funds in any way they saw fit.

reverse discrimination The assertion that affirmative action programs that require preferential treatment or quotas discriminate against those who have no minority status.

review courts See *appellate courts*.

revolution The popular overthrow of an established government or political system and its replacement with a new system of government. Famous revolutions include the American (1775–83), the French (1789–99), Russian [February Revolution (March 17, 1917) and October Revolution (November 7, 1917)], and the Second Russian Revolution, which occurred in August of 1991.

rider An amendment or provision attached to a bill that is not related to the subject of the bill.

roll-call vote See *record vote*.

rule of law A basic principle of government that accompanies constitutional supremacy which states that government shall be carried out according to established law, and that both those who govern and those who are governed will be bound by this law.

run-off election A repeat election between the two front runners in a prior election when no candidate has received a majority of votes. Run-off elections are usually held in places where the law requires a majority vote.

sabotage A destructive act intended to hinder a nation's defense efforts.

sacrifice principle A principle of taxation that holds that the sacrifices people make to pay their taxes should be fair.

samples Small numbers of people who represent a cross-section of the total population that has been polled on a specific issue.

sampling error The level of confidence in the findings of a public opinion poll.

search warrant An order issued and authorized by a judge that gives police the power to search a specific place in connection with a particular crime.

searches and seizures The methods used by law enforcement officials to look for and collect the evidence they need to convict individuals suspected of crimes as referred to in the Fourth Amendment.

secession The act of formally withdrawing from membership in an alliance; the withdrawal of a state from the federal union.

Second Continental Congress The congress of the colonies that met in 1775 to assume the powers of a central government and establish an army.

seditious speech Speech intended to promote resistance to lawful authority and that especially advocates the violent overthrow of a government.

segregation The enforced separation, often by discriminatory means, of racial, ethnic, or other groups from the rest of the population in education, housing, or other areas.

select committees Temporary legislative committees established for a special purpose.

selectmen Individuals chosen by a township to serve on the local board and manage the daily affairs of the town.

self-incrimination Providing damaging information or testimony against oneself in a court of law.

self-nomination Announcing one's own desire to run for public office.

senatorial courtesy An unwritten rule that an executive appointment to a certain state must first be approved by the senators of that state.

seniority An unwritten rule followed in both houses of Congress that specifies that members with longer terms of continuous service will be given preference when committee chairpersons and holders of other significant posts are selected.

sentence The punishment imposed by a court of law on an individual who is found guilty of a crime.

separate-but-equal doctrine A doctrine long held by the Supreme Court, which declared that segregation in schools and public accommodations did not imply the superiority of one race over another. It held that the Equal Protection Clause of the Fourteenth Amendment did not forbid racial segregation as long as the facilities for blacks were equal to those provided for whites. The doctrine was overturned in the *Brown v. Board of Education* decision of 1954.

sessions Regular periods of time during which legislative bodies assemble and conduct business.

shield laws Laws that protect reporters in courts of law against disclosing their sources and revealing other confidential information.

simple resolution Legislation that deals with matters affecting only one house of Congress and is passed by that house alone.

single-member district system A method of election in which only one candidate can win election to each office.

single-member districts Electoral districts from which single officeholders are chosen by voters.

slander The public utterance of a statement that holds a person up for contempt, ridicule, or hatred and thus damages the person's reputation.

social conflict Friction between groups within a society. Sometimes social conflict is resolved by violence, other times by the judicial system, and other times by changes in customs and traditions.

social contract theory A theory of society that states that individuals voluntarily agree to create an organized society in order to secure mutual protection and welfare. A theory derived from Hobbes, Locke, and Rousseau.

Social Security A government insurance program of obligatory saving financed from payroll taxes imposed on both employers and employees. Workers pay for the benefits while working and receive the benefits after they retire.

socioeconomic factors Social and economic factors such as age, income, education, and occupation.

Solid South A term used to describe the tendency of the southern states to vote Democratic after the Civil War.

solidarity Mutual agreement within a group.

sovereignty The supreme and independent authority that a government possesses within its own territory.

speaker The presiding officer in the lower house of a state legislature.

Speaker of the House The presiding officer in the House of Representatives, always a long-time member of the majority party and often the most powerful and influential member of the House.

special election An election held whenever an issue must be decided before the next regular election is held.

special sessions Unscheduled sessions of Congress ordered by the president.

speech plus A verbal expression of opinions, ideas, or beliefs combined with some sort of action such as marching or demonstrating.

split-ticket voting The act of voting for candidates from more than one political party in the same election.

spoils system An arrangement under which the political party that wins an election gives government jobs to its own party members.

sponsor A legislator who drafts and proposes bills.

Stamp Act An act passed by the British Parliament in 1765 which placed the first direct tax on the colonies. The Stamp Act required the use of tax stamps on all legal documents, newspapers, pamphlets, playing cards, and certain business agreements.

standing committees Permanent committees within the House or Senate that consider bills within a subject area.

standing vote A method of voting in the legislature in which those who favor a measure and those who oppose it are required to stand up to show their vote.

State of the Union Address An annual message from the president to Congress in which a legislative program is proposed. The message is aimed not only at Congress but to the American people and to the world.

status quo The existing state of affairs.

statutory law A law passed by a legislature.

straight-ticket voting The act of voting exclusively for candidates of the same party in an election.

straw poll A survey of opinions taken to estimate the strength of opposing candidates or the popularity of a proposed law.

strict constructionists Those who believe that the Constitution should be interpreted strictly and feel that the federal government should have only those powers specifically named in the Constitution.

strong mayor-council plan A plan for city government in which the mayor is the chief executive and has almost complete control over hiring and firing employees and preparing the budget.

subcommittees Divisions of larger committees that deal with a particular part of the committee's policy area.

subpoena A legal writ that requires a person to give a testimony in court.

substantive due process The Constitutional requirement that the laws used in accusing and convicting persons of crimes must be fair.

succession The legal procedure by which government leaders succeed the presidency should the president die, become disabled, or be removed from office.

suffrage See *franchise.*

suffragists Those who advocated for women's right to vote.

summit meeting A conference between the heads of two or more nations.

summons A notice that calls on a defendant to appear in court.

super-majority vote Used by the General Assembly of the United Nations. Important questions are decided by a majority vote or by a super-majority vote of two-thirds, depending on the importance of the matter.

superpowers The nations with the greatest economic and military power.

Supplemental Security Income (SSI) A government program that establishes a minimum income for the aged, the blind, and the disabled.

supremacy clause Article VI, Section 2 of the Constitution, which establishes the Constitution and federal laws as superior to all state and local legislation.

suspect classification A test used by the Supreme Court to determine if the classification of individuals based on race, national origin, or sex has in any way denied those individuals equal protection of the law.

symbolic speech The expression of beliefs, opinions, or ideas through forms other than speech or print.

teller vote A method of voting in a legislature in which those who favor a measure and those who oppose it are required to walk down an aisle to show their vote.

tenure The period of time during which a public official holds office.

term See *tenure.*

testimonials A propaganda technique that involves persuading people to support an issue or candidate because well-known individuals, such as a prominent government official or famous entertainers, offer such support.

third parties Political parties other than the two major parties, usually composed of dissatisfied groups that have split from the major parties.

Three-Fifths Compromise A compromise reached during the Constitutional Convention in which it was agreed that three-fifths of all slaves were to be counted both for tax purposes and for representation in the House of Representatives.

tight monetary policy A policy designed to slow the economy by making credit expensive and in short supply.

tolerance A fair and objective attitude toward those whose opinions, race, religion, and nationality differ from one's own.

totalitarian A ruler who rules without the consent of the governed.

town manager system A system adopted by some New England towns in which voters elect selectmen who then appoint professional town managers.

town meeting A traditional form of New England town government at which direct democracy is practiced.

townships Local government units that are subdivisions of counties and have similar governing procedures.

tracking polls Polls that track public opinion of candidates on nearly a daily basis as election day approaches.

trade and product organizations Organizations that usually support policies that benefit business in general and work toward seeking policy goals that benefit their particular membership.

transfer A propaganda technique that involves associating a candidate with a respected person, group, or symbol.

treason Article III, Section 3 of the Constitution states that treason "shall consist in levying war against (the United States), or in adhering to their enemies, giving them aid and comfort."

treaty A formal agreement between the governments of two or more countries.

trial balloon The practice of testing public reaction to a new idea by unofficially publicizing it.

trial courts A court of original jurisdiction that hears civil and criminal cases.

trial jury See *petit jury*.

two-party system A political system in which two strong and established parties compete for political offices.

tyranny The arbitrary or unrestrained exercise of power by an oppressive individual or government.

unanimous Being of one mind; agreement.

unanimous opinion Agreement by all judges on the same court decision.

unconstitutional Contrary to constitutional provisions and so invalid.

undocumented aliens illegal aliens.

unicameral legislature A legislature with only one legislative body. (Compared with *bicameral legislature*.)

unincorporated areas Areas not located within municipal boundaries.

unitary government A centralized governmental system in which local or subdivisional governments exercise only those powers given to them by the central government.

unitary system A centralized governmental system in which local or subdivisional governments exercise only those powers given to them by the central government.

United States Treasury Bonds See *government bonds*.

urban areas Highly populated communities.

value-added tax A tax on the difference between the costs that go into producing a product and the revenues received from selling the product.

veto A latin word meaning "I forbid"; the refusal by an official, such as the president or governor, to sign a bill into law.

veto power A constitutional power that enables the chief executive (president or governor) to reject legislation and return it to the legislature with reasons for the objection. This prevents or delays the bill from becoming law.

veto session A session in which state legislators can consider bills vetoed by the governor and attempt to override the governor's veto, if enough popular support within the legislature exists.

visa A permit to enter another country, issued from the country one wishes to enter.

voice vote A method of voting in a legislature.

voir dire A French phrase meaning "to speak the truth"; refers to the process by which prospective jurors are examined to ensure their judgments will be impartial.

vote of confidence Support from the parliament for the existing government.

voter turnout The percentage of eligible citizens who actually take part, or "turn out" in the election process.

waive To relinquish or give up.

War Powers Act The law passed in 1973 that spells out the conditions under which the president can commit troops to war without congressional approval.

wards The local units of a party organization.

warrant An order issued by a court authorizing a public official to proceed in a specified manner, such as a search warrant.

weak mayor-council plan Plan for city government in which the mayor is elected as chief executive officer; the council is elected as the legislative body. The mayor has only limited powers and little control over staffing and budgeting, and is often elected for a two-year term.

Western Bloc The democratic nations that emerged victorious after World War II, led by the United States.

whips Assistant floor leaders who aid the majority and minority floor leaders.

whistle-blower A government employee who calls public attention to fraud, mismanagement, or waste in his or her own agency or department.

White House Press Corps A group of reporters assigned to cover the presidency full time.

winner-take-all system A system in which the presidential candidate who wins the preference vote in a primary automatically wins the support of all the delegates chosen in the primary.

writ of certiorari A written order issued by a higher court to a lower court to send up the record of a case for review.

writ of mandamus A written order issued by a court commanding an official of the government to perform a specified lawful duty or act.

write-in candidate Someone who will campaign without being listed on the ballot, and will ask voters to write his or her name on the ballot on election day.

zoning The method by which local governments regulate how property may be used.

INDEX

A

Abelman v. *Booth*, 94
Ability-to-pay principle of taxation, 469–470
Abortion issue, 451, 452
Abridgement of civil liberties, 103
Abridgement of English Law (Bacon), 440
Absentee ballots, 270, 272
Absolute monarchy, 11
Abstain (from voting), 635
ACCESS, 498
Access, equal, for differently abled persons, 149
Accuracy in Media (AIM), 252
Accused persons, rights of, 131–139, 433, 575–578. *See also* Criminal process;
Due process
Acquired immune deficiency syndrome (AIDS), 224, 478, 649
Acquittal, 136
Act of admission, 88
Action for Children's Television (ACT), 252
Adams, John, 32, 33, 40, 46, 60, 181, 191, 363, 440, 521
Adams, John Quincy, 53, 249, 322
Adams, Samuel, 31, 46
Administrative agencies. *See also* Bureaucracy
budgets of, reviewed by Congress, 326
created by Congress, 67
lobbying directed at, 224
Administrative assistant, 305
Administrative councils (Britain), 631
Adulateur, The (Warren), 33
Advertising:
freedom of speech and, 120–121
political, 250–253, 269, 350–353
of state-run lotteries, 613
Advice and consent, by Senate, 317, 322, 324, 372, 377, 383, 387, 388, 418, 439, 447–448, 496
Affirmative action, 148, 150
Afghanistan, Soviet invasion of, 388, 493, 507, 510
AFL-CIO, 220
Africa, famine in, 212, 326

African Americans:
civil rights movement and, 144–147
in Civil Service, 425
number of, 165, 174–176
political offices held by, 185, 502–503
poverty among, 475
segregation laws and, 139–144
single-mother families among, 475
separate-but-equal doctrine and, 68, 143
voting choices of, 276
voting rights and, 266–268
African National Congress (ANC), 509
Age:
discrimination based on, 408
minimum,
for congresspersons, 291, 293
for drinking, 617, 619
for president, 357
for state governor, 546
for voting, 263, 268
political affiliation and, 190
political attitudes and, 214
of Supreme Court justices, 448
voter turnout and, 271–272
voters' choices and, 276
Age Discrimination in Employment Act of 1967, 408
Agencies, government. *See* Administrative agencies; Bureaucracy
Agency for International Development (AID), 498, 507
Agenda:
defined, 40
president's ability to set, 389
Agents of political socialization, 210–214
Agnew, Spiro, 359
Agriculture, Chinese system of, 640
Aid to Families with Dependent Children (AFDC), 477
AIDS. *See* Acquired immune deficiency syndrome (AIDS)
Air Force, U.S., 6, 173, 321, 501, 502
Air Force One, 358
Air pollution, 479–484
Air Pollution Control Act of 1955, 479
Air Quality Act of 1967, 480
Airline Deregulation Act of 1978, 417
Alcohol, 596
Alien and Sedition Acts of 1798,

115–116, 164
Aliens:
defined, 85, 161
illegal (undocumented), 161, 164, 168, 177
rights of, 164
types of, 161, 164, 168, 177
Allegiance:
to nation, as citizen's responsibility, 170
Pledge of, 112, 211
Alliances, 507–510
Almanac of American Politics (Borone et al.), 298
Altgeld, William, 87
Ambassador, 388, 501
Amendments, constitutional. *See* Constitutional amendments
American Association of Retired Persons (AARP), 218, 219, 221
American Bar Association, 568–569
American Battle Monuments Commission, 413
American Civil Liberties Union (ACLU), 111, 123, 433
American Creed, 34
American economic system, 641–644
American Farm Bureau Federation, 220, 344, 423
American Federation of Labor (AFL), 220
American Federation of Labor– Congress of Industrial Organizations (AFL-CIO), 220
American Federation of Teachers, 223
American Friends Service Committee, 498
American Independent Party, 187–188, 197
American Indians. *See* Native Americans
American Medical Association (AMA), 223
American Nazi Party, 123
American Revolution, 8, 9, 29–34, 36, 38, 432, 461
Americans for Common Cents, 465
Americans with Disabilities Act of 1990, 149, 408, 418
Amnesty, 168, 386
Amnesty International USA, 498, 637

AMTRAK, 419
Anderson, John B., 198
Anthony, Susan B., 64, 262
   dollar, 465
   Profile of, 264–265
Anti-Federalists, 44–46, 184, 190, 687
Antislavery movement, 64
Anzus Pact of 1951, 508, 510
Apartheid, 510
Appellate courts, 438–439, 563, 565
Appellate jurisdiction, 436
Appointment powers:
   of president, 322, 324, 377, 383, 386,
      418, 447–448, 452, 453
   of state governor, 550–551
Apportionment, 285–289, 530
Appropriation power of Congress, 314
Archer, Bill, 323
Arguments, before Supreme Court,
   443–445
Arizona Committee to Re-elect the
   President, 446
Arizona v. *Fulminante*, 134
Armistice, 387
Arms Control and Disarmament
   Agency, 497
Arms race, 492–493, 495
Army, U.S., 6, 43, 173, 501, 502
Arraignment, 576
Arrest, 132, 575
Arthur, Chester A., 420
Articles of Confederation, 34–39, 76–77,
   85, 86, 283, 313, 315, 355
Asian Americans:
   equality for, 148
   increasing number of, 174, 176
   voting rights for, 268
Assembly:
   freedom of, 80, 103, 122–123
   representative, 27
Assessor, county, 592
Associated Milk Producers, Inc.
   (AMPI), 220
Association of Bay Area Governments,
   603
Athenian model of democracy, 11–12, 18
Atomic bomb, 386, 491
Attachés, 501
Attainder, bills of, 104, 328
Attorney(s):
   court-appointed, 576
   district, 575
   prosecuting, 575
   right to. *See* Counsel, right to
Attorney general, 557, 575
Auditor, 592, 556
Audubon magazine, 483
Australia, Anzus Pack and, 508
Australian ballot, 246
Authoritarian government, 11

Authority, governmental, 6
Autocracy, 11
Average, mean or median versus, 642
Aviation, regulation of, 415
Aziz, Tariq, 496

B

Bacon, Francis, 440
Bad-tendency rule, 117
Bail, 138
Baker, James, 369, 496, 500
Baker v. *Carr*, 287, 451, 528, 530
Bakke, Alan, 148
Balance the ticket, 365
Ballots, 246
   Australian, 246
   absentee, 270, 272
   "bedsheet," 246
   defined, 233
   length of, 246
   office-group (Massachusetts), 246
   party-column, 246
   preparation of, 591
   secret, 245
   in state elections, 540
Baltic states, 388, 506, 648
Bandwagon effect, 256
Banking system, 417, 460, 485. *See also*
   Monetary policy
Bankruptcy laws, 315
Bar graphs, 168–169
Barkley, Alben, 363
Barron v. *Mayor of Baltimore*, 172
Bastille Day (France), 7, 8
Battle of Concord, 30
Battle of Lexington, 30
Bean, Roy, 564
Beard, Charles, 234
"Bedsheet" ballot, 246
Begging, freedom of speech and, 114
Bench trial, 137, 444, 576
Benefits-received principle of taxation,
   469
Benfield, James, 465
Bentsen, Lloyd, 277, 297, 323, 341
Berger, Victor L., 291*n*
Berlin Wall, 492, 493, 495, 504
Betts v. *Bradey*, 433
Biased sample, 208
Biases, identifying, 145, 348
Bible reading in schools, 109
Bicameral legislature, 40, 283–284, 529,
   628
Biennial session, 533
Bigelow v. *Virginia*, 120
Bill of Rights, 56, 103–105, 108, 111,
   132, 328, 433. *See also* specific
   amendments

   Anti-Federalists' argument for, 46
   citizens' rights under, 170–172
   colonial models for, 28
   English, 23, 628
   Japanese, 634
   state compliance with, 106–107,
      170–172, 433, 523
   nationalization of, 170–172
   ought versus *shall* in, 61–62
   ratification of, 61–63, 104
   in state constitutions, 523
Bills, congressional, 302
   compromise, 347
   defined, 336
   enacting into law, process of, 340–347
   House action on, 342–344
   introduction of, 333, 336, 340
   number of proposed versus passed, 338
   pigeonholed, 340
   presidential action on, 347–348
   public and private, 337
   readings of, 340, 343
   reporting, 342
   revenue, 314
   riders attached to, 339
   scheduling, for debate, 342
   Senate action on, 344–345
   sponsors of, 340
Bills of attainder, 104, 328
Bingham, George Caleb, 262
Biographies, reading, 381
Bipartisan Commission on
   Comprehensive Health Care, 338
Birth:
   citizenship by, 158
   location of *(jus soli)*, 158
Bismarck, Otto von, 7
Black, Hugo, 105, 109, 115–117, 329
Black Caucus, 333
Blackmun, Harry, 111, 120, 444
Blacks. *See* African Americans
Blakency, Sir Percy, 509*n*
Blanket primary, 236
Block grants, 616–617
Board of Education of Westside
   Community Schools v. *Mergens*,
   109
Bonds, Treasury, 315, 466, 474
Book of States, 35
Booth, John Wilkes, 360
Bork, Robert, 227, 448
Borone, Michael, 298
Boroughs, 590, 631. *See also* Counties
Borrowing:
   by state and local governments, 611, 614
   by U.S. Congress, 314–315
Boston Tea Party, 30, 227
Botswana, 140
Boycott, 30, 145
Bradley, Tom, 270

Brandeis, Louis, 431
Brandenburg v. *Ohio*, 116
Branzburg v. *Hayes*, 118
Brennan, William, 444, 453
Brewster, Henry, 64
Brookings Institute, The, 498
Brown v. *Board of Education of Topeka*,
    75, 143, 144, 147, 380, 451
Brown, Edmond G. ("Pat"), 240
Brown, Jerry, 545
Brown, Michael, 465
Brown, Ron, 201
Brown, Willie, 541
Bryan, Rich, 90
Bryson, Reid, 483
Buchanan, Bruce, 277
Buchanan, James, 358*n*, 367
Budget:
    administrative agency, 326
    defined, 370
    federal, 63, 315, 320, 464–469
    governor's, 552
    president's proposed annual, 370–371
Budget and Impoundment Control Act
    of 1974, 320, 396
Bull Moose Party, 197
Burden of proof, 134
Bureau of the Budget, U.S., 320
Bureau of the Census, U.S., 35, 162,
    285–286
Bureaucracy, 401–428
    defined, 401
    executive departments, 366, 377,
        405–410
    government corporations, 418–419
    independent executive agencies,
        410–414
    independent regulatory agencies,
        414–418
    Jacksonian reorganization of, 420, 425
    Japanese, 636
    merit system and, 420–422, 424
    nature and size of, 401–405
    organization of, 405
    spoils system and, 174, 420
    whistle-blowers and, 424
Bureaucrats, 401, 423–424
Burstyn v. *Wilson*, 120
Bush, Barbara, 384
Bush, Dorothy, 384
Bush, George, 90, 255, 290
    appointments made by, 324, 386, 425,
        453, 503
    cabinet of, 369
    campaign spending by, 244
    ceremonial duties of, 383
    a day in the life of, 384–385
    defeated by Bentsen in 1970, 323, 341
    defense spending and, 504
    as director of Central Intelligence

Agency, 497
    election of, to presidency, 274
    media and, 380, 381
    new federalism and, 96
    Panama invasion and, 379, 510
    Persian Gulf War and, 274, 371, 379,
        387, 395, 498–499, 510, 552
    reregulation and, 417
    recognition of Baltics by, 388
    Soviet Union and, 69, 495
    as vice president, 276, 363, 373
Business:
    government-operated, 611, 615
    regulation of. *See* Government
        regulation
    small, 641
Business cycles, 464
Business interest groups, 218, 220
Busing, 144

C

C-SPAN, 343
Cabinet, 68, 70, 365–369
    appointments to, 324
    British, 628, 629
    defined, 365
    foreign policy and, 496–497
    French, 632
    Japanese, 635–636
    Kitchen, 368
    members of, 366
    role and influence of, 367–369
    shadow, 630
Cable News Network (CNN), 342, 646
Caddell, Patrick, 240, 242
Calder, Ron, 86
Calendar of General Orders, 342
Calendar of the Committee of the
        Whole House on the State of the
        Union, 342
Calendars, congressional, 342
California constitution, 523
Cambodia, U.S. invasion of, 575
Camp David, 358
Campaigns, 238–244. *See also* Political
        candidates
    financing and regulation of, 242–244
    importance of money in, 257
    lengthy, and voter turnout, 271
    manager of, 238
    media and, 249–256, 269. *See also*
        Television
    nomination of candidates and, 233–238
    organization of, 238–240
    party caucus and, 234
    party nominating convention and, 234
    planning, 240–242
    running, as party function, 187
Canada, U.S. free trade agreement with,
    510

Candidates, political. *See* Political
    candidates
Canvasses, 186
Capital punishment, 137, 139, 554, 556,
    579
Capitalism, 638–644
Capitol, U.S., floor plan of, 335
Card stacking, 255–256
Caricatures, 79
Carlucci, Frank, 503
Carswell, G. Harold, 447
Carter, Jimmy, 161, 173, 196, 241–242,
    274, 303, 358, 362, 369, 373, 383,
    386, 387, 388, 421, 392, 398, 403,
    434, 621
Cartoons, political, 79
Case law, 431–432
Casework, 291
Caseworkers, 305
Castro, Fidel, 11, 177, 226
Categorical grants, 615–616
Caucuses, 234, 333–334
Cause and effect versus correlations,
    318
Cease-fire, 387
Censorship, 117
Censure, 291
Census, 162–164, 174, 184
Center for Defense Information, 498
Central Intelligence Agency (CIA), 173,
    303, 327, 371, 372, 384, 413–414,
    497
Certiorari, writ of, 442–443
Chamber of Commerce, 218
Chancellors, colonial governors as, 554
Chargé d'affaires, 501
Charles I, King of England, 23
Charter (Jamestown), 27
Chase, Samuel, 60*n*
Chávez, Cesar, 165
Cheney, Richard, 369, 497, 505
Chief administrator plan, 593
Chief diplomat, president as, 387–388
Chief executive:
    executive departments close to, 410
    governor as, 548
    president as, 356, 383, 386
Chief legislator:
    governor as, 548
    president as, 388–391
Chief of staff, president as, 369
Chief of state, president as, 382–383
Children:
    labor by, 95
    latchkey, 295
    in poverty, 475–476
    rights of, 82–83, 112, 575
China. *See* People's Republic of China
Chinese Exclusion Act of 1882, 166
Choice, freedom of, 642–643

Christian Scientists, 112
Christmas displays, 110–111
Chung, Connie, 254
Chung, Margaret, 254
Chung, William Ling, 254
Church-related interest groups, 223
Church-state issue, 108–111
Churchill, Winston, 388, 463, 492, 648
Circuit courts of appeals, U.S., 438–439
Circular flow of economic activity, 639–640
Cities:
    government of, 593–602
    growth of, 593
    incorporation of, 583, 593–594
    planning and zoning, 585–587, 589
City manager, 597
Citizens' Party, 188
Citizens' Stamp Advisory Committee, 413
Citizenship, 157–161
    African-American slaves and, 157–158
    by birth, 158
    by choice (naturalization), 158–160
    Constitution and, 157–159
    determined by federal government, 157
    diversity of, 442
    duties of, 14
    granted to Native Americans, 158
    immigrants and aliens and, 161–171
    loss of, 160–161
    rights and responsibilities of, 66, 170–174
    skills in, 38, 66, 211
Citrus Growers Association, 423
Civil Aeronautics Board (CAB), 415
Civil disobedience, 145
Civil law, 432
Civil Rights Act of 1957, 266, 345
Civil Rights Act of 1964, 140–141, 145, 147, 148, 266, 316, 408
Civil rights and liberties. See also Constitution, U.S.
    citizen's duty to defend, 173
    defined, 103, 142
Civil Rights Commission, U.S., 266, 413–414
Civil rights groups, 227
Civil rights movement, 140–142, 144–147, 214, 266–267
Civil Service, 174
    defined, 420
    examination for, 174, 175
    General Schedule (GS) ratings in, 422
    history and function of, 420–423
    merit system in, 420–422, 424
    minorities and women in, 425
Civil Service Commission, 174, 420–421
Civil Service reform acts, 420, 421, 424
Civil War, 44, 67, 87, 95, 522
    central issues of, 93–94

Dred Scott decision and, 157, 436, 452
    income taxes during, 472
Civil War amendments, 55, 142–143. See also Thirteenth Amendment; Fourteenth Amendment; Fifteenth Amendment
Civilian Conservation Corps (CCC), 464
Clay, Henry, 53, 191–192
Clean Air Act of 1963 (as amended), 411, 480–481, 483
Clean Government Party (Japan), 638
Clean Water Act of 1974, 481
Clear and present danger rule, 116–117
Clemency proceedings, 554, 556
Clergy and Laity Concerned, 499
Clerk:
    county, 592
    of the House, 334
    law, 447
    of the Senate, 340
Cleveland, Grover, 87, 276
Clinton, Bill, 70, 186, 240, 256, 356, 382, 389, 720
Clinton, George, 547
Closed primary, 235
Cloture rule, 345
CNN (Cable News Network), 342, 646
Coalitions, 186–187, 636
Coast Guard, U.S., 6, 173
Cocaine, 596
Coercive Acts of 1774, 30
Coin Coalition, 465
Coinage of money, 80, 315, 465
Cold War, 492–493, 495, 504
Colgrove v. Battin, 171
Collective farms, 640
Collective security, 492
Colonial America, 26–34. See also American Revolution
Colonial empire, of U.S., 490
Command economy, 638, 648. See also Communism
Commander-in-chief:
    governor as, 552–553
    president as, 67, 316, 377, 386–387, 496
Commentaries on the Law of Municipal Corporations (Dillon), 583
Commerce:
    federal regulation of. See Commerce clause
    interstate, 44, 67, 315. See also Commerce clause
    intrastate, 94, 522
    state regulation of, 81
Commerce clause, 68, 92, 315–316, 607–608
Commercial speech, 120–121
Commercials, political, 250–253. See also Political advertising
Commission plan, 597–598
Committee(s):

congressional. See Congressional committees; specific committees
    political action (PAC), 225, 227, 243–244, 255–256
    of state legislatures, 536–537
Committee for National Security, 498
Committee of the whole (House), 343
Committees for the Reelection of the President (CREEP), 397, 446
Commodity Credit Corporation (CCC), 418–419
Common Cause, 242
Common law, 431–432, 628
Common-law marriage, 82
Common Sense (Paine), 30–31, 261–262
Communication Workers of America (CWA), 227
Communications, regulation of, 415
Communism, 492, 638, 645–648
Communist bloc, 492
Communist Party:
    in China and Eastern Europe, 493, 495. See also People's Republic of China; Soviet Union
    in France, 633
    in Japan, 638
Community action, organizing for, 614
Community service:
    careers in, 173–174
    sentencing to, 577
Commute (a sentence), 554
Competition, economic, 641, 644
Competitive Banking and Quality Act of 1987, 485
Comprehensive Employment and Training Act (CETA), 464
Comprehensive Environmental Response, Compensation and Liability Act of 1980, 481
Compromise, as citizenship skill, 66
Comptroller, state office of the, 558
Comptroller general, 307
Computerized voting systems, 246, 343–344
Concord, Battle of, 30
Concurrent jurisdiction, 442
Concurrent majority, 93
Concurrent powers, 83–85
Concurrent resolutions, 337
Concurring (court) opinion, 443
Conduct, of congresspersons, 291, 293
Confederacy, 142
Confederal system, 76
Confederation, 35
    Articles of. See Articles of Confederation
Conference committee, 305
Confessions, criminal process and, 134–135
Confidence, vote of, 630
Confidentiality, reporters and, 118

Conflicts:
social, 3–4
solving, as purpose of government, 5–6
Congress, U.S. *See also* House of
Representatives, U.S.; Senate, U.S.
administrative agencies created by, 67
amendment process and, 63, 65–67
as bicameral legislature, 283–284
bills deliberated by. *See* Bills,
congressional
citizenship granted by, 159
committees of. *See* Congressional
committees; specific committees
constitutional amendment process and,
63, 65–67, 322
constitutional powers and duties of, 54,
56–58, 67, 78, 80, 283–286,
291–292, 296, 299, 301,
312–331, 342, 347, 395, 540
contempt of, 326
creation and evolution of, 283–289
electoral vote and, 322
expressed powers of, 313–319
first location of, 46
foreign policy and, 498–499
impeachment powers of, 321–322
implied powers of, 318–321
investigative powers of, 324–326, 329
legislative powers of, 313–321
legislative process in, 332–351. *See also*
Bills, congressional
limits on powers of, 328
members of. *See* Congresspersons
nonlegislative powers of, 321–329
number of assistants employed by, 305
obtaining information about, 298
opening day of, 334
organization of, 282–311
oversight function of, 326, 328
party caucuses in, 333
political parties and, 299–302, 304
powers of, under Articles of
Confederation, 35–36, 39
presidential and vice-presidential
succession and, 66, 70, 322, 359,
363, 364
presidential powers limited by, 394–396
presidential vetoes overridden by, 390,
395
quorum requirements in, 342
sessions of, 284–285, 342, 378
structure of, 299–307
term of, 284–285
voting by, 300, 343–344
wars declared/not declared by, 317, 379
Congress for Racial Equality (CORE),
145
Congressional Budget Office (CBO),
307, 315, 320
Congressional Caucus for Women's
Issues, 295

Congressional committees, 297, 301–305
budget, 315
campaign, 201
conference, 305, 347
joint, 303, 305, 347
markup sessions of, 342
politics of, 304
power of, 302
reasons for, 302
select, 302–303
seniority rule and, 302, 304
size and number of, 302
staff assisting, 307
standing, 302, 303, 340, 342
subcommittees of, 301–302, 340, 342
Congressional Directory, 35, 298
Congressional districts, 286–289
Congressional Quarterly (CQ), 298
Congressional Record, 35, 307, 340, 344
Congressional Research Service (CRS),
307
Congressional Steel Caucus, 333
Congressional Sunbelt Council, 333
Congressional Women's Caucus, 333
Congresspersons:
campaigns by. *See* Campaigns
communicating with, 325
compensation and benefits for, 294–296
conduct of, 291, 293
increasing workload of, 305
incumbents, 289, 291
political affiliation of members of, 68
privileges and immunities of, 291, 296
profile of, 293–294
qualifications of, 291, 293
reprimand of, 291, 293
responsibilities of, 293–299
roles of, 296–297, 299
support staff and agencies for, 305–307
term of, 289, 291, 292, 308, 541
voting records of, 344
Connecticut Compromise (Connecticut
Plan), 41, 44
Conscription, 503
Consensus, 183, 635
Consent Calendar, 342
Consent of the governed, 14, 23, 34
Conservative Party (Great Britain), 630
Conservatives, 215
Consolidation:
of local governmental units, 603
of schools, 603
Constituents:
congressperson as servant of, 297
of executive departments, 405
mobilizing, by interest groups, 227
Constitution(s):
British, 628
French, 631
Japanese, 634
state. *See* State constitutions

Constitution, U.S., 53–73
adaptability of, 318
aliens protected by, 164
amending, 56, 63, 65–68, 70
amendments to. *See* Constitutional
amendments
Article I of (legislative powers), 56, 57,
67, 78, 80, 82, 103, 162, 283,
313–315, 318–319, 328, 472,
607
Article II of (executive powers), 56, 57,
70, 78, 356, 377, 496
Article III of (judicial powers), 56, 57,
60, 67, 439, 450
Article IV of (relations among the
states), 54, 56, 85–87, 574, 583
Article V of (amendment process; equal
suffrage in Senate), 56, 63, 292
Article VI of (supremacy clause), 56, 89,
522
articles of, 54, 56
Bill of Rights of. *See* Bill of Rights;
specific amendments
brevity of, 53, 522
cabinet not mentioned in, 366
census-taking required by, 162
checks and balances under, 57–58, 328,
394
commerce clause of, 67, 92–93,
607–608
compared to British, 628
concurrent powers under, 83–85
custom and usage and, 68, 70
due process clause of, 106–107, 122,
129–131, 170–171
elastic (necessary and proper) clause of,
80, 92, 318
elections and, 245, 247
equal protection clause of, 139–147,
150, 170–171, 437, 530
establishment clause of, 108–111
executive branch and, 6, 54, 56, 57, 67,
68, 70, 78, 316–317, 356–358,
377–378, 383, 386, 389, 391,
496
foreign policy and, 495–496
founding fathers (framers) of, 40, 53, 54,
57, 59, 77
"founding mothers" of, 33
free exercise clause of, 111–112
freedom of assembly under, 80, 103,
122–123
freedom of petition under, 103, 122–123
freedom of religion under, 80, 103,
108–112, 431
freedom of speech under, 80, 103,
113–121, 444–445
freedom of the press under, 80, 103,
116–121, 138
full faith and credit clause of, 86
horizontal federalism and, 85–86

interpretation of. *See* Court(s); Supreme Court, U.S.
judicial branch and, 54, 56–60, 67, 431–455
legislative branch and, 54, 56, 57, 67, 283–286, 291–292, 296, 299, 301, 314–317, 321, 328, 342, 347, 395, 540
limited government and, 56–57, 83, 583
models for, 28, 36
national supremacy under, 54, 56, 89, 93–94, 522
necessary and proper (elastic) clause of, 80, 92, 318
political parties and, 68, 201
popular sovereignty under, 57
powers delegated (enumerated, expressed) by, 78, 80, 313–318
powers denied by, 80, 82, 84
Preamble to, 54–56, 634
principles of government expressed by, 56–61, 75, 77, 85–86
privacy rights and, 133
privileges and immunities clause of, 85–86
property rights protected by, 643–644
ratification of, 43–47, 190, 440
relations among states and, 54, 56, 62, 85–88, 574, 583
representative democracy under, 18
separation of powers under, 57
slavery issue and, 41, 44
state constitutions and, 521–522
state powers under, 62, 78, 81–82, 104, 521–522
strict versus loose construction of, 92–94, 318, 321
structure of, 53–56
as supreme law of land, 53, 56, 432
supremacy clause of, 56, 89, 93–94, 522
taxing powers under, 607–609
United Nations Charter compared to, 511
voting rights under. *See* Voting rights
writing of, 28, 39–44
Constitutional amendments, 53, 55–57, 80, 171–172, 452. *See also* Bill of Rights; specific amendments
Civil War, 55, 142–143. *See also* Thirteenth Amendment; Fourteenth Amendment; Fifteenth Amendment
defined, 56
pre-Civil War, 55
proposed
to balance federal budget, 63
to lengthen House term, 289
number of, versus those ratified, 65–67
proposing, 63, 322, 526, 528
ratification of, 63, 66

repeal of, 65
twentieth-century, 55
Constitutional Convention of 1787, 33, 39–44, 48, 283–284, 355–356
Constitutional conventions:
Congress's power to call, 322
proposed, 48
state, 526, 528
Constitutional initiative, 528
Constitutional law, 432. *See also* Constitution, U.S.
Constitutional monarchy, 11, 627–628
Consul, 501
Consulate, 501
Consumer, waste-conscious, 482
Consumer Federation of America, 344
Consumer interest groups, 221, 222
Consumer Product Safety Commission (CPSC), 417
Consumer Reports, 221
Consumers Union, 221
Containment policy, 492
Contempt of Congress, 326
Contempt of court, 135
Contiguous boundaries, 287
Continental Congresses, 30–35, 39
Contracts, understanding, 570
Controlled (command) economic system, 638. *See also* Communism
Controller, state, 558
Conventions:
delegates to, 234
nominating, 234
national, 68, 124, 146, 200–201, 237–238
Cooley, Thomas, 583
Cooley's rule, 583
Cooperative federalism, 95
Copyright laws, 317
Corn Growers Association, 423
Cornwallis, General, 43
Coroner, county, 592
Corporate income taxes, 469, 471, 609
Corporation:
government, 418–419
municipal, 583, 593–594
Correlations, 318
Council-manager plan, 597–599
Council of Economic Advisors (CEA), 371, 394, 464
Council on Environmental Quality (CEQ), 371–372, 480
Councils of government (COGs), 603
Counsel, right to, 135, 136, 433, 576–577
Counties, 590
government of, 590–593
number of, in U.S., 590
relative weakness of, 593
County board, 591
County boroughs (Great Britain), 631
County clerk, 592

County courts, 591
County Election, The (Bingham), 262
County-manager plan, 592–593
Court(s):
achieving policy goals through, 227
appellate, 438–439, 563, 565
checks on, 451–452
common law tradition in, 431–432
contempt of, 135
county, 591
decisions and opinions of, 443. *See also* Case law; Common law
docket of, 596
English, 431
exclusionary rule of, 133–134
federal, 436–442
of appeals (circuit courts), 438–439
congressional power to create, 317
constitutional authority for, 54, 56–60, 67
development of, 436–437
district, 438
jobs with, 174
judges of, 377, 383, 386. *See also* Supreme Court Justices
jurisdiction of, 439–442
Supreme Court. *See* Supreme Court, U.S.
system of, 437
interpretation of Constitution by, 68, 105–106, 453. *See also* Judicial review; Supreme Court, U.S.
judicial review by, 58–59, 67–68, 328, 396, 436, 442
jurisdiction of, 433, 436, 439–442, 563–565
justice (of the peace), 564
juvenile, 82
king's, 431
lobbying directed at, 224
magistrate, 564
probate, 564
small claims, 564, 566–567
state, 562–581
of appeal and review, 563, 565
of general jurisdiction, 563–565
highest (supreme), 563–565
judges of, 565–571
of limited jurisdiction, 563–564
supreme, 547
typical system of, 563–565
traffic, 564
trial, 438, 563–564
Cox v. New Hampshire, 122
Credentials Committee, 238
Crime(s), 571
in colonial America versus today, 132
definition of, in different cultures, 140
loss of citizenship for, 160
punishment for. *See* Punishment; Sentencing

witnessing a, 531
Criminal law, 432, 571–579. *See also*
     Criminal process
Criminal process:
   due process rights and, 129–131. *See*
        also Due process
   freedom of press and, 118, 120, 138
   illegal drugs and, 596
   rights of accused persons in, 131–139,
        433, 575–578. *See also* Criminal
        process; Due process
   speedy-trial statutes and, 596
   state, 575–579
Cruel and unusual punishment,
     138–139, 579
Crump, Edward, 600
Cuba:
   dictatorship in, 11
   emigration from, to U.S., 177
   freedom of speech and, 113
   refugees from, 161
Culture, government and, 6–7, 589
Cuomo, Mario, 552
Curia regis, 431
Currency, 80, 315, 465
Custom:
   British constitution based on, 628
   presidential powers derived from,
        379–380
   U.S. Constitution and, 68, 70
Customs (tax), U.S., 471
Czechoslovakia, political parties in, 183,
     197

D

Daley, Richard, 200, 602
Darman, Richard, 466
Das Kapital (**Marx**), 645
Daughters of Liberty, 33
Dayton, Jonathan, 40
Death penalty. *See* Capital punishment
Death taxes. *See* Inheritance taxes
Debate(s):
   analyzing a political, 362
   congressional, 343–345
   television, 249–250, 362
Debt, national (public), 315, 466–467
Decentralization, 90
Decisions:
   court, 443. *See also* Case law; Common
        law
   making, as citizenship skill, 38
Declaration of Independence, 7, 9, 32,
     34, 129, 141
Declaration of 1789 (France), 631
De facto **segregation**, 144
Defeat, The (**Warren**), 33

Defense, national. *See* National defense;
     National Security
Defense Contract Audit Agency, 424
Deficit, budget. *See* Federal budget deficit
De Gaulle, Charles, 663
De Jonge v. *Oregon*, 122, 171
De jure **segregation**, 144
Delegated (expressed) powers, 78, 80,
     313–318
Delegates, 30, 234, 297
Deliberative organ, of U.N., 511
Democracy:
   Athenian model of, 11–12, 18
   defined, 11
   direct, 11–12, 18, 27, 540
   federalism distinguished from, 77
   as foreign policy goal, 505
   parliamentary, 12
   presidential, 12
   principles of, 12, 14
   representative (indirect), 12, 18
Democracy in America (**de Tocqueville**),
     217
Democratic Party, 182, 184, 186–187,
     190, 198
   affiliation with, socioeconomic class
        and, 214, 273–276
   beginnings of, 191
   Governors' Conference of, 548
   Great Depression and, 421
   in Jacksonian era, 185
   national committee of, 201
   national convention of, 68, 146, 201
   national headquarters/address of, 188
   organizational structure of, 199–201
   presidents affiliated with, 196
   splinter parties formed from, 197
Democratic-Republicans, 190–191, 420
Demonstrations:
   by interest groups, 227–228
   in People's Republic of China, 15, 648
   protected by Constitution, 80
Denaturalization, 160–161
Deng Xiaoping, 648
Denmark, government of, 11
Dennis v. *United States*, 116
Dennison Rule, 86
Departments:
   of French government, 633–634
   of state governments, 551, 559, 575
   of U.S. government. *See* U.S.
        Department of _____
Deportation, 164
Deposit insurance, 419, 485
Depressions, 464. *See also* Great
     Depression
Deregulation, 417
de Secondat, Charles. *See* Montesquieu,
     Baron de
Desegregation, 75, 87, 143–147
D'Estaing, Valery Giscard, 633

Deterrence, 492–493
de Tocqueville, Alexis, 217, 452, 531,
     545
Détente, 493
Diamos (**Japan**), 634
Dictatorship, 11
Differently abled persons, 148, 149, 408
Dillon, John F., 583
Dillon v. *Gloss*, 66
Dillon's rule, 583
Dinkens, David, 599
Diplomacy, 507
Diplomat, 387
Direct democracy, 11–12, 18, 27, 540
Direct primary, 235–236
Direct tax, 314
"Dirty Dozen," 227
Disabled persons. *See* **Differently abled**
     persons
Discharge Calendar, 342
Discrimination:
   employment, 148, 150, 151, 316, 408
   gender, 150, 408
   prohibited by Civil Rights Act of 1964,
        147, 316, 408
   racial, 408. *See also* Desegregation;
        Segregation
   reverse, 148, 150, 151
Dissenting (court) opinion, 443
District, congressional, 286–289
District attorney, 575, 592
District court, U.S., 438
Diversity of citizenship, 442
Divine right theory, 7, 9
Division of powers, 78
Divorce, rights of children after,
     82–83
Dixiecrat (States' Rights) Party, 197
Doctrine, 116
Dole, Bob, 290
Dollar, coin replacing, 465
Domestic violence, 87
Door-to-door campaigning, 241
Door-to-door sales, 93, 415, 418
Double jeopardy, 137
Douglas, Stephen A., 360
Douglas, William O., 116, 283
Draft, 503
Draft registration:
   as citizen's responsibility, 107
   gender discrimination and, 150
Dred Scott v. *Sandford*, 157–158, 436,
     452
Drinking age, minimum, 81, 617, 619
Drugs, war on, 596
Dual federalism, 94–95
Due process, 106–107, 122, 129–131,
     170–171. *See also* Fifth
     Amendment; Fourteenth
     Amendment

challenges to, 130–131
defined, 129
government taxation and, 608
juvenile justice and, 572–573
procedural, 130
in state criminal process, 576
substantive, 130
Dukakis, Michael, 244, 251–252, 274, 341, 384, 550, 556
Duncan, Gloria, 588
Dyrstad, Joanell, 556

E
Earth First, 514
East-West Foreign Trade Board, 414
Eastern Airlines, 417
Eastern Europe, communism in, 647–648. *See also* People's Republic of China; Soviet Union
Economic activity:
circular flow of, 639–640
directing, by taxation, 473–474
Economic information, reading maps for, 527
Economic prosperity, as foreign policy goal, 505
Economic Report of the President, 371, 389
Economic sanctions, 510
Economic status:
political attitudes and, 214
political party affiliation and, 190
voters' choices and, 276
Economic system(s):
American, 641
command (controlled), 638, 648. *See also* Communism
converging, 644–648
global, 15
market (capitalist), 638–644
mixed, 640
Edison, Thomas, 246
Editor, writing letter to, 209
Education. *See also* School(s)
of congresspersons, 293
political affiliation and, 190
state and local spending on, 584, 618
state commissioner of, 558
as state responsibility, 523
of Supreme Court justices, 448–449
voting and, 271, 276
Eighteenth Amendment (Prohibition), 63, 65, 66
Eighth Amendment (cruel and unusual punishment), 138–139, 579
Eisenhower, Dwight D., 87, 89, 143, 157, 196, 274, 357, 363, 365, 367, 379, 380, 396
Elastic (necessary and proper) clause, 80, 92, 318

Elderly:
interest groups representing, 221
as percentage of population, 221
poverty among, 476
Elected chief executive plan, 593
Elections:
congressional, 289, 292
Constitution and, 245
in France, 633
general, 245, 247
in Great Britain, 630
gubernatorial, 546, 559
held at fixed intervals, 245
initiatives and, 540, 541
interest groups' involvement in, 225, 227
nonpartisan, 236, 533
off-year, of governors, 559
partisan, 533
presidential, 194–195, 247–256, 269
primary, 184, 235–237
realigning, 193
recall, 245, 540, 547
referendum, 540
role of media in, 249–256, 269
run-off, 184, 236
special, 245
of state court judges, 568
of state legislators, 533, 540, 541
structure of, in U.S., 244–249
supervision of, 591
third parties' failure to win, 198
voter turnout for, 269
Elective process, 184
Electoral college system, 247–249
Electorate, 184, 261, 277
Electors, 247
Electronic surveillance, 58–59, 67–68, 133
Elizabeth I, queen of England, 26
Elizabeth II, queen of England, 628
Ellsberg, Daniel, 117
El Salvador, refugees from, 161
Emancipation Proclamation, 360, 367
Embassy, 500
Emergency Highway Conservation Act of 1974, 617
Employment:
discrimination in, 148, 150, 151, 316, 408. *See also* Discrimination
equal opportunity in, 148
fiscal policy and, 464–469
free exercise of religion and, 431
in government jobs, 272–273, 424, 425, 621. *See also* Civil Service
rights of employees and, 408–409
wrongful discharge from, 408
Employment Act of 1946, 394, 464
Enabling act, 88
Encyclopedia of Associations, 218
Enemy aliens, 161

Enforcement powers, 387
Engel v. *Vitale*, 109
England. *See* Great Britain
Enumerated (expressed) powers, 78, 80, 313–318
Environment, 17, 479–484
Environmental Action, 344
Environmental Defense Fund, 221
Environmental impact statement, 481
Environmental interest groups, 221, 223, 227
Environmental Protection Agency (EPA), 314, 416, 484
Equal employment opportunity (EEO), 148
Equal Employment Opportunity Commission (EEOC), 416
Equal Pay Act of 1963, 408
Equal protection, 139–147, 150, 170–171, 437, 530
affirmative action policies and, 148, 150
discriminatory state laws and, 142
gender discrimination and, 148, 150
Equal Rights Amendment, **71**, **295**
Equalization, categorical grants and, 616
Error, sampling, 210
Escobedo v. *Illinois*, 135
Eskimos. *See* Native Americans
Espionage, 115
Espionage Act of 1917, 116
Establishment clause, 108–111
Estate taxes, **609**. *See also* Inheritance taxes
Ethiopians, starvation of, 212
Ethnic background, voters' choices and, 276
Ethnic organizations, 223
Everson v. *Board of Education*, 171
Evidence, in criminal process, 132–134
Evolutionary theory of government origin, 7, 9
Ex post facto **laws**, 104
Excessive bail, 138
Excessive entanglement theory, 110
Excise taxes, 469, 471, 474, 609
Exclusionary rule, 133–134
Exclusive jurisdiction, 442
Executive agreements, 67, 388, 396
Executive authority, early fear of, in U.S., 34
Executive branch. *See also* Bureaucracy; President
constitutional powers and duties of, 6, 54, 56–58, 67, 68, 70, 78, 316–317, 356, 377–378, 383, 386, 389, 391
Cabinet and. *See* Cabinet
departments of. *See* Bureaucracy; Executive departments
foreign policy and, 496–498

judicial branch checked by, 452
legislative branch checked by. *See*
  Veto(es), presidential
of state government, 550–553. *See also*
  Governor; State(s),
  administration of
Executive departments, 405–406, 410
Executive Office of the President (EOP),
  369–372
Executive orders, 379–380
Executive powers:
  of governor, 550–553
  of president. *See* President,
    constitutional powers and
    responsibilities of
Executive privilege, 396
Expansionism, 490
Expatriation, 160
Expenditures. *See* Spending
Export/Import Bank of the United
  States (Ex/Im Bank), 419
Exports:
  defined, 44, 80
  taxes and, 80, 607–608
Expressed (enumerated) powers, 78, 80,
  313–318
Expulsion, from U.S. Congress, 291
Extradition, interstate, 86, 574
Extraordinary majority, 528
Exxon Corporation, 479
Exxon *Valdez*, 479, 552

F

Fact and opinion, distinguishing
  between, 451
Fair trial. *See* Trial, fair
Family:
  law pertaining to, 82–83
  political affiliation and, 190
  political socialization by, 210–211
Faubus, Orval, 89, 143, 547
Federal Aviation Administration (FAA),
  333, 450
Federal budget, 63, 315
  control over, 320
  fiscal policy and, 464–469
Federal budget deficit, 466–467, 469
Federal Bureau of Investigation (FBI),
  173, 397, 413, 514
*Federal Career Directory: A Guide for
  College Students* (OPM), 175
Federal Child Abuse Prevention and
  Treatment Act of 1984, 82
Federal Communications Commission
  (FCC), 67, 120, 252, 415, 416
Federal courts. *See* Court(s), federal
Federal Deposit Insurance Corporation
  (FDIC), 419, 485
Federal Election Campaign Act of 1974,
  242–243

Federal Election Commission (FEC),
  242–243, 414
Federal government, defined, 7. *See also*
  Government, U.S.
Federal grants, 615–619
Federal Judgeship Act of 1984, 438–439
Federal questions, 442
Federal Regulation of Lobbying Act of
  1946, 228
Federal Reserve System, 459, 461
  Board of Governors of (Fed), 416, 461,
    464
Federal Savings and Loan Insurance
  Corporation (FSLIC), 485
Federal system, 77–85. *See also*
  Federalism
Federal Trade Commission (FTC), 93,
  222, 333, 415–416, 418, 438, 450
Federal Water Pollution Control Act of
  1955 (as amended), 479, 481
Federalism, 74–99
  changing face of, 94–96
  cooperative, 95
  democracy distinguished from, 77
  dual, 94–95
  horizontal, 85
  new, 95–96, 616, 621
  principle of, 59
  reasons for, 77–78
Federalist Papers, The, 45–46, 358, 386,
  436, 450
Federalists, 44–46, 60n, 61, 184, 190–191
Feiner v. *New York*, 122
Fellowship of Reconciliation, 499
Felonies, 131, 433
Feminist movement, 64. *See also*
  Women, rights of
Ferguson, James E., 547n
Ferguson, Miriam ("Ma"), 554
Ferraro, Geraldine, 358n
Fifteenth Amendment (voting rights for
  African-American males), 82, 86,
  266, 276, 437
Fifth Amendment:
  double jeopardy prohibited by, 137
  due process clause of, 129, 137
  privilege against self-incrimination
    under, 134–136, 329
Fighting words, 121
Filibuster, 345
Film media, 120
Financial Institution Reform, Recovery,
  and Enforcement Act (Thrift
  Bailout Act) of 1989, 485
Fire protection, provided by local
  government, 584–585
Fireside chats, 380
First Amendment, 170
  freedom of assembly and petition under,
    80, 103, 122–123
  freedom of press under, 116–121

freedom of religion under, 80, 103,
  108–112, 431
freedom of speech under, 80, 103,
  113–121, 444–445
freedom of the press under, 80, 103,
  116–121, 138
tolerance of differences and, 176
First Bank of the United States, 89
First Continental Congress, 30
Fiscal policy, 459, 464–469
Fiscal year, 370
Fitzgerald, A. Ernest, 424
Flag-burning issue, 124, 452
Flag-salute issue, 112, 211
Foley, Thomas, 186, 299
Food and Drug Administration (FDA),
  224, 417
Food stamps, 477
Force theory of government origin, 7, 9
Ford, Gerald, 248, 322, 359, 362, 363,
  365, 383, 386, 395, 397, 498
Foreign aid, 506–507
Foreign Intelligence Surveillance Act of
  1978, 134
Foreign invasion, protection against, 87
Foreign policy:
  Congress and, 316, 498–499
  defined, 489
  elections and, 274
  executive branch and, 82, 377, 387–388,
    496–498
  goals of, 505–506
  history of American, 489–493
  how to influence, 498
  making of, 495–499
  tools of, 506–510
Foreign service, 500–501
Foreigners, percentage of U.S. public
  debt held by, 469
Fortas, Abe, 447–448
Founding fathers, 40
"Founding mothers," 33
Fourteenth Amendment, 82, 86
  Bill of Rights extended to states by,
    170–172, 433, 523
  capital punishment and, 579
  citizenship defined by, 158–159,
    170–172
  congressional districting and, 530
  due process clause of, 106–107, 122,
    129–130, 170–171, 433, 608
  equal protection clause of, 142–144,
    150, 170–171, 437, 530
  gender discrimination and, 150
  government taxation limited by, 608
  nongovernmental discrimination and,
    145
Fourth Amendment (searches and
  seizures), 67, 133–134
France:

Bastille Day in, 7, 8
government and politics in, 76, 182, 631–634
Revolution of 1879 in, 8, 631
Franchise, voting, 261. *See also* Voting rights
Frankfurter, Felix, 131
Franklin, Benjamin, 9, 32, 40, 48, 181
Frazee **v.** *Illinois Department of Employment Security*, **431, 432**
Frazier, Lynn J., 540, 547
Free enterprise system, 641–642. *See also* Capitalism
Free exercise clause, 111–112. *See also* Freedom of religion
Free Soil Party, 196, 197
Freedom, individual, as principle of democracy, 14
Freedom of assembly, 80, 103, 122–123
Freedom of choice, 642–643
Freedom of Information Act of 1966, 412–413
Freedom of petition, 103, 122–123
Freedom of religion, 80, 103, 108–112, 431
Freedom of speech, 80, 103, 113–121
  advertising and, 120–121
  begging and, 114
  commercial speech and, 120–121
  in high schools, 444–445
  judicial doctrines affecting, 116–118
  limits placed on, 115–116, 121
  media and, 116–121. *See also* Freedom of the press
  pure speech and, 113
  seditious speech and, 115–116
  speech plus and, 113, 115
  symbolic speech and, 115
Freedom of the press, 80, 103, 116–121
  confidentiality and, 118
  fair trial and, 118, 120, 138
  judicial doctrines affecting, 116–118
Friday Conference, 447
Friedman, Milton, 627
Friendly, Fred W., 381
Frontiero **v.** *Richardson*, 150
Fugitives, 86, 574
Full faith and credit clause, 86
Fulton, Robert, 92–93
Functional consolidations, 603
Fundamental Orders of Connecticut, 28
Furman **v.** *Georgia*, 139

G
Gag orders, 118
Gallup, George, 208
Gallup Poll, 208, 216
Gambling, legalized, 612–613
Gandhi, Mahatma, 140

Gannet Company **v.** *De Pasquale*, 118, 120
Garfield, James, 359*n*, 363, 421
Gault **decision**, 572
Gender discrimination, 150–151, 408
Gender gap, 276
General Accounting Office (GAO), 307, 424
General elections, 245, 247
General grants-in-aid, 617. *See also* Revenue-sharing program
General jurisdiction, 563–565
General Motors Corporation, 222
General Schedule (GS) ratings and salaries, 422
General Services Administration (GSA), 413–414
Generalization, defined, 119
Geographic region, voters' choices and, 276
George III, king of England, 29, 30, 32, 283
Germany:
  multiparty system in, 182
  Nazi. *See* Nazi Germany
Gerry, Elbridge, 287
Gerrymandering, 287, 289, 530, 532
Giaratano, Joseph M., 556
Gibbons **v.** *Ogden*, 92–93, 316, 440
Gideon **v.** *Wainwright*, 136, 147, 171, 433
Gift taxes, 469, 471
Ginsburg, Douglas, 448
Gitlow **v.** *New York*, 117, 171
Glaser, Norm, 90
Glaspie, April, 342
Glittering generalities, 255
Global economy, 15
Global environmental concerns, 17
Global warming, 483–484
Goldwater, Barry, 251, 274
Gorbachev, Mikhail, 17, 507, 645
Gore, Albert, Jr., 186, 720
Government(s):
  around the world, compared, 626–652
  authoritarian, 11, 646
  authority of, 6
  autocratic, 11, 646
  defined, 4
  democratic, 11–14. *See also* Democracy
  effect of, on our everyday lives, 4–5
  employees of, 272–273, 424, 425, 621. *See also* Civil Service
  flow of power in various systems of, 77
  forms of, 9–14
  in France, 631–634
  in Great Britain, 627–631
  how to affect, 5
  limited, 23–24, 56, 57
  local. *See* Local government

  meaning of, 3–7
  necessity for, 3
  number of, in U.S. today, 75–76
  origins of, theories on, 7, 10, 24–26
  purposes of, 5–7
  representative, 23–24
  republican form of, 86
  state. *See* State(s)
  totalitarian, 11, 646
  unitary system of, 7, 76, 630, 633
  voluntary consent to, 14, 23, 34
  why study, 4–7
Government, U.S., 7, 621. *See also* Federalism
  under Articles of Confederation, 34–39, 76–77, 85, 86, 283, 313, 315, 355
  budget of, 63, 315, 320, 464–469
  in colonial era, 26–34. *See also* American Revolution
  constitutional powers and duties of, 78–89. *See also* Constitution, U.S.
  debt of, 315, 466–468
  European origins of, 26–29
  independence of, 29–34. *See also* American Revolution
  jobs with, 173–175. *See also* Government(s), employees of
  land owned by, 91
  powers of, 78–89, 92–93. *See also* Constitution, U.S.
  role of, in American economy, 641
  strong central, 34
  taxation by, 469–474, 607–608. *See also* Tax(es); Taxation
  three branches of, 313
Government Accounting Office (GAO), 326, 328
Government agencies. *See* Administrative agencies; Bureaucracy
Government bonds, 315, 466, 474
Government corporations, 418–419
Government Printing Office (GPO), 307
Government publications, using, 35
Government regulation, 417, 437, 451, 596, 640–642. *See also* Deregulation; Reregulation
  constitutional authority for, 92–93. *See also* Commerce clause
  environmental, 479–484
  of interest groups and lobbyists, 228–229
  by states, 81
Governor, 545–556
  in colonial era, 554
  compensation of, 547
  death or removal of, 547
  executive powers of, 550–553

election of, 546
judicial appointments by, 565
judicial powers of, 554–556
legislative powers of, 553–554
lieutenant. *See* Lieutenant governor
many roles of, 548–549
off-year election of, 559
qualifications of, 546
selection of, 546
state constitutional description of, 550
term of, 546–547
**Gramm-Rudman-Hollings Deficit
    Reduction Act of 1985**, 467, 469
Grand jury, 137, 575–576
Grand Old Party (GOP). *See* Republican
    Party
Grandfather clause, 266
Grant, Ulysses S., 447
Grants, federal, 615–619
Graphs, line, 468
Gray Panthers, 221
Great Britain:
    American colonies of, 26–34. *See also*
        American Revolution
    bicameral legislature in, 284
    Bill of Rights in, 23, 628
    cabinet in, 628–629
    common law tradition in, 431, 628
    constitution of, 628
    constitutional monarchy in, 11, 627–628
    elections in, 245, 630
    local government in, 630–631
    Magna Carta of, 23, 129, 628
    Norman conquest of, 431
    Parliament of, 23, 284, 336, 628–629
    parliamentary democracy in, 12
    political parties in, 630
    prime minister of, 382, 628–629
    queen's role in, 382, 627–628
    U.S. aid to, during World War II, 462
    U.S. independence from, 7. *See also*
        American Revolution
Great Compromise, 41, 44, 284
Great Depression, 95–96, 462, 545
    Civil Service reform and, 421
    fiscal policy during, 464
    impact of, on political parties, 193, 196
    no political consensus during, 183
    presidential economic powers expanded
        during, 379
    Social Security designed during, 477
Green vote, 275
Greenhouse effect, 483–484
Gregg v. *Georgia*, 139
Grenada invasion, 67, 386
Grievances, 30
Griswold, Roger, 191
Griswold v. *Connecticut*, 171
Group, The (Warren), 33

Garfield, James A., 420
Guiteau, Charles J., 420, 421
Gun control issue, 224, 225, 227. *See
    also* National Rifle Association
    (NRA)

H

Habeas corpus, **writ of**, 103–104, 328
**Habitual Criminal Sterilization Act of
    1935**, 131
Haitian refugees, 161
Hamilton, Alexander, 39, 40, 44–46, 48,
    164, 190, 318, 321, 355, 358, 366,
    386, 450
Hamilton v. *Regents of the University of
    California*, 171
Hammer v. *Dagenhart*, 95
Hancock, John, 32
Hand, Learned, 106, 563
Handicapped. *See* Differently abled
    persons
Hannighan, Tom, 541
Harding, Warren G., 359*n,* 557*n*
**Hare Krishna Festival of Giant
    Chariots**, 108
Harkin, Tom, 149
Harrison, Benjamin, 249
Harrison, William H., 318, 359
Hartnett, Thomas, 308
**Hatch Act (Political Activities Act) of
    1939**, 421
Hay, John, 490
Hayakawa, S.I., 388
Hayes, Rutherford B., 249
Haynsworth, Clement, 447
Hazelwood School District v. *Cathy
    Kuhlmeier*, 444–445
Heart, Peter, 240
Henderson v. *Mayor of New York*, 166
Hereditary peers, 629
Hereditary ruler, 627–628
Henry, Patrick, 46
Henry I, king of England, 129
Hijacking, 514
Hiroshima, 386, 491
Hispanic Caucus, 333
Hispanics:
    equality for, 148
    immigration and, 165
    congressional representative of, 336
    children of, in poverty, 475
    in Civil Service positions, 425
    increasing number of, in U.S., 174, 176
    as percentage of U.S. population, 165
    voting rights for, 268
*History of the Rise, Progress, and
    Determination of the American
    Revolution, The* (Warren), 33

Hitler, Adolf, 11
Hobbes, Thomas, 9, 24–25
Hollerith, Herman, 162
Hollings, Ernest, 301
Holmes, Oliver Wendell, 113, 115, 117,
    123, 459
Home-rule movement, 583–584
Homeless, 476
Hong Kong, 648
Hoover, Herbert, 285, 462
Hopkins, Stephen, 23
Hopper, of House, 340
Horizontal federalism, 85
Horton, Willie, 252
House Agricultural Committee, 411
House Appropriations Committee, 304,
    325, 466
House Armed Services Committee, 295,
    499
House Assassinations committees, 303
House Banking Committee, 338, 342
House Budget Committee, 315, 320
House Calendar, 342
House "committee of the whole," 343
House Committee on Agriculture, 424
**House Committee on Energy and
    Commerce**, 411
**House Committee on Interior and
    Insular Affairs**, 342
**House Committee on the Post Office
    and Civil Service**, 295
House Ethics Committee, 291
**House International Relations
    Committee**, 304, 499
House Judiciary Committee, 295, 322,
    397
House of Burgesses (Virginia), 28
House of Commons (Great Britain),
    284, 300, 529*n,* 628–629
House of Councilers (Japan), 635
House of Lords (Great Britain), 284
House of Representatives, 284, 628–629.
    See also Congress, U.S.;
        Congresspersons
    apportionment of, 285–289
    bills considered by. *See* Bills,
        congressional
    calendars in, 342
    campaign financing and, 244
    census-taking and, 162
    clerk of, 334
    committees of. *See* Congressional
        committees; specific committees
    compared to Senate, 292
    constitutional amendment process and,
        63
    constitutional number of representatives
        in, 284
    Document Room of, 298

electoral power of, 322
floor debate in, 343
hopper of, 340
impeachment proceedings initiated by, 321
Japanese, 635
Journal of, 340
leadership of, 299–300, 333
majority leader of, 300
members of. *See* Congresspersons
minority leader of, 300
organization of, 289–291
political party caucuses in, 333
presidential elections and, 248
Republican Conference of, 304
rules of, 334
size of, 18, 185, 284, 289
Speaker of, 299–300, 334, 340, 343, 344
staff of, 334
three-fifths compromise and, 41
voting in, 343–344
whips in, 300
House Rules Committee, 304, 342
House Select Committee on Children, Youth, and Families, 295, 475
House Select Committee to Investigate Covert Arms Transaction with Iran, 303
House Un-American Activities Committee (HUAC), 329
House Ways and Means Committee, 304, 314, 323, 384, 464
Hoyt v. *Florida*, 150
Human rights, 113, 505, 637
Hung jury, 137, 435, 577
Hunger Action Handbook—What You Can Do and How to Do It (Seeds), 88
Hungry, helping the, 88
Huntington Library and Art Gallery, 523
Hussein, Saddam, 11, 15, 17, 510, 646
Hyperpluralism, 521

I

Idaho Environmental Council, 90
Ideological parties, 197. *See also* Political parties
Ideologues, 216
Illegal aliens, 161, 164, 168–169, 177
Illegal drugs, 596
Image of candidate, 240, 274
Immigrants, 161, 164, 174, 176
Immigration, 164, 166–170. *See also* Aliens; Immigrants
Immigration acts, 167, 168
Immigration and Naturalization Service, 173
Immunity. *See also* Privileges and immunities

congressional, 296
granted to witnesses, 326
Impeachment:
constitutional reasons for, 395
of governor, 547
of judges or justices, 60, 570
of president, 317, 321–322, 397
president's power to pardon and, 386
Implied powers, 78, 80, 318–321
Import taxes, 607–608
Impoundment, 320, 379
In re Oliver, 171
Inalienable rights, 34. *See also* Natural rights
Income:
of congresspersons, 293–295
voting and, 276
Income-maintenance programs, 476–477
Income tax, 469, 471–474, 609
Income transfer, 477
Incorporation, municipal, 583, 593–594
Incorporation theory, 172
Incumbents:
in Congress, 289, 291
defined, 274
in state legislatures, 308, 541
Independence:
Declaration of, 7, 9, 32, 34, 129, 141
Resolution of, 31, 32
Independence Hall (Philadelphia), 40, 57
Independent executive agencies, 410–414
Independent regulatory agencies, 414–418
Independents, political, 202–203
Indian Queen, 40
Indictment, 137, 575–576
Indirect democracy, 12
Indirect tax, 314
Individual Retirement Account (IRA), 474
Information:
an, in criminal procedure, 576
analyzing, 348
economic, reading maps for, 527
Inherent powers, 78, 80
Inherent rights, 34. *See also* Natural rights
Inheritance taxes, 469, 471, 609
Initiative, 540, 541
In-kind subsidies, 475
Inouye, Daniel, 327
Institute for Policy Studies, 499
Institutions, defined, 7
Instructed delegate, 297
Insurance, deposit, 419, 485
Integration. *See* Desegregation
Intelligence, defined, 497
Inter-American Treaty of Reciprocal Assistance (Rio Pact) of 1947, 508

Interdependence of nations, 15, 17
Interest group(s), 4, 217–228
agricultural, 220–221
business, 218, 220
church-related, 223
consumer, 221, 222
criticisms of, 229
defined, 217
for the elderly, 221
environmental, 221, 227
ethnic organizations, 223
increasing number of, 218–223
labor, 220
parties compared to, 218
policy-shaping techniques used by, 223–228
professional, 223
profiles of selected, 219
regulation of, 228
view of, by the press, 228
Interest rates, 459
Intergovernmental transfers, 614–619
Interim committees, 537
Internal affairs, defined, 511
Internal Revenue Service, 174
International Brotherhood of Teamsters, 220
International Business Machines Corp., 162
International Longshoremen's Union, 220
International trade:
as foreign policy tool, 510
in global economy, 15
Interstate commerce, 44, 67, 315. *See also* Commerce clause
Interstate Commerce Commission (ICC), 414–417
Interstate compacts, 86
Interstate extradition, 86, 574
Interstate Oil and Gas Compact of 1935, 86
Interventionism, 490
Intolerable Acts of 1774, 30
Intrastate commerce, 94, 522
Investigative powers of Congress, 324–326, 329
Iran:
American hostages in, 274, 303, 328, 388. See also Iran-*contra* affair
government of, 108, 388
Iran-*contra* affair, 303, 305, 327, 328, 497
Iraq:
dictatorship in, 11
freedom of speech and, 113
invasion of Kuwait by, 7, 15, 17, 212, 379, 395, 497, 504, 510, 513, 646. *See also* Persian Gulf War
threat of worldwide terrorism by, 514

U.S. ambassador to, 342
Irish Republican Army (IRA), 514
Iron curtain, 492, 504
Iron triangle, 423–424
Islam, 108
Isolationism, 489
Israel, multiparty system in, 183
Issue-oriented parties, 196–197
Italy:
  Mussolini's dictatorship in, 11
  political parties in, 183

J

Jackson, Andrew, 94, 95, 191, 234, 368,
    378, 420, 425, 443, 447, 452, 545
Jackson, Jesse, 185
Jackson, Robert H., 112
Jamestown, Virginia, 27
Japan, government and politics in, 76,
    634–638
Japanese relocation camps, 161
Japanese Socialist Party (JSP), 638
Jay, John, 44, 45, 46, 261
Jefferson, Thomas, 9, 32, 33, 40, 48, 60,
    61, 108, 116, 181, 190, 191, 322,
    334, 336, 363, 366, 378, 420
Jeffersonians, 190, 420
Jehovah's Witnesses, 112
Jim Crow laws, 142–143
John, king of England, 23, 24
Johnson, Alma, 503
Johnson, Andrew, 395
Johnson, Eddie B., 532
Johnson, Gregory Lee, 124
Johnson, Lyndon B., 67, 87, 148, 172,
    196, 251, 266, 274, 386, 387, 447,
    615
Johnston, Henry S., 547*n*
Joint Chiefs of Staff (JCS), 371, 497,
    501
Joint Committee on Printing, 35
Joint committees:
  of state legislatures, 537
  of U.S. Congress, 303, 305, 347
Joint Economic Committee (JEC), 303,
    305
Joint resolutions, 337
Joseph Napolitan Associates, 240
Journal **(of House of Representatives)**,
    340
Joyce, James, 121
Judges. *See also* Supreme Court justices
  federal, 58, 324, 377, 383, 386, 396,
      439, 447–448
  sitting, 569*n*
  state, 565–571
Judicial activism, 450–451

Judicial branch, 431–452. *See also*
    Court(s); Supreme Court, U.S.
  constitutional powers of, 54, 56–60, 67,
    431–452
  checks on, 451–452
  presidential powers limited by, 396
Judicial circuits, 438
Judicial implementation, 443
Judicial powers. *See also* Judicial branch
  of Congress, 317
  of state governor, 554–556
Judicial restraint, 450–451
Judicial review, 58–59, 67–68, 328, 396,
    436, 442
Judiciary. *See* Judicial branch
Judiciary Act of 1789, 60
Junkets, 342
Jurisdiction:
  appellate, 436
  concurrent, 442
  diversity, 442
  exclusive, 442
  of federal courts, 439–442
  general, 563–565
  limited, 563–564
  original, 436
  over persons and property, 433, 436
  of state courts, 563–565
  of state police, 574
Jury:
  citizen's duty to serve on, 173, 434
  grand, 137, 575–576
  hung, 137, 435, 577
  petit, 576
  selection of, 576–577
  size of, 137
  trial by, 23, 130, 136–137, 576
  verdict of, 577
Jus sanguinis, 158
Jus soli, 158
Justice courts, 564
Justice of the peace, 564
Juvenile justice system, 82, 572–573

K

Katz **v.** *United States*, 133
Kennedy, Anthony, 448
Kennedy, John F., 67, 87, 173, 196, 249,
    303, 318, 338, 358, 359, 365, 497
Kennedy, Robert, 303
Kent State University, 575
Key, V. O., 190
Keynote speaker, 238
Khomeni, Ayatollah, 388
King's court, 431
King, Martin Luther, Jr., 87, 129,
    140–141, 145, 146, 151, 185, 214,
    266–267, 303, 387

as *Architect of the American Dream*,
    140–141
Kissinger, Henry, 489, 493, 497
Kitchen Cabinet, 368
Klopfer **v.** *North Carolina*, 171
Knox, Henry, 366
Komeito **(Japan)**, 638
"Koreagate," 228
Korean War, 67, 317, 379, 510
Ku Klux Klan, 123, 146
Kuwait, Iraqi invasion of, 7, 15, 17, 212,
    379, 395, 497, 504, 510, 513, 646.
    See also Persian Gulf War

L

Labor force, 220
Labor interest groups, 220
Labor theory of value, 645
Labor unions, 123, 220
Labour Party (Great Britain), 630
Landon, Alfred, 208
Laswell, Harold D., 4
Law(s):
  administration of, by state governor,
    551–552
  of the blood (*jus sanguinis*), 158
  case, 431–432
  citizen's responsibility to obey, 107
  civil, 432
  common, 431–432, 628
  constitutional, 432
  criminal, 432, 571–579. *See also*
    Criminal process
  due process of. *See* Due process
  equal protection under. *See* Equal
    protection
  ex post facto, 104
  how a bill becomes a. *See* Bills,
    congressional; Lawmaking
    process
  Jim Crow, 142–143
  rights of accused under, 131–139, 433,
    575–578. *See also* Criminal
    process; Due process
  rule of, 57
  segregation, 142–143. *See also*
    Desegregation
  shield, 118
  of the soil (*jus soli*), 158
  sources and types of, 431–432
  state, 142–144, 571–579
  statutory, 432, 522
  unconstitutional, 58–60
  victim compensation, 571, 574
Law clerks, 447
Law lords (Great Britain), 629
Lawmaking process:
  in state legislatures, 538–539
  in U.S. Congress, 332–351

Lawrence, D. H., 121
Lawyers. *See* Attorney(s); Counsel, right to
League of Nations, 324, 387, 490
League of United Latin American Citizens, 223
League of Women Voters of the United States (LWVUS), 219
Lebanon, U.S. hostages held in, 386, 497. *See also* Iran-*contra* affair
Lee, Richard Henry, 30, 32
Legal Defense and Education Fund, 223
Legal tender, 80
Legislative assistant, 305–307
Legislative branch. *See* Congress, U.S.
Legislative correspondents, 307
Legislative director, 305
Legislative powers:
  of British Parliament, 628
  defined, 283
  of U.S. Congress, 313–321. *See also* Congress, U.S., constitutional powers and duties of
Legislative Reorganization Act of 1946, 326
Legislature(s):
  bicameral, 40, 283–284, 628, 632, 634
  British, 23, 284, 336, 628–629
  colonial, 28–29
  defined, 28–29
  French, 632–633
  Japanese, 635
  state. *See* State legislatures
  unicameral, 34
  U.S. *See* Congress, U.S.
Legitimacy, defined, 31
Lemon v. *Kurtzman*, 110
Lend-Lease program, 507
L'Enfant, Pierre-Charles, 585
Letter:
  to congressperson, 325
  to editor of newspaper, 209
  to government agency, for information, 412
Leviathan **(Hobbes)**, 25
Lewis, John, 289
Lexington, Battle of, 30
Libel, 121
Liberal Democratic Party (Japan), 638
Liberalism, 215
Liberals, 215
Libertarian Party, 187, 188
Library of Congress, 296, 305, 307
Lieutenant governor, 536, 550
Lightner, Candy, 226
Lightner, Cari, 226
Limited government, 23–24, 56, 57
Limited jurisdiction, 563–564
Lincoln, Abraham, 6, 12, 67, 131, 193, 359n, 367, 378, 379

  as *Architect of the American Dream*, 360–361
Line graphs, reading, 468
Line organizations, 405, 419
Line-item veto, 390, 392, 554
Lippman, Walter, 329
Literacy tests, 266
Livingston, Robert, 92–93
Lobbying, 223–225, 229, 533, 539, 541
Local government, 583–605
  businesses operated by, 611
  at county level, 590–593
  federal grants to, 615–619
  in France, 633–634
  in Great Britain, 630–631
  legality and functions of, 583–590
  in Japan, 638
  jobs with, 174, 621. *See also* Government(s), employees of
  at municipal level, 583–590, 593–602.
    See also Cities
  New England towns and, 594
  operation of, 590–597
  overlapping units of, 603
  powers of, 82–83
  protection of life and property as responsibility of, 571
  revenues of, 609–619
  special districts and, 595, 597
  spending by, 619–621
  taxation by, 607–614
  townships and, 594–595
  in typical state constitution, 523
Local party organizations, 199
Location of birth (*jus soli*), 158
Locke, John, 9, 23–24, 27, 34, 355
Long, Huey, 345
Loose constructionists, 92–94, 321
Loose money policy, 459
Lotteries, state-run, 612–613, 621
Louis XIV, king of France, 387
Louis XVI, king of France, 8
Louisiana v. *Resweber*, 138
Luxembourg, 7
Lynch v. *Donnelly*, 110
Lyon, Matthew, 191

M

MacArthur, Douglas, 634
Macaulay, Lord Thomas Babington, 583
Machine politics, 200, 600, 602
Madigan, Edward, 411
Madison, James, 3, 9, 39, 40, 44–46, 48, 56, 57, 60–62, 142, 191, 229, 283, 313, 328, 355
Madisonian model, 57
Magistrate courts, 564
Magna Carta, 23, 24, 129, 628

Mail(s):
  franking privileges and, 291
  fraudulent use of, 317
  voting by, 270, 273
Maine, Sir Henry, 62
Major, John, 629
Majority:
  concurrent, 93
  extraordinary, 528
Majority leader:
  in British Parliament, 628
  in the House, 300
  in the Senate, 301
Majority opinion, 443
Majority party, 186, 299
Majority rule, 14
Majority vote, 511
Malapportionment, 287
Malloy v. *Hogan*, 171
Mandamus, **writ of**, 60
Mandatory preference poll, 237
Mandatory sentencing, 571
Mandela, Nelson, 509
Mandela, Winnie, 509
Mann, Thomas, 308
Mao Tse-Dung, 648
Mapp v. *Ohio*, 133–134, 171
Maps, 288, 527
Marbury v. *Madison*, 59–60, 61, 396, 440–442
March of Dimes (MD), 219
Marginal tax rate, 470
Marijuana, 596
Marine Corps, U.S., 6, 173, 501–502
Marital status, voter turnout and, 272
Market, 638–639
Market (capitalist) economy, 638–640
Markle Commission on the Media and Electorate, 277
Markup session, 342
Marriage, 82, 591
Marshall, George, 491
Marshall, John, 59, 60, 89, 92, 94, 172, 316, 436, 443, 447, 452, 607
  as *Architect of the American Dream*, 440–441
Marshall, Mary Keith, 440
Marshall, Thomas, 440
Marshall, Thurgood, 444, 453
Marshall Plan, 491–492, 507
Marx, Karl, 642–643, 645
Mass media. *See* Media
Massachusetts ballot, 246
Massachusetts Bay Colony, 28, 479
Massachusetts Body of Liberties, 28
Matching funds, 615
Mayflower, 27–28
Mayflower Compact, 27–28
Mayor, 597
Mayor-administrator plan, 598

Mayor-council plan, 599–600
Mayor of New York v. *Miln*, 166
McCarthy, Joseph, 329
McCollum v. *Board of Education*, 109
McCulloch v. *Maryland*, 89, 92, 321, 440–441, 607–608
McKinley, William, 359n
Mecham, Evan, 547
Media:
  citizen-action groups and, 252
  political campaigns and, 241–242, 249–256. *See also* Television
  political socialization by, 211–212
  presidency and, 380–381
Media Access Project, 252
Median, 642–643
Members of Parliament (MPs), 628
Memory, improving one's, 555
Menédez de Ágviles, Pedro, 27n
Merit system, 174, 420
Merit Systems Protection Board (MSPB), **421–422**, 424
Metropolitan Transit Authority of New York, 114
Metropolitan Washington Council of Governments, 603
Metzenbaum, Howard, 337
Mexican-American Legal Defense and Education Fund, 223
Mexico, undocumented aliens from, 168. *See also* Illegal aliens
Michel, Robert, 186, 300
Middle East, 7, 379, 508. *See also* Kuwait, Iraqi invasion of; Persian Gulf War
Migratory Bird Conservation Commission, 413
Military force. *See* War(s)
Military powers. *See* War powers
Military service, 174
Militia, state. *See* National Guard
Miller v. *California*, 121
Minersville School District v. *Gobitis*, 112
Minimum age. *See* Age, minimum
Minimum wage, 197, 408
Ministers (in British Parliament), 629
Minor party, 196. *See also* Third parties
Minorities. *See also* specific groups
  in Civil Service, 425
  equality for, 4
  discrimination against. *See* Discrimination
  as percentage of U.S. population, 174
  rights of, as principle of democracy, 14
  set-asides for, 148, 150
  voter turnout of, 272
Minority leader:
  of the House, 300
  of the Senate, 301
Minority party, 186

Minors. *See* Children
Minutemen, 30
Miranda Rules, 135–136
Miranda v. *Arizona*, 135–136, 147, 171
Missouri Plan, 568–570
Mistrial, 137
Mitchell, George, 182
Mitterand, François, 631, 633, 634
Mixed economic system, 640
Mnemonics, 555
Moderates, 215
Monarchy:
  constitutional, 11, 627–628
  defined, 11
  fear of, in early U.S., 34
Mondale, Walter, 254, 327
Monetary policy, 459–464
Money:
  in circulation, 459. *See also* Monetary policy
  coinage reform and, 465
  coining of, 80, 315
Monopoly, 92
Monroe, James, 191, 490
Monroe Doctrine, 490
Montesquieu, Baron de, 25–26, 57n, 355
Mormons, 112
Morris, Gouverneur, 44, 356
Mothers Against Drunk Driving (MADD), 224, 226
Mount Vernon, 43
Mueller v. *Allen*, 110
Multilateral treaties, 508
Multiparty system, 182–183, 197, 636
Municipal government, 593–602
  functions of, 584–590
  legal status of, 583–584
Municipalities, 583. *See also* Cities
Munro, William Bennet, 268
Mussolini, Benito, 11
Mutual-assured destruction (MAD), 493
Mutual defense alliance, 508
Myers, Dee Dee, 370
Myers v. *United States*, 386

N

Nader, Ralph, 221, 222
Nagasaki, 386, 491
Name calling, 256
Nast, Thomas, 192
Nation(s):
  allegiance to, 170
  characteristics of, 7–8
  citizen's duty to defend, 107, 173
  defined, 7
  interdependence of, 15, 17
  legitimacy/legal authority of, 31
  preserving culture of, 6–7
Nation, Carrie, 63
National Academy of Sciences, 483

National Aeronautics and Space Administration (NASA), 372, 414, 415
National Asian Pacific American Legal Consortium, 223
National Assembly (France), 632
National Association for the Advancement of Colored People (NAACP), 145, 146, 223
National Association of Manufacturers (NAM), 218, 220
National Association of Social Workers, 223
National Audubon Society, 221
National Black Media Coalition, 252
National Capital Planning Commission, 585
National Cattleman's Association, 423
National Center for Atmospheric Research, 484
National Commission for Economic Conversion and Disarmament, 499
National Committee for Effective Congress, 242
National conventions, 68, 124, 146, 200–201, 237–238
National Day (China), 7
National debt, 315, 466–468
National defense, 6. *See also* National security
National Diet (Japan), 635–636
National Education Association (NEA), 219, 223
National emergencies, 387
National Environmental Policy Act of 1969, 479–480
National Farmers' Union, 220
National government. *See* Government, U.S.
National Grange, 220
National Guard, 87, 89, 143, 387, 553
  creation of, 552
  history of, 574–575
National holidays, 211
National Institute of Child Health and Human Development, 478
National Journal, 298
National Labor Relations Board (NLRB), 416
National Milk Producers Association, 423
National Organization for Women (NOW), 71, 217, 223, 252
National Origins Act of 1929, 167
National Origins Quota System, 167
National party chairperson, 201
National party committee, 201
National party conventions, 68, 124, 146, 200–201, 237–238

National party organization, 200–201
National Railway Passenger
    Corporation (AMTRAK), 419
National Recycling Coalition, 589
National Republicans, 191
National Rifle Association (NRA), 218,
    219, 224, 225, 227
National security, 6, 115–118, 122, 489
National Security Act of 1947, 497, 501
National Security Council (NSC), 365,
    371, 497, 502
National Space Council, 372
National Student Campaign Against
    Hunger, 88
National Voter Registration Act, 273
National Wildlife Federation (NWF),
    218, 221
National Wildlife magazine, 483
National Woman Suffrage Association,
    64, 262, 264
National Women's Party, 71, 263
Nationalists, 39
Native Americans:
    citizenship granted to, 158, 268
    equality for, 148
    as percentage of U.S. population, 164
    voting rights for, 268
Natural aristocracy, 420
Natural rights, 9, 23, 34
Naturalization, 158–160, 317
Navigation Acts of 1651, 29
Navy, U.S., 6, 173, 501, 502
Nazi Germany, 11, 123
Nazi Party (American), 123
Near v. *Minnesota*, 117, 171
Necessary and proper (elastic) clause,
    80, 92, 318
Negative campaign advertising, 250–253
Negotiation, as citizenship skill, 66
New Deal, 95–96, 276, 368, 396, 421,
    437, 462, 545
New England towns, 12, 594
New federalism, 95–96, 616, 621
New Jersey Plan, 41
New York Stock Exchange, 316
New York Times, 344, 451
New York Times v. *United States*,
    117–118
New Zealand, Anzus Pact and, 508
News media. *See* Freedom of the press;
    Media
Newspapers, critical reading of, 119
Nicaragua, 161, 328, 497, 507, 508. *See
    also* Iran-*contra* affair 1984
    (Orwell), 90
Nineteenth Amendment (women's
    voting rights), 82, 150, 263, 264,
    276
Ninth Amendment (nonenumerated
    rights of citizens), 104

Nixon, Richard M., 95–96, 173, 228, 249,
    274, 320, 322, 359, 363, 383, 386,
    387, 395–397, 447, 489, 493, 497,
    498
No contest plea, 137
Nomination of candidates, 184, 186,
    233–234, 236–238
Nonpartisan election, 236, 533
Nonresident aliens, 161
Noriega, Manuel, 510
North, Oliver, 328
North Atlantic Treaty Organization
    (NATO), 76, 508
North Korea, 640
Northwest Ordinance, 36
Norton, Gayle, 557
Novello, Antonia Coello, 478
Nuclear arms build-up, 493, 495
Nuclear power plants, 17
Nuclear Regulatory Commission (NRC),
    416

O

Oath of office, presidential, 383
Obscenity, 120, 121
Occupation:
    of congresspersons, 293–294
    political attitudes and, 190, 214
    voters' choices and, 276
Occupational Safety and Health Act of
    1970, 408
O'Connor, Sandra Day, 109, 111, 124,
    446
Off-budget items, 469
Off-year election of governors, 559
Office of Administration, 372
Office of Management and Budget
    (OMB), 367, 370–371, 372, 464,
    466, 503
Office of National Drug Control Policy,
    372
Office of Personnel Management
    (OPM), 175, 421–422
Office of Policy Development, 371
Office of Science and Technology, 372
Office of United States Trade
    Representative, 372
Office-group ballot, 246
Oil spills, 479, 480, 552
Old-age, Survivors, and Disability
    Insurance (OASDI), 477. *See also*
    Social Security
Old-age pensions, 197
Oliver, In re, 171
Olympic Games (Moscow, 1980), 493
Omnibus Crime Control and Safe
    Streets Act of 1968, 134
One-party system, **182**

"One person—one vote" rule, 287
O'Neil, Robert M., 277
O'Neill, Thomas P. (Tip), 257
Open Door policy, 490
Open primary, 235–236
Operation Breadbasket, 185
Operation Desert Shield, 552. *See also*
    Persian Gulf War
Opinion:
    court, 443. *See also* Case law; Common
        law; Supreme Court, U.S.
    distinguishing between fact and, 451
    public, 207–214, 227
Opinion leaders, 212, 214
Opinion polls:
    private, 241–242
    public, 207–210, 213, 241–242
Opposition (Great Britain), 630
Oral arguments, before Supreme Court,
    443–445
Orczy, Baroness, 509*n*
Organization chart, reading an, 404
Organization of American States (OAS),
    508
Organization of Chinese Americans, 223
Original jurisdiction, 436
Orwell, George, 90
Oversight function of Congress, 326, 328
Ozone layer, 17, 284. *See also* Global
    warming

P

Paine, Thomas, 30–31, 261
Pan American Airways, 514
Panama, U.S. invasion of, 379, 503, 510
Panama Canal, 356, 387–388, 510
Panhandling, 114
Pardons:
    granted by governor, 554
    granted by president, 377, 386, 397
Parishes, 590. *See also* Counties
Parker v. *Gladden*, 171
Parks, Raymond, 146
Parks, Rosa, 144, 146
Parliament:
    British, 23, 284, 336, 628–629
    defined, 23
    French, 631–633
    Members of (MPs), 628
Parliamentary democracy, 12
Parole, 556, 478
Partisan election, 533
Partisan politics, 413
Party, political. *See* Political parties
Party-column ballot, 246
Party ticket, 201
Passports, 501
Patents, 317
Paterson, William, 41

Patronage, 174, 200, 391, 600, 602
Patterson, Thomas, 241
Peace Corps, 498
Pearl Harbor, 491
Peers:
  hereditary, 629
  jury of, 23. *See also* Jury
  political socialization by, 214
Penalty, for criminal act. *See*
    Punishment; Sentencing
Pendergast, Tom, 602
Pendleton Act (Civil Service Reform
    Act) of 1883, 420
Pennsylvania Charter of Privileges, 28
Pennsylvania Frame of Government, 28
Penny, getting rid of, 465
Pensions, 197
Pentagon, Defense Contract Audit
    Agency of, 424
Pentagon Papers, 117–118
People United to Save Humanity
    (PUSH), 185
People v. *Hurlbut*, 583
People's Republic of China:
  command economy in, 640, 648
  communism in, 647–648
  democratic demonstrations in, 15, 648
  freedom of religion and, 108
  freedom of speech and, 113
  National Day in, 7
  one-party system in, 182, 187
  population of, 7
  Tiananmen Square demonstration in, 15
  total area of, 7
  U.S. recognition of, 384, 388
Pepper, Claude, 336
Percentages, figuring and using, 601
Perot, Ross, 198
Persian Gulf War, 256, 317, 342, 369,
    371, 381, 387, 479, 499, 502, 503,
    505, 507, 510, 513
Personal income tax, 471–474, 609
Personal property, 610*n*
Personal staff, of congresspersons, 305
Personality parties, 17
Persons, jurisdiction over, 433, 436
Pesticide Control Act of 1972, 481
Pesticides, 17
Petit jury, 576
Petition:
  for community action, 614
  defined, 233
  filed by candidate, 233–234
  freedom of, 103, 122–123
  for recall election, 245
Petition of Rights (England), 23
Philadelphia Convention. *See*
    Constitutional Convention
Photograph, analyzing a, 275
Picketing, 115, 123

Pierce, Barbara, 384
Pigeonhole (a bill), 340
Pilgrims, 27
Pinckney, Charles, 261
Plain folks technique, 256
Plaintiff, 442
Planks, in party platform, 190
Platforms, party, 190
Plea bargaining, 577
Pledge of Allegiance, 112, 211
Plessy v. *Ferguson*, 143
Plum Book, 420
Plurality of votes, 184, 546
Plymouth Company, 27
Pocket veto, 348, 390, 553–554
Poland, Solidarity movement in, 493.
    See also Eastern Europe
Police, state, 522–523, 574, 584–585, 591
Policy and Supporting Positions (GPO),
    420
Policy voting, 274–275
Policymaking:
  by bureaucrats, 423–424
  by congresspersons, 296, 297
  coordinating, as function of political
    parties, 186
  interest groups and, 223–228
  by state governors, 548
Political action committees (PACs), 225,
    227, 243–244, 255–256
Political Activities Act (Hatch Act) of
    1939, 421
Political advertising, 250–253, 269,
    350–353
Political arrests and trials, 132
Political attitudes, 214–216, 364
Political campaigns. *See* Campaigns
Political candidates. *See also* Campaigns
  image of, and voters' choice, 274
  image building of, 240
  PAC contributions to, 243–244
  petition filed by, 233
  political advertising by, 250–253, 269,
    350–353
  presidential, 236–238
  propaganda techniques used by,
    255–256
  selecting/nominating, 184, 186,
    233–234, 236–238
  self-nomination of, 233–234
  television debates by, 249–250, 362
  write-in, 234
Political cartoons, analyzing, 79
Political caucuses, 234, 333–334
Political consensus, 183, 637
Political consultants, 240
Political debate, analyzing, 362
Political map, using a, 288
Political participation, 4, 172–173
Political parties, 68, 181–205. *See also*

  specific parties
  balancing of competing interests by,
    186–187
  caucuses of, 234, 333–334
  as coalitions, 186–187
  comparing, 190
  Congress and, 297, 299–302, 304
  congressional campaign committees of,
    201
  in Czechoslovakia, 183, 197
  defined, 181
  elections to state legislatures and, 533
  evolution of, 192
  in France, 183, 633
  functions of, 184–187
  governor as leader of, 548–549
  in Great Britain, 630
  identification with, 189, 202, 274, 367
  ideological, 197
  in-government, 182
  in-the-electorate, 182
  interest groups compared to, 218
  in Italy, 183
  issue-oriented, 196–197
  in Japan, 636, 638
  joining a, 188
  majority, 186
  membership in, 187–190
  minority, 186
  in multiparty system, 182–183, 197,
    633, 636, 638
  national chairpersons of, 201
  national committees of, 201
  national conventions of, 68, 124, 146,
    200–201, 237–238
  nomination of candidates by, 234–238
  in one-party system, 182
  opposition (Great Britain), 630
  as organization, 182
  organizational structure of, 199–201
  platforms of, 190
  president as leader of, 391–392
  primaries of, 184, 235–237
  roles of, 181
  selection of vice-presidential nominee
    by, 365
  splinter, or personality, 197
  third parties, 17, 187–188, 196–199
  in two-party system, 182–184, 190–196.
    See also Two-party system
  voting choice and, 274
  why people join, 189–190
Political patronage, 174, 200, 391, 600,
    602
Political philosophy, 26
Political socialization, 210–214
Political spectrum, 216
Political subcultures, 78
Political systems:
  converging, 645–648

types of. *See* Government(s)
Politician:
    bureaucrat's role as, 423
    congressperson's role as, 297, 299
    president's role as, 391–392
Politics:
    effect of, on everyday life, 4–5
    how to affect, 5. *See also* Political
        participation
    machine, 200, 600, 602
    meaning of, 3–7
    partisan, 413
    why study, 4–7
*Politics in America: Members of
        Congress in Washington and at
        Home*, 298
Polk, James K., 379
Poll(s):
    mandatory preference, 237
    preference, 237
    public opinion, 207–210, 213, 241–242
    straw, 208
    tracking, 242
Poll tax, 266
Polling places, for voting, 245
Pollution, 17, 479–483
Polygamy, 112, 291n
Pompidou, Georges, 633
**Popular sovereignty, under U.S.
        Constitution**, 57
Popular vote, 247
Population:
    changes in state, 1980–1990, 288
    elderly as percentage of, 221
    Hispanics as percentage of, 165
    minorities as percentage of, 174, 176
    Native Americans as percentage of, 164
    near coastal shorelines, 618
    of People's Republic of China, 7
    school-age, changes in, 176
    shifting, from Snowbelt to Sunbelt, 97
    of U.S., 7, 18
    U.S. cities with greatest, 163
Populist Party, 197
Porkbarrel, 291
Port of New York Authority, 86, 597
**Post offices, Congress's power to
        establish**, 317
Poverty, 474–477
Powell, Adam Clayton, 291n
Powell, Alma Johnson, 503
Powell, Colin, 371, 497, 502–503
Powell, Luther, 502
Powell, Maud, 502
Powell v. *McCormack*, 291
Powers. *See* specific powers
Prayer in schools, 108, 109, 452
Preamble:
    to Japanese constitution, 634
    to typical state constitution, 523
    to U.S. Constitution, 54–56, 634

Precedent, 432
Precincts, 199
Prefectures (Japan), 638
Preference poll, 237
Preferred-position doctrine, 117
Preliminary hearing, 576
President, 355–363. *See also* Executive
        branch
    annual budget proposed by, 370–371
    appointment powers of, 322, 324, 377,
        383, 386, 418, 447–448, 452,
        453
    cabinet of. *See* Cabinet
    as chief diplomat, 387–388
    as chief executive, 356, 383, 386
    as chief legislator, 388–391
    as chief of state, 382–383
    as commander in chief, 316, 377,
        386–387, 496
    compensation of, 358
    congressional power to choose, 322
    constitutional powers and duties of, 6,
        56, 67, 70, 78, 316–317,
        357–358, 377–383, 386–389,
        391, 397
    creating office of, 355–357
    disability of, 363, 364
    Economic Report of, 371, 389
    election of, 56
    Executive Office of the (EOP), 369–372,
        386
    executive agreements by, 388, 396
    executive orders of, 379–380
    executive privilege of, 396
    foreign policy and, 496–498
    in French governmental system,
        631–632
    how to contact, 395
    informal amendment of constitution by,
        67
    legislative program of, 389
    limitations on powers of, 394–396
    media and, 380–381
    military powers exercised by, 379
    oath of office taken by, 383
    pardons, reprieves, and amnesty by, 377,
        386
    political affiliation of, since Great
        Depression, 193–196
    as political party leader and politician,
        391–392
    press conferences of, 382
    qualifications for, 357–358
    recognition power of, 388
    removal powers of, 383, 386
    representative democracy and, 18
    roles of, 382–394
    state governors who became, 545
    State of the Union Address by, 334, 336,
        337, 378, 389, 616
    strong, 378–379

    succession to office of, 300, 358–359
    term of, 70, 358
    treaty power of, 377, 387–388, 496
    vetoes by, 58, 328, 348, 389–392, 395,
        464, 553
    war powers of, 87, 379, 386–387
**President's Commission on Law
    Enforcement and Administration
    of Justice**, 568
President's Day, 211
Presidential democracy, 12
Presidential Election Campaign Fund,
    244
Presidential elections. *See also* Elections
    campaigns and, 239. *See also*
        Campaigns
    nomination of candidates and, 236–238.
        See also Political candidates
    public opinion polls and, 208. *See also*
        Public opinion polls
    third parties' failure to win, 198
    vote in, by groups, 194–195
Presidential Succession Act of 1947, 359,
    363
Press, freedom of. *See* Freedom of the
    press
Press conferences, of president, 370
Press secretary, White House, 369
Pressure groups, 217. *See also* Interest
    groups
Preventive detention, 138
Price controls, 326, 387
Primaries, 184, 235–237
Primary sources, analyzing, 69
Prime minister:
    British, 628
    French, 631–632
    Japanese, 635–636
Prior restraint, 117
Prisons, 577–579, 591, 619–620
Privacy rights, 133
Private bills, 337
Private Calendar, 342
Private opinion polls, 241–242
Private property, 643–644. *See also*
    Property
Privileges and immunities, 85–86, 296,
    396
Probable cause, 132, 575
Probate courts, 564
Probation, 578
Probation officer, 578
Procedural due process, 130
Processes, defined, 129
Proclamation of 1763, 29
Professional interest groups, 223
Profit, 643
Profit incentive, 643–644
Progressive parties, 122, 197, 198
Progressive taxation, 470, 472–473
Prohibition, 63, 65

Prohibition National Committee, 188
Prohibition Party, 196
Project grant, 616
Proof, burden of, 134
Propaganda:
    used in political campaigns, 255–256
    used by totalitarian governments, 646
Property:
    jurisdiction over, 433, 436
    ownership records and, 591
    personal, 610*n*
    private, 643–644
    taxes on, 109–111, 469, 471, 609–610
    voting rights and, 261–262
Proportional taxation, 470
Proposition, 140, 541
Prosecuting attorney, 575
Pro tempore **president of Senate**, 294, 301, 364
Pro tempore **Speaker of the House**, 300
Prototype, 27
Public bills, 337
Public Citizen, Inc., 222
Public debt, 315, 466–468
Public defender, 576. *See also* Counsel, right to
Public interest groups, 218. *See also* Interest groups
Public opinion, 207–214, 227
Public opinion polls, 207–210, 213, 241–242
Public policy, 6, 136, 459
Public safety, 136, 522–523
Public services, 6, 173–174
Public welfare, 585
Punishment. *See also* Sentencing
    capital, 137, 139, 554, 556, 579
    cruel and unusual, 138–139, 579
    loss of citizenship as, 160
Pure speech, 113

Q
Quayle, Dan, 384
Quorum, 40, 342
Quota Act of 1921, 166
Quotas:
    affirmative action policies and, 148
    immigration, 166–167

R
Racial discrimination, 408
Radical left, 215–216
Radio, 120
Rainbow Coalition, 185
Raleigh, Sir Walter, 26
Rally for the Republic (France), 633
Randolph, Edmond, 40, 366
Random sample, 209
Ratification:
    of Bill of Rights, 61–63, 104

    of Constitution, 43–47, 190, 440
    of constitutional amendments, 63, 66
    defined, 44
    of state constitutional amendments, 528
Ratings system, 227
Rationing, 387
Reactionaries, 215–216
Reagan, Ronald, 67, 96, 225, 227, 240, 242, 248, 253, 268, 274*n*, 276, 290, 303, 328, 358, 362–363, 365, 369, 373, 380–381, 383–384, 386, 395, 401–402, 423–425, 446, 448, 493, 498, 503, 504, 510, 545, 554, 616–617, 621
Realigning election, 193
Reapportionment, 285–286, 530
Recall election, 245, 540, 547
Recessions, 464
Recognition power, 388
Reconstruction amendments. *See* Civil War amendments
Record vote, 343
Recreational activities, provided by local government, 589
Recycling, 588–589
Red Brigade (Italy), 514
Redcoats, 30
Reed **v.** *Reed*, 150
Referendum, 540
Reform Bill of 1832 (Great Britain), 626
Refugee Act of 1980, 167
Refugees, 161
Refuse Act of 1899, 480
Regents of the University of California **v.** *Bakke*, 148
Registration:
    draft, 107, 150
    voter, 267–269, 271–272, 591
Regressive taxation, 470, 472, 613
Regulation, government. *See* Government regulation
Rehnquist, William H., 124, 446
Released time, 109
Religion:
    freedom of, 80, 103, 108–112, 431
    of Supreme Court justices, 449–450
    voters' choices and, 276
Removal. *See also* Impeachment; Recall election
    of state governors, 547
    of state court judges, 570–571
Removal powers:
    of president, 383, 386
    of state governor, 550–551
Reorganization Act of 1970, 326
Repeal, defined, 65
Report (a bill), 342
Reporters, confidentiality and, 118
Representative, congressperson's role as, 296–297
Representative assembly, 27

Representative democracy, 12, 18
Representative government, 23–24
Reprieve:
    governor's power to grant, 554, 556
    president's power to grant, 377, 386
Reprimand, 291, 293
Republic(s):
    defined, 12
    various French, 631
Republican government, constitutional guarantee of, 86
Republican Party, 182, 184, 186–187, 190, 193, 198. *See also* Political parties
    elephant as symbol of, 193
    Governors' Conference of, 548
    national committee of, 201, 384
    national convention of, 68, 124
    national office/address of, 188
    organizational structure of, 199–201
    presidents from, 193–196
    referred to as Grand Old Party (GOP), 193
    splinter parties formed from, 197–198
    voters' choices and, 273–276
Reserved powers, 62, 78, 81–82, 521–522
Resident aliens, 161
Resolution of Independence, 31, 32
Resolutions, congressional, 336–339
Resource Conservation and Recovery Act of 1976, 481
Resulting powers, 80
Revenue Act of 1971, 244
Revenue bills, 314
Revenue-sharing program, 95–96, 617
Revenues. *See also* Tax(es); Taxation
    federal, 473
    state, 609–619, 621
Reverse discrimination, 148, 150, 151
Reviewing (appellate) courts, 438–439, 563, 565
Revolution:
    American, 8, 9, 29–34, 36, 38, 432, 461
    defined, 8
    French, 8
Revolution, The **(Stanton)**, 64
Revolutionary War. *See* American Revolution
Reynolds **v.** *Sims*, 528, 530
Reynolds **v.** *United States*, 112
Rhodes **v.** *Chapman*, 138–139
Richmond Newspapers, Inc. **v.** *Virginia*, 120
Richmond **v.** *Croson*, 150
Rider, to a bill, 339
Rights:
    of accused persons, 131–139, 433, 575–578. *See also* Criminal process; Due process
    constitutional. *See* Constitution, U.S.; specific rights

Rio Pact (Inter-American Treaty of Reciprocal Assistance) of 1947, 508
Roanoke Island, 18
Roberts, Brigham H., 291n
Robinson v. *California*, 171
Rochin v. *California*, 130
Rockefeller, Nelson, 322, 363
Rockwell, Norman, 61
Roe v. *Wade*, 451
Roll-call vote, 343
Rolling Stone, 483
Romney, George, 87
Roos, Michael, 541
Roosevelt, Franklin D., 70, 95–96, 193, 207, 208, 261, 276, 277, 348, 358, 359n, 368, 377–380, 387–388, 394, 396, 545, 615
  as *Architect of the American Dream*, 462–463
Roosevelt, Theodore, 197, 198, 356, 358, 378, 379, 382, 490
Roosevelt Corollary to the Monroe Doctrine, 490
Roper, Elmo, 208
Roper Associates, 208
Ros-Lehtinen, Ileana, 336
Rossiter, Clinton, 186
Rostker v. *Goldberg*, 150
Rousseau, Jean-Jacques, 25
Rule of four, 443
Rule of law, 57
Ruler, hereditary, 627–628. *See also* Monarchy
Run-off election, 184, 236

S

Sabotage, 115
Sacrifice principle of taxation, 470
Sagebrush Rebellion, 90–91
St. Augustine, Florida, 27n
St. Clair, Arthur, 325
Sales, door-to-door, 93, 415, 418
Sales taxes, 469, 471, 609
Salvation Army, The, 88
Salzer, William, 547n
Sampling, in opinion polls, 208–210
Samurai (Japan), 634
San Francisco Bay Area earthquake (1989), 552
Sandinistas, 497, 507–508. *See also* Iran-*contra* affair
Sanford, Terry, 545
Santa Barbara County Association of Governments, 404
Saudi Arabia, sale of spy planes to, 423
Savings and loan crisis, 485
Scarlet Pimpernel, The (Orczy), 509n

Schenck v. *United States*, 116
Schlafly, Phyllis, 71
School(s). *See also* Education
  Bible reading in, 109
  citizen's duty to attend, 107, 173
  citizenship skills learned in, 211
  consolidation of, 603
  county superintendent of, 592
  cultural and ethinic diversity in, 176
  desegregation of, 75, 143, 380, 451
  freedom of religion and, 108
  freedom of speech in, 444–445
  parochial, state aid to, 109–110
  Pledge of Allegiance in, 112, 211
  political socialization in, 211
  prayer in, 108, 109, 452
  religious meetings in, 109
  segregation of, 436–437
  state and local spending on, 584, 618
  state superintendent of, 558
School districts, 595, 597
Schroeder, Patricia, 295
Schwarzenegger, Arnold, 255
Screen Actors Guild, 223
Search warrant, 132
Searches and seizures, 67–68, 131–134
Secession, of South, 93
Second Bank of the United States, 89, 92, 321
Second Continental Congress, 30–35
Second Harvest, 88
Secret ballot, 245
Secret Service, 358
Secretary of defense, foreign policy and, 497
Secretary of state:
  foreign policy and, 496
  in state government, 557
Securities and Exchange Commission (SEC), 415–416, 448
Security:
  collective, 492
  national, 6, 115–118, 122, 489
Security Council, of United Nations, 511–513
Sedition, 115–116, 291n
Seditious speech, 115
Seeds, 88
Segregation. *See also* Desegregation
  civil rights movement and, 140–142, 144–147, 214, 266–267
  de facto, 144
  de jure, 144
  laws requiring, 142–143
  separate-but-equal doctrine and, 143
Select Committee to Study Government Operations with Respect to Intelligence Activities, 303
Select committees, 302–303
Selective Service System, 502–504
Selectmen, 594

Self-incrimination, privilege against, 134–136, 329
Self-nomination, 233–234
Senate:
  French, 642
  state, 550. *See also* State legislatures
Senate, U.S., 284. *See also* Congress, U.S.; Congresspersons
  advice and consent of, for presidential actions, 317, 322, 324, 372, 377, 383, 387, 388, 418, 439, 447–448, 496
  amendment process and, 63
  bills and resolutions considered by. *See* Bills; Resolutions
  calendar in, 342
  cloture rule of, 345
  committees of. *See* Congressional committees; specific committees
  compared to House of Representatives, 292
  confirmation hearings by, 324
  Document Room of, 298
  equal state representation in, 292
  filibusters in, 345
  floor debate in, 344–345
  governorship as stepping stone to, 545
  leadership of, 333
  majority floor leader of, 301
  members of. *See* Congresspersons
  minority floor leader of, 301
  opening day in, 334
  organization of, 291–293
  political party caucuses in, 333
  president of, 301, 364
  president *pro tempore* of, 294, 301, 364
  size of, 18, 292
  voting in, 345
Senate Agriculture Committee, 340
Senate Appropriations Committee, 304
Senate Banking Committee, 338, 342, 465
Senate Budget Committee, 315, 320, 464
Senate Committee on Agriculture, Nutrition, and Forestry, 424
Senate Finance Committee, 304, 464
Senate Foreign Relations Committee, 304, 324, 340, 342, 499
Senate Judiciary Committee, 340
Senate Select Committee on Presidential Campaign Activities (Senate Watergate Committee), 303
Senate Select Committee on Secret Military Assistance to Iran, 303
Senatorial courtesy, 324
Seniority rule, 302, 304
Sentencing, 571, 577–579. *See also* Punishment
Separate-but-equal doctrine, 68, 143
Separation of powers, 57
Sessions:

markup, 342
special, 390–391, 533
of state legislatures, 533
of U.S. Congress, 284–285, 378, 390–391
veto, 536
Seventeenth Amendment (U.S. Senators), 292
Sex discrimination. *See* Gender discrimination
Shadow cabinet, 630
Shays, Daniel, 39
Shays' Rebellion, 39
Sheppard, Samuel H., 118
Sheriff, county, 591, 592
Sherman, Roger, 41
Shield laws, 118
Shogun **(Japan)**, 634
Sierra Club (SC), 219, 221, 227
Sierra **magazine**, 483
Simple resolution, 337, 339
Simpson, Alan, 338
Single elderly people, 476
Single-member districts, 184, 287
Single-parent families, 475
Sixteenth Amendment (federal income tax), 78, 314
Sixth Amendment (right to counsel, jury trial, speedy and public trial), 136–138, 433, 576
Skinner **v.** *Oklahoma*, 131
Slander, 121
Slaughter-House **Cases**, 172
Slavery:
abolition of, 157–158. *See also* Thirteenth Amendment
abolitionist movement against, 64
citizenship status and, 157–158
Civil War and, 93–94. *See also* Civil War
Declaration of Independence and, 32
political parties' positions on, 193, 197
three-fifths compromise and, 41
U.S. Constitution and, 41, 44
voting rights and, 261
Small Business Administration (SBA), 414
Small claims court, 564, 566–567
Smith, Adam, 641
Smith, Al, 545
Smith Act of 1940, 116
Snowbelt, 97
Social and Liberal Democratic Party (Great Britain), 630
Social conflict, 3–4
Social Contract, The **(Rousseau)**, 25
Social contract theory, 9, 24–25, 27
Social Democrats, 188, 196
Social Security, 471, 476–477
Socialism, 645–647. *See also* Command economy; Communism

Socialist Labor Party, 188, 196
Socialization, political, 210
Socioeconomic factors, voters' choices and, 276. *See also* Economic status
Solid South, 276
Solid Waste Disposal Act of 1965, 480
Solidarity, defined, 189
Solidarity movement (Poland), 493
Solving conflicts, as purpose of government, 5–6
Solving problems of world, 649
Sophocles, 545
Souter, David, 324, 453
South:
Civil War and, 93. *See also* Civil War
Jim Crow (segregation) laws in, 142–143
secession of, 93
slavery in. *See* Slavery
Solid, 276
South Africa, 183, 509, 510
South Carolina **v.** *Katzenback*, 268
South Dakota constitution, 522
Southeast Asian refugees, 161
Southern Christian Leadership Conference (SCLC), 140, 145, 185
Southern Manifesto, The: A Declaration of Constitutional Principles, 75
Sovereignty, 7
popular, under U.S. Constitution, 57
Soviet Union:
Afghanistan invaded by, 388, 493, 507, 510
Anzus Pact against, 508, 510
Cold War and, 492–493, 495
command economy in, 648
communism in, 646–647
dictatorship in, 11, 646
McDonald's franchise in, 15
North Atlantic Treaty Organization (NATO) and, 508
recent developments in, 17, 69, 492–493, 495, 645–647
repression of independence movements by, 506
SALT II and, 324
as superpower, after World War II, 491
totalitarianism in, 646
unitary system of government in, 78
Spain, British colonization and, 26
Spanish-American War of 1898, 490
Spanton, George, 424
Speaker:
of the House, 299–300, 334, 340, 343–344
of state legislatures, 536
Special districts, 595, 597
Special elections, 245
Special sessions:
of Congress, 284–285, 378, 390–391

of state legislatures, 533
Speech, freedom of. *See* Freedom of speech
Speed limit, federal grants tied to, 617
Speedy-trial statutes, 596
Spencer-Roberts, 240
Spending:
federal, 313–314, 316
state and local, 584, 619–621
Spirit of the Laws **(Montesquieu)**, 25, 57n
Splinter parties, 17
Split-ticket voting, 202
"Spoiler role," of third parties, 198
Spoils system, 174, 420
Spurious correlations, 318
Stalin, Josef, 11, 463, 647
Stamp Act Congress, 30
Stamp Act of 1765, 29, 30
Standing committees, 302, 340, 342, 536–537
Standing vote, 343
Stanton, Elizabeth Cady, 64, 262, 264
State(s):
administration of, 545–559
admission of, to Union, 88
aid to parochial schools by, 109–110
businesses operated by, 611, 615
compliance of, with Bill of Rights, 106–107
courts of. *See* Court(s), state
criminal law and procedures in, 571–579
employees of, 621
federal grants to, 615–619
government of, 520–543, 545–559. *See also* Governor
governor of, 545–556. *See also* Governor
jobs with, 174
laws of,
equal protection clause and, 142–144
supremacy clause and, 89–94
lotteries run by, 612–613, 621
militia of. *See* National Guard
party organizations in, 199
police/police powers of, 522–523, 574, 584–585, 591
powers prohibited to, 82
primary elections in, 236–237
protection of life and property as responsibility of, 571
relations among, 54, 56, 62, 85–88
reserved powers of, 62, 72, 78, 81–82, 521–522
revenues of, 609–619, 621
separation of church and, 108–111. *See also* Establishment clause
spending by, 584, 619–621
taxation by, 469–474, 607–614. *See also* Tax(es); Taxation
State constitutions, 34, 522–528, 545, 550

aliens protected by, 164
amending, 526, 528
county functions and responsibilities
    determined by, 591
general information on, 524–525
framework of government under, 523
function of government under, 523
legislative process and, 540
length of, 522–523
municipal incorporation under, 593–594
ratification of amendments to, 528
state constitutional conventions and,
    526, 528
taxing powers limited by, 607–608
typical form and content of, 523–526
U.S. Constitution and, 521–522
State legislatures:
bicameral versus unicameral, 528–529
characteristics of, 532–535
committee system in, 536–537
direct democracy in, 540
elections and, 533, 540, 541
lawmaking process in, 528–532,
    538–539
lobbyists and. *See* Lobbying
members of, 532–536, 541
officers of, 536
organization of, 536–538
rating members of, system for, 227
role of, in gubernatorial elections, 546
sessions of, 533, 536, 553
size of, 529–530
state constitutions and, 526, 540
term of office in, 533, 541
State of the Union Address, 96, 334,
    336, 337, 378, 389, 616
States' Rights (Dixiecrat) Party, 197
Statistical Abstract of the United States,
    35
Statistical tables, reading, 618
Status quo, defined, 45
Statutory law, 432, 522
Steamboat travel, regulation of, 92–93
Sternlieb, George, 607
Stevens, John, 124, 453
Stevenson, Adlai E., 157, 274
Stewart, Potter, 121, 446
Stock market, regulation of, 415
Stone v. *Graham,* 109
Straight ticket, voting a, 202
**Strategic Arms Limitations Treaty
    (SALT II),** 324
Straw poll, 208
Strict constructionists, 92, 318, 321
Strikes, 123
Strong mayor-council plan, 599–600
Subcommittees, congressional, 301–302,
    340, 342
Subcultures, political, 78
Subsidies, in-kind, 475

Substantive due process, 130
Succession, presidential, 359, 363
Suffrage, 261. *See also* Voting rights
Suffragists, 150
Sugar Act of 1764, 29
*Summer Jobs: Opportunities in the
    Federal Government,* 175
Summit meeting, 506
Summons, 433
Sunbelt, 97
Sununu, John, 186
**Superintendent of public instruction
    (state),** 558
Superintendent of schools (county), 592
Superpowers, 491
**Supervisors' Inter-County Commission
    (Detroit),** 603
Supplemental Security Income (SSI), 47
Supremacy clause, 56, 89, 93–94, 522
Supreme Court, U.S., 59, 63, 317,
    439–453. *See also* Judicial branch
on affirmative action programs, 148, 150
bad-tendency rule and, 117
British equivalent of, 629
on busing, 144
on capital punishment, 139, 579
checks on, 451–452
on child labor, 95
on church-state issue, 108–111, 171
on citizenship status of slaves, 157, 436,
    452
clear and present danger rule of,
    116–117
on congressional districting, 287, 451,
    530
on constitutional amendment process, 66
on congressional investigations, 325
constitutional authority for, 439
on cruel and unusual punishment,
    138–139, 171
desegregation in schools ordered by, 75,
    143, 380, 451
decisions and opinions of, described,
    443
on double jeopardy, 171
dual federalism doctrine and, 94–95
on due process of law, 107, 131
excessive entanglement theory of, 110
exclusionary rule of, 133–134
on executive orders, 396
on freedom of religion, 108–112, 171,
    431, 432
on freedom of speech, 113–121, 171,
    444
on gender discrimination, 150
governor's judicial power and, 556
how cases reach, 442–447
on illegally obtained confessions,
    135–136
on income taxation, 472

on interstate extradition, 86
interpretation of Constitution by, 68,
    106, 453. *See also* Judicial
    review
judicial activism of, 437, 450–451
judicial restraint of, 450–451
judicial review by, 58–60, 67–68, 396,
    436, 440, 442
loose versus strict constructionism by,
    92–94, 318, 321
on national government powers, 89,
    92–93, 166, 321, 440–441,
    607–608
New Deal legislation and, 396
number of cases heard by, 442
precedents set by, 432
preferred-position doctrine and, 117
presidential power to reprieve or pardon
    upheld by, 386
preventive detention law upheld by, 138
prior restraint doctrine and, 117
on privacy rights, 133, 171
on privilege against self-incrimination,
    135–136, 171
recent conservatism of, 453
on regulation of interest groups, 228
on reverse discrimination, 148, 150
on right to counsel, 136, 171, 433
on right to jury trial, 136–137, 171
on right to speedy and public trial, 138,
    171
on rights of juveniles, 572
role of, in impeachment proceedings,
    321
"rule of four" of, 443
on seating of members-elect in
    Congress, 291
segregation in schools upheld by,
    436–437
separate-but-equal doctrine of, 143
term of, 444
on unreasonable searches and seizures,
    133–134, 171
on wiretapping, 133
writ of *certiorari* by, 442–443
writ of mandamus by, 60
Supreme Court justices, 452
appointment of, 58, 324, 377, 383, 386,
    396, 439, 447–448, 453
characteristics of, 448–450
compensation of, 450
Friday Conference of, 447
ideology of, 448, 450–451
law clerks for, 447
work of, 444–447
Supreme Court Reporter, 447
Surgeon General of the United States,
    478
Surplus value, 645
Suspect classification test, 142

Susquehanna River Basin Commission, 414
Swaggart, Jimmy, 111
Sweden, government of, 11
Symbolic speech, 115
Symbolism, in cartoons, 79

T

Tables, interpreting, 194–195
Taft, William Howard, 198, 448
Taft-Hartley Act of 1947, 123
Taiwan, 648
Tammany Society, 200
Taney, Roger B., 94, 324
Tariff Acts of 1823 and 1830, 93
Tax(es):
  burden of, 473, 621
  citizen's duty to pay, 107, 173
  corporate income, 469, 471, 609
  direct, 314
  estate and inheritance (death taxes), 469, 471, 609
  excise, 469, 471, 474, 609
  export, 44, 80, 607–608
  gift, 469, 471
  import, 607–608
  imposed on colonies, by British Crown, 29–30
  income, 469, 471–474, 609
  indirect, 314
  personal income, 471–474, 609
  poll, 266
  property, 109–110, 469, 471, 609–610
  sales, 469, 471, 609
  types of, 471, 609–610
  value-added, 621
Tax Act of 1990, 472
Taxation:
  ability-to-pay principle of, 469–470
  benefits-received principle of, 469
  church property and, 111
  constitutional authority for, 84, 313–314, 472, 607–608
  directing economic activity by, 473–474
  by federal government, 469–474
  forms of, 470–472
  principles of, 469–472
  progressive, 470
  proportional, 470
  regressive, 470, 472, 613
  sacrifice principle of, 470
  in selected countries, 473
  by state and local governments, 469, 471, 591, 607–614
  systems of, 469–474
Taylor, Zachary, 359n
Teamsters Union, 220

Technology:
  interdependence of nations and, 15, 17
  privacy rights and, 133. *See also* Electronic surveillance
  versus totalitarianism, 646
Teheran Conference, 463
Teitel Film Corporation* v. *Cusack, 120
Telephone services, deregulation of, 417
Television:
  free speech and, 120
  how to influence programming of, 252
  impact of, on public opinion, 211–212, 253–255
  news coverage by, 253, 494
  political advertising on, 250–253, 350–353
  political debates on, 249–250, 362
  regulated by FCC, 120
  role of, in campaigns and elections, 249–256
Teller vote, 343
Tennessee Valley Authority (TVA), 419
Tenth Amendment (reserved powers of states), 62, 104
Tenure. *See* Term
Tenure Office Act, 395
Term:
  of Congress, 284–285
  of congresspersons, 289, 291–292, 308, 541
  of county board members, 591
  of president, 358, 370
  of state governor, 546–547
  of state legislators, 533, 541
  of vice president, 365
Territorial integrity, of states, 87
Territories, congressional powers relating to, 318
Terrorism, 514
Testimonials, 256
Texas constitution, 522
Third parties, 17, 187–188, 196–199
Thirteenth Amendment (abolition of slavery), 41, 82, 86, 142, 157–158
Thomas, Jay, 120
Thompson, Charles, 32
Thoreau, Henry David, 140
Thornhill* v. *Alabama, 123
Three-fifths compromise, 41
Thrift Bailout Act (Financial Institution Reform, Recovery, and Enforcement Act) of 1989, 485
Thrift institutions, 417, 485
Thurmond, Strom, 345
Tiananmen Square (China), 15
Tight money policy, 459
Tocqueville, Alexis de, 217, 431, 452, 545
Tolerance of minorities, 174, 176
Totalitarian government, 11
Tower, John, 324

Town, New England, 12, 594
Town manager system, 594
Town meeting, 596
Townships, 591, 594–595
Tracking polls, 242
Trade, international, 15, 510
Trade and product organizations, 218, 220
Traffic court, 564
Transfer techniques, 256
Treason, 115
Treasurer:
  county, 592
  state, 558
Treasury bonds, 315, 466, 474
Treaty:
  citizenship granted by, 159
  defined, 387
  multilateral, 508
  presidential power to make, 82, 377, 387–388, 496
Treaty of Paris (1783), 38
Treaty of Versailles, 324, 387
Trial. *See also* Court(s); Criminal process
  bench, 137, 444, 576
  fair, 118, 120, 134–139
  freedom of the press and, 118, 120, 138
  jury, 130, 136–137, 576
  political, 132
  in small claims court, 566–567
  speedy and public, 137–138
  in state court, 566–567, 576
Trial balloon, 494
Trucking industry, deregulation of, 417
Truman, Harry S, 67, 122, 193, 355, 358, 378, 379, 386, 395, 396, 492
Tulip Growers Association, 218
TWA flight 847, hijacking of, 514
Twain, Mark, 121
Tweed, William "Boss," 200
Twentieth Amendment (congressional sessions; presidential/vice-presidential terms), 66
Twenty-fifth Amendment (presidential/vice-presidential succession), 66, 70, 322, 359, 363, 364
Twenty-first Amendment (repeal of Eighteenth Amendment), 65
Twenty-fourth Amendment (elimination of poll tax), 66, 82, 268, 276
Twenty-second Amendment (presidential tenure), 66, 70, 358
Twenty-seventh Amendment (congressional compensation), 55, 56
Twenty-sixth Amendment (voting by 18-year-olds), 56, 66, 82, 268, 276
Twenty-third Amendment (inclusion of D.C. in presidential electorate), 66, 268, 276

2 Live Crew, 121
Two-party system:
history of, in U.S., 184, 190–196
reasons for, in U.S., 182–184
weakening of, 202–203
Two Treaties of Government (Locke), 24
Tyler, John, 359
Tyranny, 57

U

U.S.A. Green Party, 188, 196
Udall, James R., 483
Unanimous (court) opinion, 443
Unconstitutional law, 58–60
Underwood-Simmons Tariff Act of 1913, 472
Undocumented aliens, 168. *See also* Illegal aliens
Unemployment rate, 475
Unicameral legislatures, 34, 529
Uniform Marriage and Divorce Act, 83
Uniform Reciprocal Enforcement of Support Act, 83
Unincorporated areas, 595
Union Calendar, 342
Union of French Democracy, 633
Union of Soviet Socialists Republics (U.S.S.R.). *See* Soviet Union
Union Oil Company, 479
Unions, labor, 123, 220
Unitary system of government, 7, 76, 630, 633
United Farm Workers, 165, 220
United Nations, 76, 510–513
U.S. Air Force, 6, 173, 321, 501, 502
U.S. Army, 6, 43, 173, 501, 502
U.S. Bureau of the Budget, 320
U.S. Bureau of the Census, 35, 162, 285–286
U.S. Coast Guard, 6, 173
U.S. Department of Agriculture, 93, 174, 405–406, 410, 419, 423, 424, 474
U.S. Department of Commerce, 162, 406
U.S. Department of Defense (DOD), 6, 67, 314, 405–406, 410, 423, 424, 500–505, 507
U.S. Department of Education, 407
U.S. Department of Energy, 407
U.S. Department of Health and Human Services (HHS), 149, 368, 407, 410
U.S. Department of Housing and Urban Development (HUD), 407, 410
U.S. Department of Justice, 268, 406, 410
U.S. Department of Labor (DOL), 290, 368, 405–406, 418
U.S. Department of State, 6, 403, 406, 410, 462, 500–501, 507

U.S. Department of the Interior, 406, 480
U.S. Department of the Navy, 501
U.S. Department of the Treasury, 403, 405–406, 410, 465–466
bonds issued by, 315, 466, 474
U.S. Department of Transportation, 407
U.S. Department of Veterans Affairs, 407
U.S. Department of War and Navy, 403, 500, 501
U.S. government. *See* Government, U.S.
U.S. Government Manual, 35
U.S. Information Agency (USIA), 497
U.S. Liaison Office, 384
U.S. Marine Corps, 6, 173, 501–502
U.S. Mint, 465
U.S. Navy, 6, 173, 501–502
U.S. Postal Service, 163, 174, 419, 469
U.S. Reports, 447
U.S. Supreme Court. *See* Supreme Court, U.S.
U.S. v. Nixon, 396
United Steelworkers of America v. *Weber*, 150
Unsafe at Any Speed (Nader), 222
Urban areas, 593
Urban Institute, 476
Utilities, regulation of, 640

V

Valdez, Exxon, 479, 552
Value-added tax, 621
Values, identifying your own, 145
Van Buren, Martin, 357*n*
Verdict, jury, 577
Versailles Treaty, 324, 387
Veteran's Day, 211
Veto(es):
gubernatorial, 553–554
line-item, 390, 392, 554
overridden by Congress, 390, 395
pocket, 390, 395, 553–554
presidential, 58, 328, 348, 389–392, 395, 464, 553
Veto session, 536
Vice president, 363–365
duties of, 364
historical view of, 363–364
political ability and experience of, 373
as president of the Senate, 301
qualifications and compensation of, 364
selection of, 364
Twenty-fifth Amendment and, 66, 70, 322, 359, 363, 364
unlimited term of, 365
Victim compensation laws, 571, 574
Vietnam, 640, 647

Vietnam War, 67, 115, 212, 274, 317, 379, 386, 387, 396, 510
Virginia Company, 26–27
Virginia House of Burgesses, 28
Virginia Plan, 40, 41
Visa, 164, 501
Vital Speechs of the Day, 451
Voice of America, 498
Voice vote, 343
Voir dire, 577
Voltaire, Franqis Marie, 103
Volunteer Opportunities Guide (Seeds), 88
Vote(s):
of confidence, 630
green, 275
plurality of, 184, 236, 546
popular, 247
types of congressional, 300, 343–345
Voting. *See also* Election(s)
ballots for. *See* Ballots
candidates' images and, 274
as citizen's responsibility, 272
congressional, 300, 343–345
current eligibility requirements for, 268
early, 270
machines used for, 246–247
by mail, 270, 273
minimum age for, 263, 268
party identification and, 187n, 273–274
policy, 274–275
political participation through, 4, 172–173
polling places for, 245
reasons for/for not, 269, 271–273
registration for, 591
socioeconomic factors and, 276
split-ticket, 202
straight-ticket, 202
turnout for, 268–273
Voting rights, 245, 268
for African Americans, 261, 266–268
Civil War amendments and, 86
early restrictions on, 261–262, 266
equality of, as principle of democracy, 14
extension of, 1824–1982, 263
grandfather clauses and, 266
for Hispanics and Asians, 268
history of, 261–268
literacy tests for, 266
for Native Americans, 268
poll taxes and, 266
for women, 64, 150, 197, 262–265
Voting Rights Act of 1965, 267–268

W

Wage and price controls, 387
Waiver:

of Fifth Amendment rights, 135
of right to jury trial, 137
Wallace, George, 197, 198
Wallace, Henry, 197
Walton, J. C., 547*n*
Walz v. *New York City Tax Commission*, 111
War(s). *See also* specific wars
declared/not declared by Congress, 317, 379
on drugs, 596
as foreign policy tool, 510
War powers:
of Congress, 87, 316–317
of president, 87, 379, 386–387
War Powers Act of 1973, 387, 396, 498
War Powers Resolution of 1973, 317
Wards:
as city political divisions, 199
of U.S. government, 158
Warehousemen's Union, 220
Warrant:
arrest, 575
search, 132
Warren, Earl, 143, 396, 437
Warren, Mercy Ottis, 33
Washington Information Directory, 175
Washington Naval Observatory, 364
Washington Post, 344, 397
Washington, D.C., as planned city, 585–587
Washington, George, 18, 30, 38, 40, 46, 48, 70, 181, 190, 321, 356, 358, 366, 367, 372, 378, 382, 386, 391, 395, 396, 441, 490, 585
as *Architect of the American Dream*, 43–44
Waste-conscious consumer, 482
Water pollution, 479–480
Water Pollution Control Act of 1948, 479
Watergate scandal, 254, 303, 326, 327, 386, 396, 397
Watt, James, 225
"We Are the World," 212
Weak mayor-council plan, 599–600, 602
Wealth of Nations, The (Smith), 641
Webster, Daniel, 191, 363
Weekly Report (**Congressional Quarterly**), 298, 344
Weinberger, Caspar, 503
Welfare, public, 585
Wesberry v. *Sanders*, 287, 288

West Publishing Company, 447
West Virginia Board of Education v. *Barnette*, 112
Western bloc, 492
Whig Party, 191–192, 363
Whips, 300
Whisky Rebellion, 386
Whistle-blowers, 424
Whitaker and Baker, 240
White, Theodore H., 233
White flight, 143
White House Office, 369
White House Press Corps, 369–370, 382
White House Staff, 369–370
Wilder, L. Douglas, 554, 556
Wilkinson v. *Jones*, 120
William the Conqueror, 431
Wilson, James Q., 189, 356
Wilson, Woodrow, 67, 68, 198, 263, 329, 333, 336, 363, 368, 378, 387, 389, 490–491
Wilson-Gorman Tariff Act of 1894, 472
Winner-take-all system, 247–249
Wiretapping, 58–59, 67, 133–134
Wirthlin, Richard, 242
Witnesses, 173, 326, 531
Women:
antislavery movement and, 64
in armed forces, 503–504, 574
in Civil Service, 425
discrimination against, 150–151, 408
as "founding mothers" of Constitution, 33
gender gap and, 276
interest groups for, 223
Mayflower Compact and, 28
most single-parent families headed by, 475
presidential and vice-presidential offices and, 358
rights of, 64, 150, 197, 262–265
voting rights for, 64, 150, 197, 262–265
Women's Declaration of Independence, 64
Women's Lobby, Inc., 344
Women's rights conventions, 64, 264
Working for the USA (OPM), 175
Works Progress Administration (WPA), 464
World, solving problems of, 649
World peace, as foreign policy goal, 505
World Policy Institute, 499
World War I:

German citizens in U.S. and, 161
National Guard and, 552, 574
no cabinet meetings held during, 368
sedition laws during, 116, 291*n*
treaty concluding, 324, 387
U.S. foreign policy during, 490–491
women's efforts during, 263
World War II:
Central Intelligence Agency and, 497
concern with communism after, 329. *See also* Cold War
Eisenhower's experience in, 357
Japanese defeat and, 634, 636
Japanese pro-American policy after, 636
Japanese relocation camps during, 161
Marshall Plan and, 491–492, 507
National Guard and, 554
Nazi death camps and, 123
New Deal interrupted by, 462
North Atlantic Treaty Organization (NATO) and, 508
rationing during, 387
Teheran Conference during, 463
United Nations and, 510
U.S. assistance to allies during, 388, 507
U.S. entry into, 379
U.S. foreign policy during, 490–492
Wright, Jim, 291
Writ of *certiorari*, 442–443
Writ of *habeas corpus*, 103–104, 328
Writ of *mandamus*, 60
Write-in candidates, 234
Wrongful discharge, 408

X
Xiaoping, Deng, 648

Y
Yard, Molly, 217
Yates v. *United States*, 116
Year Books, 431
Yeltsin, Boris, 17, 69, 493, 647
Youth. *See* Children

Z
Zapata Petroleum Corp., 384
Zoning, 585–587, 589, 591
Zorach v. *Clauson*, 109